Department of Economic
and Social Affairs

Statistics Division

WITHDRAWN

World Statistics Pocketbook 2022 edition

Containing data available
as of 31 July 2022

United Nations, New York, 2022

The **Department of Economic and Social Affairs** of the United Nations is a vital interface between global policies in the economic, social and environmental spheres and national action. The Department works in three main interlinked areas: (i) it compiles, generates and analyses a wide range of economic, social and environmental data and information on which United Nations Member States draw to review common problems and to take stock of policy options; (ii) it facilitates the negotiations of Member States in many intergovernmental bodies on joint courses of action to address ongoing or emerging global challenges; and (iii) it advises interested Governments on the ways and means of translating policy frameworks developed in United Nations conferences and summits into programmes at the country level and, through technical assistance, helps build national capacities.

Note

Visit the United Nations World Wide Web site on the Internet:
For the Department of Economic and Social Affairs,
     http://www.un.org/esa/desa/
For statistics and statistical publications,
     http://unstats.un.org/unsd/
For UN publications, https://shop.un.org/

ST/ESA/STAT/SER.V/46
United Nations Publication
Sales No. E.22.XVII.8
ISBN: **978-92-1-259198-8**
eISBN: **978-92-1-001441-0**
Print ISSN: **2411-8915**
eISSN: **2411-894X**

Contents

World, Regional and Country profiles

Contents (*continued*)

Contents (*continued*)

Explanatory notes

The following symbols and abbreviations have been used in the *World Statistics Pocketbook*:

.	A point is used to indicate decimals.
...	Data are not available or not applicable.
~0.0	Not zero, but less than half of the unit employed.
−~0.0	Not zero, but negative and less than half of the unit employed.
%	Percentage
000	Thousands
Assist.	Assistance
Bol. Rep.	Bolivarian Republic
CIF	Cost, Insurance and Freight
CO_2	Carbon dioxide
const.	Constant
CPI	Consumer price index
Dem. Rep.	Democratic Republic
est.	Estimate
F	Females
FOB	Free on board
GDP	Gross domestic product
GNI	Gross national income
GVA	Gross value added
ISIC	International Standard Industrial Classification
ISO	International Organization for Standardization
Km^2	Square kilometres
M	Males
nes	Not elsewhere specified
pop.	Population
Rep.	Republic
SAR	Special Administrative Region
UN	United Nations
UNHCR	Office of the UN High Commissioner for Refugees
United Kingdom	United Kingdom of Great Britain and Northern Ireland
United States	United States of America
UNSD	United Nations Statistics Division
US$/USD	United States dollars

The metric system of weights and measures has been employed in the *World Statistics Pocketbook*.

Introduction

The *World Statistics Pocketbook* is an annual compilation of key economic, social and environmental indicators, presented in one-page profiles. This edition includes profiles for the 30 world geographical regions and 232 countries or areas. Prepared by the United Nations Statistics Division of the Department of Economic and Social Affairs, it responds to General Assembly resolution 2626 (XXV), in which the Secretary-General is requested to supply basic national data that will increase international public awareness of countries' development efforts.

The indicators shown are selected from the wealth of international statistical information compiled regularly by the Statistics Division and the Population Division of the United Nations, the statistical services of the United Nations specialized agencies and other international organizations and institutions. Special recognition is gratefully given for their assistance in continually providing data.

Organization of the Pocketbook

The profiles are presented first with the world and its geographical regions and sub-regions, based on the M49 regional classification[1], and then countries and areas alphabetically according to their names in English. Each profile is organised into 5 sections, where relevant and/or available:

- *General information:* includes data on surface area, population and population density, sex ratio of the population, capital city and its population, national currency and its exchange rate to the US dollar, location by geographical region and the date of admission to the United Nations.

- *Economic indicators:* includes data on national accounts Gross domestic product (GDP), GDP per capita, GDP growth rate, Gross Value Added (GVA) share by industry, employment share by industry, unemployment rate, labour force participation rate, consumer price index, agricultural production index, the value of total exports, imports and the trade balance and balance of payments.

- *Major trading partners:* shows a country's main trading partners

- *Social indicators:* includes data on population (growth rates, including for the urban population), total fertility rate, life expectancy at birth, population age distribution, international migrant stock, refugees, infant mortality rate, health (expenditure and physicians), education (expenditure and gross enrolment ratios), intentional homicide rate and seats held by women in the National Parliament.

- *Environmental and infrastructure indicators:* includes data on internet users, Research & Development expenditure, threatened species, forested area, CO_2 emission estimates, energy production and energy

---

[1] See UNSD website: https://unstats.un.org/unsd/methodology/m49/

supply per capita, tourist/visitor arrivals, important sites for terrestrial biodiversity protected, population using safely managed water sources and sanitation facilities and Official Development Assitance received or disbursed.

The complete set of indicators, listed by category and in the order in which they appear in the profiles, is shown before the country profile section (see page ix). Not all indicators are shown for each country or area due to different degrees of data availability.

The technical notes section, which follows the country profile pages, contains brief descriptions of the concepts and methodologies used in the compilation of the indicators as well as information on the statistical sources for the indicators. Readers interested in longer time-series data or more detailed descriptions of the concepts or methodologies should consult the primary sources of the data and the references listed in the section following the technical notes.

For brevity the Pocketbook omits specific information on the source or methodology for individual data points, and when a data point is estimated no distinction is made between whether the estimation was done by the international or national organization. See the technical notes section for the primary source which may provide this information.

Time period

This issue of the *World Statistics Pocketbook* presents data for the economic, social, environmental and infrastructure sections for three reference years - 2010, 2015 and 2022 - when available or the most recent data previous to these years, back to 2000. These instances are footnoted in each profile. For the general information and major trading partners sections the reference year is 2022 and 2021 respectively, unless otherwise footnoted.

Acknowledgement

The *World Statistics Pocketbook* is prepared annually by the Development Data and Outreach Branch of the Statistics Division, Department of Economic and Social Affairs of the United Nations Secretariat. The programme manager is Matthias Reister and Anuradha Chimata is the editor; David Carter, Mohamed Nabassoua and Kebebush Welkema provided production assistance; Joshua Kneidl provided IT support. Comments on this publication are welcome and may be sent by e-mail to statistics@un.org.

Profile information and indicator list*

General information

Region
Population (000)
Population density (per km²)
Capital city
Capital city population (000)
UN membership date
Surface area (km²)
Sex ratio (males per 100 females)
National currency
Exchange rate (per US$)

Economic indicators

GDP: Gross domestic product (million current US$)
GDP growth rate (annual %, constant 2015 prices)
GDP per capita (current US$)
Economy: Agriculture, industry and services and other activity (% of GVA)
Employment in agriculture, industry and services & other sectors (% of employed)
Unemployment rate (% of labour force)
Labour force participation rate (% of female/male population)
CPI: Consumer Price Index (2010=100)
Agricultural production index (2014-2016=100)
International trade: Exports, imports and balance (million current US$)
Balance of payments, current account (million current US$)

Major trading partners (% of exports and imports)

Social indicators

Population growth rate (average annual %)
Urban population (% of total population)
Urban population growth rate (average annual %)
Fertility rate, total (live births per woman)
Life expectancy at birth (females/males, years)
Population age distribution (0-14/60+ years old, %)
International migrant stock (000/% of total population)
Refugees and others of concern to the UNHCR (000)
Infant mortality rate (per 1 000 live births)
Health: Current expenditure (% of GDP)
Health: Physicians (per 1 000 population)
Education: Government expenditure (% of GDP)
Education: Primary, Secondary and Upper secondary gross enrolment ratio (females/males per 100 population)
Intentional homicide rate (per 100 000 population)
Seats held by women in the National Parliament (% of total seats)

Environmental and infrastructure indicators

Individuals using the Internet (per 100 inhabitants)
Research & Development expenditure (% of GDP)
Threatened species (number)
Forested area (% of land area)
CO_2 emission estimates (million tons/tons per capita)
Energy production, primary (Petajoules)
Energy supply per capita (Gigajoules)
Tourist/visitor arrivals at national borders (000)
Important sites for terrestrial biodiversity protected (%)
Population using safely managed drinking water sources (urban/rural, %)
Population using safely managed sanitation facilities (urban/rural, %)
Net Official Development Assistance disbursed (% of GNI of donor)
Net Official Development Assistance received (% of GNI of recipient)

* The complete set of information and indicators listed here may not be shown for each country or area depending upon data availability. The technical notes provide a brief description of each information item and indicator.

World, Regional and Country /Area profiles

World

Population (000, 2022)	7 975 105[a]	Surface area (km2)	130 094 010[b]
Pop. density (per km2, 2022)	61.2[a]	Sex ratio (m per 100 f)	101.1[a]

Economic indicators	2010	2015	2022
GDP: Gross domestic product (million current US$)	66 461 443	75 133 208	85 328 323[b]
GDP growth rate (annual %, const. 2015 prices)	4.5	3.1	- 3.4[b]
GDP per capita (current US$)	9 555.7	10 183.4	10 949.5[b]
Employment in agriculture (% of employed)[c]	33.0	28.9	26.5[b]
Employment in industry (% of employed)[c]	22.6	23.2	23.1[b]
Employment in services & other sectors (% of employed)[c]	44.4	48.0	50.4[b]
Unemployment rate (% of labour force)[c]	5.9	5.6	5.9
Labour force participation rate (female/male pop. %)[c]	48.8 / 75.5	47.9 / 74.3	46.6 / 72.0
Agricultural production index (2014-2016=100)	89	100	107[b]
International trade: exports (million current US$)	15 102 218	16 384 279	22 139 630[d]
International trade: imports (million current US$)	15 275 115	16 482 346	22 252 697[d]
International trade: balance (million current US$)	- 172 897	- 98 067	- 113 067[d]

Social indicators	2010	2015	2022
Population growth rate (average annual %)	1.2	1.2	0.8[a]
Urban population (% of total population)	51.7	53.9	55.7[e]
Urban population growth rate (average annual %)[f]	2.2	2.0	...
Fertility rate, total (live births per woman)	2.6	2.5	2.3[a]
Life expectancy at birth (females/males, years)	72.7 / 67.6	74.4 / 69.3	74.4 / 69.1[a]
Population age distribution (0-14/60+ years old, %)	27.1 / 11.1	26.4 / 12.3	25.3 / 13.9[a]
International migrant stock (000/% of total pop.)	220 983.2 / 3.2	247 958.6 / 3.4	280 598.1 / 3.6[b]
Refugees and others of concern to the UNHCR (000)	...	57 959.7	92 583.5[d]
Infant mortality rate (per 1 000 live births)	37.1	31.5	27.5[a]
Education: Primary gross enrol. ratio (f/m per 100 pop.)	101.4 / 104.0	102.4 / 102.4	101.5 / 103.3[c,b]
Education: Sec. gross enrol. ratio (f/m per 100 pop.)	69.9 / 72.2	75.0 / 75.8	76.3 / 77.2[c,b]
Education: Upr. Sec. gross enrol. ratio (f/m per 100 pop.)	58.5 / 61.0	66.0 / 67.3	67.8 / 69.2[c,b]
Intentional homicide rate (per 100 000 pop.)[c]	6.0	5.9	5.6[b]
Seats held by women in the National Parliament (%)	19.0	22.3	26.2[g]

Environment and infrastructure indicators	2010	2015	2022
Individuals using the Internet (per 100 inhabitants)[c]	28.9	40.5	59.1[b]
Research & Development expenditure (% of GDP)	1.6	1.7	1.9[b]
Forested area (% of land area)	31.5	31.3	31.2[e]
Energy production, primary (Petajoules)	530 014	570 226	612 971[e]
Energy supply per capita (Gigajoules)	74	74	76[e]
Important sites for terrestrial biodiversity protected (%)	39.5	42.1	44.0[d]
Pop. using safely managed drinking water (urban/rural, %)	84.0 / 46.3	85.0 / 52.8	85.7 / 59.6[b]
Pop. using safely managed sanitation (urban/rural %)	51.6 / 27.5	56.8 / 35.8	61.5 / 44.3[b]

a Projected estimate (medium fertility variant). b 2020. c Estimate. d 2021. e 2019. f Data refers to a 5-year period preceding the reference year. g Data are as at 1 January of reporting year.

Africa

Region	World	Population (000, 2022)	1 426 736[a]
Surface area (km2)	29 648 481[b]	Pop. density (per km2, 2022)	48.3[a]
Sex ratio (m per 100 f)	99.7[a]		

Economic indicators	2010	2015	2022
GDP: Gross domestic product (million current US$)	1 979 101	2 358 404	2 414 594[b]
GDP growth rate (annual %, const. 2015 prices)	5.9	3.4	- 2.7[b]
GDP per capita (current US$)	1 907.1	1 997.3	1 803.5[b]
Employment in agriculture (% of employed)[c]	53.4	50.4	48.7[b]
Employment in industry (% of employed)[c]	12.2	13.0	13.3[b]
Employment in services & other sectors (% employed)[c]	34.3	36.7	38.1[b]
Unemployment rate (% of labour force)[c]	6.6	6.7	8.0
Labour force participation rate (female/male pop. %)[c]	55.0 / 74.0	54.3 / 72.3	53.7 / 71.1
Agricultural production index (2014-2016=100)	85	100	112[b]
International trade: exports (million current US$)	496 594	402 988	554 934[d]
International trade: imports (million current US$)	468 435	547 529	593 682[d]
International trade: balance (million current US$)	28 159	- 144 542	- 38 748[d]

Social indicators	2010	2015	2022
Population growth rate (average annual %)	2.6	2.6	2.3[a]
Urban population (% of total population)	38.9	41.2	43.0[e]
Urban population growth rate (average annual %)[f]	3.6	3.7	...
Fertility rate, total (live births per woman)	4.9	4.6	4.2[a]
Life expectancy at birth (females/males, years)	60.2 / 57.0	62.9 / 59.3	64.1 / 60.2[a]
Population age distribution (0-14/60+ years old, %)	41.5 / 5.0	41.3 / 5.2	40.1 / 5.5[a]
International migrant stock (000/% of total pop.)	17 806.7 / 1.7	22 860.8 / 1.9	25 389.5 / 1.9[b]
Refugees and others of concern to the UNHCR (000)	...	17 067.3	37 064.5[d]
Infant mortality rate (per 1 000 live births)	60.9	52.5	44.2[a]
Intentional homicide rate (per 100 000 pop.)[c]	12.0	12.2	12.1[b]

Environment and infrastructure indicators	2010	2015	2022
Forested area (% of land area)	22.7	22.0	21.4[e]
Energy production, primary (Petajoules)	47 453	44 471	48 095[e]
Energy supply per capita (Gigajoules)	27	26	26[e]

a Projected estimate (medium fertility variant). **b** 2020. **c** Estimate. **d** 2021. **e** 2019. **f** Data refers to a 5-year period preceding the reference year.

Region	Africa	Population (000, 2022)	259 970[a]
Surface area (km2)	7 769 438[b]	Pop. density (per km2, 2022)	33.8[a]
Sex ratio (m per 100 f)	101.8[a]		

Economic indicators	2010	2015	2022
GDP: Gross domestic product (million current US$)	643 263	760 531	762 151[b]
GDP growth rate (annual %, const. 2015 prices)	4.9	3.7	- 4.1[b]
GDP per capita (current US$)	3 177.2	3 405.3	3 102.8[b]
Employment in agriculture (% of employed)[c]	29.2	26.7	24.8[b]
Employment in industry (% of employed)[c]	24.5	24.6	25.6[b]
Employment in services & other sectors (% employed)[c]	46.3	48.7	49.6[b]
Unemployment rate (% of labour force)[c]	10.6	13.2	12.6
Labour force participation rate (female/male pop. %)[c]	23.2 / 72.7	23.4 / 69.8	20.1 / 66.8
Agricultural production index (2014-2016=100)	85	102	106[b]
International trade: exports (million current US$)	165 544	108 845	170 246[d]
International trade: imports (million current US$)	181 147	205 560	215 514[d]
International trade: balance (million current US$)	- 15 603	- 96 714	- 45 268[d]

Social indicators	2010	2015	2022
Population growth rate (average annual %)	1.9	2.1	1.6[a]
Urban population (% of total population)	50.5	51.4	52.2[e]
Urban population growth rate (average annual %)[f]	2.1	2.3	...
Fertility rate, total (live births per woman)	3.2	3.4	3.0[a]
Life expectancy at birth (females/males, years)	71.8 / 67.5	73.2 / 68.7	73.6 / 69.1[a]
Population age distribution (0-14/60+ years old, %)	32.4 / 6.6	32.8 / 7.3	32.5 / 8.5[a]
International migrant stock (000/% of total pop.)	1 952.0 / 1.0	2 138.9 / 1.0	3 167.9 / 1.3[b]
Infant mortality rate (per 1 000 live births)	29.5	25.3	21.4[a]
Education: Primary gross enrol. ratio (f/m per 100 pop.)	95.5 / 100.8	98.0 / 101.5[c]	101.4 / 103.5[c,b]
Education: Sec. gross enrol. ratio (f/m per 100 pop.)	70.3 / 72.0	78.2 / 78.6[c]	81.2 / 80.5[c,b]
Education: Upr. Sec. gross enrol. ratio (f/m per 100 pop.)	52.0 / 48.6	62.8 / 59.2[c]	65.1 / 59.0[c,b]
Intentional homicide rate (per 100 000 pop.)[c]	5.5	6.3	6.6[b]
Seats held by women in the National Parliament (%)	13.2	24.6	21.2[g]

Environment and infrastructure indicators	2010	2015	2022
Individuals using the Internet (per 100 inhabitants)	22.8	41.4	64.2[b]
Research & Development expenditure (% of GDP)	0.4	0.6	0.8[b]
Forested area (% of land area)	4.4	3.6	3.5[e]
Important sites for terrestrial biodiversity protected (%)	31.2	35.1	41.7[d]
Pop. using safely managed drinking water (urban/rural, %)	84.3 / ...	84.1 / ...	83.1 / ...[b]
Pop. using safely managed sanitation (urban/rural %)	35.6 / ...	38.2 / ...	40.2 / ...[b]

a Projected estimate (medium fertility variant). b 2020. c Estimate. d 2021. e 2019. f Data refers to a 5-year period preceding the reference year. g Data are as at 1 January of reporting year.

Sub-Saharan Africa

Region	Africa	Population (000, 2022)	1 166 766[a]
Surface area (km2)	21 879 043[b,c]	Pop. density (per km2, 2022)	53.4[a]
Sex ratio (m per 100 f)	99.3[a]		

Economic indicators	2010	2015	2022
GDP: Gross domestic product (million current US$)	1 335 838	1 597 872	1 652 443[c]
GDP growth rate (annual %, const. 2015 prices)	6.5	3.3	- 2.0[c]
GDP per capita (current US$)	1 599.2	1 668.9	1 511.6[c]
Employment in agriculture (% of employed)[d]	58.1	54.5	52.6[c]
Employment in industry (% of employed)[d]	9.9	10.9	11.2[c]
Employment in services & other sectors (% employed)[d]	32.1	34.5	36.2[c]
Unemployment rate (% of labour force)[d]	5.7	5.5	7.2
Labour force participation rate (female/male pop. %)[d]	64.2 / 74.4	62.8 / 73.0	62.2 / 72.1
International trade: exports (million current US$)	331 050	294 142	384 688[e]
International trade: imports (million current US$)	287 288	341 970	378 168[e]
International trade: balance (million current US$)	43 762	- 47 827	6 520[e]

Social indicators	2010	2015	2022
Population growth rate (average annual %)	2.8	2.7	2.5[a]
Urban population (% of total population)	36.1	38.8	40.9[f]
Urban population growth rate (average annual %)[g]	4.1	4.1	...
Fertility rate, total (live births per woman)	5.3	4.9	4.5[a]
Life expectancy at birth (females/males, years)	57.7 / 54.8	60.7 / 57.3	62.1 / 58.3[a]
Population age distribution (0-14/60+ years old, %)	43.7 / 4.6	43.2 / 4.7	41.8 / 4.8[a]
International migrant stock (000/% of total pop.)	15 854.6 / 1.9	20 721.9 / 2.2	22 221.5 / 2.0[c]
Infant mortality rate (per 1 000 live births)	66.2	57.2	47.5[a]
Education: Primary gross enrol. ratio (f/m per 100 pop.)	94.5 / 102.2	96.7 / 101.0	98.2 / 102.7[d,c]
Education: Sec. gross enrol. ratio (f/m per 100 pop.)	35.7 / 43.5	40.5 / 46.9	41.1 / 46.2[d,c]
Education: Upr. Sec. gross enrol. ratio (f/m per 100 pop.)	27.2 / 34.8	30.8 / 38.0	32.3 / 37.7[d,c]
Intentional homicide rate (per 100 000 pop.)[d]	13.6	13.6	13.3[c]
Seats held by women in the National Parliament (%)	18.4	22.6	26.0[h]

Environment and infrastructure indicators	2010	2015	2022
Individuals using the Internet (per 100 inhabitants)	6.1	16.1	28.6[c]
Research & Development expenditure (% of GDP)	0.3	0.3	0.3[c]
Forested area (% of land area)	29.9	28.5	27.8[f]
Important sites for terrestrial biodiversity protected (%)	39.8	41.0	43.5[e]
Pop. using safely managed drinking water (urban/rural, %)	46.8 / 9.1	51.3 / 11.1	53.5 / 13.3[c]
Pop. using safely managed sanitation (urban/rural %)	19.8 / 16.7	21.6 / 18.0	23.5 / 19.4[c]

a Projected estimate (medium fertility variant). **b** Calculated by the UNSD. **c** 2020. **d** Estimate. **e** 2021. **f** 2019. **g** Data refers to a 5-year period preceding the reference year. **h** Data are as at 1 January of reporting year.

Eastern Africa

Region	Sub-Saharan Africa	Population (000, 2022)	473 005[a]
Surface area (km2)	6 667 493[b]	Pop. density (per km2, 2022)	71.1[a]
Sex ratio (m per 100 f)	98.4[a]		

Economic indicators	2010	2015	2022
GDP: Gross domestic product (million current US$)	232 444	324 886	431 717[b]
GDP growth rate (annual %, const. 2015 prices)	9.5	6.0	0.8[b]
GDP per capita (current US$)	687.1	836.1	971.8[b]
Employment in agriculture (% of employed)[c]	69.7	66.2	63.7[b]
Employment in industry (% of employed)[c]	7.4	8.1	8.7[b]
Employment in services & other sectors (% employed)[c]	22.9	25.6	27.6[b]
Unemployment rate (% of labour force)[c]	4.0	3.4	4.7
Labour force participation rate (female/male pop. %)[c]	73.7 / 82.6	73.0 / 82.0	72.6 / 80.3
Agricultural production index (2014-2016=100)	85	101	116[b]
International trade: exports (million current US$)	31 652	40 742	51 965[d]
International trade: imports (million current US$)	62 688	94 477	98 003[d]
International trade: balance (million current US$)	- 31 036	- 53 735	- 46 038[d]

Social indicators	2010	2015	2022
Population growth rate (average annual %)	2.9	2.7	2.5[a]
Urban population (% of total population)	24.4	26.6	28.5[e]
Urban population growth rate (average annual %)[f]	4.4	4.6	...
Fertility rate, total (live births per woman)	5.2	4.7	4.2[a]
Life expectancy at birth (females/males, years)	60.3 / 56.7	64.5 / 59.8	66.2 / 61.0[e]
Population age distribution (0-14/60+ years old, %)	45.0 / 4.1	43.8 / 4.3	41.4 / 4.5[a]
International migrant stock (000/% of total pop.)	4 743.7 / 1.4	6 696.9 / 1.7	7 682.8 / 1.7[b]
Infant mortality rate (per 1 000 live births)	55.2	45.0	35.5[a]
Seats held by women in the National Parliament (%)	21.6	27.2	31.6[g]

Environment and infrastructure indicators	2010	2015	2022
Individuals using the Internet (per 100 inhabitants)	3.4	10.6	20.8[b]
Forested area (% of land area)	32.5	29.7	29.0[e]
Pop. using safely managed drinking water (urban/rural, %)	46.6 / 6.2	53.0 / 8.6	60.4 / 11.4[b]
Pop. using safely managed sanitation (urban/rural %)	24.4 / 14.9	25.6 / 16.3	27.2 / 17.9[b]

a Projected estimate (medium fertility variant). **b** 2020. **c** Estimate. **d** 2021. **e** 2019. **f** Data refers to a 5-year period preceding the reference year. **g** Data are as at 1 January of reporting year.

Middle Africa

Region	Sub-Saharan Africa	Population (000, 2022)	196 078[a]
Surface area (km2)	6 496 820[b]	Pop. density (per km2, 2022)	30.2[a]
Sex ratio (m per 100 f)	98.9[a]		

Economic indicators	2010	2015	2022
GDP: Gross domestic product (million current US$)	189 153	238 018	196 683[b]
GDP growth rate (annual %, const. 2015 prices)	4.7	1.8	- 2.4[b]
GDP per capita (current US$)	1 437.1	1 543.5	1 095.1[b]
Unemployment rate (% of labour force)[c]	5.6	5.4	6.2
Labour force participation rate (female/male pop. %)[c]	66.3 / 74.4	64.6 / 73.7	63.9 / 72.8
Agricultural production index (2014-2016=100)	85	100	109[b]
International trade: exports (million current US$)	90 717	70 653	74 496[d]
International trade: imports (million current US$)	43 623	56 081	37 474[d]
International trade: balance (million current US$)	47 094	14 572	37 022[d]

Social indicators	2010	2015	2022
Population growth rate (average annual %)	3.3	3.2	3.0[a]
Urban population (% of total population)	45.2	47.9	50.1[e]
Urban population growth rate (average annual %)[f]	4.4	4.3	...
Fertility rate, total (live births per woman)	6.2	6.0	5.6[a]
Life expectancy at birth (females/males, years)	57.5 / 54.2	60.2 / 56.6	61.8 / 57.5[a]
Population age distribution (0-14/60+ years old, %)	45.6 / 4.5	45.7 / 4.4	45.4 / 4.4[a]
International migrant stock (000/% of total pop.)	2 436.8 / 1.9	3 479.9 / 2.3	3 861.6 / 2.2[b]
Infant mortality rate (per 1 000 live births)	74.6	62.9	50.7[a]
Seats held by women in the National Parliament (%)	13.5	18.1	19.7[g]

Environment and infrastructure indicators	2010	2015	2022
Individuals using the Internet (per 100 inhabitants)	2.1	10.0	21.5[b]
Forested area (% of land area)	47.2	45.7	44.6[e]
Pop. using safely managed drinking water (urban/rural, %)	36.4 / 2.6	42.4 / 3.0	47.3 / 3.2[b]
Pop. using safely managed sanitation (urban/rural %)	27.6 / 15.9	27.4 / 14.5	26.5 / 12.7[b]

a Projected estimate (medium fertility variant). **b** 2020. **c** Estimate. **d** 2021. **e** 2019. **f** Data refers to a 5-year period preceding the reference year. **g** Data are as at 1 January of reporting year.

Southern Africa

Region	Sub-Saharan Africa	Population (000, 2022)	68 599[a]
Surface area (km2)	2 650 670[b]	Pop. density (per km2, 2022)	25.8[a]
Sex ratio (m per 100 f)	95.1[a]		

Economic indicators	2010	2015	2022
GDP: Gross domestic product (million current US$)	406 090	349 590	334 742[b]
GDP growth rate (annual %, const. 2015 prices)	3.3	1.2	- 7.0[b]
GDP per capita (current US$)	6 955.6	5 550.4	4 958.9[b]
Employment in agriculture (% of employed)[c]	6.9	7.3	6.6[b]
Employment in industry (% of employed)[c]	24.5	24.1	23.0[b]
Employment in services & other sectors (% employed)[c]	68.6	68.6	70.4[b]
Unemployment rate (% of labour force)[c]	24.5	24.8	32.2
Labour force participation rate (female/male pop. %)[c]	45.6 / 61.1	48.4 / 62.4	48.3 / 61.4
Agricultural production index (2014-2016=100)	91	101	111[b]
International trade: exports (million current US$)	95 232	93 647	143 279[d]
International trade: imports (million current US$)	97 723	104 174	117 145[d]
International trade: balance (million current US$)	- 2 491	- 10 527	26 133[d]

Social indicators	2010	2015	2022
Population growth rate (average annual %)	1.2	2.2	0.9[a]
Urban population (% of total population)	59.4	62.1	64.1[e]
Urban population growth rate (average annual %)[f]	2.1	2.3	...
Fertility rate, total (live births per woman)	2.5	2.5	2.4[a]
Life expectancy at birth (females/males, years)	60.5 / 55.2	66.0 / 59.9	63.8 / 58.1[a]
Population age distribution (0-14/60+ years old, %)	29.7 / 7.3	29.2 / 7.8	29.3 / 8.4[a]
International migrant stock (000/% of total pop.)	2 352.5 / 4.0	3 477.9 / 5.5	3 125.1 / 4.6[b]
Infant mortality rate (per 1 000 live births)	37.5	30.7	30.4[a]
Seats held by women in the National Parliament (%)	33.4	33.4	36.6[g]

Environment and infrastructure indicators	2010	2015	2022
Individuals using the Internet (per 100 inhabitants)	22.0	49.1	67.2[b]
Forested area (% of land area)	15.7	15.3	15.0[e]
Pop. using safely managed drinking water (urban/rural, %)	87.3 / ...	84.2 / ...	81.0 / ...[b]

a Projected estimate (medium fertility variant). b 2020. c Estimate. d 2021. e 2019. f Data refers to a 5-year period preceding the reference year. g Data are as at 1 January of reporting year.

Western Africa

Region	Sub-Saharan Africa	Population (000, 2022)	429 085ᵃ
Surface area (km2)	6 064 060ᵇ	Pop. density (per km2, 2022)	70.8ᵃ
Sex ratio (m per 100 f)	101.2ᵃ,ᶜ		

Economic indicators	2010	2015	2022
GDP: Gross domestic product (million current US$)	508 151	685 378	689 302ᵇ
GDP growth rate (annual %, const. 2015 prices)	7.7	3.7	- 0.8ᵇ
GDP per capita (current US$)	1 655.0	1 948.7	1 715.3ᵇ
Employment in agriculture (% of employed)ᵈ	48.2	42.6	39.9ᵇ
Employment in industry (% of employed)ᵈ	11.2	13.3	13.9ᵇ
Employment in services & other sectors (% employed)ᵈ	40.6	44.2	46.2ᵇ
Unemployment rate (% of labour force)ᵈ	4.4	4.5	6.8
Labour force participation rate (female/male pop. %)ᵈ	57.4 / 68.9	53.7 / 65.2	52.3 / 64.9
Agricultural production index (2014-2016=100)	85	100	115ᵇ
International trade: exports (million current US$)	113 448	89 100	114 948ᵉ
International trade: imports (million current US$)	83 254	87 237	125 546ᵉ
International trade: balance (million current US$)	30 194	1 863	- 10 598ᵉ

Social indicators	2010	2015	2022
Population growth rate (average annual %)ᶜ	2.8	2.6	2.5ᵃ
Urban population (% of total population)	41.1	44.5	47.0ᶠ
Urban population growth rate (average annual %)ᵍ	4.4	4.3	...
Fertility rate, total (live births per woman)ᶜ	5.7	5.4	4.9ᵃ
Life expectancy at birth (females/males, years)ᶜ	55.0 / 53.5	56.5 / 54.9	58.2 / 56.4ᵃ
Population age distribution (0-14/60+ years old, %)ᶜ	44.1 / 4.7	44.1 / 4.6	42.7 / 4.7ᵃ
International migrant stock (000/% of total pop.)	6 321.6 / 2.1	7 067.1 / 2.0	7 552.1 / 1.9ᵇ
Infant mortality rate (per 1 000 live births)ᶜ	76.7	69.6	59.7ᵃ
Seats held by women in the National Parliament (%)	11.6	14.5	17.0ʰ

Environment and infrastructure indicators	2010	2015	2022
Individuals using the Internet (per 100 inhabitants)	7.7	19.0	33.8ᵇ
Forested area (% of land area)	14.8	14.3	14.0ᶠ
Pop. using safely managed drinking water (urban/rural, %)	33.6 / 12.1	33.9 / 14.3	34.3 / 16.5ᵇ
Pop. using safely managed sanitation (urban/rural %)	20.2 / 16.2	22.9 / 17.8	25.6 / 19.5ᵇ

a Projected estimate (medium fertility variant). b 2020. c Including Saint Helena. d Estimate. e 2021. f 2019. g Data refers to a 5-year period preceding the reference year. h Data are as at 1 January of reporting year.

Region	World	Population (000, 2022)	1 037 140[a,b]
Surface area (km2)	38 791 038[b,c]	Pop. density (per km2, 2022)	26.7[a,b]
Sex ratio (m per 100 f)	97.4[a,b]		

Economic indicators	2010	2015	2022
GDP: Gross domestic product (million current US$)	22 027 585	25 281 355	27 147 970[c]
GDP growth rate (annual %, const. 2015 prices)	3.4	2.0	- 4.3[c]
GDP per capita (current US$)	23 598.7	25 804.1	26 574.8[c]
Employment in agriculture (% of employed)[d]	10.0	9.1	9.0[c]
Employment in industry (% of employed)[d]	20.9	20.9	20.0[c]
Employment in services & other sectors (% employed)[d]	69.1	70.0	71.0[c]
Unemployment rate (% of labour force)[d]	7.9	6.2	7.4
Labour force participation rate (female/male pop. %)[d]	53.3 / 74.3	52.6 / 72.9	51.8 / 70.7
Agricultural production index (2014-2016=100)	90	99	108[c]
International trade: exports (million current US$)	2 551 125	2 827 588	3 448 620[e]
International trade: imports (million current US$)	3 230 657	3 739 612	4 666 199[e]
International trade: balance (million current US$)	- 679 532	- 912 024	-1 217 579[e]

Social indicators	2010	2015	2022
Population age distribution (0-14/60+ years old, %)[b]	24.7 / 13.1	23.2 / 14.7	21.2 / 17.2[a]
Intentional homicide rate (per 100 000 pop.)[d]	16.7	16.0	15.7[c]

Environment and infrastructure indicators	2010	2015	2022
Forested area (% of land area)	42.0	41.7	41.4[f]

a Projected estimate (medium fertility variant). b Calculated by the UNSD. c 2020. d Estimate. e 2021. f 2019.

Northern America

Region	Americas	Population (000, 2022)	376 871[a]	
Surface area (km2)	18 651 660[b]	Pop. density (per km2, 2022)	20.2[a]	
Sex ratio (m per 100 f)	98.1[a,c]			

Economic indicators	2010	2015	2022
GDP: Gross domestic product (million current US$)	16 675 374	19 771 305	22 548 633[b]
GDP growth rate (annual %, const. 2015 prices)	2.7	2.5	- 3.6[b]
GDP per capita (current US$)	48 576.4	55 377.9	61 130.0[b]
Employment in agriculture (% of employed)[d]	1.5	1.5	1.3[b]
Employment in industry (% of employed)[d]	19.7	19.9	19.7[b]
Employment in services & other sectors (% employed)[d]	78.8	78.7	79.0[b]
Unemployment rate (% of labour force)[d]	9.5	5.5	4.3
Labour force participation rate (female/male pop. %)[d]	58.2 / 70.0	56.4 / 68.1	55.8 / 66.7
Agricultural production index (2014-2016=100)	92	97	105[b]
International trade: exports (million current US$)	1 665 220	1 911 491	2 256 905[e]
International trade: imports (million current US$)	2 362 932	2 736 654	3 429 541[e]
International trade: balance (million current US$)	- 697 713	- 825 163	-1 172 635[e]

Social indicators	2010	2015	2022
Population growth rate (average annual %)[c]	0.9	0.8	0.5[a]
Urban population (% of total population)	80.8	81.6	82.4[f]
Urban population growth rate (average annual %)[g]	1.1	1.0	...
Fertility rate, total (live births per woman)[c]	1.9	1.8	1.6[a]
Life expectancy at birth (females/males, years)[c]	81.4 / 76.6	81.6 / 76.8	81.4 / 76.0[a]
Population age distribution (0-14/60+ years old, %)[c]	19.5 / 18.4	19.0 / 20.5	17.7 / 23.7[a]
International migrant stock (000/% of total pop.)	50 970.5 / 14.8	55 633.7 / 15.6	58 708.8 / 15.9[b]
Refugees and others of concern to the UNHCR (000)	...	655.4	1 233.1[f]
Infant mortality rate (per 1 000 live births)[c]	6.1	5.8	4.9[a]
Education: Primary gross enrol. ratio (f/m per 100 pop.)	101.4 / 101.2[d]	100.5 / 100.5	101.4 / 100.6[d,b]
Education: Sec. gross enrol. ratio (f/m per 100 pop.)	96.5 / 95.7[d]	99.3 / 98.3	100.5 / 102.0[d,b]
Education: Upr. Sec. gross enrol. ratio (f/m per 100 pop.)	92.9 / 90.7[d]	97.8 / 96.1	98.4 / 100.8[d,b]
Intentional homicide rate (per 100 000 pop.)[d]	4.5	4.6	6.0[b]
Seats held by women in the National Parliament (%)	19.0	21.8	28.9[h]

Environment and infrastructure indicators	2010	2015	2022
Individuals using the Internet (per 100 inhabitants)	72.5	76.1	91.5[b]
Research & Development expenditure (% of GDP)	2.7	2.7	3.3[b]
Forested area (% of land area)	35.4	35.5	35.5[f]
Important sites for terrestrial biodiversity protected (%)	32.8	33.9	34.9[e]
Pop. using safely managed drinking water (urban/rural, %)	96.5 / ...	96.9 / ...	97.4 / ...[b]
Pop. using safely managed sanitation (urban/rural %)	91.3 / ...	92.1 / ...	92.7 / ...[b]

a Projected estimate (medium fertility variant). b 2020. c Including Bermuda, Greenland, and Saint Pierre and Miquelon. d Estimate. e 2021. f 2019. g Data refers to a 5-year period preceding the reference year. h Data are as at 1 January of reporting year.

Latin America & the Caribbean

Region	Americas	Population (000, 2022)	660 269[a]
Surface area (km2)	20 139 378[b]	Pop. density (per km2, 2022)	32.6[a]
Sex ratio (m per 100 f)	97.0[a]		

Economic indicators	2010	2015	2022
GDP: Gross domestic product (million current US$)	5 352 211	5 510 050	4 599 338[b]
GDP growth rate (annual %, const. 2015 prices)	5.9	0.1	- 7.3[b]
GDP per capita (current US$)	9 069.4	8 848.4	7 046.6[b]
Employment in agriculture (% of employed)[c]	15.4	13.9	13.7[b]
Employment in industry (% of employed)[c]	21.6	21.6	20.3[b]
Employment in services & other sectors (% employed)[c]	63.0	64.6	66.1[b]
Unemployment rate (% of labour force)[c]	6.8	6.6	9.3
Labour force participation rate (female/male pop. %)[c]	50.2 / 77.0	50.2 / 75.9	49.4 / 73.2
International trade: exports (million current US$)	885 906	916 097	1 191 715[d]
International trade: imports (million current US$)	867 725	1 002 958	1 236 659[d]
International trade: balance (million current US$)	18 181	- 86 861	- 44 944[d]

Social indicators	2010	2015	2022
Population growth rate (average annual %)	1.1	1.0	0.7[a]
Urban population (% of total population)	78.6	79.9	80.9[e]
Urban population growth rate (average annual %)[f]	1.6	1.5	...
Fertility rate, total (live births per woman)	2.2	2.1	1.8[a]
Life expectancy at birth (females/males, years)	76.4 / 70.1	77.8 / 71.5	77.0 / 70.6[a]
Population age distribution (0-14/60+ years old, %)	27.7 / 10.0	25.6 / 11.3	23.2 / 13.4[a]
International migrant stock (000/% of total pop.)	8 326.6 / 1.4	9 441.5 / 1.5	14 794.6 / 2.3[b]
Refugees and others of concern to the UNHCR (000)	...	7 071.2	13 430.4[e]
Infant mortality rate (per 1 000 live births)	18.3	15.5	13.1[a]
Education: Primary gross enrol. ratio (f/m per 100 pop.)	107.2 / 110.6	107.9 / 110.1	107.5 / 109.0[c,b]
Education: Sec. gross enrol. ratio (f/m per 100 pop.)	93.0 / 85.9	97.4 / 92.3	99.9 / 95.3[c,b]
Education: Upr. Sec. gross enrol. ratio (f/m per 100 pop.)	79.8 / 68.8	84.6 / 76.2	88.9 / 81.7[c,b]
Intentional homicide rate (per 100 000 pop.)[c]	23.8	22.6	21.2[b]
Seats held by women in the National Parliament (%)	22.7	27.4	34.9[g]

Environment and infrastructure indicators	2010	2015	2022
Individuals using the Internet (per 100 inhabitants)	34.7	54.4	73.1[b]
Research & Development expenditure (% of GDP)	0.7	0.7	0.6[b]
Forested area (% of land area)	48.1	47.4	46.8[e]
Important sites for terrestrial biodiversity protected (%)	35.8	38.3	39.9[d]
Pop. using safely managed drinking water (urban/rural, %)	82.7 / 45.4	81.8 / 49.1	80.6 / 53.1[b]
Pop. using safely managed sanitation (urban/rural %)	27.5 / ...	33.2 / ...	39.6 / ...[b]

a Projected estimate (medium fertility variant). b 2020. c Estimate. d 2021. e 2019. f Data refers to a 5-year period preceding the reference year. g Data are as at 1 January of reporting year.

Caribbean

Region	Latin America & Caribbean	Population (000, 2022)	44 392 [a]
Surface area (km2)	225 996 [b]	Pop. density (per km2, 2022)	200.4 [a]
Sex ratio (m per 100 f)	97.8 [a,c]		

Economic indicators	2010	2015	2022
GDP: Gross domestic product (million current US$)	295 771	352 901	375 616 [b]
GDP growth rate (annual %, const. 2015 prices)	1.7	2.6	- 7.8 [b]
GDP per capita (current US$)	7 349.7	8 469.2	8 821.9 [b]
Employment in agriculture (% of employed) [d]	18.3	17.1	16.0 [b]
Employment in industry (% of employed) [d]	15.5	15.3	15.3 [b]
Employment in services & other sectors (% employed) [d]	66.2	67.6	68.7 [b]
Unemployment rate (% of labour force) [d]	8.5	8.4	8.5
Labour force participation rate (female/male pop. %) [d]	46.9 / 68.5	49.2 / 69.8	49.6 / 69.5
Agricultural production index (2014-2016=100)	86	99	93 [b]
International trade: exports (million current US$)	24 874	26 475	25 895 [e]
International trade: imports (million current US$)	53 245	58 007	59 502 [e]
International trade: balance (million current US$)	- 28 371	- 31 533	- 33 607 [e]

Social indicators	2010	2015	2022
Population growth rate (average annual %) [c]	0.5	0.6	0.5 [a]
Urban population (% of total population)	67.8	70.0	71.8 [f]
Urban population growth rate (average annual %) [g]	1.5	1.4	...
Fertility rate, total (live births per woman) [c]	2.3	2.2	2.0 [a]
Life expectancy at birth (females/males, years) [c]	67.6 / 63.8	75.4 / 69.5	75.9 / 69.6 [a]
Population age distribution (0-14/60+ years old, %) [c]	26.3 / 11.9	24.8 / 13.1	23.2 / 15.1 [a]
International migrant stock (000/% of total pop.)	1 338.9 / 3.2	1 501.1 / 3.5	1 605.1 / 3.7 [b]
Infant mortality rate (per 1 000 live births) [c]	38.5	30.4	26.6 [a]
Seats held by women in the National Parliament (%)	29.4	33.1	40.9 [h]

Environment and infrastructure indicators	2010	2015	2022
Individuals using the Internet (per 100 inhabitants)	23.7	40.1	63.9 [b]
Forested area (% of land area)	33.2	34.8	35.3 [f]
Pop. using safely managed sanitation (urban/rural %)	31.0 / ... [i]	... / ...	... / ...

a Projected estimate (medium fertility variant). **b** 2020. **c** Including Anguilla, Bonaire, Sint Eustatius and Saba, British Virgin Islands, Cayman Islands, Dominica, Montserrat, Saint Kitts and Nevis, Sint Maarten (Dutch part) and Turks and Caicos Islands. **d** Estimate. **e** 2021. **f** 2019. **g** Data refers to a 5-year period preceding the reference year. **h** Data are as at 1 January of reporting year. **i** 2005.

Central America

Region	Latin America & Caribbean	Population (000, 2022)	179 060[a]
Surface area (km2)	2 452 270[b]	Pop. density (per km2, 2022)	72.7[a]
Sex ratio (m per 100 f)	96.1[a]		

Economic indicators	2010	2015	2022
GDP: Gross domestic product (million current US$)	1 210 015	1 403 499	1 328 176[b]
GDP growth rate (annual %, const. 2015 prices)	5.0	3.4	- 8.2[b]
GDP per capita (current US$)	7 678.2	8 307.2	7 392.3[b]
Employment in agriculture (% of employed)[c]	17.5	16.7	16.0[b]
Employment in industry (% of employed)[c]	23.3	23.7	24.2[b]
Employment in services & other sectors (% employed)[c]	59.2	59.6	59.8[b]
Unemployment rate (% of labour force)[c]	5.2	4.4	4.9
Labour force participation rate (female/male pop. %)[c]	42.6 / 79.0	43.5 / 78.4	43.9 / 76.1
Agricultural production index (2014-2016=100)	88	99	111[b]
International trade: exports (million current US$)	336 529	426 846	546 678[d]
International trade: imports (million current US$)	366 171	464 286	603 317[d]
International trade: balance (million current US$)	- 29 642	- 37 441	- 56 639[d]

Social indicators	2010	2015	2022
Population growth rate (average annual %)	1.5	1.2	0.9[a]
Urban population (% of total population)	72.1	73.7	75.0[e]
Urban population growth rate (average annual %)[f]	2.1	1.9	...
Fertility rate, total (live births per woman)	2.5	2.3	1.9[a]
Life expectancy at birth (females/males, years)	76.8 / 70.8	77.4 / 71.4	77.4 / 70.9[a]
Population age distribution (0-14/60+ years old, %)	31.3 / 8.4	28.9 / 9.5	25.8 / 11.3[a]
International migrant stock (000/% of total pop.)	1 751.0 / 1.1	1 860.2 / 1.1	2 302.0 / 1.3[b]
Infant mortality rate (per 1 000 live births)	17.9	15.1	12.2[a]
Seats held by women in the National Parliament (%)	21.6	30.1	38.4[g]

Environment and infrastructure indicators	2010	2015	2022
Forested area (% of land area)	37.0	36.5	36.0[e]
Pop. using safely managed drinking water (urban/rural, %)	... / 38.9	... / 42.1	... / 45.4[b]
Pop. using safely managed sanitation (urban/rural %)	29.0 / ...	38.7 / ...	48.9 / ...[b]

a Projected estimate (medium fertility variant). **b** 2020. **c** Estimate. **d** 2021. **e** 2019. **f** Data refers to a 5-year period preceding the reference year. **g** Data are as at 1 January of reporting year.

South America

Region	Latin America & Caribbean	Population (000, 2022)	436 817[a]
Surface area (km2)	17 461 112[b]	Pop. density (per km2, 2022)	24.8[a]
Sex ratio (m per 100 f)	97.3[a,c]		

Economic indicators	2010	2015	2022
GDP: Gross domestic product (million current US$)	3 846 425	3 753 650	2 895 546[b]
GDP growth rate (annual %, const. 2015 prices)	6.6	- 1.3	- 6.9[b]
GDP per capita (current US$)	9 804.6	9 108.6	6 726.7[b]
Employment in agriculture (% of employed)[d]	14.4	12.5	12.5[b]
Employment in industry (% of employed)[d]	21.5	21.3	19.2[b]
Employment in services & other sectors (% employed)[d]	64.1	66.1	68.3[b]
Unemployment rate (% of labour force)[d]	7.2	7.3	11.1
Labour force participation rate (female/male pop. %)[d]	53.5 / 77.1	53.0 / 75.5	51.6 / 72.4
Agricultural production index (2014-2016=100)	89	102	111[b]
International trade: exports (million current US$)	524 502	462 776	619 141[e]
International trade: imports (million current US$)	448 308	480 665	573 840[e]
International trade: balance (million current US$)	76 194	- 17 888	45 301[e]

Social indicators	2010	2015	2022
Population growth rate (average annual %)[c]	1.0	1.0	0.6[a]
Urban population (% of total population)	82.4	83.5	84.4[f]
Urban population growth rate (average annual %)[g]	1.5	1.3	...
Fertility rate, total (live births per woman)[c]	2.1	2.0	1.8[a]
Life expectancy at birth (females/males, years)[c]	77.2 / 70.5	78.2 / 71.8	77.0 / 70.6[a]
Population age distribution (0-14/60+ years old, %)[c]	26.4 / 10.5	24.4 / 11.9	22.2 / 14.1[a]
International migrant stock (000/% of total pop.)	5 236.7 / 1.3	6 080.2 / 1.5	10 887.5 / 2.5[b]
Infant mortality rate (per 1 000 live births)[c]	16.3	14.1	12.0[a]
Seats held by women in the National Parliament (%)	19.2	22.2	29.1[h]

Environment and infrastructure indicators	2010	2015	2022
Forested area (% of land area)	49.8	49.1	48.5[f]
Energy production, primary (Petajoules)	29 338	32 046	29 056[f]
Energy supply per capita (Gigajoules)	56	59	55[f]
Pop. using safely managed drinking water (urban/rural, %)	82.4 / 47.0	83.7 / 51.2	84.5 / 55.9[b]
Pop. using safely managed sanitation (urban/rural %)	28.2 / ...	33.0 / ...	38.4 / ...[b]

a Projected estimate (medium fertility variant). b 2020. c Including Falkland Islands (Malvinas). d Estimate. e 2021. f 2019. g Data refers to a 5-year period preceding the reference year. h Data are as at 1 January of reporting year.

Region	World	Population (000, 2022)	4 722 635[a]
Surface area (km2)	31 033 131[b]	Pop. density (per km2, 2022)	150.6[a]
Sex ratio (m per 100 f)	103.6[a]		

Economic indicators

	2010	2015	2022
GDP: Gross domestic product (million current US$)	21 068 942	26 810 078	33 070 906[b]
GDP growth rate (annual %, const. 2015 prices)	7.7	4.9	- 1.1[b]
GDP per capita (current US$)	5 005.5	6 047.8	7 126.4[b]
Agricultural production index (2014-2016=100)	88	100	108[b]
International trade: exports (million current US$)	5 896 164	6 827 734	9 781 352[c]
International trade: imports (million current US$)	5 459 724	6 213 020	8 877 006[c]
International trade: balance (million current US$)	436 440	614 714	904 346[c]

Social indicators

	2010	2015	2022
Population growth rate (average annual %)	1.1	1.0	0.6[a]
Urban population (% of total population)	44.8	48.0	50.5[d]
Urban population growth rate (average annual %)[e]	2.8	2.4	...
Fertility rate, total (live births per woman)	2.3	2.2	1.9[a]
Life expectancy at birth (females/males, years)	73.8 / 69.0	75.6 / 70.8	75.8 / 70.8[a]
Population age distribution (0-14/60+ years old, %)	26.0 / 10.2	25.0 / 11.7	23.2 / 13.7[a]
International migrant stock (000/% of total pop.)	66 123.6 / 1.6	77 191.2 / 1.7	85 618.5 / 1.8[b]
Refugees and others of concern to the UNHCR (000)	...	28 420.7	29 888.4[c]
Infant mortality rate (per 1 000 live births)	33.2	26.6	22.2[a]
Intentional homicide rate (per 100 000 pop.)[f]	2.7	2.4	2.0[b]
Seats held by women in the National Parliament (%)	16.8	17.8	20.2[g]

Environment and infrastructure indicators

	2010	2015	2022
Individuals using the Internet (per 100 inhabitants)	22.6	34.5	56.8[b]
Forested area (% of land area)	19.6	19.8	20.0[d]
Energy production, primary (Petajoules)	234 830	260 253	281 061[d]
Energy supply per capita (Gigajoules)	55	61	65[d]
Pop. using safely managed drinking water (urban/rural, %)	83.8 / 49.3	86.2 / 58.1	88.6 / 67.3[b]
Pop. using safely managed sanitation (urban/rural %)	46.9 / 25.4	55.4 / 36.5	62.7 / 48.5[b]

a Projected estimate (medium fertility variant). **b** 2020. **c** 2021. **d** 2019. **e** Data refers to a 5-year period preceding the reference year. **f** Estimate. **g** Data are as at 1 January of reporting year.

Central Asia

Region	Asia	Population (000, 2022)	77 040[a]
Surface area (km2)	4 103 000[b,c]	Pop. density (per km2, 2022)	19.6[a]
Sex ratio (m per 100 f)	97.9[a]		

Economic indicators	2010	2015	2022
GDP: Gross domestic product (million current US$)	227 976	317 237	287 367[d]
GDP growth rate (annual %, const. 2015 prices)	8.2	3.0	- 1.3[d]
GDP per capita (current US$)	3 629.9	4 632.5	3 865.6[d]
Employment in agriculture (% of employed)[e]	31.2	25.4	22.0[d]
Employment in industry (% of employed)[e]	23.4	25.3	26.9[d]
Employment in services & other sectors (% employed)[e]	45.3	49.3	51.1[d]
Unemployment rate (% of labour force)[e]	6.1	5.4	6.4
Labour force participation rate (female/male pop. %)[e]	51.6 / 71.8	50.2 / 70.7	47.3 / 68.5
Agricultural production index (2014-2016=100)	79	101	110[d]
International trade: exports (million current US$)	74 961	64 827	88 191[f]
International trade: imports (million current US$)	40 985	53 082	79 977[f]
International trade: balance (million current US$)	33 976	11 746	8 215[f]

Social indicators	2010	2015	2022
Population growth rate (average annual %)	1.6	1.7	1.5[a]
Urban population (% of total population)	48.0	48.1	48.2[g]
Urban population growth rate (average annual %)[h]	1.9	1.7	...
Fertility rate, total (live births per woman)	2.7	2.8	2.9[a]
Life expectancy at birth (females/males, years)	71.8 / 65.2	73.5 / 66.8	73.6 / 67.5[a]
Population age distribution (0-14/60+ years old, %)	29.1 / 7.1	29.6 / 7.8	31.3 / 9.3[a]
International migrant stock (000/% of total pop.)	5 264.9 / 8.4	5 392.8 / 7.9	5 564.0 / 7.5[d]
Infant mortality rate (per 1 000 live births)	26.2	19.9	14.8[a]
Education: Primary gross enrol. ratio (f/m per 100 pop.)	99.5 / 100.8	103.8 / 104.8	101.3 / 102.5[d]
Education: Sec. gross enrol. ratio (f/m per 100 pop.)	89.9 / 91.4	93.8 / 95.0	96.5 / 98.0[e,d]
Education: Upr. Sec. gross enrol. ratio (f/m per 100 pop.)	80.6 / 81.9	87.3 / 88.5	88.8 / 91.4[e,d]
Intentional homicide rate (per 100 000 pop.)[e]	5.5	2.9	2.0[d]
Seats held by women in the National Parliament (%)	20.0	21.8	27.5[i]

Environment and infrastructure indicators	2010	2015	2022
Individuals using the Internet (per 100 inhabitants)	18.4	43.7	63.3[d]
Research & Development expenditure (% of GDP)	0.2	0.2	0.1[d]
Forested area (% of land area)	3.1	3.2	3.3[g]
Important sites for terrestrial biodiversity protected (%)	20.7	21.1	22.4[f]
Pop. using safely managed drinking water (urban/rural, %)	87.8 / 42.2	89.6 / 49.5	90.6 / 53.0[d]
Pop. using safely managed sanitation (urban/rural %)	47.8 / ...	50.5 / ...	53.5 / ...[d]

a Projected estimate (medium fertility variant). b Calculated by the UNSD. c 2017. d 2020. e Estimate. f 2021. g 2019. h Data refers to a 5-year period preceding the reference year. i Data are as at 1 January of reporting year.

Eastern Asia

Region	Asia	Population (000, 2022)	1 663 200[a]
Surface area (km2)	11 560 456[b]	Pop. density (per km2, 2022)	141.1[a]
Sex ratio (m per 100 f)	103.0[a]		

Economic indicators	2010	2015	2022
GDP: Gross domestic product (million current US$)	13 712 623	17 809 267	22 489 652[b]
GDP growth rate (annual %, const. 2015 prices)	8.1	4.9	0.4[b]
GDP per capita (current US$)	8 545.1	10 874.6	13 403.0[b]
Employment in agriculture (% of employed)[c]	33.2	26.1	22.6[b]
Employment in industry (% of employed)[c]	28.2	28.5	27.5[b]
Employment in services & other sectors (% employed)[c]	38.6	45.4	49.8[b]
Unemployment rate (% of labour force)[c]	4.5	4.5	4.5
Labour force participation rate (female/male pop. %)[c]	61.8 / 77.2	62.0 / 76.2	60.6 / 73.7
Agricultural production index (2014-2016=100)	89	101	104[b]
International trade: exports (million current US$)	3 219 271	3 942 643	5 445 654[d]
International trade: imports (million current US$)	2 967 424	3 317 929	4 811 211[d]
International trade: balance (million current US$)	251 847	624 714	634 442[d]

Social indicators	2010	2015	2022
Population growth rate (average annual %)	0.6	0.5	---0.0[a]
Urban population (% of total population)	54.4	59.8	63.9[e]
Urban population growth rate (average annual %)[f]	2.9	2.4	...
Fertility rate, total (live births per woman)	1.7	1.6	1.2[a]
Life expectancy at birth (females/males, years)	79.6 / 73.8	80.9 / 75.2	82.4 / 76.7[a]
Population age distribution (0-14/60+ years old, %)	18.0 / 14.4	17.7 / 17.1	16.6 / 20.1[a]
International migrant stock (000/% of total pop.)	7 062.5 / 0.4	7 866.7 / 0.5	8 975.7 / 0.5[b]
Infant mortality rate (per 1 000 live births)	12.3	8.5	5.7[a]
Education: Primary gross enrol. ratio (f/m per 100 pop.)	98.4 / 100.0	96.6 / 96.4	103.1 / 102.2[b]
Education: Sec. gross enrol. ratio (f/m per 100 pop.)	89.1 / 89.3	86.5 / 84.6	91.0 / 89.6[b]
Education: Upr. Sec. gross enrol. ratio (f/m per 100 pop.)	78.4 / 79.5	83.3 / 79.8	84.4 / 82.3[b]
Intentional homicide rate (per 100 000 pop.)[c]	1.0	0.7	0.5[b]
Seats held by women in the National Parliament (%)	18.7	20.4	21.7[g]

Environment and infrastructure indicators	2010	2015	2022
Individuals using the Internet (per 100 inhabitants)	39.5	54.4	73.1[b]
Research & Development expenditure (% of GDP)	2.2	2.4	2.7[b]
Forested area (% of land area)	21.8	22.6	23.3[e]
Important sites for terrestrial biodiversity protected (%)	21.6	25.4	26.5[d]
Pop. using safely managed drinking water (urban/rural, %)	91.0 / ...	94.0 / ...	95.2 / ...[b]
Pop. using safely managed sanitation (urban/rural %)	55.9 / 19.0	69.6 / 30.8	81.7 / 44.8[b]

a Projected estimate (medium fertility variant). **b** 2020. **c** Estimate. **d** 2021. **e** 2019. **f** Data refers to a 5-year period preceding the reference year. **g** Data are as at 1 January of reporting year.

South-eastern Asia

Region	Asia	Population (000, 2022)	681 125[a]
Surface area (km2)	4 340 700[b]	Pop. density (per km2, 2022)	153.1[a]
Sex ratio (m per 100 f)	100.3[a]		

Economic indicators	2010	2015	2022
GDP: Gross domestic product (million current US$)	1 993 317	2 481 991	2 998 082[b]
GDP growth rate (annual %, const. 2015 prices)	7.8	4.7	- 4.4[b]
GDP per capita (current US$)	3 339.2	3 912.9	4 484.0[b]
Employment in agriculture (% of employed)[c]	40.5	35.2	29.8[b]
Employment in industry (% of employed)[c]	19.2	21.3	22.9[b]
Employment in services & other sectors (% employed)[c]	40.3	43.5	47.3[b]
Unemployment rate (% of labour force)[c]	3.2	2.9	3.1
Labour force participation rate (female/male pop. %)[c]	56.2 / 80.3	56.0 / 80.2	54.9 / 77.5
Agricultural production index (2014-2016=100)	90	100	108[b]
International trade: exports (million current US$)	1 054 178	1 172 850	1 888 965[d]
International trade: imports (million current US$)	953 410	1 100 730	1 750 205[d]
International trade: balance (million current US$)	100 767	72 119	138 759[d]

Social indicators	2010	2015	2022
Population growth rate (average annual %)	1.2	1.1	0.8[a]
Urban population (% of total population)	44.3	47.2	49.4[e]
Urban population growth rate (average annual %)[f]	2.7	2.5	...
Fertility rate, total (live births per woman)	2.4	2.3	2.1[a]
Life expectancy at birth (females/males, years)	72.9 / 67.7	74.1 / 68.7	74.3 / 68.7[a]
Population age distribution (0-14/60+ years old, %)	27.5 / 8.8	26.2 / 9.9	24.5 / 12.1[a]
International migrant stock (000/% of total pop.)	8 697.9 / 1.5	10 161.1 / 1.6	10 615.4 / 1.6[b]
Infant mortality rate (per 1 000 live births)	26.4	22.6	18.6[a]
Education: Primary gross enrol. ratio (f/m per 100 pop.)	107.1 / 106.8	106.1 / 108.9	104.7 / 107.2[c,b]
Education: Sec. gross enrol. ratio (f/m per 100 pop.)	71.4 / 70.5	81.2 / 80.7	84.7 / 82.1[c,b]
Education: Upr. Sec. gross enrol. ratio (f/m per 100 pop.)	54.4 / 55.3	65.9 / 67.8	69.3 / 65.9[c,b]
Intentional homicide rate (per 100 000 pop.)[c]	2.9	3.0	1.8[b]
Seats held by women in the National Parliament (%)	19.3	17.8	21.9[g]

Environment and infrastructure indicators	2010	2015	2022
Individuals using the Internet (per 100 inhabitants)	18.8	31.5	57.8[b]
Research & Development expenditure (% of GDP)	0.7	0.9	1.0[b]
Forested area (% of land area)	49.7	48.2	47.3[e]
Important sites for terrestrial biodiversity protected (%)	28.2	31.4	36.6[d]
Pop. using safely managed drinking water (urban/rural, %)	... / ...	... / 36.9	... / 38.6[b]
Pop. using safely managed sanitation (urban/rural %)	38.1 / 35.5	40.9 / 42.7	44.0 / 50.3[b]

a Projected estimate (medium fertility variant). **b** 2020. **c** Estimate. **d** 2021. **e** 2019. **f** Data refers to a 5-year period preceding the reference year. **g** Data are as at 1 January of reporting year.

Southern Asia

Region	Asia	Population (000, 2022)	2 007 550[a]
Surface area (km2)	6 688 000[b,c]	Pop. density (per km2, 2022)	313.6[a]
Sex ratio (m per 100 f)	104.6[a]		

Economic indicators	2010	2015	2022
GDP: Gross domestic product (million current US$)	2 576 364	3 154 567	4 331 153[d]
GDP growth rate (annual %, const. 2015 prices)	7.4	6.1	- 4.5[d]
GDP per capita (current US$)	1 504.4	1 725.8	2 232.1[d]
Employment in agriculture (% of employed)[e]	49.4	44.3	40.0[d]
Employment in industry (% of employed)[e]	21.5	23.7	25.5[d]
Employment in services & other sectors (% employed)[e]	29.1	32.1	34.5[d]
Unemployment rate (% of labour force)[e]	5.2	5.4	5.6
Labour force participation rate (female/male pop. %)[e]	26.3 / 79.0	23.7 / 76.2	22.3 / 72.5
Agricultural production index (2014-2016=100)	86	98	114[d]
International trade: exports (million current US$)	354 892	390 610	496 914[f]
International trade: imports (million current US$)	497 340	559 091	783 041[f]
International trade: balance (million current US$)	- 142 448	- 168 481	- 286 127[f]

Social indicators	2010	2015	2022
Population growth rate (average annual %)	1.5	1.2	0.9[a]
Urban population (% of total population)	32.5	34.5	36.2[g]
Urban population growth rate (average annual %)[h]	2.6	2.5	...
Fertility rate, total (live births per woman)	2.7	2.5	2.2[a]
Life expectancy at birth (females/males, years)	68.8 / 65.1	71.0 / 67.6	70.1 / 66.4[a]
Population age distribution (0-14/60+ years old, %)	32.0 / 7.4	30.0 / 8.4	27.0 / 9.9[a]
International migrant stock (000/% of total pop.)	14 411.8 / 0.8	13 873.5 / 0.8	13 863.5 / 0.7[d]
Infant mortality rate (per 1 000 live births)	47.8	38.4	30.1[a]
Education: Primary gross enrol. ratio (f/m per 100 pop.)	105.8 / 105.9	109.8 / 103.4	102.0 / 102.5[d]
Education: Sec. gross enrol. ratio (f/m per 100 pop.)	57.1 / 61.1	68.9 / 69.0	71.4 / 72.0[d]
Education: Upr. Sec. gross enrol. ratio (f/m per 100 pop.)	44.6 / 49.6	56.7 / 59.6	62.4 / 65.4[d]
Intentional homicide rate (per 100 000 pop.)[e]	4.0	3.5	3.0[d]
Seats held by women in the National Parliament (%)	18.2	17.6	17.6[i]

Environment and infrastructure indicators	2010	2015	2022
Individuals using the Internet (per 100 inhabitants)	7.5	15.5	40.5[d]
Research & Development expenditure (% of GDP)	0.7	0.6	0.6[d]
Forested area (% of land area)	15.3	15.5	15.7[g]
Important sites for terrestrial biodiversity protected (%)	14.5	17.8	18.6[f]
Pop. using safely managed drinking water (urban/rural, %)	59.9 / 49.5	59.4 / 55.8	59.7 / 62.4[d]
Pop. using safely managed sanitation (urban/rural %)	32.4 / 25.4	36.3 / 37.1	39.9 / 49.1[d]

a Projected estimate (medium fertility variant). b Calculated by the UNSD. c 2017. d 2020. e Estimate. f 2021. g 2019. h Data refers to a 5-year period preceding the reference year. i Data are as at 1 January of reporting year.

Western Asia

Region	Asia	Population (000, 2022)	293 720[a]
Surface area (km2)	4 805 058[b]	Pop. density (per km2, 2022)	61.3[a]
Sex ratio (m per 100 f)	109.2[a]		

Economic indicators	2010	2015	2022
GDP: Gross domestic product (million current US$)	2 558 661	2 967 016	2 964 651[b]
GDP growth rate (annual %, const. 2015 prices)	5.7	3.7	- 3.4[b]
GDP per capita (current US$)	11 021.9	11 529.3	10 614.4[b]
Employment in agriculture (% of employed)[c,d]	10.8	10.6	9.0[b]
Employment in industry (% of employed)[c,d]	27.2	26.2	25.8[b]
Employment in services & other sectors (% employed)[c,d]	62.0	63.2	65.1[b]
Unemployment rate (% of labour force)[c,e]	7.1	7.6	9.2
Labour force participation rate (female/male pop. %)[c,e]	16.8 / 74.5	18.6 / 75.7	19.3 / 76.3
Agricultural production index (2014-2016=100)	92	101	117[b]
International trade: exports (million current US$)	919 156	976 785	1 413 972[f]
International trade: imports (million current US$)	749 249	953 680	1 070 016[f]
International trade: balance (million current US$)	169 907	23 105	343 955[f]

Social indicators	2010	2015	2022
Population growth rate (average annual %)	2.2	1.9	1.5[a]
Urban population (% of total population)	68.2	70.4	72.0[g]
Urban population growth rate (average annual %)[h]	3.2	2.7	...
Fertility rate, total (live births per woman)	3.0	2.9	2.6[a]
Life expectancy at birth (females/males, years)	75.9 / 70.5	76.4 / 70.9	77.4 / 72.0[a]
Population age distribution (0-14/60+ years old, %)	31.2 / 6.7	30.3 / 7.4	28.7 / 8.6[a]
International migrant stock (000/% of total pop.)	30 686.4 / 13.2	39 897.2 / 15.5	46 599.8 / 16.7[b]
Infant mortality rate (per 1 000 live births)	21.9	20.3	17.6[a]
Education: Primary gross enrol. ratio (f/m per 100 pop.)	98.1 / 105.5	96.9 / 103.0[c]	94.2 / 100.1[c,b]
Education: Sec. gross enrol. ratio (f/m per 100 pop.)	72.2 / 79.7	80.2 / 85.3[c]	80.5 / 86.7[c,b]
Education: Upr. Sec. gross enrol. ratio (f/m per 100 pop.)	60.3 / 66.7	76.7 / 82.1[c]	74.9 / 82.5[c,b]
Intentional homicide rate (per 100 000 pop.)[c]	3.7	4.3	4.7[b]
Seats held by women in the National Parliament (%)	9.3	12.8	16.6[i]

Environment and infrastructure indicators	2010	2015	2022
Individuals using the Internet (per 100 inhabitants)	32.7	50.8	72.0[b]
Research & Development expenditure (% of GDP)	0.7	0.8	0.9[b]
Forested area (% of land area)	6.1	6.2	6.3[g]
Important sites for terrestrial biodiversity protected (%)	16.1	17.7	18.4[f]
Pop. using safely managed sanitation (urban/rural %)	57.6 / ...	61.3 / ...	64.3 / 45.9[b]

a Projected estimate (medium fertility variant). b 2020. c Estimate. d Data excludes Armenia, Azerbaijan, Cyprus, Georgia, Israel and Türkiye. e Data excludes Armenia, Azerbaijan, Cyprus, Georgia and Türkiye f 2021. g 2019. h Data refers to a 5-year period preceding the reference year. i Data are as at 1 January of reporting year.

Region	World	Population (000, 2022)	743 556[a]
Surface area (km2)	22 134 900[b]	Pop. density (per km2, 2022)	33.7[a]
Sex ratio (m per 100 f)	93.3[a]		

Economic indicators

	2010	2015	2022
GDP: Gross domestic product (million current US$)	19 903 213	19 212 558	21 010 469[b]
GDP growth rate (annual %, const. 2015 prices)	2.4	1.9	- 6.1[b]
GDP per capita (current US$)	26 963.3	25 793.1	28 031.3[b]
Agricultural production index (2014-2016=100)	90	100	103[b]
International trade: exports (million current US$)	5 904 975	6 090 837	7 923 044[c]
International trade: imports (million current US$)	5 868 691	5 730 577	7 768 375[c]
International trade: balance (million current US$)	36 284	360 260	154 669[c]

Social indicators

	2010	2015	2022
Population growth rate (average annual %)	0.2	0.2	- 0.3[a]
Urban population (% of total population)	72.9	73.9	74.7[d]
Urban population growth rate (average annual %)[e]	0.5	0.3	...
Fertility rate, total (live births per woman)	1.6	1.6	1.5[a]
Life expectancy at birth (females/males, years)	80.2 / 72.8	81.3 / 74.6	80.8 / 74.0[a]
Population age distribution (0-14/60+ years old, %)	15.5 / 22.0	15.8 / 23.8	15.7 / 26.3[a]
International migrant stock (000/% of total pop.)	70 627.2 / 9.6	74 759.1 / 10.1	86 706.1 / 11.6[b]
Refugees and others of concern to the UNHCR (000)	...	4 673.8	6 932.6[c]
Infant mortality rate (per 1 000 live births)	5.3	4.5	3.5[a]
Education: Primary gross enrol. ratio (f/m per 100 pop.)	101.5 / 102.1	100.7 / 100.6	100.9 / 101.1[f,b]
Education: Sec. gross enrol. ratio (f/m per 100 pop.)	100.3 / 101.1	106.6 / 107.0	105.7 / 106.0[f,b]
Education: Upr. Sec. gross enrol. ratio (f/m per 100 pop.)	100.2 / 101.0	112.2 / 112.0	110.8 / 110.4[f,b]
Intentional homicide rate (per 100 000 pop.)[f]	3.5	3.5	2.6[b]
Seats held by women in the National Parliament (%)	23.2	26.7	32.6[g]

Environment and infrastructure indicators

	2010	2015	2022
Individuals using the Internet (per 100 inhabitants)	62.5	74.3	85.2[b]
Research & Development expenditure (% of GDP)	1.7	1.8	2.0[b]
Forested area (% of land area)	45.8	45.9	46.0[d]
Energy production, primary (Petajoules)	102 656	101 283	107 259[d]
Energy supply per capita (Gigajoules)	152	140	142[d]
Important sites for terrestrial biodiversity protected (%)	62.5	65.7	67.2[c]
Pop. using safely managed drinking water (urban/rural, %)	95.1 / 84.2	95.2 / 87.5	95.3 / 88.2[b]
Pop. using safely managed sanitation (urban/rural %)	76.8 / 45.9	79.3 / 47.5	80.9 / 49.3[b]

a Projected estimate (medium fertility variant). b 2020. c 2021. d 2019. e Data refers to a 5-year period preceding the reference year. f Estimate. g Data are as at 1 January of reporting year.

Eastern Europe

Region	Europe	Population (000, 2022)	289 626 [a]
Surface area (km2)	18 052 768 [b]	Pop. density (per km2, 2022)	16.0 [a]
Sex ratio (m per 100 f)	88.8 [a]		

Economic indicators	2010	2015	2022
GDP: Gross domestic product (million current US$)	2 868 904	2 626 882	3 132 805 [b]
GDP growth rate (annual %, const. 2015 prices)	3.4	0.2	- 3.3 [b]
GDP per capita (current US$)	9 729.3	8 923.1	10 691.7 [b]
Employment in agriculture (% of employed) [c]	11.7	9.8	8.4 [b]
Employment in industry (% of employed) [c]	28.6	28.1	28.2 [b]
Employment in services & other sectors (% employed) [c]	59.7	62.0	63.4 [b]
Unemployment rate (% of labour force) [c]	8.0	6.6	4.9
Labour force participation rate (female/male pop. %) [c]	52.4 / 66.4	52.4 / 67.6	51.6 / 67.0
Agricultural production index (2014-2016=100)	81	98	105 [b]
International trade: exports (million current US$)	994 605	1 023 967	1 534 414 [d]
International trade: imports (million current US$)	868 649	847 926	1 369 875 [d]
International trade: balance (million current US$)	125 955	176 042	164 539 [d]

Social indicators	2010	2015	2022
Population growth rate (average annual %)	- 0.1	–0.0	- 0.7 [a]
Urban population (% of total population)	68.9	69.3	69.8 [e]
Urban population growth rate (average annual %) [f]	- 0.1	–0.0	...
Fertility rate, total (live births per woman)	1.5	1.7	1.5 [a]
Life expectancy at birth (females/males, years)	76.5 / 66.3	78.3 / 68.8	76.5 / 66.7 [a]
Population age distribution (0-14/60+ years old, %)	15.0 / 19.4	16.0 / 21.4	16.6 / 24.1 [a]
International migrant stock (000/% of total pop.)	19 110.7 / 6.5	19 834.0 / 6.7	20 835.4 / 7.1 [b]
Infant mortality rate (per 1 000 live births)	7.5	5.8	4.4 [a]
Intentional homicide rate (per 100 000 pop.) [c]	6.9	7.2	5.0 [b]
Seats held by women in the National Parliament (%)	15.2	16.9	22.5 [g]

Environment and infrastructure indicators	2010	2015	2022
Forested area (% of land area)	47.6	47.7	47.7 [e]
Pop. using safely managed drinking water (urban/rural, %)	... / 68.8	... / 75.3	... / 76.6 [b]
Pop. using safely managed sanitation (urban/rural %)	57.7 / ...	61.3 / ...	63.8 / ... [b]

a Projected estimate (medium fertility variant). b 2020. c Estimate. d 2021. e 2019. f Data refers to a 5-year period preceding the reference year. g Data are as at 1 January of reporting year.

Region	Europe	Population (000, 2022)	106 550[a]
Surface area (km2)	1 702 418[b]	Pop. density (per km2, 2022)	65.0[a]
Sex ratio (m per 100 f)	97.9[a,c]		

Economic indicators

	2010	2015	2022
GDP: Gross domestic product (million current US$)	4 302 905	4 785 125	4 862 131[b]
GDP growth rate (annual %, const. 2015 prices)	2.4	3.8	- 6.2[b]
GDP per capita (current US$)	42 983.5	46 357.5	45 889.3[b]
Employment in agriculture (% of employed)[d]	2.2	2.1	1.7[b]
Employment in industry (% of employed)[d]	19.9	19.3	18.5[b]
Employment in services & other sectors (% employed)[d]	78.0	78.7	79.8[b]
Unemployment rate (% of labour force)[d]	8.6	6.1	4.8
Labour force participation rate (female/male pop. %)[d]	56.6 / 68.3	57.4 / 67.9	58.4 / 67.5
Agricultural production index (2014-2016=100)	92	102	102[b]
International trade: exports (million current US$)	1 045 978	1 045 828	1 310 306[e]
International trade: imports (million current US$)	1 122 240	1 132 508	1 400 669[e]
International trade: balance (million current US$)	- 76 262	- 86 680	- 90 363[e]

Social indicators

	2010	2015	2022
Population growth rate (average annual %)[c]	0.7	0.6	0.3[a]
Urban population (% of total population)	80.1	81.4	82.4[f]
Urban population growth rate (average annual %)[g]	1.1	0.9	...
Fertility rate, total (live births per woman)[c]	1.9	1.8	1.6[a]
Life expectancy at birth (females/males, years)[c]	82.2 / 77.6	82.8 / 78.6	83.8 / 80.0[a]
Population age distribution (0-14/60+ years old, %)[c]	17.5 / 22.5	17.6 / 23.5	17.2 / 25.4[a]
International migrant stock (000/% of total pop.)	11 294.9 / 11.3	13 191.1 / 12.7	14 973.9 / 14.1[b]
Infant mortality rate (per 1 000 live births)[c]	4.0	3.5	2.8[a]
Intentional homicide rate (per 100 000 pop.)[d]	1.5	1.2	1.2[b]
Seats held by women in the National Parliament (%)	29.6	30.4	37.0[h]

Environment and infrastructure indicators

	2010	2015	2022
Forested area (% of land area)	44.0	44.2	44.3[f]
Pop. using safely managed sanitation (urban/rural %)	96.4 / 85.4	97.2 / 86.5	97.5 / 87.1[b]

a Projected estimate (medium fertility variant). **b** 2020. **c** Including the Faroe Islands and the Isle of Man. **d** Estimate. **e** 2021. **f** 2019. **g** Data refers to a 5-year period preceding the reference year. **h** Data are as at 1 January of reporting year.

Southern Europe

Region	Europe	Population (000, 2022)	151 760[a]
Surface area (km2)	1 294 920[b]	Pop. density (per km2, 2022)	116.5[a]
Sex ratio (m per 100 f)	95.3[a,c]		

Economic indicators	2010	2015	2022
GDP: Gross domestic product (million current US$)	4 302 464	3 622 151	3 830 526[b]
GDP growth rate (annual %, const. 2015 prices)	0.7	1.9	- 9.3[b]
GDP per capita (current US$)	28 124.1	23 669.5	25 170.9[b]
Employment in agriculture (% of employed)[d]	7.6	6.9	6.1[b]
Employment in industry (% of employed)[d]	25.8	23.5	23.4[b]
Employment in services & other sectors (% employed)[d]	66.6	69.6	70.5[b]
Unemployment rate (% of labour force)[d]	14.3	17.2	11.1
Labour force participation rate (female/male pop. %)[d]	44.7 / 62.6	45.8 / 61.4	45.9 / 60.0
Agricultural production index (2014-2016=100)	101	101	108[b]
International trade: exports (million current US$)	830 354	886 303	1 234 638[e]
International trade: imports (million current US$)	1 039 442	925 163	1 325 795[e]
International trade: balance (million current US$)	- 209 088	- 38 860	- 91 157[e]

Social indicators	2010	2015	2022
Population growth rate (average annual %)[c]	0.2	- 0.2	- 0.3[a]
Urban population (% of total population)	69.2	70.6	71.8[f]
Urban population growth rate (average annual %)[g]	0.9	0.2	...
Fertility rate, total (live births per woman)[c]	1.5	1.4	1.3[a]
Life expectancy at birth (females/males, years)[c]	83.5 / 78.0	83.9 / 78.8	84.6 / 79.8[a]
Population age distribution (0-14/60+ years old, %)[c]	14.9 / 24.0	14.6 / 25.8	13.5 / 28.6[a]
International migrant stock (000/% of total pop.)	16 206.3 / 10.6	15 815.5 / 10.3	17 665.7 / 11.6[b]
Infant mortality rate (per 1 000 live births)[c]	3.8	3.3	2.7[a]
Intentional homicide rate (per 100 000 pop.)[d]	1.1	0.8	0.7[b]
Seats held by women in the National Parliament (%)	23.0	30.0	34.8[h]

Environment and infrastructure indicators	2010	2015	2022
Forested area (% of land area)	34.9	35.3	35.5[f]
Pop. using safely managed drinking water (urban/rural, %)	96.9 / 93.4	96.8 / 93.0	96.8 / 92.7[b]
Pop. using safely managed sanitation (urban/rural %)	78.4 / 55.0	80.9 / 57.2	82.5 / 61.0[b]

a Projected estimate (medium fertility variant). b 2020. c Including Andorra, Gibraltar, Holy See, and San Marino. d Estimate. e 2021. f 2019. g Data refers to a 5-year period preceding the reference year. h Data are as at 1 January of reporting year.

Region	Europe	Population (000, 2022)	195 620[a]
Surface area (km2)	1 084 794[b]	Pop. density (per km2, 2022)	179.6[a]
Sex ratio (m per 100 f)	96.3[a,c]		

Economic indicators	2010	2015	2022
GDP: Gross domestic product (million current US$)	8 428 940	8 178 400	9 185 006[b]
GDP growth rate (annual %, const. 2015 prices)	3.0	1.5	- 5.4[b]
GDP per capita (current US$)	44 316.4	42 107.3	46 298.1[b]
Employment in agriculture (% of employed)[d]	2.4	2.1	1.8[b]
Employment in industry (% of employed)[d]	24.7	23.6	22.9[b]
Employment in services & other sectors (% employed)[d]	72.9	74.2	75.3[b]
Unemployment rate (% of labour force)[d]	7.2	6.9	4.9
Labour force participation rate (female/male pop. %)[d]	53.0 / 65.3	54.0 / 64.6	55.3 / 64.2
Agricultural production index (2014-2016=100)	95	101	96[b]
International trade: exports (million current US$)	3 034 038	3 134 738	3 843 686[e]
International trade: imports (million current US$)	2 838 360	2 824 980	3 672 036[e]
International trade: balance (million current US$)	195 679	309 758	171 650[e]

Social indicators	2010	2015	2022
Population growth rate (average annual %)[c]	0.4	0.4	0.1[a]
Urban population (% of total population)	78.5	79.4	80.0[f]
Urban population growth rate (average annual %)[g]	0.6	0.6	...
Fertility rate, total (live births per woman)[c]	1.7	1.7	1.6[a]
Life expectancy at birth (females/males, years)[c]	83.3 / 77.8	83.8 / 78.7	84.5 / 79.6[a]
Population age distribution (0-14/60+ years old, %)[c]	15.8 / 24.2	15.5 / 25.8	15.4 / 28.3[a]
International migrant stock (000/% of total pop.)	24 015.3 / 12.8	25 918.6 / 13.5	33 231.1 / 16.9[b]
Infant mortality rate (per 1 000 live births)[c]	3.6	3.4	3.1[a]
Intentional homicide rate (per 100 000 pop.)[d]	1.2	1.2	1.2[b]
Seats held by women in the National Parliament (%)	28.4	32.0	38.2[h]

Environment and infrastructure indicators	2010	2015	2022
Forested area (% of land area)	31.4	31.8	32.1[f]
Pop. using safely managed drinking water (urban/rural, %)	98.9 / ...	99.4 / ...	99.6 / ...[b]
Pop. using safely managed sanitation (urban/rural %)	97.9 / 83.6	98.2 / 84.0	98.3 / 84.3[b]

a Projected estimate (medium fertility variant). b 2020. c Including Liechtenstein and Monaco. d Estimate. e 2021. f 2019. g Data refers to a 5-year period preceding the reference year. h Data are as at 1 January of reporting year.

Oceania

Region	World	Population (000, 2022)	45 039[a]
Surface area (km2)	8 486 460[b]	Pop. density (per km2, 2022)	5.3[a]
Sex ratio (m per 100 f)	100.6[a]		

Economic indicators	2010	2015	2022
GDP: Gross domestic product (million current US$)	1 482 602	1 470 813	1 684 384[b]
GDP growth rate (annual %, const. 2015 prices)	2.4	3.0	1.0[b]
GDP per capita (current US$)	40 521.4	37 169.7	39 742.8[b]
Unemployment rate (% of labour force)[c]	5.0	5.5	4.6
Labour force participation rate (female/male pop. %)[c]	57.0 / 68.9	57.3 / 67.7	58.0 / 66.7
Agricultural production index (2014-2016=100)	86	101	92[b]
International trade: exports (million current US$)	253 360	235 133	431 679[d]
International trade: imports (million current US$)	247 608	251 607	347 434[d]
International trade: balance (million current US$)	5 752	- 16 475	84 246[d]

Social indicators	2010	2015	2022
Population growth rate (average annual %)	1.7	1.7	1.2[a]
Urban population (% of total population)	68.1	68.1	68.2[e]
Urban population growth rate (average annual %)[f]	1.8	1.5	...
Fertility rate, total (live births per woman)	2.5	2.4	2.1[a]
Life expectancy at birth (females/males, years)	79.8 / 75.0	80.7 / 75.7	81.6 / 76.8[a]
Population age distribution (0-14/60+ years old, %)	24.3 / 14.9	23.9 / 15.9	22.9 / 17.7[a]
International migrant stock (000/% of total pop.)	7 128.6 / 19.3	8 072.3 / 20.3	9 380.7 / 22.0[b]
Refugees and others of concern to the UNHCR (000)	...	71.3	167.5[d]
Infant mortality rate (per 1 000 live births)	20.0	18.1	15.7[a]
Education: Primary gross enrol. ratio (f/m per 100 pop.)	96.4 / 99.4	101.8 / 104.8	104.2 / 106.7[c,b]
Education: Sec. gross enrol. ratio (f/m per 100 pop.)	107.1 / 114.7[c]	104.2 / 116.8	101.0 / 107.4[c,b]
Education: Upr. Sec. gross enrol. ratio (f/m per 100 pop.)	111.3 / 121.0[c]	107.3 / 121.8	121.5 / 126.6[c,b]
Intentional homicide rate (per 100 000 pop.)[c]	2.9	2.9	3.1[b]
Seats held by women in the National Parliament (%)	13.2	13.2	17.9[g]

Environment and infrastructure indicators	2010	2015	2022
Individuals using the Internet (per 100 inhabitants)	57.3	65.4	71.0[b]
Research & Development expenditure (% of GDP)	2.2	1.8	1.7[b]
Forested area (% of land area)	21.3	21.7	21.8[e]
Energy production, primary (Petajoules)	14 530	17 074	19 624[e]
Energy supply per capita (Gigajoules)	176	166	160[e]
Important sites for terrestrial biodiversity protected (%)	30.2	33.2	35.3[d]
Pop. using safely managed drinking water (urban/rural, %)	93.6 / ...	94.3 / ...	94.2 / ...[b]
Pop. using safely managed sanitation (urban/rural %)	61.7 / 22.3	66.1 / 23.3	70.2 / 23.9[b]

a Projected estimate (medium fertility variant). b 2020. c Estimate. d 2021. e 2019. f Data refers to a 5-year period preceding the reference year. g Data are as at 1 January of reporting year.

Australia and New Zealand

Region	Oceania	Population (000, 2022)	31 363[a]
Surface area (km2)	7 945 610[b]	Pop. density (per km2, 2022)	3.9[a]
Sex ratio (m per 100 f)	98.6[a]		

Economic indicators	2010	2015	2022
GDP: Gross domestic product (million current US$)	1 445 981	1 425 699	1 635 517[b]
GDP growth rate (annual %, const. 2015 prices)	2.3	3.0	1.2[b]
GDP per capita (current US$)	54 514.4	49 942.1	53 938.1[b]
Agricultural production index (2014-2016=100)	86	101	91[b]
International trade: exports (million current US$)	243 502	222 149	415 402[c]
International trade: imports (million current US$)	232 319	236 642	311 468[c]
International trade: balance (million current US$)	11 183	- 14 493	103 934[c]

Social indicators	2010	2015	2022
Population growth rate (average annual %)	1.4	1.5	1.0[a]
Urban population (% of total population)	85.3	85.8	86.2[d]
Urban population growth rate (average annual %)[e]	1.8	1.5	...
Fertility rate, total (live births per woman)	2.0	1.8	1.6[a]
Life expectancy at birth (females/males, years)	84.0 / 79.7	84.5 / 80.5	85.3 / 81.6[a]
Population age distribution (0-14/60+ years old, %)	19.4 / 18.9	19.1 / 20.3	18.3 / 22.5[a]
International migrant stock (000/% of total pop.)	6 830.4 / 25.8	7 769.5 / 27.2	9 067.6 / 29.9[b]
Infant mortality rate (per 1 000 live births)	4.3	3.3	2.9[a]
Intentional homicide rate (per 100 000 pop.)[f]	1.0	1.0	1.2[b]
Seats held by women in the National Parliament (%)	30.1	28.8	39.1[g]

Environment and infrastructure indicators	2010	2015	2022
Individuals using the Internet (per 100 inhabitants)	76.7	84.7	89.9[b]
Research & Development expenditure (% of GDP)	2.2	1.8	1.8[b]
Forested area (% of land area)	17.5	18.0	18.1[d]
Important sites for terrestrial biodiversity protected (%)	46.1	50.9	54.2[c]
Pop. using safely managed drinking water (urban/rural, %)	95.7 / ...	96.5 / ...	96.5 / ...[b]

a Projected estimate (medium fertility variant). b 2020. c 2021. d 2019. e Data refers to a 5-year period preceding the reference year. f Estimate. g Data are as at 1 January of reporting year.

Melanesia

Region	Oceania	Population (000, 2022)	12 413[a]
Surface area (km2)	529 590[b]	Pop. density (per km2, 2022)	23.4[a]
Sex ratio (m per 100 f)	+05.6[a]		

Economic indicators	2010	2015	2022
GDP: Gross domestic product (million current US$)	28 350	37 207	40 223[b]
GDP growth rate (annual %, const. 2015 prices)	8.1	4.6	- 4.7[b]
GDP per capita (current US$)	3 085.6	3 676.0	3 616.2[b]
Agricultural production index (2014-2016=100)	91	101	102[b]
International trade: exports (million current US$)	8 112	10 998	12 244[c]
International trade: imports (million current US$)	9 665	7 968	10 917[c]
International trade: balance (million current US$)	- 1 553	3 030	1 327[c]

Social indicators	2010	2015	2022
Population growth rate (average annual %)	2.7	2.2	1.8[a]
Urban population (% of total population)	19.0	19.2	19.5[d]
Urban population growth rate (average annual %)[e]	2.3	2.2	...
Fertility rate, total (live births per woman)	3.8	3.5	3.1[a]
Life expectancy at birth (females/males, years)	66.6 / 62.5	68.6 / 63.2	70.0 / 64.4[a]
Population age distribution (0-14/60+ years old, %)	37.1 / 4.8	36.0 / 5.1	34.0 / 6.1[a]
International migrant stock (000/% of total pop.)	110.7 / 1.2	119.3 / 1.2	124.1 / 1.1[b]
Infant mortality rate (per 1 000 live births)	40.5	36.4	30.9[a]
Intentional homicide rate (per 100 000 pop.)[f]	8.3	8.2	8.2[b]
Seats held by women in the National Parliament (%)	1.4	4.2	5.3[g]

Environment and infrastructure indicators	2010	2015	2022
Forested area (% of land area)	77.5	77.3	77.1[d]

a Projected estimate (medium fertility variant). **b** 2020. **c** 2021. **d** 2019. **e** Data refers to a 5-year period preceding the reference year. **f** Estimate. **g** Data are as at 1 January of reporting year.

Micronesia

			Population (000, 2022)	539[a]
Region	Oceania		Pop. density (per km2, 2022)	174.8[a]
Surface area (km2)	3 170[b]			
Sex ratio (m per 100 f)	101.4[a,c]			

Economic indicators	2010	2015	2022
GDP: Gross domestic product (million current US$)	856	1 054	1 227[b]
GDP growth rate (annual %, const. 2015 prices)	2.4	7.5	- 3.4[b]
GDP per capita (current US$)	2 949.0	3 452.9	3 803.5[b]
Agricultural production index (2014-2016=100)	94	99	96[b]
International trade: exports (million current US$)	1 508	1 766	3 502[d]
International trade: imports (million current US$)	3 292	4 721	22 195[d]
International trade: balance (million current US$)	- 1 783	- 2 955	- 18 693[d]

Social indicators	2010	2015	2022
Population growth rate (average annual %)[c]	- 0.1	0.3	1.0[a]
Urban population (% of total population)	66.6	67.9	69.0[e]
Urban population growth rate (average annual %)[f]	0.2	1.0	...
Fertility rate, total (live births per woman)[c]	3.2	3.0	2.8[a]
Life expectancy at birth (females/males, years)[c]	73.7 / 68.6	74.2 / 68.7	75.7 / 69.8[a]
Population age distribution (0-14/60+ years old, %)[c]	32.1 / 7.1	30.9 / 8.9	29.6 / 12.0[a]
International migrant stock (000/% of total pop.)	114.7 / 22.8	113.5 / 21.7	118.9 / 21.7[b]
Infant mortality rate (per 1 000 live births)[c]	27.1	25.9	22.0[a]
Intentional homicide rate (per 100 000 pop.)[g]	2.9	4.1	3.9[b]
Seats held by women in the National Parliament (%)	2.4	4.7	7.1[h]

Environment and infrastructure indicators	2010	2015	2022
Forested area (% of land area)	53.5	53.7	53.2[e]
Pop. using safely managed drinking water (urban/rural, %)	72.7 / 31.6	72.7 / 30.5	72.3 / 29.4[b]

a Projected estimate (medium fertility variant). b 2020. c Including Marshall Islands, Nauru, Northern Mariana Islands and Palau. d 2021. e 2019. f Data refers to a 5-year period preceding the reference year. g Estimate. h Data are as at 1 January of reporting year.

Polynesia

Region	Oceania	Population (000, 2022)	724[a,b]
Surface area (km2)	8 090[c]	Pop. density (per km2, 2022)	89.9[a]
Sex ratio (m per 100 f)	101.4[a,b]		

Economic indicators	2010	2015	2022
GDP: Gross domestic product (million current US$)	7 416	6 852	7 418[c]
GDP growth rate (annual %, const. 2015 prices)	- 1.9	2.5	- 8.1[c]
GDP per capita (current US$)	12 670.7	11 495.0	12 074.1[c]
Agricultural production index (2014-2016=100)	107	102	96[c]
International trade: exports (million current US$)	238	219	532[d]
International trade: imports (million current US$)	2 333	2 277	2 854[d]
International trade: balance (million current US$)	- 2 095	- 2 058	- 2 322[d]

Social indicators	2010	2015	2022
Population growth rate (average annual %)[b]	0.5	0.3	0.9[a]
Urban population (% of total population)	44.3	44.5	44.4[e]
Urban population growth rate (average annual %)[f]	0.9	0.6	...
Fertility rate, total (live births per woman)[b]	3.2	2.9	2.6[a]
Life expectancy at birth (females/males, years)[b]	77.9 / 72.9	78.7 / 73.9	79.7 / 74.8[a]
Population age distribution (0-14/60+ years old, %)[b]	32.3 / 8.5	31.0 / 9.6	28.8 / 12.0[a]
International migrant stock (000/% of total pop.)[b]	72.7 / 11.1	70.0 / 10.5	70.1 / 10.3[c]
Infant mortality rate (per 1 000 live births)[b]	11.9	11.3	10.7[a]
Intentional homicide rate (per 100 000 pop.)[g]	3.8	2.3	3.0[c]
Seats held by women in the National Parliament (%)	5.2	4.4	6.4[h]

Environment and infrastructure indicators	2010	2015	2022
Forested area (% of land area)	48.7	48.4	48.1[e]
Pop. using safely managed drinking water (urban/rural, %)	87.4 / 62.7	85.2 / 61.2	82.5 / 58.8[c]
Pop. using safely managed sanitation (urban/rural %)	... / 43.1	... / 42.5	... / 42.2[c]

a Projected estimate (medium fertility variant). b Including Pitcairn. c 2020. d 2021. e 2019. f Data refers to a 5-year period preceding the reference year. g Estimate. h Data are as at 1 January of reporting year.

Afghanistan

Region	Southern Asia	UN membership date	19 November 1946
Population (000, 2022)	41 129[a]	Surface area (km2)	652 864[b]
Pop. density (per km2, 2022)	63.3[a]	Sex ratio (m per 100 f)	102.0[a]
Capital city	Kabul	National currency	Afghani (AFN)
Capital city pop. (000, 2022)	4 114.0[c]	Exchange rate (per US$)	77.1[b]

Economic indicators	2010	2015	2022
GDP: Gross domestic product (million current US$)	14 699	18 713	19 793[b]
GDP growth rate (annual %, const. 2015 prices)	5.2	- 1.4	- 1.9[b]
GDP per capita (current US$)	503.6	543.8	508.5[b]
Economy: Agriculture (% of Gross Value Added)[d]	33.2	27.3	28.3[e,b]
Economy: Industry (% of Gross Value Added)[d]	13.0	10.8	13.1[f,b]
Economy: Services and other activity (% of GVA)[d]	53.8	61.9	58.7[g,b]
Employment in agriculture (% of employed)[h]	54.7	47.1	42.4[b]
Employment in industry (% of employed)[h]	14.4	17.0	18.3[b]
Employment in services & other sectors (% employed)[h]	30.9	35.8	39.4[b]
Unemployment rate (% of labour force)[h]	11.4	11.1	18.5
Labour force participation rate (female/male pop. %)[h]	15.1 / 76.8	18.7 / 73.9	14.4 / 68.1
CPI: Consumer Price Index (2010=100)	100	133	150[c]
Agricultural production index (2014-2016=100)	93	96	118[b]
International trade: exports (million current US$)	388	571	765[h,i]
International trade: imports (million current US$)	5 154	7 723	5 493[h,i]
International trade: balance (million current US$)	- 4 766	- 7 151	- 4 728[i]
Balance of payments, current account (million US$)	- 578	- 4 193	- 3 137[b]

Major trading partners					2021
Export partners (% of exports)[h]	India	47.1	Pakistan	34.3	China	3.6
Import partners (% of imports)[h]	Iran	14.6	China	13.9	Pakistan	12.9

Social indicators	2010	2015	2022
Population growth rate (average annual %)	2.7	2.3	2.7[a]
Urban population (% of total population)	23.7	24.8	25.8[c]
Urban population growth rate (average annual %)[j]	3.7	4.0	...
Fertility rate, total (live births per woman)	6.1	5.4	4.5[a]
Life expectancy at birth (females/males, years)	62.4 / 59.3	64.6 / 60.8	66.2 / 59.8[a]
Population age distribution (0-14/60+ years old, %)	49.0 / 3.8	45.8 / 3.8	43.1 / 3.8[a]
International migrant stock (000/% of total pop.)[k]	102.3 / 0.4	339.4 / 1.0	144.1 / 0.4[b]
Refugees and others of concern to the UNHCR (000)	1 200.0	1 421.4	3 363.2[i]
Infant mortality rate (per 1 000 live births)	64.8	54.5	40.8[a]
Health: Current expenditure (% of GDP)[l]	8.6	10.1	13.2[h,c]
Health: Physicians (per 1 000 pop.)	0.2	0.3	0.3[b]
Education: Government expenditure (% of GDP)	3.5	3.3	3.2[c]
Education: Primary gross enrol. ratio (f/m per 100 pop.)	80.6 / 118.6	83.5 / 122.7	85.4 / 127.1[c]
Education: Sec. gross enrol. ratio (f/m per 100 pop.)	33.3 / 66.9	36.8 / 65.9	40.0 / 70.1[m]
Education: Upr. Sec. gross enrol. ratio (f/m per 100 pop.)	17.8 / 42.7	27.1 / 52.6	28.5 / 52.4[m]
Intentional homicide rate (per 100 000 pop.)	3.4	9.8	6.7[m]
Seats held by women in the National Parliament (%)	27.3	27.7	27.0[n,o]

Environment and infrastructure indicators	2010	2015	2022
Individuals using the Internet (per 100 inhabitants)[h]	4.0	8.3	18.4[b]
Threatened species (number)	34	38	50
Forested area (% of land area)	1.9[h]	1.9[h]	1.9[c]
Energy production, primary (Petajoules)	41	61	82[c]
Energy supply per capita (Gigajoules)	5[h]	5	5[c]
Important sites for terrestrial biodiversity protected (%)	5.8	5.8	46.4[i]
Pop. using safely managed drinking water (urban/rural, %)	28.2 / 16.3	32.4 / 20.4	36.4 / 24.5[b]
Net Official Development Assist. received (% of GNI)	39.25	21.27	21.04[b]

a Projected estimate (medium fertility variant). b 2020. c 2019. d Data classified according to ISIC Rev. 4. e Excludes irrigation canals and landscaping care. f Excludes publishing activities. Includes irrigation and canals. g Includes publishing activities and landscape care. Excludes repair of personal and household goods. h Estimate. i 2021. j Data refers to a 5-year period preceding the reference year. k Including refugees. l Data based on calendar year (January 1 to December 31). m 2018. n Data corresponds to the composition of the House of the People elected in 2018. o Data are as at 1 January of reporting year.

Albania

Region	Southern Europe	UN membership date	14 December 1955
Population (000, 2022)	2 842[a]	Surface area (km2)	28 748[b]
Pop. density (per km2, 2022)	103.7[a]	Sex ratio (m per 100 f)	99.5[a]
Capital city	Tirana	National currency	Lek (ALL)
Capital city pop. (000, 2022)	484.6[c]	Exchange rate (per US$)	106.5[d]

Economic indicators	2010	2015	2022
GDP: Gross domestic product (million current US$)	11 927	11 387	14 910[b]
GDP growth rate (annual %, const. 2015 prices)	3.7	2.2	- 3.3[b]
GDP per capita (current US$)	4 045.7	3 939.4	5 180.9[b]
Economy: Agriculture (% of Gross Value Added)[e,f]	20.7	22.5	21.9[b]
Economy: Industry (% of Gross Value Added)[f,g]	28.7	24.8	22.9[b]
Economy: Services and other activity (% of GVA)[f,h]	50.7	52.7	55.2[b]
Employment in agriculture (% of employed)	42.1	41.4	36.1[i,b]
Employment in industry (% of employed)	20.6	18.6	20.2[i,b]
Employment in services & other sectors (% employed)	37.3	40.0	43.7[i,b]
Unemployment rate (% of labour force)	14.1	17.2	10.9[i]
Labour force participation rate (female/male pop. %)	46.7 / 63.8	46.9 / 64.0	50.4 / 65.6[i]
CPI: Consumer Price Index (2010=100)[j]	100	111	123[d]
Agricultural production index (2014-2016=100)	86	100	105[b]
International trade: exports (million current US$)[k]	1 550	1 930	3 200[i,d]
International trade: imports (million current US$)[k]	4 603	4 320	7 200[i,d]
International trade: balance (million current US$)[k]	- 3 053	- 2 391	- 3 999[d]
Balance of payments, current account (million US$)	- 1 356	- 980	- 1 393[d]

Major trading partners						2021
Export partners (% of exports)[i]	Italy	45.3	Serbia	12.1	Spain	6.0
Import partners (% of imports)[i]	Italy	25.2	Türkiye	9.6	China	9.0

Social indicators	2010	2015	2022
Population growth rate (average annual %)	- 0.5	--0.0	- 0.4[a]
Urban population (% of total population)	52.2	57.4	61.2[c]
Urban population growth rate (average annual %)[l]	1.3	1.8	...
Fertility rate, total (live births per woman)	1.7	1.6	1.4[a]
Life expectancy at birth (females/males, years)	80.7 / 75.5	81.2 / 76.4	79.5 / 74.5[a]
Population age distribution (0-14/60+ years old, %)	21.0 / 16.2	18.2 / 19.0	16.1 / 23.5[a]
International migrant stock (000/% of total pop.)	52.8 / 1.8	52.0 / 1.8	48.8 / 1.7[b]
Refugees and others of concern to the UNHCR (000)	0.1[m]	8.1	2.7[d]
Infant mortality rate (per 1 000 live births)	11.9	8.6	8.2[a]
Health: Current expenditure (% of GDP)	4.7	4.9	5.2[n]
Health: Physicians (per 1 000 pop.)	1.2	1.3[o]	1.9[b]
Education: Government expenditure (% of GDP)	3.3[p]	3.4	3.9[o]
Education: Primary gross enrol. ratio (f/m per 100 pop.)	93.8 / 93.2	107.3 / 104.0	101.6 / 98.9[b]
Education: Sec. gross enrol. ratio (f/m per 100 pop.)	88.4 / 87.9	95.1 / 99.5	95.3 / 93.4[b]
Education: Upr. Sec. gross enrol. ratio (f/m per 100 pop.)	79.0 / 81.1	89.6 / 99.6	90.8 / 90.3[b]
Intentional homicide rate (per 100 000 pop.)	4.3	2.2	2.1[b]
Seats held by women in the National Parliament (%)	16.4	20.7	35.7[q]

Environment and infrastructure indicators	2010	2015	2022
Individuals using the Internet (per 100 inhabitants)	45.0	56.9[i]	72.2[r,s,b]
Research & Development expenditure (% of GDP)	0.2[t,u]	...	...
Threatened species (number)	100	112	156
Forested area (% of land area)[i]	28.5	28.8	28.8[c]
CO2 emission estimates (million tons/tons per capita)	4.1 / 1.4	4.0 / 1.3	3.5 / 1.2[b]
Energy production, primary (Petajoules)	69	87	71[c]
Energy supply per capita (Gigajoules)	31	31	32[c]
Tourist/visitor arrivals at national borders (000)[v,w]	2 191	3 784	2 604[b]
Important sites for terrestrial biodiversity protected (%)	39.3	47.7	48.6[d]
Pop. using safely managed sanitation (urban/rural %)	43.0 / 45.8	43.5 / 50.1	44.1 / 53.6[b]
Net Official Development Assist. received (% of GNI)	3.09	2.91	2.13[b]

a Projected estimate (medium fertility variant). **b** 2020. **c** 2019. **d** 2021. **e** Excludes irrigation canals and landscaping care. **f** Data classified according to ISIC Rev. 4. **g** Excludes publishing activities. Includes irrigation and canals. **h** Includes publishing activities and landscape care. Excludes repair of personal and household goods. **i** Estimate. **j** Calculated by the UNSD from national indices. **k** In 2020, the reported share of non-standard HS codes was relatively high. **l** Data refers to a 5-year period preceding the reference year. **m** Data as at the end of December. **n** 2018. **o** 2013. **p** 2007. **q** Data are as at 1 January of reporting year. **r** Users in the last 3 months. **s** Estimated based on % of internet users between 16-74. **t** Partial data. **u** 2008. **v** Excluding nationals residing abroad. **w** Including transit visitors.

Algeria

Region	Northern Africa		UN membership date		08 October 1962
Population (000, 2022)	44 903[a]		Surface area (km2)		2 381 741[b]
Pop. density (per km2, 2022)	18.9[a]		Sex ratio (m per 100 f)		103.7[a]
Capital city	Algiers		National currency		Algerian Dinar (DZD)
Capital city pop. (000, 2022)	2 729.3[c,d]		Exchange rate (per US$)		138.8[e]

Economic indicators

	2010	2015	2022
GDP: Gross domestic product (million current US$)	161 207	165 979	147 689[b]
GDP growth rate (annual %, const. 2015 prices)	3.6	3.7	- 4.9[b]
GDP per capita (current US$)	4 480.8	4 177.9	3 368.0[b]
Economy: Agriculture (% of Gross Value Added)[f]	8.6	12.1	14.6[b]
Economy: Industry (% of Gross Value Added)[f]	51.4	37.3	33.5[b]
Economy: Services and other activity (% of GVA)[f]	40.0	50.6	51.9[b]
Employment in agriculture (% of employed)[g]	11.9	10.3	9.7[b]
Employment in industry (% of employed)[g]	30.1	31.0	30.7[b]
Employment in services & other sectors (% employed)[g]	58.0	58.7	59.6[b]
Unemployment rate (% of labour force)	10.0	11.2	12.2[g]
Labour force participation rate (female/male pop. %)	14.2 / 68.9	16.3 / 66.8	16.2 / 65.6[g]
CPI: Consumer Price Index (2010=100)[h]	100	127	166[i,e]
Agricultural production index (2014-2016=100)	76	100	112[b]
International trade: exports (million current US$)	57 051	34 796	35 721[g,e]
International trade: imports (million current US$)	41 000	51 803	34 921[g,e]
International trade: balance (million current US$)	16 051	- 17 007	801[e]
Balance of payments, current account (million US$)	12 220	- 27 038	- 18 221[b]

Major trading partners

						2021
Export partners (% of exports)[g]	Italy	18.7	Spain	15.2	France	13.7
Import partners (% of imports)[g]	China	16.3	Russian Federation	11.4	France	11.3

Social indicators

	2010	2015	2022
Population growth rate (average annual %)	1.9	2.0	1.6[a]
Urban population (% of total population)	67.5	70.8	73.2[d]
Urban population growth rate (average annual %)[j]	2.8	2.9	...
Fertility rate, total (live births per woman)	2.8	3.0	2.8[a]
Life expectancy at birth (females/males, years)	74.9 / 72.8	76.8 / 74.5	78.5 / 75.9[a]
Population age distribution (0-14/60+ years old, %)	27.6 / 7.1	29.0 / 8.1	30.6 / 9.7[a]
International migrant stock (000/% of total pop.)[k]	217.3 / 0.6	239.5 / 0.6	250.4 / 0.6[b]
Refugees and others of concern to the UNHCR (000)	94.4[l]	100.0	100.1[e]
Infant mortality rate (per 1 000 live births)	23.0	21.2	16.6[a]
Health: Current expenditure (% of GDP)	5.1	7.0	6.2[d]
Health: Physicians (per 1 000 pop.)	1.2[m]	...	1.7[n]
Education: Government expenditure (% of GDP)	4.3[o]	...	6.1[g,d]
Education: Primary gross enrol. ratio (f/m per 100 pop.)	111.5 / 119.0	113.0 / 118.7	109.5 / 113.0[b]
Education: Sec. gross enrol. ratio (f/m per 100 pop.)	98.7 / 95.2	101.5 / 97.8[p]	... / ...
Education: Upr. Sec. gross enrol. ratio (f/m per 100 pop.)	69.7 / 49.2	72.8 / 52.6[p]	... / ...
Intentional homicide rate (per 100 000 pop.)	0.7	1.4	1.3[b]
Seats held by women in the National Parliament (%)	7.7	31.6	8.1[q]

Environment and infrastructure indicators

	2010	2015	2022
Individuals using the Internet (per 100 inhabitants)	12.5	38.2[g]	62.9[g,b]
Research & Development expenditure (% of GDP)	0.1[r,s]	...	0.5[t,u]
Threatened species (number)	105	114	180
Forested area (% of land area)	0.8	0.8	0.8[g,d]
CO2 emission estimates (million tons/tons per capita)	96.5 / 2.7	131.7 / 3.3	143.6 / 3.3[d]
Energy production, primary (Petajoules)	6 200	5 883	5 954[d]
Energy supply per capita (Gigajoules)	46	56	58[d]
Tourist/visitor arrivals at national borders (000)[v]	2 070	1 710	591[b]
Important sites for terrestrial biodiversity protected (%)	41.6	42.4	43.5[e]
Pop. using safely managed drinking water (urban/rural, %)	81.7 / 61.1	79.5 / 65.9	73.7 / 68.7[b]
Pop. using safely managed sanitation (urban/rural %)	18.0 / 23.6	17.0 / 23.1	15.9 / 22.6[b]
Net Official Development Assist. received (% of GNI)	0.13	0.04	0.15[b]

a Projected estimate (medium fertility variant). **b** 2020. **c** Refers to the Governorate of Grand Algiers. **d** 2019. **e** 2021. **f** Data classified according to ISIC Rev. 4. **g** Estimate. **h** Algiers **i** Calculated by the UNSD from national indices. **j** Data refers to a 5-year period preceding the reference year. **k** Including refugees. **l** Data as at the end of December. **m** 2007. **n** 2018. **o** 2008. **p** 2011. **q** Data are as at 1 January of reporting year. **r** Partial data. **s** 2005. **t** Break in the time series. **u** 2017. **v** Including nationals residing abroad.

American Samoa

Region	Polynesia	Population (000, 2022)	44 a,b
Surface area (km2)	199 c	Pop. density (per km2, 2022)	221.4 a,b
Sex ratio (m per 100 f)	97.6 a,b	Capital city	Pago Pago
National currency	US Dollar (USD)	Capital city pop. (000, 2022)	48.5 d

Economic indicators	2010	2015	2022
Employment in agriculture (% of employed)	3.0 e,f,g	...	...
Employment in industry (% of employed)	23.2 e,f,g	...	...
Employment in services & other sectors (% employed)	73.8 e,f,g	...	...
Unemployment rate (% of labour force)	9.2 f,g	...	...

Social indicators	2010	2015	2022
Population growth rate (average annual %) b	- 0.9	- 1.7	- 0.8 a
Urban population (% of total population)	87.6	87.2	87.1 h
Urban population growth rate (average annual %) i	- 1.3	- 0.1	...
Fertility rate, total (live births per woman) b	3.3	2.7	2.3 a
Life expectancy at birth (females/males, years) b	74.3 / 70.0	74.8 / 70.3	75.5 / 70.0 a
Population age distribution (0-14/60+ years old, %) b	34.6 / 6.7	31.5 / 8.3	27.1 / 12.1 a
International migrant stock (000/% of total pop.)	23.6 / 42.0	23.5 / 42.1	23.6 / 42.8 c
Infant mortality rate (per 1 000 live births) b	8.0	7.4	7.0 a
Education: Government expenditure (% of GDP)	14.7 j	...	...
Intentional homicide rate (per 100 000 pop.)	8.9	7.2	0.0 h

Environment and infrastructure indicators	2010	2015	2022
Research & Development expenditure (% of GDP)	0.4 k,j	...	...
Threatened species (number)	79	90	105
Forested area (% of land area)	87.2	86.4	85.8 h
Energy production, primary (Petajoules)	...	0	0 l,h
Energy supply per capita (Gigajoules) l	128	76	77 h
Tourist/visitor arrivals at national borders (000)	23	20	1 c
Important sites for terrestrial biodiversity protected (%)	71.1	71.1	71.1 m

a Projected estimate (medium fertility variant). b For statistical purposes, the data for United States of America do not include this area. c 2020. d 2018. e Data classified according to ISIC Rev. 3. f Break in the time series. g Population aged 16 years and over. h 2019. i Data refers to a 5-year period preceding the reference year. j 2006. k Partial data. l Estimate. m 2021.

Andorra

Region	Southern Europe	UN membership date	28 July 1993	
Population (000, 2022)	80[a]	Surface area (km2)	468[b]	
Pop. density (per km2, 2022)	169.8[a]	Sex ratio (m per 100 f)	104.5[a]	
Capital city	Andorra la Vella	National currency	Euro (EUR)	
Capital city pop. (000, 2022)	22.6[c]	Exchange rate (per US$)	0.9[d]	

Economic indicators	2010	2015	2022
GDP: Gross domestic product (million current US$)	3 447	2 789	2 864[b]
GDP growth rate (annual %, const. 2015 prices)	- 2.0	1.4	- 12.0[b]
GDP per capita (current US$)	40 812.4	35 748.3	37 072.4[b]
Economy: Agriculture (% of Gross Value Added)[e,f]	0.5	0.6	0.6[b]
Economy: Industry (% of Gross Value Added)[f,g]	14.5	11.2	12.4[b]
Economy: Services and other activity (% of GVA)[f,h]	85.0	88.2	87.0[b]
CPI: Consumer Price Index (2010=100)[i]	100	103	108[d]
International trade: exports (million current US$)	92	90	261[j,d]
International trade: imports (million current US$)	1 541	1 294	1 398[j,d]
International trade: balance (million current US$)	- 1 448	- 1 204	- 1 137[d]
Balance of payments, current account (million US$)	...	...	449[b]

Major trading partners						2021
Export partners (% of exports)[j]	Spain	31.2	France	17.7	Nigeria	7.8
Import partners (% of imports)[j]	Spain	70.5	France	16.1	Germany	4.9

Social indicators	2010	2015	2022
Population growth rate (average annual %)	- 3.3	0.1	0.3[a]
Urban population (% of total population)	88.8	88.3	88.0[k]
Urban population growth rate (average annual %)[l]	1.0	- 1.7	...
Fertility rate, total (live births per woman)	1.4	1.4	1.1[a]
Life expectancy at birth (females/males, years)	85.4 / 80.5	85.4 / 80.6	85.8 / 81.4[a]
Population age distribution (0-14/60+ years old, %)	16.3 / 15.3	15.5 / 17.6	12.8 / 21.6[a]
International migrant stock (000/% of total pop.)[m]	52.1 / 61.6	42.3 / 54.2	45.6 / 59.0[b]
Infant mortality rate (per 1 000 live births)	6.0	6.0	5.4[a]
Health: Current expenditure (% of GDP)	6.6	6.3	6.7[k]
Health: Physicians (per 1 000 pop.)	3.1[n]	3.3	...
Education: Government expenditure (% of GDP)	3.0	3.3	3.2[k]
Intentional homicide rate (per 100 000 pop.)	0.0	0.0	2.6[b]
Seats held by women in the National Parliament (%)	35.7	50.0	46.4[o]

Environment and infrastructure indicators	2010	2015	2022
Individuals using the Internet (per 100 inhabitants)	81.0	87.9[i]	91.6[p]
Threatened species (number)	8	11	15
Forested area (% of land area)	34.0	34.0	34.0[k]
Energy production, primary (Petajoules)	1	1	1[j,k]
Energy supply per capita (Gigajoules)	114	113	119[k]
Tourist/visitor arrivals at national borders (000)	1 808[q]	2 663	1 872[b]
Important sites for terrestrial biodiversity protected (%)	26.2	26.2	26.2[d]
Pop. using safely managed sanitation (urban/rural %)	86.5 / 86.5	100.0 / 100.0	100.0 / 100.0[b]

a Projected estimate (medium fertility variant). b 2020. c 2018. d 2021. e Excludes irrigation canals and landscaping care. f Data classified according to ISIC Rev. 4. g Excludes publishing activities. Includes irrigation and canals. h Includes publishing activities and landscape care. Excludes repair of personal and household goods. i Calculated by the UNSD from national indices. j Estimate. k 2019. l Data refers to a 5-year period preceding the reference year. m Refers to foreign citizens. n 2009. o Data are as at 1 January of reporting year. p 2017. q Break in the time series.

Angola

Region	Middle Africa	UN membership date	01 December 1976
Population (000, 2022)	35 589 [a]	Surface area (km2)	1 246 700 [b]
Pop. density (per km2, 2022)	28.5 [a]	Sex ratio (m per 100 f)	97.7 [a]
Capital city	Luanda	National currency	Kwanza (AOA)
Capital city pop. (000, 2022)	8 044.7 [c,d]	Exchange rate (per US$)	555.0 [e]

Economic indicators

	2010	2015	2022
GDP: Gross domestic product (million current US$)	83 799	116 194	62 307 [b]
GDP growth rate (annual %, const. 2015 prices)	4.9	0.9	- 4.0 [b]
GDP per capita (current US$)	3 587.9	4 167.0	1 895.8 [b]
Economy: Agriculture (% of Gross Value Added) [f]	6.2	9.1	9.9 [b]
Economy: Industry (% of Gross Value Added) [f]	52.1	42.1	46.8 [b]
Economy: Services and other activity (% of GVA) [f]	41.7	48.8	43.3 [b]
Employment in agriculture (% of employed) [g]	48.9	50.6	50.2 [b]
Employment in industry (% of employed) [g]	7.8	8.6	8.1 [b]
Employment in services & other sectors (% employed) [g]	43.3	40.8	41.7 [b]
Unemployment rate (% of labour force)	9.4	7.4 [g]	8.3 [g]
Labour force participation rate (female/male pop. %)	75.6 / 79.0	74.9 / 79.9 [g]	74.6 / 79.3 [g]
CPI: Consumer Price Index (2010=100) [g,h]	100	159	379 [d]
Agricultural production index (2014-2016=100)	90	100	108 [d]
International trade: exports (million current US$)	52 612	33 925	22 347 [g,e]
International trade: imports (million current US$)	18 143	21 549	12 929 [g,e]
International trade: balance (million current US$)	34 469	12 376	9 418 [e]
Balance of payments, current account (million US$)	7 506	- 10 273	8 398 [e]

Major trading partners

						2021
Export partners (% of exports) [g]	China	61.3	India	9.9	Spain	3.4
Import partners (% of imports) [g]	China	14.3	France	14.1	Portugal	12.9

Social indicators

	2010	2015	2022
Population growth rate (average annual %)	3.8	3.6	3.0 [a]
Urban population (% of total population)	59.8	63.4	66.2 [d]
Urban population growth rate (average annual %) [i]	4.9	4.7	...
Fertility rate, total (live births per woman)	6.2	5.8	5.2 [a]
Life expectancy at birth (females/males, years)	59.0 / 54.4	63.1 / 58.2	64.5 / 59.4 [a]
Population age distribution (0-14/60+ years old, %)	45.7 / 4.1	45.8 / 4.1	45.0 / 4.3 [a]
International migrant stock (000/% of total pop.) [j]	336.4 / 1.4	632.2 / 2.3	656.4 / 2.0 [b]
Refugees and others of concern to the UNHCR (000)	19.4 [k]	45.7 [k]	56.4 [e]
Infant mortality rate (per 1 000 live births)	77.2	59.4	48.2 [a]
Health: Current expenditure (% of GDP)	2.7	2.6	2.5 [d]
Health: Physicians (per 1 000 pop.)	0.1 [l]	...	0.2 [m]
Education: Government expenditure (% of GDP)	3.4	3.5 [g]	1.8 [g,d]
Education: Primary gross enrol. ratio (f/m per 100 pop.)	94.1 / 117.7	105.9 / 121.1	... / ...
Education: Sec. gross enrol. ratio (f/m per 100 pop.)	21.3 / 31.3	20.7 / 32.3 [n]	39.7 / 61.8 [o]
Education: Upr. Sec. gross enrol. ratio (f/m per 100 pop.)	13.2 / 23.7	13.7 / 24.6 [n]	24.1 / 29.9 [o]
Intentional homicide rate (per 100 000 pop.)	...	4.8 [p]	...
Seats held by women in the National Parliament (%)	38.6	36.8	29.6 [q]

Environment and infrastructure indicators

	2010	2015	2022
Individuals using the Internet (per 100 inhabitants) [g]	2.8	22.0	36.0 [b]
Research & Development expenditure (% of GDP)	...	...	~0.0 [r,s,t,o]
Threatened species (number)	117	130	225
Forested area (% of land area)	57.9	55.7	53.9 [d]
CO2 emission estimates (million tons/tons per capita)	15.9 / 0.6	23.3 / 0.8	20.6 / 0.6 [d]
Energy production, primary (Petajoules)	4 016	4 030	3 639 [d]
Energy supply per capita (Gigajoules)	20	20	17 [d]
Tourist/visitor arrivals at national borders (000)	425	592	64 [b]
Important sites for terrestrial biodiversity protected (%)	28.1	28.1	28.1 [e]
Net Official Development Assist. received (% of GNI)	0.31	0.35	0.19 [b]

a Projected estimate (medium fertility variant). **b** 2020. **c** Refers to the urban population of the province of Luanda. **d** 2019. **e** 2021. **f** Data classified according to ISIC Rev. 4. **g** Estimate. **h** Luanda **i** Data refers to a 5-year period preceding the reference year. **j** Including refugees. **k** Data as at the end of December. **l** 2009. **m** 2018. **n** 2011. **o** 2016. **p** 2012. **q** Data are as at 1 January of reporting year. **r** Excluding private non-profit. **s** Excluding business enterprise. **t** Partial data.

Anguilla

Region	Caribbean	Population (000, 2022)	16[a,b]
Surface area (km2)	91[c]	Pop. density (per km2, 2022)	180.2[a,b]
Sex ratio (m per 100 f)	95.8[a,b]	Capital city	The Valley
National currency	E. Caribbean Dollar (XCD)[d]	Capital city pop. (000, 2022)	1.4[e]
Exchange rate (per US$)	2.7[f]		

Economic indicators	2010	2015	2022
GDP: Gross domestic product (million current US$)	270	331	258[c]
GDP growth rate (annual %, const. 2015 prices)	- 4.6	3.7	- 29.9[c]
GDP per capita (current US$)	20 056.4	23 148.2	17 225.9[c]
Economy: Agriculture (% of Gross Value Added)[g]	2.0	2.3	1.0[c]
Economy: Industry (% of Gross Value Added)[g]	15.8	15.3	15.1[c]
Economy: Services and other activity (% of GVA)[g]	82.2	82.4	83.9[c]
CPI: Consumer Price Index (2010=100)	100[h]	105	109[f]
International trade: exports (million current US$)[i]	12	11	35[f]
International trade: imports (million current US$)[i]	149	204	708[f]
International trade: balance (million current US$)	- 137[i]	- 193[i]	- 673[f]
Balance of payments, current account (million US$)	- 51	- 89	- 146[f]

Major trading partners						2021
Export partners (% of exports)[i]	Chile	80.8	Armenia	3.1	Brazil	2.7
Import partners (% of imports)[i]	Chile	46.4	United States	36.8	United Kingdom	4.7

Social indicators	2010	2015	2022
Population growth rate (average annual %)[a]	1.8	2.3	0.3[b]
Urban population (% of total population)	100.0	100.0	100.0[j]
Urban population growth rate (average annual %)[k]	1.7	1.2	...
Fertility rate, total (live births per woman)[a]	1.7	1.4	1.3[b]
Life expectancy at birth (females/males, years)[a]	81.2 / 74.5	80.8 / 73.7	81.2 / 74.1[b]
Population age distribution (0-14/60+ years old, %)[a]	23.6 / 10.3	20.3 / 12.2	17.3 / 16.0[b]
International migrant stock (000/% of total pop.)[l]	5.1 / 38.0	5.5 / 38.3	5.7 / 38.1[c]
Refugees and others of concern to the UNHCR (000)	...	...	~0.0[f]
Infant mortality rate (per 1 000 live births)[a]	7.6	7.3	6.1[b]
Education: Government expenditure (% of GDP)	2.8[m]	3.0[i]	3.6[i,e]
Education: Primary gross enrol. ratio (f/m per 100 pop.)	118.9 / 124.4	119.0 / 124.2[n]	105.8 / 106.8[j]
Education: Sec. gross enrol. ratio (f/m per 100 pop.)	111.0 / 112.1	114.3 / 114.2[n]	99.2 / 102.4[j]
Education: Upr. Sec. gross enrol. ratio (f/m per 100 pop.)	113.9 / 103.2	104.2 / 120.5[n]	94.9 / 99.5[j]
Intentional homicide rate (per 100 000 pop.)	0.0	28.3[o]	...

Environment and infrastructure indicators	2010	2015	2022
Individuals using the Internet (per 100 inhabitants)[i]	49.6	76.0	81.6[p]
Threatened species (number)	33	51	71
Forested area (% of land area)[i]	61.1	61.1	61.1[j]
Energy production, primary (Petajoules)	0[i]	0	0[j]
Energy supply per capita (Gigajoules)[i]	159	155	147[j]
Tourist/visitor arrivals at national borders (000)[q]	62	73	25[c]
Important sites for terrestrial biodiversity protected (%)	18.6	18.6	18.6[f]

a For statistical purposes, the data for United Kingdom do not include this area. b Projected estimate (medium fertility variant). c 2020. d East Caribbean Dollar. e 2018. f 2021. g Data classified according to ISIC Rev. 4. h Break in the time series. i Estimate. j 2019. k Data refers to a 5-year period preceding the reference year. l Including refugees. m 2008. n 2011. o 2014. p 2016. q Excluding nationals residing abroad.

Antigua and Barbuda

Region	Caribbean	UN membership date	11 November 1981
Population (000, 2022)	94[a]	Surface area (km2)	442[b]
Pop. density (per km2, 2022)	213.1[a]	Sex ratio (m per 100 f)	91.4[a]
Capital city	Saint John's	National currency	E. Caribbean Dollar (XCD)[c]
Capital city pop. (000, 2022)	20.8[d]	Exchange rate (per US$)	2.7[e]

Economic indicators

	2010	2015	2022
GDP: Gross domestic product (million current US$)	1 149	1 337	1 370[b]
GDP growth rate (annual %, const. 2015 prices)	- 7.8	3.8	- 20.2[b]
GDP per capita (current US$)	13 049.3	14 286.1	13 993.3[b]
Economy: Agriculture (% of Gross Value Added)[f]	1.8	1.8	2.5[b]
Economy: Industry (% of Gross Value Added)[f]	18.3	18.7	23.8[b]
Economy: Services and other activity (% of GVA)[f]	79.9	79.5	73.7[b]
Employment in agriculture (% of employed)	2.8[g,h]	...	...
Employment in industry (% of employed)	15.6[g,h]	...	...
Employment in services & other sectors (% employed)	81.6[g,h]	...	...
CPI: Consumer Price Index (2010=100)	100	110	119[e]
Agricultural production index (2014-2016=100)	102	100	88[b]
International trade: exports (million current US$)	35	26	23[i,e]
International trade: imports (million current US$)	501	465	714[i,e]
International trade: balance (million current US$)	- 466	- 439	- 691[e]
Balance of payments, current account (million current US$)	- 167	30	- 221[e]

Major trading partners

						2021
Export partners (% of exports)[i]	United Arab Emirates	52.7	United States	9.8	Netherlands	7.6
Import partners (% of imports)[i]	United States	48.2	China	7.4	Japan	4.4

Social indicators

	2010	2015	2022
Population growth rate (average annual %)	1.2	0.8	0.6[a]
Urban population (% of total population)	26.2	25.0	24.5[j]
Urban population growth rate (average annual %)[k]	- 1.0	0.1	...
Fertility rate, total (live births per woman)	1.8	1.6	1.6[a]
Life expectancy at birth (females/males, years)	79.4 / 74.0	80.4 / 75.1	81.6 / 76.5[a]
Population age distribution (0-14/60+ years old, %)	23.8 / 10.4	21.2 / 12.2	18.5 / 16.1[a]
International migrant stock (000/% of total pop.)[l]	26.4 / 30.0	28.1 / 30.0	29.4 / 30.0[b]
Refugees and others of concern to the UNHCR (000)	...	~0.0	~0.0[b]
Infant mortality rate (per 1 000 live births)	8.2	6.3	5.0[a]
Health: Current expenditure (% of GDP)[i,m,n]	5.4	5.3	4.4[j]
Health: Physicians (per 1 000 pop.)	0.5[h]	...	2.8[o]
Education: Government expenditure (% of GDP)	2.5[p]	...	3.3[i,b]
Education: Primary gross enrol. ratio (f/m per 100 pop.)	107.3 / 117.2	103.2 / 106.8	104.6 / 105.4[d]
Education: Sec. gross enrol. ratio (f/m per 100 pop.)	115.7 / 109.9	109.3 / 107.1	109.1 / 113.3[d]
Education: Upr. Sec. gross enrol. ratio (f/m per 100 pop.)	104.2 / 68.1	90.7 / 79.0	110.2 / 97.5[d]
Intentional homicide rate (per 100 000 pop.)	6.8	11.1[q]	9.2[b]
Seats held by women in the National Parliament (%)	10.5	11.1	11.1[r]

Environment and infrastructure indicators

	2010	2015	2022
Individuals using the Internet (per 100 inhabitants)[i]	47.0	70.0	73.0[s]
Threatened species (number)	38	53	75
Forested area (% of land area)[l]	20.0	19.2	18.6[j]
Energy production, primary (Petajoules)	...	0	0[i,j]
Energy supply per capita (Gigajoules)[l]	74	74	74[j]
Tourist/visitor arrivals at national borders (000)[t,u]	230	250	125[b]
Important sites for terrestrial biodiversity protected (%)	8.7	9.1	14.0[e]
Net Official Development Assist. received (% of GNI)	1.75	0.12	1.85[b]

a Projected estimate (medium fertility variant). b 2020. c East Caribbean Dollar. d 2018. e 2021. f Data classified according to ISIC Rev. 4. g Data classified according to ISIC Rev. 3. h 2008. i Estimate. j 2019. k Data refers to a 5-year period preceding the reference year. l Including refugees. m Data based on calendar year (January 1 to December 31). n Estimates should be viewed with caution as these are derived from scarce data. o 2017. p 2009. q 2012. r Data are as at 1 January of reporting year. s 2016. t Arrivals by air. u Excluding nationals residing abroad.

Argentina

Region	South America	
Population (000, 2022)	45 510[a]	
Pop. density (per km2, 2022)	16.3[a]	
Capital city	Buenos Aires	
Capital city pop. (000, 2022)	15 057.3[d,e]	

UN membership date	24 October 1945
Surface area (km2)	2 796 427[b,c]
Sex ratio (m per 100 f)	98.0[a]
National currency	Argentine Peso (ARS)
Exchange rate (per US$)	102.6[f]

Economic indicators	2010	2015	2022
GDP: Gross domestic product (million current US$)	426 487	644 903	383 067[c]
GDP growth rate (annual %, const. 2015 prices)	10.1	2.7	- 9.9[c]
GDP per capita (current US$)	10 428.6	14 971.5	8 475.7[c]
Economy: Agriculture (% of Gross Value Added)	8.5	6.1	8.2[c]
Economy: Industry (% of Gross Value Added)	30.1	27.5	26.9[c]
Economy: Services and other activity (% of GVA)	61.4	66.3	65.0[c]
Employment in agriculture (% of employed)	1.3	0.3[g]	0.1[g,c]
Employment in industry (% of employed)	23.3	23.7[g]	21.0[g]
Employment in services & other sectors (% employed)	75.4	76.1[g]	78.9[g,c]
Unemployment rate (% of labour force)	7.7	7.5[g]	10.6[g]
Labour force participation rate (female/male pop. %)	47.9 / 73.6	47.7 / 71.7[g]	50.0 / 71.2[g]
CPI: Consumer Price Index (2010=100)	...	...	491[h,f]
Agricultural production index (2014-2016=100)	88	104	110[c]
International trade: exports (million current US$)	68 174	56 784	77 934[f]
International trade: imports (million current US$)	56 792	60 203	63 184[f]
International trade: balance (million current US$)	11 382	- 3 419	14 751[f]
Balance of payments, current account (million US$)	- 1 623	- 17 622	6 800[f]

Major trading partners						2021
Export partners (% of exports)	Brazil	15.1	China	7.9	United States	6.4
Import partners (% of imports)	China	21.4	Brazil	19.6	United States	9.4

Social indicators	2010	2015	2022
Population growth rate (average annual %)	1.0	1.0	0.5[a]
Urban population (% of total population)	90.8	91.5	92.0[e]
Urban population growth rate (average annual %)[i]	1.2	1.2	...
Fertility rate, total (live births per woman)	2.3	2.3	1.9[a]
Life expectancy at birth (females/males, years)	78.8 / 72.5	80.2 / 73.3	79.3 / 72.9[a]
Population age distribution (0-14/60+ years old, %)	25.6 / 14.6	24.7 / 15.3	23.1 / 16.2[a]
International migrant stock (000/% of total pop.)[j]	1 806.0 / 4.4	2 086.3 / 4.8	2 281.7 / 5.0[c]
Refugees and others of concern to the UNHCR (000)	4.2[k]	4.4	182.7[f]
Infant mortality rate (per 1 000 live births)	13.1	11.1	8.8[a]
Health: Current expenditure (% of GDP)[g,l]	9.4	10.2	9.5[m,e]
Health: Physicians (per 1 000 pop.)	...	4.0	4.1[c]
Education: Government expenditure (% of GDP)	5.0	5.8	4.8[e]
Education: Primary gross enrol. ratio (f/m per 100 pop.)	116.2 / 117.7	111.2 / 111.4	109.6 / 109.4[e]
Education: Sec. gross enrol. ratio (f/m per 100 pop.)	104.2 / 95.0	110.2 / 103.8	110.4 / 106.1[e]
Education: Upr. Sec. gross enrol. ratio (f/m per 100 pop.)	77.8 / 64.7	91.1 / 79.4	93.3 / 84.5[e]
Intentional homicide rate (per 100 000 pop.)	5.8	6.6	5.3[c]
Seats held by women in the National Parliament (%)	38.5	36.2	44.8[n]

Environment and infrastructure indicators	2010	2015	2022
Individuals using the Internet (per 100 inhabitants)	45.0[g]	68.0[o]	85.5[p,c]
Research & Development expenditure (% of GDP)	0.6	0.6	0.5[e]
Threatened species (number)	213	243	321
Forested area (% of land area)[g]	11.0	10.6	10.5[e]
CO2 emission estimates (million tons/tons per capita)	164.2 / 4.0	181.8 / 4.2	154.9 / 3.4[c]
Energy production, primary (Petajoules)	3 331	3 059	3 292[e]
Energy supply per capita (Gigajoules)	81	79	74[e]
Tourist/visitor arrivals at national borders (000)	6 800[q]	6 816	2 090[c]
Important sites for terrestrial biodiversity protected (%)	30.3	31.6	32.6[f]
Pop. using safely managed sanitation (urban/rural %)	45.9 / ...	46.7 / ...	47.1 / ...[c]
Net Official Development Assist. received (% of GNI)	0.03	0.00	0.03[c]

a Projected estimate (medium fertility variant). b The total area includes continental areas and islands, and excludes Antarctic area. c 2020. d Refers to Gran Buenos Aires. e 2019. f 2021. g Estimate. h Index base: December 2016=100. i Data refers to a 5-year period preceding the reference year. j Including refugees. k Data as at the end of December. l Data based on calendar year (January 1 to December 31). m Estimates should be viewed with caution as these are derived from scarce data. n Data are as at 1 January of reporting year. o Population aged 10 years and over. p Population aged 4 and over. q Break in the time series.

Armenia

Region	Western Asia	UN membership date	02 March 1992
Population (000, 2022)	2 780[a]	Surface area (km2)	29 743[b]
Pop. density (per km2, 2022)	97.7[a]	Sex ratio (m per 100 f)	81.7[a]
Capital city	Yerevan	National currency	Armenian Dram (AMD)
Capital city pop. (000, 2022)	1 083.3[c]	Exchange rate (per US$)	480.1[d]

Economic indicators

	2010	2015	2022
GDP: Gross domestic product (million current US$)	9 875	10 553	12 641[b]
GDP growth rate (annual %, const. 2015 prices)	2.2	3.2	- 7.4[b]
GDP per capita (current US$)	3 432.1	3 607.3	4 266.0[b]
Economy: Agriculture (% of Gross Value Added)[e,f]	17.8	18.9	12.3[b]
Economy: Industry (% of Gross Value Added)[f,g]	34.7	28.2	29.6[b]
Economy: Services and other activity (% of GVA)[f,h]	47.4	52.9	58.1[b]
Employment in agriculture (% of employed)	38.6	35.3	28.9[i,b]
Employment in industry (% of employed)	17.4	15.9	17.5[i,b]
Employment in services & other sectors (% employed)	44.0	48.8	53.6[i,b]
Unemployment rate (% of labour force)	19.0	18.3	20.8[i]
Labour force participation rate (female/male pop. %)	46.9 / 67.6	48.8 / 66.6	43.3 / 63.5[i]
CPI: Consumer Price Index (2010=100)[i]	100[j]	125	140[d]
Agricultural production index (2014-2016=100)	74	106	86[b]
International trade: exports (million current US$)	1 011	1 483	2 971[d]
International trade: imports (million current US$)	3 782	3 257	5 319[d]
International trade: balance (million current US$)	- 2 770	- 1 774	- 2 348[d]
Balance of payments, current account (million US$)	- 1 261	- 285	- 511[d]

Major trading partners

					2021		
Export partners (% of exports)	Russian Federation	26.9	China	13.2	Switzerland	12.1
Import partners (% of imports)	Russian Federation	33.5	China	16.0	Iran	8.2

Social indicators

	2010	2015	2022
Population growth rate (average annual %)	- 0.6	- 0.4	- 0.2[a]
Urban population (% of total population)	63.4	63.1	63.2[c]
Urban population growth rate (average annual %)[k]	- 0.9	0.2	...
Fertility rate, total (live births per woman)	1.5	1.6	1.6[a]
Life expectancy at birth (females/males, years)	77.4 / 68.6	78.8 / 69.6	78.4 / 67.9[a]
Population age distribution (0-14/60+ years old, %)	19.3 / 14.0	19.6 / 15.8	20.5 / 20.3[a]
International migrant stock (000/% of total pop.)[l]	211.1 / 7.3	191.2 / 6.5	190.3 / 6.4[b]
Refugees and others of concern to the UNHCR (000)	85.8[m]	16.0	46.4[d]
Infant mortality rate (per 1 000 live births)	16.3	12.6	8.1[a]
Health: Current expenditure (% of GDP)	9.2	10.1	11.3[c]
Health: Physicians (per 1 000 pop.)	2.8	2.9	4.4[n]
Education: Government expenditure (% of GDP)	3.2	2.8	2.7[b]
Education: Primary gross enrol. ratio (f/m per 100 pop.)	100.7 / 97.7	95.8 / 94.3	91.8 / 90.8[b]
Education: Sec. gross enrol. ratio (f/m per 100 pop.)	103.7 / 105.6	88.3 / 84.0	89.3 / 85.5[b]
Education: Upr. Sec. gross enrol. ratio (f/m per 100 pop.)	97.7 / 101.7	95.0 / 85.3	85.7 / 78.2[b]
Intentional homicide rate (per 100 000 pop.)	1.9	2.6	1.8[b]
Seats held by women in the National Parliament (%)	9.2	10.7	34.6[o]

Environment and infrastructure indicators

	2010	2015	2022
Individuals using the Internet (per 100 inhabitants)	25.0[i]	59.1	76.5[b]
Research & Development expenditure (% of GDP)	0.2[p]	0.2[q,r]	0.2[q,r,b]
Threatened species (number)	36	111	117
Forested area (% of land area)	11.6	11.6[i]	11.5[i,c]
CO2 emission estimates (million tons/tons per capita)	4.1 / 1.4	5.2 / 1.7	6.5 / 2.2[b]
Energy production, primary (Petajoules)	39	45	38[c]
Energy supply per capita (Gigajoules)	37[i]	46	48[c]
Tourist/visitor arrivals at national borders (000)	684	1 192	375[b]
Important sites for terrestrial biodiversity protected (%)	21.6	22.6	22.6[d]
Pop. using safely managed sanitation (urban/rural %)	52.6 / ...	62.0 / ...	71.4 / ...[b]
Net Official Development Assist. received (% of GNI)	3.30	2.82	0.85[b]

a Projected estimate (medium fertility variant). b 2020. c 2019. d 2021. e Excludes irrigation canals and landscaping care. f Data classified according to ISIC Rev. 4. g Excludes publishing activities. Includes irrigation and canals. h Includes publishing activities and landscape care. Excludes repair of personal and household goods. i Estimate. j Break in the time series. k Data refers to a 5-year period preceding the reference year. l Including refugees. m Data as at the end of December. n 2017. o Data are as at 1 January of reporting year. p Partial data. q Excluding private non-profit. r Excluding business enterprise.

Region	Caribbean	Population (000, 2022)	106[a,b]
Surface area (km2)	180[c]	Pop. density (per km2, 2022)	591.4[a,b]
Sex ratio (m per 100 f)	89.2[a,b]	Capital city	Oranjestad
National currency	Aruban Florin (AWG)	Capital city pop. (000, 2022)	29.9[d]
Exchange rate (per US$)	1.8[e]		

Economic indicators

	2010	2015	2022
GDP: Gross domestic product (million current US$)	2 454	2 963	2 497[c]
GDP growth rate (annual %, const. 2015 prices)	- 2.8	6.3	- 22.3[c]
GDP per capita (current US$)	24 133.2	28 396.4	23 385.6[c]
Economy: Agriculture (% of Gross Value Added)[f,g,h]	0.0	0.0	0.0[c]
Economy: Industry (% of Gross Value Added)[f]	12.8	10.5	10.6[c]
Economy: Services and other activity (% of GVA)[f,i]	87.2	89.5	89.4[c]
Employment in agriculture (% of employed)[j,l]	0.6[k]	0.6[m]	...
Employment in industry (% of employed)[j,l]	14.5[k]	14.0[m]	...
Employment in services & other sectors (% employed)[j,l]	84.4[k]	85.1[m]	...
Unemployment rate (% of labour force)	10.6[k,l]	...	...
Labour force participation rate (female/male pop. %)	59.5 / 68.9[k,l,n]	58.8 / 69.6[l,m]	... / ...
CPI: Consumer Price Index (2010=100)[o]	100	103	109[e]
International trade: exports (million current US$)	125	80	88[e]
International trade: imports (million current US$)	1 071	1 165	1 170[e]
International trade: balance (million current US$)	- 947	- 1 085	- 1 081[e]
Balance of payments, current account (million US$)	- 460	111	43[e]

Major trading partners

						2021
Export partners (% of exports)	Colombia	49.4	United States	23.0	Curaçao	9.6
Import partners (% of imports)	United States	50.8	Netherlands	15.6	Areas nes[p]	11.3

Social indicators

	2010	2015	2022
Population growth rate (average annual %)[b]	1.0	0.6	- 0.2[a]
Urban population (% of total population)	43.1	43.1	43.5[q]
Urban population growth rate (average annual %)[r]	- 0.5	0.5	...
Fertility rate, total (live births per woman)[b]	1.9	2.0	1.2[a]
Life expectancy at birth (females/males, years)[b]	78.6 / 72.1	78.6 / 72.6	77.7 / 72.1[a]
Population age distribution (0-14/60+ years old, %)[b]	20.7 / 14.7	18.8 / 18.2	16.2 / 23.9[a]
International migrant stock (000/% of total pop.)[s]	34.3 / 33.8	36.1 / 34.6	53.6 / 50.2[c]
Refugees and others of concern to the UNHCR (000)	~0.0[t]	~0.0	17.2[e]
Infant mortality rate (per 1 000 live births)[b]	15.5	14.2	12.6[a]
Education: Government expenditure (% of GDP)	6.9	5.9	5.5[u]
Education: Primary gross enrol. ratio (f/m per 100 pop.)	113.0 / 114.5	115.2 / 118.9[v]	... / ...
Education: Sec. gross enrol. ratio (f/m per 100 pop.)	98.3 / 93.5	112.1 / 110.2[w]	... / ...
Education: Upr. Sec. gross enrol. ratio (f/m per 100 pop.)	91.2 / 78.5	107.0 / 105.6[w]	... / ...
Intentional homicide rate (per 100 000 pop.)	3.9	1.9[v]	...

Environment and infrastructure indicators

	2010	2015	2022
Individuals using the Internet (per 100 inhabitants)[x]	62.0	88.7	97.2[y]
Threatened species (number)	22	29	62
Forested area (% of land area)[x]	2.3	2.3	2.3[q]
Energy production, primary (Petajoules)[x]	5	1	1[q]
Energy supply per capita (Gigajoules)[x]	550	122	123[q]
Tourist/visitor arrivals at national borders (000)[z]	824	1 225	1 119[q]
Important sites for terrestrial biodiversity protected (%)	37.1	37.1	37.1[e]

a Projected estimate (medium fertility variant). b For statistical purposes, the data for Netherlands do not include this area. c 2020. d 2018. e 2021. f Data classified according to ISIC Rev. 4. g Excludes irrigation canals and landscaping care. h Including mining and quarrying. i Includes publishing activities and landscape care. Excludes repair of personal and household goods. j Data classified according to ISIC Rev. 3. k Population aged 14 years and over. l Break in the time series. m 2011. n Resident population (de jure). o Calculated by the UNSD from national indices. p Areas nes q 2019. r Data refers to a 5-year period preceding the reference year. s Including refugees. t Data as at the end of December. u 2016. v 2014. w 2012. x Estimate. y 2017. z Arrivals by air.

Australia

Region	Oceania	UN membership date	01 November 1945
Population (000, 2022)	26 177[a,b]	Surface area (km2)	7 692 024[c,d]
Pop. density (per km2, 2022)	3.4[a,b]	Sex ratio (m per 100 f)	98.6[a,b]
Capital city	Canberra	National currency	Australian Dollar (AUD)
Capital city pop. (000, 2022)	452.5[e,f]	Exchange rate (per US$)	1.4[g]

Economic indicators

	2010	2015	2022
GDP: Gross domestic product (million current US$)	1 299 463	1 247 634	1 423 473[d]
GDP growth rate (annual %, const. 2015 prices)	2.5	2.8	1.4[d]
GDP per capita (current US$)	58 654.1	52 131.4	55 822.7[d]
Economy: Agriculture (% of Gross Value Added)[h,i]	2.5	2.6	2.4[d]
Economy: Industry (% of Gross Value Added)[h,j]	28.4	24.0	27.3[d]
Economy: Services and other activity (% of GVA)[h,k]	69.2	73.4	70.3[d]
Employment in agriculture (% of employed)	3.2	2.6	2.5[l,d]
Employment in industry (% of employed)	21.0	19.4	19.8[l,d]
Employment in services & other sectors (% employed)	75.8	78.0	77.7[l,d]
Unemployment rate (% of labour force)	5.2	6.0	5.0[l]
Labour force participation rate (female/male pop. %)	58.6 / 72.3	59.1 / 71.0	60.4 / 70.0[l]
CPI: Consumer Price Index (2010=100)[n,o]	100[m]	112	124[g]
Agricultural production index (2014-2016=100)	86	100	86[d]
International trade: exports (million current US$)	212 109	187 792	342 036[g]
International trade: imports (million current US$)	201 703	200 114	261 586[g]
International trade: balance (million current US$)	10 405	- 12 322	80 450[g]
Balance of payments, current account (million US$)	- 44 714	- 56 959	56 691[g]

Major trading partners

							2021
Export partners (% of exports)	China	34.2	Areas nes[p]	18.1	Japan	8.9
Import partners (% of imports)	China	27.9	United States	10.2	Japan	6.0

Social indicators

	2010	2015	2022
Population growth rate (average annual %)[a]	1.5	1.5	1.0[b]
Urban population (% of total population)[a]	85.2	85.7	86.1[f]
Urban population growth rate (average annual %)[a,q]	1.9	1.6	...
Fertility rate, total (live births per woman)[a]	2.0	1.8	1.6[b]
Life expectancy at birth (females/males, years)[a]	84.2 / 79.8	84.7 / 80.6	85.5 / 81.7[b]
Population age distribution (0-14/60+ years old, %)[a]	19.1 / 19.0	18.9 / 20.3	18.2 / 22.6[b]
International migrant stock (000/% of total pop.)[a]	5 883.0 / 26.6	6 729.7 / 28.1	7 685.9 / 30.1[d]
Refugees and others of concern to the UNHCR (000)	25.6[r]	58.4	138.1[g]
Infant mortality rate (per 1 000 live births)[a]	4.1	3.1	2.8[b]
Health: Current expenditure (% of GDP)	8.4	9.3	9.9[f]
Health: Physicians (per 1 000 pop.)	3.3	3.5	4.1[d]
Education: Government expenditure (% of GDP)	5.6	5.3	5.1[s]
Education: Primary gross enrol. ratio (f/m per 100 pop.)	105.5 / 105.7	101.6 / 101.6	99.7 / 99.8[f]
Education: Sec. gross enrol. ratio (f/m per 100 pop.)	... / ...	145.9 / 167.9	135.7 / 145.3[f]
Education: Upr. Sec. gross enrol. ratio (f/m per 100 pop.)	... / ...	202.7 / 239.8	191.7 / 206.0[f]
Intentional homicide rate (per 100 000 pop.)	1.0	1.0	0.9[d]
Seats held by women in the National Parliament (%)	27.3	26.7	31.1[t]

Environment and infrastructure indicators

	2010	2015	2022
Individuals using the Internet (per 100 inhabitants)	76.0[l]	84.6[u]	89.6[l,d]
Research & Development expenditure (% of GDP)[l]	2.4	1.9	1.8[f]
Threatened species (number)[v]	853	909	1 828
Forested area (% of land area)	16.9	17.3	17.4[f]
CO2 emission estimates (million tons/tons per capita)[v,w]	387.7 / 17.4	376.8 / 15.6	380.4 / 14.6[d]
Energy production, primary (Petajoules)[v]	13 646	16 033	18 623[f]
Energy supply per capita (Gigajoules)[v]	244	223	215[f]
Tourist/visitor arrivals at national borders (000)[x]	5 790	7 449	1 828[d]
Important sites for terrestrial biodiversity protected (%)	46.0	52.6	57.2[g]
Pop. using safely managed drinking water (urban/rural, %)	98.7 / ...	99.0 / ...	99.0 / ...[d]
Net Official Development Assist. disbursed (% of GNI)[y]	1.23	1.15	0.22[d]

a Including Christmas Island, Cocos (Keeling) Islands and Norfolk Island. b Projected estimate (medium fertility variant). c Including Norfolk Island. d 2020. e Refers to Significant Urban Areas as of 2001. f 2019. g 2021. h Data classified according to ISIC Rev. 4. i Excludes irrigation canals and landscaping care. j Excludes publishing activities. Includes irrigation and canals. k Includes publishing activities and landscape care. Excludes repair of personal and household goods. l Estimate. m Break in the time series. n Weighted average of index values computed for the 8 capital cities. o Calculated by the UNSD from national indices. p Areas nes q Data refers to a 5-year period preceding the reference year. r Data as at the end of December. s 2018. t Data are as at 1 January of reporting year. u Population aged 15 years and over. Accessed the internet for personal use in a typical week. v Excluding overseas territories. w Data refer to fiscal years beginning 1 July. x Excluding nationals residing abroad and crew members. y DAC member (OECD).

Region	Western Europe	UN membership date	14 December 1955
Population (000, 2022)	8 940[a]	Surface area (km2)	83 878[b]
Pop. density (per km2, 2022)	108.3[a]	Sex ratio (m per 100 f)	97.0[a]
Capital city	Vienna	National currency	Euro (EUR)
Capital city pop. (000, 2022)	1 915.3[c]	Exchange rate (per US$)	0.9[d]

Economic indicators

	2010	2015	2022
GDP: Gross domestic product (million current US$)	391 893	381 818	433 258[b]
GDP growth rate (annual %, const. 2015 prices)	1.8	1.0	- 6.7[b]
GDP per capita (current US$)	46 598.7	43 995.0	48 105.6[b]
Economy: Agriculture (% of Gross Value Added)[e,f]	1.4	1.3	1.2[b]
Economy: Industry (% of Gross Value Added)[e,g]	28.7	28.2	28.4[b]
Economy: Services and other activity (% of GVA)[e,h]	69.9	70.5	70.4[b]
Employment in agriculture (% of employed)	5.2	4.5	3.5[i,b]
Employment in industry (% of employed)	24.9	25.8	25.0[i,b]
Employment in services & other sectors (% employed)	69.9	69.7	71.5[i,b]
Unemployment rate (% of labour force)	4.8	5.7	5.4[i]
Labour force participation rate (female/male pop. %)	54.2 / 67.1	55.4 / 66.4	55.3 / 66.0[i]
CPI: Consumer Price Index (2010=100)	100	111	123[d]
Agricultural production index (2014-2016=100)	95	97	102[b]
International trade: exports (million current US$)	144 882	145 276	201 647[d]
International trade: imports (million current US$)	150 593	147 928	218 972[d]
International trade: balance (million current US$)	- 5 711	- 2 652	- 17 325[d]
Balance of payments, current account (million US$)	11 472	6 634	- 2 541[d]

Major trading partners

							2021
Export partners (% of exports)	Germany	29.5	Italy	6.6	United States	6.1
Import partners (% of imports)	Germany	39.7	Italy	6.2	Switzerland	5.1

Social indicators

	2010	2015	2022
Population growth rate (average annual %)	0.3	1.3	0.2[a]
Urban population (% of total population)	57.4	57.7	58.5[c]
Urban population growth rate (average annual %)[j]	- 0.1	0.7	...
Fertility rate, total (live births per woman)	1.4	1.5	1.5[a]
Life expectancy at birth (females/males, years)	83.1 / 77.7	83.6 / 78.6	84.6 / 80.2[a]
Population age distribution (0-14/60+ years old, %)	14.8 / 23.2	14.3 / 24.0	14.4 / 26.7[a]
International migrant stock (000/% of total pop.)	1 274.9 / 15.2	1 483.1 / 17.1	1 738.2 / 19.3[b]
Refugees and others of concern to the UNHCR (000)	68.7[k]	92.2[l]	165.5[d]
Infant mortality rate (per 1 000 live births)	4.0	3.1	2.5[a]
Health: Current expenditure (% of GDP)	10.2	10.4	10.4[c]
Health: Physicians (per 1 000 pop.)	4.8	5.1	5.3[b]
Education: Government expenditure (% of GDP)	5.7	5.5	5.2[m]
Education: Primary gross enrol. ratio (f/m per 100 pop.)	99.1 / 100.4	101.5 / 102.4	102.7 / 103.4[c]
Education: Sec. gross enrol. ratio (f/m per 100 pop.)	96.8 / 100.7	98.5 / 102.1	98.9 / 101.4[c]
Education: Upr. Sec. gross enrol. ratio (f/m per 100 pop.)	92.3 / 99.6	97.3 / 103.6	96.2 / 101.2[c]
Intentional homicide rate (per 100 000 pop.)	0.7	0.5	0.7[b]
Seats held by women in the National Parliament (%)	27.9	30.6	41.5[n]

Environment and infrastructure indicators

	2010	2015	2022
Individuals using the Internet (per 100 inhabitants)	75.2[o]	83.9[o,p]	87.5[b]
Research & Development expenditure (% of GDP)	2.7[i]	3.0	3.2[i,b]
Threatened species (number)	82	106	224
Forested area (% of land area)	46.8	47.0	47.2[c]
CO2 emission estimates (million tons/tons per capita)	70.1 / 8.2	63.3 / 7.1	58.9 / 6.4[b]
Energy production, primary (Petajoules)	498	497	498[c]
Energy supply per capita (Gigajoules)	169	158	156[c]
Tourist/visitor arrivals at national borders (000)[q]	22 004	26 728	15 091[b]
Important sites for terrestrial biodiversity protected (%)	65.7	66.9	67.4[d]
Pop. using safely managed sanitation (urban/rural %)	100.0 / 99.2	100.0 / 99.2	100.0 / 99.2[b]
Net Official Development Assist. disbursed (% of GNI)[r]	1.70	1.25	- 0.02[b]

a Projected estimate (medium fertility variant). **b** 2020. **c** 2019. **d** 2021. **e** Data classified according to ISIC Rev. 4. **f** Excludes irrigation canals and landscaping care. **g** Excludes publishing activities. Includes irrigation and canals. **h** Includes publishing activities and landscape care. Excludes repair of personal and household goods. **i** Estimate. **j** Data refers to a 5-year period preceding the reference year. **k** Data as at the end of December. **l** Data relates to the end of 2014. **m** 2018. **n** Data are as at 1 January of reporting year. **o** Population aged 16 to 74 years. **p** Users in the last 3 months. **q** Only paid accommodation; excluding stays at friends and relatives and second homes. **r** DAC member (OECD).

Azerbaijan

Region	Western Asia	UN membership date	02 March 1992
Population (000, 2022)	10 358[a,b]	Surface area (km2)	86 600[c]
Pop. density (per km2, 2022)	125.3[a,b]	Sex ratio (m per 100 f)	97.4[a,b]
Capital city	Baku	National currency	Azerbaijan manat (AZN)
Capital city pop. (000, 2022)	2 313.1[d,e]	Exchange rate (per US$)	1.7[f]

Economic indicators	2010	2015	2022
GDP: Gross domestic product (million current US$)	52 906	53 076	42 607[c]
GDP growth rate (annual %, const. 2015 prices)	4.8	1.0	-4.3[c]
GDP per capita (current US$)	5 857.3	5 515.7	4 202.2[c]
Economy: Agriculture (% of Gross Value Added)[g,h]	5.9	6.7	7.6[c]
Economy: Industry (% of Gross Value Added)[g,i]	64.0	48.9	45.6[c]
Economy: Services and other activity (% of GVA)[g,j]	30.1	44.3	46.8[c]
Employment in agriculture (% of employed)	38.2	36.4	35.5[k,c]
Employment in industry (% of employed)	13.7	14.1	15.0[k,c]
Employment in services & other sectors (% employed)	48.1	49.6	49.5[k,c]
Unemployment rate (% of labour force)	5.6	5.0	6.6[k]
Labour force participation rate (female/male pop. %)	62.0 / 67.8	62.5 / 68.7	61.7 / 68.1[k]
CPI: Consumer Price Index (2010=100)	100	118	172[f]
Agricultural production index (2014-2016=100)	86	101	128[c]
International trade: exports (million current US$)	21 278	12 646	22 207[f]
International trade: imports (million current US$)	6 597	9 214	11 698[f]
International trade: balance (million current US$)	14 682	3 432	10 508[f]
Balance of payments, current account (million US$)	15 040	-222	8 292[f]

Major trading partners						2021
Export partners (% of exports)	Italy	41.6	Türkiye	12.7	Russian Federation	4.1
Import partners (% of imports)	Russian Federation	17.7	Türkiye	15.8	China	14.0

Social indicators	2010	2015	2022
Population growth rate (average annual %)[a]	1.3	1.2	0.6[b]
Urban population (% of total population)[a]	53.4	54.7	56.0[e]
Urban population growth rate (average annual %)[a,l]	1.5	1.7	...
Fertility rate, total (live births per woman)[a]	2.1	2.1	1.7[b]
Life expectancy at birth (females/males, years)[a]	72.8 / 66.3	74.8 / 68.1	76.2 / 70.6[b]
Population age distribution (0-14/60+ years old, %)[a]	23.9 / 7.9	24.4 / 8.8	23.5 / 12.5[b]
International migrant stock (000/% of total pop.)[a,m]	276.9 / 3.1	264.4 / 2.7	252.2 / 2.5[c]
Refugees and others of concern to the UNHCR (000)	596.9[n]	628.1	659.1[f]
Infant mortality rate (per 1 000 live births)[a]	32.3	23.1	16.4[b]
Health: Current expenditure (% of GDP)	2.5	4.1	4.0[e]
Health: Physicians (per 1 000 pop.)	3.7	3.4	3.2[e]
Education: Government expenditure (% of GDP)	2.8	3.0	2.7[e]
Education: Primary gross enrol. ratio (f/m per 100 pop.)[k]	93.2 / 94.2	105.6 / 107.4	98.0 / 93.9[c]
Education: Sec. gross enrol. ratio (f/m per 100 pop.)	... / ...	... / ...	93.1 / 95.0[k,c]
Education: Upr. Sec. gross enrol. ratio (f/m per 100 pop.)	... / ...	... / ...	74.8 / 79.0[k,c]
Intentional homicide rate (per 100 000 pop.)	2.3	2.2	2.3[c]
Seats held by women in the National Parliament (%)	11.4	15.6	18.3[o]

Environment and infrastructure indicators	2010	2015	2022
Individuals using the Internet (per 100 inhabitants)	46.0[p]	77.0	84.6[c]
Research & Development expenditure (% of GDP)	0.2	0.2	0.2[c]
Threatened species (number)	45	92	101
Forested area (% of land area)	12.5	13.0	13.6[e]
CO2 emission estimates (million tons/tons per capita)	23.6 / 2.6	30.8 / 3.2	33.7 / 3.3[c]
Energy production, primary (Petajoules)	2 759	2 474	2 475[e]
Energy supply per capita (Gigajoules)	54	63	66[e]
Tourist/visitor arrivals at national borders (000)	1 280	1 922	587[c]
Important sites for terrestrial biodiversity protected (%)	36.1	36.1	36.6[f]
Pop. using safely managed drinking water (urban/rural, %)	93.0 / 58.0	95.5 / 72.2	96.2 / 78.1[c]
Pop. using safely managed sanitation (urban/rural, %)	13.5 / ...	12.4 / ...	8.9 / ...[c]
Net Official Development Assist. received (% of GNI)	0.32	0.14	0.29[c]

a Including Nagorno-Karabakh. b Projected estimate (medium fertility variant). c 2020. d Including communities under the authority of the Town Council. e 2019. f 2021. g Data classified according to ISIC Rev. 4. h Excludes irrigation canals and landscaping care. i Excludes publishing activities. Includes irrigation and canals. j Includes publishing activities and landscape care. Excludes repair of personal and household goods. k Estimate. l Data refers to a 5-year period preceding the reference year. m Including refugees. n Data as at the end of December. o Data are as at 1 January of reporting year. p Population aged 7 years and over.

Region	Caribbean	UN membership date	18 September 1973
Population (000, 2022)	410[a]	Surface area (km2)	13 940[b]
Pop. density (per km2, 2022)	76.5[a]	Sex ratio (m per 100 f)	91.4[a]
Capital city	Nassau	National currency	Bahamian Dollar (BSD)
Capital city pop. (000, 2022)	279.7[c]	Exchange rate (per US$)	1.0[d]

Economic indicators

	2010	2015	2022
GDP: Gross domestic product (million current US$)	10 096	11 891	9 908[b]
GDP growth rate (annual %, const. 2015 prices)	1.5	1.6	- 14.5[b]
GDP per capita (current US$)	28 443.5	31 775.6	25 194.3[b]
Economy: Agriculture (% of Gross Value Added)[e,f]	1.2	0.9	0.5[b]
Economy: Industry (% of Gross Value Added)[e,g]	12.3	12.4	13.3[b]
Economy: Services and other activity (% of GVA)[e,h]	86.6	86.7	86.2[b]
Employment in agriculture (% of employed)[i]	2.8	2.4	2.1[b]
Employment in industry (% of employed)[i]	16.1	14.7	14.0[b]
Employment in services & other sectors (% employed)[i]	81.1	82.9	83.9[b]
Unemployment rate (% of labour force)	14.3[i]	12.0	12.9[i]
Labour force participation rate (female/male pop. %)[i]	69.4 / 76.8	69.9 / 75.7	67.8 / 72.9
CPI: Consumer Price Index (2010=100)[i]	100	110	116[b]
Agricultural production index (2014-2016=100)	93	101	101[b]
International trade: exports (million current US$)	620	443	1 067[i,d]
International trade: imports (million current US$)	2 862	3 161	3 797[i,d]
International trade: balance (million current US$)	- 2 242	- 2 719	- 2 729[d]
Balance of payments, current account (million US$)	- 814	- 1 203	- 2 376[b]

Major trading partners

						2021
Export partners (% of exports)[i]	United States	32.3	Singapore	23.0	Germany	11.9
Import partners (% of imports)[i]	United States	36.5	Singapore	14.3	Germany	8.1

Social indicators

	2010	2015	2022
Population growth rate (average annual %)	1.4	0.9	0.7[a]
Urban population (% of total population)	82.4	82.7	83.1[i]
Urban population growth rate (average annual %)[k]	1.9	1.5	...
Fertility rate, total (live births per woman)	1.8	1.6	1.4[a]
Life expectancy at birth (females/males, years)	76.1 / 69.3	76.4 / 69.8	77.8 / 70.8[a]
Population age distribution (0-14/60+ years old, %)	26.4 / 9.1	23.3 / 10.5	19.1 / 13.9[a]
International migrant stock (000/% of total pop.)[l]	54.7 / 15.4	59.2 / 15.8	63.6 / 16.2[b]
Refugees and others of concern to the UNHCR (000)	~0.0[m]	0.1	~0.0[d]
Infant mortality rate (per 1 000 live births)	13.4	12.4	10.1[a]
Health: Current expenditure (% of GDP)[i,n]	5.3	5.2	5.7[j]
Health: Physicians (per 1 000 pop.)	2.8[o]	2.3[p]	1.9[q]
Education: Government expenditure (% of GDP)[i]	...	2.3	2.5[b]
Education: Primary gross enrol. ratio (f/m per 100 pop.)	94.5 / 97.6[r]	... / ...	... / ...
Education: Sec. gross enrol. ratio (f/m per 100 pop.)	91.2 / 87.6	78.9 / 74.9[s]	... / ...
Education: Upr. Sec. gross enrol. ratio (f/m per 100 pop.)	89.8 / 84.0	78.5 / 72.6[s]	... / ...
Intentional homicide rate (per 100 000 pop.)	26.5	39.0	18.6[b]
Seats held by women in the National Parliament (%)	12.2	13.2	18.0[t]

Environment and infrastructure indicators

	2010	2015	2022
Individuals using the Internet (per 100 inhabitants)[i]	43.0	78.0	87.0[b]
Threatened species (number)	62	81	128
Forested area (% of land area)[i]	50.9	50.9	50.9[i]
Energy production, primary (Petajoules)	0	0	0[i]
Energy supply per capita (Gigajoules)	78	82	94[i]
Tourist/visitor arrivals at national borders (000)	1 378	1 496	453[b]
Important sites for terrestrial biodiversity protected (%)	11.2	29.8	29.8[d]

a Projected estimate (medium fertility variant). b 2020. c 2018. d 2021. e Data classified according to ISIC Rev. 4. f Excludes irrigation canals and landscaping care. g Excludes publishing activities. Includes irrigation and canals. h Includes publishing activities and landscape care. Excludes repair of personal and household goods. i Estimate. j 2019. k Data refers to a 5-year period preceding the reference year. l Including refugees. m Data as at the end of December. n Data refer to fiscal years beginning 1 July. o 2008. p 2011. q 2017. r 2006. s 2013. t Data are as at 1 January of reporting year.

Bahrain

Region	Western Asia	UN membership date	21 September 1971
Population (000, 2022)	1 472[a]	Surface area (km2)	778[b]
Pop. density (per km2, 2022)	1 880.2[a]	Sex ratio (m per 100 f)	162.9[a]
Capital city	Manama	National currency	Bahraini Dinar (BHD)
Capital city pop. (000, 2022)	600.4[c,d]	Exchange rate (per US$)	0.4[e]

Economic indicators

	2010	2015	2022
GDP: Gross domestic product (million current US$)	25 713	31 051	33 904[b]
GDP growth rate (annual %, const. 2015 prices)	4.3	2.5	- 5.4[b]
GDP per capita (current US$)	20 722.1	22 634.1	19 925.0[b]
Economy: Agriculture (% of Gross Value Added)[f,g]	0.3	0.3	0.3[b]
Economy: Industry (% of Gross Value Added)[f,g]	45.5	40.7	42.7[b]
Economy: Services and other activity (% of GVA)[f,g]	54.2	59.0	57.0[b]
Employment in agriculture (% of employed)	1.1	1.1	1.0[h,b]
Employment in industry (% of employed)	35.7	35.2	35.1[h,b]
Employment in services & other sectors (% employed)	63.2	63.8	64.0[h,b]
Unemployment rate (% of labour force)	1.1	1.2[h]	1.8[h]
Labour force participation rate (female/male pop. %)	43.6 / 87.2	43.6 / 87.0	43.2 / 84.2[h]
CPI: Consumer Price Index (2010=100)[i]	100	111	115[e]
Agricultural production index (2014-2016=100)	34	105	131[b]
International trade: exports (million current US$)	16 059	13 882	16 734[h,e]
International trade: imports (million current US$)	16 002	16 390	14 268[h,e]
International trade: balance (million current US$)	58	- 2 508	2 466[e]
Balance of payments, current account (million US$)	770	- 752	- 2 435[i]

Major trading partners

2021

Export partners (% of exports)[h]	Areas nes[k]	42.0	Saudi Arabia	14.3	United Arab Emirates	10.1
Import partners (% of imports)[h]	Saudi Arabia	33.7	China	11.1	Australia	5.0

Social indicators

	2010	2015	2022
Population growth rate (average annual %)	0.0	3.5	0.9[a]
Urban population (% of total population)	88.6	89.0	89.4[d]
Urban population growth rate (average annual %)[l]	6.7	2.1	...
Fertility rate, total (live births per woman)	2.1	2.1	1.8[a]
Life expectancy at birth (females/males, years)	80.0 / 77.7	80.8 / 78.3	80.5 / 78.2[a]
Population age distribution (0-14/60+ years old, %)	20.5 / 3.5	20.4 / 5.0	20.2 / 6.9[a]
International migrant stock (000/% of total pop.)[m,n]	666.4 / 53.7	722.5 / 52.7	936.1 / 55.0[b]
Refugees and others of concern to the UNHCR (000)	0.2[o]	0.4	0.4[e]
Infant mortality rate (per 1 000 live births)	7.3	6.5	5.4[a]
Health: Current expenditure (% of GDP)[p]	3.8	5.0	4.0[h,d]
Health: Physicians (per 1 000 pop.)	0.9	0.9	...
Education: Government expenditure (% of GDP)	2.5[q]	2.7	2.3[r]
Education: Primary gross enrol. ratio (f/m per 100 pop.)	101.0 / 96.1[s]	101.7 / 100.7	97.7 / 98.3[d]
Education: Sec. gross enrol. ratio (f/m per 100 pop.)	93.5 / 92.2	101.8 / 102.5	101.5 / 93.2[d]
Education: Upr. Sec. gross enrol. ratio (f/m per 100 pop.)	92.9 / 88.5	104.2 / 101.5	101.9 / 90.9[d]
Intentional homicide rate (per 100 000 pop.)	0.2	0.6	0.1[d]
Seats held by women in the National Parliament (%)	2.5	7.5	15.0[t]

Environment and infrastructure indicators

	2010	2015	2022
Individuals using the Internet (per 100 inhabitants)	55.0	93.5	99.7[b]
Research & Development expenditure (% of GDP)	...	0.1[u]	...
Threatened species (number)	32	32	63
Forested area (% of land area)[h]	0.7	0.8	0.9[d]
CO2 emission estimates (million tons/tons per capita)	25.6 / 20.6	30.2 / 21.9	32.7 / 19.9[d]
Energy production, primary (Petajoules)	849	957	1 045[d]
Energy supply per capita (Gigajoules)	413	421	408[d]
Tourist/visitor arrivals at national borders (000)[v]	11 952	9 670[w]	1 909[b]
Important sites for terrestrial biodiversity protected (%)	0.0	0.0	0.0[e]

a Projected estimate (medium fertility variant). b 2020. c Refers to the urban area of the municipality of Al-Manamah. d 2019. e 2021. f Data classified according to ISIC Rev. 4. g At producers' prices. h Estimate. i Calculated by the UNSD from national indices. j 2018. k Areas nes l Data refers to a 5-year period preceding the reference year. m Including refugees. n Refers to foreign citizens. o Data as at the end of December. p Data based on calendar year (January 1 to December 31). q 2008. r 2017. s 2006. t Data are as at 1 January of reporting year. u 2014. v Excluding nationals residing abroad. w Break in the time series.

Bangladesh

Region	Southern Asia	UN membership date	17 September 1974	
Population (000, 2022)	171 186[a]	Surface area (km2)	148 460[b]	
Pop. density (per km2, 2022)	1 315.1[a]	Sex ratio (m per 100 f)	98.3[a]	
Capital city	Dhaka	National currency	Taka (BDT)	
Capital city pop. (000, 2022)	20 283.6[c,d]	Exchange rate (per US$)	85.8[e]	

Economic indicators

	2010	2015	2022
GDP: Gross domestic product (million current US$)	114 508	194 466	329 484[b]
GDP growth rate (annual %, const. 2015 prices)	5.6	6.6	5.2[b]
GDP per capita (current US$)	775.9	1 244.5	2 000.6[b]
Economy: Agriculture (% of Gross Value Added)[f]	17.8	15.3	13.0[b]
Economy: Industry (% of Gross Value Added)[f]	26.1	27.8	31.1[b]
Economy: Services and other activity (% of GVA)[f]	56.0	57.0	55.9[b]
Employment in agriculture (% of employed)	47.3	43.5[g]	37.7[g,b]
Employment in industry (% of employed)	17.6	19.9[g]	21.6[g,b]
Employment in services & other sectors (% employed)	35.1	36.6[g]	40.6[g,b]
Unemployment rate (% of labour force)	3.4	4.4[g]	5.0[g]
Labour force participation rate (female/male pop. %)[g]	30.5 / 83.3	32.5 / 79.6	35.5 / 79.2
CPI: Consumer Price Index (2010=100)[h]	100	145	200[e]
Agricultural production index (2014-2016=100)	90	101	111[b]
International trade: exports (million current US$)	19 231	31 734	39 249[g,e]
International trade: imports (million current US$)	30 504	48 059	67 283[g,e]
International trade: balance (million current US$)	- 11 273	- 16 325	- 28 034[e]
Balance of payments, current account (million US$)	2 108	2 580	- 15 563[e]

Major trading partners

						2021
Export partners (% of exports)[g]	United States	16.9	Germany	16.3	Spain	6.9
Import partners (% of imports)[g]	China	31.0	India	18.2	Singapore	5.2

Social indicators

	2010	2015	2022
Population growth rate (average annual %)	1.2	1.2	1.0[a]
Urban population (% of total population)	30.5	34.3	37.4[d]
Urban population growth rate (average annual %)[i]	3.7	3.5	...
Fertility rate, total (live births per woman)	2.3	2.1	2.0[a]
Life expectancy at birth (females/males, years)	70.3 / 67.2	72.7 / 68.5	76.0 / 71.5[a]
Population age distribution (0-14/60+ years old, %)	33.4 / 6.7	30.2 / 7.5	26.0 / 9.3[a]
International migrant stock (000/% of total pop.)[i]	1 345.5 / 0.9	1 422.2 / 0.9	2 115.4 / 1.3[b]
Refugees and others of concern to the UNHCR (000)	229.3[k]	233.0	1 361.8[e]
Infant mortality rate (per 1 000 live births)	39.0	30.9	20.4[a]
Health: Current expenditure (% of GDP)[l]	2.7	2.6	2.5[d]
Health: Physicians (per 1 000 pop.)	0.4	0.5	0.7[b]
Education: Government expenditure (% of GDP)	1.9[m]	2.0[g,n]	1.3[d]
Education: Primary gross enrol. ratio (f/m per 100 pop.)	109.3 / 102.8[g]	... / ...	125.0 / 114.4[b]
Education: Sec. gross enrol. ratio (f/m per 100 pop.)	54.7 / 48.7	69.7 / 61.8	81.5 / 67.5[b]
Education: Upr. Sec. gross enrol. ratio (f/m per 100 pop.)	40.0 / 41.1	49.8 / 50.3	66.9 / 59.8[b]
Intentional homicide rate (per 100 000 pop.)	2.7	2.6	2.4[o]
Seats held by women in the National Parliament (%)	18.6	20.0	20.9[p]

Environment and infrastructure indicators

	2010	2015	2022
Individuals using the Internet (per 100 inhabitants)[g]	3.7	12.9	24.8[b]
Threatened species (number)	122	137	218
Forested area (% of land area)[g]	14.5	14.5	14.5[d]
CO2 emission estimates (million tons/tons per capita)[l]	53.3 / 0.3	74.4 / 0.5	92.7 / 0.5[d]
Energy production, primary (Petajoules)	1 304	1 510	1 561[d]
Energy supply per capita (Gigajoules)	10	12	13[d]
Tourist/visitor arrivals at national borders (000)	139	126	168[b]
Important sites for terrestrial biodiversity protected (%)	41.5	41.5	41.5
Pop. using safely managed drinking water (urban/rural, %)	42.3 / 60.5	46.9 / 61.2	52.8 / 62.1[b]
Pop. using safely managed sanitation (urban/rural %)	30.6 / 27.5	32.1 / 34.5	33.5 / 41.9[b]
Net Official Development Assist. received (% of GNI)	1.06	1.25	1.59[b]

a Projected estimate (medium fertility variant). b 2020. c Mega city. d 2019. e 2021. f Data classified according to ISIC Rev. 4. g Estimate. h Calculated by the UNSD from national indices. i Data refers to a 5-year period preceding the reference year. j Including refugees. k Data as at the end of December. l Data refer to fiscal years beginning 1 July. m 2009. n 2013. o 2018. p Data are as at 1 January of reporting year.

Barbados

Region	Caribbean	UN membership date	09 December 1966
Population (000, 2022)	282[a]	Surface area (km2)	431[b]
Pop. density (per km2, 2022)	655.0[a]	Sex ratio (m per 100 f)	92.2[a]
Capital city	Bridgetown	National currency	Barbados Dollar (BBD)
Capital city pop. (000, 2022)	89.2[c]	Exchange rate (per US$)	2.0[d]

Economic indicators

	2010	2015	2022
GDP: Gross domestic product (million current US$)	4 530	4 715	4 440[b]
GDP growth rate (annual %, const. 2015 prices)	- 2.3	2.5	- 17.6[b]
GDP per capita (current US$)	16 056.1	16 525.1	15 449.2[b]
Economy: Agriculture (% of Gross Value Added)[e,f]	1.5	1.5	1.6[b]
Economy: Industry (% of Gross Value Added)[f,g]	15.8	15.4	14.3[b]
Economy: Services and other activity (% of GVA)[f,h]	82.7	83.1	84.2[b]
Employment in agriculture (% of employed)	2.8	2.9	2.6[i,b]
Employment in industry (% of employed)	18.8	19.4	18.9[i,b]
Employment in services & other sectors (% employed)	78.4	77.8	78.5[i,b]
Unemployment rate (% of labour force)	10.7	9.8	9.8[i]
Labour force participation rate (female/male pop. %)	61.9 / 71.8	60.8 / 67.4	56.7 / 63.9[i]
CPI: Consumer Price Index (2010=100)[k]	100[l]	168[l]	204[l,m,d]
Agricultural production index (2014-2016=100)	107	103	101[b]
International trade: exports (million current US$)	314	483	350[d]
International trade: imports (million current US$)	1 196	1 618	1 673[d]
International trade: balance (million current US$)	- 883	- 1 135	- 1 323[d]
Balance of payments, current account (million US$)	- 272	- 99	- 453[n]

Major trading partners

						2021
Export partners (% of exports)	Areas nes[o]	20.9	United States	19.2	Jamaica	7.7
Import partners (% of imports)	United States	47.0	Trinidad and Tobago	12.5	United Kingdom	4.4

Social indicators

	2010	2015	2022
Population growth rate (average annual %)	0.3	0.2	0.1[a]
Urban population (% of total population)	31.9	31.2	31.2[p]
Urban population growth rate (average annual %)[q]	- 0.2	- 0.1	...
Fertility rate, total (live births per woman)	1.7	1.6	1.6[a]
Life expectancy at birth (females/males, years)	77.7 / 73.6	78.6 / 74.5	79.6 / 75.7[a]
Population age distribution (0-14/60+ years old, %)	20.1 / 16.6	18.8 / 18.7	16.9 / 23.1[a]
International migrant stock (000/% of total pop.)[r]	32.8 / 11.6	34.5 / 12.1	34.9 / 12.1[b]
Refugees and others of concern to the UNHCR (000)	...	~0.0	~0.0[d]
Infant mortality rate (per 1 000 live births)	13.5	12.7	10.4[a]
Health: Current expenditure (% of GDP)[i,s]	6.8	6.8	6.3[p]
Health: Physicians (per 1 000 pop.)	1.8[t]	...	2.5[u]
Education: Government expenditure (% of GDP)	6.1	5.4[i]	4.3[b]
Education: Primary gross enrol. ratio (f/m per 100 pop.)	100.4 / 98.8[i]	95.6 / 96.2	98.1 / 101.2[b]
Education: Sec. gross enrol. ratio (f/m per 100 pop.)	102.1 / 101.7[i]	109.5 / 105.7	105.7 / 102.4[b]
Education: Upr. Sec. gross enrol. ratio (f/m per 100 pop.)	109.4 / 101.7[i]	113.5 / 107.8	115.3 / 102.3[b]
Intentional homicide rate (per 100 000 pop.)	11.0	10.9	14.3[b]
Seats held by women in the National Parliament (%)	10.0	16.7	20.0[v]

Environment and infrastructure indicators

	2010	2015	2022
Individuals using the Internet (per 100 inhabitants)[i]	65.1	76.1	81.8[u]
Threatened species (number)	36	51	76
Forested area (% of land area)	14.7	14.7	14.7[p]
Energy production, primary (Petajoules)	4	3	3[p]
Energy supply per capita (Gigajoules)	71	59	55[p]
Tourist/visitor arrivals at national borders (000)	532	592	207[b]
Important sites for terrestrial biodiversity protected (%)	1.8	1.8	1.8[d]
Net Official Development Assist. received (% of GNI)	0.35	...	...

a Projected estimate (medium fertility variant). b 2020. c 2018. d 2021. e Excludes irrigation canals and landscaping care. f Data classified according to ISIC Rev. 4. g Excludes publishing activities. Includes irrigation and canals. h Excludes repair of personal and household goods. i Estimate. j Calculated by the UNSD from national indices. k Data refer to the Retail Price Index. l Index base: July 2001=100. m Average for 11 months excluding data for February. n 2016. o Areas nes p 2019. q Data refers to a 5-year period preceding the reference year. r Including refugees. s Data refer to fiscal years beginning 1 April. t 2005. u 2017. v Data are as at 1 January of reporting year.

Belarus

Region	Eastern Europe	UN membership date	24 October 1945
Population (000, 2022)	9 535[a]	Surface area (km2)	207 600[b]
Pop. density (per km2, 2022)	47.0[a]	Sex ratio (m per 100 f)	85.3[a]
Capital city	Minsk	National currency	Belarusian Ruble (BYN)
Capital city pop. (000, 2022)	2 016.7[c,d]	Exchange rate (per US$)	2.5[e]

Economic indicators

	2010	2015	2022
GDP: Gross domestic product (million current US$)	57 232	56 455	60 259[b]
GDP growth rate (annual %, const. 2015 prices)	7.8	- 3.8	- 0.9[b]
GDP per capita (current US$)	6 075.2	5 980.7	6 377.1[b]
Economy: Agriculture (% of Gross Value Added)[f,g]	10.1	7.2	7.8[b]
Economy: Industry (% of Gross Value Added)[g,h]	40.3	37.7	35.9[b]
Economy: Services and other activity (% of GVA)[g,i]	49.5	55.1	56.3[b]
Employment in agriculture (% of employed)	11.0[j]	9.7	10.8[j,b]
Employment in industry (% of employed)	32.2[j]	31.1	30.2[j,b]
Employment in services & other sectors (% employed)	56.8[j]	59.2	59.0[j,b]
Unemployment rate (% of labour force)[j]	6.3	5.8	4.6
Labour force participation rate (female/male pop. %)[j]	56.7 / 69.2	58.4 / 70.8	57.3 / 71.2
CPI: Consumer Price Index (2010=100)	100[j]	387	587[e]
Agricultural production index (2014-2016=100)	97	100	106[b]
International trade: exports (million current US$)	25 283	26 660	39 889[e]
International trade: imports (million current US$)	34 884	30 291	41 811[e]
International trade: balance (million current US$)	- 9 601	- 3 631	- 1 922[e]
Balance of payments, current account (million US$)	- 8 280	- 1 831	1 843[e]

Major trading partners

						2021
Export partners (% of exports)	Areas nes[k]	40.3	Russian Federation	35.0	Poland	4.0
Import partners (% of imports)	Areas nes[k]	37.0	Russian Federation	28.6	China	8.1

Social indicators

	2010	2015	2022
Population growth rate (average annual %)	- 0.3	0.1	- 0.3[a]
Urban population (% of total population)	74.7	77.2	79.0[d]
Urban population growth rate (average annual %)[l]	0.3	0.7	...
Fertility rate, total (live births per woman)	1.5	1.7	1.5[a]
Life expectancy at birth (females/males, years)	77.0 / 65.5	78.8 / 68.9	78.4 / 68.1[a]
Population age distribution (0-14/60+ years old, %)	14.9 / 19.7	16.3 / 21.4	16.8 / 24.5[a]
International migrant stock (000/% of total pop.)	1 090.4 / 11.6	1 082.9 / 11.5	1 067.1 / 11.3[b]
Refugees and others of concern to the UNHCR (000)	8.4[m]	7.9	9.2[e]
Infant mortality rate (per 1 000 live births)	4.4	3.1	1.9[a]
Health: Current expenditure (% of GDP)	5.7	6.1	5.9[d]
Health: Physicians (per 1 000 pop.)	...	5.2	4.5[d]
Education: Government expenditure (% of GDP)	5.2	4.8	5.0[b]
Education: Primary gross enrol. ratio (f/m per 100 pop.)	104.3 / 104.5	99.2 / 99.1	100.4 / 100.6[n]
Education: Sec. gross enrol. ratio (f/m per 100 pop.)	106.4 / 109.9	104.6 / 106.3	101.7 / 103.1[n]
Education: Upr. Sec. gross enrol. ratio (f/m per 100 pop.)	123.0 / 132.3	110.1 / 115.9	112.0 / 118.7[n]
Intentional homicide rate (per 100 000 pop.)	4.3	3.5	2.4[d]
Seats held by women in the National Parliament (%)	31.8	27.3	40.0[o]

Environment and infrastructure indicators

	2010	2015	2022
Individuals using the Internet (per 100 inhabitants)	31.8[p]	62.2[q]	85.1[r,b]
Research & Development expenditure (% of GDP)	0.7[s]	0.5[s]	0.5[b]
Threatened species (number)	16	21	35
Forested area (% of land area)	42.5	42.5	43.1[d]
CO2 emission estimates (million tons/tons per capita)	60.3 / 6.3	53.3 / 5.5	56.2 / 5.9[b]
Energy production, primary (Petajoules)	167	163	177[d]
Energy supply per capita (Gigajoules)	122	113	114[d]
Tourist/visitor arrivals at national borders (000)	5 674[t]	4 386[t]	3 598[u,b]
Important sites for terrestrial biodiversity protected (%)	75.8	87.9	87.9[e]
Pop. using safely managed sanitation (urban/rural %)	85.5 / 62.6	82.1 / 55.1	80.3 / 49.0[b]
Net Official Development Assist. received (% of GNI)	0.24	0.19	1.43[b]

a Projected estimate (medium fertility variant). b 2020. c Including communities under the authority of the Town Council. d 2019. e 2021. f Excludes irrigation canals and landscaping care. g Data classified according to ISIC Rev. 4. h Excludes publishing activities. Includes irrigation and canals. i Includes publishing activities and landscape care. Excludes repair of personal and household goods. j Estimate. k Areas nes l Data refers to a 5-year period preceding the reference year. m Data as at the end of December. n 2018. o Data are as at 1 January of reporting year. p Population aged 16 years and over. q Users in the last 12 months. r Population aged 6 to 72 years. s Data have been converted from the former national currency using the appropriate conversion rate. t Excludes the Belarusian-Russian border segment. u Includes estimation of the Belarusian-Russian border segment.

Belgium

Region	Western Europe	UN membership date	27 December 1945
Population (000, 2022)	11 656[a]	Surface area (km2)	30 528[b]
Pop. density (per km2, 2022)	385.0[a]	Sex ratio (m per 100 f)	97.7[a]
Capital city	Brussels	National currency	Euro (EUR)
Capital city pop. (000, 2022)	2 065.3[c,d]	Exchange rate (per US$)	0.9[e]

Economic indicators

	2010	2015	2022
GDP: Gross domestic product (million current US$)	480 952	462 150	521 861[b]
GDP growth rate (annual %, const. 2015 prices)	2.9	2.0	- 5.7[b]
GDP per capita (current US$)	43 967.7	40 941.9	45 028.3[b]
Economy: Agriculture (% of Gross Value Added)[f,g]	0.9	0.8	0.7[b]
Economy: Industry (% of Gross Value Added)[g,h]	23.4	22.0	21.7[b]
Economy: Services and other activity (% of GVA)[g,i]	75.7	77.3	77.6[b]
Employment in agriculture (% of employed)	1.4	1.2	0.9[j,b]
Employment in industry (% of employed)	23.4	21.4	20.6[j,b]
Employment in services & other sectors (% employed)	75.3	77.4	78.4[j,b]
Unemployment rate (% of labour force)	8.3	8.5	6.2[j]
Labour force participation rate (female/male pop. %)	47.7 / 60.8	48.0 / 58.9	50.1 / 58.9[j]
CPI: Consumer Price Index (2010=100)	100[k]	109[k]	121[e]
Agricultural production index (2014-2016=100)	96	101	102[b]
International trade: exports (million current US$)	407 596	397 739	336 468[e]
International trade: imports (million current US$)	391 256	371 025	344 685[e]
International trade: balance (million current US$)	16 340	26 714	- 8 216[e]
Balance of payments, current account (million US$)	7 338	6 363	- 2 157[e]

Major trading partners

						2021
Export partners (% of exports)	Germany	17.1	France	13.4	Netherlands	12.1
Import partners (% of imports)	Netherlands	21.0	Germany	15.9	France	10.2

Social indicators

	2010	2015	2022
Population growth rate (average annual %)	0.7	0.6	0.3[a]
Urban population (% of total population)	97.7	97.9	98.0[d]
Urban population growth rate (average annual %)[l]	0.8	0.7	...
Fertility rate, total (live births per woman)	1.9	1.7	1.6[a]
Life expectancy at birth (females/males, years)	82.6 / 77.4	83.1 / 78.6	84.4 / 80.2[a]
Population age distribution (0-14/60+ years old, %)	16.9 / 23.1	17.0 / 24.1	16.5 / 26.2[a]
International migrant stock (000/% of total pop.)	1 503.8 / 13.7	1 783.5 / 15.8	2 005.5 / 17.3[b]
Refugees and others of concern to the UNHCR (000)	36.9[m]	45.8	89.3[e]
Infant mortality rate (per 1 000 live births)	3.6	3.2	2.9[a]
Health: Current expenditure (% of GDP)	10.2	10.4	10.7[d]
Health: Physicians (per 1 000 pop.)	2.9	3.0	6.1[b]
Education: Government expenditure (% of GDP)	6.4	6.5	6.4[n]
Education: Primary gross enrol. ratio (f/m per 100 pop.)	101.8 / 102.0	103.1 / 103.2	103.2 / 102.1[d]
Education: Sec. gross enrol. ratio (f/m per 100 pop.)	167.3 / 146.9	174.7 / 153.6	165.7 / 146.9[d]
Education: Upr. Sec. gross enrol. ratio (f/m per 100 pop.)	180.6 / 152.6	168.7 / 142.8	162.2 / 138.3[d]
Seats held by women in the National Parliament (%)	38.0	39.3	42.0[o]

Environment and infrastructure indicators

	2010	2015	2022
Individuals using the Internet (per 100 inhabitants)	75.0	85.1[p]	91.5[b]
Research & Development expenditure (% of GDP)	2.1	2.4	3.5[b]
Threatened species (number)	27	30	78
Forested area (% of land area)	22.8	22.8[j]	22.8[j,d]
CO2 emission estimates (million tons/tons per capita)	105.4 / 9.6	94.0 / 8.2	84.5 / 7.2[b]
Energy production, primary (Petajoules)	650	446	656[d]
Energy supply per capita (Gigajoules)	228	193	198[d]
Tourist/visitor arrivals at national borders (000)	7 186	8 355[q]	2 584[b]
Important sites for terrestrial biodiversity protected (%)	72.8	74.2	75.9[e]
Net Official Development Assist. disbursed (% of GNI)[r]	1.68	0.79	0.85[b]

a Projected estimate (medium fertility variant). b 2020. c Refers to the population of Brussels-Capital Region and "communes" of the agglomeration and suburbs. d 2019. e 2021. f Excludes irrigation canals and landscaping care. g Data classified according to ISIC Rev. 4. h Excludes publishing activities. Includes irrigation and canals. i Includes publishing activities and landscape care. Excludes repair of personal and household goods. j Estimate. k Calculated by the UNSD from national indices. l Data refers to a 5-year period preceding the reference year. m Data as at the end of December. n 2018. o Data are as at 1 January of reporting year. p Users in the last 3 months. q Break in the time series. r DAC member (OECD).

Region	Central America	UN membership date	25 September 1981
Population (000, 2022)	405[a]	Surface area (km2)	22 965[b]
Pop. density (per km2, 2022)	17.8[a]	Sex ratio (m per 100 f)	101.1[a]
Capital city	Belmopan	National currency	Belize Dollar (BZD)
Capital city pop. (000, 2022)	23.0[c]	Exchange rate (per US$)	2.0[d]

Economic indicators

	2010	2015	2022
GDP: Gross domestic product (million current US$)	1 388	1 734	1 586[b]
GDP growth rate (annual %, const. 2015 prices)	3.3	2.9	- 16.7[b]
GDP per capita (current US$)	4 304.1	4 805.1	3 987.7[b]
Economy: Agriculture (% of Gross Value Added)[e]	12.7	14.8	13.3[b]
Economy: Industry (% of Gross Value Added)[e]	20.8	16.2	16.3[b]
Economy: Services and other activity (% of GVA)[e]	66.5	69.0	70.4[b]
Employment in agriculture (% of employed)	18.9[f]	18.1	16.6[f,b]
Employment in industry (% of employed)	16.5[f]	15.4	15.7[f,b]
Employment in services & other sectors (% employed)	64.5[f]	66.5	67.7[f,b]
Unemployment rate (% of labour force)	8.2[f]	7.6	7.8[f]
Labour force participation rate (female/male pop. %)[f]	45.0 / 79.0	48.4 / 79.7	48.2 / 77.8
CPI: Consumer Price Index (2010=100)[g]	100	104	110[d]
Agricultural production index (2014-2016=100)	96	102	95[b]
International trade: exports (million current US$)	282	314	264[d]
International trade: imports (million current US$)	700	996	1 060[d]
International trade: balance (million current US$)	- 418	- 682	- 796[d]
Balance of payments, current account (million US$)	- 46	- 175	- 166[d]

Major trading partners

					2021
Export partners (% of exports)	United Kingdom	22.9	United States	22.2	Mexico	8.4
Import partners (% of imports)	United States	35.9	China	15.9	Mexico	12.9

Social indicators

	2010	2015	2022
Population growth rate (average annual %)	2.3	2.1	1.3[a]
Urban population (% of total population)	45.2	45.4	45.9[h]
Urban population growth rate (average annual %)[i]	2.5	2.3	
Fertility rate, total (live births per woman)	2.6	2.4	2.0[a]
Life expectancy at birth (females/males, years)	75.4 / 69.6	76.5 / 70.4	74.7 / 67.7[a]
Population age distribution (0-14/60+ years old, %)	35.5 / 5.9	31.8 / 6.6	27.7 / 8.0[a]
International migrant stock (000/% of total pop.)[j]	46.4 / 14.4	54.6 / 15.1	62.0 / 15.6[b]
Refugees and others of concern to the UNHCR (000)	0.2[k]	0.1	5.7[d]
Infant mortality rate (per 1 000 live births)	16.0	13.0	10.1[a]
Health: Current expenditure (% of GDP)[f,l]	5.7	5.9	6.0[h]
Health: Physicians (per 1 000 pop.)	0.8[m]	1.1[n]	1.1[c]
Education: Government expenditure (% of GDP)	6.7	6.9	7.9[f,b]
Education: Primary gross enrol. ratio (f/m per 100 pop.)	110.3 / 114.8	110.2 / 115.5	105.2 / 110.1[b]
Education: Sec. gross enrol. ratio (f/m per 100 pop.)	78.2 / 72.4	81.7 / 79.6	86.9 / 83.7[b]
Education: Upr. Sec. gross enrol. ratio (f/m per 100 pop.)	56.6 / 47.3	63.3 / 56.1	67.3 / 57.6[b]
Intentional homicide rate (per 100 000 pop.)	40.0	33.0	25.7[b]
Seats held by women in the National Parliament (%)	0.0	3.1	12.5[o]

Environment and infrastructure indicators

	2010	2015	2022
Individuals using the Internet (per 100 inhabitants)	28.2[p]	41.6[f]	50.8[f,h]
Threatened species (number)	92	117	184
Forested area (% of land area)[f]	61.0	58.4	56.5[h]
Energy production, primary (Petajoules)	14	9	7[h]
Energy supply per capita (Gigajoules)	40	43	44[h]
Tourist/visitor arrivals at national borders (000)	242	341	144[b]
Important sites for terrestrial biodiversity protected (%)	41.1	43.3	43.3[d]
Net Official Development Assist. received (% of GNI)	1.95	1.74	4.31[b]

a Projected estimate (medium fertility variant). b 2020. c 2018. d 2021. e Data classified according to ISIC Rev. 4. f Estimate. g Calculated by the UNSD from national indices. h 2019. i Data refers to a 5-year period preceding the reference year. j Including refugees. k Data as at the end of December. l Data refer to fiscal years beginning 1 April. m 2009. n 2012. o Data are as at 1 January of reporting year. p Population aged 5 years and over.

Benin

Region	Western Africa	UN membership date	20 September 1960
Population (000, 2022)	13 353[a]	Surface area (km2)	114 763[b]
Pop. density (per km2, 2022)	118.4[a]	Sex ratio (m per 100 f)	100.4[a]
Capital city	Porto-Novo[c]	National currency	CFA Franc, BCEAO (XOF)[d]
Capital city pop. (000, 2022)	285.3[e]	Exchange rate (per US$)	579.2[f]

Economic indicators

	2010	2015	2022
GDP: Gross domestic product (million current US$)	6 970	11 380	15 205[b]
GDP growth rate (annual %, const. 2015 prices)	2.1	13.0	2.0[b]
GDP per capita (current US$)	757.7	1 076.0	1 254.2[b]
Economy: Agriculture (% of Gross Value Added)[g]	25.4	28.7[h]	30.4[h,b]
Economy: Industry (% of Gross Value Added)[g]	24.7	17.8[i]	16.8[i,b]
Economy: Services and other activity (% of GVA)[g]	49.9	53.5[j]	52.9[j,b]
Employment in agriculture (% of employed)[k]	44.0	41.2	38.0[b]
Employment in industry (% of employed)[k]	18.7	18.6	19.1[b]
Employment in services & other sectors (% employed)[k]	37.3	40.2	42.9[b]
Unemployment rate (% of labour force)	1.0	2.0[k]	1.5[k]
Labour force participation rate (female/male pop. %)[k]	69.1 / 74.8	69.8 / 73.7	69.7 / 72.7
CPI: Consumer Price Index (2010=100)[k,l]	100	110	116[f]
Agricultural production index (2014-2016=100)	77	93	123[b]
International trade: exports (million current US$)	534	626	1 024[f]
International trade: imports (million current US$)	2 134	2 475	3 186[f]
International trade: balance (million current US$)	- 1 600	- 1 849	- 2 163[f]
Balance of payments, current account (million US$)	- 531	- 679	- 274[b]

Major trading partners

						2021
Export partners (% of exports)	Bangladesh	41.7	India	10.0	China	9.8
Import partners (% of imports)	India	17.2	China	11.7	France	11.0

Social indicators

	2010	2015	2022
Population growth rate (average annual %)	2.9	2.9	2.7[a]
Urban population (% of total population)	43.1	45.7	47.9[m]
Urban population growth rate (average annual %)[n]	4.1	4.0	...
Fertility rate, total (live births per woman)	5.4	5.3	4.9[a]
Life expectancy at birth (females/males, years)	59.7 / 57.0	60.7 / 58.1	61.7 / 58.3[a]
Population age distribution (0-14/60+ years old, %)	43.7 / 4.8	43.2 / 4.8	42.4 / 4.9[a]
International migrant stock (000/% of total pop.)[o,p]	309.2 / 3.4	366.3 / 3.5	394.3 / 3.3[b]
Refugees and others of concern to the UNHCR (000)	7.3[q]	0.6	1.9[f]
Infant mortality rate (per 1 000 live births)	69.6	63.1	54.4[a]
Health: Current expenditure (% of GDP)	3.0	2.9	2.4[m]
Health: Physicians (per 1 000 pop.)	0.1	0.1[r]	0.1[m]
Education: Government expenditure (% of GDP)	3.7	3.2	3.0[k,m]
Education: Primary gross enrol. ratio (f/m per 100 pop.)	113.2 / 126.9	127.6 / 137.2	109.7 / 118.5[b]
Education: Sec. gross enrol. ratio (f/m per 100 pop.)	... / ...	48.9 / 68.5	42.4 / 52.4[b]
Education: Upr. Sec. gross enrol. ratio (f/m per 100 pop.)	15.2 / 29.6[k,s]	25.8 / 51.5	24.9 / 38.5[b]
Seats held by women in the National Parliament (%)	10.8	8.4	7.4[t]

Environment and infrastructure indicators

	2010	2015	2022
Individuals using the Internet (per 100 inhabitants)	3.1	11.3[k]	25.8[k,b]
Threatened species (number)	62	74	133
Forested area (% of land area)[k]	32.2	30.0	28.2[m]
CO2 emission estimates (million tons/tons per capita)	5.1 / 0.5	6.0 / 0.5	8.4 / 0.6[b]
Energy production, primary (Petajoules)	82	104	121[m]
Energy supply per capita (Gigajoules)	16	17	19[m]
Tourist/visitor arrivals at national borders (000)	199	255	325[b]
Important sites for terrestrial biodiversity protected (%)	66.7	66.7	66.7[f]
Net Official Development Assist. received (% of GNI)	7.27	3.86	6.77[b]

a Projected estimate (medium fertility variant). b 2020. c Porto-Novo is the constitutional capital and Cotonou is the economic capital. d African Financial Community (CFA) Franc, Central Bank of West African States (BCEAO). e 2018. f 2021. g Data classified according to ISIC Rev. 4. h Excludes irrigation canals and landscaping care. i Excludes publishing activities. Includes irrigation and canals. j Includes publishing activities and landscape care. Excludes repair of personal and household goods. k Estimate. l For Cotonou only. m 2019. n Data refers to a 5-year period preceding the reference year. o Refers to foreign citizens. p Including refugees. q Data as at the end of December. r 2011. s 2005. t Data are as at 1 January of reporting year.

Bermuda

Region	Northern America	Population (000, 2022)	64 [a,b]
Surface area (km2)	54 [c]	Pop. density (per km2, 2022)	1 188.6 [a,b]
Sex ratio (m per 100 f)	93.0 [a,b]	Capital city	Hamilton
National currency	Bermudian Dollar (BMD)	Capital city pop. (000, 2022)	10.1 [d]
Exchange rate (per US$)	1.0 [e]		

Economic indicators

	2010	2015	2022
GDP: Gross domestic product (million current US$)	6 635	6 655	7 719 [c]
GDP growth rate (annual %, const. 2015 prices)	0.6	0.8	0.7 [c]
GDP per capita (current US$)	101 462.4	104 480.0	123 944.9 [c]
Economy: Agriculture (% of Gross Value Added) [f,g]	0.3	0.2	0.3 [c]
Economy: Industry (% of Gross Value Added) [f]	6.9	5.4	5.9 [c]
Economy: Services and other activity (% of GVA) [f,h]	92.8	94.4	93.9 [c]
Employment in agriculture (% of employed) [i,j,k]	1.4	1.6 [l]	...
Employment in industry (% of employed) [i,j,k]	12.9	10.3 [l]	...
Employment in services & other sectors (% employed) [i,j,k]	85.7	87.6 [l]	...
Unemployment rate (% of labour force) [k]	4.5 [j,m]	6.7 [n,l]	...
Labour force participation rate (female/male pop. %)	81.0 / 87.0 [k]	72.6 / 80.0 [k,n,o]	... / ...
CPI: Consumer Price Index (2010=100)	...	148 [p,q]	...
International trade: exports (million current US$)	15 [r]	9	28 [r,e]
International trade: imports (million current US$)	970	929	1 021 [r,e]
International trade: balance (million current US$)	- 955	- 920	- 993 [e]
Balance of payments, current account (million US$)	696	943	854 [c]

Major trading partners

						2021
Export partners (% of exports) [r]	United States	94.2	United Kingdom	1.5	Germany	1.3
Import partners (% of imports) [r]	United States	69.9	Canada	7.9	United Kingdom	5.0

Social indicators

	2010	2015	2022
Population growth rate (average annual %) [a]	0.2	- 0.4	- 0.2 [b]
Urban population (% of total population)	100.0	100.0	100.0 [s]
Urban population growth rate (average annual %) [t]	- 0.4	- 0.6	...
Fertility rate, total (live births per woman) [a]	1.7	1.4	1.4 [b]
Life expectancy at birth (females/males, years) [a]	85.3 / 75.9	85.8 / 76.4	84.5 / 78.4 [b]
Population age distribution (0-14/60+ years old, %) [a]	16.2 / 19.0	15.1 / 22.6	14.7 / 28.6 [b]
International migrant stock (000/% of total pop.)	18.5 / 28.4	19.2 / 30.2	19.7 / 31.7 [c]
Infant mortality rate (per 1 000 live births) [a]	1.9	3.1	2.1 [b]
Education: Government expenditure (% of GDP)	2.3	1.5	1.3 [u]
Education: Primary gross enrol. ratio (f/m per 100 pop.)	101.2 / 93.8 [v]	100.2 / 102.1	... / ...
Education: Sec. gross enrol. ratio (f/m per 100 pop.)	83.7 / 71.2	81.5 / 72.6	... / ...
Education: Upr. Sec. gross enrol. ratio (f/m per 100 pop.)	76.6 / 63.9	78.2 / 64.1	... / ...
Intentional homicide rate (per 100 000 pop.)	10.7	6.3	0.0 [s]

Environment and infrastructure indicators

	2010	2015	2022
Individuals using the Internet (per 100 inhabitants) [r]	84.2	98.3	98.4 [u]
Research & Development expenditure (% of GDP) [x]	0.2 [w]	0.2	0.2 [c]
Threatened species (number)	50	64	84
Forested area (% of land area) [r]	18.5	18.5	18.5 [s]
Energy production, primary (Petajoules) [r]	1	1	1 [s]
Energy supply per capita (Gigajoules)	135 [r]	127	138 [s]
Tourist/visitor arrivals at national borders (000) [y,z]	232	220	42 [c]
Important sites for terrestrial biodiversity protected (%)	52.0	52.0	52.0 [e]

a For statistical purposes, the data for United Kingdom do not include this area. b Projected estimate (medium fertility variant). c 2020. d 2018. e 2021. f Data classified according to ISIC Rev. 4. g Excludes irrigation canals and landscaping care. h Excludes repair of personal and household goods. i Data classified according to ISIC Rev. 3. j Break in the time series. k Population aged 16 years and over. l 2013. m 2009. n Excluding the institutional population. o 2012. p Base: 2000=100. q 2014. r Estimate. s 2019. t Data refers to a 5-year period preceding the reference year. u 2017. v 2006. w Excluding most or all capital expenditures. x Overestimated or based on overestimated data. y Arrivals by air. z Excluding nationals residing abroad.

Bhutan

Region	Southern Asia	UN membership date	21 September 1971
Population (000, 2022)	782[a]	Surface area (km2)	38 394[b]
Pop. density (per km2, 2022)	20.4[a]	Sex ratio (m per 100 f)	112.3[a]
Capital city	Thimphu	National currency	Ngultrum (BTN)
Capital city pop. (000, 2022)	203.3[c]	Exchange rate (per US$)	75.3[d]

Economic indicators

	2010	2015	2022
GDP: Gross domestic product (million current US$)	1 548	2 004	2 483[b]
GDP growth rate (annual %, const. 2015 prices)	11.9	6.6	- 0.8[b]
GDP per capita (current US$)	2 258.2	2 752.7	3 218.0[b]
Economy: Agriculture (% of Gross Value Added)[e]	15.4	15.1	16.5[b]
Economy: Industry (% of Gross Value Added)[e]	45.7	44.5	40.9[b]
Economy: Services and other activity (% of GVA)[e]	38.9	40.4	42.7[b]
Employment in agriculture (% of employed)	59.6	58.0	54.6[f,b]
Employment in industry (% of employed)	6.6	9.7	11.1[f,b]
Employment in services & other sectors (% employed)	33.8	32.4	34.3[f,b]
Unemployment rate (% of labour force)	3.3	2.4	4.4[f]
Labour force participation rate (female/male pop. %)	63.4 / 72.3	55.1 / 70.1	52.6 / 68.0[f]
CPI: Consumer Price Index (2010=100)	100	88[g]	114[g,d]
Agricultural production index (2014-2016=100)	97	97	103[b]
International trade: exports (million current US$)	413	549[f]	855[f,d]
International trade: imports (million current US$)	854	1 062[f]	3 534[f,d]
International trade: balance (million current US$)	- 440	- 512[f]	- 2 679[d]
Balance of payments, current account (million US$)	- 323	- 548	- 381[b]

Major trading partners

							2021
Export partners (% of exports)[f]	India	92.3	Nepal	4.5	Italy	1.7
Import partners (% of imports)[f]	India	76.8	China	9.6	Thailand	5.2

Social indicators

	2010	2015	2022
Population growth rate (average annual %)	1.1	0.9	0.6[a]
Urban population (% of total population)	34.8	38.7	41.6[h]
Urban population growth rate (average annual %)[i]	4.4	3.7	...
Fertility rate, total (live births per woman)	2.3	2.0	1.4[a]
Life expectancy at birth (females/males, years)	70.1 / 67.0	72.1 / 68.9	74.2 / 70.6[a]
Population age distribution (0-14/60+ years old, %)	29.6 / 7.5	27.0 / 8.3	22.1 / 9.3[a]
International migrant stock (000/% of total pop.)	48.4 / 7.1	51.1 / 7.0	53.6 / 6.9[b]
Infant mortality rate (per 1 000 live births)	34.2	27.3	20.7[a]
Health: Current expenditure (% of GDP)[j]	3.6	3.8	3.6[b]
Health: Physicians (per 1 000 pop.)	0.3[k]	0.3	0.5[b]
Education: Government expenditure (% of GDP)	4.1	7.6	6.9[f,c]
Education: Primary gross enrol. ratio (f/m per 100 pop.)	109.4 / 107.0	104.8 / 103.7	106.6 / 105.0[b]
Education: Sec. gross enrol. ratio (f/m per 100 pop.)	64.7 / 62.5	86.8 / 81.3	95.7 / 84.7[f,c]
Education: Upr. Sec. gross enrol. ratio (f/m per 100 pop.)	39.8 / 43.7	67.4 / 69.1	75.0 / 71.0[f,c]
Intentional homicide rate (per 100 000 pop.)	2.3	1.6	2.5[b]
Seats held by women in the National Parliament (%)	8.5	8.5	17.4[l]

Environment and infrastructure indicators

	2010	2015	2022
Individuals using the Internet (per 100 inhabitants)[f]	13.6	39.8	53.5[b]
Threatened species (number)	59	71	121
Forested area (% of land area)	71.0	71.2	71.4[h]
Energy production, primary (Petajoules)	73	77	85[h]
Energy supply per capita (Gigajoules)	83	88	94[h]
Tourist/visitor arrivals at national borders (000)[m]	41[n]	155	30[b]
Important sites for terrestrial biodiversity protected (%)	45.4	47.0	47.0[d]
Pop. using safely managed drinking water (urban/rural, %)	48.8 / 25.4	48.9 / 27.2	49.0 / 27.6[b]
Pop. using safely managed sanitation (urban/rural %)	69.1 / 62.1	60.4 / 64.5	63.1 / 66.8[b]
Net Official Development Assist. received (% of GNI)	6.66	5.23	9.22[b]

a Projected estimate (medium fertility variant). b 2020. c 2018. d 2021. e Data classified according to ISIC Rev. 4. f Estimate. g Base: April 2019 = 100 h 2019. i Data refers to a 5-year period preceding the reference year. j Data refer to fiscal years beginning 1 July. k 2008. l Data are as at 1 January of reporting year. m Including regional high end tourists. n Break in the time series.

Bolivia (Plurinational State of)

Region	South America	
Population (000, 2022)	12 224[a]	
Pop. density (per km2, 2022)	11.3[a]	
Capital city	Sucre[d]	
Capital city pop. (000, 2022)	277.9[e]	

UN membership date	14 November 1945	
Surface area (km2)	1 098 581[b,c]	
Sex ratio (m per 100 f)	100.5[a]	
National currency	Boliviano (BOB)	
Exchange rate (per US$)	6.9[f]	

Economic indicators	2010	2015	2022
GDP: Gross domestic product (million current US$)	19 650	33 000	36 573[c]
GDP growth rate (annual %, const. 2015 prices)	4.1	4.9	- 8.8[c]
GDP per capita (current US$)	1 955.5	3 036.0	3 133.1[c]
Economy: Agriculture (% of Gross Value Added)[g]	12.4	12.6	13.5[c]
Economy: Industry (% of Gross Value Added)[g]	35.8	31.0	29.7[c]
Economy: Services and other activity (% of GVA)[g]	51.8	56.5	56.8[c]
Employment in agriculture (% of employed)	30.0[h]	27.8	30.4[h,c]
Employment in industry (% of employed)	20.7[h]	22.5	19.4[h,c]
Employment in services & other sectors (% employed)	49.3[h]	49.6	50.3[h,c]
Unemployment rate (% of labour force)	2.6[h]	3.1	5.6[h]
Labour force participation rate (female/male pop. %)	62.3 / 81.9[h]	54.6 / 79.6	66.0 / 83.1[h]
CPI: Consumer Price Index (2010=100)[i]	100	134	151[f]
Agricultural production index (2014-2016=100)	79	103	109[c]
International trade: exports (million current US$)	7 051	8 923	11 080[f]
International trade: imports (million current US$)	5 604	9 843	9 618[f]
International trade: balance (million current US$)	1 448	- 920	1 462[f]
Balance of payments, current account (million US$)	874	- 1 936	815[f]

Major trading partners						2021
Export partners (% of exports)	India	16.7	Brazil	13.1	Argentina	9.4
Import partners (% of imports)	China	20.5	Brazil	17.7	Argentina	13.2

Social indicators	2010	2015	2022
Population growth rate (average annual %)	1.7	1.6	1.2[a]
Urban population (% of total population)	66.4	68.4	69.8[i]
Urban population growth rate (average annual %)[k]	2.4	2.1	...
Fertility rate, total (live births per woman)	3.2	2.9	2.6[a]
Life expectancy at birth (females/males, years)	68.7 / 63.8	69.9 / 64.9	67.9 / 62.3[a]
Population age distribution (0-14/60+ years old, %)	34.8 / 7.2	33.1 / 7.3	30.8 / 7.6[a]
International migrant stock (000/% of total pop.)[l]	122.8 / 1.2	143.0 / 1.3	164.1 / 1.4[c]
Refugees and others of concern to the UNHCR (000)	0.7[m]	0.8	11.9[f]
Infant mortality rate (per 1 000 live births)	36.7	30.6	24.9[a]
Health: Current expenditure (% of GDP)[n,o]	5.2	6.6	6.9[i]
Health: Physicians (per 1 000 pop.)	0.4	0.5[p]	1.0[q]
Education: Primary gross enrol. ratio (f/m per 100 pop.)	104.2 / 104.8	94.9 / 96.9	98.2 / 98.8[i]
Education: Sec. gross enrol. ratio (f/m per 100 pop.)	88.5 / 88.9	90.7 / 92.0	89.2 / 90.8[i]
Education: Upr. Sec. gross enrol. ratio (f/m per 100 pop.)	83.7 / 82.9	88.0 / 87.7	85.4 / 85.0[i]
Intentional homicide rate (per 100 000 pop.)	...	6.2	7.0[i]
Seats held by women in the National Parliament (%)	22.3	53.1	46.2[r]

Environment and infrastructure indicators	2010	2015	2022
Individuals using the Internet (per 100 inhabitants)	22.4[h]	37.5[s,t]	59.9[c]
Research & Development expenditure (% of GDP)[u,v]	0.2[u,v]	...	...
Threatened species (number)	163	216	458
Forested area (% of land area)[h]	49.0	48.0	47.1[i]
CO2 emission estimates (million tons/tons per capita)	14.4 / 1.4	19.6 / 1.8	21.2 / 1.8[i]
Energy production, primary (Petajoules)	657	937	733[i]
Energy supply per capita (Gigajoules)	27	32	33[i]
Tourist/visitor arrivals at national borders (000)	679	882	323[c]
Important sites for terrestrial biodiversity protected (%)	45.4	45.4	45.4[f]
Pop. using safely managed sanitation (urban/rural %)	47.0 / ...	53.3 / ...	59.9 / ...[c]
Net Official Development Assist. received (% of GNI)	2.99	2.48	0.94[c]

a Projected estimate (medium fertility variant). b Data updated according to "Superintendencia Agraria". Interior waters correspond to natural or artificial bodies of water or snow. c 2020. d La Paz is the seat of government and Sucre is the constitutional capital. e 2018. f 2021. g Data classified according to ISIC Rev. 4. h Estimate. i Calculated by the UNSD from national indices. j 2019. k Data refers to a 5-year period preceding the reference year. l Including refugees. m Data as at the end of December. n Data based on calendar year (January 1 to December 31). o Data are based on SHA2011. p 2011. q 2017. r Data are as at 1 January of reporting year. s Users in the last 3 months. t Population aged 5 years and over. u Break in the time series. v 2009.

Bonaire, Sint Eustatius and Saba

Region	Caribbean	Population (000, 2022)	27 [a,b]
Pop. density (per km2, 2022)	82.4 [a,b]	Sex ratio (m per 100 f)	104.8 [a,b]
Capital city	Kralendijk	National currency	US Dollar (USD)
Capital city pop. (000, 2022)	11.3 [c,d]		

Social indicators	2010	2015	2022
Population growth rate (average annual %) [b]	3.5	2.6	0.4 [a]
Urban population (% of total population)	74.7	74.8	75.0 [e]
Urban population growth rate (average annual %) [f]	7.5	3.2	...
Fertility rate, total (live births per woman) [b]	1.7	1.7	1.6 [a]
Life expectancy at birth (females/males, years) [b]	78.3 / 72.8	79.8 / 75.5	78.2 / 73.2 [a]
Population age distribution (0-14/60+ years old, %) [b]	18.9 / 13.9	17.5 / 16.4	16.8 / 21.1 [a]
International migrant stock (000/% of total pop.)	20.9 / 100.0	24.6 / 100.0	26.2 / 100.0 [g]
Refugees and others of concern to the UNHCR (000)	~0.0 [h,i]	...	...
Infant mortality rate (per 1 000 live births) [b]	14.5	10.9	12.8 [a]

Environment and infrastructure indicators	2010	2015	2022
Threatened species (number)	...	55	80
Forested area (% of land area) [j]	...	~0.0	5.9 [e]
Energy production, primary (Petajoules)	...	0	0 [j,e]
Energy supply per capita (Gigajoules) [j]	...	61	66 [e]
Important sites for terrestrial biodiversity protected (%)	39.3	62.5	62.5 [k]

a Projected estimate (medium fertility variant). b For statistical purposes, the data for Netherlands do not include this area. c Refers to the island of Bonaire. d 2018. e 2019. f Data refers to a 5-year period preceding the reference year. g 2020. h Bonaire only. i Data as at the end of December. j Estimate. k 2021.

Bosnia and Herzegovina

Region	Southern Europe	UN membership date	22 May 1992
Population (000, 2022)	3 234[a]	Surface area (km2)	51 209[b]
Pop. density (per km2, 2022)	63.2[a]	Sex ratio (m per 100 f)	97.0[a]
Capital city	Sarajevo	National currency	Convertible Mark (BAM)
Capital city pop. (000, 2022)	342.7[c,d]	Exchange rate (per US$)	1.7[e]

Economic indicators

	2010	2015	2022
GDP: Gross domestic product (million current US$)	17 176	16 212	19 801[b]
GDP growth rate (annual %, const. 2015 prices)	0.9	3.1	- 4.3[b]
GDP per capita (current US$)	4 635.4	4 727.3	6 035.5[b]
Economy: Agriculture (% of Gross Value Added)[f,g]	8.0	7.3	7.3[b]
Economy: Industry (% of Gross Value Added)[g,h]	26.5	26.6	28.0[b]
Economy: Services and other activity (% of GVA)[g,i]	65.5	66.1	64.7[b]
Employment in agriculture (% of employed)	19.7	17.5[j]	15.1[j,b]
Employment in industry (% of employed)	30.9	30.6[j]	32.3[j,b]
Employment in services & other sectors (% employed)	49.4	51.9[j]	52.6[j,b]
Unemployment rate (% of labour force)	27.3	27.7	15.0[j]
Labour force participation rate (female/male pop. %)	33.0 / 55.9	33.5 / 54.9	31.9 / 51.6[j]
CPI: Consumer Price Index (2010=100)	100	104	106[e]
Agricultural production index (2014-2016=100)	100	99	115[b]
International trade: exports (million current US$)	4 803	5 099	8 614[e]
International trade: imports (million current US$)	9 223	8 994	13 029[e]
International trade: balance (million current US$)	- 4 420	- 3 895	- 4 415[e]
Balance of payments, current account (million US$)	- 1 031	- 826	- 485[e]

Major trading partners

						2021
Export partners (% of exports)	Germany	15.0	Croatia	13.1	Serbia	12.7
Import partners (% of imports)	Italy	12.0	Germany	11.9	Serbia	11.4

Social indicators

	2010	2015	2022
Population growth rate (average annual %)	- 1.8	- 1.3	- 0.8[a]
Urban population (% of total population)	45.6	47.2	48.6[d]
Urban population growth rate (average annual %)[k]	0.4	- 0.3	...
Fertility rate, total (live births per woman)	1.3	1.3	1.3[a]
Life expectancy at birth (females/males, years)	79.7 / 74.3	78.1 / 74.2	77.5 / 73.1[a]
Population age distribution (0-14/60+ years old, %)	15.9 / 19.5	15.1 / 21.9	14.9 / 25.8[a]
International migrant stock (000/% of total pop.)[l,i]	38.9 / 1.1	38.6 / 1.1	36.0 / 1.1[b]
Refugees and others of concern to the UNHCR (000)	179.0[m]	143.9	100.5[e]
Infant mortality rate (per 1 000 live births)	6.3	5.5	4.9[a]
Health: Current expenditure (% of GDP)	9.0	9.4	9.0[d]
Health: Physicians (per 1 000 pop.)	1.8	2.2	...
Education: Upr. Sec. gross enrol. ratio (f/m per 100 pop.)	... / ...	... / ...	86.9 / 83.4[b]
Intentional homicide rate (per 100 000 pop.)	1.5	1.7	1.3[b]
Seats held by women in the National Parliament (%)	19.0	21.4	26.2[n]

Environment and infrastructure indicators

	2010	2015	2022
Individuals using the Internet (per 100 inhabitants)	42.8[j]	52.6[j]	73.2[b]
Research & Development expenditure (% of GDP)	~0.0[o,p]	0.2	0.2[b]
Threatened species (number)	67	85	130
Forested area (% of land area)[j]	41.1	42.2	42.7[d]
CO2 emission estimates (million tons/tons per capita)	20.7 / 5.5	19.6 / 5.6	22.9 / 6.4[b]
Energy production, primary (Petajoules)	182	173	226[d]
Energy supply per capita (Gigajoules)	73	73	92[d]
Tourist/visitor arrivals at national borders (000)	365	678	197[b]
Important sites for terrestrial biodiversity protected (%)	28.9	29.0	29.0[e]
Pop. using safely managed sanitation (urban/rural %)	7.0 / ...	19.4 / ...	29.8 / ...[b]
Net Official Development Assist. received (% of GNI)	2.93	2.18	2.21[b]

a Projected estimate (medium fertility variant). b 2020. c Refers to the municipalities of Stari Grad Sarajevo, Centar Sarajevo, Novo Sarajevo, Novi Grad Sarajevo and Ilidza. d 2019. e 2021. f Excludes irrigation canals and landscaping care. g Data classified according to ISIC Rev. 4. h Excludes publishing activities. Includes irrigation and canals. i Includes publishing activities and landscape care. Excludes repair of personal and household goods. j Estimate. k Data refers to a 5-year period preceding the reference year. l Including refugees. m Data as at the end of December. n Data are as at 1 January of reporting year. o Partial data. p 2009.

Botswana

Region	Southern Africa	UN membership date	17 October 1966
Population (000, 2022)	2 630[a]	Surface area (km2)	582 000[b]
Pop. density (per km2, 2022)	4.6[a]	Sex ratio (m per 100 f)	97.5[a]
Capital city	Gaborone	National currency	Pula (BWP)
Capital city pop. (000, 2022)	269.3[c]	Exchange rate (per US$)	11.7[d]

Economic indicators

	2010	2015	2022
GDP: Gross domestic product (million current US$)	12 787	14 421	15 782[b]
GDP growth rate (annual %, const. 2015 prices)	8.6	- 1.7	- 7.9[b]
GDP per capita (current US$)	6 434.8	6 799.9	6 711.0[b]
Economy: Agriculture (% of Gross Value Added)[e]	2.8	2.4	2.4[b]
Economy: Industry (% of Gross Value Added)[e]	35.7	33.2	27.7[b]
Economy: Services and other activity (% of GVA)[e]	61.6	64.4	69.9[b]
Employment in agriculture (% of employed)[f]	24.6	22.3	20.4[b]
Employment in industry (% of employed)[f]	18.2	18.3	18.1[b]
Employment in services & other sectors (% employed)[f]	57.1	59.5	61.5[b]
Unemployment rate (% of labour force)	17.9	20.6[f]	23.7[f]
Labour force participation rate (female/male pop. %)	52.7 / 66.1	54.9 / 65.3[f]	56.4 / 64.9[f]
CPI: Consumer Price Index (2010=100)[g]	100	133	163[d]
Agricultural production index (2014-2016=100)	125	105	102[b]
International trade: exports (million current US$)	4 693	6 330	7 379[f,d]
International trade: imports (million current US$)	5 657	8 048	8 626[f,d]
International trade: balance (million current US$)	- 964	- 1 718	- 1 247[d]
Balance of payments, current account (million US$)	- 744	301	- 1 620[b]

Major trading partners

						2021
Export partners (% of exports)[f]	United Arab Emirates	21.5	Belgium	21.4	India	21.0
Import partners (% of imports)[f]	South Africa	58.6	Belgium	7.8	Namibia	7.6

Social indicators

	2010	2015	2022
Population growth rate (average annual %)	2.1	2.0	1.7[a]
Urban population (% of total population)	62.4	67.2	70.2[h]
Urban population growth rate (average annual %)[i]	3.8	3.3	...
Fertility rate, total (live births per woman)	3.0	2.9	2.8[a]
Life expectancy at birth (females/males, years)	61.8 / 58.1	66.3 / 61.3	68.4 / 63.3[a]
Population age distribution (0-14/60+ years old, %)	34.8 / 4.8	34.2 / 5.1	32.6 / 5.9[a]
International migrant stock (000/% of total pop.)[j]	94.9 / 4.8	103.1 / 4.9	110.3 / 4.7[b]
Refugees and others of concern to the UNHCR (000)	3.3[k]	2.4	0.7[d]
Infant mortality rate (per 1 000 live births)	38.6	37.4	33.1[a]
Health: Current expenditure (% of GDP)	6.2	5.7	6.0[h]
Health: Physicians (per 1 000 pop.)	0.4	0.4[l]	0.4[c]
Education: Government expenditure (% of GDP)	9.6[m]	7.8[f]	6.9[f,h]
Education: Primary gross enrol. ratio (f/m per 100 pop.)	106.6 / 109.8[m]	102.1 / 104.4	... / ...
Education: Sec. gross enrol. ratio (f/m per 100 pop.)	83.5 / 76.4[n]	... / ...	... / ...
Education: Upr. Sec. gross enrol. ratio (f/m per 100 pop.)	62.9 / 54.5[n]	... / ...	... / ...
Intentional homicide rate (per 100 000 pop.)	15.2	...	...
Seats held by women in the National Parliament (%)	7.9	9.5	11.1[o]

Environment and infrastructure indicators

	2010	2015	2022
Individuals using the Internet (per 100 inhabitants)	6.0	37.3[f]	64.0[b]
Research & Development expenditure (% of GDP)	0.5[p]	0.5[q]	...
Threatened species (number)	18	24	35
Forested area (% of land area)[f]	29.0	28.0	27.1[h]
CO2 emission estimates (million tons/tons per capita)	3.5 / 1.6	7.2 / 3.3	7.5 / 3.1[h]
Energy production, primary (Petajoules)	30	56	56[h]
Energy supply per capita (Gigajoules)	37	38	42[h]
Tourist/visitor arrivals at national borders (000)	1 973	1 528	1 655[c]
Important sites for terrestrial biodiversity protected (%)	51.1	51.1	51.1[d]
Pop. using safely managed drinking water (urban/rural, %)	83.7 / ...	83.4 / ...	83.1 / ...[b]
Net Official Development Assist. received (% of GNI)	1.27	0.47	0.54[b]

a Projected estimate (medium fertility variant). **b** 2020. **c** 2018. **d** 2021. **e** Data classified according to ISIC Rev. 4. **f** Estimate. **g** Calculated by the UNSD from national indices. **h** 2019. **i** Data refers to a 5-year period preceding the reference year. **j** Including refugees. **k** Data as at the end of December. **l** 2012. **m** 2009. **n** 2008. **o** Data are as at 1 January of reporting year. **p** 2005. **q** 2013.

Brazil

Region	South America	UN membership date	24 October 1945
Population (000, 2022)	215 314[a]	Surface area (km2)	8 515 767[b]
Pop. density (per km2, 2022)	25.8[a]	Sex ratio (m per 100 f)	96.5[a]
Capital city	Brasilia	National currency	Brazilian Real (BRL)
Capital city pop. (000, 2022)	4 559.0[c,d]	Exchange rate (per US$)	5.6[e]

Economic indicators

	2010	2015	2022
GDP: Gross domestic product (million current US$)	2 208 838	1 802 212	1 444 733[b]
GDP growth rate (annual %, const. 2015 prices)	7.5	- 3.5	- 4.1[b]
GDP per capita (current US$)	11 286.1	8 814.0	6 796.8[b]
Economy: Agriculture (% of Gross Value Added)[f,g]	4.8	5.0	6.5[b]
Economy: Industry (% of Gross Value Added)[f,h]	27.4	22.5	20.8[b]
Economy: Services and other activity (% of GVA)[f,i]	67.8	72.5	72.7[b]
Employment in agriculture (% of employed)	12.6[j]	10.2	9.1[j,b]
Employment in industry (% of employed)	22.5[j]	22.2	19.6[j,b]
Employment in services & other sectors (% employed)	64.8[j]	67.6	71.3[j,b]
Unemployment rate (% of labour force)	7.3[j]	8.4	13.6[j]
Labour force participation rate (female/male pop. %)	52.9 / 75.5[j]	51.7 / 73.3	50.7 / 69.6[j]
CPI: Consumer Price Index (2010=100)[k]	100	138	187[e]
Agricultural production index (2014-2016=100)	89	102	113[b]
International trade: exports (million current US$)	201 915	191 127	280 815[e]
International trade: imports (million current US$)	181 768	171 446	234 690[e]
International trade: balance (million current US$)	20 147	19 681	46 124[e]
Balance of payments, current account (million US$)	- 79 237	- 54 789	- 27 925[e]

Major trading partners

						2021
Export partners (% of exports)	China	31.3	United States	11.2	Argentina	4.2
Import partners (% of imports)	China	22.8	United States	17.7	Argentina	5.3

Social indicators

	2010	2015	2022
Population growth rate (average annual %)	0.9	0.8	0.5[a]
Urban population (% of total population)	84.3	85.8	86.8[d]
Urban population growth rate (average annual %)[l]	1.4	1.2	...
Fertility rate, total (live births per woman)	1.8	1.8	1.6[a]
Life expectancy at birth (females/males, years)	76.6 / 69.8	77.6 / 71.1	76.6 / 70.3[a]
Population age distribution (0-14/60+ years old, %)	24.8 / 10.3	22.5 / 11.9	20.3 / 14.6[a]
International migrant stock (000/% of total pop.)[m]	592.6 / 0.3	710.3 / 0.3	1 079.1 / 0.5[b]
Refugees and others of concern to the UNHCR (000)	5.2[n]	66.0	446.6[e]
Infant mortality rate (per 1 000 live births)	16.5	14.1	12.3[a]
Health: Current expenditure (% of GDP)[o,p]	7.9	8.9	9.6[d]
Health: Physicians (per 1 000 pop.)	...	1.9[q]	2.3[d]
Education: Government expenditure (% of GDP)	5.6	6.2	6.1[r]
Education: Primary gross enrol. ratio (f/m per 100 pop.)[j]	128.2 / 133.9[s]	111.0 / 115.7	109.4 / 114.5[d]
Education: Sec. gross enrol. ratio (f/m per 100 pop.)[j]	102.1 / 91.5[s]	103.4 / 97.9	106.8 / 101.3[d]
Education: Upr. Sec. gross enrol. ratio (f/m per 100 pop.)[j]	99.5 / 79.5[s]	99.3 / 84.8	101.4 / 89.5[d]
Intentional homicide rate (per 100 000 pop.)	26.7	28.5	22.5[b]
Seats held by women in the National Parliament (%)	8.8	9.0	14.8[t]

Environment and infrastructure indicators

	2010	2015	2022
Individuals using the Internet (per 100 inhabitants)	40.6[u,v]	58.3	81.3[b]
Research & Development expenditure (% of GDP)	1.2	1.4	1.2[d]
Threatened species (number)	773	966	2 040
Forested area (% of land area)[j]	61.2	60.3	59.6[d]
CO2 emission estimates (million tons/tons per capita)	389.6 / 1.9	474.0 / 2.2	402.9 / 1.8[b]
Energy production, primary (Petajoules)	10 116	11 567	12 975[d]
Energy supply per capita (Gigajoules)	56	61	58[d]
Tourist/visitor arrivals at national borders (000)[w]	5 161	6 306	2 146[b]
Important sites for terrestrial biodiversity protected (%)	42.0	42.8	43.7[e]
Pop. using safely managed drinking water (urban/rural, %)	83.4 / 56.4	85.1 / 62.9	87.8 / 71.8[b]
Pop. using safely managed sanitation (urban/rural %)	42.2 / ...	46.1 / ...	50.7 / ...[b]
Net Official Development Assist. received (% of GNI)	0.02	0.04	0.04[b]

a Projected estimate (medium fertility variant). b 2020. c Refers to the "Região Integrada de Desenvolvimento do Distrito Federal e Entorno". d 2019. e 2021. f Data classified according to ISIC Rev. 4. g Excludes irrigation canals and landscaping care. h Excludes publishing activities. Includes irrigation and canals. i Includes publishing activities and landscape care. Excludes repair of personal and household goods. j Estimate. k Calculated by the UNSD from national indices. l Data refers to a 5-year period preceding the reference year. m Including refugees. n Data as at the end of December. o Data based on calendar year (January 1 to December 31). p Health expenditure data 2000-2019 based on health satellite accounts and converted to SHA 2011 HC, HF, and HK series by the country. q 2013. r 2018. s 2009. t Data are as at 1 January of reporting year. u Population aged 10 years and over. v Users in the last 3 months. w Including nationals residing abroad.

British Virgin Islands

Region	Caribbean	Population (000, 2022)	31 [a,b]
Surface area (km2)	151 [c]	Pop. density (per km2, 2022)	203.3 [a,b]
Sex ratio (m per 100 f)	92.7 [a,b]	Capital city	Road Town
National currency	US Dollar (USD)	Capital city pop. (000, 2022)	15.1 [d]

Economic indicators	2010	2015	2022
GDP: Gross domestic product (million current US$)	1 114	1 279	1 492 [c]
GDP growth rate (annual %, const. 2015 prices)	1.7	0.8	1.7 [c]
GDP per capita (current US$)	40 085.3	43 878.3	49 357.2 [c]
Economy: Agriculture (% of Gross Value Added) [e,f]	0.1	0.1	0.1 [c]
Economy: Industry (% of Gross Value Added) [e,g]	4.4	6.2	6.7 [c]
Economy: Services and other activity (% of GVA) [e,h]	95.4	93.7	93.2 [c]
Employment in agriculture (% of employed)	0.5 [i]	...	...
Employment in industry (% of employed)	11.1 [i]	...	...
Employment in services & other sectors (% employed)	87.4 [i]	...	...
International trade: exports (million current US$) [i]	~0	~0	0 [k]
International trade: imports (million current US$) [i]	313	430	628 [k]
International trade: balance (million current US$)	- 313 [i]	- 430 [i]	- 628 [k]

Major trading partners						2021
Export partners (% of exports) [i]	Seychelles	32.7	Austria	15.2	Cyprus	10.7
Import partners (% of imports) [i]	Germany	42.7	United States	11.7	Cyprus	10.2

Social indicators	2010	2015	2022
Population growth rate (average annual %) [b]	0.4	1.4	0.8 [a]
Urban population (% of total population)	44.8	46.6	48.1 [l]
Urban population growth rate (average annual %) [m]	4.0	2.8	...
Fertility rate, total (live births per woman) [b]	1.2	1.2	1.0 [a]
Life expectancy at birth (females/males, years) [b]	78.2 / 72.9	78.6 / 73.0	79.3 / 73.6 [a]
Population age distribution (0-14/60+ years old, %) [b]	22.1 / 9.5	19.1 / 11.6	14.5 / 16.1 [a]
International migrant stock (000/% of total pop.) [n]	17.1 / 61.4	19.5 / 67.0	22.2 / 73.3 [c]
Refugees and others of concern to the UNHCR (000)	~0.0 [o]	...	~0.0 [k]
Infant mortality rate (per 1 000 live births) [b]	17.9	16.4	13.7 [a]
Education: Government expenditure (% of GDP)	3.8	5.1	2.9 [i]
Education: Primary gross enrol. ratio (f/m per 100 pop.)	107.2 / 110.0	114.5 / 122.3	123.1 / 121.3 [c]
Education: Sec. gross enrol. ratio (f/m per 100 pop.)	109.1 / 107.1	96.9 / 89.3	97.4 / 98.5 [c]
Education: Upr. Sec. gross enrol. ratio (f/m per 100 pop.)	99.7 / 83.1	83.4 / 69.1	102.7 / 98.2 [c]
Intentional homicide rate (per 100 000 pop.)	8.3 [p]	...	...

Environment and infrastructure indicators	2010	2015	2022
Individuals using the Internet (per 100 inhabitants)	37.0	37.6 [q]	77.7 [r]
Threatened species (number)	43	61	102
Forested area (% of land area) [i]	24.3	24.1	24.1 [l]
Energy production, primary (Petajoules)	0	0	0 [l]
Energy supply per capita (Gigajoules) [i]	101	103	79 [l]
Tourist/visitor arrivals at national borders (000)	330	393	83 [c]
Important sites for terrestrial biodiversity protected (%)	7.4	7.4	7.4 [k]

a Projected estimate (medium fertility variant). b For statistical purposes, the data for United Kingdom do not include this area. c 2020. d 2018. e Data classified according to ISIC Rev. 4. f Excludes irrigation canals and landscaping care. g Excludes publishing activities. Includes irrigation and canals. h Includes publishing activities and landscape care. Excludes repair of personal and household goods. i Data classified according to ISIC Rev. 3. j Estimate. k 2021. l 2019. m Data refers to a 5-year period preceding the reference year. n Including refugees. o Data as at the end of December. p 2006. q 2012. r 2017.

Brunei Darussalam

Region	South-eastern Asia	UN membership date	21 September 1984
Population (000, 2022)	449[a]	Surface area (km2)	5 765[b]
Pop. density (per km2, 2022)	77.9[a]	Sex ratio (m per 100 f)	107.1[a]
Capital city	Bandar Seri Begawan	National currency	Brunei Dollar (BND)
Capital city pop. (000, 2022)	40.8[c]	Exchange rate (per US$)	1.4[d]

Economic indicators

	2010	2015	2022
GDP: Gross domestic product (million current US$)	13 707	12 930	12 003[b]
GDP growth rate (annual %, const. 2015 prices)	2.6	- 0.4	1.1[b]
GDP per capita (current US$)	35 268.9	31 164.3	27 436.7[b]
Economy: Agriculture (% of Gross Value Added)[e,f]	0.7	1.1	1.2[b]
Economy: Industry (% of Gross Value Added)[e,g]	67.4	60.2	58.1[b]
Economy: Services and other activity (% of GVA)[e,h]	31.9	38.7	40.7[b]
Employment in agriculture (% of employed)[i]	0.7	0.7	1.3[b]
Employment in industry (% of employed)[i]	19.3	17.8	15.8[b]
Employment in services & other sectors (% employed)[i]	80.0	81.5	82.8[b]
Unemployment rate (% of labour force)[i]	6.8	7.8	7.4
Labour force participation rate (female/male pop. %)[i]	56.4 / 76.1	56.3 / 71.0	53.9 / 72.0
CPI: Consumer Price Index (2010=100)	100	100	103[d]
Agricultural production index (2014-2016=100)	89	97	106[b]
International trade: exports (million current US$)	8 908	6 353	11 172[i,d]
International trade: imports (million current US$)	2 539	3 229	8 147[i,d]
International trade: balance (million current US$)	6 369	3 124	3 025[d]
Balance of payments, current account (million US$)	5 016	2 157	514[b]

Major trading partners

							2021
Export partners (% of exports)[i]	Japan	25.6	Singapore	21.3	China	17.7
Import partners (% of imports)[i]	Malaysia	17.4	Singapore	14.2	China	10.8

Social indicators

	2010	2015	2022
Population growth rate (average annual %)	1.5	1.1	0.8[a]
Urban population (% of total population)	75.0	76.7	77.9[i]
Urban population growth rate (average annual %)[k]	1.7	1.9	...
Fertility rate, total (live births per woman)	1.9	1.9	1.8[a]
Life expectancy at birth (females/males, years)	77.1 / 72.8	77.0 / 72.7	76.8 / 72.5[a]
Population age distribution (0-14/60+ years old, %)	26.0 / 5.5	24.2 / 7.0	22.1 / 10.4[a]
International migrant stock (000/% of total pop.)	100.6 / 25.9	102.7 / 24.8	112.0 / 25.6[b]
Refugees and others of concern to the UNHCR (000)	21.0[l]	20.5	20.9[d]
Infant mortality rate (per 1 000 live births)	7.8	8.5	9.3[a]
Health: Current expenditure (% of GDP)[m]	2.3	2.4	2.2[i]
Health: Physicians (per 1 000 pop.)	1.4	1.8	1.6[n]
Education: Government expenditure (% of GDP)	2.0	3.4[o]	4.4[p]
Education: Primary gross enrol. ratio (f/m per 100 pop.)	106.3 / 106.8	105.3 / 105.7	98.5 / 98.1[b]
Education: Sec. gross enrol. ratio (f/m per 100 pop.)	99.5 / 98.9	97.5 / 95.5	92.9 / 89.9[b]
Education: Upr. Sec. gross enrol. ratio (f/m per 100 pop.)	97.7 / 96.6	95.0 / 91.6	87.8 / 83.7[b]
Intentional homicide rate (per 100 000 pop.)	0.3	0.5[q]	...
Seats held by women in the National Parliament (%)	...	...	9.1[r]

Environment and infrastructure indicators

	2010	2015	2022
Individuals using the Internet (per 100 inhabitants)	53.0[i]	71.2[i]	95.0[b]
Research & Development expenditure (% of GDP)	...	...	0.3[s,t,c]
Threatened species (number)	170	189	339
Forested area (% of land area)[i]	72.1	72.1	72.1[i]
CO2 emission estimates (million tons/tons per capita)	6.9 / 17.6	6.0 / 14.4	6.6 / 15.2[i]
Energy production, primary (Petajoules)	775	673	637[i]
Energy supply per capita (Gigajoules)	349	274	390[i]
Tourist/visitor arrivals at national borders (000)[u]	214	218	62[b]
Important sites for terrestrial biodiversity protected (%)	41.7	41.7	41.7[d]

a Projected estimate (medium fertility variant). b 2020. c 2018. d 2021. e Data classified according to ISIC Rev. 4. f Excludes irrigation canals and landscaping care. g Excludes publishing activities. Includes irrigation and canals. h Includes publishing activities and landscape care. Excludes repair of personal and household goods. i Estimate. j 2019. k Data refers to a 5-year period preceding the reference year. l Data as at the end of December. m Data refer to fiscal years beginning 1 April. n 2017. o 2014. p 2016. q 2013. r Data are as at 1 January of reporting year. s Break in the time series. t Higher Education only. u Arrivals by air.

Bulgaria

Region	Eastern Europe	UN membership date	14 December 1955
Population (000, 2022)	6 782[a]	Surface area (km2)	110 372[b]
Pop. density (per km2, 2022)	62.6[a]	Sex ratio (m per 100 f)	94.1[a]
Capital city	Sofia	National currency	Bulgarian Lev (BGN)
Capital city pop. (000, 2022)	1 276.9[c]	Exchange rate (per US$)	1.7[d]

Economic indicators

	2010	2015	2022
GDP: Gross domestic product (million current US$)	50 682	50 782	69 888[b]
GDP growth rate (annual %, const. 2015 prices)	1.5	3.4	- 4.4[b]
GDP per capita (current US$)	6 825.9	7 053.3	10 058.1[b]
Economy: Agriculture (% of Gross Value Added)[e,f]	4.6	4.7	4.0[b]
Economy: Industry (% of Gross Value Added)[e,g]	27.2	27.8	25.3[b]
Economy: Services and other activity (% of GVA)[e,h]	68.2	67.5	70.7[b]
Employment in agriculture (% of employed)	6.8	6.9	6.3[i,b]
Employment in industry (% of employed)	33.0	29.9	30.1[i,b]
Employment in services & other sectors (% employed)	60.2	63.2	63.7[i,b]
Unemployment rate (% of labour force)	10.3	9.1	4.9[i]
Labour force participation rate (female/male pop. %)[j]	47.8 / 59.4	48.6 / 60.0	49.3 / 62.7[i]
CPI: Consumer Price Index (2010=100)[j]	100	107	120[d]
Agricultural production index (2014-2016=100)	92	98	90[b]
International trade: exports (million current US$)	20 608	25 779	40 894[i,d]
International trade: imports (million current US$)	25 360	29 265	46 011[i,d]
International trade: balance (million current US$)	- 4 752	- 3 486	- 5 117[d]
Balance of payments, current account (million US$)	- 965	- 123	- 257[d]

Major trading partners

							2021
Export partners (% of exports)[i]	Germany	16.0	Romania	9.1	Italy	6.9
Import partners (% of imports)[i]	Germany	12.1	Romania	7.3	Türkiye	7.1

Social indicators

	2010	2015	2022
Population growth rate (average annual %)	- 0.6	- 0.9	- 1.5[a]
Urban population (% of total population)	72.3	74.0	75.3[c]
Urban population growth rate (average annual %)[k]	- 0.3	- 0.2	...
Fertility rate, total (live births per woman)	1.6	1.5	1.6[a]
Life expectancy at birth (females/males, years)	77.4 / 70.4	78.1 / 71.2	75.1 / 68.3[a]
Population age distribution (0-14/60+ years old, %)	13.7 / 25.4	14.1 / 27.4	14.0 / 29.2[a]
International migrant stock (000/% of total pop.)	76.3 / 1.0	123.8 / 1.7	184.4 / 2.7[b]
Refugees and others of concern to the UNHCR (000)	6.9[l]	19.0	23.6[d]
Infant mortality rate (per 1 000 live births)	9.1	6.5	5.3[a]
Health: Current expenditure (% of GDP)	7.1	7.4	7.1[c]
Health: Physicians (per 1 000 pop.)	3.8	4.0	4.2[m]
Education: Government expenditure (% of GDP)	3.9	4.1[n]	4.1[o]
Education: Primary gross enrol. ratio (f/m per 100 pop.)	108.2 / 108.5	93.7 / 94.7	85.6 / 86.2[c]
Education: Sec. gross enrol. ratio (f/m per 100 pop.)	88.2 / 92.1	100.6 / 103.9	91.5 / 93.2[c]
Education: Upr. Sec. gross enrol. ratio (f/m per 100 pop.)	91.7 / 94.5	111.8 / 114.1	114.8 / 117.7[c]
Intentional homicide rate (per 100 000 pop.)	2.0	1.8	1.0[b]
Seats held by women in the National Parliament (%)	20.8	20.4	22.5[p]

Environment and infrastructure indicators

	2010	2015	2022
Individuals using the Internet (per 100 inhabitants)	46.2[q]	56.7	70.2[b]
Research & Development expenditure (% of GDP)	0.6	0.9	0.9[b]
Threatened species (number)	66	85	143
Forested area (% of land area)[i]	34.4	35.3	35.7[c]
CO2 emission estimates (million tons/tons per capita)	44.6 / 5.9	44.2 / 6.1	35.1 / 5.0[b]
Energy production, primary (Petajoules)	441	507	492[c]
Energy supply per capita (Gigajoules)	100	108	110[c]
Tourist/visitor arrivals at national borders (000)	6 047	7 099	2 688[b]
Important sites for terrestrial biodiversity protected (%)	98.3	98.3	99.3[d]
Pop. using safely managed sanitation (urban/rural %)	56.9 / 43.4	66.3 / 52.2	76.1 / 60.1[b]
Net Official Development Assist. disbursed (% of GNI)	...	0.09[r]	...

a Projected estimate (medium fertility variant). b 2020. c 2019. d 2021. e Data classified according to ISIC Rev. 4. f Excludes irrigation canals and landscaping care. g Excludes publishing activities. Includes irrigation and canals. h Includes publishing activities and landscape care. Excludes repair of personal and household goods. i Estimate. j Calculated by the UNSD from national indices. k Data refers to a 5-year period preceding the reference year. l Data as at the end of December. m 2018. n 2013. o 2017. p Data are as at 1 January of reporting year. q Population aged 16 to 74 years. r 2014.

Burkina Faso

Region	Western Africa	UN membership date	20 September 1960
Population (000, 2022)	22 674[a]	Surface area (km2)	274 200[b]
Pop. density (per km2, 2022)	82.9[a]	Sex ratio (m per 100 f)	99.3[a]
Capital city	Ouagadougou	National currency	CFA Franc, BCEAO (XOF)[c]
Capital city pop. (000, 2022)	2 652.7[d]	Exchange rate (per US$)	579.2[e]

Economic indicators

	2010	2015	2022
GDP: Gross domestic product (million current US$)	10 100	11 823	17 369[b]
GDP growth rate (annual %, const. 2015 prices)	8.4	3.9	2.0[b]
GDP per capita (current US$)	647.2	652.8	830.9[b]
Economy: Agriculture (% of Gross Value Added)[f,g]	26.2	24.9	22.3[b]
Economy: Industry (% of Gross Value Added)[f,h]	28.2	26.8	32.7[b]
Economy: Services and other activity (% of GVA)[f,i]	45.6	48.3	45.0[b]
Employment in agriculture (% of employed)[j]	48.2	29.1	24.7[b]
Employment in industry (% of employed)[j]	20.9	32.0	33.9[b]
Employment in services & other sectors (% employed)[j]	31.0	38.9	41.4[b]
Unemployment rate (% of labour force)[j]	3.6	4.3	4.7
Labour force participation rate (female/male pop. %)[j]	59.0 / 80.2	57.7 / 73.8	57.2 / 72.7
CPI: Consumer Price Index (2010=100)[k]	100	108	114[e]
Agricultural production index (2014-2016=100)	89	96	106[b]
International trade: exports (million current US$)	1 288	2 177	5 060[e]
International trade: imports (million current US$)	2 048	2 980	4 710[e]
International trade: balance (million current US$)	- 760	- 802	350[e]
Balance of payments, current account (million US$)	- 182	- 895	743[b]

Major trading partners

						2021
Export partners (% of exports)	Switzerland	72.7	India	9.6	Singapore	3.8
Import partners (% of imports)	China	13.9	Ivory Coast	8.5	France	7.8

Social indicators

	2010	2015	2022
Population growth rate (average annual %)	2.9	2.9	2.5[a]
Urban population (% of total population)	24.6	27.5	30.0[d]
Urban population growth rate (average annual %)[l]	5.7	5.2	...
Fertility rate, total (live births per woman)	5.9	5.5	4.7[a]
Life expectancy at birth (females/males, years)	57.9 / 55.0	60.4 / 57.2	61.5 / 58.0[a]
Population age distribution (0-14/60+ years old, %)	45.6 / 4.2	45.6 / 4.1	43.7 / 4.1[a]
International migrant stock (000/% of total pop.)[m]	674.4 / 4.3	704.7 / 3.9	724.0 / 3.5[b]
Refugees and others of concern to the UNHCR (000)	1.1[n]	34.2	1 334.4[e]
Infant mortality rate (per 1 000 live births)	67.8	58.3	47.4[a]
Health: Current expenditure (% of GDP)	5.2	5.1	5.5[d]
Health: Physicians (per 1 000 pop.)	~0.0	0.1	0.1[d]
Education: Government expenditure (% of GDP)	3.5	3.7	5.8[j,d]
Education: Primary gross enrol. ratio (f/m per 100 pop.)	74.3 / 81.6	87.2 / 89.5	93.1 / 92.2[b]
Education: Sec. gross enrol. ratio (f/m per 100 pop.)	18.9 / 24.8	32.3 / 35.1	41.8 / 39.4[b]
Education: Upr. Sec. gross enrol. ratio (f/m per 100 pop.)	7.6 / 12.4	10.6 / 16.1	21.1 / 25.4[b]
Intentional homicide rate (per 100 000 pop.)	0.8	0.6	1.3[o]
Seats held by women in the National Parliament (%)	15.3	13.3	6.3[p,q]

Environment and infrastructure indicators

	2010	2015	2022
Individuals using the Internet (per 100 inhabitants)[j]	2.4	8.0	22.0[b]
Research & Development expenditure (% of GDP)	0.2[r]	0.2[s,t,u]	0.2[t,v,b]
Threatened species (number)	24	29	40
Forested area (% of land area)[j]	24.5	23.6	22.9[d]
Energy production, primary (Petajoules)	118	126	132[d]
Energy supply per capita (Gigajoules)	9	10	10[d]
Tourist/visitor arrivals at national borders (000)	274	163	67[b]
Important sites for terrestrial biodiversity protected (%)	78.8	78.8	78.8[e]
Net Official Development Assist. received (% of GNI)	10.65	8.84	10.39[b]

a Projected estimate (medium fertility variant). b 2020. c African Financial Community (CFA) Franc, Central Bank of West African States (BCEAO). d 2019. e 2021. f Data classified according to ISIC Rev. 4. g Excludes irrigation canals and landscaping care. h Excludes publishing activities. Includes irrigation and canals. i Includes publishing activities and landscape care. Excludes repair of personal and household goods. j Estimate. k Ouagadougou l Data refers to a 5-year period preceding the reference year. m Including refugees. n Data as at the end of December. o 2017. p Data corresponds to the National Assembly that was dissolved by a coup d'état on 24 January 2022. q Data are as at 1 January of reporting year. r 2009. s Break in the time series. t Excluding business enterprise. u 2014. v Excluding private non-profit.

Burundi

Region	Eastern Africa	UN membership date	18 September 1962
Population (000, 2022)	12 890 [a]	Surface area (km2)	27 834 [b]
Pop. density (per km2, 2022)	496.7 [a]	Sex ratio (m per 100 f)	98.6 [a]
Capital city	Gitega	National currency	Burundi Franc (BIF)
Capital city pop. (000, 2022)	899.0 [c]	Exchange rate (per US$)	2 006.1 [d]

Economic indicators	2010	2015	2022
GDP: Gross domestic product (million current US$)	2 032	2 811	3 399 [b]
GDP growth rate (annual %, const. 2015 prices)	5.1	- 0.4	- 1.0 [b]
GDP per capita (current US$)	234.2	276.6	285.9 [b]
Economy: Agriculture (% of Gross Value Added) [e]	40.7	37.5	37.2 [b]
Economy: Industry (% of Gross Value Added) [e]	16.3	16.4	18.8 [b]
Economy: Services and other activity (% of GVA) [e]	43.0	46.2	44.0 [b]
Employment in agriculture (% of employed) [f]	92.1	92.0	92.0 [b]
Employment in industry (% of employed) [f]	1.8	1.6	1.4 [b]
Employment in services & other sectors (% employed) [f]	6.1	6.4	6.5 [b]
Unemployment rate (% of labour force) [f]	1.6	1.6	1.7
Labour force participation rate (female/male pop. %) [f]	81.6 / 79.8	79.9 / 78.0	79.1 / 77.3
CPI: Consumer Price Index (2010=100) [g]	100	154	212 [d]
Agricultural production index (2014-2016=100)	99	96	136 [b]
International trade: exports (million current US$)	118	114	242 [f,d]
International trade: imports (million current US$)	404	561	1 085 [f,d]
International trade: balance (million current US$)	- 286	- 447	- 843 [d]
Balance of payments, current account (million US$)	- 301	- 373	- 363 [c]

Major trading partners						2021
Export partners (% of exports) [f]	United Arab Emirates	32.2	Dem. Rep. of Congo	19.6	Pakistan	5.6
Import partners (% of imports) [f]	China	15.6	Saudi Arabia	11.8	India	9.5

Social indicators	2010	2015	2022
Population growth rate (average annual %)	3.7	1.1	2.7 [a]
Urban population (% of total population)	10.6	12.1	13.4 [h]
Urban population growth rate (average annual %) [i]	5.9	5.6	...
Fertility rate, total (live births per woman)	6.3	5.7	5.0 [a]
Life expectancy at birth (females/males, years)	58.4 / 55.7	62.2 / 58.2	63.9 / 60.1 [a]
Population age distribution (0-14/60+ years old, %)	44.9 / 3.7	46.8 / 3.8	45.8 / 3.8 [a]
International migrant stock (000/% of total pop.) [j]	247.3 / 2.9	298.3 / 2.9	344.8 / 2.9 [b]
Refugees and others of concern to the UNHCR (000)	200.8 [k]	137.7	150.5 [d]
Infant mortality rate (per 1 000 live births)	59.4	46.3	36.3 [a]
Health: Current expenditure (% of GDP) [l]	11.3	6.4	8.0 [h]
Health: Physicians (per 1 000 pop.)	~0.0	~0.0	0.1 [b]
Education: Government expenditure (% of GDP)	6.8	6.4 [f]	5.1 [c]
Education: Primary gross enrol. ratio (f/m per 100 pop.)	136.4 / 138.0	132.8 / 129.0	115.9 / 114.4 [d]
Education: Sec. gross enrol. ratio (f/m per 100 pop.)	19.5 / 27.1	42.9 / 45.8	52.2 / 43.0 [d]
Education: Upr. Sec. gross enrol. ratio (f/m per 100 pop.)	9.2 / 15.5	22.6 / 30.4	51.6 / 44.5 [d]
Intentional homicide rate (per 100 000 pop.)	...	4.5	6.1 [m]
Seats held by women in the National Parliament (%)	31.4	30.5	38.2 [n]

Environment and infrastructure indicators	2010	2015	2022
Individuals using the Internet (per 100 inhabitants) [f]	1.0	2.0	9.4 [b]
Research & Development expenditure (% of GDP) [o]	0.1	0.1 [p]	0.2 [q,c]
Threatened species (number)	52	60	198
Forested area (% of land area) [f]	7.6	10.9	10.9 [h]
Energy production, primary (Petajoules)	54 [f]	56	56 [h]
Energy supply per capita (Gigajoules)	7 [f]	6	6 [h]
Tourist/visitor arrivals at national borders (000) [r]	142 [q]	131	299 [s]
Important sites for terrestrial biodiversity protected (%)	56.8	56.8	56.8 [d]
Net Official Development Assist. received (% of GNI)	31.05	11.81	14.62 [b]

a Projected estimate (medium fertility variant). b 2020. c 2018. d 2021. e Data classified according to ISIC Rev. 4. f Estimate. g Bujumbura h 2019. i Data refers to a 5-year period preceding the reference year. j Including refugees. k Data as at the end of December. l Data revision. m 2016. n Data are as at 1 January of reporting year. o Partial data. p 2012. q Break in the time series. r Including nationals residing abroad. s 2017.

Cabo Verde

Region	Western Africa	
Population (000, 2022)	593[a]	
Pop. density (per km2, 2022)	147.2[a]	
Capital city	Praia	
Capital city pop. (000, 2022)	167.5[c]	

UN membership date	16 September 1975	
Surface area (km2)	4 033[b]	
Sex ratio (m per 100 f)	98.9[a]	
National currency	Cabo Verde Escudo (CVE)	
Exchange rate (per US$)	97.6[d]	

Economic indicators	2010	2015	2022
GDP: Gross domestic product (million current US$)	1 664	1 596	1 704[b]
GDP growth rate (annual %, const. 2015 prices)	1.5	1.0	- 14.8[b]
GDP per capita (current US$)	3 378.3	3 041.8	3 064.3[b]
Economy: Agriculture (% of Gross Value Added)[e,f]	9.2	10.0	5.6[b]
Economy: Industry (% of Gross Value Added)[f,g]	20.8	20.7	26.6[b]
Economy: Services and other activity (% of GVA)[f,h]	70.1	69.3	67.8[b]
Employment in agriculture (% of employed)[i]	16.2	14.6	11.1[b]
Employment in industry (% of employed)[i]	22.2	21.6	22.1[b]
Employment in services & other sectors (% employed)[i]	61.5	63.8	66.8[b]
Unemployment rate (% of labour force)	10.7	11.8[i]	15.1[i]
Labour force participation rate (female/male pop. %)[i]	47.4 / 70.0	50.3 / 67.2	48.7 / 62.9
CPI: Consumer Price Index (2010=100)[j]	100	109	113[d]
Agricultural production index (2014-2016=100)	93	101	81[b]
International trade: exports (million current US$)	220	67	64[i,d]
International trade: imports (million current US$)	731	603	1 169[i,d]
International trade: balance (million current US$)	- 511	- 537	- 1 105[d]
Balance of payments, current account (million US$)	- 223	- 51	- 257[d]

Major trading partners						2021
Export partners (% of exports)[i]	Spain	63.0	Portugal	15.1	Italy	11.6
Import partners (% of imports)[i]	Portugal	41.9	Netherlands	16.2	Spain	8.4

Social indicators	2010	2015	2022
Population growth rate (average annual %)	1.2	1.1	0.9[a]
Urban population (% of total population)	61.8	64.3	66.2[k]
Urban population growth rate (average annual %)[l]	2.5	2.0	...
Fertility rate, total (live births per woman)	2.5	2.1	1.9[a]
Life expectancy at birth (females/males, years)	78.1 / 69.0	79.0 / 70.1	79.0 / 70.3[a]
Population age distribution (0-14/60+ years old, %)	32.0 / 7.6	29.1 / 7.4	26.2 / 8.7[a]
International migrant stock (000/% of total pop.)[m]	14.4 / 2.9	14.9 / 2.8	15.8 / 2.8[b]
Refugees and others of concern to the UNHCR (000)	~0.0[n,o]	0.1	0.1[d]
Infant mortality rate (per 1 000 live births)	21.7	16.4	11.4[a]
Health: Current expenditure (% of GDP)	4.5	4.8	4.9[k]
Health: Physicians (per 1 000 pop.)	0.6	0.8	0.8[c]
Education: Government expenditure (% of GDP)	5.6	5.3	4.7[k]
Education: Primary gross enrol. ratio (f/m per 100 pop.)	107.0 / 115.2	101.7 / 109.2	97.9 / 103.9[k]
Education: Sec. gross enrol. ratio (f/m per 100 pop.)	94.3 / 79.6	100.0 / 89.6	92.7 / 85.3[k]
Education: Upr. Sec. gross enrol. ratio (f/m per 100 pop.)	74.8 / 56.5	86.5 / 67.7	79.9 / 64.7[k]
Intentional homicide rate (per 100 000 pop.)	7.5[p]	8.8	6.5[b]
Seats held by women in the National Parliament (%)	18.1	20.8	38.9[q]

Environment and infrastructure indicators	2010	2015	2022
Individuals using the Internet (per 100 inhabitants)	30.0[i]	42.7	64.5[i,b]
Research & Development expenditure (% of GDP)	...	0.1[r,s,t]	...
Threatened species (number)	31	51	129
Forested area (% of land area)	10.6	11.0	11.3[k]
Energy production, primary (Petajoules)	1	2[i]	2[i,k]
Energy supply per capita (Gigajoules)	19	17[i]	19[i,k]
Tourist/visitor arrivals at national borders (000)[u]	336	520	180[b]
Important sites for terrestrial biodiversity protected (%)	12.0	12.0	12.0[d]
Net Official Development Assist. received (% of GNI)	20.55	9.96	9.46[b]

a Projected estimate (medium fertility variant). b 2020. c 2018. d 2021. e Excludes irrigation canals and landscaping care. f Data classified according to ISIC Rev. 4. g Excludes publishing activities. Includes irrigation and canals. h Includes publishing activities and landscape care. Excludes repair of personal and household goods. i Estimate. j Calculated by the UNSD from national indices. k 2019. l Data refers to a 5-year period preceding the reference year. m Including refugees. n Data as at the end of December. o 2005. p 2006. q Data are as at 1 January of reporting year. r Higher Education only. s Partial data. t 2011. u Non-resident tourists staying in hotels and similar establishments.

Cambodia

Region	South-eastern Asia	UN membership date	14 December 1955	
Population (000, 2022)	16 768[a]	Surface area (km2)	181 035[b]	
Pop. density (per km2, 2022)	92.6[a]	Sex ratio (m per 100 f)	98.0	
Capital city	Phnom Penh	National currency	Riel (KHR)	
Capital city pop. (000, 2022)	2 014.0[c,d]	Exchange rate (per US$)	4 113.5[e]	

Economic indicators	2010	2015	2022
GDP: Gross domestic product (million current US$)	11 242	18 050	25 291[b]
GDP growth rate (annual %, const. 2015 prices)	6.0	7.0	- 3.1[b]
GDP per capita (current US$)	785.5	1 162.9	1 512.7[b]
Economy: Agriculture (% of Gross Value Added)[f]	36.0	28.2	24.4[b]
Economy: Industry (% of Gross Value Added)[f]	23.3	29.4	37.0[b]
Economy: Services and other activity (% of GVA)[f]	40.7	42.3	38.6[b]
Employment in agriculture (% of employed)	57.3[g]	42.5	31.2[g,b]
Employment in industry (% of employed)	16.0[g]	24.9	29.6[g,b]
Employment in services & other sectors (% employed)	26.7[g]	32.6	39.2[g,b]
Unemployment rate (% of labour force)	0.8	0.4	0.6[g]
Labour force participation rate (female/male pop. %)	81.3 / 88.6	73.4 / 86.4	74.9 / 86.2[g]
CPI: Consumer Price Index (2010=100)[h]	100	117	138[e]
Agricultural production index (2014-2016=100)	82	98	112[e]
International trade: exports (million current US$)	5 590	8 542	18 210[g,e]
International trade: imports (million current US$)	4 903	10 669	28 318[g,e]
International trade: balance (million current US$)	688	- 2 126	- 10 108[e]
Balance of payments, current account (million US$)	- 981	- 1 598	- 12 339[e]

Major trading partners						2021
Export partners (% of exports)[g]	United States	30.1	Singapore	14.8	China	6.1
Import partners (% of imports)[g]	China	37.1	Thailand	15.0	Viet Nam	13.9

Social indicators	2010	2015	2022
Population growth rate (average annual %)	1.5	1.3	1.0[a]
Urban population (% of total population)	20.3	22.2	23.8[d]
Urban population growth rate (average annual %)[i]	2.6	3.4	...
Fertility rate, total (live births per woman)	2.8	2.6	2.3[a]
Life expectancy at birth (females/males, years)	69.8 / 65.4	72.0 / 67.6	72.6 / 67.1[a]
Population age distribution (0-14/60+ years old, %)	32.1 / 5.7	30.9 / 7.0	28.9 / 9.7[a]
International migrant stock (000/% of total pop.)[j]	82.0 / 0.6	74.0 / 0.5	79.3 / 0.5[b]
Refugees and others of concern to the UNHCR (000)	0.2[k]	0.2	57.5[e]
Infant mortality rate (per 1 000 live births)	35.7	26.4	20.6[a]
Health: Current expenditure (% of GDP)[l]	6.9	6.2	7.0[d]
Health: Physicians (per 1 000 pop.)	0.2	0.2[m]	...
Education: Government expenditure (% of GDP)	1.5	1.9[m]	2.2[n]
Education: Primary gross enrol. ratio (f/m per 100 pop.)	120.2 / 127.4	116.7 / 117.5	103.7 / 106.9[b]
Education: Sec. gross enrol. ratio (f/m per 100 pop.)	41.6 / 48.7[g,o]	... / ...	57.1 / 52.6[b]
Education: Upr. Sec. gross enrol. ratio (f/m per 100 pop.)	24.3 / 33.0[g,o]	... / ...	38.2 / 38.5[b]
Intentional homicide rate (per 100 000 pop.)	2.3	1.8[p]	...
Seats held by women in the National Parliament (%)	21.1	20.3	20.8[q]

Environment and infrastructure indicators	2010	2015	2022
Individuals using the Internet (per 100 inhabitants)	1.3	18.0[g]	32.9[r]
Research & Development expenditure (% of GDP)	...	0.1[s]	...
Threatened species (number)	204	243	331
Forested area (% of land area)[g]	60.0	50.1	46.6[d]
CO2 emission estimates (million tons/tons per capita)	5.6 / 0.3	8.7 / 0.5	13.9 / 0.8[d]
Energy production, primary (Petajoules)	124	143	162[d]
Energy supply per capita (Gigajoules)	14	16	21[d]
Tourist/visitor arrivals at national borders (000)[t]	2 508	4 775	1 306[b]
Important sites for terrestrial biodiversity protected (%)	24.7	25.8	54.5[e]
Pop. using safely managed drinking water (urban/rural, %)	51.1 / 14.5	54.2 / 16.4	57.1 / 18.4[b]
Net Official Development Assist. received (% of GNI)	6.35	4.01	5.66[b]

a Projected estimate (medium fertility variant). b 2020. c Refers to the municipality of Phnom Penh including suburban areas. d 2019. e 2021. f Data classified according to ISIC Rev. 4. g Estimate. h Phnom Penh i Data refers to a 5-year period preceding the reference year. j Including refugees. k Data as at the end of December. l Data refer to fiscal years beginning 1 July. m 2014. n 2018. o 2008. p 2011. q Data are as at 1 January of reporting year. r 2017. s Break in the time series. t Arrivals by all means of transport.

Cameroon

Region	Middle Africa	
Population (000, 2022)	27 914[a]	
Pop. density (per km2, 2022)	59.9[a]	
Capital city	Yaoundé	
Capital city pop. (000, 2022)	3 822.4[d]	

UN membership date	20 September 1960
Surface area (km2)	475 650[b]
Sex ratio (m per 100 f)	99.5[a]
National currency	CFA Franc, BEAC (XAF)[c]
Exchange rate (per US$)	579.2[e]

Economic indicators

	2010	2015	2022
GDP: Gross domestic product (million current US$)	26 144	30 905	39 881[b]
GDP growth rate (annual %, const. 2015 prices)	3.4	5.7	- 1.5[b]
GDP per capita (current US$)	1 285.3	1 326.5	1 502.3[b]
Economy: Agriculture (% of Gross Value Added)[f,g]	15.1	16.1	16.5[b]
Economy: Industry (% of Gross Value Added)[g,h]	29.1	27.4	27.2[b]
Economy: Services and other activity (% of GVA)[g,i]	55.8	56.6	56.2[b]
Employment in agriculture (% of employed)[i]	55.1	46.5	42.9[b]
Employment in industry (% of employed)[i]	12.2	14.3	15.1[b]
Employment in services & other sectors (% employed)[i]	32.8	39.1	42.1[b]
Unemployment rate (% of labour force)	4.1	3.6[i]	3.8[i]
Labour force participation rate (female/male pop. %)	70.5 / 82.1	70.6 / 81.8[i]	70.4 / 80.9[i]
CPI: Consumer Price Index (2010=100)[i]	100	113	124[b]
Agricultural production index (2014-2016=100)	82	101	104[b]
International trade: exports (million current US$)	3 878	4 053	4 512[i,e]
International trade: imports (million current US$)	5 133	6 037	7 534[i,e]
International trade: balance (million current US$)	- 1 255	- 1 984	- 3 023[e]
Balance of payments, current account (million US$)	- 857	- 1 174	- 1 512[b]

Major trading partners

						2021
Export partners (% of exports)[i]	China	29.8	Netherlands	13.4	India	8.8
Import partners (% of imports)[i]	China	34.4	France	8.0	Nigeria	7.0

Social indicators

	2010	2015	2022
Population growth rate (average annual %)	2.9	3.0	2.6[a]
Urban population (% of total population)	51.6	54.6	57.0[d]
Urban population growth rate (average annual %)[k]	3.9	3.8	...
Fertility rate, total (live births per woman)	5.2	4.8	4.4[a]
Life expectancy at birth (females/males, years)	58.0 / 55.2	61.2 / 58.1	62.6 / 59.4[a]
Population age distribution (0-14/60+ years old, %)	43.8 / 4.5	43.3 / 4.3	42.2 / 4.2[a]
International migrant stock (000/% of total pop.)[l]	291.5 / 1.4	508.3 / 2.2	579.2 / 2.2[b]
Refugees and others of concern to the UNHCR (000)	106.7[m]	391.8	1 486.3[e]
Infant mortality rate (per 1 000 live births)	71.4	59.1	45.8[a]
Health: Current expenditure (% of GDP)[i]	3.8	3.7	3.6[d]
Health: Physicians (per 1 000 pop.)	0.1	0.1[n]	0.1[o]
Education: Government expenditure (% of GDP)	3.0	2.8[i]	3.1[i,d]
Education: Primary gross enrol. ratio (f/m per 100 pop.)	100.2 / 116.0	109.9 / 122.4	100.2 / 111.2[d]
Education: Sec. gross enrol. ratio (f/m per 100 pop.)	36.8 / 44.1[p]	54.4 / 63.6	55.4 / 64.6[q]
Education: Upr. Sec. gross enrol. ratio (f/m per 100 pop.)	26.0 / 31.9[p]	39.7 / 49.0	39.0 / 44.8[b]
Intentional homicide rate (per 100 000 pop.)	4.9	1.2	1.4[r]
Seats held by women in the National Parliament (%)	13.9	31.1	33.9[s]

Environment and infrastructure indicators

	2010	2015	2022
Individuals using the Internet (per 100 inhabitants)[i]	4.3	18.3	37.8[b]
Threatened species (number)	624	697	1 178
Forested area (% of land area)[i]	44.2	43.6	43.1[d]
CO2 emission estimates (million tons/tons per capita)	6.7 / 0.2	8.0 / 0.3	8.7 / 0.3[d]
Energy production, primary (Petajoules)	353	495	544[d]
Energy supply per capita (Gigajoules)	14	16	16[d]
Tourist/visitor arrivals at national borders (000)	573	897	1 021[d]
Important sites for terrestrial biodiversity protected (%)	35.0	35.5	35.5[e]
Net Official Development Assist. received (% of GNI)	2.08	2.18	3.57[b]

a Projected estimate (medium fertility variant). b 2020. c African Financial Community (CFA) Franc, Bank of Central African States (BEAC). d 2019. e 2021. f Excludes irrigation canals and landscaping care. g Data classified according to ISIC Rev. 4. h Excludes publishing activities. Includes irrigation and canals. i Includes publishing activities and landscape care. Excludes repair of personal and household goods. j Estimate. k Data refers to a 5-year period preceding the reference year. l Including refugees. m Data as at the end of December. n 2011. o 2018. p 2009. q 2016. r 2017. s Data are as at 1 January of reporting year.

Canada

Region	Northern America	UN membership date	09 November 1945
Population (000, 2022)	38 454 [a]	Surface area (km2)	9 984 670 [b]
Pop. density (per km2, 2022)	4.2 [a]	Sex ratio (m per 100 f)	98.8 [a]
Capital city	Ottawa	National currency	Canadian Dollar (CAD)
Capital city pop. (000, 2022)	1 378.2 [c,d]	Exchange rate (per US$)	1.3 [e]

Economic indicators

	2010	2015	2022
GDP: Gross domestic product (million current US$)	1 617 267	1 556 129	1 644 037 [b]
GDP growth rate (annual %, const. 2015 prices)	3.1	0.7	- 5.3 [b]
GDP per capita (current US$)	47 361.1	43 193.8	43 559.7 [b]
Economy: Agriculture (% of Gross Value Added) [f,g]	1.6	2.0	1.9 [b]
Economy: Industry (% of Gross Value Added) [g,h]	27.9	25.8	25.7 [b]
Economy: Services and other activity (% of GVA) [g,i]	70.5	72.1	72.4 [b]
Employment in agriculture (% of employed)	1.8	1.6	1.4 [i,b]
Employment in industry (% of employed)	20.2	19.9	19.4 [i,b]
Employment in services & other sectors (% employed)	78.0	78.4	79.2 [i,b]
Unemployment rate (% of labour force)	8.1	6.9	6.1 [i]
Labour force participation (female/male pop. %)	62.4 / 71.6	61.2 / 70.6	60.6 / 69.4 [i]
CPI: Consumer Price Index (2010=100) [k]	100	109	122 [e]
Agricultural production index (2014-2016=100)	86	99	113 [b]
International trade: exports (million current US$)	386 580	408 697	501 201 [e]
International trade: imports (million current US$)	392 109	419 375	489 490 [e]
International trade: balance (million current US$)	- 5 529	- 10 677	11 711 [e]
Balance of payments, current account (million US$)	- 58 163	- 54 696	1 217 [e]

Major trading partners

						2021
Export partners (% of exports)	United States	75.5	China	4.5	United Kingdom	2.6
Import partners (% of imports)	United States	48.5	China	14.0	Mexico	5.5

Social indicators

	2010	2015	2022
Population growth rate (average annual %)	1.1	1.0	0.8 [a]
Urban population (% of total population)	80.9	81.3	81.5 [d]
Urban population growth rate (average annual %) [l]	1.3	1.1	...
Fertility rate, total (live births per woman)	1.6	1.6	1.5 [a]
Life expectancy at birth (females/males, years)	83.5 / 79.1	83.9 / 79.9	84.8 / 80.9 [a]
Population age distribution (0-14/60+ years old, %)	16.6 / 19.9	16.2 / 22.3	15.6 / 25.9 [a]
International migrant stock (000/% of total pop.)	6 761.2 / 19.8	7 428.7 / 20.6	8 049.3 / 21.3 [b]
Refugees and others of concern to the UNHCR (000)	216.6 [m]	155.8 [m]	202.5 [e]
Infant mortality rate (per 1 000 live births)	5.0	4.5	3.9 [a]
Health: Current expenditure (% of GDP) [n]	10.7	10.7	10.8 [d]
Health: Physicians (per 1 000 pop.)	...	...	2.4 [d]
Education: Government expenditure (% of GDP)	5.4	5.3 [o]	...
Education: Primary gross enrol. ratio (f/m per 100 pop.)	98.9 / 98.4	102.9 / 102.1	100.7 / 101.3 [d]
Education: Sec. gross enrol. ratio (f/m per 100 pop.)	101.2 / 103.6	110.9 / 109.9	114.8 / 113.9 [d]
Education: Upr. Sec. gross enrol. ratio (f/m per 100 pop.)	102.0 / 105.0	119.9 / 118.2	120.3 / 119.1 [d]
Intentional homicide rate (per 100 000 pop.)	1.6	1.7	2.0 [b]
Seats held by women in the National Parliament (%)	22.1	25.2	30.5 [p]

Environment and infrastructure indicators

	2010	2015	2022
Individuals using the Internet (per 100 inhabitants)	80.3 [q,r]	90.0 [i]	97.0 [i,b]
Research & Development expenditure (% of GDP)	1.8	1.7	1.7 [s,b]
Threatened species (number)	77	97	187
Forested area (% of land area)	38.7	38.7	38.7 [d]
CO2 emission estimates (million tons/tons per capita)	534.3 / 15.5	557.3 / 15.4	531.2 / 13.8 [b]
Energy production, primary (Petajoules)	16 662	19 766	22 413 [d]
Energy supply per capita (Gigajoules)	319	325	342 [d]
Tourist/visitor arrivals at national borders (000)	16 219	17 971	2 960 [b]
Important sites for terrestrial biodiversity protected (%)	27.0	27.6	30.0 [e]
Pop. using safely managed sanitation (urban/rural %)	80.9 / 80.6	82.9 / 82.5	84.4 / 84.1 [b]
Net Official Development Assist. disbursed (% of GNI) [t]	1.46	0.24	0.17 [b]

a Projected estimate (medium fertility variant). b 2020. c Refers to the Census Metropolitan Area. d 2019. e 2021. f Excludes irrigation canals and landscaping care. g Data classified according to ISIC Rev. 4. h Excludes publishing activities. Includes irrigation and canals. i Includes publishing activities and landscape care. Excludes repair of personal and household goods. j Estimate. k Calculated by the UNSD from national indices. l Data refers to a 5-year period preceding the reference year. m Data as at the end of December. n Data are based on SHA2011. o 2011. p Data are as at 1 January of reporting year. q Break in the time series. r Population aged 16 years and over. s Provisional data. t DAC member (OECD).

Region	Caribbean	Population (000, 2022)	69[a,b]
Surface area (km2)	264[c]	Pop. density (per km2, 2022)	285.1[a,b]
Sex ratio (m per 100 f)	101.9[a,b]	Capital city	George Town
National currency	Cayman Islands Dollar (KYD)	Capital city pop. (000, 2022)	34.9[d]
Exchange rate (per US$)	0.8[e]		

Economic indicators	2010	2015	2022
GDP: Gross domestic product (million current US$)	4 277	4 785	6 256[c]
GDP growth rate (annual %, const. 2015 prices)	- 2.7	2.8	3.5[c]
GDP per capita (current US$)	75 460.8	77 517.7	95 190.9[c]
Economy: Agriculture (% of Gross Value Added)[f,g]	0.3	0.4	0.4[c]
Economy: Industry (% of Gross Value Added)[f,h]	7.4	7.4	8.0[c]
Economy: Services and other activity (% of GVA)[f,i]	92.2	92.2	91.6[c]
Employment in agriculture (% of employed)[j]	0.6	0.8[k]	...
Employment in industry (% of employed)[j]	14.9	15.5[k]	...
Employment in services & other sectors (% employed)[j]	84.2	83.6[k]	...
Unemployment rate (% of labour force)	6.7	6.3[k]	...
Labour force participation rate (female/male pop. %)	80.6 / 88.0[j,l,m]	80.6 / 85.6[k]	... / ...
CPI: Consumer Price Index (2010=100)[n]	100	104	116[c]
International trade: exports (million current US$)	24[o]	65[o]	17[c]
International trade: imports (million current US$)	828[o]	915	1 538[e]
International trade: balance (million current US$)	- 804[o]	- 851	- 1 521[e]
Balance of payments, current account (million US$)	...	...	- 764[c]

Major trading partners						2021
Export partners (% of exports)	United States	77.8	Jamaica	13.1	United Kingdom	9.1
Import partners (% of imports)	United States	81.5	Jamaica	3.4	United Kingdom	2.5

Social indicators	2010	2015	2022
Population growth rate (average annual %)[b]	2.7	2.2	0.9[a]
Urban population (% of total population)	100.0	100.0	100.0[p]
Urban population growth rate (average annual %)[q]	2.6	1.5	...
Fertility rate, total (live births per woman)[b]	1.8	1.2	1.2[a]
Life expectancy at birth (females/males, years)[b]	78.8 / 73.0	77.3 / 72.5	78.1 / 73.2[a]
Population age distribution (0-14/60+ years old, %)[b]	18.3 / 8.5	17.5 / 10.0	16.8 / 13.1[a]
International migrant stock (000/% of total pop.)[r,s]	24.1 / 42.5	26.2 / 42.4	29.2 / 44.5[c]
Refugees and others of concern to the UNHCR (000)	~0.0[t]	0.1	0.1[a]
Infant mortality rate (per 1 000 live births)[b]	7.2	8.7	7.3[a]
Education: Primary gross enrol. ratio (f/m per 100 pop.)	92.8 / 98.9[u]	88.4 / 86.7[k]	92.2 / 94.2[c]
Education: Sec. gross enrol. ratio (f/m per 100 pop.)	84.1 / 76.5[u]	84.4 / 82.8[k]	75.5 / 73.0[o]
Education: Upr. Sec. gross enrol. ratio (f/m per 100 pop.)	81.4 / 71.2[u]	74.3 / 73.9[k]	71.2 / 66.1[c]
Intentional homicide rate (per 100 000 pop.)	15.9	8.2[v]	...

Environment and infrastructure indicators	2010	2015	2022
Individuals using the Internet (per 100 inhabitants)[o]	66.0	77.0	81.1[w]
Threatened species (number)	34	71	94
Forested area (% of land area)[o]	53.0	53.0	53.0[p]
Energy supply per capita (Gigajoules)	141	130	152[p]
Tourist/visitor arrivals at national borders (000)[x]	288	385	122[c]
Important sites for terrestrial biodiversity protected (%)	31.7	32.5	32.5[c]

a Projected estimate (medium fertility variant). **b** For statistical purposes, the data for United Kingdom do not include this area. **c** 2020. **d** 2018. **e** 2021. **f** Data classified according to ISIC Rev. 4. **g** Excludes irrigation canals and landscaping care. **h** Excludes publishing activities. Includes irrigation and canals. **i** Includes publishing activities and landscape care. Excludes repair of personal and household goods. **j** Break in the time series. **k** 2013. **l** Resident population (de jure). **m** 2009. **n** Calculated by the UNSD from national indices. **o** Estimate. **p** 2019. **q** Data refers to a 5-year period preceding the reference year. **r** Refers to foreign citizens. **s** Including refugees. **t** Data as at the end of December. **u** 2008. **v** 2014. **w** 2017. **x** Arrivals by air.

Central African Republic

Region	Middle Africa	UN membership date	20 September 1960
Population (000, 2022)	5 579[a]	Surface area (km2)	622 984[b]
Pop. density (per km2, 2022)	9.0[a]	Sex ratio (m per 100 f)	99.9[a]
Capital city	Bangui	National currency	CFA Franc, BEAC (XAF)[c]
Capital city pop. (000, 2022)	869.6[d]	Exchange rate (per US$)	579.2[e]

Economic indicators

	2010	2015	2022
GDP: Gross domestic product (million current US$)	2 141	1 695	2 323[b]
GDP growth rate (annual %, const. 2015 prices)	4.6	4.3	1.0[b]
GDP per capita (current US$)	487.9	377.1	481.0[b]
Economy: Agriculture (% of Gross Value Added)[f]	39.8	32.5	33.4[b]
Economy: Industry (% of Gross Value Added)[f]	26.1	22.8	21.7[b]
Economy: Services and other activity (% of GVA)[f]	34.1	44.6	44.9[b]
Employment in agriculture (% of employed)[g]	78.8	78.5	77.1[b]
Employment in industry (% of employed)[g]	6.2	5.3	5.4[b]
Employment in services & other sectors (% employed)[g]	15.1	16.2	17.5[b]
Unemployment rate (% of labour force)	5.7	5.6	6.4
Labour force participation rate (female/male pop. %)[g]	63.9 / 79.8	63.6 / 80.7	63.7 / 79.6
CPI: Consumer Price Index (2010=100)[g,h]	100	133	161[e]
Agricultural production index (2014-2016=100)	94	99	105[b]
International trade: exports (million current US$)	90	97	72[g,e]
International trade: imports (million current US$)	210	457	530[g,e]
International trade: balance (million current US$)	- 120	- 360	- 458[e]

Major trading partners

					2021
Export partners (% of exports)[g]	United Arab Emirates 35.7	China	25.9	Italy	12.3
Import partners (% of imports)[g]	Dem. Rep. of Congo 20.8	China	12.1	France	10.8

Social indicators

	2010	2015	2022
Population growth rate (average annual %)	2.0	1.6	2.8[a]
Urban population (% of total population)	38.9	40.3	41.8[d]
Urban population growth rate (average annual %)[i]	1.9	1.1	...
Fertility rate, total (live births per woman)	5.9	6.0	5.9[a]
Life expectancy at birth (females/males, years)	50.5 / 48.1	54.5 / 51.2	56.8 / 52.3[a]
Population age distribution (0-14/60+ years old, %)	46.0 / 3.5	48.8 / 3.9	48.1 / 4.1[a]
International migrant stock (000/% of total pop.)[i,k]	94.7 / 2.2	81.6 / 1.8	88.5 / 1.8[b]
Refugees and others of concern to the UNHCR (000)	215.3[l]	517.2	893.9[e]
Infant mortality rate (per 1 000 live births)	97.3	84.7	67.7[a]
Health: Current expenditure (% of GDP)[m]	3.8	5.0	7.8[d]
Health: Physicians (per 1 000 pop.)	~0.0[n]	0.1	0.1[o]
Education: Government expenditure (% of GDP)	1.1	1.99	1.8[g,d]
Education: Primary gross enrol. ratio (f/m per 100 pop.)	73.4 / 101.2	75.7 / 99.8[p]	89.4 / 114.6[q]
Education: Sec. gross enrol. ratio (f/m per 100 pop.)	9.8 / 17.4[n]	11.9 / 22.9[p]	13.8 / 20.5[r]
Education: Upr. Sec. gross enrol. ratio (f/m per 100 pop.)	5.6 / 10.0[n]	6.9 / 11.7[p]	7.0 / 11.8[r]
Seats held by women in the National Parliament (%)	9.6	12.5[s]	12.9[t]

Environment and infrastructure indicators

	2010	2015	2022
Individuals using the Internet (per 100 inhabitants)[g]	2.0	2.9	10.4[b]
Threatened species (number)	36	54	98
Forested area (% of land area)	36.3	36.0	35.8[d]
Energy production, primary (Petajoules)	33	33	34[g,d]
Energy supply per capita (Gigajoules)	8	8	8[g,d]
Tourist/visitor arrivals at national borders (000)[u]	54	120	87[d]
Important sites for terrestrial biodiversity protected (%)	74.2	74.2	74.2[e]
Pop. using safely managed drinking water (urban/rural, %)	14.2 / 2.8	12.8 / 2.6	11.5 / 2.3[b]
Pop. using safely managed sanitation (urban/rural %)	31.5 / 8.0	27.7 / 7.0	24.1 / 5.9[b]
Net Official Development Assist. received (% of GNI)	12.13	28.35	33.78[b]

a Projected estimate (medium fertility variant). b 2020. c African Financial Community (CFA) Franc, Bank of Central African States (BEAC). d 2019. e 2021. f Data classified according to ISIC Rev. 4. g Estimate. h Bangui. i Data refers to a 5-year period preceding the reference year. j Including refugees. k Refers to foreign citizens. l Data as at the end of December. m Estimates should be viewed with caution as these are derived from scarce data. n 2009. o 2018. p 2012. q 2016. r 2017. s 2013. t Data are as at 1 January of reporting year. u Arrivals by air at Bangui only.

Chad

Region	Middle Africa	UN membership date	20 September 1960	
Population (000, 2022)	17 723[a]	Surface area (km2)	1 284 000[b]	
Pop. density (per km2, 2022)	14.1[a]	Sex ratio (m per 100 f)	100.8[a]	
Capital city	N'Djamena	National currency	CFA Franc, BEAC (XAF)[c]	
Capital city pop. (000, 2022)	1 371.5[d]	Exchange rate (per US$)	579.2[e]	

Economic indicators

	2010	2015	2022
GDP: Gross domestic product (million current US$)	10 971	11 690	11 154[b]
GDP growth rate (annual %, const. 2015 prices)	15.0	1.8	- 0.8[b]
GDP per capita (current US$)	917.9	828.5	679.1[b]
Economy: Agriculture (% of Gross Value Added)[f]	35.9	29.5	27.7[b]
Economy: Industry (% of Gross Value Added)[f]	36.7	31.7	19.3[b]
Economy: Services and other activity (% of GVA)[f]	27.4	38.8	53.0[b]
Employment in agriculture (% of employed)[g]	78.5	77.0	76.3[b]
Employment in industry (% of employed)[g]	2.4	2.4	2.1[b]
Employment in services & other sectors (% employed)[g]	19.1	20.7	21.6[b]
Unemployment rate (% of labour force)[g]	1.0	1.1	1.8
Labour force participation rate (female/male pop. %)[g]	53.7 / 74.7	50.4 / 72.7	47.4 / 70.2
CPI: Consumer Price Index (2010=100)	100[g,h]	117[g,h]	122[i,e]
Agricultural production index (2014-2016=100)	88	97	119[b]
International trade: exports (million current US$)[g]	3 410	2 900	1 974[e]
International trade: imports (million current US$)[g]	2 507	2 200	1 055[e]
International trade: balance (million current US$)	904[g]	700[g]	919[e]

Major trading partners
2021

Export partners (% of exports)[g]	Germany	42.4	Other Asia, nes	18.6	United Arab Emirates	11.5
Import partners (% of imports)[g]	China	30.9	United Arab Emirates	21.8	France	7.0

Social indicators

	2010	2015	2022
Population growth rate (average annual %)	3.4	2.9	3.1[a]
Urban population (% of total population)	22.0	22.5	23.3[d]
Urban population growth rate (average annual %)[j]	3.5	3.8	...
Fertility rate, total (live births per woman)	7.0	6.7	6.2[a]
Life expectancy at birth (females/males, years)	50.8 / 48.4	53.1 / 50.1	54.8 / 51.3[a]
Population age distribution (0-14/60+ years old, %)	48.6 / 3.4	48.4 / 3.3	47.5 / 3.4[a]
International migrant stock (000/% of total pop.)[k]	417.0 / 3.5	467.0 / 3.3	547.5 / 3.3[b]
Refugees and others of concern to the UNHCR (000)	533.0[l]	473.5	1 022.2[e]
Infant mortality rate (per 1 000 live births)	91.1	80.6	65.5[a]
Health: Current expenditure (% of GDP)[m]	4.1	4.5	4.4[d]
Health: Physicians (per 1 000 pop.)	~0.0[n]	~0.0	0.1[b]
Education: Government expenditure (% of GDP)	2.0	2.4	2.4[g,d]
Education: Primary gross enrol. ratio (f/m per 100 pop.)	89.1 / 94.6	79.4 / 103.7	78.0 / 100.3[d]
Education: Sec. gross enrol. ratio (f/m per 100 pop.)	13.4 / 31.7	13.9 / 30.9	14.3 / 26.8[d]
Education: Upr. Sec. gross enrol. ratio (f/m per 100 pop.)	8.7 / 24.2	9.0 / 25.3	10.2 / 23.5[d]
Seats held by women in the National Parliament (%)	5.2	14.9	31.2[o]

Environment and infrastructure indicators

	2010	2015	2022
Individuals using the Internet (per 100 inhabitants)[g]	1.7	3.5	10.4[b]
Research & Development expenditure (% of GDP)	...	...	0.3[p,q,r]
Threatened species (number)	30	38	55
Forested area (% of land area)	4.4	3.9[g]	3.5[g,d]
Energy production, primary (Petajoules)	324	375	358[d]
Energy supply per capita (Gigajoules)	7	6	6[d]
Tourist/visitor arrivals at national borders (000)	71[s]	120[s]	10[t,b]
Important sites for terrestrial biodiversity protected (%)	67.3	67.3	67.3[e]
Pop. using safely managed drinking water (urban/rural, %)	16.2 / 2.6	16.8 / 2.3	17.4 / 2.0[b]
Pop. using safely managed sanitation (urban/rural, %)	23.5 / 4.8	27.7 / 4.0	32.3 / 3.3[b]
Net Official Development Assist. received (% of GNI)	4.75	5.71	10.42[b]

a Projected estimate (medium fertility variant). b 2020. c African Financial Community (CFA) Franc, Bank of Central African States (BEAC). d 2019. e 2021. f Data classified according to ISIC Rev. 4. g Estimate. h N'Djamena i Calculated by the UNSD from national indices. j Data refers to a 5-year period preceding the reference year. k Including refugees. l Data as at the end of December. m Estimates should be viewed with caution as these are derived from scarce data. n 2006. o Data are as at 1 January of reporting year. p Excluding business enterprise. q Excluding private non-profit. r 2016. s Arrivals by air. t Non-resident tourists staying in hotels and similar establishments.

Channel Islands

Region	Northern Europe	Surface area (km2)	180[a,b]
Capital city	Saint Helier[c]	National currency	Pound Sterling (GBP)
Capital city pop. (000, 2022)	34.4[d]	Exchange rate (per US$)	0.7[e]

Economic indicators	2010	2015	2022
Employment in agriculture (% of employed)[f]	4.7	4.0	3.5[g]
Employment in industry (% of employed)[f]	26.7	24.9	22.9[g]
Employment in services & other sectors (% employed)[f]	68.6	71.1	73.6[g]
Unemployment rate (% of labour force)[f]	7.2	8.2	6.8
Labour force participation rate (female/male pop. %)[f]	51.4 / 67.7	51.2 / 68.2	51.8 / 67.2

Social indicators	2010	2015	2022
Urban population (% of total population)[a]	31.1	31.0	30.9[h]
Urban population growth rate (average annual %)[a,i]	0.9	0.5	...
International migrant stock (000/% of total pop.)[j]	77.6 / 48.6	82.3 / 49.8	84.1 / 48.4[g]
Intentional homicide rate (per 100 000 pop.)	0.0	...	...

Environment and infrastructure indicators	2010	2015	2022
Forested area (% of land area)	5.2[f]	5.2	5.2[h]

a Refers to Guernsey and Jersey. **b** 2017. **c** The capital of the Bailiwick of Jersey. **d** 2018. **e** 2021. **f** Estimate. **g** 2020. **h** 2019. **i** Data refers to a 5-year period preceding the reference year. **j** Refers to Guernsey and Jersey. For statistical purposes, the data for United Kingdom do not include this area.

Region	South America	UN membership date	24 October 1945
Population (000, 2022)	19 604[a]	Surface area (km2)	756 102[b]
Pop. density (per km2, 2022)	26.0[a]	Sex ratio (m per 100 f)	98.5[a]
Capital city	Santiago	National currency	Chilean Peso (CLP)
Capital city pop. (000, 2022)	6 723.5[c,d]	Exchange rate (per US$)	866.2[e]

Economic indicators

	2010	2015	2022
GDP: Gross domestic product (million current US$)	218 538	243 919	252 940[b]
GDP growth rate (annual %, const. 2015 prices)	5.8	2.3	- 5.8[b]
GDP per capita (current US$)	12 808.0	13 574.2	13 231.7[b]
Economy: Agriculture (% of Gross Value Added)[f,g]	3.9	4.0	4.2[b]
Economy: Industry (% of Gross Value Added)[f,h]	38.8	32.6	34.2[b]
Economy: Services and other activity (% of GVA)[f,i]	57.3	63.4	61.5[b]
Employment in agriculture (% of employed)	10.6	9.4	8.8[j,b]
Employment in industry (% of employed)	23.0	23.3	22.0[j,b]
Employment in services & other sectors (% employed)	66.4	67.3	69.2[j,b]
Unemployment rate (% of labour force)	8.4	6.5	8.2[j]
Labour force participation rate (female/male pop. %)	45.6 / 72.4	48.5 / 71.8	46.4 / 67.1[j]
CPI: Consumer Price Index (2010=100)	100	118	142[e]
Agricultural production index (2014-2016=100)	93	101	108[b]
International trade: exports (million current US$)	71 106	62 033	94 705[e]
International trade: imports (million current US$)	59 007	62 387	91 837[e]
International trade: balance (million current US$)	12 099	- 354	2 868[e]
Balance of payments, current account (million US$)	3 069	- 5 735	3 370[b]

Major trading partners

						2021
Export partners (% of exports)	China	38.8	United States	15.8	Japan	7.7
Import partners (% of imports)	China	29.9	United States	17.4	Brazil	8.4

Social indicators

	2010	2015	2022
Population growth rate (average annual %)	1.0	1.0	0.1[a]
Urban population (% of total population)	87.1	87.4	87.6[d]
Urban population growth rate (average annual %)[k]	1.1	1.0	...
Fertility rate, total (live births per woman)	1.8	1.7	1.5[a]
Life expectancy at birth (females/males, years)	81.2 / 75.7	82.4 / 77.0	81.9 / 77.2[a]
Population age distribution (0-14/60+ years old, %)	21.5 / 13.9	20.0 / 15.8	18.3 / 18.3[a]
International migrant stock (000/% of total pop.)	375.4 / 2.2	639.7 / 3.6	1 645.0 / 8.6[b]
Refugees and others of concern to the UNHCR (000)	1.9[l]	2.5	493.7[e]
Infant mortality rate (per 1 000 live births)	7.3	6.8	4.9[a]
Health: Current expenditure (% of GDP)[n]	6.8[m]	8.3[o]	9.3[o,d]
Health: Physicians (per 1 000 pop.)	1.4	2.1	2.8[b]
Education: Government expenditure (% of GDP)	4.2	4.9	5.4[p]
Education: Primary gross enrol. ratio (f/m per 100 pop.)	102.2 / 105.2	99.1 / 102.2	100.9 / 103.8[d]
Education: Sec. gross enrol. ratio (f/m per 100 pop.)	91.4 / 88.7	102.1 / 101.5	103.3 / 104.1[d]
Education: Upr. Sec. gross enrol. ratio (f/m per 100 pop.)	88.3 / 84.1	101.0 / 99.1	105.0 / 104.8[d]
Intentional homicide rate (per 100 000 pop.)	3.2	3.4	4.8[b]
Seats held by women in the National Parliament (%)	14.2	15.8	35.5[q]

Environment and infrastructure indicators

	2010	2015	2022
Individuals using the Internet (per 100 inhabitants)	45.0[j,r]	76.6	88.3[j,b]
Research & Development expenditure (% of GDP)	0.3	0.4	0.3[j,d]
Threatened species (number)	145	182	278
Forested area (% of land area)	22.5	23.7[j]	24.3[j,d]
CO2 emission estimates (million tons/tons per capita)	70.5 / 4.0	83.0 / 4.5	81.7 / 4.1[b]
Energy production, primary (Petajoules)	386	541	572[d]
Energy supply per capita (Gigajoules)	75	84	91[d]
Tourist/visitor arrivals at national borders (000)[s]	2 801	4 478	1 119[b]
Important sites for terrestrial biodiversity protected (%)	26.9	28.9	32.5[e]
Pop. using safely managed drinking water (urban/rural, %)	98.6 / ...	98.7 / ...	98.8 / ...[b]
Pop. using safely managed sanitation (urban/rural %)	64.8 / ...	73.3 / ...	81.4 / ...[b]
Net Official Development Assist. received (% of GNI)	0.09	0.02	0.03[t]

a Projected estimate (medium fertility variant). **b** 2020. **c** Refers to the urban population of Santiago Metropolitan Area Region. **d** 2019. **e** 2021. **f** Data classified according to ISIC Rev. 4. **g** Excludes irrigation canals and landscaping care. **h** Excludes publishing activities. Includes irrigation and canals. **i** Includes publishing activities and landscape care. Excludes repair of personal and household goods. **j** Estimate. **k** Data refers to a 5-year period preceding the reference year. **l** Data as at the end of December. **m** Country is still reporting data based on SHA 1.0. **n** Data based on calendar year (January 1 to December 31). **o** Data are based on SHA2011. **p** 2018. **q** Data are as at 1 January of reporting year. **r** Population aged 5 years and over. **s** Including nationals residing abroad. **t** 2017.

China

Region	Eastern Asia	
Population (000, 2022)	1 425 887 [a,b]	
Pop. density (per km2, 2022)	148.5 [a,b]	
Capital city	Beijing	
Capital city pop. (000, 2022)	20 035.5 [d,e]	

UN membership date	24 October 1945	
Surface area (km2)	9 600 000 [c]	
Sex ratio (m per 100 f)	104.2 [a,b]	
National currency	Yuan Renminbi (CNY)	
Exchange rate (per US$)	6.4 [b,f]	

Economic indicators

	2010	2015	2022
GDP: Gross domestic product (million current US$)[b]	6 087 188	11 061 570	14 722 801 [c]
GDP growth rate (annual %, const. 2015 prices)[b]	10.6	7.0	2.3 [c]
GDP per capita (current US$)[b]	4 447.1	7 862.7	10 229.0 [c]
Economy: Agriculture (% of Gross Value Added)[g]	9.9	8.7 [h]	8.0 [h,c]
Economy: Industry (% of Gross Value Added)[g,i]	46.4	41.0 [i]	38.0 [i,c]
Economy: Services and other activity (% of GVA)[g,i,k]	43.7	50.3 [l]	54.0 [l,c]
Employment in agriculture (% of employed)[b,m]	36.7	28.6	24.7 [c]
Employment in industry (% of employed)[b,m]	28.7	29.2	28.2 [c]
Employment in services & other sectors (% employed)[b,m]	34.6	42.2	47.1 [c]
Unemployment rate (% of labour force)[b,m]	4.5	4.6	4.7
Labour force participation rate (female/male pop. %)[b,m]	63.6 / 78.0	63.6 / 76.9	61.5 / 74.0
CPI: Consumer Price Index (2010=100)	100	115	113 [n,f]
Agricultural production index (2014-2016=100)[b]	89	101	104 [c]
International trade: exports (million current US$)[b]	1 577 764	2 273 468	3 362 302 [f]
International trade: imports (million current US$)[b]	1 396 002	1 679 564	2 684 363 [f]
International trade: balance (million current US$)[b]	181 762	593 904	677 939 [f]
Balance of payments, current account (million US$)[b]	237 810	293 022	317 301 [f]

Major trading partners

						2021
Export partners (% of exports)	United States	17.2	China, Hong Kong SAR	10.4	Japan	4.9
Import partners (% of imports)	Other Asia, nes	9.3	Republic of Korea	8.0	Japan	7.7

Social indicators

	2010	2015	2022
Population growth rate (average annual %)[b]	0.7	0.6	~-0.0 [a]
Urban population (% of total population)[b]	49.2	55.5	60.3 [e]
Urban population growth rate (average annual %)[b,o]	3.5	2.9	...
Fertility rate, total (live births per woman)[b]	1.7	1.7	1.2 [a]
Life expectancy at birth (females/males, years)[b]	78.3 / 73.1	79.8 / 74.4	81.3 / 76.0 [a]
Population age distribution (0-14/60+ years old, %)[b]	18.5 / 12.8	18.4 / 15.6	17.2 / 18.6 [a]
International migrant stock (000/% of total pop.)[b,p]	849.9 / 0.1	978.0 / 0.1	1 039.7 / 0.1 [c]
Refugees and others of concern to the UNHCR (000)	301.1 [b,p]	301.6 [b]	304.1 [f]
Infant mortality rate (per 1 000 live births)[b]	13.0	8.9	5.9 [a]
Health: Current expenditure (% of GDP)	4.2	4.9	5.4 [e]
Health: Physicians (per 1 000 pop.)	1.4	1.8	2.2 [e]
Education: Government expenditure (% of GDP)	3.8	3.8	3.5 [q]
Education: Primary gross enrol. ratio (f/m per 100 pop.)	98.0 / 99.8	96.4 / 96.2	103.7 / 102.7 [c]
Education: Sec. gross enrol. ratio (f/m per 100 pop.)	88.0 / 88.3	... / ...	... / ...
Education: Upr. Sec. gross enrol. ratio (f/m per 100 pop.)	76.1 / 77.5	81.1 / 77.4	82.3 / 80.1 [c]
Intentional homicide rate (per 100 000 pop.)	1.0	0.7	0.5 [q]
Seats held by women in the National Parliament (%)	21.3	23.6	24.9 [r]

Environment and infrastructure indicators

	2010	2015	2022
Individuals using the Internet (per 100 inhabitants)[b]	34.3	50.3 [m,s,t,u]	70.4 [c]
Research & Development expenditure (% of GDP)[b]	1.7	2.1	2.4 [c]
Threatened species (number)[b]	859	1 040	1 346
Forested area (% of land area)	21.3	22.3	23.1 [e]
CO2 emission estimates (million tons/tons per capita)[b]	7 943.8 / 5.9	9 249.9 / 6.7	9 985.3 / 7.1 [e]
Energy production, primary (Petajoules)[b]	88 642	100 963	109 745 [e]
Energy supply per capita (Gigajoules)[b]	74	86	95 [e]
Tourist/visitor arrivals at national borders (000)[b]	55 664	56 886	7 967 [c]
Important sites for terrestrial biodiversity protected (%)	8.6	9.5	10.1 [f]
Pop. using safely managed drinking water (urban/rural, %)	89.2 / ...	93.1 / ...	95.0 / ... [c]
Pop. using safely managed sanitation (urban/rural %)[b]	53.6 / 17.3	70.7 / 29.5	85.6 / 43.9 [c]
Net Official Development Assist. received (% of GNI)[b]	0.01	0.00	0.00 [c]

a Projected estimate (medium fertility variant). b For statistical purposes, the data for China do not include those for the Hong Kong Special Administrative Region (Hong Kong SAR), Macao Special Administrative Region (Macao SAR) and Taiwan Province of China. c 2020. d Refers to all city districts (excluding Yanqing District) meeting the criteria such as contiguous built-up areas, being the location of the local government, being a Street or Having a Resident Committee. e 2019. f 2021. g Data classified according to ISIC Rev. 4. h Excludes irrigation canals and landscaping care. i Including taxes less subsidies on production and imports. j Excludes publishing activities. Includes irrigation and canals. k Excludes repair of motor vehicles and motorcycles, personal and household goods. l Excludes repair of personal and household goods. m Estimate. n Index base: 2015=100. o Data refers to a 5-year period preceding the reference year. p Refers to foreign citizens. q 2018. r Data are as at 1 January of reporting year. s Population aged 6 years and over. t Data refer to permanent residents. u Users in the last 6 months.

China, Hong Kong SAR

Region	Eastern Asia	
Surface area (km2)	1 107[b]	
Sex ratio (m per 100 f)	85.4[a]	
National currency	Hong Kong Dollar (HKD)	
Exchange rate (per US$)	7.8[e]	

Population (000, 2022)	7 489[a]
Pop. density (per km2, 2022)	6 814.3[a]
Capital city	Hong Kong
Capital city pop. (000, 2022)	7 490.8[c,d]

Economic indicators

	2010	2015	2022
GDP: Gross domestic product (million current US$)	228 639	309 386	349 445[b]
GDP growth rate (annual %, const. 2015 prices)	6.8	2.4	- 6.1[b]
GDP per capita (current US$)	32 820.5	43 054.0	46 611.4[b]
Economy: Agriculture (% of Gross Value Added)[f,g,h]	0.1	0.1	0.1[b]
Economy: Industry (% of Gross Value Added)[g,i,j]	7.0	7.3	6.4[b]
Economy: Services and other activity (% of GVA)[g,k]	93.0	92.7	93.5[b]
Employment in agriculture (% of employed)[l]	0.2	0.2	0.2[b]
Employment in industry (% of employed)[l]	12.8	12.0	11.5[b]
Employment in services & other sectors (% employed)[l]	87.0	87.8	88.3[b]
Unemployment rate (% of labour force)	4.3	3.3	4.2[l]
Labour force participation rate (female/male pop. %)	51.9 / 68.5	54.7 / 68.8	53.4 / 65.4[l]
CPI: Consumer Price Index (2010=100)	100	123	137[e]
Agricultural production index (2014-2016=100)	101	97	221[b]
International trade: exports (million current US$)	400 692	510 553	670 926[e]
International trade: imports (million current US$)	441 369	559 306	713 173[e]
International trade: balance (million current US$)	- 40 677	- 48 753	- 42 247[e]
Balance of payments, current account (million US$)	16 012	10 264	41 356[e]

Major trading partners

					2021
Export partners (% of exports)	China	59.9	United States	6.0	Other Asia, nes	2.8
Import partners (% of imports)	China	44.3	Other Asia, nes	9.9	Singapore	7.6

Social indicators

	2010	2015	2022
Population growth rate (average annual %)	0.5	0.6	---0.0[a]
Urban population (% of total population)	100.0	100.0	100.0[d]
Urban population growth rate (average annual %)[m]	0.6	0.6	...
Fertility rate, total (live births per woman)	1.1	1.2	0.8[a]
Life expectancy at birth (females/males, years)	85.9 / 80.2	87.2 / 81.5	86.9 / 81.8[a]
Population age distribution (0-14/60+ years old, %)	12.3 / 18.5	11.6 / 21.9	12.0 / 28.7[a]
International migrant stock (000/% of total pop.)[n]	2 780.0 / 39.9	2 841.1 / 39.5	2 962.5 / 39.5[b]
Refugees and others of concern to the UNHCR (000)	0.6[o]	10.1	0.3[e]
Infant mortality rate (per 1 000 live births)	1.7	1.4	1.4[a]
Education: Government expenditure (% of GDP)	3.5	3.3	4.4[b]
Education: Primary gross enrol. ratio (f/m per 100 pop.)	... / ...	111.2 / 109.3	110.2 / 105.7[b]
Education: Sec. gross enrol. ratio (f/m per 100 pop.)	88.2 / 87.9	101.4 / 103.1	107.6 / 109.1[b]
Education: Upr. Sec. gross enrol. ratio (f/m per 100 pop.)	77.7 / 76.4	97.9 / 99.2	105.4 / 109.5[b]
Intentional homicide rate (per 100 000 pop.)	0.5	0.3	0.3[b]

Environment and infrastructure indicators

	2010	2015	2022
Individuals using the Internet (per 100 inhabitants)	72.0[p]	84.9[p,q]	92.4[b]
Research & Development expenditure (% of GDP)	0.7	0.8	1.0[b]
Threatened species (number)	49	60	96
CO2 emission estimates (million tons/tons per capita)	41.7 / 5.9	43.5 / 5.9	35.4 / 4.7[b]
Energy supply per capita (Gigajoules)	78	80	79[d]
Tourist/visitor arrivals at national borders (000)	20 085	26 686	1 359[b]
Important sites for terrestrial biodiversity protected (%)	48.9	48.9	48.9[e]
Pop. using safely managed drinking water (urban/rural, %)	99.4 / ...	100.0 / ...	100.0 / ...[b]
Pop. using safely managed sanitation (urban/rural, %)	86.0 / ...	86.0 / ...	85.9 / ...[b]

a Projected estimate (medium fertility variant). b 2020. c Consists of the population of Hong Kong Island, New Kowloon the new towns in New Territories and the marine areas. d 2019. e 2021. f Including mining and quarrying. g Data classified according to ISIC Rev. 4. h Excluding hunting and forestry. i Includes waste management. j Excluding mining and quarrying. k Excluding waste management. l Estimate. m Data refers to a 5-year period preceding the reference year. n Including refugees. o Data as at the end of December. p Population aged 10 years and over. q Users in the last 12 months.

China, Macao SAR

Region	Eastern Asia
Surface area (km2)	33[b,c]
Sex ratio (m per 100 f)	88.4[a]
National currency	Pataca (MOP)
Exchange rate (per US$)	8.0[e]

Population (000, 2022)	695[a]
Pop. density (per km2, 2022)	21 724.0[a]
Capital city	Macao
Capital city pop. (000, 2022)	642.1[d]

Economic indicators

	2010	2015	2022
GDP: Gross domestic product (million current US$)	28 242	45 060	24 333[c]
GDP growth rate (annual %, const. 2015 prices)	25.1	- 21.5	- 56.3[c]
GDP per capita (current US$)	52 472.7	74 840.7	37 473.8[c]
Economy: Industry (% of Gross Value Added)	7.4	10.4	6.2[c]
Economy: Services and other activity (% of GVA)	92.6	89.6	93.8[c]
Employment in agriculture (% of employed)	0.4	0.4	0.4[f,c]
Employment in industry (% of employed)	13.7	15.8	9.5[f,c]
Employment in services & other sectors (% employed)	85.9	83.8	90.1[f,c]
Unemployment rate (% of labour force)	2.8	1.8	2.5[f]
Labour force participation rate (female/male pop. %)	66.0 / 77.5	68.2 / 79.8	65.0 / 72.2[f]
CPI: Consumer Price Index (2010=100)	100	131[g]	145[g,a]
Agricultural production index (2014-2016=100)	107	87	89[c]
International trade: exports (million current US$)	870	1 339	1 392[e]
International trade: imports (million current US$)	5 629	10 603	19 347[e]
International trade: balance (million current US$)	- 4 760	- 9 264	- 17 954[e]
Balance of payments, current account (million US$)	10 992	10 515	3 879[c]

Major trading partners

						2021
Export partners (% of exports)	China, Hong Kong SAR	79.2	China	13.0	United States	5.0
Import partners (% of imports)	China	31.8	France	18.1	Italy	11.0

Social indicators

	2010	2015	2022
Population growth rate (average annual %)	2.6	1.8	1.3[a]
Urban population (% of total population)	100.0	100.0	100.0[d]
Urban population growth rate (average annual %)[h]	2.1	2.3	...
Fertility rate, total (live births per woman)	1.0	1.2	1.1[a]
Life expectancy at birth (females/males, years)	86.2 / 80.0	86.8 / 81.1	88.0 / 82.8[a]
Population age distribution (0-14/60+ years old, %)	12.9 / 11.4	12.9 / 14.5	14.8 / 19.5[a]
International migrant stock (000/% of total pop.)	318.5 / 59.2	376.1 / 62.5	403.5 / 62.1[c]
Refugees and others of concern to the UNHCR (000)	~0.0[i]	~0.0	~0.0[c]
Infant mortality rate (per 1 000 live births)	3.4	2.8	2.2[a]
Education: Government expenditure (% of GDP)	2.6	3.0	3.1[d]
Education: Primary gross enrol. ratio (f/m per 100 pop.)	94.0 / 95.8	98.5 / 100.1	98.0 / 100.5[c]
Education: Sec. gross enrol. ratio (f/m per 100 pop.)	86.4 / 89.2	93.8 / 95.2	102.7 / 102.5[c]
Education: Upr. Sec. gross enrol. ratio (f/m per 100 pop.)	75.3 / 73.3	87.4 / 86.7	97.2 / 96.9[c]
Intentional homicide rate (per 100 000 pop.)	0.4	0.2	0.3[c]

Environment and infrastructure indicators

	2010	2015	2022
Individuals using the Internet (per 100 inhabitants)	55.2[j]	77.6[k]	88.1[f,c]
Research & Development expenditure (% of GDP)[l]	0.1	0.1	0.4[m,c]
Threatened species (number)	9	11	26
Energy production, primary (Petajoules)	4[f]	3	4[d]
Energy supply per capita (Gigajoules)	60	71	63[d]
Tourist/visitor arrivals at national borders (000)[n]	11 926	14 308	2 822[c]
Important sites for terrestrial biodiversity protected (%)	0.0	0.0	0.0[e]
Pop. using safely managed drinking water (urban/rural, %)	100.0 / ...	100.0 / ...	100.0 / ...[c]
Pop. using safely managed sanitation (urban/rural %)	55.8 / ...	61.2 / ...	66.6 / ...[c]

a Projected estimate (medium fertility variant). b Inland waters include the reservoirs. c 2020. d 2019. e 2021. f Estimate. g Calculated by the UNSD from national indices. h Data refers to a 5-year period preceding the reference year. i Data as at the end of December. j Population aged 3 years and over. k Users in the last 3 months. l Partial data. m Break in the time series. n Does not include other non-residents namely workers, students, etc.

Colombia

Region	South America	UN membership date	05 November 1945
Population (000, 2022)	51 874[a]	Surface area (km2)	1 141 748[b]
Pop. density (per km2, 2022)	46.2[a]	Sex ratio (m per 100 f)	97.3[a]
Capital city	Bogota	National currency	Colombian Peso (COP)
Capital city pop. (000, 2022)	10 779.4[c,d]	Exchange rate (per US$)	3 997.7[e]

Economic indicators

	2010	2015	2022
GDP: Gross domestic product (million current US$)	286 563	293 482	271 347[b]
GDP growth rate (annual %, const. 2015 prices)	4.5	3.0	- 6.8[b]
GDP per capita (current US$)	6 336.7	6 175.9	5 332.8[b]
Economy: Agriculture (% of Gross Value Added)[f,g]	6.9	6.6	8.4[b]
Economy: Industry (% of Gross Value Added)[g,h]	34.4	31.5	26.1[b]
Economy: Services and other activity (% of GVA)[g,i]	58.6	61.9	65.5[b]
Employment in agriculture (% of employed)	18.4	16.0	16.5[j,b]
Employment in industry (% of employed)	20.0	19.8	20.0[j,b]
Employment in services & other sectors (% employed)	61.6	64.2	63.5[j,b]
Unemployment rate (% of labour force)	11.0	8.3	13.1[j]
Labour force participation rate (female/male pop. %)	55.4 / 81.0	58.2 / 81.6	53.2 / 78.6[j]
CPI: Consumer Price Index (2010=100)[k]	100	118	150[e]
Agricultural production index (2014-2016=100)	81	101	103[b]
International trade: exports (million current US$)	39 820	35 691	41 390[e]
International trade: imports (million current US$)	40 683	54 036	61 099[e]
International trade: balance (million current US$)	- 863	- 18 345	- 19 709[e]
Balance of payments, current account (million US$)	- 8 583	- 18 702	- 17 833[e]

Major trading partners

						2021
Export partners (% of exports)	United States	28.1	China	8.8	Panama	5.8
Import partners (% of imports)	China	24.2	United States	23.2	Mexico	6.2

Social indicators

	2010	2015	2022
Population growth rate (average annual %)	1.1	1.0	0.3[a]
Urban population (% of total population)	78.0	79.8	81.1[d]
Urban population growth rate (average annual %)[l]	1.7	1.4	...
Fertility rate, total (live births per woman)	2.0	1.9	1.7[a]
Life expectancy at birth (females/males, years)	78.3 / 71.8	79.3 / 73.3	77.1 / 70.3[a]
Population age distribution (0-14/60+ years old, %)	27.1 / 9.0	24.4 / 10.8	21.3 / 13.5[a]
International migrant stock (000/% of total pop.)	130.3 / 0.3	159.4 / 0.3	1 905.4 / 3.7[b]
Refugees and others of concern to the UNHCR (000)	3 672.4[m]	6 520.6	11 205.7[e]
Infant mortality rate (per 1 000 live births)	15.5	13.2	10.9[a]
Health: Current expenditure (% of GDP)[n]	7.1	7.5	7.7[d]
Health: Physicians (per 1 000 pop.)	1.6	2.0	2.3[b]
Education: Government expenditure (% of GDP)	4.8	4.5	4.5[d]
Education: Primary gross enrol. ratio (f/m per 100 pop.)	119.3 / 121.3	113.4 / 117.0	112.1 / 115.9[d]
Education: Sec. gross enrol. ratio (f/m per 100 pop.)	102.3 / 93.0	98.1 / 91.5	103.4 / 98.4[d]
Education: Upr. Sec. gross enrol. ratio (f/m per 100 pop.)	87.0 / 72.6	85.2 / 72.0	87.6 / 77.0[d]
Intentional homicide rate (per 100 000 pop.)	34.2	26.9	22.6[b]
Seats held by women in the National Parliament (%)	8.4	19.9	18.6[o]

Environment and infrastructure indicators

	2010	2015	2022
Individuals using the Internet (per 100 inhabitants)	36.5[p]	55.9	69.8[p,b]
Research & Development expenditure (% of GDP)	0.2	0.4	0.3[j,b]
Threatened species (number)	681	751	1 511
Forested area (% of land area)	54.8	54.2	53.5[d]
CO2 emission estimates (million tons/tons per capita)	60.3 / 1.3	75.7 / 1.6	72.6 / 1.4[b]
Energy production, primary (Petajoules)	4 406	5 815	5 507[d]
Energy supply per capita (Gigajoules)	31	43	41[d]
Tourist/visitor arrivals at national borders (000)[q]	1 405	3 099[r,s]	1 262[r,s,b]
Important sites for terrestrial biodiversity protected (%)	35.3	43.6	50.2[e]
Pop. using safely managed drinking water (urban/rural, %)	81.4 / 37.0	81.1 / 38.6	80.5 / 40.2[b]
Pop. using safely managed sanitation (urban/rural %)	15.4 / ...	16.0 / ...	16.6 / ...[b]
Net Official Development Assist. received (% of GNI)	0.24	0.47	0.70[b]

a Projected estimate (medium fertility variant). **b** 2020. **c** Refers to the nuclei of Santa Fe de Bogotá, Soacha, Chia and Funza. **d** 2019. **e** 2021. **f** Excludes irrigation canals and landscaping care. **g** Data classified according to ISIC Rev. 4. **h** Excludes publishing activities. Includes irrigation and canals. **i** Includes publishing activities and landscape care. Excludes repair of personal and household goods. **j** Estimate. **k** Calculated by the UNSD from national indices. **l** Data refers to a 5-year period preceding the reference year. **m** Data as at the end of December. **n** Data based on calendar year (January 1 to December 31). **o** Data are as at 1 January of reporting year. **p** Population aged 5 years and over. **q** Arrivals of non-resident travellers by immigration checkpoints. **r** Including nationals residing abroad. **s** The nationals residing abroad are calculated with the country of residence reported at the exit.

Comoros

Region	Eastern Africa	UN membership date	12 November 1975	
Population (000, 2022)	837[a]	Surface area (km2)	2 235[b]	
Pop. density (per km2, 2022)	449.6[a]	Sex ratio (m per 100 f)	100.9[a]	
Capital city	Moroni	National currency	Comorian Franc (KMF)	
Capital city pop. (000, 2022)	62.4[c]	Exchange rate (per US$)	434.4[d]	

Economic indicators

	2010	2015	2022
GDP: Gross domestic product (million current US$)	907	966	1 235[b]
GDP growth rate (annual %, const. 2015 prices)	4.8	2.0	3.9[b]
GDP per capita (current US$)	1 315.2	1 242.1	1 420.7[b]
Economy: Agriculture (% of Gross Value Added)[e]	31.6	31.7	38.1[b]
Economy: Industry (% of Gross Value Added)[e]	12.2	10.8	8.7[b]
Economy: Services and other activity (% of GVA)[e]	56.1	57.5	53.2[b]
Employment in agriculture (% of employed)[f]	53.7	51.8	49.9[b]
Employment in industry (% of employed)[f]	13.7	13.4	13.0[b]
Employment in services & other sectors (% employed)[f]	32.6	34.8	37.0[b]
Unemployment rate (% of labour force)[f]	6.7	8.1	9.1
Labour force participation rate (female/male pop. %)[f]	32.5 / 53.9	32.7 / 56.1	32.6 / 54.9
CPI: Consumer Price Index (2010=100)	100	104[g]	...
Agricultural production index (2014-2016=100)	99	98	105[b]
International trade: exports (million current US$)	14	15	18[f,d]
International trade: imports (million current US$)	181	173	311[f,d]
International trade: balance (million current US$)	- 167	- 158	- 294[d]
Balance of payments, current account (million US$)	- 39	- 2	- 24[b]

Major trading partners

						2021
Export partners (% of exports)[f]	France	26.6	India	22.8	Germany	12.4
Import partners (% of imports)[f]	United Arab Emirates	19.0	France	15.7	Pakistan	13.2

Social indicators

	2010	2015	2022
Population growth rate (average annual %)	2.1	2.2	1.8[a]
Urban population (% of total population)	28.0	28.5	29.2[h]
Urban population growth rate (average annual %)[i]	2.5	2.7	...
Fertility rate, total (live births per woman)	4.8	4.4	3.9[a]
Life expectancy at birth (females/males, years)	63.1 / 59.3	65.2 / 60.8	66.1 / 61.5[a]
Population age distribution (0-14/60+ years old, %)	42.0 / 6.0	39.8 / 6.2	38.0 / 6.5[a]
International migrant stock (000/% of total pop.)	12.6 / 1.8	12.6 / 1.6	12.5 / 1.4[b]
Refugees and others of concern to the UNHCR (000)	~0.0[j,k]	...	...
Infant mortality rate (per 1 000 live births)	62.4	54.4	45.5[a]
Health: Current expenditure (% of GDP)[l]	5.0	4.6	5.2[h]
Health: Physicians (per 1 000 pop.)	0.2[m]	0.2[n]	0.3[c]
Education: Government expenditure (% of GDP)	4.4[o]	2.5	...
Education: Primary gross enrol. ratio (f/m per 100 pop.)	104.1 / 113.0[o]	101.2 / 108.6[p]	99.4 / 99.6[c]
Education: Sec. gross enrol. ratio (f/m per 100 pop.)	... / ...	63.1 / 59.1[p]	61.4 / 57.6[c]
Education: Upr. Sec. gross enrol. ratio (f/m per 100 pop.)	... / ...	55.1 / 50.0[p]	47.8 / 42.9[c]
Seats held by women in the National Parliament (%)	3.0	3.0[p]	16.7[q]

Environment and infrastructure indicators

	2010	2015	2022
Individuals using the Internet (per 100 inhabitants)[f]	5.1	7.5	8.5[r]
Threatened species (number)	89	106	143
Forested area (% of land area)	20.0	18.9	17.9[h]
Energy production, primary (Petajoules)[f]	3	4	4[h]
Energy supply per capita (Gigajoules)[f]	8	8	10[h]
Tourist/visitor arrivals at national borders (000)[s]	15	24	7[b]
Important sites for terrestrial biodiversity protected (%)	57.4	57.4	57.4[d]
Net Official Development Assist. received (% of GNI)	7.71	6.78	10.75[b]

a Projected estimate (medium fertility variant). b 2020. c 2018. d 2021. e Data classified according to ISIC Rev. 4. f Estimate. g 2013. h 2019. i Data refers to a 5-year period preceding the reference year. j Data as at the end of December. k 2005. l Data revision. m 2009. n 2012. o 2008. p 2014. q Data are as at 1 January of reporting year. r 2017. s Arrivals by air.

Region	Middle Africa	UN membership date	20 September 1960
Population (000, 2022)	5 970 [a]	Surface area (km2)	342 000 [b]
Pop. density (per km2, 2022)	17.5 [a]	Sex ratio (m per 100 f)	99.8 [a]
Capital city	Brazzaville	National currency	CFA Franc, BEAC (XAF) [c]
Capital city pop. (000, 2022)	2 308.1 [d]	Exchange rate (per US$)	579.2 [e]

Economic indicators

	2010	2015	2022
GDP: Gross domestic product (million current US$)	13 678	11 751	10 100 [b]
GDP growth rate (annual %, const. 2015 prices)	9.9	- 3.2	- 8.2 [b]
GDP per capita (current US$)	3 200.5	2 419.8	1 830.4 [b]
Economy: Agriculture (% of Gross Value Added) [f]	4.2	6.3	7.5 [b]
Economy: Industry (% of Gross Value Added) [f]	68.0	50.0	47.2 [b]
Economy: Services and other activity (% of GVA) [f]	27.8	43.7	45.3 [b]
Employment in agriculture (% of employed) [g]	37.4	35.0	33.8 [b]
Employment in industry (% of employed) [g]	23.3	23.0	21.7 [b]
Employment in services & other sectors (% employed) [g]	39.2	42.0	44.5 [b]
Unemployment rate (% of labour force) [g]	20.1	20.4	22.5
Labour force participation rate (female/male pop. %) [g]	66.9 / 68.8	66.7 / 69.3	66.2 / 68.0
CPI: Consumer Price Index (2010=100) [g,h]	100	116	129 [e]
Agricultural production index (2014-2016=100)	85	102	101 [b]
International trade: exports (million current US$)	6 918	8 623	6 667 [g,e]
International trade: imports (million current US$)	4 369	10 550	2 437 [g,e]
International trade: balance (million current US$)	2 548	- 1 927	4 230 [e]
Balance of payments, current account (million US$)	900	- 4 629	- 3 594 [i]

Major trading partners

						2021
Export partners (% of exports) [g]	China	63.8	Spain	8.6	Gabon	4.6
Import partners (% of imports) [g]	China	18.7	France	14.5	Belgium	7.4

Social indicators

	2010	2015	2022
Population growth rate (average annual %)	3.3	2.4	2.3 [a]
Urban population (% of total population)	63.3	65.5	67.4 [d]
Urban population growth rate (average annual %) [j]	4.0	3.3	...
Fertility rate, total (live births per woman)	4.8	4.6	4.1 [a]
Life expectancy at birth (females/males, years)	62.8 / 60.6	64.3 / 62.1	64.6 / 61.5 [a]
Population age distribution (0-14/60+ years old, %)	40.6 / 4.1	42.0 / 4.1	41.1 / 4.6 [a]
International migrant stock (000/% of total pop.) [k]	425.2 / 9.9	390.1 / 8.0	387.6 / 7.0 [b]
Refugees and others of concern to the UNHCR (000)	138.7 [l]	65.8	196.6 [e]
Infant mortality rate (per 1 000 live births)	43.6	37.6	36.7 [a]
Health: Current expenditure (% of GDP)	1.9	2.5	2.1 [d]
Health: Physicians (per 1 000 pop.)	0.1	0.2 [m]	0.1 [n]
Education: Government expenditure (% of GDP)	5.7	3.3 [g]	3.9 [g,d]
Education: Primary gross enrol. ratio (f/m per 100 pop.)	106.1 / 112.2	110.5 / 102.8 [o]	92.4 / 95.0 [n]
Education: Sec. gross enrol. ratio (f/m per 100 pop.)	... / ...	48.8 / 56.3 [o]	... / ...
Education: Upr. Sec. gross enrol. ratio (f/m per 100 pop.)	... / ...	26.7 / 46.9 [o]	... / ...
Seats held by women in the National Parliament (%)	7.3	7.4	11.3 [p]

Environment and infrastructure indicators

	2010	2015	2022
Individuals using the Internet (per 100 inhabitants) [g]	5.0	7.6	8.6 [q]
Threatened species (number)	103	119	234
Forested area (% of land area) [g]	64.6	64.5	64.3 [d]
CO2 emission estimates (million tons/tons per capita)	2.1 / 0.4	3.6 / 0.7	4.1 / 0.7 [d]
Energy production, primary (Petajoules)	724	607	834 [d]
Energy supply per capita (Gigajoules)	16	24	25 [d]
Tourist/Visitor arrivals at national borders (000)	194	220	156 [n]
Important sites for terrestrial biodiversity protected (%)	58.3	61.6	72.0 [e]
Pop. using safely managed drinking water (urban/rural, %)	55.4 / 12.4	58.5 / 17.0	58.6 / 19.1 [b]
Net Official Development Assist. received (% of GNI)	10.77	0.74	2.31 [b]

a Projected estimate (medium fertility variant). b 2020. c African Financial Community (CFA) Franc, Bank of Central African States (BEAC). d 2019. e 2021. f Data classified according to ISIC Rev. 4. g Estimate. h Brazzaville i 2016. j Data refers to a 5-year period preceding the reference year. k Including refugees. l Data as at the end of December. m 2011. n 2018. o 2012. p Data are as at 1 January of reporting year. q 2017.

Cook Islands

Region	Polynesia	Population (000, 2022)	17[a,b]
Surface area (km2)	236[c,d]	Pop. density (per km2, 2022)	70.9[a,b]
Sex ratio (m per 100 f)	90.8[a,b]	Capital city	Avarua
National currency	New Zealand Dollar (NZD)	Capital city pop. (000, 2022)	13.1[e,f]
Exchange rate (per US$)	1.5[g]		

Economic indicators	2010	2015	2022
GDP: Gross domestic product (million current US$)	241	302	283[d]
GDP growth rate (annual %, const. 2015 prices)	- 4.9	5.7	- 25.4[d]
GDP per capita (current US$)	13 092.7	17 182.6	16 135.0[d]
Economy: Agriculture (% of Gross Value Added)[h,i]	3.4	3.2	3.1[d]
Economy: Industry (% of Gross Value Added)[i,j]	7.9	11.3	9.7[d]
Economy: Services and other activity (% of GVA)[i,k]	88.7	85.4	87.2[d]
Employment in agriculture (% of employed)	...	4.3[l,m]	
Employment in industry (% of employed)	...	11.7[l,m]	...
Employment in services & other sectors (% employed)	...	84.0[l,m]	...
Unemployment rate (% of labour force)[l]	6.9[n,o]	8.2[m]	...
Labour force participation rate (female/male pop. %)	64.2 / 76.1[l,n,o]	65.4 / 76.6[l,m]	... / ...
CPI: Consumer Price Index (2010=100)[e,p]	100	109	110[d]
Agricultural production index (2014-2016=100)	107	100	83[d]
International trade: exports (million current US$)	5	14[q]	4[q,g]
International trade: imports (million current US$)	91	109[q]	66[q,g]
International trade: balance (million current US$)	- 85	- 95[q]	- 63[g]

Major trading partners						2021
Export partners (% of exports)[q]	Japan	41.7	France	17.3	Thailand	16.3
Import partners (% of imports)[q]	New Zealand	58.1	Türkiye	13.4	Italy	10.9

Social indicators	2010	2015	2022
Population growth rate (average annual %)[b]	3.4	- 0.8	0.3[a]
Urban population (% of total population)	73.3	74.4	75.3[r]
Urban population growth rate (average annual %)[s]	- 0.6	- 0.9	...
Fertility rate, total (live births per woman)[b]	2.6	2.4	2.2[a]
Life expectancy at birth (females/males, years)[b]	77.8 / 69.9	78.3 / 70.6	79.0 / 71.4[a]
Population age distribution (0-14/60+ years old, %)[b]	28.1 / 12.1	26.2 / 14.0	23.6 / 17.5[a]
International migrant stock (000/% of total pop.)[t]	3.8 / 20.5	4.2 / 23.7	4.6 / 26.1[d]
Infant mortality rate (per 1 000 live births)[b]	9.2	7.5	5.7[a]
Health: Current expenditure (% of GDP)[u]	3.7	2.7	3.1[r]
Health: Physicians (per 1 000 pop.)	1.3[v]	1.4[w]	...
Education: Government expenditure (% of GDP)	...	3.9	3.5[q,r]
Education: Primary gross enrol. ratio (f/m per 100 pop.)	85.4 / 89.8	99.8 / 104.2	113.7 / 115.9[d]
Education: Sec. gross enrol. ratio (f/m per 100 pop.)	86.4 / 78.3	90.6 / 85.4	98.6 / 99.4[d]
Education: Upr. Sec. gross enrol. ratio (f/m per 100 pop.)	77.8 / 61.7	82.7 / 71.5	80.2 / 69.2[d]
Intentional homicide rate (per 100 000 pop.)	...	3.5[x]	...

Environment and infrastructure indicators	2010	2015	2022
Individuals using the Internet (per 100 inhabitants)	35.7	51.0[q]	54.0[q,y]
Threatened species (number)	53	73	82
Forested area (% of land area)	65.0	65.0	65.0[r]
Energy production, primary (Petajoules)	...	0	0[r]
Energy supply per capita (Gigajoules)[q]	47	58	68[r]
Tourist/visitor arrivals at national borders (000)[z]	104	125	25[d]
Important sites for terrestrial biodiversity protected (%)	24.4	24.4	30.9[g]

a Projected estimate (medium fertility variant). b For statistical purposes, the data for New Zealand do not include this area. c Excluding Niue, shown separately, which is part of Cook Islands, but because of remoteness is administered separately. d 2020. e Refers to the island of Rarotonga. f 2018. g 2021. h Excludes irrigation canals and landscaping care. i Data classified according to ISIC Rev. 4. j Excludes publishing activities. Includes irrigation and canals. k Includes publishing activities and landscape care. Excludes repair of personal and household goods. l Resident population (de jure). m 2011. n Break in the time series. o 2006. p Calculated by the UNSD from national indices. q Estimate. r 2019. s Data refers to a 5-year period preceding the reference year. t Including refugees. u Data refer to fiscal years beginning 1 July. v 2009. w 2014. x 2012. y 2016. z Air and sea arrivals.

Costa Rica

Region	Central America	UN membership date	02 November 1945	
Population (000, 2022)	5 181[a]	Surface area (km2)	51 100[b]	
Pop. density (per km2, 2022)	101.5[a]	Sex ratio (m per 100 f)	100.0[a]	
Capital city	San José	National currency	Costa Rican Colon (CRC)	
Capital city pop. (000, 2022)	1 378.5[c,d]	Exchange rate (per US$)	642.2[e]	

Economic indicators

	2010	2015	2022
GDP: Gross domestic product (million current US$)	37 659	56 442	61 521[b]
GDP growth rate (annual %, const. 2015 prices)	5.4	3.7	-4.5[b]
GDP per capita (current US$)	8 227.1	11 642.8	12 076.8[b]
Economy: Agriculture (% of Gross Value Added)[f,g]	7.1	5.2	4.7[b]
Economy: Industry (% of Gross Value Added)[g,h]	25.4	21.7	21.2[b]
Economy: Services and other activity (% of GVA)[g,i]	67.5	73.1	74.1[b]
Employment in agriculture (% of employed)	11.4[j]	12.3	11.9[j,b]
Employment in industry (% of employed)	20.0[j]	19.2	19.8[j,b]
Employment in services & other sectors (% employed)	68.6[j]	68.5	68.3[j,b]
Unemployment rate (% of labour force)	7.2	9.0	17.1[j]
Labour force participation rate (female/male pop. %)	43.9 / 74.6	47.7 / 74.2	47.7 / 71.0[j]
CPI: Consumer Price Index (2010=100)[k,l]	100	122	132[e]
Agricultural production index (2014-2016=100)	88	98	98[b]
International trade: exports (million current US$)	9 045	9 578	16 060[j,e]
International trade: imports (million current US$)	13 920	15 504	17 659[j,e]
International trade: balance (million current US$)	- 4 875	- 5 926	- 1 599[e]
Balance of payments, current account (million US$)	- 1 214	- 1 921	- 2 106[e]

Major trading partners

						2021
Export partners (% of exports)[j]	United States	43.5	Netherlands	7.7	Belgium	5.3
Import partners (% of imports)[j]	United States	37.4	China	14.5	Mexico	6.8

Social indicators

	2010	2015	2022
Population growth rate (average annual %)	1.3	1.0	0.5[a]
Urban population (% of total population)	71.7	76.9	80.1[d]
Urban population growth rate (average annual %)[m]	3.1	2.5	...
Fertility rate, total (live births per woman)	1.9	1.8	1.5[a]
Life expectancy at birth (females/males, years)	81.1 / 76.3	81.6 / 76.7	80.0 / 74.8[a]
Population age distribution (0-14/60+ years old, %)	24.7 / 10.9	22.6 / 12.7	20.2 / 15.8[a]
International migrant stock (000/% of total pop.)[n]	405.8 / 8.9	411.7 / 8.5	520.7 / 10.2[b]
Refugees and others of concern to the UNHCR (000)	19.9[o]	7.9	127.5[e]
Infant mortality rate (per 1 000 live births)	9.1	7.8	6.8[a]
Health: Current expenditure (% of GDP)[p]	8.0	7.6[q]	7.3[q,d]
Health: Physicians (per 1 000 pop.)	2.3	2.7	3.3[b]
Education: Government expenditure (% of GDP)	6.6	6.9	6.7[b]
Education: Primary gross enrol. ratio (f/m per 100 pop.)	115.7 / 118.0	111.0 / 111.6	116.0 / 114.1[b]
Education: Sec. gross enrol. ratio (f/m per 100 pop.)	103.2 / 99.0	125.3 / 120.4	148.0 / 136.3[b]
Education: Upr. Sec. gross enrol. ratio (f/m per 100 pop.)	82.2 / 70.6	118.2 / 99.9	162.1 / 137.1[b]
Intentional homicide rate (per 100 000 pop.)	11.5	11.5	11.2[b]
Seats held by women in the National Parliament (%)	36.8	33.3	45.6[r]

Environment and infrastructure indicators

	2010	2015	2022
Individuals using the Internet (per 100 inhabitants)	36.5[s,t]	59.8	80.5[b]
Research & Development expenditure (% of GDP)	0.5	0.4	0.4[u]
Threatened species (number)	285	323	571
Forested area (% of land area)[j]	56.2	57.8	59.1[d]
CO2 emission estimates (million tons/tons per capita)	6.9 / 1.4	7.2 / 1.4	7.7 / 1.5[d]
Energy production, primary (Petajoules)	104	110	106[d]
Energy supply per capita (Gigajoules)	44	43	42[d]
Tourist/visitor arrivals at national borders (000)	2 100	2 660	1 012[b]
Important sites for terrestrial biodiversity protected (%)	41.5	41.6	41.7[e]
Pop. using safely managed drinking water (urban/rural, %)	80.2 / 77.0	80.3 / 79.9	80.4 / 81.1[b]
Pop. using safely managed sanitation (urban/rural %)	34.4 / 37.0	30.7 / 36.6	28.7 / 36.6[b]
Net Official Development Assist. received (% of GNI)	0.28	0.21	0.36[b]

a Projected estimate (medium fertility variant). **b** 2020. **c** Refers to the urban population of cantons. **d** 2019. **e** 2021. **f** Excludes irrigation canals and landscaping care. **g** Data classified according to ISIC Rev. 4. **h** Excludes publishing activities. Includes irrigation and canals. **i** Includes publishing activities and landscape care. Excludes repair of personal and household goods. **j** Estimate. **k** Central area. **l** Calculated by the UNSD from national indices. **m** Data refers to a 5-year period preceding the reference year. **n** Including refugees. **o** Data as at the end of December. **p** Data based on calendar year (January 1 to December 31). **q** Data are based on SHA2011. **r** Data are as at 1 January of reporting year. **s** Users in the last 3 months. **t** Population aged 5 years and over. **u** 2018.

Côte d'Ivoire

Region	Western Africa	UN membership date	20 September 1960
Population (000, 2022)	28 160[a]	Surface area (km2)	322 462[b]
Pop. density (per km2, 2022)	88.6[a]	Sex ratio (m per 100 f)	101.9[a]
Capital city	Yamoussoukro[c]	National currency	CFA Franc, BCEAO (XOF)[d]
Capital city pop. (000, 2022)	231.1[e]	Exchange rate (per US$)	579.2[f]

Economic indicators

	2010	2015	2022
GDP: Gross domestic product (million current US$)[g]	26 264	45 780	61 143[b]
GDP growth rate (annual %, const. 2015 prices)	7.7	14.9	2.0[b]
GDP per capita (current US$)	1 279.1	1 971.1	2 317.9[b]
Economy: Agriculture (% of Gross Value Added)	25.2	19.8	21.5[b]
Economy: Industry (% of Gross Value Added)	22.6	21.1	22.4[b]
Economy: Services and other activity (% of GVA)	52.2	59.1	56.2[b]
Employment in agriculture (% of employed)[h]	47.3	43.6	39.3[b]
Employment in industry (% of employed)[h]	11.4	12.1	13.4[b]
Employment in services & other sectors (% employed)[h]	41.4	44.4	47.3[b]
Unemployment rate (% of labour force)[h]	6.8	3.1	3.4
Labour force participation rate (female/male pop. %)[h]	46.6 / 71.7	46.3 / 67.4	45.9 / 64.8
CPI: Consumer Price Index (2010=100)[h,i]	100	111	119[f]
Agricultural production index (2014-2016=100)	75	104	123[b]
International trade: exports (million current US$)	10 284	12 560	15 384[h,f]
International trade: imports (million current US$)	7 849	10 406	14 043[h,f]
International trade: balance (million current US$)	2 434	2 154	1 341[f]
Balance of payments, current account (million US$)	465	- 201	- 1 974[b]

Major trading partners

						2021
Export partners (% of exports)[h]	Netherlands	10.7	United States	6.0	France	5.9
Import partners (% of imports)[h]	China	17.2	Nigeria	13.5	France	10.7

Social indicators

	2010	2015	2022
Population growth rate (average annual %)	2.1	2.6	2.5[a]
Urban population (% of total population)	47.3	49.4	51.2[j]
Urban population growth rate (average annual %)[k]	3.0	3.4	...
Fertility rate, total (live births per woman)	5.1	4.8	4.3[a]
Life expectancy at birth (females/males, years)	56.2 / 53.9	58.9 / 56.7	60.3 / 57.7[a]
Population age distribution (0-14/60+ years old, %)	44.0 / 3.8	43.6 / 3.8	41.5 / 3.8[a]
International migrant stock (000/% of total pop.)[l,m]	2 366.5 / 11.5	2 470.6 / 10.6	2 564.9 / 9.7[b]
Refugees and others of concern to the UNHCR (000)	564.5[n]	726.8	955.8[f]
Infant mortality rate (per 1 000 live births)	76.6	66.6	56.8[a]
Health: Current expenditure (% of GDP)	4.4	3.2	3.3[j]
Health: Physicians (per 1 000 pop.)	0.1[o]	0.2[p]	0.2[j]
Education: Government expenditure (% of GDP)	4.6	3.5[h]	3.7[h,j]
Education: Primary gross enrol. ratio (f/m per 100 pop.)	64.1 / 79.5[q]	84.9 / 96.4	97.5 / 103.4[b]
Education: Sec. gross enrol. ratio (f/m per 100 pop.)	... / ...	35.1 / 49.9	52.0 / 62.9[b]
Education: Upr. Sec. gross enrol. ratio (f/m per 100 pop.)	... / ...	21.6 / 32.4	30.9 / 41.2[b]
Seats held by women in the National Parliament (%)	8.9	9.2	14.2[r]

Environment and infrastructure indicators

	2010	2015	2022
Individuals using the Internet (per 100 inhabitants)	2.7[h]	16.7	36.3[j]
Research & Development expenditure (% of GDP)	...	...	0.1[s,t,u]
Threatened species (number)	210	226	332
Forested area (% of land area)[h]	12.5	10.7	9.3[j]
CO2 emission estimates (million tons/tons per capita)	7.7 / 0.3	11.1 / 0.4	12.3 / 0.4[j]
Energy production, primary (Petajoules)	389	395	436[j]
Energy supply per capita (Gigajoules)	17	18	17[j]
Tourist/visitor arrivals at national borders (000)	252[v]	1 441[w,x]	668[b]
Important sites for terrestrial biodiversity protected (%)	73.8	73.8	73.8[f]
Pop. using safely managed drinking water (urban/rural, %)	55.7 / 15.8	55.1 / 15.2	54.5 / 14.6[b]
Net Official Development Assist. received (% of GNI)	3.52	1.45	2.62[b]

a Projected estimate (medium fertility variant). b 2020. c Yamoussoukro is the capital and Abidjan is the administrative capital. d African Financial Community (CFA) Franc, Central Bank of West African States (BCEAO). e 2018. f 2021. g Data compiled in accordance with the System of National Accounts 1968 (1968 SNA). h Estimate. i Including refugees. j 2019. k Data refers to a 5-year period preceding the reference year. l Refers to foreign citizens. m Abidjan j 2019. k Data refers to a 5-year period preceding the reference year. l Refers to foreign citizens. m Including refugees. n Data as at the end of December. o 2008. p 2014. q 2009. r Data are as at 1 January of reporting year. s Excluding business enterprise. t Partial data. u 2016. v Arrivals to Félix Houphouët Boigny Airport only. w Break in the time series. x Figures include arrivals by land (road and railway).

Croatia

Region	Southern Europe	UN membership date	22 May 1992
Population (000, 2022)	4 030[a]	Surface area (km2)	56 594[b]
Pop. density (per km2, 2022)	72.1[a]	Sex ratio (m per 100 f)	95.0[a]
Capital city	Zagreb	National currency	Kuna (HRK)
Capital city pop. (000, 2022)	685.2[c,d]	Exchange rate (per US$)	6.6[e]

Economic indicators

	2010	2015	2022
GDP: Gross domestic product (million current US$)	60 426	50 163	57 204[b]
GDP growth rate (annual %, const. 2015 prices)	- 1.3	2.5	- 8.1[b]
GDP per capita (current US$)	13 961.1	11 850.9	13 934.2[b]
Economy: Agriculture (% of Gross Value Added)[f,g]	4.3	3.6	3.8[b]
Economy: Industry (% of Gross Value Added)[g,h]	25.2	24.8	25.3[b]
Economy: Services and other activity (% of GVA)[g,i]	70.4	71.6	70.9[b]
Employment in agriculture (% of employed)	14.3	9.2	5.8[j,b]
Employment in industry (% of employed)	27.5	26.7	27.5[j,b]
Employment in services & other sectors (% employed)	58.3	64.1	66.8[j,b]
Unemployment rate (% of labour force)	11.6	16.2	7.2[j]
Labour force participation rate (female/male pop. %)	46.1 / 59.7	46.9 / 59.2	45.9 / 58.7[j]
CPI: Consumer Price Index (2010=100)	100	107	113[e]
Agricultural production index (2014-2016=100)	94	97	86[b]
International trade: exports (million current US$)	11 811	12 844	22 674[e]
International trade: imports (million current US$)	20 067	20 580	33 646[e]
International trade: balance (million current US$)	- 8 256	- 7 737	- 10 972[e]
Balance of payments, current account (million US$)	- 1 485	1 673	2 251[e]

Major trading partners

						2021
Export partners (% of exports)	Slovenia	12.7	Italy	12.5	Germany	11.8
Import partners (% of imports)	Germany	14.8	Italy	12.6	Slovenia	11.0

Social indicators

	2010	2015	2022
Population growth rate (average annual %)	- 0.3	- 0.8	- 0.5[a]
Urban population (% of total population)	55.2	56.2	57.2[d]
Urban population growth rate (average annual %)[k]	0.1	- 0.1	...
Fertility rate, total (live births per woman)	1.5	1.4	1.4[a]
Life expectancy at birth (females/males, years)	80.0 / 73.6	80.5 / 74.5	82.0 / 76.4[a]
Population age distribution (0-14/60+ years old, %)	15.3 / 23.8	14.4 / 26.3	14.1 / 29.6[a]
International migrant stock (000/% of total pop.)	573.2 / 13.2	561.1 / 13.3	528.1 / 12.9[b]
Refugees and others of concern to the UNHCR (000)	25.5[l]	17.5	5.7[e]
Infant mortality rate (per 1 000 live births)	3.9	3.8	3.0[a]
Health: Current expenditure (% of GDP)	8.1	6.8	7.0[d]
Health: Physicians (per 1 000 pop.)	2.8	3.2	3.5[d]
Education: Government expenditure (% of GDP)	4.2	4.6[m]	3.9[n]
Education: Primary gross enrol. ratio (f/m per 100 pop.)	92.0 / 91.9	100.6 / 100.6	93.6 / 92.9[d]
Education: Sec. gross enrol. ratio (f/m per 100 pop.)	103.4 / 96.6	101.0 / 96.5	102.8 / 97.5[d]
Education: Upr. Sec. gross enrol. ratio (f/m per 100 pop.)	98.9 / 88.3	94.4 / 89.8	93.9 / 89.2[d]
Intentional homicide rate (per 100 000 pop.)	1.4	0.9	1.0[b]
Seats held by women in the National Parliament (%)	23.5	25.8	31.8[o]

Environment and infrastructure indicators

	2010	2015	2022
Individuals using the Internet (per 100 inhabitants)	56.6[p]	69.8[p,q]	78.3[b]
Research & Development expenditure (% of GDP)	0.7	0.8	1.2[b]
Threatened species (number)	101	159	240
Forested area (% of land area)	34.3	34.3	34.6[d]
CO2 emission estimates (million tons/tons per capita)	18.9 / 4.2	16.0 / 3.7	14.9 / 3.5[b]
Energy production, primary (Petajoules)	215	184	164[d]
Energy supply per capita (Gigajoules)	90	83	87[d]
Tourist/visitor arrivals at national borders (000)[r]	9 111	12 683	5 545[b]
Important sites for terrestrial biodiversity protected (%)	24.4	80.8	80.8
Pop. using safely managed drinking water (urban/rural, %)	93.5 / 68.5[s]	93.5 / ...	93.5 / ...[b]
Pop. using safely managed sanitation (urban/rural %)	89.5 / ...	84.0 / ...	75.6 / ...[b]
Net Official Development Assist. disbursed (% of GNI)	...	0.08[m]	...
Net Official Development Assist. received (% of GNI)	0.23	...	...

a Projected estimate (medium fertility variant). b 2020. c Refers to the settlement of Zagreb. d 2019. e 2021. f Excludes irrigation canals and landscaping care. g Data classified according to ISIC Rev. 4. h Excludes publishing activities. Includes irrigation and canals. i Includes publishing activities and landscape care. Excludes repair of personal and household goods. j Estimate. k Data refers to a 5-year period preceding the reference year. l Data as at the end of December. m 2013. n 2017. o Data are as at 1 January of reporting year. p Population aged 16 to 74 years. q Users in the last 3 months. r Excluding arrivals in ports of nautical tourism. s 2007.

Cuba

Region	Caribbean	UN membership date	24 October 1945
Population (000, 2022)	11 212[a]	Surface area (km2)	109 884[b]
Pop. density (per km2, 2022)	105.0[a]	Sex ratio (m per 100 f)	98.5[a]
Capital city	Havana	National currency	Cuban Peso (CUP)[c]
Capital city pop. (000, 2022)	2 138.4[d]	Exchange rate (per US$)	24.0[e,f]

Economic indicators

	2010	2015	2022
GDP: Gross domestic product (million current US$)	64 328	87 206	107 352[b]
GDP growth rate (annual %, const. 2015 prices)	2.4	4.4	- 10.9[b]
GDP per capita (current US$)	5 730.4	7 700.4	9 477.9[b]
Economy: Agriculture (% of Gross Value Added)[g]	3.7	3.9	3.7[b]
Economy: Industry (% of Gross Value Added)[g]	23.1	22.6	24.9[b]
Economy: Services and other activity (% of GVA)[g]	73.2	73.5	71.3[b]
Employment in agriculture (% of employed)	18.6	18.6[h]	17.3[h,b]
Employment in industry (% of employed)	17.1	17.1[h]	16.8[h,b]
Employment in services & other sectors (% employed)	64.3	64.3[h]	65.9[h,b]
Unemployment rate (% of labour force)	2.5	2.4	2.5[h]
Labour force participation rate (female/male pop. %)	41.9 / 68.4	42.3 / 70.0[h]	41.2 / 69.3[h]
Agricultural production index (2014-2016=100)	86	100	74[b]
International trade: exports (million current US$)[h]	4 914	3 618	1 006[f]
International trade: imports (million current US$)[h]	11 488	12 638	5 292[f]
International trade: balance (million current US$)	- 6 574[h]	- 9 020[h]	- 4 285[f]

Major trading partners

						2021
Export partners (% of exports)[h]	Canada	30.5	China	24.4	Spain	6.6
Import partners (% of imports)[h]	Spain	17.6	China	13.6	Argentina	7.8

Social indicators

	2010	2015	2022
Population growth rate (average annual %)	0.1	0.1	- 0.2[a]
Urban population (% of total population)	76.6	76.9	77.1[d]
Urban population growth rate (average annual %)[i]	0.2	0.3	...
Fertility rate, total (live births per woman)	1.7	1.7	1.4[a]
Life expectancy at birth (females/males, years)	80.0 / 75.5	80.1 / 75.5	80.6 / 75.8[a]
Population age distribution (0-14/60+ years old, %)	17.7 / 17.6	16.7 / 19.3	15.7 / 22.0[a]
International migrant stock (000/% of total pop.)	7.4 / 0.1	4.6 / ~0.0	3.0 / ~0.0[b]
Refugees and others of concern to the UNHCR (000)	0.4[j]	0.3	0.2[f]
Infant mortality rate (per 1 000 live births)	5.2	4.6	4.0[a]
Health: Current expenditure (% of GDP)[h,k]	10.7	12.8	11.1[d]
Health: Physicians (per 1 000 pop.)	6.8	7.8	8.4[i]
Education: Government expenditure (% of GDP)	12.8	...	...
Education: Primary gross enrol. ratio (f/m per 100 pop.)	100.2 / 102.6	96.5 / 102.3	101.6 / 104.6[b]
Education: Sec. gross enrol. ratio (f/m per 100 pop.)	92.4 / 92.1	99.1 / 96.7	100.3 / 99.6[b]
Education: Upr. Sec. gross enrol. ratio (f/m per 100 pop.)	91.1 / 88.8	101.2 / 91.4	111.7 / 104.0[b]
Intentional homicide rate (per 100 000 pop.)	4.5	5.5	5.0[m]
Seats held by women in the National Parliament (%)	43.2	48.9	53.4[n]

Environment and infrastructure indicators

	2010	2015	2022
Individuals using the Internet (per 100 inhabitants)	15.9[o]	37.3	74.0[h,b]
Research & Development expenditure (% of GDP)	0.6	0.4	0.5[b]
Threatened species (number)	304	337	400
Forested area (% of land area)	27.5[h]	30.6	31.2[h,d]
CO2 emission estimates (million tons/tons per capita)	27.3 / 2.4	28.6 / 2.5	25.4 / 2.2[d]
Energy production, primary (Petajoules)	200	212	184[d]
Energy supply per capita (Gigajoules)	45	41	32[d]
Tourist/visitor arrivals at national borders (000)[p]	2 507	3 506	1 085[b]
Important sites for terrestrial biodiversity protected (%)	51.2	54.5	54.5[f]
Pop. using safely managed sanitation (urban/rural %)	32.9 / 54.6	32.6 / 52.8	32.4 / 51.0[b]
Net Official Development Assist. received (% of GNI)	0.21	0.24	2.60[m]

a Projected estimate (medium fertility variant). b 2020. c The national currency of Cuba is the Cuban Peso (CUP). The convertible peso (CUC) is used by foreigners and tourists in Cuba. d 2019. e UN operational exchange rate. f 2021. g Data classified according to ISIC Rev. 4. h Estimate. i Data refers to a 5-year period preceding the reference year. j Data as at the end of December. k Data based on calendar year (January 1 to December 31). l 2018. m 2016. n Data are as at 1 January of reporting year. o Including users of the international network and also those having access only to the Cuban network. p Arrivals by air.

Curaçao

Region	Caribbean
Surface area (km2)	444 c
Sex ratio (m per 100 f)	92.1 a,b
National currency	Neth. Ant. Guilder (ANG) d
Exchange rate (per US$)	1.9 g

Population (000, 2022)	191 a,b
Pop. density (per km2, 2022)	450.9 a,b
Capital city	Willemstad
Capital city pop. (000, 2022)	144.0 e,f

Economic indicators	2010	2015	2022
GDP: Gross domestic product (million current US$)	2 951	3 152	2 596 c
GDP growth rate (annual %, const. 2015 prices)	0.1	0.3	- 18.4 c
GDP per capita (current US$)	19 782.2	19 718.3	15 819.2 c
Economy: Agriculture (% of Gross Value Added) h,i,j	0.4	0.2	0.2 c
Economy: Industry (% of Gross Value Added) i,k	16.3	19.3	16.6 c
Economy: Services and other activity (% of GVA) i,l	83.3	80.5	83.1 c
Employment in agriculture (% of employed)	1.1 m,n	...	...
Employment in industry (% of employed)	17.6 m,n	...	...
Employment in services & other sectors (% employed)	81.3 m,n	...	...
Unemployment rate (% of labour force) p	9.6 o,q	13.0 r	...
Labour force participation rate (female/male pop. %)	53.2 / 66.5 n	... / ...	... / ...
CPI: Consumer Price Index (2010=100) s	100	108	122 g
Balance of payments, current account (million US$)	...	- 519	- 689 g

Social indicators	2010	2015	2022
Population growth rate (average annual %) a	1.5	0.8	0.5 b
Urban population (% of total population)	89.9	89.4	89.1 t
Urban population growth rate (average annual %) u	2.5	1.2	...
Fertility rate, total (live births per woman) a	2.2	1.9	1.6 b
Life expectancy at birth (females/males, years) a	78.0 / 71.4	79.8 / 72.1	80.3 / 72.7 b
Population age distribution (0-14/60+ years old, %) a	22.1 / 17.3	20.8 / 19.5	17.2 / 21.4 b
International migrant stock (000/% of total pop.) v	34.6 / 23.2	37.6 / 23.5	57.2 / 34.9 c
Refugees and others of concern to the UNHCR (000)	~0.0	0.1	17.1 g
Infant mortality rate (per 1 000 live births) a	11.6	9.5	7.8 b
Education: Government expenditure (% of GDP)	...	4.9 r	...
Education: Primary gross enrol. ratio (f/m per 100 pop.)	... / ...	157.7 / 164.2 r	100.9 / 106.6 c
Education: Sec. gross enrol. ratio (f/m per 100 pop.)	... / ...	90.8 / 83.8 r	122.5 / 100.7 c
Education: Upr. Sec. gross enrol. ratio (f/m per 100 pop.)	... / ...	86.1 / 76.8 r	... / 107.6
Intentional homicide rate (per 100 000 pop.)	19.0 w	...	...

Environment and infrastructure indicators	2010	2015	2022
Individuals using the Internet (per 100 inhabitants)	...	...	68.1 x
Threatened species (number)	...	49	71 g
Forested area (% of land area) y	...	~0.0	0.2 t
CO2 emission estimates (million tons/tons per capita)	4.4 / 19.1	5.3 / 33.4	2.2 / 13.7 t
Energy production, primary (Petajoules)	...	1	1 t
Energy supply per capita (Gigajoules)	...	630	195 t
Tourist/visitor arrivals at national borders (000) z	342	468	175 c
Important sites for terrestrial biodiversity protected (%)	6.1	40.4	44.8 g

a For statistical purposes, the data for Netherlands do not include this area. b Projected estimate (medium fertility variant). c 2020. d Netherlands Antillean Guilder. e Total population of Curaçao excluding some neighborhoods (see source). f 2018. g 2021. h Including mining and quarrying. i Data classified according to ISIC Rev. 4. j Excludes irrigation canals and landscaping care. k Excludes publishing activities. Includes irrigation and canals. l Includes publishing activities and landscape care. Excludes repair of personal and household goods. m Data classified according to ISIC Rev. 3. n 2008. o Break in the time series. p Excluding the institutional population. q 2009. r 2013. s Calculated by the UNSD from national indices. t 2019. u Data refers to a 5-year period preceding the reference year. v Including refugees. w 2007. x 2017. y Estimate. z Arrivals by air.

Cyprus

Region	Western Asia	UN membership date	20 September 1960
Population (000, 2022)	1 252[a,b]	Surface area (km2)	9 251[c]
Pop. density (per km2, 2022)	135.4[a,b]	Sex ratio (m per 100 f)	100.3[a,b]
Capital city	Nicosia	National currency	Euro (EUR)
Capital city pop. (000, 2022)	269.5[d]	Exchange rate (per US$)	0.9[e]

Economic indicators

	2010	2015	2022
GDP: Gross domestic product (million current US$)[f]	25 707	19 835	24 612[c]
GDP growth rate (annual %, const. 2015 prices)[f]	2.0	3.4	- 5.2[c]
GDP per capita (current US$)[f]	30 993.1	23 398.1	28 133.1[c]
Economy: Agriculture (% of Gross Value Added)[g,h]	2.3	2.1	2.2[c]
Economy: Industry (% of Gross Value Added)[h,i]	16.4	11.7	14.2[c]
Economy: Services and other activity (% of GVA)[h,j]	81.2	86.2	83.6[c]
Employment in agriculture (% of employed)	3.8	4.0	2.0[k,c]
Employment in industry (% of employed)	20.4	16.2	16.3[k,c]
Employment in services & other sectors (% employed)	75.8	79.8	81.7[k,c]
Unemployment rate (% of labour force)	6.3	14.9	6.0[k]
Labour force participation rate (female/male pop. %)	57.6 / 71.1	57.5 / 67.1	56.9 / 68.4[k]
CPI: Consumer Price Index (2010=100)[l,m]	100	102	104[c]
Agricultural production index (2014-2016=100)	107	103	106[c]
International trade: exports (million current US$)	1 506	3 367	3 887[e]
International trade: imports (million current US$)	8 645	7 133	10 089[e]
International trade: balance (million current US$)	- 7 138	- 3 766	- 6 202[e]
Balance of payments, current account (million US$)	- 2 799	- 84	- 2 031[e]

Major trading partners

						2021
Export partners (% of exports)	Lebanon	8.7	Greece	7.7	Marshall Islands	7.6
Import partners (% of imports)	Greece	23.9	Italy	10.2	Germany	6.2

Social indicators

	2010	2015	2022
Population growth rate (average annual %)[b]	1.7	0.9	0.7[a]
Urban population (% of total population)[b]	67.6	66.9	66.8[n]
Urban population growth rate (average annual %)[b,o]	1.4	0.7	...
Fertility rate, total (live births per woman)[b]	1.4	1.3	1.3[a]
Life expectancy at birth (females/males, years)[b]	82.0 / 77.4	82.9 / 79.1	83.7 / 80.1[a]
Population age distribution (0-14/60+ years old, %)[b]	17.0 / 15.9	16.1 / 17.6	15.9 / 20.4[a]
International migrant stock (000/% of total pop.)[b]	188.5 / 16.9	176.7 / 15.2	190.4 / 15.8[c]
Refugees and others of concern to the UNHCR (000)	8.8[p]	14.1	41.1[e]
Infant mortality rate (per 1 000 live births)[b]	2.9	2.5	2.1[a]
Health: Current expenditure (% of GDP)[q]	6.5	6.8	7.0[n]
Health: Physicians (per 1 000 pop.)	2.2	2.6	3.1[n]
Education: Government expenditure (% of GDP)	6.5	6.3	5.8[r]
Education: Primary gross enrol. ratio (f/m per 100 pop.)[k]	101.6 / 101.6	99.3 / 99.3	100.1 / 100.8[n]
Education: Sec. gross enrol. ratio (f/m per 100 pop.)[k]	92.0 / 90.9	99.4 / 100.1	99.2 / 102.4[n]
Education: Upr. Sec. gross enrol. ratio (f/m per 100 pop.)[k]	88.1 / 86.0	99.6 / 100.3	96.4 / 100.7[n]
Intentional homicide rate (per 100 000 pop.)	0.7	1.3	1.2[c]
Seats held by women in the National Parliament (%)	12.5	12.5	14.3[s]

Environment and infrastructure indicators

	2010	2015	2022
Individuals using the Internet (per 100 inhabitants)	53.0[t]	71.7	90.8[c]
Research & Development expenditure (% of GDP)	0.4	0.5	0.8[u,c]
Threatened species (number)	43	60	106
Forested area (% of land area)	18.7	18.7	18.7[n]
CO2 emission estimates (million tons/tons per capita)[f]	7.4 / 9.0	6.0 / 7.1	6.0 / 6.7[c]
Energy production, primary (Petajoules)	4	5	7[n]
Energy supply per capita (Gigajoules)	93	74	79[n]
Tourist/visitor arrivals at national borders (000)	2 173	2 659	632[c]
Important sites for terrestrial biodiversity protected (%)	58.6	69.1	74.1[e]
Pop. using safely managed sanitation (urban/rural %)	86.3 / ...	86.3 / ...	86.3 / ...[c]

a Projected estimate (medium fertility variant). b Refers to the whole country. c 2020. d 2018. e 2021. f Excluding northern Cyprus. g Excludes irrigation canals and landscaping care. h Data classified according to ISIC Rev. 4. i Excludes publishing activities. Includes irrigation and canals. j Includes publishing activities and landscape care. Excludes repair of personal and household goods. k Estimate. l Data refer to government controlled areas. m Calculated by the UNSD from national indices. n 2019. o Data refers to a 5-year period preceding the reference year. p Data as at the end of December. q Since 2016 health expenditure data do not include foreign health insurance provided insurance to the country's residents is missing. r 2017. s Data are as at 1 January of reporting year. t Population aged 16 to 74 years. u Provisional data.

Czechia

Region	Eastern Europe	UN membership date	19 January 1993
Population (000, 2022)	10 494[a]	Surface area (km2)	78 871[b]
Pop. density (per km2, 2022)	135.9[a]	Sex ratio (m per 100 f)	97.1[a]
Capital city	Prague	National currency	Czech Koruna (CZK)
Capital city pop. (000, 2022)	1 298.8[c]	Exchange rate (per US$)	22.0[d]

Economic indicators

	2010	2015	2022
GDP: Gross domestic product (million current US$)	209 070	188 033	245 349[b]
GDP growth rate (annual %, const. 2015 prices)	2.4	5.4	- 5.8[b]
GDP per capita (current US$)	19 842.4	17 736.6	22 910.6[b]
Economy: Agriculture (% of Gross Value Added)[e,f]	1.7	2.5	2.1[b]
Economy: Industry (% of Gross Value Added)[f,g]	36.7	37.5	33.8[b]
Economy: Services and other activity (% of GVA)[f,h]	61.6	60.0	64.1[b]
Employment in agriculture (% of employed)	3.1	2.9	2.6[i,b]
Employment in industry (% of employed)	38.0	38.0	37.1[i,b]
Employment in services & other sectors (% employed)	58.9	59.0	60.2[i,b]
Unemployment rate (% of labour force)	7.3	5.0	2.3[i]
Labour force participation rate (female/male pop. %)	49.3 / 68.0	51.2 / 68.0	52.0 / 68.4[i]
CPI: Consumer Price Index (2010=100)	100	108	125[d]
Agricultural production index (2014-2016=100)	89	97	97[d]
International trade: exports (million current US$)	132 141	157 194	227 161[d]
International trade: imports (million current US$)	125 691	140 716	211 839[d]
International trade: balance (million current US$)	6 450	16 478	15 322[d]
Balance of payments, current account (million US$)	- 7 351	845	- 2 282[d]

Major trading partners

						2021
Export partners (% of exports)	Germany	32.4	Slovakia	8.1	Poland	6.7
Import partners (% of imports)	Germany	22.4	China	16.7	Poland	8.2

Social indicators

	2010	2015	2022
Population growth rate (average annual %)	0.4	~0.0	- 0.1[a]
Urban population (% of total population)	73.3	73.5	73.9[c]
Urban population growth rate (average annual %)[j]	0.4	0.2	...
Fertility rate, total (live births per woman)	1.5	1.6	1.7[a]
Life expectancy at birth (females/males, years)	80.6 / 74.4	81.5 / 75.6	81.2 / 75.1[a]
Population age distribution (0-14/60+ years old, %)	14.4 / 22.5	15.3 / 25.0	16.0 / 26.3[a]
International migrant stock (000/% of total pop.)[k]	398.5 / 3.8	416.5 / 3.9	540.9 / 5.1[b]
Refugees and others of concern to the UNHCR (000)	3.5[l]	5.0	5.5[d]
Infant mortality rate (per 1 000 live births)	2.6	2.5	2.4[a]
Health: Current expenditure (% of GDP)	6.9	7.2	7.8[c]
Health: Physicians (per 1 000 pop.)	3.6	4.0	4.2[b]
Education: Government expenditure (% of GDP)	4.0	5.8	4.3[m]
Education: Primary gross enrol. ratio (f/m per 100 pop.)	103.6 / 104.0	99.7 / 99.3	100.5 / 100.1[c]
Education: Sec. gross enrol. ratio (f/m per 100 pop.)	94.9 / 94.4	105.6 / 104.6	101.8 / 100.8[c]
Education: Upr. Sec. gross enrol. ratio (f/m per 100 pop.)	92.9 / 91.6	110.2 / 108.0	106.5 / 104.6[c]
Intentional homicide rate (per 100 000 pop.)	1.0	0.8	0.7[b]
Seats held by women in the National Parliament (%)	15.5	19.0	25.5[n]

Environment and infrastructure indicators

	2010	2015	2022
Individuals using the Internet (per 100 inhabitants)	68.8[o]	75.7	81.3[b]
Research & Development expenditure (% of GDP)	1.3	1.9	2.0[p,b]
Threatened species (number)	33	45	126
Forested area (% of land area)	34.4	34.6	34.7[c]
CO2 emission estimates (million tons/tons per capita)	112.6 / 10.5	99.4 / 9.3	86.2 / 7.9[b]
Energy production, primary (Petajoules)	1 340	1 207	1 119[c]
Energy supply per capita (Gigajoules)	180	166	167[c]
Tourist/visitor arrivals at national borders (000)	8 629	11 619	14 651[i,c]
Important sites for terrestrial biodiversity protected (%)	94.7	94.7	94.7[d]
Pop. using safely managed drinking water (urban/rural, %)	97.7 / 96.4	98.0 / 97.7	98.0 / 97.7[b]
Net Official Development Assist. disbursed (% of GNI)[q]	0.13	0.16	0.13[b]

a Projected estimate (medium fertility variant). b 2020. c 2019. d 2021. e Excludes irrigation canals and landscaping care. f Data classified according to ISIC Rev. 4. g Excludes publishing activities. Includes irrigation and canals. h Includes publishing activities and landscape care. Excludes repair of personal and household goods. i Estimate. j Data refers to a 5-year period preceding the reference year. k Refers to foreign citizens. l Data as at the end of December. m 2018. n Data are as at 1 January of reporting year. o Population aged 16 to 74 years. p Provisional data. q DAC member (OECD).

Democratic People's Republic of Korea

Region	Eastern Asia	UN membership date	17 September 1991
Population (000, 2022)	26 069[a]	Surface area (km2)	120 538[b]
Pop. density (per km2, 2022)	216.5[a]	Sex ratio (m per 100 f)	98.0[a]
Capital city	Pyongyang	National currency	North Korean Won (KPW)
Capital city pop. (000, 2022)	3 060.9[c]	Exchange rate (per US$)	110.0[d,e]

Economic indicators

	2010	2015	2022
GDP: Gross domestic product (million current US$)[f]	13 945	16 283	15 847[b]
GDP growth rate (annual %, const. 2015 prices)[f]	- 0.5	- 1.1	- 4.5[b]
GDP per capita (current US$)[f]	571.0	649.9	617.9[b]
Economy: Agriculture (% of Gross Value Added)[g]	20.8	21.6	22.4[b]
Economy: Industry (% of Gross Value Added)[g]	48.2	46.2	43.8[b]
Economy: Services and other activity (% of GVA)[g]	31.0	32.2	33.8[b]
Employment in agriculture (% of employed)[h]	53.5	52.0	51.1[b]
Employment in industry (% of employed)[h]	15.4	14.5	13.2[b]
Employment in services & other sectors (% employed)[h]	31.1	33.5	35.7[b]
Unemployment rate (% of labour force)[h]	2.7	2.7	2.2
Labour force participation rate (female/male pop. %)[h]	78.1 / 86.8	78.1 / 86.8	77.1 / 86.0
Agricultural production index (2014-2016=100)	99	99	95[b]
International trade: exports (million current US$)[h]	882	987	247[e]
International trade: imports (million current US$)[h]	1 957	2 604	308[e]
International trade: balance (million current US$)	- 1 075[h]	- 1 617[h]	- 62[e]

Major trading partners

							2021
Export partners (% of exports)[h]	China	25.3	Senegal	18.1	Angola	6.3
Import partners (% of imports)[h]	China	71.5	Russian Federation	17.3	Dem. Rep. of Congo	4.0

Social indicators

	2010	2015	2022
Population growth rate (average annual %)	0.4	0.5	0.4[a]
Urban population (% of total population)	60.4	61.3	62.1[c]
Urban population growth rate (average annual %)[i]	0.8	0.8	...
Fertility rate, total (live births per woman)	1.8	1.9	1.8[a]
Life expectancy at birth (females/males, years)	73.5 / 66.5	75.5 / 69.7	76.1 / 71.0[a]
Population age distribution (0-14/60+ years old, %)	21.7 / 13.9	19.8 / 14.2	18.9 / 17.3[a]
International migrant stock (000/% of total pop.)[h]	44.0 / 0.2	48.5 / 0.2	49.5 / 0.2[b]
Infant mortality rate (per 1 000 live births)	23.1	16.8	13.6[a]
Health: Physicians (per 1 000 pop.)	3.3[j]	3.5[k]	3.7[l]
Education: Primary gross enrol. ratio (f/m per 100 pop.)	99.4 / 99.4[m]	... / ...	89.3 / 89.3[n]
Education: Sec. gross enrol. ratio (f/m per 100 pop.)	... / ...	92.9 / 91.7	... / ...
Education: Upr. Sec. gross enrol. ratio (f/m per 100 pop.)	... / ...	94.9 / 93.1	95.4 / 93.4[n]
Seats held by women in the National Parliament (%)	15.6	16.3	17.6[o]

Environment and infrastructure indicators

	2010	2015	2022
Individuals using the Internet (per 100 inhabitants)[h]	0.0	0.0[p]	...
Threatened species (number)	52	64	118
Forested area (% of land area)[h]	51.8	51.0	50.3[c]
CO2 emission estimates (million tons/tons per capita)	49.9 / 11.1	22.9 / 11.4	54.4 / 11.0
Energy production, primary (Petajoules)	699	788	606[c]
Energy supply per capita (Gigajoules)	25	13	25[c]
Important sites for terrestrial biodiversity protected (%)	0.0	0.0	0.0[e]
Pop. using safely managed drinking water (urban/rural, %)	78.0 / 52.4	77.4 / 50.4	77.0 / 48.8[b]
Pop. using safely managed sanitation (urban/rural %)	... / 18.4	... / 9.0	... / 1.2[b]

a Projected estimate (medium fertility variant). b 2020. c 2019. d UN operational exchange rate. e 2021. f Data compiled in accordance with the System of National Accounts 1968 (1968 SNA). g Data classified according to ISIC Rev. 4. h Estimate. i Data refers to a 5-year period preceding the reference year. j 2008. k 2014. l 2017. m 2009. n 2018. o Data are as at 1 January of reporting year. p 2012.

Democratic Republic of the Congo

Region	Middle Africa	UN membership date	20 September 1960
Population (000, 2022)	99 010[a]	Surface area (km2)	2 345 410[b]
Pop. density (per km2, 2022)	43.7[a]	Sex ratio (m per 100 f)	98.4[a]
Capital city	Kinshasa	National currency	Congolese Franc (CDF)
Capital city pop. (000, 2022)	13 743.3[c]	Exchange rate (per US$)	2 000.0[d]

Economic indicators

	2010	2015	2022
GDP: Gross domestic product (million current US$)	21 566	37 918	45 308[b]
GDP growth rate (annual %, const. 2015 prices)	7.1	6.9	1.7[b]
GDP per capita (current US$)	334.0	497.3	505.9[b]
Economy: Agriculture (% of Gross Value Added)[e]	22.4	19.7	21.6[b]
Economy: Industry (% of Gross Value Added)[e]	40.5	44.8	40.7[b]
Economy: Services and other activity (% of GVA)[e,f]	37.0	35.5	37.7[b]
Employment in agriculture (% of employed)[g]	70.0	67.0	65.1[b]
Employment in industry (% of employed)[g]	8.6	9.5	9.8[b]
Employment in services & other sectors (% employed)[g]	21.4	23.5	25.1[b]
Unemployment rate (% of labour force)[g]	4.0	4.5	5.4
Labour force participation rate (female/male pop. %)[g]	65.1 / 70.9	62.4 / 69.7	61.7 / 69.2
CPI: Consumer Price Index (2010=100)	100	130	134[h]
Agricultural production index (2014-2016=100)	82	100	110[b]
International trade: exports (million current US$)[g]	5 300	5 800	29 245[d]
International trade: imports (million current US$)[g]	4 500	6 200	9 697[d]
International trade: balance (million current US$)	800[g]	- 400[g]	19 548[d]
Balance of payments, current account (million US$)	- 2 174	- 1 484	- 1 095[b]

Major trading partners

						2021
Export partners (% of exports)[g]	China	41.0	United Rep. Tanzania	11.8	Zambia	8.8
Import partners (% of imports)[g]	China	25.3	United States	21.3	South Africa	9.2

Social indicators

	2010	2015	2022
Population growth rate (average annual %)	3.3	3.4	3.2[a]
Urban population (% of total population)	40.0	42.7	45.0[c]
Urban population growth rate (average annual %)[j]	4.6	4.6	...
Fertility rate, total (live births per woman)	6.6	6.4	6.1[a]
Life expectancy at birth (females/males, years)	58.0 / 54.8	60.3 / 56.7	62.0 / 57.5[a]
Population age distribution (0-14/60+ years old, %)	46.2 / 4.9	46.3 / 4.7	46.5 / 4.6[a]
International migrant stock (000/% of total pop.)[j]	589.9 / 0.9	810.0 / 1.1	952.9 / 1.1[b]
Refugees and others of concern to the UNHCR (000)	2 363.9[k]	2 001.0	6 025.3[d]
Infant mortality rate (per 1 000 live births)	72.2	62.2	50.0[a]
Health: Current expenditure (% of GDP)	3.9	4.0	3.5[c]
Health: Physicians (per 1 000 pop.)	0.1[l]	0.1[m]	0.4[n]
Education: Government expenditure (% of GDP)	1.5	2.2	1.5[g,o]
Education: Primary gross enrol. ratio (f/m per 100 pop.)	93.0 / 106.9	107.6 / 108.4	114.7 / 122.2[n]
Education: Sec. gross enrol. ratio (f/m per 100 pop.)	30.1 / 52.2	36.0 / 56.3	... / ...
Education: Upr. Sec. gross enrol. ratio (f/m per 100 pop.)	24.2 / 46.4	29.5 / 47.6	... / ...
Seats held by women in the National Parliament (%)	8.4	8.9	12.8[p]

Environment and infrastructure indicators

	2010	2015	2022
Individuals using the Internet (per 100 inhabitants)[g]	0.7	3.8	13.6[b]
Research & Development expenditure (% of GDP)	0.1[q,r,l]	0.4[s,t,u]	...
Threatened species (number)	296	333	709
Forested area (% of land area)[g]	60.5	58.1	56.1[c]
CO2 emission estimates (million tons/tons per capita)	7.3 / ~0.0	8.8 / ~0.0	8.3 / ~0.0[c]
Energy production, primary (Petajoules)	856	1 218	1 285[c]
Energy supply per capita (Gigajoules)	13	16	15[c]
Tourist/visitor arrivals at national borders (000)	81[v]	354[w]	351[w,h]
Important sites for terrestrial biodiversity protected (%)	50.3	50.3	52.7[d]
Pop. using safely managed drinking water (urban/rural, %)	33.7 / 0.7	37.0 / 0.9	40.4 / 1.0[b]
Pop. using safely managed sanitation (urban/rural, %)	18.0 / 17.4	16.2 / 14.2	14.5 / 11.2[b]
Net Official Development Assist. received (% of GNI)	16.87	7.40	6.95[b]

a Projected estimate (medium fertility variant). b 2020. c 2019. d 2021. e Data classified according to ISIC Rev. 4. f Including restaurants and hotels. g Estimate. h 2016. i Data refers to a 5-year period preceding the reference year. j Including refugees. k Data as at the end of December. l 2009. m 2013. n 2018. o 2017. p Data are as at 1 January of reporting year. q Government only. r S&T budget instead of R&D expenditure. s Excluding business enterprise. t Break in the time series. u Overestimated or based on overestimated data. v Arrivals by air. w The arrivals data relate only to three border posts (N'Djili airport in Kinshasa, the Luano airport in Lubumbashi, and the land border-crossing of Kasumbalesa in Katanga province).

Denmark

Region	Northern Europe	UN membership date	24 October 1945
Population (000, 2022)	5 882[a,b]	Surface area (km2)	42 938[c,d]
Pop. density (per km2, 2022)	138.8[a,b]	Sex ratio (m per 100 f)	99.0[a,b]
Capital city	Copenhagen	National currency	Danish Krone (DKK)
Capital city pop. (000, 2022)	1 333.9[e,f]	Exchange rate (per US$)	6.6[g]

Economic indicators

	2010	2015	2022
GDP: Gross domestic product (million current US$)	321 995	302 673	356 085[d]
GDP growth rate (annual %, const. 2015 prices)	1.9	2.3	- 2.1[d]
GDP per capita (current US$)	57 966.6	53 206.1	61 476.6[d]
Economy: Agriculture (% of Gross Value Added)[h,i]	1.4	1.1	1.5[d]
Economy: Industry (% of Gross Value Added)[i,j]	22.8	23.0	24.3[d]
Economy: Services and other activity (% of GVA)[i,k]	75.8	75.9	74.2[d]
Employment in agriculture (% of employed)	2.4	2.5	2.1[l,d]
Employment in industry (% of employed)	19.6	19.3	18.3[l,d]
Employment in services & other sectors (% employed)	78.0	78.2	79.6[l,d]
Unemployment rate (% of labour force)	7.8	6.3	4.3[l]
Labour force participation rate (female/male pop. %)	58.8 / 68.3	56.7 / 66.0	57.9 / 66.5[l]
CPI: Consumer Price Index (2010=100)[m]	100	107	113[g]
Agricultural production index (2014-2016=100)	97	101	103[d]
International trade: exports (million current US$)	96 217	94 619	125 200[g]
International trade: imports (million current US$)	82 724	85 327	121 628[g]
International trade: balance (million current US$)	13 492	9 291	3 572[g]
Balance of payments, current account (million US$)	21 051	24 953	32 957[g]

Major trading partners

						2021
Export partners (% of exports)	Undisclosed[n]	18.2	Germany	12.9	Sweden	9.3
Import partners (% of imports)	Germany	20.6	Sweden	12.6	Netherlands	8.2

Social indicators

	2010	2015	2022
Population growth rate (average annual %)[a]	0.5	0.5	0.5[b]
Urban population (% of total population)	86.8	87.5	88.0[f]
Urban population growth rate (average annual %)[o]	0.7	0.6	...
Fertility rate, total (live births per woman)[a]	1.9	1.7	1.7[b]
Life expectancy at birth (females/males, years)[a]	81.3 / 77.1	82.7 / 78.8	83.8 / 80.0[b]
Population age distribution (0-14/60+ years old, %)[a]	18.0 / 23.2	16.9 / 24.7	16.1 / 26.5[b]
International migrant stock (000/% of total pop.)[a]	500.8 / 9.0	595.9 / 10.5	717.6 / 12.4[d]
Refugees and others of concern to the UNHCR (000)	24.5[p]	27.3	45.9[q]
Infant mortality rate (per 1 000 live births)[a]	3.4	3.7	2.9[b]
Health: Current expenditure (% of GDP)	10.3	10.2	10.0[f]
Health: Physicians (per 1 000 pop.)	3.7	3.9 .	4.2[q]
Education: Government expenditure (% of GDP)	8.6	7.6[r]	7.8[s]
Education: Primary gross enrol. ratio (f/m per 100 pop.)	99.7 / 99.5	100.8 / 102.1	100.2 / 100.3[f]
Education: Sec. gross enrol. ratio (f/m per 100 pop.)	120.0 / 119.0	133.4 / 127.3	129.3 / 130.4[f]
Education: Upr. Sec. gross enrol. ratio (f/m per 100 pop.)	121.8 / 121.5	148.1 / 137.6	137.9 / 137.2[f]
Intentional homicide rate (per 100 000 pop.)	0.8	1.1	0.9[d]
Seats held by women in the National Parliament (%)	38.0	38.0	39.7[t]

Environment and infrastructure indicators

	2010	2015	2022
Individuals using the Internet (per 100 inhabitants)	88.7[u]	96.3[v]	96.5[d]
Research & Development expenditure (% of GDP)	2.9	3.1	3.0[d]
Threatened species (number)	33	36	90
Forested area (% of land area)	14.7	15.6	15.7[f]
CO2 emission estimates (million tons/tons per capita)[w]	48.3 / 8.5	33.5 / 5.7	26.6 / 4.4[d]
Energy production, primary (Petajoules)[w]	974	672	512[f]
Energy supply per capita (Gigajoules)[w]	147	120	116[f]
Tourist/visitor arrivals at national borders (000)	8 744	10 424	5 935[d]
Important sites for terrestrial biodiversity protected (%)	88.8	88.8	88.8[g]
Net Official Development Assist. disbursed (% of GNI)[x]	1.52	0.97	0.96[d]

a For statistical purposes, the data for Denmark do not include Faroe Islands, and Greenland. b Projected estimate (medium fertility variant). c Excluding Faeroe Islands and Greenland shown separately, if available. d 2020. e Refers to the Greater Copenhagen Region, consisting of (parts of) 16 municipalities. f 2019. g 2021. h Excludes irrigation canals and landscaping care. i Data classified according to ISIC Rev. 4. j Excludes publishing activities. Includes irrigation and canals. k Includes publishing activities and landscape care. Excludes repair of personal and household goods. l Estimate. m Calculated by the UNSD from national indices. n Undisclosed (Special categories). o Data refers to a 5-year period preceding the reference year. p Data as at the end of December. q 2018. r 2014. s 2017. t Data are as at 1 January of reporting year. u Population aged 16 to 74 years. v Users in the last 3 months. w Excluding the Faroe Islands and Greenland. x DAC member (OECD).

Djibouti

Region	Eastern Africa	UN membership date	20 September 1977
Population (000, 2022)	1 121 a	Surface area (km2)	23 200 b
Pop. density (per km2, 2022)	48.4 a	Sex ratio (m per 100 f)	98.5 a
Capital city	Djibouti	National currency	Djibouti Franc (DJF)
Capital city pop. (000, 2022)	568.8 c,d	Exchange rate (per US$)	177.7 e

Economic indicators	2010	2015	2022
GDP: Gross domestic product (million current US$)	1 244	2 445	3 423 b
GDP growth rate (annual %, const. 2015 prices)	11.7	7.7	1.2 b
GDP per capita (current US$)	1 480.2	2 675.6	3 465.0 b
Economy: Agriculture (% of Gross Value Added)	2.8	1.3	1.4 b
Economy: Industry (% of Gross Value Added)	16.1	12.1	12.0 b
Economy: Services and other activity (% of GVA)	81.1	86.6	86.6 b
Employment in agriculture (% of employed) f	40.7	36.5	32.4 b
Employment in industry (% of employed) f	11.5	12.3	13.3 b
Employment in services & other sectors (% employed) f	47.8	51.2	54.3 b
Unemployment rate (% of labour force) f	27.1	26.3	27.9
Labour force participation rate (female/male pop. %) f	16.8 / 47.5	17.4 / 45.9	17.4 / 44.3
CPI: Consumer Price Index (2010=100)	100	112	122 b
Agricultural production index (2014-2016=100)	118	84	122 b
International trade: exports (million current US$) f	470	132	381 e
International trade: imports (million current US$) f	603	890	1 591 e
International trade: balance (million current US$)	- 133 f	- 758 f	- 1 209 e
Balance of payments, current account (million US$)	50	714	366 b

Major trading partners						2021
Export partners (% of exports) f	China	25.9	India	17.5	United States	15.2
Import partners (% of imports) f	China	38.3	United Arab Emirates	15.6	India	9.6

Social indicators	2010	2015	2022
Population growth rate (average annual %)	1.9	1.7	1.4 a
Urban population (% of total population)	77.0	77.4	77.9 d
Urban population growth rate (average annual %) g	1.7	1.8	...
Fertility rate, total (live births per woman)	3.4	3.1	2.8 a
Life expectancy at birth (females/males, years)	62.3 / 58.3	64.3 / 59.7	65.5 / 60.3 a
Population age distribution (0-14/60+ years old, %)	36.1 / 5.9	33.9 / 6.3	30.4 / 7.1 a
International migrant stock (000/% of total pop.) h	102.3 / 12.2	112.4 / 12.3	119.7 / 12.1 b
Refugees and others of concern to the UNHCR (000)	15.8 i	17.4	34.9 e
Infant mortality rate (per 1 000 live births)	51.3	45.2	36.5 a
Health: Current expenditure (% of GDP) f,j	3.1	3.1 k	1.8 k,d
Health: Physicians (per 1 000 pop.)	0.2 l	0.2 m	...
Education: Government expenditure (% of GDP)	4.5	3.6 f	3.6 f,n
Education: Primary gross enrol. ratio (f/m per 100 pop.)	58.5 / 58.9 o	72.8 / 67.9	70.0 / 76.3 e
Education: Sec. gross enrol. ratio (f/m per 100 pop.)	31.1 / 38.5 o	45.3 / 48.0	55.5 / 54.9 e
Education: Upr. Sec. gross enrol. ratio (f/m per 100 pop.)	19.8 / 26.8 o	37.2 / 41.9	41.8 / 40.8 e
Seats held by women in the National Parliament (%)	13.8	12.7	26.2 p

Environment and infrastructure indicators	2010	2015	2022
Individuals using the Internet (per 100 inhabitants) f	6.5	22.9	59.0 b
Threatened species (number)	81	94	127
Forested area (% of land area) f	0.2	0.2	0.2 d
Energy production, primary (Petajoules)	3	4	4 d
Energy supply per capita (Gigajoules)	13	11	10 f,d
Tourist/visitor arrivals at national borders (000)	51	63 q	...
Important sites for terrestrial biodiversity protected (%)	0.0	0.8	0.8 e
Pop. using safely managed sanitation (urban/rural %)	34.2 / 14.9	38.4 / 18.2	41.6 / 20.9 b
Net Official Development Assist. received (% of GNI)	11.52	6.73	7.79 b

a Projected estimate (medium fertility variant). b 2020. c Refers to the population of the "cercle". d 2019. e 2021. f Estimate. g Data refers to a 5-year period preceding the reference year. h Including refugees. i Data as at the end of December. j Data based on calendar year (January 1 to December 31). k Estimates should be viewed with caution as these are derived from scarce data. l 2006. m 2014. n 2018. o 2009. p Data are as at 1 January of reporting year. q 2013.

Dominica

Region	Caribbean	UN membership date	18 December 1978
Population (000, 2022)	73[a]	Surface area (km2)	750[b]
Pop. density (per km2, 2022)	97.0[a]	Sex ratio (m per 100 f)	98.9[a]
Capital city	Roseau	National currency	E. Caribbean Dollar (XCD)[c]
Capital city pop. (000, 2022)	14.9[d]	Exchange rate (per US$)	2.7[e]

Economic indicators

	2010	2015	2022
GDP: Gross domestic product (million current US$)	494	541	507[b]
GDP growth rate (annual %, const. 2015 prices)	0.7	- 2.4	- 16.1[b]
GDP per capita (current US$)	6 967.3	7 596.4	7 037.7[b]
Economy: Agriculture (% of Gross Value Added)[f]	13.7	16.5	17.8[b]
Economy: Industry (% of Gross Value Added)[f]	14.0	14.7	14.3[b]
Economy: Services and other activity (% of GVA)[f]	72.2	68.8	67.9[b]
CPI: Consumer Price Index (2010=100)	100	102	105[e]
Agricultural production index (2014-2016=100)	98	99	100[b]
International trade: exports (million current US$)	34	30[g]	29[g,e]
International trade: imports (million current US$)	225	214[g]	865[g,e]
International trade: balance (million current US$)	- 190	- 184[g]	- 835[e]
Balance of payments, current account (million US$)	- 80	- 25	- 179[e]

Major trading partners

						2021
Export partners (% of exports)[g]	Saudi Arabia	19.4	Jordan	15.8	United States	5.8
Import partners (% of imports)[g]	United States	73.6	China	4.9	Trinidad and Tobago	4.0

Social indicators

	2010	2015	2022
Population growth rate (average annual %)	- 0.1	- 0.3	0.4[a]
Urban population (% of total population)	68.1	69.6	70.8[h]
Urban population growth rate (average annual %)[i]	0.7	0.9	...
Fertility rate, total (live births per woman)	1.9	1.7	1.6[a]
Life expectancy at birth (females/males, years)	74.9 / 68.7	71.1 / 66.6	76.5 / 69.9[a]
Population age distribution (0-14/60+ years old, %)	23.6 / 14.8	21.7 / 13.4	19.6 / 14.5[a]
International migrant stock (000/% of total pop.)	8.1 / 11.4	8.1 / 11.4	8.3 / 11.5[b]
Refugees and others of concern to the UNHCR (000)	...	...	~0.0[b]
Infant mortality rate (per 1 000 live births)	21.2	33.9	11.4[a]
Health: Current expenditure (% of GDP)[g,j]	5.2	5.2	5.5[h]
Health: Physicians (per 1 000 pop.)	...	...	1.1[d]
Education: Government expenditure (% of GDP)	...	3.4	5.0[b]
Education: Primary gross enrol. ratio (f/m per 100 pop.)	101.8 / 103.6	115.2 / 117.1	98.7 / 105.8[b]
Education: Sec. gross enrol. ratio (f/m per 100 pop.)	93.0 / 85.1	93.8 / 94.7	102.9 / 100.3[b]
Education: Upr. Sec. gross enrol. ratio (f/m per 100 pop.)	88.5 / 63.9	80.1 / 71.7	95.5 / 83.2[b]
Intentional homicide rate (per 100 000 pop.)	21.2	12.6	20.8[b]
Seats held by women in the National Parliament (%)	14.3	21.9	34.4[k]

Environment and infrastructure indicators

	2010	2015	2022
Individuals using the Internet (per 100 inhabitants)	47.4	65.0[g]	69.6[g,l]
Threatened species (number)	48	62	90
Forested area (% of land area)	63.8	63.8	63.8[h]
Energy production, primary (Petajoules)	0	0	0[h]
Energy supply per capita (Gigajoules)	36	37[g]	35[g,h]
Tourist/visitor arrivals at national borders (000)	77	75	22[b]
Important sites for terrestrial biodiversity protected (%)	33.3	33.3	33.3[e]
Net Official Development Assist. received (% of GNI)	6.71	2.24	13.26[b]

a Projected estimate (medium fertility variant). b 2020. c East Caribbean Dollar. d 2018. e 2021. f Data classified according to ISIC Rev. 4. g Estimate. h 2019. i Data refers to a 5-year period preceding the reference year. j Data refer to fiscal years beginning 1 July. k Data are as at 1 January of reporting year. l 2017.

Dominican Republic

Region	Caribbean	UN membership date	24 October 1945
Population (000, 2022)	11 229[a]	Surface area (km2)	48 671[b]
Pop. density (per km2, 2022)	232.4[a]	Sex ratio (m per 100 f)	100.7[a]
Capital city	Santo Domingo	National currency	Dominican Peso (DOP)
Capital city pop. (000, 2022)	3 245.0[c,d]	Exchange rate (per US$)	57.5[e]

Economic indicators

	2010	2015	2022
GDP: Gross domestic product (million current US$)	53 160	71 155	78 845[b]
GDP growth rate (annual %, const. 2015 prices)	8.3	6.9	- 6.7[b]
GDP per capita (current US$)	5 483.1	6 920.6	7 268.2[b]
Economy: Agriculture (% of Gross Value Added)[f,g]	6.5	5.9	6.5[b]
Economy: Industry (% of Gross Value Added)[f,h]	29.9	30.6	32.4[b]
Economy: Services and other activity (% of GVA)[f,i]	63.6	63.5	61.2[b]
Employment in agriculture (% of employed)	12.4	10.0	8.8[j,b]
Employment in industry (% of employed)	18.5	18.5	19.9[j,b]
Employment in services & other sectors (% employed)	69.1	71.5	71.3[j,b]
Unemployment rate (% of labour force)	5.2	7.6	7.5[j]
Labour force participation rate (female/male pop. %)	41.6 / 71.9	48.1 / 76.1	51.0 / 76.2[j]
CPI: Consumer Price Index (2010=100)[k]	100	122	152[e]
Agricultural production index (2014-2016=100)	79	100	117[b]
International trade: exports (million current US$)	4 767	8 384	11 725[e]
International trade: imports (million current US$)	15 138	17 348	26 875[e]
International trade: balance (million current US$)	- 10 371	- 8 964	- 15 150[e]
Balance of payments, current account (million US$)	- 4 024	- 1 280	- 2 689[e]

Major trading partners

						2021
Export partners (% of exports)	United States	55.6	Switzerland	8.2	Haiti	8.1
Import partners (% of imports)	United States	42.8	China	17.3	Mexico	3.5

Social indicators

	2010	2015	2022
Population growth rate (average annual %)	1.3	1.2	0.9[a]
Urban population (% of total population)	73.8	78.6	81.8[d]
Urban population growth rate (average annual %)[l]	3.2	2.5	...
Fertility rate, total (live births per woman)	2.5	2.4	2.2[a]
Life expectancy at birth (females/males, years)	75.7 / 68.9	76.4 / 69.8	77.5 / 71.0[a]
Population age distribution (0-14/60+ years old, %)	30.7 / 8.1	29.0 / 9.1	27.1 / 11.2[a]
International migrant stock (000/% of total pop.)[m]	395.5 / 4.1	549.3 / 5.3	603.8 / 5.6[b]
Refugees and others of concern to the UNHCR (000)	2.4[n]	135.1[o]	116.1[e]
Infant mortality rate (per 1 000 live births)	28.5	28.3	24.4[a]
Health: Current expenditure (% of GDP)[j,p]	5.6	5.8	5.9[d]
Health: Physicians (per 1 000 pop.)	1.1[q]	1.5[r]	1.5[d]
Education: Government expenditure (% of GDP)	1.9	3.8[j]	4.0[j,d]
Education: Primary gross enrol. ratio (f/m per 100 pop.)[j]	103.4 / 117.3	106.2 / 116.4	103.3 / 108.0[b]
Education: Sec. gross enrol. ratio (f/m per 100 pop.)[j]	82.8 / 73.6	83.8 / 76.2	83.1 / 76.5[b]
Education: Upr. Sec. gross enrol. ratio (f/m per 100 pop.)[j]	78.0 / 65.4	80.5 / 70.0	73.5 / 62.2[b]
Intentional homicide rate (per 100 000 pop.)	25.5	17.8[s]	8.9[b]
Seats held by women in the National Parliament (%)	19.7	20.8	27.9[t]

Environment and infrastructure indicators

	2010	2015	2022
Individuals using the Internet (per 100 inhabitants)	31.4[j]	54.2[u]	76.9[j,b]
Threatened species (number)	126	153	267
Forested area (% of land area)	42.9	43.5[j]	44.2[j,d]
CO2 emission estimates (million tons/tons per capita)	19.5 / 2.0	22.0 / 2.1	25.7 / 2.3[d]
Energy production, primary (Petajoules)	28	23	29[j,d]
Energy supply per capita (Gigajoules)	31	32	37[d]
Tourist/visitor arrivals at national borders (000)[v]	4 125	5 600	2 405[b]
Important sites for terrestrial biodiversity protected (%)	74.1	76.9	76.9
Net Official Development Assist. received (% of GNI)	0.37	0.41	0.74[b]

a Projected estimate (medium fertility variant). b 2020. c Refers to the urban population of the Municipalities of Santo Domingo de Guzmán, Santo Domingo Este, Santo Domingo Oeste, and Santo Domingo Norte. d 2019. e 2021. f Data classified according to ISIC Rev. 4. g Excludes irrigation canals and landscaping care. h Excludes publishing activities. Includes irrigation and canals. i Includes publishing activities and landscape care. Excludes repair of personal and household goods. j Estimate. k Calculated by the UNSD from national indices. l Data refers to a 5-year period preceding the reference year. m Including refugees. n Data as at the end of December. o Revised estimate includes only individuals born in the country where both parents were born abroad. p Data based on calendar year (January 1 to December 31). q 2008. r 2011. s 2014. t Data are as at 1 January of reporting year. u Users in the last 3 months. v Arrivals by air only.

Ecuador

Region	South America	UN membership date	21 December 1945
Population (000, 2022)	18 001[a]	Surface area (km2)	257 217[b]
Pop. density (per km2, 2022)	72.5[a]	Sex ratio (m per 100 f)	99.6[a]
Capital city	Quito	National currency	US Dollar (USD)
Capital city pop. (000, 2022)	1 847.7[c]		

Economic indicators

	2010	2015	2022
GDP: Gross domestic product (million current US$)	69 555	99 290	98 808[b]
GDP growth rate (annual %, const. 2015 prices)	3.5	0.1	- 7.8[b]
GDP per capita (current US$)	4 633.6	6 124.5	5 600.4[b]
Economy: Agriculture (% of Gross Value Added)[d,e]	10.2	10.2	10.4[b]
Economy: Industry (% of Gross Value Added)[e,f]	36.3	34.4	33.9[b]
Economy: Services and other activity (% of GVA)[e,g]	53.5	55.4	55.7[b]
Employment in agriculture (% of employed)	27.9	26.2	29.4[h,b]
Employment in industry (% of employed)	18.5	19.7	18.2[h,b]
Employment in services & other sectors (% employed)	53.6	54.1	52.5[h,b]
Unemployment rate (% of labour force)	4.1	3.6	6.1[h]
Labour force participation rate (female/male pop. %)	48.0 / 77.6	51.9 / 79.6	53.4 / 76.7[h]
CPI: Consumer Price Index (2010=100)	100	121	124[i]
Agricultural production index (2014-2016=100)	102	104	96[b]
International trade: exports (million current US$)	17 490	18 331	26 699[i]
International trade: imports (million current US$)	20 591	21 387	25 687[i]
International trade: balance (million current US$)	- 3 101	- 3 057	1 012[i]
Balance of payments, current account (million US$)	- 1 582	- 2 221	3 060[i]

Major trading partners

						2021
Export partners (% of exports)	United States	24.0	China	15.3	Panama	14.9
Import partners (% of imports)	China	23.5	United States	22.1	Colombia	7.0

Social indicators

	2010	2015	2022
Population growth rate (average annual %)	1.6	1.5	1.1[a]
Urban population (% of total population)	62.7	63.4	64.0[c]
Urban population growth rate (average annual %)[j]	2.0	1.8	...
Fertility rate, total (live births per woman)	2.6	2.3	2.0[a]
Life expectancy at birth (females/males, years)	78.5 / 72.5	79.2 / 74.4	80.5 / 75.3[a]
Population age distribution (0-14/60+ years old, %)	31.2 / 8.6	29.0 / 9.8	25.7 / 11.3[a]
International migrant stock (000/% of total pop.)[k]	375.3 / 2.5	387.5 / 2.4	784.8 / 4.4[b]
Refugees and others of concern to the UNHCR (000)	171.1[l]	133.1[l]	508.7[i]
Infant mortality rate (per 1 000 live births)	16.0	13.0	10.7[a]
Health: Current expenditure (% of GDP)[m,n]	6.1	7.5	7.8[c]
Health: Physicians (per 1 000 pop.)	2.1	2.1	2.2[o]
Education: Government expenditure (% of GDP)	4.5	5.0	4.1[b]
Education: Primary gross enrol. ratio (f/m per 100 pop.)	113.2 / 112.9	107.9 / 107.4	100.1 / 98.0[b]
Education: Sec. gross enrol. ratio (f/m per 100 pop.)	94.5 / 90.3	106.2 / 102.0	101.8 / 99.4[b]
Education: Upr. Sec. gross enrol. ratio (f/m per 100 pop.)	82.9 / 76.5	98.5 / 93.3	97.5 / 93.6[b]
Intentional homicide rate (per 100 000 pop.)	17.5	6.5	7.8[b]
Seats held by women in the National Parliament (%)	32.3	41.6	38.7[p]

Environment and infrastructure indicators

	2010	2015	2022
Individuals using the Internet (per 100 inhabitants)	29.0[q]	48.9[q]	64.6[b]
Research & Development expenditure (% of GDP)	0.4	0.4[r]	...
Threatened species (number)	2 255	2 308	2 608
Forested area (% of land area)	52.5	51.6[h]	50.6[c]
CO2 emission estimates (million tons/tons per capita)	32.1 / 2.1	37.8 / 2.3	36.0 / 2.0[c]
Energy production, primary (Petajoules)	1 110	1 260	1 281[c]
Energy supply per capita (Gigajoules)	35	37	36[c]
Tourist/visitor arrivals at national borders (000)[s]	1 047	1 676	507[b]
Important sites for terrestrial biodiversity protected (%)	22.2	23.9	27.0[i]
Pop. using safely managed drinking water (urban/rural, %)	72.1 / 47.9	74.0 / 50.3	74.7 / 52.8[b]
Pop. using safely managed sanitation (urban/rural %)	35.2 / 50.8	33.7 / 55.5	31.2 / 60.3[b]
Net Official Development Assist. received (% of GNI)	0.25	0.33	0.36[b]

a Projected estimate (medium fertility variant). b 2020. c 2019. d Excludes irrigation canals and landscaping care. e Data classified according to ISIC Rev. 4. f Excludes publishing activities. Includes irrigation and canals. g Includes publishing activities and landscape care. Excludes repair of personal and household goods. h Estimate. i 2021. j Data refers to a 5-year period preceding the reference year. k Including refugees. l Data as at the end of December. m Data based on calendar year (January 1 to December 31). n Data are based on SHA2011. o 2017. p Data are as at 1 January of reporting year. q Population aged 5 years and over. r 2014. s Including nationals residing abroad.

Egypt

Region	Northern Africa	UN membership date	24 October 1945
Population (000, 2022)	110 990[a]	Surface area (km2)	1 002 000[b]
Pop. density (per km2, 2022)	111.5[a]	Sex ratio (m per 100 f)	102.3[a]
Capital city	Cairo	National currency	Egyptian Pound (EGP)
Capital city pop. (000, 2022)	20 485.0[c,d]	Exchange rate (per US$)	15.7[e]

Economic indicators

	2010	2015	2022
GDP: Gross domestic product (million current US$)	214 630	317 745	369 309[b]
GDP growth rate (annual %, const. 2015 prices)	5.1	4.4	3.6[b]
GDP per capita (current US$)	2 593.4	3 437.2	3 608.8[b]
Economy: Agriculture (% of Gross Value Added)[f,g]	14.0	11.3	12.1[b]
Economy: Industry (% of Gross Value Added)[f,g]	37.5	36.2	33.5[b]
Economy: Services and other activity (% of GVA)[f,g]	48.5	52.5	54.4[b]
Employment in agriculture (% of employed)	28.3	25.8	23.3[h,b]
Employment in industry (% of employed)	25.4	25.1	28.2[h,b]
Employment in services & other sectors (% employed)	46.3	49.1	48.6[h,b]
Unemployment rate (% of labour force)	8.8	13.0	9.0[h]
Labour force participation rate (female/male pop. %)	23.2 / 75.4	22.8 / 71.1	15.4 / 67.3[h]
CPI: Consumer Price Index (2010=100)[i]	100	157	319[i,e]
Agricultural production index (2014-2016=100)	91	101	100[b]
International trade: exports (million current US$)	26 332	21 852	40 702[e]
International trade: imports (million current US$)	53 003	73 975	73 781[e]
International trade: balance (million current US$)	- 26 672	- 52 123	- 33 080[e]
Balance of payments, current account (million US$)	- 4 504	- 17 243	- 14 236[b]

Major trading partners

						2021
Export partners (% of exports)	Areas nes[k]	6.7	Türkiye	6.5	Italy	6.3
Import partners (% of imports)	China	13.6	Areas nes[k]	9.4	Saudi Arabia	8.5

Social indicators

	2010	2015	2022
Population growth rate (average annual %)	2.1	2.1	1.5[a]
Urban population (% of total population)	43.0	42.8	42.7[d]
Urban population growth rate (average annual %)[l]	1.8	2.1	...
Fertility rate, total (live births per woman)	3.2	3.4	2.9[a]
Life expectancy at birth (females/males, years)	72.3 / 67.1	73.1 / 68.0	72.6 / 67.9[a]
Population age distribution (0-14/60+ years old, %)	33.3 / 6.6	33.5 / 6.9	32.9 / 7.7[a]
International migrant stock (000/% of total pop.)[m]	310.0 / 0.4	353.6 / 0.4	543.9 / 0.5[b]
Refugees and others of concern to the UNHCR (000)	109.9[n]	256.4	335.0[e]
Infant mortality rate (per 1 000 live births)	23.8	19.6	16.0[a]
Health: Current expenditure (% of GDP)[o]	4.2	5.3[p]	4.7[h,d]
Health: Physicians (per 1 000 pop.)	...	0.8	0.7[d]
Education: Government expenditure (% of GDP)	3.5	3.9	...
Education: Primary gross enrol. ratio (f/m per 100 pop.)	100.7 / 103.7	103.7 / 104.0[q]	106.9 / 106.0[d]
Education: Sec. gross enrol. ratio (f/m per 100 pop.)	67.9 / 69.8	80.6 / 81.0[q]	89.0 / 89.9[d]
Education: Upr. Sec. gross enrol. ratio (f/m per 100 pop.)	46.6 / 49.7	66.5 / 68.0[q]	76.9 / 78.2[d]
Intentional homicide rate (per 100 000 pop.)	2.2	2.6[r]	...
Seats held by women in the National Parliament (%)	...	...	27.7[s]

Environment and infrastructure indicators

	2010	2015	2022
Individuals using the Internet (per 100 inhabitants)	21.6[t]	37.8	71.9[b]
Research & Development expenditure (% of GDP)	0.4[u,v]	0.7	1.0[b]
Threatened species (number)	121	141	207
Forested area (% of land area)[h]	0.1	~0.0	~0.0[d]
CO2 emission estimates (million tons/tons per capita)[o]	178.7 / 2.1	201.6 / 2.2	227.6 / 2.2[d]
Energy production, primary (Petajoules)	3 602	3 051	3 982[d]
Energy supply per capita (Gigajoules)	39	37	41[d]
Tourist/visitor arrivals at national borders (000)	14 051	9 139	12 876[d]
Important sites for terrestrial biodiversity protected (%)	39.6	39.6	39.6[d]
Pop. using safely managed sanitation (urban/rural %)	67.5 / 52.8	69.7 / 57.7	72.8 / 62.7[b]
Net Official Development Assist. received (% of GNI)	0.28	0.78	0.45[b]

a Projected estimate (medium fertility variant). b 2020. c Refers to Greater Cairo as the sum of the Governorate of Al-Qahirah (Cairo) and the surrounding districts of the Governorates of Al-Jizah (Giza) and Al-Qalyûbyah (Qalyubia). d 2019. e 2021. f Data classified according to ISIC Rev. 4. g At factor cost. h Estimate. i For urban population only. j Calculated by the UNSD from national indices. k Areas nes l Data refers to a 5-year period preceding the reference year. m Including refugees. n Data as at the end of December. o Data refer to fiscal years beginning 1 July. p Data are based on SHA2011. q 2014. r 2012. s Data are as at 1 January of reporting year. t Population aged 6 years and over. u Excluding private non-profit. v Excluding business enterprise.

El Salvador

Region	Central America	UN membership date	24 October 1945
Population (000, 2022)	6 336[a]	Surface area (km2)	21 041[b]
Pop. density (per km2, 2022)	305.8[a]	Sex ratio (m per 100 f)	90.9[a]
Capital city	San Salvador	National currency	US Dollar (USD)
Capital city pop. (000, 2022)	1 105.7[c,d]		

Economic indicators	2010	2015	2022
GDP: Gross domestic product (million current US$)	18 448	23 438	24 639[b]
GDP growth rate (annual %, const. 2015 prices)	2.1	2.4	- 7.9[b]
GDP per capita (current US$)	2 983.2	3 705.6	3 798.6[b]
Economy: Agriculture (% of Gross Value Added)[e,f]	7.6	6.1	5.7[b]
Economy: Industry (% of Gross Value Added)[e,g]	27.5	27.8	26.3[b]
Economy: Services and other activity (% of GVA)[e,h]	64.8	66.1	68.0[b]
Employment in agriculture (% of employed)	20.8	18.1	16.0[i,b]
Employment in industry (% of employed)	21.4	22.2	22.1[i,b]
Employment in services & other sectors (% employed)	57.9	59.7	62.0[i,b]
Unemployment rate (% of labour force)	4.9	4.0	5.8[i]
Labour force participation rate (female/male pop. %)	45.7 / 76.1	44.8 / 74.4	44.7 / 73.7[i]
CPI: Consumer Price Index (2010=100)[j]	100	108	115[k]
Agricultural production index (2014-2016=100)	102	97	104[b]
International trade: exports (million current US$)	4 499	5 509	6 629[k]
International trade: imports (million current US$)	8 416	10 293	15 076[k]
International trade: balance (million current US$)	- 3 917	- 4 784	- 8 447[k]
Balance of payments, current account (million US$)	- 533	- 754	- 1 456[k]

Major trading partners						2021
Export partners (% of exports)	United States	39.9	Guatemala	17.3	Honduras	16.4
Import partners (% of imports)	United States	27.2	China	16.8	Guatemala	10.6

Social indicators	2010	2015	2022
Population growth rate (average annual %)	0.4	0.3	0.4[a]
Urban population (% of total population)	65.5	69.7	72.7[d]
Urban population growth rate (average annual %)[l]	1.6	1.7	...
Fertility rate, total (live births per woman)	2.2	2.1	1.8[a]
Life expectancy at birth (females/males, years)	76.2 / 67.2	76.6 / 66.8	75.8 / 66.8[a]
Population age distribution (0-14/60+ years old, %)	31.8 / 9.7	28.4 / 10.4	25.4 / 11.6[a]
International migrant stock (000/% of total pop.)[m]	40.3 / 0.7	42.1 / 0.7	42.8 / 0.7[b]
Refugees and others of concern to the UNHCR (000)	0.1[n]	~0.0	71.9[k]
Infant mortality rate (per 1 000 live births)	16.3	13.1	9.9[a]
Health: Current expenditure (% of GDP)[o]	8.2	7.6	8.5[p,q,d]
Health: Physicians (per 1 000 pop.)	1.9[r]	...	2.9[s]
Education: Government expenditure (% of GDP)	4.0	3.9	3.4[d]
Education: Primary gross enrol. ratio (f/m per 100 pop.)	112.3 / 117.6	100.4 / 104.8	89.2 / 91.4[d]
Education: Sec. gross enrol. ratio (f/m per 100 pop.)	69.0 / 69.3	75.6 / 75.0	69.0 / 68.4[d]
Education: Upr. Sec. gross enrol. ratio (f/m per 100 pop.)	47.3 / 46.6	58.6 / 55.9	56.8 / 54.6[d]
Intentional homicide rate (per 100 000 pop.)	64.5	105.2	37.2[d]
Seats held by women in the National Parliament (%)	19.0	27.4	27.4[t]

Environment and infrastructure indicators	2010	2015	2022
Individuals using the Internet (per 100 inhabitants)	15.9[u]	26.8	54.6[b]
Research & Development expenditure (% of GDP)	0.1	0.1[p]	0.2[d]
Threatened species (number)	72	83	158
Forested area (% of land area)[i]	30.4	29.3	28.4[d]
CO2 emission estimates (million tons/tons per capita)	6.3 / 1.0	6.8 / 1.0	7.6 / 1.1[d]
Energy production, primary (Petajoules)	92	79	82[d]
Energy supply per capita (Gigajoules)	28	27	29[d]
Tourist/visitor arrivals at national borders (000)	1 150	1 402	549[b]
Important sites for terrestrial biodiversity protected (%)	22.8	28.0	28.0[k]
Pop. using safely managed drinking water (urban/rural, %)	80.7 / ...	79.2 / ...	77.4 / ...[b]
Pop. using safely managed sanitation (urban/rural %)	18.0 / ...	17.6 / ...	17.1 / ...[b]
Net Official Development Assist. received (% of GNI)	1.69	0.40	2.69[b]

a Projected estimate (medium fertility variant). b 2020. c Refers to the urban parts of the municipalities San Salvador, Mejicanos, Soyapango, Delgado, Ilopango, Cuscatancingo, Ayutuxtepeque and San Marcos. d 2019. e Data classified according to ISIC Rev. 4. f Excludes irrigation canals and landscaping care. g Excludes publishing activities. Includes irrigation and canals. h Includes publishing activities and landscape care. Excludes repair of personal and household goods. i Estimate. j Urban areas. k 2021. l Data refers to a 5-year period preceding the reference year. m Including refugees. n Data as at the end of December. o Data based on calendar year (January 1 to December 31). p Break in the time series. q Last available data reported by the country using Government reports and national accounts data. r 2008. s 2018. t Data are as at 1 January of reporting year. u Population aged 10 years and over.

Equatorial Guinea

Region	Middle Africa	UN membership date	12 November 1968
Population (000, 2022)	1 675[a]	Surface area (km2)	28 052[b]
Pop. density (per km2, 2022)	59.7[a]	Sex ratio (m per 100 f)	111.8[a]
Capital city	Malabo	National currency	CFA Franc, BEAC (XAF)[c]
Capital city pop. (000, 2022)	296.8[d]	Exchange rate (per US$)	579.2[e]

Economic indicators

	2010	2015	2022
GDP: Gross domestic product (million current US$)	16 299	13 176	10 022[b]
GDP growth rate (annual %, const. 2015 prices)	- 8.9	- 9.1	- 4.9[b]
GDP per capita (current US$)	17 272.0	11 274.9	7 143.2[b]
Economy: Agriculture (% of Gross Value Added)[f]	1.1	1.9	3.0[b]
Economy: Industry (% of Gross Value Added)[f]	74.3	59.0	45.3[b]
Economy: Services and other activity (% of GVA)[f]	24.6	39.1	51.8[b]
Employment in agriculture (% of employed)[g]	41.7	42.0	42.5[b]
Employment in industry (% of employed)[g]	22.9	20.9	18.5[b]
Employment in services & other sectors (% employed)[g]	35.4	37.1	38.9[b]
Unemployment rate (% of labour force)[g]	8.8	8.5	8.9
Labour force participation rate (female/male pop. %)[g]	50.6 / 60.5	51.0 / 59.5	50.5 / 58.7
CPI: Consumer Price Index (2010=100)	100[h]	119	130[b]
Agricultural production index (2014-2016=100)	93	103	101[b]
International trade: exports (million current US$)[g]	9 964	9 570	4 423[e]
International trade: imports (million current US$)[g]	5 679	6 010	820[e]
International trade: balance (million current US$)	4 285[g]	3 560[g]	3 603[e]

Major trading partners

						2021
Export partners (% of exports)[g]	China	25.1	India	17.6	Spain	16.6
Import partners (% of imports)[g]	Spain	21.4	China	13.8	Nigeria	12.9

Social indicators

	2010	2015	2022
Population growth rate (average annual %)	4.7	3.9	2.4[a]
Urban population (% of total population)	65.9	70.6	72.6[i]
Urban population growth rate (average annual %)[j]	7.2	5.6	...
Fertility rate, total (live births per woman)	5.2	4.8	4.2[a]
Life expectancy at birth (females/males, years)	59.6 / 56.3	62.1 / 58.3	63.3 / 59.4[a]
Population age distribution (0-14/60+ years old, %)	38.9 / 5.0	38.7 / 5.0	38.5 / 5.1[a]
International migrant stock (000/% of total pop.)[k]	8.7 / 0.9	209.6 / 17.9	230.6 / 16.4[b]
Infant mortality rate (per 1 000 live births)	79.6	68.1	53.8[a]
Health: Current expenditure (% of GDP)[g]	1.8	2.9	3.1[i]
Health: Physicians (per 1 000 pop.)	...	...	0.4[i]
Education: Primary gross enrol. ratio (f/m per 100 pop.)	68.9 / 69.8	61.6 / 62.0	... / ...
Education: Sec. gross enrol. ratio (f/m per 100 pop.)	22.1 / 29.9[m]	... / ...	... / ...
Education: Upr. Sec. gross enrol. ratio (f/m per 100 pop.)	5.6 / 13.3[m]	... / ...	... / ...
Seats held by women in the National Parliament (%)	10.0	24.0	22.0[n]

Environment and infrastructure indicators

	2010	2015	2022
Individuals using the Internet (per 100 inhabitants)	6.0	21.3[g]	26.2[g,l]
Threatened species (number)	130	155	285
Forested area (% of land area)	90.3	88.8	87.6[i]
CO2 emission estimates (million tons/tons per capita)	8.0 / 8.4	5.5 / 4.7	4.8 / 3.5[i]
Energy production, primary (Petajoules)	884	820	570[i]
Energy supply per capita (Gigajoules)	82	93	56[i]
Important sites for terrestrial biodiversity protected (%)	100.0	100.0	100.0[e]
Net Official Development Assist. received (% of GNI)	0.89	0.08	0.08[b]

a Projected estimate (medium fertility variant). b 2020. c African Financial Community (CFA) Franc, Bank of Central African States (BEAC). d 2018. e 2021. f Data classified according to ISIC Rev. 4. g Estimate. h Break in the time series. i 2019. j Data refers to a 5-year period preceding the reference year. k Refers to foreign citizens. l 2017. m 2005. n Data are as at 1 January of reporting year.

Eritrea

Region	Eastern Africa
Population (000, 2022)	3 684[a]
Pop. density (per km2, 2022)	30.4[a]
Capital city	Asmara
Capital city pop. (000, 2022)	928.8[c]

UN membership date	28 May 1993
Surface area (km2)	121 144[b]
Sex ratio (m per 100 f)	97.4[a]
National currency	Nakfa (ERN)
Exchange rate (per US$)	15.1[d]

Economic indicators	2010	2015	2022
GDP: Gross domestic product (million current US$)[e]	1 590	2 013	2 084[b]
GDP growth rate (annual %, const. 2015 prices)[e]	10.9	- 20.6	- 0.6[b]
GDP per capita (current US$)[e]	501.4	602.2	587.6[b]
Economy: Agriculture (% of Gross Value Added)[f]	19.1	17.2	17.3[b]
Economy: Industry (% of Gross Value Added)[f]	30.9	31.2	31.3[b]
Economy: Services and other activity (% of GVA)[f]	50.0	51.6	51.4[b]
Employment in agriculture (% of employed)[g]	64.7	63.1	60.8[b]
Employment in industry (% of employed)[g]	9.1	8.5	8.5[b]
Employment in services & other sectors (% employed)[g]	26.3	28.5	30.7[b]
Unemployment rate (% of labour force)[g]	5.5	5.8	7.9
Labour force participation rate (female/male pop. %)[g]	73.4 / 85.7	72.9 / 87.3	72.6 / 84.7
Agricultural production index (2014-2016=100)	95	99	103[b]
International trade: exports (million current US$)[g]	13	15	489[d]
International trade: imports (million current US$)[g]	1 187	2 801	357[d]
International trade: balance (million current US$)	- 1 175[g]	- 2 786[g]	132[d]

Major trading partners					2021
Export partners (% of exports)[g]	China	47.4	United Arab Emirates 43.1	Republic of Korea	8.2
Import partners (% of imports)[g]	United Arab Emirates 32.3		China 21.1	Türkiye	7.1

Social indicators	2010	2015	2022
Population growth rate (average annual %)	2.2	0.8	1.7[a]
Urban population (% of total population)	35.2	38.2	40.7[c]
Urban population growth rate (average annual %)[h]	4.5	3.6	...
Fertility rate, total (live births per woman)	4.6	4.2	3.8[a]
Life expectancy at birth (females/males, years)	65.5 / 62.0	68.0 / 64.0	68.7 / 64.5[a]
Population age distribution (0-14/60+ years old, %)	42.7 / 5.5	42.2 / 5.7	39.2 / 6.1[a]
International migrant stock (000/% of total pop.)[g,i]	15.8 / 0.5	15.9 / 0.5	13.9 / 0.4[b]
Refugees and others of concern to the UNHCR (000)	5.0[j]	3.0	0.1[d]
Infant mortality rate (per 1 000 live births)	39.0	33.9	28.6[a]
Health: Current expenditure (% of GDP)[g]	4.9	4.5	4.5[c]
Health: Physicians (per 1 000 pop.)	−0.0	0.1	0.1[b]
Education: Government expenditure (% of GDP)	2.1[k]	...	...
Education: Primary gross enrol. ratio (f/m per 100 pop.)	76.9 / 90.2	70.4 / 81.7	63.1 / 73.6[l]
Education: Sec. gross enrol. ratio (f/m per 100 pop.)	45.1 / 58.8	47.5 / 56.0	45.4 / 49.9[l]
Education: Upr. Sec. gross enrol. ratio (f/m per 100 pop.)	28.1 / 39.5	36.5 / 42.8	29.6 / 31.3[l]
Seats held by women in the National Parliament (%)	22.0	22.0	22.0[c]

Environment and infrastructure indicators	2010	2015	2022
Individuals using the Internet (per 100 inhabitants)[g]	0.6	1.1	1.3[m]
Threatened species (number)	97	113	158
Forested area (% of land area)	9.0	8.8	8.7[g,c]
CO2 emission estimates (million tons/tons per capita)	0.6 / 0.2	0.7 / 0.1	0.9 / 0.2[c]
Energy production, primary (Petajoules)	24	26	27[c]
Energy supply per capita (Gigajoules)	10	10	11[c]
Tourist/visitor arrivals at national borders (000)[n]	84	114	142[o]
Important sites for terrestrial biodiversity protected (%)	0.0	0.0	0.0[d]
Net Official Development Assist. received (% of GNI)	10.34	6.54[p]	

a Projected estimate (medium fertility variant). b 2020. c 2019. d 2021. e Data compiled in accordance with the System of National Accounts 1968 (1968 SNA). f Data classified according to ISIC Rev. 4. g Estimate. h Data refers to a 5-year period preceding the reference year. i Including refugees. j Data as at the end of December. k 2006. l 2018. m 2017. n Including nationals residing abroad. o 2016. p 2011.

Estonia

Region	Northern Europe	UN membership date	17 September 1991
Population (000, 2022)	1 326 [a]	Surface area (km2)	45 261 [b]
Pop. density (per km2, 2022)	30.5 [a]	Sex ratio (m per 100 f)	90.4 [a]
Capital city	Tallinn	National currency	Euro (EUR)
Capital city pop. (000, 2022)	441.3 [c]	Exchange rate (per US$)	0.9 [d]

Economic indicators

	2010	2015	2022
GDP: Gross domestic product (million current US$)	19 535	22 882	30 650 [b]
GDP growth rate (annual %, const. 2015 prices)	2.4	1.9	- 3.0 [b]
GDP per capita (current US$)	14 664.9	17 396.1	23 105.5 [b]
Economy: Agriculture (% of Gross Value Added) [e,f]	3.6	3.3	2.5 [b]
Economy: Industry (% of Gross Value Added) [e,g]	27.9	27.5	25.9 [b]
Economy: Services and other activity (% of GVA) [e,h]	68.5	69.2	71.6 [b]
Employment in agriculture (% of employed)	4.2	3.9	3.1 [i,b]
Employment in industry (% of employed)	30.3	30.7	29.4 [i,b]
Employment in services & other sectors (% employed)	65.5	65.4	67.6 [i,b]
Unemployment rate (% of labour force)	16.7	6.2	5.2 [i]
Labour force participation rate (female/male pop. %)	55.1 / 66.9	55.9 / 69.4	57.1 / 69.6 [i]
CPI: Consumer Price Index (2010=100)	100	111	127 [d]
Agricultural production index (2014-2016=100)	79	111	108 [b]
International trade: exports (million current US$) [j]	12 811	13 908	22 280 [d]
International trade: imports (million current US$) [j]	13 197	15 732	24 161 [d]
International trade: balance (million current US$) [j]	- 385	- 1 824	- 1 881 [d]
Balance of payments, current account (million US$)	340	403	- 453 [d]

Major trading partners

						2021
Export partners (% of exports)	Finland	13.9	Latvia	9.6	United States	9.0
Import partners (% of imports)	Russian Federation	11.6	Germany	9.3	China	8.7

Social indicators

	2010	2015	2022
Population growth rate (average annual %)	- 0.3	0.2	- 0.2 [a]
Urban population (% of total population)	68.1	68.4	69.1 [c]
Urban population growth rate (average annual %) [k]	- 0.5	- 0.2	...
Fertility rate, total (live births per woman)	1.7	1.6	1.7 [a]
Life expectancy at birth (females/males, years)	80.4 / 70.7	81.7 / 73.1	83.0 / 75.0 [a]
Population age distribution (0-14/60+ years old, %)	15.2 / 23.3	16.0 / 25.2	16.4 / 27.0 [a]
International migrant stock (000/% of total pop.)	217.9 / 16.4	194.7 / 14.8	199.3 / 15.0 [b]
Refugees and others of concern to the UNHCR (000)	101.0 [l]	86.8	72.2 [d]
Infant mortality rate (per 1 000 live births)	4.1	2.8	1.8 [a]
Health: Current expenditure (% of GDP)	6.3	6.3	6.7 [c]
Health: Physicians (per 1 000 pop.)	3.2	3.4	3.5 [c]
Education: Government expenditure (% of GDP)	5.5	5.1	5.2 [m]
Education: Primary gross enrol. ratio (f/m per 100 pop.)	102.2 / 103.8	97.1 / 97.1	98.3 / 97.6 [c]
Education: Sec. gross enrol. ratio (f/m per 100 pop.)	105.3 / 105.2	110.8 / 111.3	117.7 / 113.6 [c]
Education: Upr. Sec. gross enrol. ratio (f/m per 100 pop.)	109.1 / 105.6	116.1 / 113.1	134.1 / 124.5 [c]
Intentional homicide rate (per 100 000 pop.)	5.3	3.4	3.2 [b]
Seats held by women in the National Parliament (%)	22.8	19.8	25.7 [n]

Environment and infrastructure indicators

	2010	2015	2022
Individuals using the Internet (per 100 inhabitants)	74.1 [o,p]	88.4	89.1 [b]
Research & Development expenditure (% of GDP)	1.6	1.5	1.8 [b]
Threatened species (number)	11	17	56
Forested area (% of land area)	55.1	55.7	56.1 [i,c]
CO2 emission estimates (million tons/tons per capita)	19.0 / 14.0	15.6 / 11.7	9.0 / 6.5 [b]
Energy production, primary (Petajoules)	206	234	226 [c]
Energy supply per capita (Gigajoules)	178	175	166 [c]
Tourist/visitor arrivals at national borders (000) [q]	2 511	2 961	1 023 [b]
Important sites for terrestrial biodiversity protected (%)	94.7	94.8	94.9 [a]

a Projected estimate (medium fertility variant). b 2020. c 2019. d 2021. e Data classified according to ISIC Rev. 4. f Excludes irrigation canals and landscaping care. g Excludes publishing activities. Includes irrigation and canals. h Includes publishing activities and landscape care. Excludes repair of personal and household goods. i Estimate. j General Extra-EU/Special Intra-EU k Data refers to a 5-year period preceding the reference year. l Data as at the end of December. m 2018. n Data are as at 1 January of reporting year. o Users in the last 3 months. p Population aged 16 to 74 years. q Based on mobile positioning data by the Bank of Estonia and Positium LBS.

Eswatini

Region	Southern Africa	UN membership date	24 September 1968
Population (000, 2022)	1 202[a]	Surface area (km2)	17 363[b]
Pop. density (per km2, 2022)	69.2[a]	Sex ratio (m per 100 f)	98.5[a]
Capital city	Mbabane[c]	National currency	Lilangeni (SZL)
Capital city pop. (000, 2022)	68.0[c,d]	Exchange rate (per US$)	15.2[e]

Economic indicators	2010	2015	2022
GDP: Gross domestic product (million current US$)	4 439	4 059	3 835[b]
GDP growth rate (annual %, const. 2015 prices)	3.8	2.2	- 5.6[b]
GDP per capita (current US$)	4 168.5	3 676.2	3 305.8[b]
Economy: Agriculture (% of Gross Value Added)[f,g]	10.4	9.8	8.9[b]
Economy: Industry (% of Gross Value Added)[f,h]	38.7	37.6	35.5[b]
Economy: Services and other activity (% of GVA)[f,i]	50.9	52.6	55.6[b]
Employment in agriculture (% of employed)[j]	15.2	13.5	12.3[b]
Employment in industry (% of employed)[j]	25.3	24.6	23.5[b]
Employment in services & other sectors (% employed)[j]	59.5	61.8	64.2[b]
Unemployment rate (% of labour force)[j]	26.4	23.3	25.2
Labour force participation rate (female/male pop. %)[j]	46.6 / 57.6	46.9 / 56.2	46.6 / 54.1
CPI: Consumer Price Index (2010=100)	100	135	167[k]
Agricultural production index (2014-2016=100)	95	100	103[b]
International trade: exports (million current US$)	1 557[j]	1 820	3 282[j,e]
International trade: imports (million current US$)	1 710[j]	1 508	2 029[j,e]
International trade: balance (million current US$)	- 153[j]	312	1 253[e]
Balance of payments, current account (million US$)	- 388	533	255[b]

Major trading partners						2021
Export partners (% of exports)[j]	South Africa	65.0	Kenya	7.2	Nigeria	5.9
Import partners (% of imports)[j]	South Africa	71.4	China	7.3	India	3.4

Social indicators	2010	2015	2022
Population growth rate (average annual %)	0.5	0.7	0.7[a]
Urban population (% of total population)	22.5	23.3	24.0[k]
Urban population growth rate (average annual %)[l]	2.1	2.6	...
Fertility rate, total (live births per woman)	3.4	3.1	2.8[a]
Life expectancy at birth (females/males, years)	48.3 / 44.9	58.1 / 52.1	60.6 / 52.6[a]
Population age distribution (0-14/60+ years old, %)	38.8 / 4.7	37.5 / 5.3	34.7 / 6.2[a]
International migrant stock (000/% of total pop.)[m]	32.6 / 3.1	32.4 / 2.9	32.9 / 2.8[b]
Refugees and others of concern to the UNHCR (000)	0.8[n]	0.9	2.1[e]
Infant mortality rate (per 1 000 live births)	61.3	43.0	39.2[a]
Health: Current expenditure (% of GDP)	8.6	7.1	6.8[k]
Health: Physicians (per 1 000 pop.)	0.2[o]	0.1[p]	0.1[b]
Education: Government expenditure (% of GDP)	6.1	5.4[j]	5.3[j,b]
Education: Primary gross enrol. ratio (f/m per 100 pop.)	118.8 / 131.0	113.5 / 124.9	109.8 / 119.0[k]
Education: Sec. gross enrol. ratio (f/m per 100 pop.)	63.7 / 67.3	76.0 / 76.0	82.2 / 82.6[q]
Education: Upr. Sec. gross enrol. ratio (f/m per 100 pop.)	49.5 / 53.9	61.7 / 62.1	71.4 / 73.0[q]
Intentional homicide rate (per 100 000 pop.)	19.5	10.1	11.6[r]
Seats held by women in the National Parliament (%)	13.6	6.2	12.2[s]

Environment and infrastructure indicators	2010	2015	2022
Individuals using the Internet (per 100 inhabitants)	11.0	25.6[j]	30.3[j,r]
Research & Development expenditure (% of GDP)	...	0.3	...
Threatened species (number)	29	34	48
Forested area (% of land area)[j]	28.2	28.6	28.9[k]
Energy production, primary (Petajoules)	29	33	31[k]
Energy supply per capita (Gigajoules)	39	41	40[k]
Tourist/visitor arrivals at national borders (000)	868	873	194[b]
Important sites for terrestrial biodiversity protected (%)	20.9	21.2	22.7[e]
Pop. using safely managed drinking water (urban/rural, %)	82.5 / ...	87.1 / ...	88.7 / ...[b]
Net Official Development Assist. received (% of GNI)	2.16	2.37	2.80[b]

a Projected estimate (medium fertility variant). b 2020. c Mbabane is the administrative capital and Lobamba is the legislative capital. d 2018. e 2021. f Data classified according to ISIC Rev. 4. g Excludes irrigation canals and landscaping care. h Excludes publishing activities. Includes irrigation and canals. i Includes publishing activities and landscape care. Excludes repair of personal and household goods. j Estimate. k 2019. l Data refers to a 5-year period preceding the reference year. m Including refugees. n Data as at the end of December. o 2009. p 2011. q 2016. r 2017. s Data are as at 1 January of reporting year.

Ethiopia

Region	Eastern Africa	UN membership date	13 November 1945
Population (000, 2022)	123 380[a]	Surface area (km2)	1 104 300[b]
Pop. density (per km2, 2022)	123.4[a]	Sex ratio (m per 100 f)	100.9[a]
Capital city	Addis Ababa	National currency	Ethiopian Birr (ETB)
Capital city pop. (000, 2022)	4 592.0[c]	Exchange rate (per US$)	39.2[b]

Economic indicators	2010	2015	2022
GDP: Gross domestic product (million current US$)	26 311	63 079	96 611[b]
GDP growth rate (annual %, const. 2015 prices)	12.6	10.4	6.1[b]
GDP per capita (current US$)	300.2	625.6	840.4[b]
Economy: Agriculture (% of Gross Value Added)[d]	45.3	38.8	37.2[b]
Economy: Industry (% of Gross Value Added)[d]	10.4	17.5	24.2[b]
Economy: Services and other activity (% of GVA)[d]	44.3	43.7	38.6[b]
Employment in agriculture (% of employed)[e]	74.0	69.1	65.6[b]
Employment in industry (% of employed)[e]	8.0	9.1	10.4[b]
Employment in services & other sectors (% employed)[e]	18.0	21.8	24.0[b]
Unemployment rate (% of labour force)[e]	2.3	2.3	4.0
Labour force participation rate (female/male pop. %)[e]	74.4 / 88.9	74.5 / 87.7	73.9 / 85.2
CPI: Consumer Price Index (2010=100)[f]	100	205	487[g]
Agricultural production index (2014-2016=100)	82	101	120[b]
International trade: exports (million current US$)	2 330	2 024	1 835[e,g]
International trade: imports (million current US$)	8 602	17 686	7 373[e,g]
International trade: balance (million current US$)	- 6 272	- 15 662	- 5 538[g]
Balance of payments, current account (million US$)	- 635	- 7 567	- 2 719[b]

Major trading partners						2021
Export partners (% of exports)[e]	Somalia	11.6	United States	10.2	Netherlands	7.5
Import partners (% of imports)[e]	China	29.5	India	10.5	Türkiye	5.7

Social indicators	2010	2015	2022
Population growth rate (average annual %)	2.8	2.7	2.5[a]
Urban population (% of total population)	17.3	19.4	21.2[c]
Urban population growth rate (average annual %)[h]	4.6	4.9	...
Fertility rate, total (live births per woman)	5.2	4.5	4.1[a]
Life expectancy at birth (females/males, years)	61.8 / 57.7	66.3 / 61.1	68.9 / 62.6[a]
Population age distribution (0-14/60+ years old, %)	45.1 / 4.4	42.5 / 4.6	39.6 / 4.9[a]
International migrant stock (000/% of total pop.)[i]	568.7 / 0.6	1 161.6 / 1.2	1 085.5 / 0.9[b]
Refugees and others of concern to the UNHCR (000)	155.4[j]	705.7	4 740.6[g]
Infant mortality rate (per 1 000 live births)	54.4	43.2	31.9[a]
Health: Current expenditure (% of GDP)	5.5	3.8	3.2[c]
Health: Physicians (per 1 000 pop.)	~0.0[k]	...	0.1[b]
Education: Government expenditure (% of GDP)	4.5	4.7	5.1[e,l]
Education: Primary gross enrol. ratio (f/m per 100 pop.)	88.0 / 95.2	96.1 / 105.8	113.5 / 125.2[b]
Education: Sec. gross enrol. ratio (f/m per 100 pop.)	31.6 / 38.0	34.2 / 35.6	... / ...
Education: Upr. Sec. gross enrol. ratio (f/m per 100 pop.)	13.4 / 19.1	17.4 / 17.7	... / ...
Intentional homicide rate (per 100 000 pop.)	...	8.8[m]	...
Seats held by women in the National Parliament (%)	21.9	27.8	41.5[n]

Environment and infrastructure indicators	2010	2015	2022
Individuals using the Internet (per 100 inhabitants)	0.8[e]	13.9	24.0[e,b]
Research & Development expenditure (% of GDP)	0.2[o]	0.6[p]	0.3[o,q]
Threatened species (number)	120	145	228
Forested area (% of land area)	15.8	15.4	15.2[e,c]
CO2 emission estimates (million tons/tons per capita)[r,s]	16.4 / 0.1	22.1 / 0.1	28.0 / 0.1[c]
Energy production, primary (Petajoules)	1 212	1 330	1 420[c]
Energy supply per capita (Gigajoules)	15	14	14[c]
Tourist/visitor arrivals at national borders (000)[t,u]	468	864	518[b]
Important sites for terrestrial biodiversity protected (%)	13.1	15.0	16.4[g]
Pop. using safely managed drinking water (urban/rural, %)	37.0 / 1.6	38.0 / 3.2	39.0 / 5.2[b]
Pop. using safely managed sanitation (urban/rural %)	14.0 / 2.6	15.0 / 3.4	15.9 / 4.1[b]
Net Official Development Assist. received (% of GNI)	11.58	5.04	4.95[b]

a Projected estimate (medium fertility variant). b 2020. c 2019. d Data classified according to ISIC Rev. 4. e Estimate. f Calculated by the UNSD from national indices. g 2021. h Data refers to a 5-year period preceding the reference year. i Including refugees. j Data as at the end of December. k 2009. l 2018. m 2012. n Data are as at 1 January of reporting year. o Break in the time series. p 2013. q 2017. r Data refer to fiscal years beginning 1 July. s Excluding Eritrea. t Arrivals through all ports of entry. u Including nationals residing abroad.

Falkland Islands (Malvinas)

Region	South America	Population (000, 2022)	4 [a,b]
Surface area (km2)	12 173 [c,d]	Pop. density (per km2, 2022)	0.3 [a,b]
Sex ratio (m per 100 f)	100.7 [a,b]	Capital city	Stanley
National currency	Falkland Islands Pound (FKP)	Capital city pop. (000, 2022)	2.3 [c,e]
Exchange rate (per US$)	0.7 [f]		

Economic indicators

	2010	2015	2022
Unemployment rate (% of labour force)	...	1.2 [g,h]	...
Labour force participation rate (female/male pop. %)	... / ...	77.2 / 86.0 [g,i,h]	... / ...
International trade: exports (million current US$) [j]	9	4	300 [f]
International trade: imports (million current US$) [j]	50	21	151 [f]
International trade: balance (million current US$)	- 41 [j]	- 17 [j]	149 [f]

Major trading partners

							2021
Export partners (% of exports) [j]	Spain	80.6	United States	4.0	Morocco	3.4
Import partners (% of imports) [j]	United Kingdom	60.0	Spain	31.9	Greece	5.1

Social indicators

	2010	2015	2022
Population growth rate (average annual %) [b]	- 0.3	2.3	0.4 [a]
Urban population (% of total population) [c]	73.7	76.3	78.1 [k]
Urban population growth rate (average annual %) [c,l]	0.2	1.0	...
Fertility rate, total (live births per woman) [b]	1.5	1.6	1.6 [a]
Life expectancy at birth (females/males, years) [b]	79.8 / 75.9	80.1 / 76.6	81.2 / 77.4 [a]
Population age distribution (0-14/60+ years old, %) [b]	17.6 / 15.9	17.9 / 14.8	17.7 / 17.4 [a]
International migrant stock (000/% of total pop.) [b]	1.4 / 49.5	1.6 / 55.4	2.0 / 56.2 [d]
Infant mortality rate (per 1 000 live births) [b]	10.7	10.1	9.0 [a]

Environment and infrastructure indicators

	2010	2015	2022
Individuals using the Internet (per 100 inhabitants)	95.8	98.3 [i]	99.0 [j,m]
Threatened species (number)	23	23	30
Forested area (% of land area) [j]	0.0	0.0	0.0 [k]
Energy production, primary (Petajoules)	0 [j]	0 [j]	0 [k]
Energy supply per capita (Gigajoules)	197 [j]	202	172 [k]
Important sites for terrestrial biodiversity protected (%)	20.8	20.8	20.8 [f]

a Projected estimate (medium fertility variant). b A dispute exists between the Governments of Argentina and the United Kingdom of Great Britain and Northern Ireland concerning sovereignty over the Falkland Islands (Malvinas). For statistical purposes, the data for United Kingdom do not include this area. c A dispute exists between the Governments of Argentina and the United Kingdom of Great Britain and Northern Ireland concerning sovereignty over the Falkland Islands (Malvinas). d 2020. e 2018. f 2021. g Population aged 16 to 65 years. h 2013. i Break in the time series. j Estimate. k 2019. l Data refers to a 5-year period preceding the reference year. m 2016.

Faroe Islands

Region	Northern Europe	Population (000, 2022)	53[a,b]
Surface area (km2)	1 393[c]	Pop. density (per km2, 2022)	38.3[a,b]
Sex ratio (m per 100 f)	107.3[a,b]	Capital city	Tórshavn
National currency	Danish Krone (DKK)	Capital city pop. (000, 2022)	20.8[d]
Exchange rate (per US$)	6.6[e]		

Economic indicators	2010	2015	2022
Employment in agriculture (% of employed)	11.1[f,g,h]	...	...
Employment in industry (% of employed)	22.2[f,g,h]	...	...
Employment in services & other sectors (% employed)	66.7[f,g,h]	...	...
Unemployment rate (% of labour force)[i,j]	6.4[k]	4.0[l]	...
Labour force participation rate (female/male pop. %)	77.5 / 85.3[i,j]	79.4 / 86.0[i,j,l]	... / ...
Agricultural production index (2014-2016=100)	93	98	90[c]
International trade: exports (million current US$)[m]	839	1 024	1 685[e]
International trade: imports (million current US$)[m]	780	911	1 519[e]
International trade: balance (million current US$)	59[m]	113[m]	166[e]
Balance of payments, current account (million US$)	144	194[n]	...

Major trading partners						2021
Export partners (% of exports)[m]	Russian Federation	21.9	United Kingdom	17.9	Denmark	16.4
Import partners (% of imports)[m]	Denmark	51.9	Netherlands	11.0	Norway	10.1

Social indicators	2010	2015	2022
Population growth rate (average annual %)[b]	- 0.1	1.3	0.4[a]
Urban population (% of total population)	40.9	41.6	42.2[o]
Urban population growth rate (average annual %)[p]	0.7	0.5	...
Fertility rate, total (live births per woman)[b]	2.5	2.4	2.7[a]
Life expectancy at birth (females/males, years)[b]	78.9 / 75.7	82.0 / 77.7	80.7 / 77.3[a]
Population age distribution (0-14/60+ years old, %)[b]	21.8 / 20.5	21.0 / 22.8	20.7 / 23.6[a]
International migrant stock (000/% of total pop.)	5.1 / 10.7	5.5 / 11.4	6.8 / 13.9[c]
Infant mortality rate (per 1 000 live births)[b]	6.1	5.3	5.3[a]
Education: Government expenditure (% of GDP)[m]	...	7.7	8.2[q]

Environment and infrastructure indicators	2010	2015	2022
Individuals using the Internet (per 100 inhabitants)	75.2	94.2[m]	97.6[m,q]
Threatened species (number)	13	14	34
Forested area (% of land area)	0.1	0.1	0.1[o]
Energy production, primary (Petajoules)	0	1	1[o]
Energy supply per capita (Gigajoules)[m]	187	189	221[o]
Important sites for terrestrial biodiversity protected (%)	0.0	15.8	15.8[e]

a Projected estimate (medium fertility variant). **b** For statistical purposes, the data for Denmark do not include this area. **c** 2020. **d** 2018. **e** 2021. **f** Data classified according to ISIC Rev. 2. **g** Population aged 16 years and over. **h** 2005. **i** Population aged 15 to 74 years. **j** Excluding the institutional population. **k** Break in the time series. **l** 2013. **m** Estimate. **n** 2011. **o** 2019. **p** Data refers to a 5-year period preceding the reference year. **q** 2017.

Fiji

Region	Melanesia	UN membership date	13 October 1970
Population (000, 2022)	930[a]	Surface area (km2)	18 272[b]
Pop. density (per km2, 2022)	50.9[a]	Sex ratio (m per 100 f)	100.5[a]
Capital city	Suva	National currency	Fiji Dollar (FJD)
Capital city pop. (000, 2022)	178.3[c]	Exchange rate (per US$)	2.1[d]

Economic indicators	2010	2015	2022
GDP: Gross domestic product (million current US$)	3 141	4 682	4 494[b]
GDP growth rate (annual %, const. 2015 prices)	3.0	4.7	- 15.7[b]
GDP per capita (current US$)	3 652.5	5 390.6	5 013.2[b]
Economy: Agriculture (% of Gross Value Added)[e,f]	10.2	10.0	17.6[b]
Economy: Industry (% of Gross Value Added)[e,g]	19.9	19.3	21.0[b]
Economy: Services and other activity (% of GVA)[e,h]	69.9	70.6	61.4[b]
Employment in agriculture (% of employed)[i]	43.9	39.4	35.7[b]
Employment in industry (% of employed)[i]	14.4	13.2	13.3[b]
Employment in services & other sectors (% employed)[i]	41.7	47.4	51.0[b]
Unemployment rate (% of labour force)[i]	4.3	4.3	4.9
Labour force participation rate (female/male pop. %)[i]	43.7 / 79.7	39.8 / 76.2	37.8 / 75.3
CPI: Consumer Price Index (2010=100)[j]	100	116	129[d]
Agricultural production index (2014-2016=100)	89	109	115[b]
International trade: exports (million current US$)	841	895	815[d]
International trade: imports (million current US$)	1 808	2 081	2 116[d]
International trade: balance (million current US$)	- 967	- 1 186	- 1 300[d]
Balance of payments, current account (million US$)	- 149	- 163	- 597[d]

Major trading partners						2021
Export partners (% of exports)	United States	20.5	Australia	16.5	New Zealand	8.2
Import partners (% of imports)	Singapore	17.1	Australia	16.9	China	15.0

Social indicators	2010	2015	2022
Population growth rate (average annual %)	0.4	0.1	0.7[a]
Urban population (% of total population)	52.2	54.7	56.8[k]
Urban population growth rate (average annual %)[l]	1.8	1.7	...
Fertility rate, total (live births per woman)	2.7	2.6	2.5[a]
Life expectancy at birth (females/males, years)	69.3 / 65.5	68.9 / 64.9	70.2 / 66.5[a]
Population age distribution (0-14/60+ years old, %)	31.1 / 6.9	30.2 / 7.8	28.6 / 9.7[a]
International migrant stock (000/% of total pop.)[m]	13.4 / 1.6	13.8 / 1.6	14.1 / 1.6[b]
Refugees and others of concern to the UNHCR (000)	~0.0[n]	~0.0	~0.0[d]
Infant mortality rate (per 1 000 live births)	19.8	20.3	17.9[a]
Health: Current expenditure (% of GDP)	3.4	3.3	3.8[o,k]
Health: Physicians (per 1 000 pop.)	0.4[p]	0.9	...
Education: Government expenditure (% of GDP)	4.8	4.8[i]	5.1[i,k]
Education: Primary gross enrol. ratio (f/m per 100 pop.)	104.0 / 105.6[p]	105.5 / 107.9	114.2 / 118.6[k]
Education: Sec. gross enrol. ratio (f/m per 100 pop.)	90.7 / 82.9[p]	94.3 / 85.7[q]	... / ...
Education: Upr. Sec. gross enrol. ratio (f/m per 100 pop.)	75.3 / 63.8[p]	81.9 / 71.9[q]	... / ...
Intentional homicide rate (per 100 000 pop.)	2.3	2.3[r]	2.2[b]
Seats held by women in the National Parliament (%)	8.5[s]	14.0	19.6[t]

Environment and infrastructure indicators	2010	2015	2022
Individuals using the Internet (per 100 inhabitants)[l]	20.0	42.5	68.9[c]
Threatened species (number)	192	278	349
Forested area (% of land area)[l]	58.7	60.6	62.0[k]
Energy production, primary (Petajoules)	5	7	7[k]
Energy supply per capita (Gigajoules)	24	29	29[i,k]
Tourist/visitor arrivals at national borders (000)[u]	632	755	147[b]
Important sites for terrestrial biodiversity protected (%)	11.2	11.2	11.2[d]
Net Official Development Assist. received (% of GNI)	2.49	2.33	4.71[b]

a Projected estimate (medium fertility variant). b 2020. c 2018. d 2021. e Data classified according to ISIC Rev. 4. f Excludes irrigation canals and landscaping care. g Excludes publishing activities. Includes irrigation and canals. h Includes publishing activities and landscape care. Excludes repair of personal and household goods. i Estimate. j Calculated by the UNSD from national indices. k 2019. l Data refers to a 5-year period preceding the reference year. m Including refugees. n Data as at the end of December. o Data refer to fiscal years beginning 1 April. p 2009. q 2012. r 2014. s 2006. t Data are as at 1 January of reporting year. u Excluding nationals residing abroad.

Finland

Region	Northern Europe	UN membership date	14 December 1955
Population (000, 2022)	5 541 [a,b]	Surface area (km2)	336 884 [c,d]
Pop. density (per km2, 2022)	18.3 [a,b]	Sex ratio (m per 100 f)	97.7 [a,b]
Capital city	Helsinki	National currency	Euro (EUR)
Capital city pop. (000, 2022)	1 292.2 [e]	Exchange rate (per US$)	0.9 [f]

Economic indicators

	2010	2015	2022
GDP: Gross domestic product (million current US$)	249 181	234 440	269 751 [d]
GDP growth rate (annual %, const. 2015 prices)	3.2	0.5	- 2.9 [d]
GDP per capita (current US$)	46 438.9	42 772.3	48 685.2 [d]
Economy: Agriculture (% of Gross Value Added) [g,h]	2.8	2.6	2.8 [d]
Economy: Industry (% of Gross Value Added) [g,i]	29.9	27.0	27.8 [d]
Economy: Services and other activity (% of GVA) [g,j]	67.3	70.4	69.4 [d]
Employment in agriculture (% of employed)	4.4	4.2	3.5 [k,d]
Employment in industry (% of employed)	23.3	21.7	22.0 [k,d]
Employment in services & other sectors (% employed)	72.3	74.1	74.5 [k,d]
Unemployment rate (% of labour force)	8.4	9.4	6.8 [k]
Labour force participation rate (female/male pop. %)	56.0 / 64.1	55.6 / 62.4	56.1 / 63.6 [k]
CPI: Consumer Price Index (2010=100)	100 [l]	109 [l]	115 [f]
Agricultural production index (2014-2016=100)	94	100	99 [d]
International trade: exports (million current US$)	70 117	59 682	81 327 [f]
International trade: imports (million current US$)	68 767	60 174	85 993 [f]
International trade: balance (million current US$)	1 349	- 492	- 4 666 [f]
Balance of payments, current account (million US$)	2 792	- 2 209	2 115 [f]

Major trading partners

						2021
Export partners (% of exports)	Germany	13.2	Sweden	10.2	United States	6.6
Import partners (% of imports)	Germany	14.5	Russian Federation	11.7	Sweden	11.5

Social indicators

	2010	2015	2022
Population growth rate (average annual %) [b]	0.4	0.3	0.1 [a]
Urban population (% of total population) [b]	83.8	85.2	85.4 [e]
Urban population growth rate (average annual %) [b,m]	0.6	0.8	...
Fertility rate, total (live births per woman) [b]	1.9	1.6	1.4 [a]
Life expectancy at birth (females/males, years) [b]	83.2 / 76.7	84.2 / 78.6	84.9 / 79.8 [a]
Population age distribution (0-14/60+ years old, %) [b]	16.6 / 24.7	16.4 / 27.0	15.2 / 29.7 [a]
International migrant stock (000/% of total pop.) [b]	228.5 / 4.3	314.9 / 5.7	386.1 / 7.0 [d]
Refugees and others of concern to the UNHCR (000)	14.0 [n]	16.3	32.1 [f]
Infant mortality rate (per 1 000 live births) [b]	2.3	1.7	1.6 [a]
Health: Current expenditure (% of GDP)	9.1	9.6	9.2 [e]
Health: Physicians (per 1 000 pop.)	3.3	3.3	4.6 [o]
Education: Government expenditure (% of GDP)	6.5	7.0	6.3 [o]
Education: Primary gross enrol. ratio (f/m per 100 pop.)	99.1 / 99.8	100.3 / 100.8	99.6 / 100.2 [e]
Education: Sec. gross enrol. ratio (f/m per 100 pop.)	110.1 / 105.2	157.5 / 142.9	152.1 / 138.9 [e]
Education: Upr. Sec. gross enrol. ratio (f/m per 100 pop.)	120.5 / 110.2	210.2 / 181.8	200.9 / 172.8 [e]
Intentional homicide rate (per 100 000 pop.)	2.2	1.5	1.6 [d]
Seats held by women in the National Parliament (%)	40.0	42.5	45.5 [p]

Environment and infrastructure indicators

	2010	2015	2022
Individuals using the Internet (per 100 inhabitants)	86.9 [q]	86.4	92.2 [d]
Research & Development expenditure (% of GDP)	3.7	2.9	2.9 [d]
Threatened species (number)	18	25	68
Forested area (% of land area)	73.2	73.7	73.7 [e]
CO2 emission estimates (million tons/tons per capita)	63.6 / 11.6	43.9 / 7.7	37.3 / 6.5 [d]
Energy production, primary (Petajoules)	725	732	796 [e]
Energy supply per capita (Gigajoules)	285	247	251 [e]
Tourist/visitor arrivals at national borders (000)	3 670	2 622 [r]	896 [d]
Important sites for terrestrial biodiversity protected (%)	68.8	71.7	71.8 [f]
Net Official Development Assist. disbursed (% of GNI) [s]	1.78	- 0.02	0.96 [d]

a Projected estimate (medium fertility variant). **b** Including Åland Islands. **c** Excluding Åland Islands. **d** 2020. **e** 2019. **f** 2021. **g** Data classified according to ISIC Rev. 4. **h** Excludes irrigation canals and landscaping care. **i** Excludes publishing activities. Includes irrigation and canals. **j** Includes publishing activities and landscape care. Excludes repair of personal and household goods. **k** Estimate. **l** Calculated by the UNSD from national indices. **m** Data refers to a 5-year period preceding the reference year. **n** Data as at the end of December. **o** 2018. **p** Data are as at 1 January of reporting year. **q** Population aged 16 to 74 years. **r** Non-resident tourists staying in all types of accommodation establishments. **s** DAC member (OECD).

France

Region	Western Europe	UN membership date	24 October 1945
Population (000, 2022)	64 627[a,b]	Surface area (km2)	551 500[c]
Pop. density (per km2, 2022)	117.2[a,b]	Sex ratio (m per 100 f)	93.5[a,b]
Capital city	Paris	National currency	Euro (EUR)
Capital city pop. (000, 2022)	10 958.2[d]	Exchange rate (per US$)	0.9[e]

Economic indicators

	2010	2015	2022
GDP: Gross domestic product (million current US$)[f]	2 642 610	2 438 208	2 630 318[c]
GDP growth rate (annual %, const. 2015 prices)[f]	1.9	1.1	- 7.9[c]
GDP per capita (current US$)[f]	40 685.3	36 611.8	38 958.6[c]
Economy: Agriculture (% of Gross Value Added)[g]	1.8	1.8	1.8[c]
Economy: Industry (% of Gross Value Added)[h,i]	19.8	19.8	18.4[c]
Economy: Services and other activity (% of GVA)[h,j]	78.4	78.5	79.8[c]
Employment in agriculture (% of employed)	2.9	2.7	2.4[k,c]
Employment in industry (% of employed)	22.3	20.4	19.9[k,c]
Employment in services & other sectors (% employed)	74.8	76.9	77.7[k,c]
Unemployment rate (% of labour force)	8.9	10.4	7.5[k]
Labour force participation rate (female/male pop. %)	51.5 / 62.0	51.6 / 60.8	51.5 / 59.4[k]
CPI: Consumer Price Index (2010=100)[l,m]	100	106	112[e]
Agricultural production index (2014-2016=100)	97	102	93[c]
International trade: exports (million current US$)	511 651	493 941	585 148[e]
International trade: imports (million current US$)	599 172	563 398	714 842[e]
International trade: balance (million current US$)	- 87 520	- 69 457	- 129 694[e]
Balance of payments, current account (million US$)	- 22 031	- 9 130	- 17 669[e]

Major trading partners

						2021
Export partners (% of exports)	Germany	14.0	Italy	7.9	Belgium	7.6
Import partners (% of imports)	Germany	16.8	Belgium	10.7	Netherlands	8.9

Social indicators

	2010	2015	2022
Population growth rate (average annual %)[a]	0.6	0.3	0.2[b]
Urban population (% of total population)	78.4	79.7	80.7[d]
Urban population growth rate (average annual %)[n]	0.9	0.8	...
Fertility rate, total (live births per woman)[a]	2.0	1.9	1.8[b]
Life expectancy at birth (females/males, years)[a]	84.7 / 78.0	85.2 / 79.0	86.0 / 80.4[b]
Population age distribution (0-14/60+ years old, %)[a]	18.3 / 23.2	18.2 / 25.3	17.2 / 27.8[b]
International migrant stock (000/% of total pop.)	7 310.0 / 11.6	7 878.3 / 12.2	8 524.9 / 13.1[c]
Refugees and others of concern to the UNHCR (000)	250.4[o]	320.1	540.9[e]
Infant mortality rate (per 1 000 live births)[a]	3.6	3.6	3.3[b]
Health: Current expenditure (% of GDP)[p]	11.2	11.4	11.1[d]
Health: Physicians (per 1 000 pop.)	3.4	3.2	3.3[d]
Education: Government expenditure (% of GDP)	...	...	5.4[q]
Education: Primary gross enrol. ratio (f/m per 100 pop.)[k]	102.1 / 103.4	101.7 / 102.3	102.3 / 102.8[d]
Education: Sec. gross enrol. ratio (f/m per 100 pop.)[k]	107.0 / 105.9	103.9 / 102.9	104.4 / 104.2[d]
Education: Upr. Sec. gross enrol. ratio (f/m per 100 pop.)[k]	112.7 / 109.6	108.6 / 105.4	108.8 / 107.3[d]
Intentional homicide rate (per 100 000 pop.)	1.3	1.6	1.3[c]
Seats held by women in the National Parliament (%)	18.9	26.2	39.5[r]

Environment and infrastructure indicators

	2010	2015	2022
Individuals using the Internet (per 100 inhabitants)	77.3[s]	78.0[t,u,v]	84.8[k,c]
Research & Development expenditure (% of GDP)	2.2[t]	2.2	2.4[k,c]
Threatened species (number)	168	236	460
Forested area (% of land area)[k]	30.0	30.7	31.4[d]
CO2 emission estimates (million tons/tons per capita)	347.1 / 5.2	311.7 / 4.6[w]	264.4 / 3.8[w,c]
Energy production, primary (Petajoules)[w]	5 632	5 768	5 444[d]
Energy supply per capita (Gigajoules)[w]	174	158	150[d]
Tourist/visitor arrivals at national borders (000)[x]	76 647	84 452	41 684[c]
Important sites for terrestrial biodiversity protected (%)	63.3	68.1	80.9[e]
Pop. using safely managed drinking water (urban/rural, %)	98.9 / ...	99.4 / ...	99.6 / ...[c]
Net Official Development Assist. disbursed (% of GNI)[y]	1.35	0.05	0.59[c]

a For statistical purposes, the data for France do not include the five overseas departments and French Polynesia, New Caledonia, St. Pierre and Miquelon, St. Barthélemy, St. Martin (French part), Wallis and Futuna Islands. **b** Projected estimate (medium fertility variant). **c** 2020. **d** 2019. **e** 2021. **f** Including French Guiana, Guadeloupe, Martinique and Réunion. **g** Excludes irrigation canals and landscaping care. Data classified according to ISIC Rev. 4. **h** Data classified according to ISIC Rev. 4. **i** Excludes publishing activities. Includes irrigation and canals. **j** Includes publishing activities and landscape care. Excludes repair of personal and household goods. **k** Estimate. **l** Calculated by the UNSD from national indices. **m** All households. Metropolitan France and overseas departments. **n** Data refers to a 5-year period preceding the reference year. **o** Data as at the end of December. **p** Data are based on SHA2011. **q** 2018. **r** Data are as at 1 January of reporting year. **s** Population aged 16 to 74 years. **t** Break in the time series. **u** Population aged 15 years and over. **v** Users in the last 3 months. **w** From 2011 onwards, data include Monaco, and the five overseas departments and exclude New Caledonia, French Polynesia, St. Barthélemy, St. Martin, St. Pierre and Miquelon, and Wallis and Futuna. **x** Arrivals of non-resident visitors. **y** DAC member (OECD).

French Guiana

Region	South America	Population (000, 2022)	305[a,b]	
Surface area (km2)	83 534[c]	Pop. density (per km2, 2022)	3.7[a,b]	
Sex ratio (m per 100 f)	98.8[a,b]	Capital city	Cayenne	
National currency	Euro (EUR)	Capital city pop. (000, 2022)	57.5[d]	
Exchange rate (per US$)	0.9[e]			

Economic indicators	2010	2015	2022
Employment in industry (% of employed)[f,g]	14.1	14.9[h]	...
Employment in services & other sectors (% employed)[f,g]	51.5	58.3[h]	...
Unemployment rate (% of labour force)[f]	21.0	21.3[i,j]	...
Labour force participation rate (female/male pop. %)	43.2 / 54.9[f]	48.4 / 58.8[f,i,j]	... / ...
CPI: Consumer Price Index (2010=100)[k]	100	105	108[l,c]

Social indicators	2010	2015	2022
Population growth rate (average annual %)[b]	2.2	2.2	2.5[a]
Urban population (% of total population)	82.9	84.5	85.6[m]
Urban population growth rate (average annual %)[n]	3.2	3.1	...
Fertility rate, total (live births per woman)[b]	3.5	3.5	3.5[a]
Life expectancy at birth (females/males, years)[b]	79.1 / 72.8	79.6 / 74.1	80.3 / 74.8[a]
Population age distribution (0-14/60+ years old, %)[b]	35.2 / 6.2	33.7 / 7.6	32.1 / 9.4[a]
International migrant stock (000/% of total pop.)[o]	96.3 / 41.3	106.1 / 40.7	119.2 / 39.9[c]
Infant mortality rate (per 1 000 live births)[b]	9.7	8.9	7.6[a]
Intentional homicide rate (per 100 000 pop.)	13.2[p]	...	...

Environment and infrastructure indicators	2010	2015	2022
Individuals using the Internet (per 100 inhabitants)	25.7[q,p]	...	...
Threatened species (number)	56	67	118
Forested area (% of land area)	97.1[q]	96.8	96.7[q,m]
Energy production, primary (Petajoules)	3[r]	...	...
Tourist/visitor arrivals at national borders (000)[s]	83[p]	87	111[t]
Important sites for terrestrial biodiversity protected (%)	81.0	81.3	83.1[e]

a Projected estimate (medium fertility variant). b For statistical purposes, the data for France do not include this area. c 2020. d 2018. e 2021. f Excluding the institutional population. g Population aged 15 to 64 years. h 2012. i Break in the time series. j 2013. k Calculated by the UNSD from national indices. l Average for 6 months excluding data for April to September. m 2019. n Data refers to a 5-year period preceding the reference year. o Including refugees. p 2009. q Estimate. r Data after 2010 are included in France. s Survey at Cayenne-Rochambeau airport on departure. t 2017.

French Polynesia

Region	Polynesia	Population (000, 2022)	306[a,b]
Surface area (km2)	3 687[c,d]	Pop. density (per km2, 2022)	83.1[a,b]
Sex ratio (m per 100 f)	102.2[a,b]	Capital city	Papeete
National currency	CFP Franc (XPF)[e]	Capital city pop. (000, 2022)	136.0[f,g]
Exchange rate (per US$)	105.4[h]		

Economic indicators

	2010	2015	2022
GDP: Gross domestic product (million current US$)	6 081	5 324	5 817[d]
GDP growth rate (annual %, const. 2015 prices)	- 2.5	1.8	- 7.6[d]
GDP per capita (current US$)	22 820.8	19 491.9	20 707.5[d]
Economy: Agriculture (% of Gross Value Added)[i]	2.5	3.6	3.5[d]
Economy: Industry (% of Gross Value Added)[i]	12.3	12.0	11.7[d]
Economy: Services and other activity (% of GVA)[i]	85.2	84.4	84.8[d]
Employment in agriculture (% of employed)[i]	8.7	7.7	6.8[d]
Employment in industry (% of employed)[i]	16.4	15.1	14.6[d]
Employment in services & other sectors (% employed)[i]	74.9	77.1	78.6[d]
Unemployment rate (% of labour force)[i]	12.2	12.2	14.2
Labour force participation rate (female/male pop. %)[i]	48.3 / 63.9	49.2 / 63.3	48.2 / 62.1
CPI: Consumer Price Index (2010=100)	...	122[k,l]	...
Agricultural production index (2014-2016=100)	97	102	103[d]
International trade: exports (million current US$)	153	130	157[j,h]
International trade: imports (million current US$)	1 726	1 527	2 092[j,h]
International trade: balance (million current US$)	- 1 573	- 1 397	- 1 936[h]
Balance of payments, current account (million US$)	- 18	291	412[m]

Major trading partners

							2021
Export partners (% of exports)[j]	France	29.7	United States	19.8	Japan		13.7
Import partners (% of imports)[j]	France	25.9	China	13.7	United States		9.6

Social indicators

	2010	2015	2022
Population growth rate (average annual %)[b]	0.5	0.6	0.9[a]
Urban population (% of total population)	60.3	61.7	61.9[n]
Urban population growth rate (average annual %)[o]	2.0	1.2	...
Fertility rate, total (live births per woman)[b]	2.2	1.9	1.7[a]
Life expectancy at birth (females/males, years)[b]	83.8 / 78.6	85.1 / 80.0	86.0 / 81.3[a]
Population age distribution (0-14/60+ years old, %)[b]	25.7 / 9.5	24.1 / 11.3	21.3 / 15.2[a]
International migrant stock (000/% of total pop.)[p]	31.6 / 11.9	30.1 / 11.0	30.1 / 10.7[d]
Infant mortality rate (per 1 000 live births)[b]	7.4	6.3	5.4[a]
Intentional homicide rate (per 100 000 pop.)	0.4[q]	...	...

Environment and infrastructure indicators

	2010	2015	2022
Individuals using the Internet (per 100 inhabitants)	49.0	64.6[j]	72.7[j,r]
Threatened species (number)	160	175	196
Forested area (% of land area)[i]	43.1	43.1	43.1[n]
Energy production, primary (Petajoules)	1	1	1[n]
Energy supply per capita (Gigajoules)	52	47	47[n]
Tourist/visitor arrivals at national borders (000)[s,t]	154	184	77[d]
Important sites for terrestrial biodiversity protected (%)	0.0	0.0	0.0[h]

a Projected estimate (medium fertility variant). **b** For statistical purposes, the data for France do not include this area. **c** Including water bodies of lake Vaihiria, lake Temae and the Maiao lagoons, but not lake Maeva and the lagoons of Raiatea and Tahaa from the upper islands. No lagoons from lower islands are included. **d** 2020. **e** Communauté financière du Pacifique (CFP) Franc. **f** Refers to the total population in the communes of Arue, Faaa, Mahina, Papara, Papeete, Pirae and Punaauia. **g** 2018. **h** 2021. **i** Data classified according to ISIC Rev. 4. **j** Estimate. **k** Base: 2000=100. **l** 2014. **m** 2016. **n** 2019. **o** Data refers to a 5-year period preceding the reference year. **p** Including refugees. **q** 2009. **r** 2017. **s** Arrivals by air. **t** Excluding nationals residing abroad.

Gabon

Region	Middle Africa	UN membership date	20 September 1960
Population (000, 2022)	2 389[a]	Surface area (km2)	267 668[b]
Pop. density (per km2, 2022)	9.3[a]	Sex ratio (m per 100 f)	103.6[a]
Capital city	Libreville	National currency	CFA Franc, BEAC (XAF)[c]
Capital city pop. (000, 2022)	823.9[d]	Exchange rate (per US$)	579.2[e]

Economic indicators

	2010	2015	2022
GDP: Gross domestic product (million current US$)	14 359	14 372	15 111[b]
GDP growth rate (annual %, const. 2015 prices)	7.1	3.9	- 0.8[b]
GDP per capita (current US$)	8 840.8	7 379.2	6 789.4[b]
Economy: Agriculture (% of Gross Value Added)[f]	4.2	4.7	7.0[b]
Economy: Industry (% of Gross Value Added)[f]	59.6	51.9	41.3[b]
Economy: Services and other activity (% of GVA)[f]	36.2	43.4	51.7[b]
Employment in agriculture (% of employed)[g]	37.2	34.9	32.4[b]
Employment in industry (% of employed)[g]	10.2	10.6	10.8[b]
Employment in services & other sectors (% employed)[g]	52.6	54.5	56.9[b]
Unemployment rate (% of labour force)	20.4	20.6[g]	21.8[g]
Labour force participation rate (female/male pop. %)	39.6 / 57.7	40.0 / 56.5[g]	39.4 / 57.2[g]
CPI: Consumer Price Index (2010=100)[g,h]	100	109	124[b]
Agricultural production index (2014-2016=100)	88	100	103[b]
International trade: exports (million current US$)[g]	8 539	5 677	5 237[e]
International trade: imports (million current US$)[g]	2 969	2 938	2 306[e]
International trade: balance (million current US$)	5 570[g]	2 739[g]	2 931[e]
Balance of payments, current account (million US$)	2 453	141	...

Major trading partners

						2021
Export partners (% of exports)[g]	China	40.0	India	15.4	Indonesia	4.8
Import partners (% of imports)[g]	France	18.8	China	17.3	Congo	12.2

Social indicators

	2010	2015	2022
Population growth rate (average annual %)	3.5	2.9	2.0[a]
Urban population (% of total population)	85.5	88.1	89.7[d]
Urban population growth rate (average annual %)[i]	3.9	3.9	
Fertility rate, total (live births per woman)	4.2	3.9	3.5[a]
Life expectancy at birth (females/males, years)	65.8 / 62.1	67.8 / 63.4	68.4 / 63.4[a]
Population age distribution (0-14/60+ years old, %)	37.4 / 6.1	36.7 / 5.9	36.3 / 6.0[a]
International migrant stock (000/% of total pop.)[j,k]	270.8 / 16.7	378.7 / 19.4	416.7 / 18.7[b]
Refugees and others of concern to the UNHCR (000)	13.2[l]	2.9	0.4[e]
Infant mortality rate (per 1 000 live births)	42.4	35.6	29.5[a]
Health: Current expenditure (% of GDP)	2.5	2.7	2.8[d]
Health: Physicians (per 1 000 pop.)	0.1[m]	...	0.6[n]
Education: Government expenditure (% of GDP)	3.1	2.9	2.8[g,d]
Education: Primary gross enrol. ratio (f/m per 100 pop.)	... / ...	137.7 / 142.1[o]	... / ...
Seats held by women in the National Parliament (%)	14.7	14.2	15.4[p]

Environment and infrastructure indicators

	2010	2015	2022
Individuals using the Internet (per 100 inhabitants)[g]	13.0	45.8	62.0[b]
Research & Development expenditure (% of GDP)	0.6[q]	...	...
Threatened species (number)	204	231	599
Forested area (% of land area)	91.8	91.6	91.4[d]
CO2 emission estimates (million tons/tons per capita)	3.3 / 1.6	3.9 / 1.7	3.1 / 1.1[d]
Energy production, primary (Petajoules)	589	561	535[d]
Energy supply per capita (Gigajoules)	57	57	48[d]
Tourist/visitor arrivals at national borders (000)	269[r,s]	...	...
Important sites for terrestrial biodiversity protected (%)	61.2	61.2	61.7[e]
Net Official Development Assist. received (% of GNI)	0.05	0.75	0.37[b]

a Projected estimate (medium fertility variant). b 2020. c African Financial Community (CFA) Franc, Bank of Central African States (BEAC). d 2019. e 2021. f Data classified according to ISIC Rev. 4. g Estimate. h Libreville and Owendo. i Data refers to a 5-year period preceding the reference year. j Including refugees. k Refers to foreign citizens. l Data as at the end of December. m 2008. n 2018. o 2011. p Data are as at 1 January of reporting year. q 2009. r Arrivals by air only. s 2005.

Gambia

Region	Western Africa	UN membership date	21 September 1965
Population (000, 2022)	2 706[a]	Surface area (km2)	11 295[b]
Pop. density (per km2, 2022)	267.4[a]	Sex ratio (m per 100 f)	99.0[a]
Capital city	Banjul	National currency	Dalasi (GMD)
Capital city pop. (000, 2022)	443.4[c,d]	Exchange rate (per US$)	52.6[e]

Economic indicators

	2010	2015	2022
GDP: Gross domestic product (million current US$)	1 543	1 378	1 830[b]
GDP growth rate (annual %, const. 2015 prices)	5.9	4.1	- 6.2[b]
GDP per capita (current US$)	860.6	660.7	757.4[b]
Economy: Agriculture (% of Gross Value Added)[f,g]	37.4	24.3	22.8[b]
Economy: Industry (% of Gross Value Added)[f,h]	10.4	18.8	20.6[b]
Economy: Services and other activity (% of GVA)[f,i]	52.2	56.9	56.6[b]
Employment in agriculture (% of employed)[j]	31.0	29.2	26.6[b]
Employment in industry (% of employed)[j]	16.4	15.8	15.8[b]
Employment in services & other sectors (% employed)[j]	52.6	54.9	57.7[b]
Unemployment rate (% of labour force)[j]	9.4	9.5	11.0
Labour force participation rate (female/male pop. %)[j]	49.6 / 68.4	50.3 / 67.8	49.9 / 66.8
CPI: Consumer Price Index (2010=100)[k]	100	131	196[e]
Agricultural production index (2014-2016=100)	138	106	101[b]
International trade: exports (million current US$)	68	83	29[j,e]
International trade: imports (million current US$)	284	391	672[j,e]
International trade: balance (million current US$)	- 215	- 308	- 643[e]
Balance of payments, current account (million US$)	18	- 54	- 94[e]

Major trading partners

							2021
Export partners (% of exports)[j]	Senegal	50.5	Mali	25.4	Guinea-Bissau	9.1
Import partners (% of imports)[j]	Norway	13.6	China	10.4	Ivory Coast	9.2

Social indicators

	2010	2015	2022
Population growth rate (average annual %)	3.1	2.8	2.4[a]
Urban population (% of total population)	55.7	59.2	61.9[d]
Urban population growth rate (average annual %)[l]	4.5	4.4	...
Fertility rate, total (live births per woman)	5.7	5.3	4.6[a]
Life expectancy at birth (females/males, years)	61.6 / 59.8	63.6 / 61.4	64.3 / 61.5[a]
Population age distribution (0-14/60+ years old, %)	45.7 / 4.2	45.4 / 3.8	43.1 / 4.0[a]
International migrant stock (000/% of total pop.)[m]	185.8 / 10.4	192.5 / 9.2	215.7 / 8.9[b]
Refugees and others of concern to the UNHCR (000)	8.5[n]	11.8	4.6[e]
Infant mortality rate (per 1 000 live births)	43.9	36.9	28.0[a]
Health: Current expenditure (% of GDP)	5.1	3.2	3.8[d]
Health: Physicians (per 1 000 pop.)	0.1[o]	0.1	0.1[b]
Education: Government expenditure (% of GDP)	2.6	2.2	2.9[i,d]
Education: Primary gross enrol. ratio (f/m per 100 pop.)	80.8 / 78.8	93.0 / 87.1	109.4 / 97.8[b]
Education: Sec. gross enrol. ratio (f/m per 100 pop.)	49.1 / 51.2[j]	... / ...	... / ...
Education: Upr. Sec. gross enrol. ratio (f/m per 100 pop.)	38.2 / 44.1[j]	... / ...	... / ...
Seats held by women in the National Parliament (%)	7.5	9.4	10.3[p]

Environment and infrastructure indicators

	2010	2015	2022
Individuals using the Internet (per 100 inhabitants)	9.2	18.2[i]	36.5[i,b]
Research & Development expenditure (% of GDP)	~0.0[q,r]	0.1[s,t]	0.1[q,u,v,w,x]
Threatened species (number)	43	55	125
Forested area (% of land area)	29.6	26.8[i]	24.5[i,d]
Energy production, primary (Petajoules)	6	7	7[d]
Energy supply per capita (Gigajoules)	7	7	7[i,d]
Tourist/visitor arrivals at national borders (000)[z]	91[y]	449	246[b]
Important sites for terrestrial biodiversity protected (%)	41.7	41.7	41.7[e]
Pop. using safely managed drinking water (urban/rural, %)	55.9 / 5.9	61.8 / 6.7	66.9 / 7.6[b]
Pop. using safely managed sanitation (urban/rural %)	30.0 / 41.0	31.5 / 32.7	31.8 / 24.2[b]
Net Official Development Assist. received (% of GNI)	8.00	8.47	16.09[b]

a Projected estimate (medium fertility variant). b 2020. c Refers to the local government areas of Banjul and Kanifing. d 2019. e 2021. f Data classified according to ISIC Rev. 4. g Excludes irrigation canals and landscaping care. h Excludes publishing activities. Includes irrigation and canals. i Includes publishing activities and landscape care. Excludes repair of personal and household goods. j Estimate. k Banjul, Kombo St. Mary I. Data refers to a 5-year period preceding the reference year. m Including refugees. n Data as at the end of December. o 2008. p Data are as at 1 January of reporting year. q Partial data. r 2009. s Overestimated or based on overestimated data. t 2011. u Excluding private non-profit. v Excluding Higher Education. w Break in the time series. x 2018. y Arrivals by air only. z Including nationals residing abroad.

Georgia

Region	Western Asia	UN membership date	31 July 1992	
Population (000, 2022)	3 744 [a,b]	Surface area (km2)	69 700 [c]	
Pop. density (per km2, 2022)	53.9 [a,b]	Sex ratio (m per 100 f)	88.7 [a,b]	
Capital city	Tbilisi	National currency	Lari (GEL)	
Capital city pop. (000, 2022)	1 077.3 [d]	Exchange rate (per US$)	3.1 [e]	

Economic indicators	2010	2015	2022
GDP: Gross domestic product (million current US$)	12 243	14 954	15 892 [c]
GDP growth rate (annual %, const. 2015 prices)	6.2	3.0	- 6.2 [c]
GDP per capita (current US$)	2 986.8	3 716.0	3 983.7 [c]
Economy: Agriculture (% of Gross Value Added) [f,g]	9.6	8.8	8.4 [c]
Economy: Industry (% of Gross Value Added) [f,h]	19.1	21.5	24.7 [c]
Economy: Services and other activity (% of GVA) [f,i]	71.4	69.7	66.9 [c]
Employment in agriculture (% of employed)	48.1	44.0	41.3 [i,c]
Employment in industry (% of employed)	10.6	11.0	14.2 [i,c]
Employment in services & other sectors (% employed)	41.3	44.9	44.5 [i,c]
Unemployment rate (% of labour force)	20.2	16.5	11.8 [i]
Labour force participation rate (female/male pop. %)	55.7 / 76.8	58.9 / 80.1	52.8 / 69.7 [i]
CPI: Consumer Price Index (2010=100) [k]	100	115	154 [e]
Agricultural production index (2014-2016=100)	89	102	116 [c]
International trade: exports (million current US$)	1 677	2 205	4 242 [e]
International trade: imports (million current US$)	5 236	7 281	10 105 [e]
International trade: balance (million current US$)	- 3 558	- 5 077	- 5 862 [e]
Balance of payments, current account (million US$)	- 1 199	- 1 767	- 1 966 [c]

Major trading partners						2021
Export partners (% of exports)	China	14.5	Russian Federation	14.4	Azerbaijan	12.5
Import partners (% of imports)	Türkiye	18.1	Russian Federation	10.1	China	8.6

Social indicators	2010	2015	2022
Population growth rate (average annual %) [b]	- 0.4	--0.0	- 0.5 [a]
Urban population (% of total population) [b]	55.5	57.4	59.0 [d]
Urban population growth rate (average annual %) [b,l]	- 0.5	- 0.7	...
Fertility rate, total (live births per woman) [b]	1.9	2.2	2.1 [a]
Life expectancy at birth (females/males, years) [b]	76.6 / 67.6	78.1 / 68.5	76.5 / 66.8 [a]
Population age distribution (0-14/60+ years old, %) [b]	18.7 / 17.8	19.4 / 19.5	21.3 / 21.0 [a]
International migrant stock (000/% of total pop.) [b,m]	73.1 / 1.8	76.7 / 1.9	79.4 / 2.0 [c]
Refugees and others of concern to the UNHCR (000)	362.2 [n]	268.3	292.8 [e]
Infant mortality rate (per 1 000 live births) [b]	12.7	9.5	8.2 [a]
Health: Current expenditure (% of GDP)	9.1	7.4	6.7 [d]
Health: Physicians (per 1 000 pop.)	4.4	5.0	5.1 [c]
Education: Government expenditure (% of GDP)	2.8	3.2	3.8 [c]
Education: Primary gross enrol. ratio (f/m per 100 pop.)	104.1 / 102.7	102.8 / 102.7	99.7 / 99.2 [c]
Education: Sec. gross enrol. ratio (f/m per 100 pop.)	100.9 / 97.8 [o]	100.8 / 98.1	103.1 / 102.1 [c]
Education: Upr. Sec. gross enrol. ratio (f/m per 100 pop.)	104.6 / 100.4 [o]	97.6 / 92.9	105.3 / 104.7 [c]
Intentional homicide rate (per 100 000 pop.)	4.6	...	1.9 [d]
Seats held by women in the National Parliament (%)	5.1	11.3	19.1 [p]

Environment and infrastructure indicators	2010	2015	2022
Individuals using the Internet (per 100 inhabitants)	26.9	47.6 [q]	72.5 [c]
Research & Development expenditure (% of GDP)	0.2 [r]	0.3 [s,t,u]	0.3 [s,t,u,c]
Threatened species (number)	46	114	127
Forested area (% of land area)	40.6 [j]	40.6	40.6 [d]
CO2 emission estimates (million tons/tons per capita)	5.2 / 1.3	8.8 / 2.3	9.0 / 2.3 [c]
Energy production, primary (Petajoules)	58	55	46 [d]
Energy supply per capita (Gigajoules)	34	49	54 [d]
Tourist/visitor arrivals at national borders (000)	1 067	3 012	1 087 [c]
Important sites for terrestrial biodiversity protected (%)	34.4	40.3	40.3 [e]
Pop. using safely managed drinking water (urban/rural, %)	83.9 / 39.4	84.0 / 39.9	84.1 / 40.3 [c]
Pop. using safely managed sanitation (urban/rural %)	33.1 / 50.6	29.6 / 47.5	27.6 / 44.5 [c]
Net Official Development Assist. received (% of GNI)	4.90	3.07	6.88 [c]

a Projected estimate (medium fertility variant). b Including Abkhazia and South Ossetia. c 2020. d 2019. e 2021. f Data classified according to ISIC Rev. 4. g Excludes irrigation canals and landscaping care. h Excludes publishing activities. Includes irrigation and canals. i Includes publishing activities and landscape care. Excludes repair of personal and household goods. j Estimate. k Data refer to 5 cities only. l Data refers to a 5-year period preceding the reference year. m Including refugees. n Data as at the end of December. o 2008. p Data are as at 1 January of reporting year. q Population aged 6 years and over. r 2005. s Excluding private non-profit. t Excluding business enterprise. u Partial data.

Germany

Region	Western Europe	UN membership date	18 September 1973
Population (000, 2022)	83 370[a]	Surface area (km2)	357 581[b]
Pop. density (per km2, 2022)	239.2[a]	Sex ratio (m per 100 f)	97.4[a]
Capital city	Berlin	National currency	Euro (EUR)
Capital city pop. (000, 2022)	3 556.8[c]	Exchange rate (per US$)	0.9[d]

Economic indicators

	2010	2015	2022
GDP: Gross domestic product (million current US$)	3 396 354	3 356 236	3 846 414[b]
GDP growth rate (annual %, const. 2015 prices)	4.2	1.5	- 4.6[b]
GDP per capita (current US$)	42 020.0	41 036.1	45 908.7[b]
Economy: Agriculture (% of Gross Value Added)[e,f]	0.9	0.8	0.8[b]
Economy: Industry (% of Gross Value Added)[e,g]	29.9	30.1	29.2[b]
Economy: Services and other activity (% of GVA)[e,h]	69.2	69.1	69.9[b]
Employment in agriculture (% of employed)	1.6	1.4	1.2[i,b]
Employment in industry (% of employed)	28.3	27.7	26.8[i,b]
Employment in services & other sectors (% employed)	70.0	70.9	72.1[i,b]
Unemployment rate (% of labour force)	7.0	4.6	3.2[i]
Labour force participation rate (female/male pop. %)	53.0 / 66.0	54.7 / 65.9	57.0 / 66.1[i]
CPI: Consumer Price Index (2010=100)	100	107	109[i,d]
Agricultural production index (2014-2016=100)	95	99	95[b]
International trade: exports (million current US$)	1 267 743	1 328 500	1 630 918[d]
International trade: imports (million current US$)	1 060 672	1 057 536	1 422 819[d]
International trade: balance (million current US$)	207 071	270 964	208 099[d]
Balance of payments, current account (million US$)	196 172	288 621	314 087[d]

Major trading partners

						2021
Export partners (% of exports)	United States	8.9	China	7.6	France	7.4
Import partners (% of imports)	China	11.9	Netherlands	7.6	United States	6.1

Social indicators

	2010	2015	2022
Population growth rate (average annual %)	0.1	0.3	- 0.1[a]
Urban population (% of total population)	77.0	77.2	77.4[c]
Urban population growth rate (average annual %)[k]	0.1	0.3	...
Fertility rate, total (live births per woman)	1.4	1.5	1.5[a]
Life expectancy at birth (females/males, years)	82.6 / 77.4	83.0 / 78.1	83.5 / 78.5[a]
Population age distribution (0-14/60+ years old, %)	13.6 / 25.9	13.2 / 27.3	14.0 / 29.7[a]
International migrant stock (000/% of total pop.)	9 812.3 / 12.1	10 220.4 / 12.5	15 762.5 / 18.8[b]
Refugees and others of concern to the UNHCR (000)	670.6[l]	573.8	1 482.5[d]
Infant mortality rate (per 1 000 live births)	3.5	3.3	3.0[a]
Health: Current expenditure (% of GDP)	11.1	11.2	11.7[c]
Health: Physicians (per 1 000 pop.)	3.8	4.1	4.4[b]
Education: Government expenditure (% of GDP)	4.9	4.9	5.0[m]
Education: Primary gross enrol. ratio (f/m per 100 pop.)	102.7 / 103.3	101.6 / 101.7	103.0 / 102.1[c]
Education: Sec. gross enrol. ratio (f/m per 100 pop.)	101.2 / 106.7	96.4 / 101.1	94.8 / 100.1[c]
Education: Upr. Sec. gross enrol. ratio (f/m per 100 pop.)	100.8 / 113.9	96.0 / 106.7	90.2 / 103.0[c]
Intentional homicide rate (per 100 000 pop.)	1.0	0.8	0.9[b]
Seats held by women in the National Parliament (%)	32.8	36.5	34.9[n]

Environment and infrastructure indicators

	2010	2015	2022
Individuals using the Internet (per 100 inhabitants)	82.0[o]	87.6[o]	89.8[b]
Research & Development expenditure (% of GDP)	2.7	2.9	3.1[p,b]
Threatened species (number)	79	107	251
Forested area (% of land area)	32.7	32.7	32.7[c]
CO2 emission estimates (million tons/tons per capita)	769.6 / 9.5	739.9 / 8.9	594.7 / 7.0[b]
Energy production, primary (Petajoules)	5 490	5 016	4 362[c]
Energy supply per capita (Gigajoules)	171	158	147[c]
Tourist/visitor arrivals at national borders (000)[q]	26 875	34 970	12 449[b]
Important sites for terrestrial biodiversity protected (%)	77.9	78.5	79.1[d]
Pop. using safely managed sanitation (urban/rural %)	98.1 / 91.1	98.5 / 91.4	98.7 / 91.6[b]
Net Official Development Assist. disbursed (% of GNI)[r]	1.24	1.39	1.14[b]

a Projected estimate (medium fertility variant). b 2020. c 2019. d 2021. e Data classified according to ISIC Rev. 4. f Excludes irrigation canals and landscaping care. g Excludes publishing activities. Includes irrigation and canals. h Includes publishing activities and landscape care. Excludes repair of personal and household goods. i Estimate. j Index base: 2015=100. k Data refers to a 5-year period preceding the reference year. l Data as at the end of December. m 2018. n Data are as at 1 January of reporting year. o Population aged 16 to 74 years. p Provisional data. q Non-resident tourists staying in all types of accommodation establishments. r DAC member (OECD).

Ghana

Region	Western Africa	UN membership date	08 March 1957	
Population (000, 2022)	33 476[a]	Surface area (km2)	238 537[b]	
Pop. density (per km2, 2022)	147.1[a]	Sex ratio (m per 100 f)	99.5[a]	
Capital city	Accra	National currency	Ghana Cedi (GHS)	
Capital city pop. (000, 2022)	2 475.2[c]	Exchange rate (per US$)	6.0[d]	

Economic indicators

	2010	2015	2022
GDP: Gross domestic product (million current US$)	42 587	50 034	68 532[b]
GDP growth rate (annual %, const. 2015 prices)	7.9	2.1	0.4[b]
GDP per capita (current US$)	1 718.6	1 796.5	2 205.5[b]
Economy: Agriculture (% of Gross Value Added)[e,f]	28.9	21.8	20.5[b]
Economy: Industry (% of Gross Value Added)[e,g]	28.2	34.0	31.6[b]
Economy: Services and other activity (% of GVA)[e,h]	43.0	44.2	47.9[b]
Employment in agriculture (% of employed)	50.2[i]	35.2	28.5[i,b]
Employment in industry (% of employed)	13.7[i]	18.7	22.2[i,b]
Employment in services & other sectors (% employed)	36.1[i]	46.1	49.4[i,b]
Unemployment rate (% of labour force)	5.4	6.8	4.5[i]
Labour force participation rate (female/male pop. %)	67.6 / 74.5[i]	65.0 / 73.5	64.7 / 72.3[i]
CPI: Consumer Price Index (2010=100)	100	183	336[d]
Agricultural production index (2014-2016=100)	84	100	116[b]
International trade: exports (million current US$)[j]	5 233	13 756	19 500[i,d]
International trade: imports (million current US$)[j]	8 057	14 687	14 234[i,d]
International trade: balance (million current US$)[j]	- 2 824	- 932	5 266[d]
Balance of payments, current account (million US$)	- 2 747	- 2 824	- 2 134[b]

Major trading partners

							2021
Export partners (% of exports)[i]	China	16.7	Switzerland	14.7	India	14.2	
Import partners (% of imports)[i]	China	18.2	United States	9.4	United Kingdom	6.6	

Social indicators

	2010	2015	2022
Population growth rate (average annual %)	2.4	2.3	1.9[a]
Urban population (% of total population)	50.7	54.1	56.7[c]
Urban population growth rate (average annual %)[k]	4.0	3.6	...
Fertility rate, total (live births per woman)	4.2	4.0	3.5[a]
Life expectancy at birth (females/males, years)	62.5 / 59.8	65.0 / 61.4	66.1 / 61.8[a]
Population age distribution (0-14/60+ years old, %)	39.2 / 4.8	38.9 / 5.0	36.9 / 5.9[a]
International migrant stock (000/% of total pop.)[l]	337.8 / 1.4	414.7 / 1.5	476.4 / 1.5[b]
Refugees and others of concern to the UNHCR (000)	14.8[m]	21.3	14.3[d]
Infant mortality rate (per 1 000 live births)	47.0	38.7	31.6[a]
Health: Current expenditure (% of GDP)	4.3	4.6	3.4[c]
Health: Physicians (per 1 000 pop.)	0.1	0.1	0.2[b]
Education: Government expenditure (% of GDP)	5.5	4.6[i]	4.0[i,n]
Education: Primary gross enrol. ratio (f/m per 100 pop.)	99.5 / 101.1[o]	108.3 / 108.4	104.4 / 102.6[b]
Education: Sec. gross enrol. ratio (f/m per 100 pop.)	45.7 / 51.7[o]	66.1 / 69.6	77.8 / 77.5[b]
Education: Upr. Sec. gross enrol. ratio (f/m per 100 pop.)	23.6 / 29.0[o]	45.8 / 50.9	66.2 / 68.2[b]
Intentional homicide rate (per 100 000 pop.)	1.7	1.9	2.1[p]
Seats held by women in the National Parliament (%)	8.3	10.9	14.6[q]

Environment and infrastructure indicators

	2010	2015	2022
Individuals using the Internet (per 100 inhabitants)	7.8[r,s]	23.0[i]	58.0[i,b]
Research & Development expenditure (% of GDP)	0.4[s]	...	...
Threatened species (number)	202	223	294
Forested area (% of land area)	34.9	34.6[i]	35.1[i,c]
CO2 emission estimates (million tons/tons per capita)	11.1 / 0.4	15.0 / 0.5	20.6 / 0.6[b]
Energy production, primary (Petajoules)	168	424	686[c]
Energy supply per capita (Gigajoules)	12	14	15[c]
Tourist/visitor arrivals at national borders (000)[t]	931	897	...
Important sites for terrestrial biodiversity protected (%)	68.9	68.9	68.9[d]
Pop. using safely managed drinking water (urban/rural, %)	43.9 / 6.3	51.9 / 10.9	60.3 / 16.1[b]
Pop. using safely managed sanitation (urban/rural %)	9.4 / 7.8	10.8 / 11.2	12.1 / 15.0[b]
Net Official Development Assist. received (% of GNI)	5.36	3.69	3.11[b]

a Projected estimate (medium fertility variant). **b** 2020. **c** 2019. **d** 2021. **e** Data classified according to ISIC Rev. 4. **f** Excludes irrigation canals and landscaping care. **g** Excludes publishing activities. Includes irrigation and canals. **h** Includes publishing activities and landscape care. Excludes repair of personal and household goods. **i** Estimate. **j** Since 2011, Ghana have been exporting crude petroleum & natural gas in relatively larger quantities. **k** Data refers to a 5-year period preceding the reference year. **l** Including refugees. **m** Data as at the end of December. **n** 2018. **o** 2009. **p** 2017. **q** Data are as at 1 January of reporting year. **r** Population aged 12 years and over. **s** Break in the time series. **t** Including nationals residing abroad.

Gibraltar

Region	Southern Europe	Population (000, 2022)	33 [a,b]
Surface area (km2)	6 [c]	Pop. density (per km2, 2022)	3 264.9 [a,b]
Sex ratio (m per 100 f)	99.8 [a,b]	Capital city	Gibraltar
National currency	Gibraltar Pound (GIP)	Capital city pop. (000, 2022)	34.7 [d]
Exchange rate (per US$)	0.7 [e]		

Economic indicators	2010	2015	2022
CPI: Consumer Price Index (2010=100)	...	142 [f,g]	...
International trade: exports (million current US$) [h]	259	295	156 [e]
International trade: imports (million current US$) [h]	627	815	8 449 [e]
International trade: balance (million current US$)	- 368 [h]	- 520 [h]	- 8 293 [e]

Major trading partners						2021
Export partners (% of exports) [h]	Netherlands	27.2	Poland	17.3	Spain	7.8
Import partners (% of imports) [h]	Spain	13.5	Italy	13.3	Russian Federation	10.1

Social indicators	2010	2015	2022
Population growth rate (average annual %) [b]	1.4	0.2	0.1 [a]
Urban population (% of total population)	100.0	100.0	100.0 [i]
Urban population growth rate (average annual %) [j]	0.7	0.6	...
Fertility rate, total (live births per woman) [b]	1.8	2.2	1.8 [a]
Life expectancy at birth (females/males, years) [b]	84.1 / 77.8	84.2 / 76.9	84.7 / 80.9 [a]
Population age distribution (0-14/60+ years old, %) [b]	18.1 / 22.0	17.8 / 23.7	17.0 / 27.2 [a]
International migrant stock (000/% of total pop.)	10.4 / 30.9	11.1 / 32.8	11.2 / 33.2 [c]
Infant mortality rate (per 1 000 live births) [b]	10.9	11.4	8.9 [a]
Education: Primary gross enrol. ratio (f/m per 100 pop.)	112.8 / 110.9 [k]	... / ...	113.7 / 104.0 [c]
Education: Sec. gross enrol. ratio (f/m per 100 pop.)	83.2 / 85.2 [k]	... / ...	94.6 / 96.8 [c]
Education: Upr. Sec. gross enrol. ratio (f/m per 100 pop.)	79.8 / 83.7 [k]	... / ...	97.4 / 99.8 [c]
Intentional homicide rate (per 100 000 pop.)	3.0	...	...

Environment and infrastructure indicators	2010	2015	2022
Individuals using the Internet (per 100 inhabitants)	65.0	65.0 [h,l]	94.4 [h,m]
Threatened species (number)	22	26	59
Forested area (% of land area) [h]	0.0	0.0	0.0 [i]
CO2 emission estimates (million tons/tons per capita)	0.5 / 13.9	0.6 / 17.3	0.7 / 21.1 [i]
Energy production, primary (Petajoules)	...	...	0 [h,i]
Energy supply per capita (Gigajoules)	218	264	332 [i]
Important sites for terrestrial biodiversity protected (%)	0.0	0.0	0.0 [e]
Pop. using safely managed drinking water (urban/rural, %)	100.0 / ...	100.0 / ...	100.0 / ... [c]

a Projected estimate (medium fertility variant). b For statistical purposes, the data for United Kingdom do not include this area. c 2020. d 2018. e 2021. f Base: 2000=100. g 2014. h Estimate. i 2019. j Data refers to a 5-year period preceding the reference year. k 2009. l 2012. m 2016.

Greece

Region	Southern Europe	UN membership date	25 October 1945
Population (000, 2022)	10 385[a]	Surface area (km2)	131 957[b]
Pop. density (per km2, 2022)	79.4[a]	Sex ratio (m per 100 f)	95.8[a]
Capital city	Athens	National currency	Euro (EUR)
Capital city pop. (000, 2022)	3 154.2[c,d]	Exchange rate (per US$)	0.9[e]

Economic indicators

	2010	2015	2022
GDP: Gross domestic product (million current US$)	296 835	195 605	188 835[b]
GDP growth rate (annual %, const. 2015 prices)	- 5.5	- 0.2	- 9.0[b]
GDP per capita (current US$)	27 263.5	18 349.9	18 117.1[b]
Economy: Agriculture (% of Gross Value Added)[f,g]	3.4	4.4	4.8[b]
Economy: Industry (% of Gross Value Added)[f,h]	16.9	16.4	17.1[b]
Economy: Services and other activity (% of GVA)[f,i]	79.7	79.2	78.1[b]
Employment in agriculture (% of employed)	12.4	12.9	11.7[j,b]
Employment in industry (% of employed)	19.6	14.9	15.2[j,b]
Employment in services & other sectors (% employed)	68.0	72.2	73.1[j,b]
Unemployment rate (% of labour force)	12.7	24.9	14.8[j]
Labour force participation rate (female/male pop. %)	44.0 / 63.5	44.7 / 59.7	43.4 / 58.2[j]
CPI: Consumer Price Index (2010=100)[k]	100	101	102[e]
Agricultural production index (2014-2016=100)	102	104	100[b]
International trade: exports (million current US$)	27 586	28 289	47 206[e]
International trade: imports (million current US$)	66 453	47 264	75 984[e]
International trade: balance (million current US$)	- 38 867	- 18 975	- 28 778[e]
Balance of payments, current account (million US$)	- 30 263	- 1 611	- 12 694[e]

Major trading partners

							2021
Export partners (% of exports)	Italy	9.8	Germany	7.2	Cyprus	5.9
Import partners (% of imports)	Germany	10.6	Italy	8.0	China	7.8

Social indicators

	2010	2015	2022
Population growth rate (average annual %)	- 0.2	- 0.6	- 0.5[a]
Urban population (% of total population)	76.3	78.0	79.4[d]
Urban population growth rate (average annual %)[l]	0.7	0.1	...
Fertility rate, total (live births per woman)	1.4	1.3	1.4[a]
Life expectancy at birth (females/males, years)	83.4 / 77.7	83.6 / 77.9	83.3 / 78.0[a]
Population age distribution (0-14/60+ years old, %)	14.6 / 25.0	14.6 / 26.7	13.9 / 29.4[a]
International migrant stock (000/% of total pop.)	1 321.1 / 12.1	1 242.9 / 11.7	1 340.5 / 12.9[b]
Refugees and others of concern to the UNHCR (000)	57.4[m]	37.6	166.1[e]
Infant mortality rate (per 1 000 live births)	3.4	3.8	3.4[a]
Health: Current expenditure (% of GDP)	9.6	8.1[n]	7.8[d]
Health: Physicians (per 1 000 pop.)	5.9	6.0	6.3[d]
Education: Government expenditure (% of GDP)	4.0[o]	3.7	3.6[p]
Education: Primary gross enrol. ratio (f/m per 100 pop.)	97.4 / 99.6	99.1 / 100.0	100.2 / 99.7[d]
Education: Sec. gross enrol. ratio (f/m per 100 pop.)	104.4 / 108.1	98.4 / 105.8	105.2 / 110.8[d]
Education: Upr. Sec. gross enrol. ratio (f/m per 100 pop.)	106.2 / 107.6	99.4 / 109.1	110.3 / 117.6[d]
Intentional homicide rate (per 100 000 pop.)	1.6	0.9	0.7[b]
Seats held by women in the National Parliament (%)	17.3	23.0	21.0[q]

Environment and infrastructure indicators

	2010	2015	2022
Individuals using the Internet (per 100 inhabitants)	44.4[r]	66.8	78.1[b]
Research & Development expenditure (% of GDP)	0.6[j]	1.0	1.5[b]
Threatened species (number)	156	291	592
Forested area (% of land area)[j]	30.3	30.3	30.3[d]
CO2 emission estimates (million tons/tons per capita)	84.5 / 7.5	65.5 / 6.0	47.4 / 4.4[b]
Energy production, primary (Petajoules)	397	357	252[d]
Energy supply per capita (Gigajoules)	106	91	87[d]
Tourist/visitor arrivals at national borders (000)[s]	15 007	23 599	7 374[b]
Important sites for terrestrial biodiversity protected (%)	87.3	87.3	87.3[e]
Pop. using safely managed sanitation (urban/rural %)	90.7 / ...	94.0 / ...	97.3 / ...[b]
Net Official Development Assist. disbursed (% of GNI)[t]	0.26	- 0.04	0.24[b]

a Projected estimate (medium fertility variant). b 2020. c Refers to the localities of Calithèa, Peristérion and Piraeus, among others. d 2019. e 2021. f Data classified according to ISIC Rev. 4. g Excludes irrigation canals and landscaping care. h Excludes publishing activities. Includes irrigation and canals. i Includes publishing activities and landscape care. Excludes repair of personal and household goods. j Estimate. k Calculated by the UNSD from national indices. l Data refers to a 5-year period preceding the reference year. m Data as at the end of December. n Break in the time series. o 2005. p 2018. q Data are as at 1 January of reporting year. r Population aged 16 to 74 years. s Information is based on the border survey conducted by the Bank of Greece. t DAC member (OECD).

Greenland

Region	Northern America	Population (000, 2022)	56 [a,b]
Surface area (km2)	2 166 086 [c]	Pop. density (per km2, 2022)	0.1 [a,b]
Sex ratio (m per 100 f)	110.6 [a,b]	Capital city	Nuuk
National currency	Danish Krone (DKK)	Capital city pop. (000, 2022)	18.4 [d]
Exchange rate (per US$)	6.6 [e]		

Economic indicators

	2010	2015	2022
GDP: Gross domestic product (million current US$)	2 503	2 499	3 130 [c]
GDP growth rate (annual %, const. 2015 prices)	1.7	- 2.5	1.2 [c]
GDP per capita (current US$)	44 195.9	44 328.6	55 138.6 [c]
Economy: Agriculture (% of Gross Value Added) [f]	13.8	17.6	19.2 [c]
Economy: Industry (% of Gross Value Added) [g]	18.6	17.6	18.7 [c]
Economy: Services and other activity (% of GVA) [h]	67.6	64.9	62.1 [c]
Employment in agriculture (% of employed)	...	4.6 [i,j,k]	...
Employment in industry (% of employed)	...	12.6 [i,j,k]	...
Employment in services & other sectors (% employed)	...	82.5 [i,j,k]	...
Unemployment rate (% of labour force)	8.4 [l]	9.7 [i,m,n,o,p]	...
International trade: exports (million current US$)	389	406	954 [q,e]
International trade: imports (million current US$)	847	667	1 046 [q,e]
International trade: balance (million current US$)	- 458	- 261	- 92 [e]

Major trading partners

						2021
Export partners (% of exports) [q]	Denmark	52.6	China	17.3	Japan	5.3
Import partners (% of imports) [q]	Denmark	64.2	Sweden	14.0	Spain	11.9

Social indicators

	2010	2015	2022
Population growth rate (average annual %) [b]	- 0.1	0.1	0.4 [a]
Urban population (% of total population)	84.4	86.1	87.1 [r]
Urban population growth rate (average annual %) [s]	0.3	0.3	...
Fertility rate, total (live births per woman)	2.2	2.1	2.0 [a]
Life expectancy at birth (females/males, years) [b]	73.8 / 67.8	75.7 / 69.5	76.0 / 70.1 [a]
Population age distribution (0-14/60+ years old, %) [b]	22.4 / 10.9	21.1 / 12.8	20.9 / 16.9 [a]
International migrant stock (000/% of total pop.)	6.1 / 10.8	6.0 / 10.7	5.9 / 10.4 [c]
Infant mortality rate (per 1 000 live births) [b]	9.3	9.6	8.6 [a]
Education: Government expenditure (% of GDP) [q]	...	12.0	10.6 [d]
Intentional homicide rate (per 100 000 pop.)	19.4	7.1	5.3 [t]

Environment and infrastructure indicators

	2010	2015	2022
Individuals using the Internet (per 100 inhabitants)	63.0	67.6 [q]	69.5 [q,u]
Threatened species (number)	14	17	30
Forested area (% of land area)	~0.0	~0.0	~0.0 [r]
Energy production, primary (Petajoules)	1	2	2 [q,r]
Energy supply per capita (Gigajoules)	186	155	140 [q,r]
Important sites for terrestrial biodiversity protected (%)	26.3	29.7	29.7 [e]

a Projected estimate (medium fertility variant). b For statistical purposes, the data for Denmark do not include this area. c 2020. d 2018. e 2021. f Excludes irrigation canals and landscaping care. g Excludes publishing activities. Includes irrigation and canals. h Includes publishing activities and landscape care. Excludes repair of personal and household goods. i Nationals, residents. j Population aged 15 to 64 years. k 2011. l 2006. m Excluding the institutional population. n Population aged 18 to 64 years. o Break in the time series. p 2013. q Estimate. r 2019. s Data refers to a 5-year period preceding the reference year. t 2016. u 2017.

Grenada

Region	Caribbean	UN membership date	17 September 1974
Population (000, 2022)	125[a]	Surface area (km2)	345[b]
Pop. density (per km2, 2022)	368.9[a]	Sex ratio (m per 100 f)	100.0[a]
Capital city	Saint George's	National currency	E. Caribbean Dollar (XCD)[c]
Capital city pop. (000, 2022)	39.3[d,e]	Exchange rate (per US$)	2.7[f]

Economic indicators

	2010	2015	2022
GDP: Gross domestic product (million current US$)	771	997	1 043[b]
GDP growth rate (annual %, const. 2015 prices)	- 0.5	6.4	- 13.8[b]
GDP per capita (current US$)	7 257.8	9 096.9	9 272.9[b]
Economy: Agriculture (% of Gross Value Added)[g]	5.2	8.6	5.8[b]
Economy: Industry (% of Gross Value Added)[g]	16.8	14.2	15.4[b]
Economy: Services and other activity (% of GVA)[g]	78.1	77.2	78.8[b]
CPI: Consumer Price Index (2010=100)	100	104	109[f]
Agricultural production index (2014-2016=100)	77	104	92[b]
International trade: exports (million current US$)	25[h]	33[h]	35[f]
International trade: imports (million current US$)	306[h]	372[h]	447[f]
International trade: balance (million current US$)	- 281[h]	- 339[h]	- 412[f]
Balance of payments, current account (million US$)	- 204	- 125	- 294[f]

Major trading partners

							2021
Export partners (% of exports)	Areas nes[i]	57.4	United States	16.8	St. Vin. & Grenadines	4.9
Import partners (% of imports)	United States	39.1	Trinidad and Tobago	17.2	Cayman Islands	9.3

Social indicators

	2010	2015	2022
Population growth rate (average annual %)	0.7	0.8	0.6[a]
Urban population (% of total population)	35.9	36.0	36.4[j]
Urban population growth rate (average annual %)[k]	0.3	0.5	...
Fertility rate, total (live births per woman)	2.2	2.1	2.0[a]
Life expectancy at birth (females/males, years)	77.6 / 72.5	78.1 / 72.2	78.3 / 72.6[a]
Population age distribution (0-14/60+ years old, %)	24.7 / 12.1	24.0 / 12.9	24.0 / 14.9[a]
International migrant stock (000/% of total pop.)	7.0 / 6.6	7.1 / 6.4	7.2 / 6.4[b]
Refugees and others of concern to the UNHCR (000)	~0.0[l]	...	0.2[f]
Infant mortality rate (per 1 000 live births)	12.4	13.3	12.3[a]
Health: Current expenditure (% of GDP)[h,m]	5.4	4.6	5.0[j]
Health: Physicians (per 1 000 pop.)	0.7[n]	...	1.4[e]
Education: Government expenditure (% of GDP)[h]	...	4.2	3.6[e]
Education: Primary gross enrol. ratio (f/m per 100 pop.)	113.9 / 119.1	116.3 / 120.6	106.0 / 107.7[e]
Education: Sec. gross enrol. ratio (f/m per 100 pop.)	118.6 / 114.9	110.7 / 112.8	122.1 / 118.2[e]
Education: Upr. Sec. gross enrol. ratio (f/m per 100 pop.)	107.1 / 85.2	113.4 / 103.3	119.2 / 110.3[e]
Intentional homicide rate (per 100 000 pop.)	9.4	5.5	12.4[b]
Seats held by women in the National Parliament (%)	13.3	33.3	46.7[o]

Environment and infrastructure indicators

	2010	2015	2022
Individuals using the Internet (per 100 inhabitants)[h]	27.0	52.5	56.9[b]
Threatened species (number)	37	51	78
Forested area (% of land area)	52.1	52.1	52.1[j]
Energy production, primary (Petajoules)	0	0	0[j]
Energy supply per capita (Gigajoules)	38	37	46[j]
Tourist/visitor arrivals at national borders (000)	110	155	54[b]
Important sites for terrestrial biodiversity protected (%)	34.5	34.5	34.5[f]
Net Official Development Assist. received (% of GNI)	4.63	2.74	7.06[b]

a Projected estimate (medium fertility variant). b 2020. c East Caribbean Dollar. d Refers to Saint George Parish. e 2018. f 2021. g Data classified according to ISIC Rev. 4. h Estimate. i Areas nes j 2019. k Data refers to a 5-year period preceding the reference year. l Data as at the end of December. m Data based on calendar year (January 1 to December 31). n 2006. o Data are as at 1 January of reporting year.

Guadeloupe

Region	Caribbean	Population (000, 2022)	396 a,b
Surface area (km2)	1 639 c	Pop. density (per km2, 2022)	243.1 a,b
Sex ratio (m per 100 f)	82.6 a,b	Capital city	Basse-Terre
National currency	Euro (EUR)	Capital city pop. (000, 2022)	58.4 d
Exchange rate (per US$)	0.9 e		

Economic indicators	2010	2015	2022
Employment in agriculture (% of employed)	...	3.3 f,g,h	...
Employment in industry (% of employed) f,g	13.8	13.5 h	...
Employment in services & other sectors (% employed) f,g	64.4	65.5 h	...
Unemployment rate (% of labour force) g	23.8	26.1 i,j	...
Labour force participation rate (female/male pop. %)	39.5 / 44.2 g	49.6 / 56.5 g,i,j	... / ...
CPI: Consumer Price Index (2010=100) k	100	106	110 l,c

Social indicators	2010	2015	2022
Population growth rate (average annual %) b	0.1	- 0.4	- 0.1 a
Urban population (% of total population) m	98.4	98.4	98.5 n
Urban population growth rate (average annual %) m,o	0.5	--0.0	...
Fertility rate, total (live births per woman) b	2.2	2.2	2.0 a
Life expectancy at birth (females/males, years) b	83.9 / 76.9	85.3 / 78.1	83.9 / 77.3 a
Population age distribution (0-14/60+ years old, %) b	22.0 / 18.8	20.5 / 22.2	18.1 / 27.0 a
International migrant stock (000/% of total pop.)	94.9 / 23.4	91.0 / 22.7	90.2 / 22.5 c
Infant mortality rate (per 1 000 live births) b	6.3	5.2	4.4 a
Intentional homicide rate (per 100 000 pop.)	8.9 p	9.7	5.8 q

Environment and infrastructure indicators	2010	2015	2022
Individuals using the Internet (per 100 inhabitants)	23.4 r,p	...	...
Threatened species (number) s	54	70	101
Forested area (% of land area) r	43.2	44.6	44.4 n
Energy production, primary (Petajoules)	2 r,t	...	...
Tourist/visitor arrivals at national borders (000) s,u	392	512	735 d
Important sites for terrestrial biodiversity protected (%)	82.3	82.4	82.4 e

a Projected estimate (medium fertility variant). b For statistical purposes, the data for France do not include this area. c 2020. d 2018. e 2021. f Population aged 15 to 64 years. g Excluding the institutional population. h 2012. i Break in the time series. j 2013. k Calculated by the UNSD from national indices. l Average for 9 months excluding data for April to June. m Including Saint Barthélemy and Saint Martin (French part). n 2019. o Data refers to a 5-year period preceding the reference year. p 2009. q 2016. r Estimate. s Excluding the north islands, Saint Barthélemy and Saint Martin (French part). t Data after 2010 are included in France. u Arrivals by air.

Guam

Region	Micronesia	Population (000, 2022)	172[a,b]
Surface area (km2)	541[c]	Pop. density (per km2, 2022)	317.5[a,b]
Sex ratio (m per 100 f)	101.3[a,b]	Capital city	Hagåtña
National currency	US Dollar (USD)	Capital city pop. (000, 2022)	146.9[d]

Economic indicators	2010	2015	2022
Employment in agriculture (% of employed)	0.3	0.3[e]	0.2[e,c]
Employment in industry (% of employed)	15.1	14.8[e]	14.3[e,c]
Employment in services & other sectors (% employed)	84.6	84.9[e]	85.5[e,c]
Unemployment rate (% of labour force)	8.2	6.9	6.8[e]
Labour force participation rate (female/male pop. %)	56.5 / 66.2	56.4 / 68.6[e]	54.5 / 67.5[e]
CPI: Consumer Price Index (2010=100)[f]	100	106	127[g]

Social indicators	2010	2015	2022
Population growth rate (average annual %)[a]	0.5	0.2	0.7[b]
Urban population (% of total population)	94.1	94.5	94.9[h]
Urban population growth rate (average annual %)[i]	0.2	0.4	...
Fertility rate, total (live births per woman)[a]	3.0	2.9	2.6[b]
Life expectancy at birth (females/males, years)[a]	80.5 / 73.6	80.5 / 73.1	82.0 / 74.8[b]
Population age distribution (0-14/60+ years old, %)[a]	27.1 / 10.6	26.9 / 13.2	26.1 / 17.0[b]
International migrant stock (000/% of total pop.)	75.4 / 47.3	76.1 / 47.0	80.5 / 47.7[c]
Infant mortality rate (per 1 000 live births)[a]	11.6	11.7	9.7[b]
Intentional homicide rate (per 100 000 pop.)	1.9	2.5[i]	4.2[h]

Environment and infrastructure indicators	2010	2015	2022
Individuals using the Internet (per 100 inhabitants)[e]	54.0	73.1	80.5[k]
Research & Development expenditure (% of GDP)	0.3[l]	...	...
Threatened species (number)	34	95	111
Forested area (% of land area)	44.4	46.3	51.9[h]
Energy production, primary (Petajoules)	...	0	0[h]
Energy supply per capita (Gigajoules)	...	0	1[h]
Tourist/visitor arrivals at national borders (000)[m]	1 197	1 409	328[c]
Important sites for terrestrial biodiversity protected (%)	2.4	2.4	2.4[g]

a For statistical purposes, the data for United States of America do not include this area. b Projected estimate (medium fertility variant). c 2020. d 2018. e Estimate. f Calculated by the UNSD from national indices. g 2021. h 2019. i Data refers to a 5-year period preceding the reference year. j 2011. k 2017. l 2005. m Air and sea arrivals.

Guatemala

Region	Central America	UN membership date	21 November 1945
Population (000, 2022)	17 844[a]	Surface area (km2)	108 889[b]
Pop. density (per km2, 2022)	166.5[a]	Sex ratio (m per 100 f)	98.0[a]
Capital city	Guatemala City	National currency	Quetzal (GTQ)
Capital city pop. (000, 2022)	2 891.2[c]	Exchange rate (per US$)	7.7[d]

Economic indicators

	2010	2015	2022
GDP: Gross domestic product (million current US$)	40 682	62 186	77 605[b]
GDP growth rate (annual %, const. 2015 prices)	2.9	4.1	- 1.5[b]
GDP per capita (current US$)	2 780.7	3 826.3	4 331.7[b]
Economy: Agriculture (% of Gross Value Added)[e,f]	11.4	10.6	10.9[b]
Economy: Industry (% of Gross Value Added)[f,g]	24.2	24.1	23.4[b]
Economy: Services and other activity (% of GVA)[f,h]	64.4	65.3	65.7[b]
Employment in agriculture (% of employed)	33.5	31.9	31.3[i,b]
Employment in industry (% of employed)	22.0	18.9	18.4[i,b]
Employment in services & other sectors (% employed)	44.5	49.2	50.3[i,b]
Unemployment rate (% of labour force)	3.5	2.5	3.5[i]
Labour force participation rate (female/male pop. %)	40.7 / 84.4[i]	38.7 / 84.2	38.6 / 81.7[i]
CPI: Consumer Price Index (2010=100)	100[j]	122	154[d]
Agricultural production index (2014-2016=100)	78	101	108[b]
International trade: exports (million current US$)	8 460	10 677	13 736[d]
International trade: imports (million current US$)	13 830	17 637	26 594[d]
International trade: balance (million current US$)	- 5 370	- 6 960	- 12 858[d]
Balance of payments, current account (million US$)	- 767	- 774	2 177[d]

Major trading partners

						2021
Export partners (% of exports)	United States	31.8	El Salvador	12.6	Honduras	10.2
Import partners (% of imports)	United States	32.8	China	15.6	Mexico	10.4

Social indicators

	2010	2015	2022
Population growth rate (average annual %)	2.0	1.8	1.4[a]
Urban population (% of total population)	48.4	50.0	51.4[c]
Urban population growth rate (average annual %)[k]	2.8	2.7	...
Fertility rate, total (live births per woman)	3.4	3.0	2.4[a]
Life expectancy at birth (females/males, years)	74.3 / 67.6	75.2 / 69.1	71.8 / 65.7[a]
Population age distribution (0-14/60+ years old, %)	39.1 / 6.0	36.2 / 6.5	32.4 / 7.1[a]
International migrant stock (000/% of total pop.)[l]	66.4 / 0.5	74.9 / 0.5	84.3 / 0.5[b]
Refugees and others of concern to the UNHCR (000)	0.1[m]	0.3	103.7[d]
Infant mortality rate (per 1 000 live births)	28.3	23.3	19.8[a]
Health: Current expenditure (% of GDP)[n]	6.1[o]	6.0	6.2[c]
Health: Physicians (per 1 000 pop.)	0.9[p]	...	1.2[b]
Education: Government expenditure (% of GDP)	2.8	3.0	3.3[b]
Education: Primary gross enrol. ratio (f/m per 100 pop.)	114.3 / 116.6	99.9 / 103.1	99.7 / 101.5[b]
Education: Sec. gross enrol. ratio (f/m per 100 pop.)	50.7 / 53.9	52.6 / 55.8	49.9 / 50.9[b]
Education: Upr. Sec. gross enrol. ratio (f/m per 100 pop.)	35.3 / 34.9	37.2 / 36.1	36.6 / 34.0[b]
Intentional homicide rate (per 100 000 pop.)	40.7	33.0[q]	17.5[b]
Seats held by women in the National Parliament (%)	12.0	13.3	19.4[r]

Environment and infrastructure indicators

	2010	2015	2022
Individuals using the Internet (per 100 inhabitants)[i]	10.5	28.8	50.0[b]
Research & Development expenditure (% of GDP)[s]	~0.0	~0.0	~0.0[c]
Threatened species (number)	230	282	592
Forested area (% of land area)[i]	34.7	33.5	33.0[c]
CO2 emission estimates (million tons/tons per capita)	12.5 / 0.7	17.5 / 1.0	20.8 / 1.1[c]
Energy production, primary (Petajoules)	279	311	350[c]
Energy supply per capita (Gigajoules)	27	30	32[c]
Tourist/visitor arrivals at national borders (000)	1 119	1 473	396[b]
Important sites for terrestrial biodiversity protected (%)	25.3	28.9	30.1[d]
Pop. using safely managed drinking water (urban/rural, %)	61.5 / 42.5	64.5 / 44.0	65.4 / 45.5[b]
Net Official Development Assist. received (% of GNI)	1.01	0.68	0.62[b]

a Projected estimate (medium fertility variant). b 2020. c 2019. d 2021. e Excludes irrigation canals and landscaping care. f Data classified according to ISIC Rev. 4. g Excludes publishing activities. Includes irrigation and canals. h Includes publishing activities and landscape care. Excludes repair of personal and household goods. i Estimate. j Break in the time series. k Data refers to a 5-year period preceding the reference year. l Including refugees. m Data as at the end of December. n Data based on calendar year (January 1 to December 31). o Country is still reporting data based on SHA 1.0. p 2009. q 2014. r Data are as at 1 January of reporting year. s Partial data.

Guinea

Region	Western Africa	UN membership date	12 December 1958
Population (000, 2022)	13 859[a]	Surface area (km2)	245 836[b]
Pop. density (per km2, 2022)	56.4[a]	Sex ratio (m per 100 f)	97.8[a]
Capital city	Conakry	National currency	Guinean Franc (GNF)
Capital city pop. (000, 2022)	1 889.2[c]	Exchange rate (per US$)	9 990.0[b]

Economic indicators

	2010	2015	2022
GDP: Gross domestic product (million current US$)	6 853	8 794	15 490[b]
GDP growth rate (annual %, const. 2015 prices)	4.8	3.8	7.1[b]
GDP per capita (current US$)	672.4	769.3	1 179.5[b]
Economy: Agriculture (% of Gross Value Added)[d]	18.6	20.1	25.1[b]
Economy: Industry (% of Gross Value Added)[d]	34.3	28.6	34.8[b]
Economy: Services and other activity (% of GVA)[d]	47.1	51.3	40.1[b]
Employment in agriculture (% of employed)[e]	67.5	64.9	61.3[b]
Employment in industry (% of employed)[e]	5.3	5.4	6.2[b]
Employment in services & other sectors (% employed)[e]	27.2	29.7	32.5[b]
Unemployment rate (% of labour force)[e]	4.8	4.9	6.2
Labour force participation rate (female/male pop. %)[e]	63.0 / 65.8	63.4 / 64.6	63.0 / 62.5
CPI: Consumer Price Index (2010=100)[f]	100	186	327[b]
Agricultural production index (2014-2016=100)	82	100	134[b]
International trade: exports (million current US$)	1 471[e]	1 574	7 551[e,g]
International trade: imports (million current US$)	1 402[e]	2 139	3 892[e,g]
International trade: balance (million current US$)	69[e]	- 565	3 660[g]
Balance of payments, current account (million US$)	- 327	- 1 020	4 639[g]

Major trading partners

						2021
Export partners (% of exports)[e]	United Arab Emirates	54.3	India	20.6	China	16.7
Import partners (% of imports)[e]	China	38.3	India	10.6	United Arab Emirates	6.5

Social indicators

	2010	2015	2022
Population growth rate (average annual %)	2.5	2.6	2.4[a]
Urban population (% of total population)	33.7	35.1	36.5[c]
Urban population growth rate (average annual %)[h]	3.0	3.1	...
Fertility rate, total (live births per woman)	5.4	5.0	4.3[a]
Life expectancy at birth (females/males, years)	57.8 / 55.5	59.3 / 56.9	60.2 / 57.6[a]
Population age distribution (0-14/60+ years old, %)	44.5 / 5.4	43.3 / 5.2	41.5 / 5.1[a]
International migrant stock (000/% of total pop.)[i,j]	178.8 / 1.8	126.7 / 1.1	121.4 / 0.9[b]
Refugees and others of concern to the UNHCR (000)	15.0[k]	9.0	8.9[g]
Infant mortality rate (per 1 000 live births)	78.8	72.7	63.9[a]
Health: Current expenditure (% of GDP)	3.4	5.8	4.0[c]
Health: Physicians (per 1 000 pop.)	0.1[l]	0.1	0.2[m]
Education: Government expenditure (% of GDP)	2.6	2.5	2.2[b]
Education: Primary gross enrol. ratio (f/m per 100 pop.)	76.0 / 92.3	85.0 / 100.4[n]	92.4 / 109.0[b]
Education: Sec. gross enrol. ratio (f/m per 100 pop.)	24.6 / 43.1[o]	31.0 / 47.5[n]	... / ...
Education: Upr. Sec. gross enrol. ratio (f/m per 100 pop.)	16.0 / 32.5[o]	24.2 / 38.5[n]	... / ...
Seats held by women in the National Parliament (%)	19.3[o]	21.9	16.7[p,g]

Environment and infrastructure indicators

	2010	2015	2022
Individuals using the Internet (per 100 inhabitants)[e]	1.0	9.2	26.0[b]
Threatened species (number)	134	163	413
Forested area (% of land area)[e]	26.7	26.0	25.4[c]
Energy production, primary (Petajoules)	112	116	118[c]
Energy supply per capita (Gigajoules)	14	13	14[c]
Tourist/visitor arrivals at national borders (000)[q]	12	35	99[r]
Important sites for terrestrial biodiversity protected (%)	71.7	71.7	71.7[g]
Net Official Development Assist. received (% of GNI)	3.26	6.16	5.04[b]

a Projected estimate (medium fertility variant). b 2020. c 2019. d Data classified according to ISIC Rev. 4. e Estimate. f Conakry g 2021. h Data refers to a 5-year period preceding the reference year. i Refers to foreign citizens. j Including refugees. k Data as at the end of December. l 2005. m 2018. n 2014. o 2008. p Data are as at 1 January of reporting year. q Arrivals by air at Conakry airport. r 2017.

Guinea-Bissau

Region	Western Africa	UN membership date		17 September 1974
Population (000, 2022)	2 106[a]	Surface area (km2)		36 125[b]
Pop. density (per km2, 2022)	74.9[a]	Sex ratio (m per 100 f)		97.6[a]
Capital city	Bissau	National currency		CFA Franc, BCEAO (XOF)[c]
Capital city pop. (000, 2022)	578.8[d]	Exchange rate (per US$)		579.2[e]

Economic indicators	2010	2015	2022	
GDP: Gross domestic product (million current US$)	849	1 047	1 315[b]	
GDP growth rate (annual %, const. 2015 prices)	4.6	6.1	- 1.4[b]	
GDP per capita (current US$)	557.6	602.9	668.2[b]	
Economy: Agriculture (% of Gross Value Added)[f]	46.2	49.0	32.6[b]	
Economy: Industry (% of Gross Value Added)[f]	13.5	12.8	14.2[b]	
Economy: Services and other activity (% of GVA)[f]	40.3	38.2	53.2[b]	
Employment in agriculture (% of employed)[g]	71.0	69.7	67.8[b]	
Employment in industry (% of employed)[g]	7.1	6.9	7.0[b]	
Employment in services & other sectors (% employed)[g]	21.8	23.4	25.2[b]	
Unemployment rate (% of labour force)[g]	6.1	5.9	6.6	
Labour force participation rate (female/male pop. %)[g]	64.4 / 79.4	64.5 / 79.0	64.2 / 78.4	
CPI: Consumer Price Index (2010=100)[h]	100	109	113[d]	
Agricultural production index (2014-2016=100)	92	103	105[b]	
International trade: exports (million current US$)[g]	120	548	189[e]	
International trade: imports (million current US$)[g]	197	221	345[e]	
International trade: balance (million current US$)	- 77[g]	327[g]	- 156[e]	
Balance of payments, current account (million US$)	- 71	21	- 39[b]	

Major trading partners						2021
Export partners (% of exports)[g]	India	63.3	Ivory Coast	12.3	Pakistan	9.7
Import partners (% of imports)[g]	Portugal	25.9	China	21.1	Senegal	17.7

Social indicators	2010	2015	2022
Population growth rate (average annual %)	2.6	2.6	2.1[a]
Urban population (% of total population)	40.1	42.1	43.8[d]
Urban population growth rate (average annual %)[i]	3.4	3.6	...
Fertility rate, total (live births per woman)	5.1	4.7	3.9[a]
Life expectancy at birth (females/males, years)	58.4 / 53.9	61.2 / 56.9	61.9 / 57.7[a]
Population age distribution (0-14/60+ years old, %)	43.6 / 4.2	42.8 / 4.3	40.1 / 4.5[a]
International migrant stock (000/% of total pop.)[j]	21.4 / 1.4	22.3 / 1.3	17.9 / 0.9[b]
Refugees and others of concern to the UNHCR (000)	8.0[k]	8.8	1.9[e]
Infant mortality rate (per 1 000 live births)	73.6	61.2	50.1[a]
Health: Current expenditure (% of GDP)[g]	6.3	8.1	8.3[d]
Health: Physicians (per 1 000 pop.)	0.1[l]	0.2	0.2[b]
Education: Government expenditure (% of GDP)	1.9	2.3	2.9[g,d]
Education: Primary gross enrol. ratio (f/m per 100 pop.)	114.5 / 122.9	... / ...	... / ...
Intentional homicide rate (per 100 000 pop.)	...	...	1.1[m]
Seats held by women in the National Parliament (%)	10.0	13.7	13.7[n]

Environment and infrastructure indicators	2010	2015	2022
Individuals using the Internet (per 100 inhabitants)[g]	2.4	6.1	22.9[b]
Threatened species (number)	52	66	124
Forested area (% of land area)[g]	73.4	71.9	70.7[d]
Energy production, primary (Petajoules)	24	25	26[d]
Energy supply per capita (Gigajoules)	18	17	17[d]
Tourist/visitor arrivals at national borders (000)[o]	22	44	52[d]
Important sites for terrestrial biodiversity protected (%)	39.8	59.5	59.5[e]
Pop. using safely managed drinking water (urban/rural, %)	40.8 / 7.6	40.9 / 9.3	40.9 / 11.2[b]
Pop. using safely managed sanitation (urban/rural, %)	14.8 / 2.3	18.4 / 3.2	22.2 / 4.2[b]
Net Official Development Assist. received (% of GNI)	15.25	8.85	10.11[b]

a Projected estimate (medium fertility variant). b 2020. c African Financial Community (CFA) Franc, Central Bank of West African States (BCEAO). d 2019. e 2021. f Data classified according to ISIC Rev. 4. g Estimate. h Bissau i Data refers to a 5-year period preceding the reference year. j Including refugees. k Data as at the end of December. l 2009. m 2017. n Data are as at 1 January of reporting year. o Arrivals at "Osvaldo Vieira" Airport.

Guyana

Region	South America	UN membership date	20 September 1966
Population (000, 2022)	809[a]	Surface area (km2)	214 969[b]
Pop. density (per km2, 2022)	4.1[a]	Sex ratio (m per 100 f)	95.9[a]
Capital city	Georgetown	National currency	Guyana Dollar (GYD)
Capital city pop. (000, 2022)	109.9[c]	Exchange rate (per US$)	208.5[d]

Economic indicators

	2010	2015	2022
GDP: Gross domestic product (million current US$)	3 433	4 280	5 471[b]
GDP growth rate (annual %, const. 2015 prices)	4.1	0.7	43.5[b]
GDP per capita (current US$)	4 580.7	5 576.8	6 956.0[b]
Economy: Agriculture (% of Gross Value Added)[e,f]	30.0	27.0	17.8[b]
Economy: Industry (% of Gross Value Added)[e,g]	26.2	26.2	41.0[b]
Economy: Services and other activity (% of GVA)[e,h]	43.8	46.8	41.2[b]
Employment in agriculture (% of employed)[i]	20.6	18.0	16.8[b]
Employment in industry (% of employed)[i]	23.5	23.2	22.9[b]
Employment in services & other sectors (% employed)[i]	55.9	58.7	60.3[b]
Unemployment rate (% of labour force)[i]	11.8	13.2	14.9
Labour force participation rate (female/male pop. %)[i]	38.1 / 72.7	40.6 / 68.6	41.4 / 65.0
CPI: Consumer Price Index (2010=100)[i,j]	100	109	123[d]
Agricultural production index (2014-2016=100)	76	109	114[b]
International trade: exports (million current US$)	901	1 169	4 257[d]
International trade: imports (million current US$)	1 452	1 484	4 160[d]
International trade: balance (million current US$)	- 551	- 315	98[d]
Balance of payments, current account (million US$)	- 246	- 39	- 448[b]

Major trading partners

						2021
Export partners (% of exports)	United States	42.0	Singapore	16.5	United Arab Emirates	6.9
Import partners (% of imports)	Singapore	40.1	United States	19.8	Trinidad and Tobago	8.0

Social indicators

	2010	2015	2022
Population growth rate (average annual %)	- 0.5	0.5	0.5[a]
Urban population (% of total population)	26.6	26.4	26.7[k]
Urban population growth rate (average annual %)[l]	- 1.0	0.4	...
Fertility rate, total (live births per woman)	2.7	2.5	2.4[a]
Life expectancy at birth (females/males, years)	70.2 / 63.6	71.6 / 65.0	69.4 / 62.8[a]
Population age distribution (0-14/60+ years old, %)	32.3 / 7.1	30.1 / 8.3	28.6 / 9.9[a]
International migrant stock (000/% of total pop.)[m]	8.2 / 1.1	8.7 / 1.1	31.2 / 4.0[b]
Refugees and others of concern to the UNHCR (000)	~0.0[n]	~0.0	23.4[d]
Infant mortality rate (per 1 000 live births)	30.1	26.9	23.6[a]
Health: Current expenditure (% of GDP)[i,o]	4.2	4.0	4.9[k]
Health: Physicians (per 1 000 pop.)	0.7	...	1.4[b]
Education: Government expenditure (% of GDP)	2.4	3.9	4.5[i,c]
Education: Primary gross enrol. ratio (f/m per 100 pop.)	95.0 / 97.9	96.0 / 99.6[p]	... / ...
Education: Sec. gross enrol. ratio (f/m per 100 pop.)	91.9 / 88.4	99.2 / 96.3[p]	... / ...
Education: Upr. Sec. gross enrol. ratio (f/m per 100 pop.)	74.0 / 69.6	90.0 / 83.8[p]	... / ...
Intentional homicide rate (per 100 000 pop.)	18.7	19.4	20.0[b]
Seats held by women in the National Parliament (%)	30.0	31.3	35.7[q]

Environment and infrastructure indicators

	2010	2015	2022
Individuals using the Internet (per 100 inhabitants)	29.9	34.0[i]	37.3[i,r]
Threatened species (number)	69	87	181
Forested area (% of land area)[i]	94.1	93.8	93.6[k]
CO2 emission estimates (million tons/tons per capita)	1.8 / 2.3	2.1 / 2.7	2.7 / 3.4[k]
Energy production, primary (Petajoules)	8	7	4[k]
Energy supply per capita (Gigajoules)	46	45	52[k]
Tourist/visitor arrivals at national borders (000)	152	207	86[b]
Net Official Development Assist. received (% of GNI)	3.09	0.75	1.22[b]

a Projected estimate (medium fertility variant). b 2020. c 2018. d 2021. e Data classified according to ISIC Rev. 4. f Excludes irrigation canals and landscaping care. g Excludes publishing activities. Includes irrigation and canals. h Includes publishing activities and landscape care. Excludes repair of personal and household goods. i Estimate. j Georgetown k 2019. l Data refers to a 5-year period preceding the reference year. m Including refugees. n Data as at the end of December. o Data based on calendar year (January 1 to December 31). p 2012. q Data are as at 1 January of reporting year. r 2017.

Haiti

Region	Caribbean	UN membership date	24 October 1945
Population (000, 2022)	11 585[a]	Surface area (km2)	27 750[b]
Pop. density (per km2, 2022)	420.2[a]	Sex ratio (m per 100 f)	98.2[a]
Capital city	Port-au-Prince	National currency	Gourde (HTG)
Capital city pop. (000, 2022)	2 704.2[c]	Exchange rate (per US$)	99.9[d]

Economic indicators

	2010	2015	2022
GDP: Gross domestic product (million current US$)	11 812	14 228	15 505[b]
GDP growth rate (annual %, const. 2015 prices)	- 3.8	1.6	- 3.3[b]
GDP per capita (current US$)	1 187.2	1 330.2	1 359.8[b]
Economy: Agriculture (% of Gross Value Added)[e,f]	21.0	18.0	20.9[b]
Economy: Industry (% of Gross Value Added)[f,g]	24.4	27.1	23.9[b]
Economy: Services and other activity (% of GVA)[f,h]	54.5	54.9	55.2[b]
Employment in agriculture (% of employed)[i]	33.6	30.3	28.3[b]
Employment in industry (% of employed)[i]	6.5	7.1	6.6[b]
Employment in services & other sectors (% employed)[i]	59.9	62.6	65.0[b]
Unemployment rate (% of labour force)[i]	15.4	14.0	15.4
Labour force participation rate (female/male pop. %)	60.7 / 70.9	62.2 / 69.9[i]	61.5 / 69.2[i]
CPI: Consumer Price Index (2010=100)	100	139	176[j,d]
Agricultural production index (2014-2016=100)	90	100	78[b]
International trade: exports (million current US$)[i]	579	1 018	1 277[d]
International trade: imports (million current US$)[i]	3 147	3 523	2 551[d]
International trade: balance (million current US$)	- 2 568[i]	- 2 505[i]	- 1 274[d]
Balance of payments, current account (million US$)	- 102	- 271	141[d]

Major trading partners

						2021
Export partners (% of exports)[i]	United States	82.9	Canada	4.2	Mexico	3.5
Import partners (% of imports)[i]	United States	29.8	Dominican Rep.	21.1	China	17.6

Social indicators

	2010	2015	2022
Population growth rate (average annual %)	0.7	1.4	1.2[a]
Urban population (% of total population)	47.5	52.4	56.2[c]
Urban population growth rate (average annual %)[k]	3.7	3.3	...
Fertility rate, total (live births per woman)	3.5	3.1	2.8[a]
Life expectancy at birth (females/males, years)	46.3 / 45.8	66.0 / 60.6	66.7 / 60.9[a]
Population age distribution (0-14/60+ years old, %)	36.0 / 6.1	34.2 / 6.5	32.1 / 7.1[a]
International migrant stock (000/% of total pop.)[l]	17.2 / 0.2	18.0 / 0.2	18.9 / 0.2[b]
Refugees and others of concern to the UNHCR (000)	~0.0[m]	~0.0	~0.0[d]
Infant mortality rate (per 1 000 live births)	75.9	52.8	43.4[a]
Health: Current expenditure (% of GDP)[i,n]	4.6[o]	5.1	4.7[c]
Health: Physicians (per 1 000 pop.)	...	0.1	0.2[p]
Education: Government expenditure (% of GDP)	...	1.9	1.7[p]
Intentional homicide rate (per 100 000 pop.)	6.8	10.0	6.7[p]
Seats held by women in the National Parliament (%)	4.1	4.2	2.5[q,r,b]

Environment and infrastructure indicators

	2010	2015	2022
Individuals using the Internet (per 100 inhabitants)[i]	8.4	14.2	34.5[b]
Threatened species (number)	137	169	426
Forested area (% of land area)[i]	13.7	13.2	12.7[c]
CO2 emission estimates (million tons/tons per capita)	3.1 / 0.2	4.0 / 0.3	4.1 / 0.3[c]
Energy production, primary (Petajoules)	131	139	147[c]
Energy supply per capita (Gigajoules)	16	16	17[c]
Tourist/visitor arrivals at national borders (000)[s,t]	255	516	203[b]
Important sites for terrestrial biodiversity protected (%)	14.7	26.8	31.7[d]
Net Official Development Assist. received (% of GNI)	24.73	7.02	6.59[b]

a Projected estimate (medium fertility variant). b 2020. c 2019. d 2021. e Excludes irrigation canals and landscaping care. f Data classified according to ISIC Rev. 4. g Excludes publishing activities. Includes irrigation and canals. h Includes publishing activities and landscape care. Excludes repair of personal and household goods. i Estimate. j Base: October 2017-September 2018=100. k Data refers to a 5-year period preceding the reference year. l Including refugees. m Data as at the end of December. n Data refer to fiscal years beginning 1 October. o Estimates should be viewed with caution as these are derived from scarce data. p 2018. q The term of all members in the 119-member Chamber of Deputies and 20 of 30 senators expired on 13 January 2020. There are currently only 10 sitting senators. r Data are as at 1 January of reporting year. s Including nationals residing abroad. t Arrivals by air.

Holy See

Region	Southern Europe	Surface area (km2)	~0[a,b]
Pop. density (per km2, 2022)	1 160.2[c,d]	Capital city	Vatican City
National currency	Euro (EUR)	Capital city pop. (000, 2022)	0.8[e]
Exchange rate (per US$)	0.9[f]		

Social indicators	2010	2015	2022
Population growth rate (average annual %)[c]	- 0.5	- 1.1	1.0[d]
Urban population (% of total population)	100.0	100.0	100.0[g]
Urban population growth rate (average annual %)[h]	- 0.1	0.2	...
International migrant stock (000/% of total pop.)[c,i]	0.8 / 100.0	0.8 / 100.0	0.8 / 100.0[b]

Environment and infrastructure indicators	2010	2015	2022
Threatened species (number)	1	1	2
Forested area (% of land area)[i]	0.0	0.0	0.0[g]

a Surface area is 0.44 Km2. **b** 2020. **c** Data refer to the Vatican City State. **d** Projected estimate (medium fertility variant). **e** 2018. **f** 2021. **g** 2019. **h** Data refers to a 5-year period preceding the reference year. **i** Estimate.

Honduras

Region	Central America	UN membership date	17 December 1945
Population (000, 2022)	10 433 [a]	Surface area (km2)	112 492 [b]
Pop. density (per km2, 2022)	95.6 [a]	Sex ratio (m per 100 f)	102.0 [a]
Capital city	Tegucigalpa	National currency	Lempira (HNL)
Capital city pop. (000, 2022)	1 403.2 [c]	Exchange rate (per US$)	24.3 [d]

Economic indicators	2010	2015	2022
GDP: Gross domestic product (million current US$)	15 839	20 980	23 828 [b]
GDP growth rate (annual %, const. 2015 prices)	3.7	3.8	- 9.0 [b]
GDP per capita (current US$)	1 904.3	2 302.2	2 405.7 [b]
Economy: Agriculture (% of Gross Value Added) [e]	11.9	12.6	12.6 [b]
Economy: Industry (% of Gross Value Added) [e]	26.2	26.5	26.9 [b]
Economy: Services and other activity (% of GVA) [e]	62.0	60.8	60.5 [b]
Employment in agriculture (% of employed)	36.5	28.7	30.1 [f,b]
Employment in industry (% of employed)	19.1	21.8	19.7 [f,b]
Employment in services & other sectors (% employed)	44.5	49.5	50.2 [f,b]
Unemployment rate (% of labour force)	4.1	6.2	8.4 [f]
Labour force participation rate (female/male pop. %)	42.9 / 81.6	46.7 / 81.9	43.4 / 79.9 [f]
CPI: Consumer Price Index (2010=100) [f]	100	129	163 [d]
Agricultural production index (2014-2016=100)	91	100	106 [b]
International trade: exports (million current US$)	3 104	4 201	5 117 [f,d]
International trade: imports (million current US$)	6 895	8 381	13 223 [f,d]
International trade: balance (million current US$)	- 3 791	- 4 179	- 8 105 [d]
Balance of payments, current account (million US$)	- 804	- 980	- 1 385 [d]

Major trading partners						2021
Export partners (% of exports) [f]	United States	33.3	Areas nes [g]	18.0	Germany	6.8
Import partners (% of imports) [f]	United States	36.2	China	16.1	Mexico	7.9

Social indicators	2010	2015	2022
Population growth rate (average annual %)	2.0	1.8	1.5 [a]
Urban population (% of total population)	51.9	55.2	57.7 [c]
Urban population growth rate (average annual %) [h]	3.4	3.0	...
Fertility rate, total (live births per woman)	3.0	2.6	2.3 [a]
Life expectancy at birth (females/males, years)	73.3 / 69.0	75.0 / 70.2	73.2 / 68.5 [a]
Population age distribution (0-14/60+ years old, %)	37.7 / 6.5	34.2 / 5.7	30.1 / 6.6 [a]
International migrant stock (000/% of total pop.) [i]	27.3 / 0.3	38.3 / 0.4	39.2 / 0.4 [b]
Refugees and others of concern to the UNHCR (000)	~0.0 [j]	~0.0	252.3 [d]
Infant mortality rate (per 1 000 live births)	19.7	16.2	12.8 [a]
Health: Current expenditure (% of GDP) [f,k]	8.7	7.5	7.3 [c]
Health: Physicians (per 1 000 pop.)	0.3	...	0.5 [b]
Education: Government expenditure (% of GDP)	6.8	6.4	4.9 [f,c]
Education: Primary gross enrol. ratio (f/m per 100 pop.)	100.7 / 100.6	92.5 / 93.0	90.6 / 89.9 [b]
Education: Sec. gross enrol. ratio (f/m per 100 pop.)	72.8 / 59.1	55.4 / 46.2	62.9 / 54.7 [b]
Education: Upr. Sec. gross enrol. ratio (f/m per 100 pop.)	76.7 / 55.0	43.9 / 32.5	61.3 / 48.7 [b]
Intentional homicide rate (per 100 000 pop.)	75.0	56.5	36.3 [b]
Seats held by women in the National Parliament (%)	18.0	25.8	27.3 [l]

Environment and infrastructure indicators	2010	2015	2022
Individuals using the Internet (per 100 inhabitants)	11.1	27.1 [m]	42.0 [f,b]
Research & Development expenditure (% of GDP)	...	~0.0 [n,o]	~0.0 [p]
Threatened species (number)	240	294	448
Forested area (% of land area) [f]	58.8	57.8	57.0 [c]
CO2 emission estimates (million tons/tons per capita)	8.3 / 0.9	10.1 / 1.0	10.2 / 1.0 [c]
Energy production, primary (Petajoules)	97	99	98 [c]
Energy supply per capita (Gigajoules)	24	26	25 [c]
Tourist/visitor arrivals at national borders (000)	863	880	204 [b]
Important sites for terrestrial biodiversity protected (%)	72.1	72.1	72.3 [d]
Pop. using safely managed drinking water (urban/rural, %)	... / 17.3	... / 18.0	... / 18.7 [b]
Pop. using safely managed sanitation (urban/rural %)	34.0 / 58.3	34.5 / 64.0	34.7 / 70.6 [b]
Net Official Development Assist. received (% of GNI)	3.11	2.77	6.45 [b]

a Projected estimate (medium fertility variant). b 2020. c 2019. d 2021. e Data classified according to ISIC Rev. 4. f Estimate. g Areas nes h Data refers to a 5-year period preceding the reference year. i Including refugees. j Data as at the end of December. k Data based on calendar year (January 1 to December 31). l Data are as at 1 January of reporting year. m Users in the last 3 months. n Partial data. o Break in the time series. p 2017.

Hungary

Region	Eastern Europe	UN membership date	14 December 1955
Population (000, 2022)	9 967[a]	Surface area (km2)	93 023[b]
Pop. density (per km2, 2022)	110.1[a]	Sex ratio (m per 100 f)	92.3[a]
Capital city	Budapest	National currency	Forint (HUF)
Capital city pop. (000, 2022)	1 763.9[c]	Exchange rate (per US$)	325.7[d]

Economic indicators

	2010	2015	2022
GDP: Gross domestic product (million current US$)	132 231	125 210	155 808[b]
GDP growth rate (annual %, const. 2015 prices)	1.1	3.7	- 4.7[b]
GDP per capita (current US$)	13 319.9	12 805.4	16 128.7[b]
Economy: Agriculture (% of Gross Value Added)[e,f]	3.6	4.5	4.0[b]
Economy: Industry (% of Gross Value Added)[e,g]	29.7	31.3	29.0[b]
Economy: Services and other activity (% of GVA)[e,h]	66.8	64.2	67.0[b]
Employment in agriculture (% of employed)	4.5	4.9	4.6[i,b]
Employment in industry (% of employed)	30.7	30.3	32.8[i,b]
Employment in services & other sectors (% employed)	64.8	64.8	62.6[i,b]
Unemployment rate (% of labour force)	11.2	6.8	3.8[i]
Labour force participation rate (female/male pop. %)	43.8 / 57.8	47.4 / 63.1	51.3 / 67.0[i]
CPI: Consumer Price Index (2010=100)	100	111	132[d]
Agricultural production index (2014-2016=100)	79	95	94[b]
International trade: exports (million current US$)	94 749	100 297	141 257[d]
International trade: imports (million current US$)	87 432	90 761	138 905[d]
International trade: balance (million current US$)	7 317	9 536	2 352[d]
Balance of payments, current account (million US$)	342	2 926	- 5 243[d]

Major trading partners

					2021
Export partners (% of exports)	Germany	26.7	Italy	5.9	Romania	5.3
Import partners (% of imports)	Germany	23.8	China	7.1	Austria	6.1

Social indicators

	2010	2015	2022
Population growth rate (average annual %)	- 0.3	- 0.3	5.6[a]
Urban population (% of total population)	68.9	70.5	71.6[c]
Urban population growth rate (average annual %)[j]	0.4	0.2	...
Fertility rate, total (live births per woman)	1.3	1.4	1.6[a]
Life expectancy at birth (females/males, years)	78.3 / 70.6	78.9 / 72.2	78.3 / 71.6[a]
Population age distribution (0-14/60+ years old, %)	14.7 / 22.6	14.5 / 25.4	14.4 / 25.8[a]
International migrant stock (000/% of total pop.)	436.6 / 4.4	475.5 / 4.9	584.6 / 6.1[b]
Refugees and others of concern to the UNHCR (000)	5.8[k]	28.8	5.8[d]
Infant mortality rate (per 1 000 live births)	5.2	4.1	3.3[a]
Health: Current expenditure (% of GDP)	7.5[l]	6.9[l]	6.4[c]
Health: Physicians (per 1 000 pop.)	2.9	3.1	6.1[b]
Education: Government expenditure (% of GDP)	4.7	4.5	4.6[m]
Education: Primary gross enrol. ratio (f/m per 100 pop.)	100.5 / 101.2	102.2 / 102.5	94.8 / 96.1[c]
Education: Sec. gross enrol. ratio (f/m per 100 pop.)	96.4 / 97.7	103.3 / 102.7	86.5 / 74.5[c]
Education: Upr. Sec. gross enrol. ratio (f/m per 100 pop.)	96.7 / 96.8	107.6 / 105.4	105.1 / 105.3[c]
Intentional homicide rate (per 100 000 pop.)	1.4	2.3	0.8[b]
Seats held by women in the National Parliament (%)	11.1	10.1	13.1[n]

Environment and infrastructure indicators

	2010	2015	2022
Individuals using the Internet (per 100 inhabitants)	65.0[o]	72.8[p]	84.8[b]
Research & Development expenditure (% of GDP)	1.1	1.3	1.6[b]
Threatened species (number)	47	67	141
Forested area (% of land area)	22.6	22.6	22.5[c]
CO2 emission estimates (million tons/tons per capita)	48.3 / 4.7	43.9 / 4.3	44.6 / 4.5[c]
Energy production, primary (Petajoules)	495	471	458[c]
Energy supply per capita (Gigajoules)	112	108	115[c]
Tourist/visitor arrivals at national borders (000)	9 510	14 316	7 417[i,b]
Important sites for terrestrial biodiversity protected (%)	84.3	84.3	84.3
Pop. using safely managed drinking water (urban/rural, %)	94.0 / 88.9	94.0 / 88.9	94.0 / 89.0[b]
Pop. using safely managed sanitation (urban/rural %)	77.6 / 69.4	88.3 / 77.2	90.5 / 80.7[b]
Net Official Development Assist. disbursed (% of GNI)[q]	0.09	0.13	2.25[b]

a Projected estimate (medium fertility variant). **b** 2020. **c** 2019. **d** 2021. **e** Data classified according to ISIC Rev. 4. **f** Excludes irrigation canals and landscaping care. **g** Excludes publishing activities. Includes irrigation and canals. **h** Includes publishing activities and landscape care. Excludes repair of personal and household goods. **i** Estimate. **j** Data refers to a 5-year period preceding the reference year. **k** Data as at the end of December. **l** Break in the time series. **m** 2018. **n** Data are as at 1 January of reporting year. **o** Population aged 16 to 74 years. **p** Users in the last 3 months. **q** DAC member (OECD).

Iceland

Region	Northern Europe	UN membership date		19 November 1946
Population (000, 2022)	373[a]	Surface area (km2)		103 000[b]
Pop. density (per km2, 2022)	3.7[a]	Sex ratio (m per 100 f)		105.2[a]
Capital city	Reykjavik	National currency		Iceland Krona (ISK)
Capital city pop. (000, 2022)	216.4[c]	Exchange rate (per US$)		130.4[d]

Economic indicators

	2010	2015	2022
GDP: Gross domestic product (million current US$)	13 751	17 517	21 718[b]
GDP growth rate (annual %, const. 2015 prices)	- 2.8	4.4	- 6.5[b]
GDP per capita (current US$)	42 928.4	53 043.4	63 644.0[b]
Economy: Agriculture (% of Gross Value Added)[e,f]	7.0	5.9	4.8[b]
Economy: Industry (% of Gross Value Added)[e,g]	24.4	22.5	21.8[b]
Economy: Services and other activity (% of GVA)[e,h]	68.6	71.6	73.4[b]
Employment in agriculture (% of employed)	5.6	4.2	3.8[i,b]
Employment in industry (% of employed)	18.4	17.8	16.1[i,b]
Employment in services & other sectors (% employed)	76.0	77.9	80.1[i,b]
Unemployment rate (% of labour force)	7.6	4.0	3.7[i]
Labour force participation rate (female/male pop. %)	70.6 / 79.1	73.1 / 80.9	62.7 / 71.5[i]
CPI: Consumer Price Index (2010=100)	100	118	139[d]
Agricultural production index (2014-2016=100)	89	100	103[b]
International trade: exports (million current US$)	4 603	4 722	5 974[d]
International trade: imports (million current US$)	3 914	5 285	7 838[d]
International trade: balance (million current US$)	689	- 563	- 1 864[d]
Balance of payments, current account (million US$)	- 845	986	- 708[d]

Major trading partners

							2021
Export partners (% of exports)	Netherlands	27.2	Spain	11.8	United Kingdom	9.6
Import partners (% of imports)	Norway	9.7	China	8.9	Germany	8.5

Social indicators

	2010	2015	2022
Population growth rate (average annual %)	0.3	1.0	0.7[a]
Urban population (% of total population)	93.6	93.7	93.9[a]
Urban population growth rate (average annual %)[k]	1.8	0.6	...
Fertility rate, total (live births per woman)	2.2	1.8	1.7[a]
Life expectancy at birth (females/males, years)	83.8 / 79.6	83.6 / 81.1	84.3 / 81.4[a]
Population age distribution (0-14/60+ years old, %)	20.9 / 17.0	20.2 / 19.1	18.5 / 21.0[a]
International migrant stock (000/% of total pop.)	35.1 / 11.0	39.1 / 11.8	65.4 / 19.2[b]
Refugees and others of concern to the UNHCR (000)	0.2[i]	0.4	1.8[d]
Infant mortality rate (per 1 000 live births)	2.1	2.0	1.4[a]
Health: Current expenditure (% of GDP)	8.4	8.1	8.6[j]
Health: Physicians (per 1 000 pop.)	3.6	3.8	4.1[i]
Education: Government expenditure (% of GDP)	6.9	7.5	7.6[c]
Education: Primary gross enrol. ratio (f/m per 100 pop.)	99.6 / 99.0	98.6 / 98.7	101.2 / 100.8[i]
Education: Sec. gross enrol. ratio (f/m per 100 pop.)	108.2 / 106.5	119.6 / 118.6	113.7 / 117.1[i]
Education: Upr. Sec. gross enrol. ratio (f/m per 100 pop.)	118.1 / 114.2	132.9 / 131.7	123.5 / 129.1[i]
Intentional homicide rate (per 100 000 pop.)	0.6	0.9	1.5[b]
Seats held by women in the National Parliament (%)	42.9	41.3	47.6[m]

Environment and infrastructure indicators

	2010	2015	2022
Individuals using the Internet (per 100 inhabitants)	93.4[n,o]	98.2[i]	99.0[i,b]
Research & Development expenditure (% of GDP)	2.6[p]	2.2	2.5[b]
Threatened species (number)	17	21	40
Forested area (% of land area)	0.4	0.5[i]	0.5[i]
CO2 emission estimates (million tons/tons per capita)	2.0 / 6.1	2.1 / 6.2	1.5 / 4.0[b]
Energy production, primary (Petajoules)	259	292	335[i]
Energy supply per capita (Gigajoules)	891	970	1 072[i]
Tourist/visitor arrivals at national borders (000)	489	1 289	486[b]
Important sites for terrestrial biodiversity protected (%)	16.7	19.1	19.1[d]
Net Official Development Assist. disbursed (% of GNI)[q]	0.26	0.24	0.27[b]

a Projected estimate (medium fertility variant). b 2020. c 2018. d 2021. e Data classified according to ISIC Rev. 4. f Excludes irrigation canals and landscaping care. g Excludes publishing activities. Includes irrigation and canals. h Includes publishing activities and landscape care. Excludes repair of personal and household goods. i Estimate. j 2019. k Data refers to a 5-year period preceding the reference year. l Data as at the end of December. m Data are as at 1 January of reporting year. n Population aged 16 to 74 years. o Users in the last 3 months. p 2009. q DAC member (OECD).

India

Region	Southern Asia	UN membership date	30 October 1945	
Population (000, 2022)	1 417 173[a]	Surface area (km2)	3 287 263[b]	
Pop. density (per km2, 2022)	476.7[a]	Sex ratio (m per 100 f)	106.6[a]	
Capital city	New Delhi	National currency	Indian Rupee (INR)	
Capital city pop. (000, 2022)	29 399.1[c,d]	Exchange rate (per US$)	74.3[e]	

Economic indicators

	2010	2015	2022
GDP: Gross domestic product (million current US$)	1 669 620	2 146 759	2 664 749[b]
GDP growth rate (annual %, const. 2015 prices)	8.5	8.0	- 7.3[b]
GDP per capita (current US$)	1 352.7	1 638.6	1 931.0[b]
Economy: Agriculture (% of Gross Value Added)[f,g]	18.4	17.7	18.1[b]
Economy: Industry (% of Gross Value Added)[f,h]	33.1	30.0	28.3[b]
Economy: Services and other activity (% of GVA)[f,i]	48.5	52.3	53.6[b]
Employment in agriculture (% of employed)	51.5	45.7[i]	41.5[i,b]
Employment in industry (% of employed)	21.8	24.1[i]	26.2[i,b]
Employment in services & other sectors (% employed)	26.7	30.3[i]	32.3[i,b]
Unemployment rate (% of labour force)[i]	5.5	5.4	5.4
Labour force participation rate (female/male pop. %)	26.0 / 79.3	21.8 / 75.9[i]	19.9 / 71.1[i]
CPI: Consumer Price Index (2010=100)[k]	100	149	200[e]
Agricultural production index (2014-2016=100)	86	98	116[b]
International trade: exports (million current US$)	220 408	264 381	394 814[e]
International trade: imports (million current US$)	350 029	390 745	570 402[e]
International trade: balance (million current US$)	- 129 621	- 126 364	- 175 588[e]
Balance of payments, current account (million US$)	- 54 516	- 22 457	- 34 648[e]

Major trading partners

						2021
Export partners (% of exports)	United States	18.1	United Arab Emirates	6.4	China	5.8
Import partners (% of imports)	China	15.3	United Arab Emirates	7.6	United States	7.3

Social indicators

	2010	2015	2022
Population growth rate (average annual %)	1.4	1.2	0.7[a]
Urban population (% of total population)	30.9	32.8	34.5[d]
Urban population growth rate (average annual %)[l]	2.6	2.4	...
Fertility rate, total (live births per woman)	2.6	2.3	2.0[a]
Life expectancy at birth (females/males, years)	68.6 / 65.3	71.1 / 68.3	69.4 / 66.3[a]
Population age distribution (0-14/60+ years old, %)	31.0 / 7.8	28.6 / 8.9	25.3 / 10.5[a]
International migrant stock (000/% of total pop.)[m]	5 574.0 / 0.5	5 210.8 / 0.4	4 878.7 / 0.4[b]
Refugees and others of concern to the UNHCR (000)	193.7[n]	205.8	208.7[e]
Infant mortality rate (per 1 000 live births)	45.2	34.7	26.3[a]
Health: Current expenditure (% of GDP)[o]	3.3	3.6	3.0[d]
Health: Physicians (per 1 000 pop.)	...	...	0.7[b]
Education: Government expenditure (% of GDP)	3.4	3.3	3.5[p]
Education: Primary gross enrol. ratio (f/m per 100 pop.)	110.7 / 107.7[i]	114.8 / 102.8	100.9 / 99.0[b]
Education: Sec. gross enrol. ratio (f/m per 100 pop.)	61.1 / 64.9	74.7 / 73.1	75.3 / 75.7[b]
Education: Upr. Sec. gross enrol. ratio (f/m per 100 pop.)	47.4 / 52.5	62.6 / 64.2	66.5 / 70.0[b]
Intentional homicide rate (per 100 000 pop.)	3.8	3.4	2.9[b]
Seats held by women in the National Parliament (%)	10.8	12.0	14.9[q]

Environment and infrastructure indicators

	2010	2015	2022
Individuals using the Internet (per 100 inhabitants)	7.5[i]	14.9[i]	43.0[b]
Research & Development expenditure (% of GDP)	0.8	0.7	0.7[i,r]
Threatened species (number)	758	1 039	1 286
Forested area (% of land area)[i]	23.4	23.8	24.2[d]
CO2 emission estimates (million tons/tons per capita)[o]	1 625.1 / 1.3	2 094.1 / 1.6	2 371.9 / 1.7[d]
Energy production, primary (Petajoules)	21 105	21 875	24 030[d]
Energy supply per capita (Gigajoules)	22	27	30[d]
Tourist/visitor arrivals at national borders (000)	5 776	13 284[s]	6 337[s,b]
Important sites for terrestrial biodiversity protected (%)	1.4	6.1	6.2[e]
Pop. using safely managed drinking water (urban/rural, %)	... / 43.1	... / 50.7	... / 56.1[b]
Pop. using safely managed sanitation (urban/rural %)	29.2 / 23.7	33.4 / 36.8	37.3 / 50.5[b]
Net Official Development Assist. received (% of GNI)	0.17	0.15	0.07[b]

a Projected estimate (medium fertility variant). b 2020. c Refers to the Delhi metropolitan area that is not restricted to state boundaries (National Capital Territory), includes contiguous suburban cities and towns, such as Faridabad, Gurgaon, and Ghaziabad. d 2019. e 2021. f Data classified according to ISIC Rev. 4. g Excludes irrigation canals and landscaping care. h Excludes publishing activities. Includes irrigation and canals. i Includes publishing activities and landscape care. Excludes repair of personal and household goods. j Estimate. k Industrial workers. l Data refers to a 5-year period preceding the reference year. m Including refugees. n Data as at the end of December. o Data refer to fiscal years beginning 1 April. p 2016. q Data are as at 1 January of reporting year. r 2018. s Including nationals residing abroad.

Indonesia

Region	South-eastern Asia	UN membership date	28 September 1950	
Population (000, 2022)	275 501 [a]	Surface area (km2)	1 910 931 [b]	
Pop. density (per km2, 2022)	144.2 [a]	Sex ratio (m per 100 f)	101.4 [a]	
Capital city	Jakarta	National currency	Rupiah (IDR)	
Capital city pop. (000, 2022)	10 638.7 [c,d]	Exchange rate (per US$)	14 269.0 [e]	

Economic indicators	2010	2015	2022
GDP: Gross domestic product (million current US$)	755 094	860 854	1 058 424 [b]
GDP growth rate (annual %, const. 2015 prices)	6.2	4.9	- 2.1 [b]
GDP per capita (current US$)	3 122.4	3 331.7	3 869.6 [b]
Economy: Agriculture (% of Gross Value Added) [f,g]	14.3	13.9	14.2 [b]
Economy: Industry (% of Gross Value Added) [f,h]	43.9	41.4	39.7 [b]
Economy: Services and other activity (% of GVA) [f,i]	41.8	44.7	46.1 [b]
Employment in agriculture (% of employed)	39.1	33.0	27.7 [j,b]
Employment in industry (% of employed)	18.7	22.0	22.7 [j,b]
Employment in services & other sectors (% employed)	42.2	44.9	49.6 [j,b]
Unemployment rate (% of labour force)	5.6	4.5	4.4 [j]
Labour force participation rate (female/male pop. %)	50.9 / 82.3	50.7 / 82.4	53.7 / 81.6 [j]
CPI: Consumer Price Index (2010=100)	100	132	156 [e]
Agricultural production index (2014-2016=100)	91	101	119 [b]
International trade: exports (million current US$)	157 779	150 366	231 522 [e]
International trade: imports (million current US$)	135 663	142 695	196 190 [e]
International trade: balance (million current US$)	22 116	7 671	35 333 [e]
Balance of payments, current account (million US$)	5 144	- 17 519	3 430 [e]

Major trading partners						2021
Export partners (% of exports)	China	23.2	United States	11.2	Japan	7.7
Import partners (% of imports)	China	28.7	Singapore	7.9	Japan	7.5

Social indicators	2010	2015	2022
Population growth rate (average annual %)	1.2	1.1	0.6 [a]
Urban population (% of total population)	49.9	53.3	56.0 [d]
Urban population growth rate (average annual %) [k]	3.0	2.6	...
Fertility rate, total (live births per woman)	2.5	2.3	2.2 [a]
Life expectancy at birth (females/males, years)	70.4 / 66.9	71.6 / 67.8	70.4 / 66.2 [a]
Population age distribution (0-14/60+ years old, %)	27.9 / 8.7	26.9 / 9.3	25.2 / 10.9 [a]
International migrant stock (000/% of total pop.) [l]	307.5 / 0.1	338.1 / 0.1	355.5 / 0.1 [b]
Refugees and others of concern to the UNHCR (000)	2.9 [m]	13.2	13.6 [e]
Infant mortality rate (per 1 000 live births)	27.6	22.8	17.7 [a]
Health: Current expenditure (% of GDP)	2.8	2.9	2.9 [d]
Health: Physicians (per 1 000 pop.)	0.1	0.3	0.6 [b]
Education: Government expenditure (% of GDP)	2.8	3.6	2.8 [d]
Education: Primary gross enrol. ratio (f/m per 100 pop.)	111.0 / 107.4	104.4 / 107.4	104.6 / 108.1 [n]
Education: Sec. gross enrol. ratio (f/m per 100 pop.)	76.7 / 76.2	86.3 / 86.0	90.0 / 87.8 [n]
Education: Upr. Sec. gross enrol. ratio (f/m per 100 pop.)	63.1 / 64.5	74.4 / 77.8	81.9 / 78.7 [n]
Seats held by women in the National Parliament (%)	18.0	17.1	21.9 [o]

Environment and infrastructure indicators	2010	2015	2022
Individuals using the Internet (per 100 inhabitants)	10.9 [p]	22.1	53.7 [b]
Research & Development expenditure (% of GDP)	0.1 [j,q,r,s]	0.1 [j,t]	0.3 [b]
Threatened species (number)	1 142	1 246	2 168
Forested area (% of land area) [j]	53.1	50.6	49.4 [d]
CO2 emission estimates (million tons/tons per capita)	409.9 / 1.6	474.0 / 1.8	641.5 / 2.4 [b]
Energy production, primary (Petajoules) [u]	16 605	17 364	21 267 [d]
Energy supply per capita (Gigajoules) [u]	33	34	41 [d]
Tourist/visitor arrivals at national borders (000)	7 003	10 407	4 053 [b]
Important sites for terrestrial biodiversity protected (%)	19.4	22.8	25.9 [e]
Net Official Development Assist. received (% of GNI)	0.18	0.00	0.12 [b]

a Projected estimate (medium fertility variant). b 2020. c Refers to the functional urban area. d 2019. e 2021. f Data classified according to ISIC Rev. 4. g Excludes irrigation canals and landscaping care. h Excludes publishing activities. Includes irrigation and canals. i Includes publishing activities and landscape care. Excludes repair of personal and household goods. j Estimate. k Data refers to a 5-year period preceding the reference year. l Including refugees. m Data as at the end of December. n 2018. o Data are as at 1 January of reporting year. p Refers to total population. q Partial data. r Break in the time series. s 2009. t 2013. u Data include Timor-Leste.

Iran (Islamic Republic of)

Region	Southern Asia	UN membership date	24 October 1945
Population (000, 2022)	88 551[a]	Surface area (km2)	1 630 848[b]
Pop. density (per km2, 2022)	54.4[a]	Sex ratio (m per 100 f)	102.0[a]
Capital city	Tehran	National currency	Iranian Rial (IRR)
Capital city pop. (000, 2022)	9 013.7[c]	Exchange rate (per US$)	42 000.0[d]

Economic indicators

	2010	2015	2022
GDP: Gross domestic product (million current US$)	523 804	417 210	939 316[b]
GDP growth rate (annual %, const. 2015 prices)	6.9	- 1.4	3.4[b]
GDP per capita (current US$)	7 101.2	5 315.3	11 183.3[b]
Economy: Agriculture (% of Gross Value Added)[e,f]	5.6	10.4	14.7[b]
Economy: Industry (% of Gross Value Added)[f,g]	43.3	33.0	32.5[b]
Economy: Services and other activity (% of GVA)[f,h]	51.1	56.6	52.8[b]
Employment in agriculture (% of employed)	19.2	18.0	17.8[i,b]
Employment in industry (% of employed)	32.2	32.5	30.3[i,b]
Employment in services & other sectors (% employed)	48.6	49.4	51.9[i,b]
Unemployment rate (% of labour force)	13.7	11.2	11.1[i]
Labour force participation rate (female/male pop. %)	15.2 / 67.7	14.3 / 68.0	15.1 / 69.1[i]
CPI: Consumer Price Index (2010=100)[j]	...	92	328[d]
Agricultural production index (2014-2016=100)	90	99	99[b]
International trade: exports (million current US$)	83 785	60 041	17 204[i,d]
International trade: imports (million current US$)	54 697	40 037	23 030[i,d]
International trade: balance (million current US$)	29 088	20 003	- 5 826[d]

Major trading partners

							2021
Export partners (% of exports)[i]	Other Asia, nes	39.0	Türkiye	16.9	Russian Federation	6.1
Import partners (% of imports)[i]	China	26.1	United Arab Emirates	19.8	Türkiye	8.7

Social indicators

	2010	2015	2022
Population growth rate (average annual %)	1.4	2.2	0.7[a]
Urban population (% of total population)	70.6	73.4	75.4[c]
Urban population growth rate (average annual %)[k]	2.0	2.0	...
Fertility rate, total (live births per woman)	1.8	2.1	1.7[a]
Life expectancy at birth (females/males, years)	75.7 / 70.6	77.8 / 72.7	77.5 / 71.9[a]
Population age distribution (0-14/60+ years old, %)	22.3 / 7.8	23.5 / 9.2	23.6 / 11.6[a]
International migrant stock (000/% of total pop.)[l,m]	2 722.4 / 3.7	2 729.9 / 3.5	2 797.2 / 3.3[b]
Refugees and others of concern to the UNHCR (000)	1 085.3[n]	979.5	800.1[d]
Infant mortality rate (per 1 000 live births)	16.3	13.1	10.3[a]
Health: Current expenditure (% of GDP)[o,p]	6.7	7.5	6.7[c]
Health: Physicians (per 1 000 pop.)	0.5[q]	1.2	1.6[r]
Education: Government expenditure (% of GDP)	3.7	2.8	3.7[c]
Education: Primary gross enrol. ratio (f/m per 100 pop.)	99.6 / 101.7	112.3 / 105.7	113.9 / 107.7[s]
Education: Sec. gross enrol. ratio (f/m per 100 pop.)	78.0 / 83.2	83.0 / 88.7	84.7 / 87.9[s]
Education: Upr. Sec. gross enrol. ratio (f/m per 100 pop.)	70.4 / 74.5	77.3 / 83.3[t]	76.3 / 79.3[s]
Intentional homicide rate (per 100 000 pop.)	3.0[u]	2.5[t]	2.2[r]
Seats held by women in the National Parliament (%)	2.8	3.1	5.6[v]

Environment and infrastructure indicators

	2010	2015	2022
Individuals using the Internet (per 100 inhabitants)	15.9[w]	45.3[w]	84.1[b]
Research & Development expenditure (% of GDP)	0.3[x,y]	0.4	0.9[c]
Threatened species (number)	102	121	189
Forested area (% of land area)	6.6	6.6	6.6[i,c]
CO2 emission estimates (million tons/tons per capita)[o]	503.0 / 6.8	560.8 / 7.1	588.6 / 7.0[c]
Energy production, primary (Petajoules)	14 283	13 637	14 786[c]
Energy supply per capita (Gigajoules)	116	128	138[c]
Tourist/visitor arrivals at national borders (000)	2 938	5 237	1 550[b]
Important sites for terrestrial biodiversity protected (%)	43.5	43.5	43.5[c]
Pop. using safely managed drinking water (urban/rural, %)	95.9 / 84.1	96.0 / 85.6	96.1 / 87.2[b]
Net Official Development Assist. received (% of GNI)	0.02	0.03	0.12[b]

a Projected estimate (medium fertility variant). b 2020. c 2019. d 2021. e Excludes irrigation canals and landscaping care. f Data classified according to ISIC Rev. 4. g Excludes publishing activities. Includes irrigation and canals. h Includes publishing activities and landscape care. Excludes repair of personal and household goods. i Estimate. j Index base: fiscal (solar) year 2016 (21 March 2016 - 20 March 2017)=100. k Data refers to a 5-year period preceding the reference year. l Refers to foreign citizens. m Including refugees. n Data as at the end of December. o Data refer to fiscal years beginning 21 March. p Country is still reporting data based on SHA 1.0. q 2006. r 2018. s 2017. t 2014. u 2009. v Data are as at 1 January of reporting year. w Population aged 6 years and over. x Excluding private non-profit. y Excluding government.

Iraq

Region	Western Asia	UN membership date	21 December 1945
Population (000, 2022)	44 496[a]	Surface area (km2)	435 052[b]
Pop. density (per km2, 2022)	102.5[a]	Sex ratio (m per 100 f)	100.4[a]
Capital city	Baghdad	National currency	Iraqi Dinar (IQD)
Capital city pop. (000, 2022)	6 974.4[c]	Exchange rate (per US$)	1 450.0[d]

Economic indicators

	2010	2015	2022
GDP: Gross domestic product (million current US$)[e]	138 517	166 774	166 757[b]
GDP growth rate (annual %, const. 2015 prices)[e]	6.4	4.7	- 15.7[b]
GDP per capita (current US$)[e]	4 657.3	4 688.3	4 145.9[b]
Economy: Agriculture (% of Gross Value Added)[f]	5.1	4.2	5.8[b]
Economy: Industry (% of Gross Value Added)[f]	55.4	45.0	40.6[b]
Economy: Services and other activity (% of GVA)[f]	39.4	50.9	53.6[b]
Employment in agriculture (% of employed)[g]	21.9	19.4	17.8[b]
Employment in industry (% of employed)[g]	21.7	22.8	22.4[b]
Employment in services & other sectors (% employed)[g]	56.4	57.9	59.9[b]
Unemployment rate (% of labour force)[g]	8.3	10.7	13.3
Labour force participation rate (female/male pop. %)[g]	11.9 / 70.8	14.0 / 72.0	11.2 / 72.3
CPI: Consumer Price Index (2010=100)	100	119	128[d]
Agricultural production index (2014-2016=100)	121	81	148[b]
International trade: exports (million current US$)	52 483	49 403	80 611[g,d]
International trade: imports (million current US$)	43 915	32 667	41 008[g,d]
International trade: balance (million current US$)	8 568	16 736	39 602[d]
Balance of payments, current account (million US$)	6 488	- 2 762	- 6 197[b]

Major trading partners

						2021
Export partners (% of exports)[g]	China	30.6	India	30.5	Republic of Korea	6.5
Import partners (% of imports)[g]	United Arab Emirates	31.4	Türkiye	19.3	China	18.5

Social indicators

	2010	2015	2022
Population growth rate (average annual %)	3.2	2.6	2.2[a]
Urban population (% of total population)	69.1	69.9	70.7[c]
Urban population growth rate (average annual %)[h]	2.7	3.4	...
Fertility rate, total (live births per woman)	4.4	4.1	3.4[a]
Life expectancy at birth (females/males, years)	70.1 / 63.9	71.2 / 67.5	73.4 / 69.2[a]
Population age distribution (0-14/60+ years old, %)	41.2 / 4.7	40.3 / 5.0	37.7 / 5.1[a]
International migrant stock (000/% of total pop.)[i,j]	120.5 / 0.4	359.4 / 1.0	365.8 / 0.9[b]
Refugees and others of concern to the UNHCR (000)	1 796.3[k]	4 311.7	1 565.5[d]
Infant mortality rate (per 1 000 live births)	28.6	24.5	17.6[a]
Health: Current expenditure (% of GDP)[l]	3.2	3.1	4.5[c]
Health: Physicians (per 1 000 pop.)	0.7	1.0[m]	1.0[b]
Education: Primary gross enrol. ratio (f/m per 100 pop.)	99.1 / 117.8[n]	... / ...	... / ...
Education: Sec. gross enrol. ratio (f/m per 100 pop.)	46.0 / 61.4[n]	... / ...	... / ...
Education: Upr. Sec. gross enrol. ratio (f/m per 100 pop.)	35.3 / 44.8[n]	... / ...	... / ...
Intentional homicide rate (per 100 000 pop.)	9.0	10.1[o]	...
Seats held by women in the National Parliament (%)	25.5	26.5	28.9[p]

Environment and infrastructure indicators

	2010	2015	2022
Individuals using the Internet (per 100 inhabitants)	2.5	16.8[g]	60.0[q,c]
Research & Development expenditure (% of GDP)	~0.0[r,s,t]	~0.0	~0.0[b]
Threatened species (number)	60	69	99
Forested area (% of land area)	1.9[g]	1.9	1.9[c]
CO2 emission estimates (million tons/tons per capita)	90.1 / 3.0	100.8 / 2.8	139.4 / 3.5[c]
Energy production, primary (Petajoules)	5 274	7 565	10 308[c]
Energy supply per capita (Gigajoules)	48	56	58[c]
Tourist/visitor arrivals at national borders (000)	1 518	892[o]	...
Important sites for terrestrial biodiversity protected (%)	2.8	5.5	5.6[d]
Pop. using safely managed drinking water (urban/rural, %)	62.7 / 37.8	63.7 / 42.8	64.6 / 47.6[b]
Pop. using safely managed sanitation (urban/rural %)	36.7 / 41.0	40.1 / 43.3	42.3 / 44.4[b]
Net Official Development Assist. received (% of GNI)	1.55	0.90	1.43[b]

a Projected estimate (medium fertility variant). b 2020. c 2019. d 2021. e Data compiled in accordance with the System of National Accounts 1968 (1968 SNA). f Data classified according to ISIC Rev. 4. g Estimate. h Data refers to a 5-year period preceding the reference year. i Including refugees. j Refers to foreign citizens. k Data as at the end of December. l Data based on calendar year (January 1 to December 31). m 2014. n 2007. o 2013. p Data are as at 1 January of reporting year. q Includes Kurdistan. r Excluding business enterprise. s Based on R&D budget instead of R&D expenditure. t Excluding private non-profit.

Ireland

Region	Northern Europe	UN membership date	14 December 1955	
Population (000, 2022)	5 023 [a]	Surface area (km2)	69 825 [b]	
Pop. density (per km2, 2022)	73.5 [a]	Sex ratio (m per 100 f)	98.3 [a]	
Capital city	Dublin	National currency	Euro (EUR)	
Capital city pop. (000, 2022)	1 214.7 [c]	Exchange rate (per US$)	0.9 [d]	

Economic indicators

	2010	2015	2022
GDP: Gross domestic product (million current US$)	221 660	291 463	425 889 [b]
GDP growth rate (annual %, const. 2015 prices)	1.8	25.2	5.9 [b]
GDP per capita (current US$)	48 670.2	62 647.5	86 251.0 [b]
Economy: Agriculture (% of Gross Value Added) [e,f]	1.0	1.0	1.0 [b]
Economy: Industry (% of Gross Value Added) [f,g]	25.7	41.4	40.5 [b]
Economy: Services and other activity (% of GVA) [f,h]	73.3	57.7	58.5 [b]
Employment in agriculture (% of employed)	5.8	5.3	4.5 [i,b]
Employment in industry (% of employed)	18.1	18.1	18.5 [i,b]
Employment in services & other sectors (% employed)	76.2	76.6	77.0 [i,b]
Unemployment rate (% of labour force)	14.5	9.9	6.0 [i]
Labour force participation rate (female/male pop. %)	55.2 / 70.2	54.9 / 69.1	56.3 / 68.4 [i]
CPI: Consumer Price Index (2010=100) [j]	100	105	109 [d]
Agricultural production index (2014-2016=100)	88	101	116 [b]
International trade: exports (million current US$)	120 645	124 731	194 264 [i,d]
International trade: imports (million current US$)	64 601	77 795	117 334 [i,d]
International trade: balance (million current US$)	56 045	46 935	76 930 [d]
Balance of payments, current account (million US$)	2 320	12 912	70 249 [d]

Major trading partners

						2021
Export partners (% of exports) [i]	United States	30.9	Belgium	11.1	Germany	10.8
Import partners (% of imports) [i]	United Kingdom	22.9	United States	15.1	France	11.1

Social indicators

	2010	2015	2022
Population growth rate (average annual %)	0.5	1.0	0.7 [a]
Urban population (% of total population)	61.5	62.5	63.4 [c]
Urban population growth rate (average annual %) [k]	2.2	0.6	...
Fertility rate, total (live births per woman)	2.1	1.9	1.8 [a]
Life expectancy at birth (females/males, years)	82.7 / 78.3	83.3 / 79.5	84.4 / 81.0 [a]
Population age distribution (0-14/60+ years old, %)	21.1 / 16.1	21.4 / 18.1	19.6 / 20.5 [a]
International migrant stock (000/% of total pop.)	730.5 / 16.0	759.3 / 16.3	871.3 / 17.6 [b]
Refugees and others of concern to the UNHCR (000)	14.2 [l]	10.5 [l]	16.5 [d]
Infant mortality rate (per 1 000 live births)	3.7	3.5	2.5 [a]
Health: Current expenditure (% of GDP)	10.5	7.3	6.7 [c]
Health: Physicians (per 1 000 pop.)	4.1	3.2	3.5 [b]
Education: Government expenditure (% of GDP)	6.0	3.8	3.4 [m]
Education: Primary gross enrol. ratio (f/m per 100 pop.) [i]	103.3 / 103.2	101.0 / 101.4	100.9 / 101.0 [c]
Education: Sec. gross enrol. ratio (f/m per 100 pop.) [i]	121.7 / 114.8	118.7 / 115.4	144.5 / 132.0 [c]
Education: Upr. Sec. gross enrol. ratio (f/m per 100 pop.) [i]	141.6 / 126.9	141.5 / 133.7	194.2 / 167.0 [c]
Intentional homicide rate (per 100 000 pop.)	1.2	0.7	0.7 [b]
Seats held by women in the National Parliament (%)	13.9	16.3	23.1 [n]

Environment and infrastructure indicators

	2010	2015	2022
Individuals using the Internet (per 100 inhabitants)	69.8 [o]	83.5	92.0 [b]
Research & Development expenditure (% of GDP)	1.6 [i]	1.2 [i]	1.2 [p,b]
Threatened species (number)	27	39	90
Forested area (% of land area)	10.5	11.0	11.3 [c]
CO2 emission estimates (million tons/tons per capita)	39.7 / 8.6	35.9 / 7.5	32.1 / 6.4 [b]
Energy production, primary (Petajoules)	78	81	171 [c]
Energy supply per capita (Gigajoules)	134	120	118 [c]
Tourist/visitor arrivals at national borders (000) [q]	7 134	9 528	10 951 [c]
Important sites for terrestrial biodiversity protected (%)	77.7	80.7	83.5 [d]
Pop. using safely managed sanitation (urban/rural %)	72.1 / 67.2	84.2 / 70.7	88.6 / 73.0 [b]
Net Official Development Assist. disbursed (% of GNI) [r]	1.57	0.54	0.31 [b]

a Projected estimate (medium fertility variant). b 2020. c 2019. d 2021. e Excludes irrigation canals and landscaping care. f Data classified according to ISIC Rev. 4. g Excludes publishing activities. Includes irrigation and canals. h Includes publishing activities and landscape care. Excludes repair of personal and household goods. i Estimate. j Calculated by the UNSD from national indices. k Data refers to a 5-year period preceding the reference year. l Data as at the end of December. m 2018. n Data are as at 1 January of reporting year. o Population aged 16 to 74 years. p Provisional data. q Including tourists from Northern Ireland. r DAC member (OECD).

Isle of Man

Region	Northern Europe	Population (000, 2022)	84 [a,b]
Surface area (km2)	572 [c]	Pop. density (per km2, 2022)	147.8 [a,b]
Sex ratio (m per 100 f)	98.1 [a,b]	Capital city	Douglas
National currency	Pound Sterling (GBP)	Capital city pop. (000, 2022)	27.2 [d]
Exchange rate (per US$)	0.7 [e]		

Economic indicators	2010	2015	2022
Employment in agriculture (% of employed)	1.9 [f,g]	...	...
Employment in industry (% of employed)	14.8 [f,g]	...	...
Employment in services & other sectors (% employed)	83.3 [f,g]	...	...
Unemployment rate (% of labour force)	2.4 [g]	2.6 [h,i,j]	...
Labour force participation rate (female/male pop. %)	56.3 / 69.9 [g]	57.5 / 69.3 [i,k,l]	... / ...
CPI: Consumer Price Index (2010=100)	...	161 [m,n]	...

Social indicators	2010	2015	2022
Population growth rate (average annual %) [b]	1.1	- 0.4	0.2 [a]
Urban population (% of total population)	52.0	52.2	52.7 [o]
Urban population growth rate (average annual %) [p]	1.0	0.9	...
Fertility rate, total (live births per woman) [b]	2.2	1.7	1.6 [a]
Life expectancy at birth (females/males, years) [b]	81.4 / 76.6	80.8 / 77.1	82.7 / 78.8 [a]
Population age distribution (0-14/60+ years old, %) [b]	16.7 / 24.4	16.1 / 26.5	14.7 / 29.4 [a]
International migrant stock (000/% of total pop.)	43.4 / 51.2	42.2 / 50.7	43.0 / 50.6 [c]
Infant mortality rate (per 1 000 live births) [b]	13.0	13.1	10.4 [a]
Intentional homicide rate (per 100 000 pop.)	...	1.2	0.0 [q]

Environment and infrastructure indicators	2010	2015	2022
Threatened species (number)	2	3	8
Forested area (% of land area) [r]	6.1	6.1	6.1 [o]
Energy production, primary (Petajoules) [r]	0	0	1 [o]
Energy supply per capita (Gigajoules)	47	49	58 [o]

a Projected estimate (medium fertility variant). b For statistical purposes, the data for United Kingdom do not include this area. c 2020. d 2018. e 2021. f Data classified according to ISIC Rev. 3. g 2006. h Population aged 15 to 64 years. i Break in the time series. j 2013. k Population aged 16 years and over. l 2011. m Base: 2000=100. n 2014. o 2019. p Data refers to a 5-year period preceding the reference year. q 2016. r Estimate.

Israel

Region	Western Asia	
Population (000, 2022)	9 038[a]	
Pop. density (per km2, 2022)	417.6[a]	
Capital city	Jerusalem[c]	
Capital city pop. (000, 2022)	919.4[d,e]	

UN membership date	11 May 1949
Surface area (km2)	22 072[b]
Sex ratio (m per 100 f)	99.5[a]
National currency	New Israeli Sheqel (ILS)
Exchange rate (per US$)	3.1[f]

Economic indicators

	2010	2015	2022
GDP: Gross domestic product (million current US$)	234 655	300 078	407 101[b]
GDP growth rate (annual %, const. 2015 prices)	5.7	2.3	- 2.2[b]
GDP per capita (current US$)	31 941.3	37 610.9	47 033.6[b]
Economy: Agriculture (% of Gross Value Added)[g,h]	1.7	1.3	1.2[b]
Economy: Industry (% of Gross Value Added)[h,i]	23.6	22.5	20.6[b]
Economy: Services and other activity (% of GVA)[h,j]	74.7	76.2	78.1[b]
Employment in agriculture (% of employed)	1.3[k]	1.0	0.9[k,b]
Employment in industry (% of employed)	19.1[k]	17.6	16.8[k,b]
Employment in services & other sectors (% employed)	79.6[k]	81.4	82.3[k,b]
Unemployment rate (% of labour force)	8.5	5.2	4.7[k]
Labour force participation rate (female/male pop. %)	57.5 / 69.4	59.1 / 69.3	59.1 / 66.4[k]
CPI: Consumer Price Index (2010=100)	100	107	109[f]
Agricultural production index (2014-2016=100)	91	99	101[b]
International trade: exports (million current US$)	58 413	64 062	60 157[f]
International trade: imports (million current US$)	59 194	62 068	92 148[f]
International trade: balance (million current US$)	- 781	1 994	- 31 991[f]
Balance of payments, current account (million US$)	8 103	15 724	22 266[f]

Major trading partners

							2021
Export partners (% of exports)	United States	27.1	Areas nes[l]	9.0	China	7.3
Import partners (% of imports)	China	18.1	United States	10.2	Areas nes	10.1

Social indicators

	2010	2015	2022
Population growth rate (average annual %)	1.8	1.9	1.5[a]
Urban population (% of total population)	91.8	92.2	92.5[e]
Urban population growth rate (average annual %)[m]	2.4	1.7	...
Fertility rate, total (live births per woman)	3.0	3.2	2.9[a]
Life expectancy at birth (females/males, years)	83.6 / 79.8	84.0 / 80.1	84.5 / 80.6[a]
Population age distribution (0-14/60+ years old, %)	27.8 / 14.3	28.1 / 15.2	28.1 / 16.1[a]
International migrant stock (000/% of total pop.)[n]	1 956.2 / 26.6	2 011.7 / 25.2	1 953.6 / 22.6[b]
Refugees and others of concern to the UNHCR (000)	31.1[o]	45.2	41.5[f]
Infant mortality rate (per 1 000 live births)	3.8	3.3	2.9[a]
Health: Current expenditure (% of GDP)	7.0	7.1	7.5[e]
Health: Physicians (per 1 000 pop.)	3.5	3.5	3.6[b]
Education: Government expenditure (% of GDP)	5.5	5.9	6.2[p]
Education: Primary gross enrol. ratio (f/m per 100 pop.)	105.7 / 105.2	106.0 / 105.3	105.2 / 103.9[e]
Education: Sec. gross enrol. ratio (f/m per 100 pop.)	104.5 / 102.0	104.2 / 103.2	105.9 / 104.1[e]
Education: Upr. Sec. gross enrol. ratio (f/m per 100 pop.)	103.9 / 101.5	102.6 / 101.0	107.0 / 104.5[e]
Intentional homicide rate (per 100 000 pop.)	2.0	1.4	1.5[e]
Seats held by women in the National Parliament (%)	19.2	22.5	30.0[q]

Environment and infrastructure indicators

	2010	2015	2022
Individuals using the Internet (per 100 inhabitants)	67.5[r]	77.4	90.1[b]
Research & Development expenditure (% of GDP)[s]	3.9	4.3	5.4[b]
Threatened species (number)	131	152	246
Forested area (% of land area)	7.1	7.6	6.5[e]
CO2 emission estimates (million tons/tons per capita)	69.1 / 9.0	64.5 / 7.6	58.6 / 6.3[b]
Energy production, primary (Petajoules)	162	273	336[e]
Energy supply per capita (Gigajoules)	132	115	107[e]
Tourist/visitor arrivals at national borders (000)[t]	2 803	2 799	831[b]
Important sites for terrestrial biodiversity protected (%)	16.1	16.4	17.1[f]
Pop. using safely managed drinking water (urban/rural, %)	99.7 / 99.7	99.5 / 99.4	99.3 / 99.1[b]
Pop. using safely managed sanitation (urban/rural %)	87.5 / 85.7	91.3 / 89.2	95.1 / 92.7[b]
Net Official Development Assist. disbursed (% of GNI)	...	0.07[u]	...

a Projected estimate (medium fertility variant). **b** 2020. **c** Designation and data provided by Israel. The position of the UN on Jerusalem is stated in A/RES/181 (II) and subsequent General Assembly and Security Council resolutions. **d** Including East Jerusalem. **e** 2019. **f** 2021. **g** Excludes irrigation canals and landscaping care. **h** Data classified according to ISIC Rev. 4. **i** Excludes publishing activities. Includes irrigation and canals. **j** Includes publishing activities and landscape care. Excludes repair of personal and household goods. **k** Estimate. **l** Areas nes **m** Data refers to a 5-year period preceding the reference year. **n** Including refugees. **o** Data as at the end of December. **p** 2018. **q** Data are as at 1 January of reporting year. **r** Population aged 20 years and over. **s** Do not correspond exactly to Frascati Manual recommendations. **t** Excluding nationals residing abroad. **u** 2014.

Italy

Region	Southern Europe	UN membership date	14 December 1955
Population (000, 2022)	59 038 [a]	Surface area (km2)	302 068 [b]
Pop. density (per km2, 2022)	199.5 [a]	Sex ratio (m per 100 f)	95.2 [a]
Capital city	Rome	National currency	Euro (EUR)
Capital city pop. (000, 2022)	4 234.0 [c,d]	Exchange rate (per US$)	0.9 [a]

Economic indicators

	2010	2015	2022
GDP: Gross domestic product (million current US$)	2 134 018	1 835 899	1 888 709 [b]
GDP growth rate (annual %, const. 2015 prices)	1.7	0.8	- 8.9 [b]
GDP per capita (current US$)	35 971.5	30 306.1	31 238.0 [b]
Economy: Agriculture (% of Gross Value Added) [f,g]	2.0	2.3	2.2 [b]
Economy: Industry (% of Gross Value Added) [g,h]	24.3	23.2	23.9 [b]
Economy: Services and other activity (% of GVA) [g,i]	73.7	74.5	73.9 [b]
Employment in agriculture (% of employed)	3.8	3.8	3.6 [j,b]
Employment in industry (% of employed)	28.6	26.6	25.6 [j,b]
Employment in services & other sectors (% employed)	67.6	69.6	70.8 [j,b]
Unemployment rate (% of labour force)	8.4	11.9	9.5 [j]
Labour force participation rate (female/male pop. %)	38.2 / 59.1	39.8 / 58.9	40.4 / 58.1 [j]
CPI: Consumer Price Index (2010=100)	100	107	113 [k,e]
Agricultural production index (2014-2016=100)	109	103	100 [b]
International trade: exports (million current US$)	446 840	456 989	601 663 [e]
International trade: imports (million current US$)	486 984	410 933	557 228 [e]
International trade: balance (million current US$)	- 40 145	46 055	44 435 [e]
Balance of payments, current account (million US$)	- 70 819	26 183	53 095 [e]

Major trading partners

						2021
Export partners (% of exports)	Germany	13.1	France	10.3	United States	9.5
Import partners (% of imports)	Germany	16.1	France	8.3	China	8.2

Social indicators

	2010	2015	2022
Population growth rate (average annual %)	0.4	- 0.2	- 0.3 [a]
Urban population (% of total population)	68.3	69.6	70.7 [d]
Urban population growth rate (average annual %) [l]	0.5	0.3	...
Fertility rate, total (live births per woman)	1.4	1.3	1.3 [a]
Life expectancy at birth (females/males, years)	84.5 / 79.5	84.7 / 80.2	86.0 / 82.0 [a]
Population age distribution (0-14/60+ years old, %)	14.1 / 26.7	13.7 / 28.0	12.4 / 31.0 [a]
International migrant stock (000/% of total pop.)	5 787.9 / 9.8	5 805.3 / 9.6	6 387.0 / 10.6 [b]
Refugees and others of concern to the UNHCR (000)	61.3 [m]	142.6	191.1 [e]
Infant mortality rate (per 1 000 live births)	3.2	2.9	2.1 [a]
Health: Current expenditure (% of GDP)	8.9	8.9	8.7 [d]
Health: Physicians (per 1 000 pop.)	3.8	3.8	3.9 [b]
Education: Government expenditure (% of GDP)	4.3	4.1	4.3 [n]
Education: Primary gross enrol. ratio (f/m per 100 pop.)	102.5 / 103.5	100.2 / 100.6	100.0 / 101.9 [d]
Education: Sec. gross enrol. ratio (f/m per 100 pop.)	102.4 / 103.4	102.1 / 102.4	100.4 / 101.9 [d]
Education: Upr. Sec. gross enrol. ratio (f/m per 100 pop.)	99.9 / 99.9	100.9 / 100.2	99.8 / 100.1 [d]
Intentional homicide rate (per 100 000 pop.)	0.9	0.8	0.5 [b]
Seats held by women in the National Parliament (%)	21.3	31.0	36.3 [o]

Environment and infrastructure indicators

	2010	2015	2022
Individuals using the Internet (per 100 inhabitants)	53.7 [p]	58.1	70.5 [b]
Research & Development expenditure (% of GDP)	1.2	1.3	1.5 [b]
Threatened species (number)	174	279	557
Forested area (% of land area)	30.5 [j]	31.4 [j]	32.2 [d]
CO2 emission estimates (million tons/tons per capita) [q]	398.4 / 6.6	335.5 / 5.4	285.7 / 4.7 [b]
Energy production, primary (Petajoules) [q]	1 378	1 509	1 437 [d]
Energy supply per capita (Gigajoules) [q]	123	105	103 [d]
Tourist/visitor arrivals at national borders (000) [r]	43 626	50 732	25 190 [b]
Important sites for terrestrial biodiversity protected (%)	72.3	73.2	75.9 [e]
Pop. using safely managed sanitation (urban/rural %)	96.4 / 94.3	96.4 / 94.3	96.4 / 94.3 [b]
Net Official Development Assist. disbursed (% of GNI) [s]	0.47	0.86	0.34 [b]

a Projected estimate (medium fertility variant). b 2020. c Refers to the official Metropolitan City. d 2019. e 2021. f Excludes irrigation canals and landscaping care. g Data classified according to ISIC Rev. 4. h Excludes publishing activities. Includes irrigation and canals. i Includes publishing activities and landscape care. Excludes repair of personal and household goods. j Estimate. k Calculated by the UNSD from national indices. l Data refers to a 5-year period preceding the reference year. m Data as at the end of December. n 2018. o Data are as at 1 January of reporting year. p Population aged 16 to 74 years. q Data include San Marino and the Holy See. r Excluding seasonal and border workers. s DAC member (OECD).

Jamaica

Region	Caribbean	UN membership date	18 September 1962
Population (000, 2022)	2 827[a]	Surface area (km2)	10 990[b]
Pop. density (per km2, 2022)	261.1[a]	Sex ratio (m per 100 f)	98.4[a]
Capital city	Kingston	National currency	Jamaican Dollar (JMD)
Capital city pop. (000, 2022)	589.5[c]	Exchange rate (per US$)	153.9[d]

Economic indicators

	2010	2015	2022
GDP: Gross domestic product (million current US$)	13 221	14 198	13 812[b]
GDP growth rate (annual %, const. 2015 prices)	- 1.5	0.9	- 10.2[b]
GDP per capita (current US$)	4 704.1	4 911.0	4 664.5[b]
Economy: Agriculture (% of Gross Value Added)[e]	5.9	7.2	9.8[b]
Economy: Industry (% of Gross Value Added)[e]	20.0	22.0	23.0[b]
Economy: Services and other activity (% of GVA)[e]	74.1	70.7	67.3[b]
Employment in agriculture (% of employed)	17.8[f]	17.7	15.7[f,b]
Employment in industry (% of employed)	16.2[f]	14.9	16.2[f,b]
Employment in services & other sectors (% employed)	66.0[f]	67.3	68.1[f,b]
Unemployment rate (% of labour force)	12.4	13.5	8.3[f]
Labour force participation rate (female/male pop. %)	54.7 / 70.3	56.3 / 70.3	54.9 / 68.8[f]
CPI: Consumer Price Index (2010=100)[g]	100	141	181[d]
Agricultural production index (2014-2016=100)	91	98	101[b]
International trade: exports (million current US$)	1 328	1 263	1 381[f,d]
International trade: imports (million current US$)	5 225	4 993	5 420[f,d]
International trade: balance (million current US$)	- 3 898	- 3 730	- 4 039[d]
Balance of payments, current account (million US$)	- 934	- 430	- 43[b]

Major trading partners

						2021
Export partners (% of exports)[f]	United States	46.6	Canada	9.7	Netherlands	8.1
Import partners (% of imports)[f]	United States	39.7	China	8.3	Brazil	6.5

Social indicators

	2010	2015	2022
Population growth rate (average annual %)	0.4	0.3	- 0.1[a]
Urban population (% of total population)	53.7	54.8	56.0[c]
Urban population growth rate (average annual %)[h]	0.9	0.8	...
Fertility rate, total (live births per woman)	1.7	1.6	1.3[a]
Life expectancy at birth (females/males, years)	74.7 / 70.6	74.0 / 70.8	72.7 / 68.5[a]
Population age distribution (0-14/60+ years old, %)	26.6 / 8.4	23.3 / 9.4	19.8 / 11.9[a]
International migrant stock (000/% of total pop.)[i]	23.7 / 0.8	23.2 / 0.8	23.6 / 0.8[b]
Refugees and others of concern to the UNHCR (000)	~0.0[j]	~0.0	0.1[d]
Infant mortality rate (per 1 000 live births)	15.2	13.2	11.3[a]
Health: Current expenditure (% of GDP)[f,k]	5.3	5.6	6.1[c]
Health: Physicians (per 1 000 pop.)	0.4[l]	0.4	0.5[m]
Education: Government expenditure (% of GDP)	6.4	5.5	5.4[f,b]
Education: Primary gross enrol. ratio (f/m per 100 pop.)	90.8 / 90.4[n]	... / ...	... / ...
Education: Sec. gross enrol. ratio (f/m per 100 pop.)	95.5 / 88.2	83.8 / 78.2	83.4 / 82.7[b]
Education: Upr. Sec. gross enrol. ratio (f/m per 100 pop.)	102.8 / 86.0	78.6 / 74.0	77.2 / 74.7[b]
Intentional homicide rate (per 100 000 pop.)	51.5	41.8	44.9[b]
Seats held by women in the National Parliament (%)	13.3	12.7	28.6[o]

Environment and infrastructure indicators

	2010	2015	2022
Individuals using the Internet (per 100 inhabitants)	27.7[p]	42.2	68.2[m]
Threatened species (number)	282	298	342
Forested area (% of land area)[f]	51.6	53.3	54.8[c]
CO2 emission estimates (million tons/tons per capita)	7.3 / 2.5	6.8 / 2.3	8.2 / 2.7[c]
Energy production, primary (Petajoules)	8	10	8[c]
Energy supply per capita (Gigajoules)	40	41	39[c]
Tourist/visitor arrivals at national borders (000)[q,r]	1 922	2 123	880[b]
Important sites for terrestrial biodiversity protected (%)	15.9	15.9	15.9[d]
Net Official Development Assist. received (% of GNI)	1.11	0.43	0.50[b]

a Projected estimate (medium fertility variant). b 2020. c 2019. d 2021. e Data classified according to ISIC Rev. 4. f Estimate. g Calculated by the UNSD from national indices. h Data refers to a 5-year period preceding the reference year. i Including refugees. j Data as at the end of December. k Data refer to fiscal years beginning 1 April. l 2008. m 2018. n 2007. o Data are as at 1 January of reporting year. p Population aged 14 years and over. q Including nationals residing abroad; E/D cards. r Arrivals of non-resident tourists by air.

Japan

Region	Eastern Asia	UN membership date	18 December 1956	
Population (000, 2022)	123 952[a]	Surface area (km2)	377 930[b,c]	
Pop. density (per km2, 2022)	328.9[a]	Sex ratio (m per 100 f)	94.6[a]	
Capital city	Tokyo	National currency	Yen (JPY)	
Capital city pop. (000, 2022)	37 435.2[d,e]	Exchange rate (per US$)	114.2[f]	

Economic indicators

	2010	2015	2022
GDP: Gross domestic product (million current US$)	5 759 072	4 444 931	5 057 759[c]
GDP growth rate (annual %, const. 2015 prices)	4.1	1.6	- 4.6[c]
GDP per capita (current US$)	44 802.9	34 730.1	39 989.7[c]
Economy: Agriculture (% of Gross Value Added)[g,h,i]	1.1	1.0	1.1[c]
Economy: Industry (% of Gross Value Added)[g,h,j]	28.3	28.8	28.9[c]
Economy: Services and other activity (% of GVA)[g,h,k]	70.6	70.2	70.0[c]
Employment in agriculture (% of employed)	4.1	3.6	3.4[l,c]
Employment in industry (% of employed)	25.6	25.0	24.1[l,c]
Employment in services & other sectors (% employed)	70.4	71.4	72.6[l,c]
Unemployment rate (% of labour force)	5.1	3.4	2.6[l]
Labour force participation rate (female/male pop. %)	48.3 / 71.5	49.6 / 70.3	53.1 / 70.8[l]
CPI: Consumer Price Index (2010=100)[m]	100	104	105[f]
Agricultural production index (2014-2016=100)	96	100	99[c]
International trade: exports (million current US$)	769 774	624 874	757 066[f]
International trade: imports (million current US$)	694 059	625 568	772 276[f]
International trade: balance (million current US$)	75 715	- 695	- 15 210[f]
Balance of payments, current account (million US$)	220 888	136 472	142 491[f]

Major trading partners

							2021
Export partners (% of exports)	China	21.6	United States	18.0	Other Asia, nes	7.2	
Import partners (% of imports)	China	24.0	United States	10.7	Australia	6.8	

Social indicators

	2010	2015	2022
Population growth rate (average annual %)	--0.0	- 0.2	- 0.5[a]
Urban population (% of total population)	90.8	91.4	91.7[e]
Urban population growth rate (average annual %)[n]	1.1	-0.0	...
Fertility rate, total (live births per woman)	1.4	1.4	1.3[a]
Life expectancy at birth (females/males, years)	86.2 / 79.5	87.0 / 80.7	87.8 / 81.8[a]
Population age distribution (0-14/60+ years old, %)	13.2 / 31.5	12.7 / 33.9	11.6 / 35.8[a]
International migrant stock (000/% of total pop.)[o]	2 134.2 / 1.7	2 232.2 / 1.7	2 771.0 / 2.2[c]
Refugees and others of concern to the UNHCR (000)	7.0[p]	13.8[l]	25.6[f]
Infant mortality rate (per 1 000 live births)	2.3	2.0	1.7[a]
Health: Current expenditure (% of GDP)	9.1	10.7	10.7[e]
Health: Physicians (per 1 000 pop.)	2.2	2.3[q]	2.5[r]
Education: Primary gross enrol. ratio (f/m per 100 pop.)	... / ...	... / ...	97.7 / 97.5[r]
Education: Sec. gross enrol. ratio (f/m per 100 pop.)	... / ...	... / ...	102.2 / 101.7[r]
Education: Upr. Sec. gross enrol. ratio (f/m per 100 pop.)	... / ...	... / ...	... / 103.4
Intentional homicide rate (per 100 000 pop.)	0.4	0.3	0.3[c]
Seats held by women in the National Parliament (%)	11.2	9.5	9.7[s]

Environment and infrastructure indicators

	2010	2015	2022
Individuals using the Internet (per 100 inhabitants)	78.2[t]	91.1	90.2[c]
Research & Development expenditure (% of GDP)	3.1	3.2	3.3[c]
Threatened species (number)	330	364	588
Forested area (% of land area)[l]	68.5	68.4	68.4[e]
CO2 emission estimates (million tons/tons per capita)[u]	1 142.4 / 8.8	1 163.5 / 9.1	1 033.2 / 8.1[c]
Energy production, primary (Petajoules)[u]	4 205	1 322	2 079[e]
Energy supply per capita (Gigajoules)[u]	163	142	137[e]
Tourist/visitor arrivals at national borders (000)[v]	8 611	19 737	4 116[c]
Important sites for terrestrial biodiversity protected (%)	50.0	63.0	64.8[f]
Net Official Development Assist. disbursed (% of GNI)[w]	0.86	0.83	0.62[c]

a Projected estimate (medium fertility variant). b Data refer to 1 October 2007. c 2020. d Major metropolitan areas. e 2019. f 2021. g Data classified according to ISIC Rev. 4. h At producers' prices. i Excludes irrigation canals and landscaping care. j Excludes publishing activities. Includes irrigation and canals. k Includes publishing activities and landscape care. Excludes repair of personal and household goods. l Estimate. m Calculated by the UNSD from national indices. n Data refers to a 5-year period preceding the reference year. o Refers to foreign citizens. p Data as at the end of December. q 2014. r 2018. s Data are as at 1 January of reporting year. t Population aged 6 years and over. u Data include Okinawa. v Excluding nationals residing abroad. w DAC member (OECD).

Region	Western Asia	UN membership date	14 December 1955
Population (000, 2022)	11 286[a]	Surface area (km2)	89 318[b]
Pop. density (per km2, 2022)	127.1[a]	Sex ratio (m per 100 f)	107.5[a]
Capital city	Amman	National currency	Jordanian Dinar (JOD)
Capital city pop. (000, 2022)	2 108.5[c]	Exchange rate (per US$)	0.7[d]

Economic indicators

	2010	2015	2022
GDP: Gross domestic product (million current US$)	27 134	38 587	43 697[b]
GDP growth rate (annual %, const. 2015 prices)	2.3	2.5	- 1.6[b]
GDP per capita (current US$)	3 736.6	4 164.1	4 282.7[b]
Economy: Agriculture (% of Gross Value Added)[e,f]	4.0	4.9	5.7[b]
Economy: Industry (% of Gross Value Added)[f,g]	29.5	28.1	26.4[b]
Economy: Services and other activity (% of GVA)[f,h]	66.5	67.0	67.9[b]
Employment in agriculture (% of employed)[i]	3.5	3.3	3.0[b]
Employment in industry (% of employed)[i]	26.4	25.4	24.4[b]
Employment in services & other sectors (% employed)[i]	70.1	71.3	72.6[b]
Unemployment rate (% of labour force)	12.5	13.1	18.8[i]
Labour force participation rate (female/male pop. %)[i]	16.1 / 61.3	16.6 / 62.7	13.7 / 63.1
CPI: Consumer Price Index (2010=100)	100	116	102[j,d]
Agricultural production index (2014-2016=100)	88	101	99[b]
International trade: exports (million current US$)	7 023	7 833	15 353[i,d]
International trade: imports (million current US$)	15 262	20 475	19 246[i,d]
International trade: balance (million current US$)	- 8 239	- 12 642	- 3 893[d]
Balance of payments, current account (million US$)	- 1 882	- 3 470	- 3 707[b]

Major trading partners

						2021
Export partners (% of exports)[i]	United States	22.1	India	10.9	Saudi Arabia	10.5
Import partners (% of imports)[i]	China	15.9	Saudi Arabia	12.3	United States	8.3

Social indicators

	2010	2015	2022
Population growth rate (average annual %)	2.6	7.2	0.5[a]
Urban population (% of total population)	86.1	90.3	91.2[c]
Urban population growth rate (average annual %)[k]	6.2	5.8	...
Fertility rate, total (live births per woman)	3.8	3.2	2.8[a]
Life expectancy at birth (females/males, years)	76.1 / 72.1	77.3 / 73.0	76.7 / 72.1[a]
Population age distribution (0-14/60+ years old, %)	36.6 / 5.3	35.1 / 4.9	32.1 / 6.3[a]
International migrant stock (000/% of total pop.)[l,m]	2 786.9 / 38.4	3 167.0 / 34.2	3 457.7 / 33.9[b]
Refugees and others of concern to the UNHCR (000)	453.2	684.8	757.7[d]
Infant mortality rate (per 1 000 live births)	17.0	14.9	12.4[a]
Health: Current expenditure (% of GDP)[n]	8.2	7.5[o]	7.6[i,c]
Health: Physicians (per 1 000 pop.)	2.2	2.8	2.7[c]
Education: Government expenditure (% of GDP)	3.1	3.5[p]	3.0[c]
Education: Primary gross enrol. ratio (f/m per 100 pop.)	81.1 / 82.7	79.1 / 79.9[q]	79.8 / 80.9[b]
Education: Sec. gross enrol. ratio (f/m per 100 pop.)	81.6 / 78.6	70.3 / 68.0[q]	68.8 / 66.8[b]
Education: Upr. Sec. gross enrol. ratio (f/m per 100 pop.)	71.9 / 63.1	65.7 / 58.5[q]	60.2 / 54.2[b]
Intentional homicide rate (per 100 000 pop.)	1.6	1.6	1.2[b]
Seats held by women in the National Parliament (%)	6.4	12.0	12.3[r]

Environment and infrastructure indicators

	2010	2015	2022
Individuals using the Internet (per 100 inhabitants)	27.2[s]	54.2[i]	66.1[i,t]
Research & Development expenditure (% of GDP)	0.4[u]	...	0.7[v,w,x]
Threatened species (number)	90	102	131
Forested area (% of land area)	1.1	1.1[i]	1.1[c]
CO2 emission estimates (million tons/tons per capita)	19.0 / 2.6	24.0 / 2.6	23.1 / 2.3[c]
Energy production, primary (Petajoules)	9	8	17[c]
Energy supply per capita (Gigajoules)	42	40	40[c]
Tourist/visitor arrivals at national borders (000)[y]	4 207	3 761	1 067[b]
Important sites for terrestrial biodiversity protected (%)	6.5	9.4	12.7[d]
Pop. using safely managed sanitation (urban/rural %)	83.6 / ...	84.0 / ...	84.4 / ...[b]
Net Official Development Assist. received (% of GNI)	3.55	5.60	7.15[b]

a Projected estimate (medium fertility variant). **b** 2020. **c** 2019. **d** 2021. **e** Excludes irrigation canals and landscaping care. **f** Data classified according to ISIC Rev. 4. **g** Excludes publishing activities. Includes irrigation and canals. **h** Includes publishing activities and landscape care. Excludes repair of personal and household goods. **i** Estimate. **j** Base: 2018=100. **k** Data refers to a 5-year period preceding the reference year. **l** Refers to foreign citizens. **m** Including refugees. **n** Data based on calendar year (January 1 to December 31). **o** Data are based on SHA2011. **p** 2013. **q** 2014. **r** Data are as at 1 January of reporting year. **s** Population aged 5 years and over. **t** 2018. **u** 2008. **v** Break in the time series. **w** Overestimated or based on overestimated data. **x** 2016. **y** Including nationals residing abroad.

Kazakhstan

Region	Central Asia
Population (000, 2022)	19 398[a]
Pop. density (per km2, 2022)	7.2[a]
Capital city	Nur-Sultan
Capital city pop. (000, 2022)	1 117.6[c]

UN membership date	02 March 1992
Surface area (km2)	2 724 902[b]
Sex ratio (m per 100 f)	92.8[a]
National currency	Tenge (KZT)
Exchange rate (per US$)	431.8[d]

Economic indicators	2010	2015	2022
GDP: Gross domestic product (million current US$)	148 047	184 388	171 082[b]
GDP growth rate (annual %, const. 2015 prices)	7.3	1.2	- 2.5[b]
GDP per capita (current US$)	9 109.3	10 493.3	9 111.4[b]
Economy: Agriculture (% of Gross Value Added)[e,f]	4.7	5.0	5.8[b]
Economy: Industry (% of Gross Value Added)[e,g]	41.9	32.5	35.4[b]
Economy: Services and other activity (% of GVA)[e,h]	53.4	62.5	58.9[b]
Employment in agriculture (% of employed)	28.3	18.0	15.4[i,b]
Employment in industry (% of employed)	18.7	20.6	20.5[i,b]
Employment in services & other sectors (% employed)	53.0	61.4	64.1[i,b]
Unemployment rate (% of labour force)	5.8	4.9	4.9[i]
Labour force participation rate (female/male pop. %)	65.4 / 75.9	65.4 / 77.0	63.2 / 75.5[i]
CPI: Consumer Price Index (2010=100)	100	137	201[b]
Agricultural production index (2014-2016=100)	77	99	118[b]
International trade: exports (million current US$)	57 244	45 954	62 621[i,d]
International trade: imports (million current US$)	24 024	30 567	42 355[i,d]
International trade: balance (million current US$)	33 220	15 387	20 266[d]
Balance of payments, current account (million US$)	1 386	- 6 012	- 5 736[d]

Major trading partners						2021
Export partners (% of exports)[i]	China	19.2	Italy	14.2	Russian Federation	10.4
Import partners (% of imports)[i]	Russian Federation	34.9	China	16.7	Republic of Korea	12.8

Social indicators	2010	2015	2022
Population growth rate (average annual %)	1.4	1.3	1.1[a]
Urban population (% of total population)	56.8	57.2	57.5[c]
Urban population growth rate (average annual %)[i]	1.2	1.7	...
Fertility rate, total (live births per woman)	2.6	2.7	3.0[a]
Life expectancy at birth (females/males, years)	72.5 / 63.6	74.8 / 66.4	73.0 / 65.8[a]
Population age distribution (0-14/60+ years old, %)	24.6 / 10.1	27.0 / 11.0	29.7 / 12.8[a]
International migrant stock (000/% of total pop.)[k]	3 334.9 / 20.5	3 546.1 / 20.2	3 732.1 / 19.9[b]
Refugees and others of concern to the UNHCR (000)	12.7[l]	7.8	8.6[d]
Infant mortality rate (per 1 000 live births)	18.1	10.6	8.5[a]
Health: Current expenditure (% of GDP)	2.7	3.0	2.8[c]
Health: Physicians (per 1 000 pop.)	3.9	4.0	4.1[b]
Education: Government expenditure (% of GDP)	3.5	2.8	2.9[c]
Education: Primary gross enrol. ratio (f/m per 100 pop.)	109.1 / 108.5	111.7 / 111.5	100.2 / 100.4[b]
Education: Sec. gross enrol. ratio (f/m per 100 pop.)	98.8 / 98.2	112.2 / 108.5	103.8 / 103.7[b]
Education: Upr. Sec. gross enrol. ratio (f/m per 100 pop.)	95.2 / 92.1	109.0 / 99.8	112.4 / 112.6[b]
Intentional homicide rate (per 100 000 pop.)	8.5	4.9	3.2[b]
Seats held by women in the National Parliament (%)	17.8	26.2	27.4[m]

Environment and infrastructure indicators	2010	2015	2022
Individuals using the Internet (per 100 inhabitants)	31.6[n]	70.8	85.9[b]
Research & Development expenditure (% of GDP)	0.2	0.2	0.1[d]
Threatened species (number)	73	78	92
Forested area (% of land area)[i]	1.1	1.2	1.3[c]
CO2 emission estimates (million tons/tons per capita)	223.0 / 13.5	181.7 / 10.2	207.7 / 11.1[c]
Energy production, primary (Petajoules)	6 770	6 812	6 984[c]
Energy supply per capita (Gigajoules)	207	181	162[c]
Tourist/visitor arrivals at national borders (000)	4 097	6 430	2 035[b]
Important sites for terrestrial biodiversity protected (%)	26.2	26.9	28.5[d]
Pop. using safely managed sanitation (urban/rural %)	91.7 / ...	91.0 / ...	91.0 / ...[b]
Net Official Development Assist. received (% of GNI)	0.17	0.05	0.05[b]

a Projected estimate (medium fertility variant). b 2020. c 2019. d 2021. e Data classified according to ISIC Rev. 4. f Excludes irrigation canals and landscaping care. g Excludes publishing activities. Includes irrigation and canals. h Includes publishing activities and landscape care. Excludes repair of personal and household goods. i Estimate. j Data refers to a 5-year period preceding the reference year. k Including refugees. l Data as at the end of December. m Data are as at 1 January of reporting year. n Population aged 16 to 74 years.

Kenya

Region	Eastern Africa	UN membership date	16 December 1963
Population (000, 2022)	54 028[a]	Surface area (km2)	591 958[b]
Pop. density (per km2, 2022)	93.0[a]	Sex ratio (m per 100 f)	98.3[a]
Capital city	Nairobi	National currency	Kenyan Shilling (KES)
Capital city pop. (000, 2022)	4 556.4[c]	Exchange rate (per US$)	113.1[d]

Economic indicators

	2010	2015	2022
GDP: Gross domestic product (million current US$)	43 820	70 120	101 014[b]
GDP growth rate (annual %, const. 2015 prices)	8.4	5.7	- 0.3[b]
GDP per capita (current US$)	1 042.6	1 464.6	1 878.6[b]
Economy: Agriculture (% of Gross Value Added)[e,f]	17.0	20.6	24.5[b]
Economy: Industry (% of Gross Value Added)[e,g]	21.4	20.0	18.5[b]
Economy: Services and other activity (% of GVA)[e,h]	61.6	59.4	57.0[b]
Employment in agriculture (% of employed)[i]	60.3	57.3	53.8[b]
Employment in industry (% of employed)[i]	6.3	6.7	7.4[b]
Employment in services & other sectors (% employed)[i]	33.4	36.0	38.7[b]
Unemployment rate (% of labour force)[i]	2.8	2.8	5.5
Labour force participation rate (female/male pop. %)[i]	71.1 / 76.4	71.4 / 77.3	71.5 / 75.7
CPI: Consumer Price Index (2010=100)	100	150	212[d]
Agricultural production index (2014-2016=100)	96	101	110[b]
International trade: exports (million current US$)	5 169	5 907	6 751[d]
International trade: imports (million current US$)	12 093	16 058	19 594[d]
International trade: balance (million current US$)	- 6 924	- 10 151	- 12 843[d]
Balance of payments, current account (million US$)	- 2 369	- 4 421	- 4 797[b]

Major trading partners

						2021
Export partners (% of exports)	Uganda	12.3	Netherlands	8.3	United States	8.0
Import partners (% of imports)	China	20.5	India	10.8	United Arab Emirates	8.3

Social indicators

	2010	2015	2022
Population growth rate (average annual %)	2.7	2.2	2.0[a]
Urban population (% of total population)	23.6	25.7	27.5[c]
Urban population growth rate (average annual %)[j]	4.4	4.4	...
Fertility rate, total (live births per woman)	4.4	3.8	3.3[a]
Life expectancy at birth (females/males, years)	62.4 / 58.9	64.1 / 59.7	64.7 / 59.6[a]
Population age distribution (0-14/60+ years old, %)	43.3 / 3.3	41.6 / 3.8	37.8 / 4.6[a]
International migrant stock (000/% of total pop.)[k]	954.9 / 2.3	1 126.9 / 2.4	1 050.1 / 2.0[b]
Refugees and others of concern to the UNHCR (000)	751.0[l]	613.8	582.0[d]
Infant mortality rate (per 1 000 live births)	40.2	34.9	28.0[a]
Health: Current expenditure (% of GDP)	6.1	5.2	4.6[c]
Health: Physicians (per 1 000 pop.)	0.2	0.2[m]	0.2[n]
Education: Government expenditure (% of GDP)	5.5	5.3	5.1[i,b]
Education: Primary gross enrol. ratio (f/m per 100 pop.)	102.7 / 105.1[o]	103.6 / 103.7	103.4 / 103.0[p]
Education: Sec. gross enrol. ratio (f/m per 100 pop.)	53.7 / 59.9[o]	... / ...	... / ...
Education: Upr. Sec. gross enrol. ratio (f/m per 100 pop.)	39.1 / 45.1[o]	... / ...	... / ...
Intentional homicide rate (per 100 000 pop.)	4.6	4.7	3.5[b]
Seats held by women in the National Parliament (%)	9.8	19.7	21.4[q]

Environment and infrastructure indicators

	2010	2015	2022
Individuals using the Internet (per 100 inhabitants)	7.2	16.6	29.5[i,b]
Research & Development expenditure (% of GDP)	0.7[r]	...	...
Threatened species (number)	338	463	636
Forested area (% of land area)[i]	6.4	6.2	6.3[c]
CO2 emission estimates (million tons/tons per capita)	14.5 / 0.3	18.6 / 0.3	24.3 / 0.4[c]
Energy production, primary (Petajoules)	650[i]	761	772[i,c]
Energy supply per capita (Gigajoules)	19[i]	20	19[i,c]
Tourist/visitor arrivals at national borders (000)[s,t]	1 470	1 114	1 364[u]
Important sites for terrestrial biodiversity protected (%)	33.8	34.0	34.0[d]
Pop. using safely managed drinking water (urban/rural, %)	59.3 / ...	58.3 / ...	57.7 / ...[b]
Pop. using safely managed sanitation (urban/rural %)	... / 28.4	... / 29.0	... / 29.5[b]
Net Official Development Assist. received (% of GNI)	4.09	3.90	4.11[b]

a Projected estimate (medium fertility variant). b 2020. c 2019. d 2021. e Data classified according to ISIC Rev. 4. f Excludes irrigation canals and landscaping care. g Excludes publishing activities. Includes irrigation and canals. h Includes publishing activities and landscape care. Excludes repair of personal and household goods. i Estimate. j Data refers to a 5-year period preceding the reference year. k Including refugees. l Data as at the end of December. m 2014. n 2018. o 2009. p 2016. q Data are as at 1 January of reporting year. r Break in the time series. s Excluding nationals residing abroad. t Arrivals of non-resident visitors from all border entry points. u 2017.

Kiribati

Region	Micronesia		UN membership date	14 September 1999	
Population (000, 2022)	131[a]		Surface area (km2)	726[b,c]	
Pop. density (per km2, 2022)	180.8[a]		Sex ratio (m per 100 f)	95.0[a]	
Capital city	Bairiki		National currency	Australian Dollar (AUD)	
Capital city pop. (000, 2022)	3.2[d]		Exchange rate (per US$)	1.4[e]	

Economic indicators	2010	2015	2022
GDP: Gross domestic product (million current US$)	155	170	181[c]
GDP growth rate (annual %, const. 2015 prices)	- 1.1	9.9	- 0.5[c]
GDP per capita (current US$)	1 508.9	1 535.1	1 514.6[c]
Economy: Agriculture (% of Gross Value Added)[f,g]	24.3	22.2	25.2[c]
Economy: Industry (% of Gross Value Added)[f,g]	12.0	15.7	9.4[c]
Economy: Services and other activity (% of GVA)[f,g]	63.7	62.1	65.4[c]
Employment in agriculture (% of employed)	22.1	...	...
Employment in industry (% of employed)	16.1	...	...
Employment in services & other sectors (% employed)	61.8	...	...
Unemployment rate (% of labour force)	30.6[h]	...	...
Labour force participation rate (female/male pop. %)	52.3 / 66.8[i]	... / ...	... / ...
CPI: Consumer Price Index (2010=100)[j]	100	100	101[k]
Agricultural production index (2014-2016=100)	97	100	94[c]
International trade: exports (million current US$)	4	10	13[i,e]
International trade: imports (million current US$)	73	111	147[i,e]
International trade: balance (million current US$)	- 69	- 101	- 134[e]
Balance of payments, current account (million US$)	~0	56	71[c]

Major trading partners						2021
Export partners (% of exports)[j]	Japan	31.8	Malaysia	17.3	Australia	11.5
Import partners (% of imports)[j]	Fiji	18.0	Australia	15.6	China	14.1

Social indicators	2010	2015	2022
Population growth rate (average annual %)	1.8	1.5	1.8[a]
Urban population (% of total population)	47.4	51.6	54.8[k]
Urban population growth rate (average annual %)[l]	3.8	3.5	...
Fertility rate, total (live births per woman)	3.9	3.5	3.3[a]
Life expectancy at birth (females/males, years)	66.6 / 63.2	67.6 / 64.3	69.4 / 65.7[a]
Population age distribution (0-14/60+ years old, %)	36.4 / 5.2	35.6 / 5.5	36.1 / 6.3[a]
International migrant stock (000/% of total pop.)	2.9 / 2.8	2.9 / 2.6	3.1 / 2.6[c]
Infant mortality rate (per 1 000 live births)	49.2	44.9	37.4[a]
Health: Current expenditure (% of GDP)[m,n]	9.2	8.0	10.3[k]
Health: Physicians (per 1 000 pop.)	0.4	0.2[o]	...
Education: Government expenditure (% of GDP)	...	9.9	12.4[k]
Education: Primary gross enrol. ratio (f/m per 100 pop.)	113.2 / 107.2[p]	106.6 / 104.5	111.1 / 105.1[c]
Education: Sec. gross enrol. ratio (f/m per 100 pop.)	91.4 / 82.7[q]	... / ...	... / ...
Education: Upr. Sec. gross enrol. ratio (f/m per 100 pop.)	81.4 / 67.5[q]	... / ...	... / ...
Intentional homicide rate (per 100 000 pop.)	3.9	7.5[r]	...
Seats held by women in the National Parliament (%)	4.3	8.7	6.7[s]

Environment and infrastructure indicators	2010	2015	2022
Individuals using the Internet (per 100 inhabitants)	9.1	14.9[j]	38.0[j,c]
Threatened species (number)	90	100	115
Forested area (% of land area)[j]	1.5	1.5	1.5[k]
Energy production, primary (Petajoules)[j]	1	1	1[k]
Energy supply per capita (Gigajoules)	13	12	13[j,k]
Tourist/visitor arrivals at national borders (000)[t]	5	4	1[c]
Important sites for terrestrial biodiversity protected (%)	40.0	40.0	40.0[e]
Pop. using safely managed drinking water (urban/rural, %)	18.8 / 5.9	19.9 / 6.3	21.1 / 6.7[c]
Pop. using safely managed sanitation (urban/rural %)	25.5 / 20.2	25.9 / 23.8	26.1 / 27.4[c]
Net Official Development Assist. received (% of GNI)	10.38	18.45	16.53[c]

a Projected estimate (medium fertility variant). b Land area only. Excluding 84 square km of uninhabited islands. c 2020. d 2015. e 2021. f Data classified according to ISIC Rev. 4. g At factor cost. h De facto population. i Persons present (de facto). j Estimate. k 2019. l Data refers to a 5-year period preceding the reference year. m General government expenditure (GGE) can be larger than the Gross domestic product (GDP) because government accounts for a very large part of domestic consumption and because a large part of domestic consumption in the country is accounted for by imports. n Data refer to fiscal years beginning 1 July. o 2013. p 2009. q 2008. r 2012. s Data are as at 1 January of reporting year. t Air arrivals. Tarawa and Christmas Island.

Kuwait

Region	Western Asia	UN membership date	14 May 1963
Population (000, 2022)	4 269[a]	Surface area (km2)	17 818[b]
Pop. density (per km2, 2022)	239.6[a]	Sex ratio (m per 100 f)	155.2[a]
Capital city	Kuwait City	National currency	Kuwaiti Dinar (KWD)
Capital city pop. (000, 2022)	3 052.5[c,d]	Exchange rate (per US$)	0.3[e]

Economic indicators	2010	2015	2022
GDP: Gross domestic product (million current US$)	115 416	114 585	105 949[b]
GDP growth rate (annual %, const. 2015 prices)	- 2.4	0.6	- 8.9[b]
GDP per capita (current US$)	38 576.4	29 874.0	24 809.0[b]
Economy: Agriculture (% of Gross Value Added)[f]	0.4	0.5	0.4[b]
Economy: Industry (% of Gross Value Added)[f]	58.2	48.7	39.5[b]
Economy: Services and other activity (% of GVA)[f]	41.4	50.9	60.1[b]
Employment in agriculture (% of employed)[g]	2.5	2.2	2.0[b]
Employment in industry (% of employed)[g]	24.5	24.8	24.4[b]
Employment in services & other sectors (% employed)[g]	73.0	73.0	73.7[b]
Unemployment rate (% of labour force)	1.8	2.2	3.4[g]
Labour force participation rate (female/male pop. %)[g]	48.5 / 85.3	50.1 / 88.3	49.2 / 85.8
CPI: Consumer Price Index (2010=100)	100	118	134[e]
Agricultural production index (2014-2016=100)	64	95	118[b]
International trade: exports (million current US$)	62 698	54 121	83 720[g,a]
International trade: imports (million current US$)	22 691	30 957	34 301[g,e]
International trade: balance (million current US$)	40 007	23 164	49 418[e]
Balance of payments, current account (million US$)	36 989	8 584	22 030[b]

Major trading partners						2021
Export partners (% of exports)[g]	Areas nes[h]	89.3	Saudi Arabia	1.7	China	1.5
Import partners (% of imports)[g]	China	17.4	United States	8.5	United Arab Emirates	8.2

Social indicators	2010	2015	2022
Population growth rate (average annual %)	5.1	8.1	1.0[a]
Urban population (% of total population)	100.0	100.0	100.0[d]
Urban population growth rate (average annual %)[i]	5.5	5.4	...
Fertility rate, total (live births per woman)	2.3	2.2	2.1[a]
Life expectancy at birth (females/males, years)	80.1 / 76.4	82.0 / 77.9	82.8 / 78.9[a]
Population age distribution (0-14/60+ years old, %)	23.0 / 3.2	21.7 / 4.6	20.7 / 9.3[a]
International migrant stock (000/% of total pop.)[j,k]	1 874.8 / 62.7	2 866.1 / 74.7	3 110.2 / 72.8[b]
Refugees and others of concern to the UNHCR (000)	96.5[l]	94.6	93.8[b]
Infant mortality rate (per 1 000 live births)	8.9	7.5	6.7[a]
Health: Current expenditure (% of GDP)[m]	2.7	4.2	5.5[d]
Health: Physicians (per 1 000 pop.)	2.4	2.6	2.3[b]
Education: Government expenditure (% of GDP)[g]	3.8[n]	4.8	6.6[b]
Education: Primary gross enrol. ratio (f/m per 100 pop.)	101.2 / 103.2	104.3 / 101.0	93.0 / 82.5[b]
Education: Sec. gross enrol. ratio (f/m per 100 pop.)	98.8 / 97.0	101.0 / 94.9	... / ...
Education: Upr. Sec. gross enrol. ratio (f/m per 100 pop.)	92.9 / 86.4	100.8 / 86.5[o]	... / ...
Intentional homicide rate (per 100 000 pop.)	2.0	1.8[o]	...
Seats held by women in the National Parliament (%)	7.7	1.5	1.6[p]

Environment and infrastructure indicators	2010	2015	2022
Individuals using the Internet (per 100 inhabitants)	61.4[g]	82.0[g]	99.1[b]
Research & Development expenditure (% of GDP)	0.1[q,r]	0.1[r,s,t,u]	0.2[q,b]
Threatened species (number)	41	42	72
Forested area (% of land area)[g]	0.4	0.4	0.4[d]
CO2 emission estimates (million tons/tons per capita)	77.6 / 25.8	86.7 / 22.5	90.0 / 21.3[d]
Energy production, primary (Petajoules)[v]	5 557	7 014	6 766[d]
Energy supply per capita (Gigajoules)[v]	451	366	380[d]
Tourist/visitor arrivals at national borders (000)[w]	5 208	6 941	2 161[b]
Important sites for terrestrial biodiversity protected (%)	31.0	42.1	51.6[e]

a Projected estimate (medium fertility variant). **b** 2020. **c** Data refers to the Governorates of Capital, Hawalli, Al-Farwaniya and Mubarak Al-Kabeer. **d** 2019. **e** 2021. **f** Data classified according to ISIC Rev. 4. **g** Estimate. **h** Areas nes **i** Data refers to a 5-year period preceding the reference year. **j** Including refugees. **k** Refers to foreign citizens. **l** Data as at the end of December. **m** Data refer to fiscal years beginning 1 April. **n** 2006. **o** 2012. **p** Data are as at 1 January of reporting year. **q** Government only. **r** Partial data. **s** Excluding private non-profit. **t** Break in the time series. **u** Excluding business enterprise. **v** The data for crude oil production include 50 per cent of the output of the Neutral Zone. **w** Non-resident tourists staying in hotels and similar establishments.

Kyrgyzstan

Region	Central Asia	UN membership date	02 March 1992
Population (000, 2022)	6 631 [a]	Surface area (km2)	199 949 [b]
Pop. density (per km2, 2022)	34.6 [a]	Sex ratio (m per 100 f)	96.5 [a]
Capital city	Bishkek	National currency	Som (KGS)
Capital city pop. (000, 2022)	1 017.2 [c]	Exchange rate (per US$)	84.8 [d]

Economic indicators	2010	2015	2022
GDP: Gross domestic product (million current US$)	4 794	6 678	7 736 [b]
GDP growth rate (annual %, const. 2015 prices)	- 0.5	3.9	- 8.6 [b]
GDP per capita (current US$)	884.2	1 120.7	1 185.7 [b]
Economy: Agriculture (% of Gross Value Added) [e,f]	18.8	15.4	14.6 [b]
Economy: Industry (% of Gross Value Added) [f,g]	28.2	27.5	31.8 [b]
Economy: Services and other activity (% of GVA) [f,h]	53.0	57.1	53.6 [b]
Employment in agriculture (% of employed)	32.3 [i]	29.3	20.4 [i,b]
Employment in industry (% of employed)	21.0 [i]	20.9	24.7 [i,b]
Employment in services & other sectors (% employed)	46.7 [i]	49.8	54.9 [i,b]
Unemployment rate (% of labour force)	8.6	7.6	8.8 [i]
Labour force participation rate (female/male pop. %)	52.4 / 76.8	49.9 / 75.5	43.0 / 72.4 [i]
CPI: Consumer Price Index (2010=100)	100	146	185 [d]
Agricultural production index (2014-2016=100)	89	102	110 [b]
International trade: exports (million current US$)	1 488	1 441	1 688 [d]
International trade: imports (million current US$)	3 223	4 068	5 448 [d]
International trade: balance (million current US$)	- 1 734	- 2 627	- 3 760 [d]
Balance of payments, current account (million US$)	- 475	- 1 052	374 [b]

Major trading partners						2021
Export partners (% of exports)	Kazakhstan	25.5	Russian Federation	22.9	United Kingdom	13.9
Import partners (% of imports)	Russian Federation	32.8	China	26.8	Kazakhstan	12.0

Social indicators	2010	2015	2022
Population growth rate (average annual %)	1.1	1.7	1.6 [a]
Urban population (% of total population)	35.3	35.8	36.6 [c]
Urban population growth rate (average annual %) [j]	1.3	1.8	...
Fertility rate, total (live births per woman)	3.1	3.2	2.9 [a]
Life expectancy at birth (females/males, years)	72.2 / 64.3	73.4 / 66.6	74.9 / 66.2 [a]
Population age distribution (0-14/60+ years old, %)	30.7 / 6.1	32.5 / 6.4	34.4 / 7.9 [a]
International migrant stock (000/% of total pop.) [k]	232.1 / 4.3	204.4 / 3.4	199.0 / 3.1 [b]
Refugees and others of concern to the UNHCR (000)	304.2 [l]	14.3	0.8 [d]
Infant mortality rate (per 1 000 live births)	25.8	19.7	13.1 [a]
Health: Current expenditure (% of GDP)	7.0	7.1	4.5 [c]
Health: Physicians (per 1 000 pop.)	2.3	2.2 [m]	...
Education: Government expenditure (% of GDP)	5.8	6.0	5.4 [c]
Education: Primary gross enrol. ratio (f/m per 100 pop.)	99.1 / 99.8	105.0 / 105.8	102.4 / 102.8 [b]
Education: Sec. gross enrol. ratio (f/m per 100 pop.)	87.4 / 87.7	91.7 / 90.5	98.1 / 98.1 [b]
Education: Upr. Sec. gross enrol. ratio (f/m per 100 pop.)	73.7 / 72.8	84.4 / 79.2	85.3 / 83.1 [b]
Intentional homicide rate (per 100 000 pop.)	16.8	5.1	1.7 [b]
Seats held by women in the National Parliament (%)	25.6	23.3	20.5 [n]

Environment and infrastructure indicators	2010	2015	2022
Individuals using the Internet (per 100 inhabitants) [i]	16.3	30.2	51.0 [c]
Research & Development expenditure (% of GDP)	0.2	0.1 [o]	0.1 [o,b]
Threatened species (number)	40	41	51
Forested area (% of land area) [i]	6.4	6.5	6.8 [c]
CO2 emission estimates (million tons/tons per capita)	6.1 / 1.1	9.9 / 1.6	9.5 / 1.4 [c]
Energy production, primary (Petajoules)	53	75	100 [c]
Energy supply per capita (Gigajoules)	21	28	25 [c]
Tourist/visitor arrivals at national borders (000)	1 224	4 000	2 079 [b]
Important sites for terrestrial biodiversity protected (%)	23.6	23.6	23.6 [d]
Pop. using safely managed drinking water (urban/rural, %)	87.7 / 41.1	90.6 / 52.7	91.8 / 57.4 [b]
Pop. using safely managed sanitation (urban/rural %)	81.5 / 93.5	83.7 / 95.8	85.6 / 96.5 [b]
Net Official Development Assist. received (% of GNI)	8.29	7.04	6.01 [b]

a Projected estimate (medium fertility variant). b 2020. c 2019. d 2021. e Excludes irrigation canals and landscaping care. f Data classified according to ISIC Rev. 4. g Excludes publishing activities. Includes irrigation and canals. h Includes publishing activities and landscape care. Excludes repair of personal and household goods. i Estimate. j Data refers to a 5-year period preceding the reference year. k Including refugees. l Data as at the end of December. m 2014. n Data are as at 1 January of reporting year. o Excluding private non-profit.

Lao People's Democratic Republic

Region	South-eastern Asia	UN membership date	14 December 1955
Population (000, 2022)	7 530 [a]	Surface area (km2)	236 800 [b]
Pop. density (per km2, 2022)	32.6 [a]	Sex ratio (m per 100 f)	101.6 [a]
Capital city	Vientiane	National currency	Lao Kip (LAK)
Capital city pop. (000, 2022)	673.1 [c]	Exchange rate (per US$)	11 041.0 [d]

Economic indicators	2010	2015	2022
GDP: Gross domestic product (million current US$)	7 313	14 390	19 082 [b]
GDP growth rate (annual %, const. 2015 prices)	8.1	7.3	3.3 [b]
GDP per capita (current US$)	1 170.3	2 134.7	2 622.8 [b]
Economy: Agriculture (% of Gross Value Added) [e,f]	23.6	19.7	18.5 [b]
Economy: Industry (% of Gross Value Added) [e,g]	30.9	31.0	37.2 [b]
Economy: Services and other activity (% of GVA) [e,h]	45.5	49.4	44.3 [b]
Employment in agriculture (% of employed)	71.5	65.9 [i]	61.7 [i,b]
Employment in industry (% of employed)	8.3	10.6 [i]	12.2 [i,b]
Employment in services & other sectors (% employed)	20.2	23.5 [i]	26.2 [i,b]
Unemployment rate (% of labour force)	0.7	0.8 [i]	1.3 [i]
Labour force participation rate (female/male pop. %)	76.7 / 79.8	76.1 / 79.1 [i]	75.1 / 78.2 [i]
CPI: Consumer Price Index (2010=100) [i]	100 [j]	126	148 [d]
Agricultural production index (2014-2016=100)	61	104	107 [b]
International trade: exports (million current US$)	1 909	2 985	6 228 [i,d]
International trade: imports (million current US$)	1 837	3 778	5 658 [i,d]
International trade: balance (million current US$)	72	- 793	571 [d]
Balance of payments, current account (million US$)	29	- 2 268	- 115 [b]

Major trading partners						2021
Export partners (% of exports) [i]	Thailand	34.7	China	28.8	Viet Nam	19.6
Import partners (% of imports) [i]	Thailand	49.6	China	25.8	Viet Nam	8.0

Social indicators	2010	2015	2022
Population growth rate (average annual %)	1.5	1.5	1.4 [a]
Urban population (% of total population)	30.1	33.1	35.6 [c]
Urban population growth rate (average annual %) [k]	3.7	3.2	...
Fertility rate, total (live births per woman)	3.1	2.8	2.4 [a]
Life expectancy at birth (females/males, years)	66.2 / 61.9	68.7 / 64.7	71.2 / 66.9 [a]
Population age distribution (0-14/60+ years old, %)	35.9 / 5.8	33.1 / 6.4	30.6 / 7.2 [a]
International migrant stock (000/% of total pop.) [l,m]	33.0 / 0.5	45.5 / 0.7	48.7 / 0.7 [b]
Refugees and others of concern to the UNHCR (000)	...	...	~0.0 [b]
Infant mortality rate (per 1 000 live births)	51.8	42.3	30.6 [a]
Health: Current expenditure (% of GDP) [n]	2.9	2.5 [o]	2.6 [o,c]
Health: Physicians (per 1 000 pop.)	0.2 [p]	0.5 [q]	0.4 [b]
Education: Government expenditure (% of GDP)	1.7	2.9 [q]	...
Education: Primary gross enrol. ratio (f/m per 100 pop.)	117.9 / 128.9	111.3 / 116.6	97.2 / 100.4 [b]
Education: Sec. gross enrol. ratio (f/m per 100 pop.)	42.3 / 51.5	60.7 / 66.1	61.0 / 64.5 [b]
Education: Upr. Sec. gross enrol. ratio (f/m per 100 pop.)	28.4 / 35.2	42.6 / 47.8	46.6 / 52.2 [b]
Seats held by women in the National Parliament (%)	25.2	25.0	22.0 [r]

Environment and infrastructure indicators	2010	2015	2022
Individuals using the Internet (per 100 inhabitants)	7.0	18.2 [i]	33.8 [i,b]
Threatened species (number)	132	210 [i]	278
Forested area (% of land area) [i]	73.4	72.7	72.1 [c]
CO2 emission estimates (million tons/tons per capita)	3.0 / 0.4	8.3 / 1.1	17.8 / 2.4 [c]
Energy production, primary (Petajoules)	98	162	276 [c]
Energy supply per capita (Gigajoules)	16	25	34 [c]
Tourist/visitor arrivals at national borders (000)	1 670	3 543	812 [b]
Important sites for terrestrial biodiversity protected (%)	36.2	38.1	49.7 [d]
Pop. using safely managed drinking water (urban/rural, %)	24.3 / 9.2	25.8 / 11.0	27.0 / 12.4 [b]
Pop. using safely managed sanitation (urban/rural, %)	55.7 / 39.1	60.9 / 50.7	63.3 / 60.3 [b]
Net Official Development Assist. received (% of GNI)	5.83	3.43	2.92 [b]

a Projected estimate (medium fertility variant). b 2020. c 2019. d 2021. e Data classified according to ISIC Rev. 4. f Excludes irrigation canals and landscaping care. g Excludes publishing activities. Includes irrigation and canals. h Includes publishing activities and landscape care. Excludes repair of personal and household goods. i Estimate. j Break in the time series. k Data refers to a 5-year period preceding the reference year. l Including refugees. m Refers to foreign citizens. n Data refer to fiscal years beginning 1 October. o Data are based on SHA2011. p 2009. q 2014. r Data are as at 1 January of reporting year.

Latvia

Region	Northern Europe	UN membership date	17 September 1991
Population (000, 2022)	1 851[a]	Surface area (km2)	64 594[b]
Pop. density (per km2, 2022)	29.7[a]	Sex ratio (m per 100 f)	86.5[a]
Capital city	Riga	National currency	Euro (EUR)
Capital city pop. (000, 2022)	633.8[c]	Exchange rate (per US$)	0.9[c]

Economic indicators

	2010	2015	2022
GDP: Gross domestic product (million current US$)	23 964	27 252	33 707[b]
GDP growth rate (annual %, const. 2015 prices)	- 4.5	3.9	- 3.6[b]
GDP per capita (current US$)	11 309.9	13.641.9	17 870.5[b]
Economy: Agriculture (% of Gross Value Added)[e,f]	4.6	4.0	4.6[b]
Economy: Industry (% of Gross Value Added)[f,g]	23.0	21.7	22.4[b]
Economy: Services and other activity (% of GVA)[f,h]	72.5	74.3	73.0[b]
Employment in agriculture (% of employed)	8.6	7.9	6.5[i,b]
Employment in industry (% of employed)	23.1	23.6	23.7[i,b]
Employment in services & other sectors (% employed)	68.3	68.4	69.8[i,b]
Unemployment rate (% of labour force)	19.5	9.9	7.1[i]
Labour force participation rate (female/male pop. %)	53.9 / 65.0	54.1 / 67.4	54.7 / 66.9[i]
CPI: Consumer Price Index (2010=100)	100	108	121[d]
Agricultural production index (2014-2016=100)	73	107	111[b]
International trade: exports (million current US$)	8 851	11 650	19 448[d]
International trade: imports (million current US$)	11 143	14 096	23 086[d]
International trade: balance (million current US$)	- 2 292	- 2 446	- 3 638[d]
Balance of payments, current account (million US$)	413	- 166	- 1 133[d]

Major trading partners

						2021
Export partners (% of exports)	Lithuania	17.8	Estonia	10.6	United Kingdom	7.7
Import partners (% of imports)	Lithuania	17.2	Germany	10.5	Poland	9.6

Social indicators

	2010	2015	2022
Population growth rate (average annual %)	- 1.2	- 0.9	- 1.1[a]
Urban population (% of total population)	67.8	68.0	68.2[c]
Urban population growth rate (average annual %)[j]	- 1.3	- 1.2	...
Fertility rate, total (live births per woman)	1.4	1.7	1.6[a]
Life expectancy at birth (females/males, years)	77.9 / 67.8	79.2 / 69.9	80.1 / 71.5[a]
Population age distribution (0-14/60+ years old, %)	14.2 / 24.3	15.0 / 26.2	15.6 / 29.1[a]
International migrant stock (000/% of total pop.)	313.8 / 14.8	265.4 / 13.3	239.4 / 12.7[b]
Refugees and others of concern to the UNHCR (000)	327.0[k]	263.2	209.9[d]
Infant mortality rate (per 1 000 live births)	5.2	4.0	2.8[a]
Health: Current expenditure (% of GDP)	6.1	5.7	6.6[c]
Health: Physicians (per 1 000 pop.)	3.1	3.2	3.4[b]
Education: Government expenditure (% of GDP)	5.1	5.3	4.2[l]
Education: Primary gross enrol. ratio (f/m per 100 pop.)[i]	101.9 / 103.9	99.4 / 99.4	100.0 / 100.0[c]
Education: Sec. gross enrol. ratio (f/m per 100 pop.)[i]	102.1 / 103.5	111.2 / 113.5	107.6 / 107.6[c]
Education: Upr. Sec. gross enrol. ratio (f/m per 100 pop.)[i]	100.7 / 100.0	121.4 / 122.9	114.2 / 113.4[c]
Intentional homicide rate (per 100 000 pop.)	...	3.4	3.7[b]
Seats held by women in the National Parliament (%)	22.0	18.0	27.0[m]

Environment and infrastructure indicators

	2010	2015	2022
Individuals using the Internet (per 100 inhabitants)	68.4[n]	79.2[o]	88.9[b]
Research & Development expenditure (% of GDP)	0.6	0.6	0.7[b]
Threatened species (number)	18	25	46
Forested area (% of land area)	54.2	54.5	54.7[c]
CO2 emission estimates (million tons/tons per capita)	8.5 / 3.9	7.2 / 3.5	6.8 / 3.4[b]
Energy production, primary (Petajoules)	83	98	118[c]
Energy supply per capita (Gigajoules)	89	90	99[c]
Tourist/visitor arrivals at national borders (000)[p]	1 373	2 024	636[b]
Important sites for terrestrial biodiversity protected (%)	97.2	97.2	97.2[d]
Net Official Development Assist. disbursed (% of GNI)	...	0.08[q]	...

a Projected estimate (medium fertility variant). b 2020. c 2019. d 2021. e Excludes irrigation canals and landscaping care. f Data classified according to ISIC Rev. 4. g Excludes publishing activities. Includes irrigation and canals. h Includes publishing activities and landscape care. Excludes repair of personal and household goods. i Estimate. j Data refers to a 5-year period preceding the reference year. k Data as at the end of December. l 2018. m Data are as at 1 January of reporting year. n Population aged 16 to 74 years. o Users in the last 3 months. p Non-resident departures. Survey of persons crossing the state border. q 2014.

Lebanon

Region	Western Asia	UN membership date	24 October 1945
Population (000, 2022)	5 490[a]	Surface area (km2)	10 452[b]
Pop. density (per km2, 2022)	536.6[a]	Sex ratio (m per 100 f)	94.2[a]
Capital city	Beirut	National currency	Lebanese Pound (LBP)
Capital city pop. (000, 2022)	2 406.9[c,d,e]	Exchange rate (per US$)	1 507.5[f]

Economic indicators

	2010	2015	2022
GDP: Gross domestic product (million current US$)	38 444	50 066	63 546[b]
GDP growth rate (annual %, const. 2015 prices)	8.0	0.6	- 25.0[b]
GDP per capita (current US$)	7 761.6	7 663.9	9 310.2[b]
Economy: Agriculture (% of Gross Value Added)[g,h]	4.3	3.6	2.6[b]
Economy: Industry (% of Gross Value Added)[g,i]	15.4	16.9	7.5[b]
Economy: Services and other activity (% of GVA)[g,j]	80.3	79.5	89.9[b]
Employment in agriculture (% of employed)[k]	14.7	14.4	13.4[b]
Employment in industry (% of employed)[k]	25.2	23.5	22.3[b]
Employment in services & other sectors (% employed)[k]	60.1	62.1	64.3[b]
Unemployment rate (% of labour force)[k]	6.8	9.3	14.2
Labour force participation rate (female/male pop. %)[k]	20.9 / 63.3	21.1 / 65.7	21.2 / 65.0
CPI: Consumer Price Index (2010=100)[k]	100	115	612[f]
Agricultural production index (2014-2016=100)	89	99	100[b]
International trade: exports (million current US$)	4 254	2 953	4 230[f]
International trade: imports (million current US$)	17 970	18 600	13 857[f]
International trade: balance (million current US$)	- 13 716	- 15 646	- 9 627[f]
Balance of payments, current account (million US$)	- 7 552	- 8 542	- 2 959[b]

Major trading partners

						2021
Export partners (% of exports)	United Arab Emirates	24.3	Switzerland	10.1	Cameroon	6.7
Import partners (% of imports)	Türkiye	11.0	Greece	9.9	China	9.2

Social indicators

	2010	2015	2022
Population growth rate (average annual %)	0.5	- 2.1	- 2.3[a]
Urban population (% of total population)	87.3	88.1	88.8[e]
Urban population growth rate (average annual %)[l]	1.8	6.2	...
Fertility rate, total (live births per woman)	2.1	2.2	2.1[a]
Life expectancy at birth (females/males, years)	79.9 / 76.1	81.0 / 77.2	76.6 / 72.2[a]
Population age distribution (0-14/60+ years old, %)	25.8 / 9.0	24.8 / 10.9	27.4 / 14.4[a]
International migrant stock (000/% of total pop.)[m]	793.2 / 16.0	1 916.3 / 29.3	1 712.8 / 25.1[b]
Refugees and others of concern to the UNHCR (000)	9.5[n]	1 189.1	872.7[f]
Infant mortality rate (per 1 000 live births)	8.7	7.2	6.2[a]
Health: Current expenditure (% of GDP)[c,o]	7.4	7.4	8.6[k,e]
Health: Physicians (per 1 000 pop.)	2.3	2.1	2.2[e]
Education: Government expenditure (% of GDP)	1.6	2.1	2.6[k,e]
Intentional homicide rate (per 100 000 pop.)	3.3	3.5	1.9[b]
Seats held by women in the National Parliament (%)	3.1	3.1	4.7[p]

Environment and infrastructure indicators

	2010	2015	2022
Individuals using the Internet (per 100 inhabitants)[k]	43.7[q]	74.0	84.1[b]
Threatened species (number)	50	69	192
Forested area (% of land area)[k]	13.4	13.7	14.0[e]
CO2 emission estimates (million tons/tons per capita)	18.6 / 3.7	25.0 / 3.8	25.9 / 3.7[e]
Energy production, primary (Petajoules)	9	8	10[e]
Energy supply per capita (Gigajoules)	53	52	51[e]
Tourist/visitor arrivals at national borders (000)[r]	2 168	1 518	414[b]
Important sites for terrestrial biodiversity protected (%)	4.4	4.4	4.7[f]
Net Official Development Assist. received (% of GNI)	1.17	1.96	4.37[b]

a Projected estimate (medium fertility variant). b 2020. c Estimates should be viewed with caution as these are derived from scarce data. d Excluding Syrian refugees. e 2019. f 2021. g Data classified according to ISIC Rev. 4. h Excludes irrigation canals and landscaping care. i Excludes publishing activities. Includes irrigation and canals. j Includes publishing activities and landscape care. Excludes repair of personal and household goods. k Estimate. l Data refers to a 5-year period preceding the reference year. m Including refugees. n Data as at the end of December. o Data based on calendar year (January 1 to December 31). p Data are as at 1 January of reporting year. q Population aged 15 years and over. r Excluding the Lebanon, Syria and Palestine nationalities.

Lesotho

Region	Southern Africa	UN membership date	17 October 1966
Population (000, 2022)	2 306[a]	Surface area (km2)	30 355[b]
Pop. density (per km2, 2022)	75.9[a]	Sex ratio (m per 100 f)	97.4[a]
Capital city	Maseru	National currency	Loti (LSL)
Capital city pop. (000, 2022)	201.9[c]	Exchange rate (per US$)	15.9[d]

Economic indicators

	2010	2015	2022
GDP: Gross domestic product (million current US$)	2 234	2 360	2 273[b]
GDP growth rate (annual %, const. 2015 prices)	5.3	3.1	- 6.5[b]
GDP per capita (current US$)	1 119.6	1 146.0	1 061.3[b]
Economy: Agriculture (% of Gross Value Added)[e,f]	5.4	4.2	5.2[b]
Economy: Industry (% of Gross Value Added)[f,g]	34.9	37.9	39.2[b]
Economy: Services and other activity (% of GVA)[f,h]	59.7	57.9	55.5[b]
Employment in agriculture (% of employed)[i]	11.3	9.4	8.4[b]
Employment in industry (% of employed)[i]	42.4	42.9	41.9[b]
Employment in services & other sectors (% employed)[i]	46.3	47.7	49.6[b]
Unemployment rate (% of labour force)[i]	27.1	23.8	23.9
Labour force participation rate (female/male pop. %)[i]	59.5 / 75.1	57.4 / 73.2	56.8 / 71.6
CPI: Consumer Price Index (2010=100)	100	127	174[d]
Agricultural production index (2014-2016=100)	105	101	99[b]
International trade: exports (million current US$)	503	604	955[i,d]
International trade: imports (million current US$)	1 277	1 410	1 659[i,d]
International trade: balance (million current US$)	- 773	- 806	- 705[d]
Balance of payments, current account (million US$)	- 158	- 78	- 100[d]

Major trading partners

						2021
Export partners (% of exports)[i]	South Africa	33.4	Belgium	32.7	United States	29.5
Import partners (% of imports)[i]	South Africa	71.1	China	8.5	Other Asia, nes	5.5

Social indicators

	2010	2015	2022
Population growth rate (average annual %)	0.7	1.2	1.0[a]
Urban population (% of total population)	24.8	26.9	28.6[j]
Urban population growth rate (average annual %)[k]	3.1	2.9	...
Fertility rate, total (live births per woman)	3.2	3.3	3.0[a]
Life expectancy at birth (females/males, years)	48.2 / 43.2	53.9 / 48.5	55.9 / 50.3[a]
Population age distribution (0-14/60+ years old, %)	36.1 / 6.3	35.1 / 6.3	34.0 / 6.6[a]
International migrant stock (000/% of total pop.)[l,m]	6.4 / 0.3	9.2 / 0.4	12.1 / 0.6[b]
Refugees and others of concern to the UNHCR (000)	...	~0.0	0.5[d]
Infant mortality rate (per 1 000 live births)	73.9	72.6	69.0[a]
Health: Current expenditure (% of GDP)[i]	8.4	9.0	11.3[i]
Health: Physicians (per 1 000 pop.)	0.1	...	0.5[c]
Education: Government expenditure (% of GDP)	12.3[n]	9.0	7.4[i,b]
Education: Primary gross enrol. ratio (f/m per 100 pop.)	122.1 / 127.4	113.7 / 119.6	117.8 / 124.1[o]
Education: Sec. gross enrol. ratio (f/m per 100 pop.)	65.4 / 47.1	69.7 / 51.8	71.3 / 52.8[o]
Education: Upr. Sec. gross enrol. ratio (f/m per 100 pop.)	39.5 / 29.2	53.6 / 39.9	51.1 / 35.7[o]
Intentional homicide rate (per 100 000 pop.)	38.3	43.6	...
Seats held by women in the National Parliament (%)	24.2	26.7	24.4[p]

Environment and infrastructure indicators

	2010	2015	2022
Individuals using the Internet (per 100 inhabitants)[i]	3.9	25.0	43.0[b]
Research & Development expenditure (% of GDP)	~0.0[q,r]	0.1[s,t]	...
Threatened species (number)	16	17	21
Forested area (% of land area)	1.1[i]	1.1	1.1[j]
Energy production, primary (Petajoules)	27	20[i]	16[i,j]
Energy supply per capita (Gigajoules)	26	22[i]	21[i,j]
Tourist/visitor arrivals at national borders (000)	426	1 082	1 142[j]
Important sites for terrestrial biodiversity protected (%)	16.5	16.5	16.5[d]
Pop. using safely managed drinking water (urban/rural, %)	59.1 / 4.9	68.5 / 6.9	77.7 / 8.9[b]
Pop. using safely managed sanitation (urban/rural %)	28.4 / 28.6	34.0 / 40.0	39.4 / 51.0[b]
Net Official Development Assist. received (% of GNI)	8.92	3.28	8.13[b]

a Projected estimate (medium fertility variant). b 2020. c 2018. d 2021. e Excludes irrigation canals and landscaping care. f Data classified according to ISIC Rev. 4. g Excludes publishing activities. Includes irrigation and canals. h Includes publishing activities and landscape care. Excludes repair of personal and household goods. i Estimate. j 2019. k Data refers to a 5-year period preceding the reference year. l Refers to foreign citizens. m Including refugees. n 2008. o 2017. p Data are as at 1 January of reporting year. q Partial data. r 2009. s Excluding business enterprise. t Excluding private non-profit.

Liberia

Region	Western Africa	
Population (000, 2022)	5 303	
Pop. density (per km2, 2022)	55.1 [a]	
Capital city	Monrovia	
Capital city pop. (000, 2022)	1 467.0 [c]	

UN membership date	02 November 1945
Surface area (km2)	111 369 [b]
Sex ratio (m per 100 f)	99.2 [a]
National currency	Liberian Dollar (LRD)
Exchange rate (per US$)	164.2 [b]

Economic indicators

	2010	2015	2022
GDP: Gross domestic product (million current US$)	1 292	2 669	2 481 [b]
GDP growth rate (annual %, const. 2015 prices)	7.3	9.3	- 2.9 [b]
GDP per capita (current US$)	332.0	596.8	490.5 [b]
Economy: Agriculture (% of Gross Value Added) [d]	64.5	69.5	75.6 [b]
Economy: Industry (% of Gross Value Added) [d]	12.5	10.5	7.9 [b]
Economy: Services and other activity (% of GVA) [d]	17.9	20.0	16.4 [b]
Employment in agriculture (% of employed)	47.3	44.2 [e]	43.0 [e,b]
Employment in industry (% of employed)	10.8	11.0 [e]	10.1 [e,b]
Employment in services & other sectors (% employed)	41.9	44.9 [e]	46.9 [e,b]
Unemployment rate (% of labour force)	2.3	2.1	3.9 [e]
Labour force participation rate (female/male pop. %) [e]	71.6 / 82.9	71.8 / 82.2	71.1 / 80.2
CPI: Consumer Price Index (2010=100)	100	148	223 [f]
Agricultural production index (2014-2016=100)	93	97	105 [b]
International trade: exports (million current US$) [e]	222	627	459 [g]
International trade: imports (million current US$) [e]	710	901	2 698 [g]
International trade: balance (million current US$)	- 488 [e]	- 273 [e]	- 2 239 [g]
Balance of payments, current account (million US$)	- 853	171	- 653 [c]

Major trading partners

							2021
Export partners (% of exports) [e]	Switzerland	21.2	Poland	14.2	France	11.9
Import partners (% of imports) [e]	China	30.5	Singapore	26.0	Republic of Korea	14.4

Social indicators

	2010	2015	2022
Population growth rate (average annual %)	2.9	2.1	2.1 [a]
Urban population (% of total population)	47.8	49.8	51.6 [c]
Urban population growth rate (average annual %) [h]	4.6	3.4	...
Fertility rate, total (live births per woman)	5.1	4.5	4.0 [a]
Life expectancy at birth (females/males, years)	60.6 / 58.2	60.4 / 57.9	62.4 / 59.8 [a]
Population age distribution (0-14/60+ years old, %)	43.3 / 5.4	42.6 / 5.2	40.5 / 5.1 [a]
International migrant stock (000/% of total pop.) [i]	99.2 / 2.5	112.1 / 2.5	87.9 / 1.7 [b]
Refugees and others of concern to the UNHCR (000)	26.6 [j]	40.4	38.5 [g]
Infant mortality rate (per 1 000 live births)	74.0	67.7	57.3 [a]
Health: Current expenditure (% of GDP) [k]	8.9	10.6	8.5 [c]
Health: Physicians (per 1 000 pop.)	~0.0	~0.0	0.1 [f]
Education: Government expenditure (% of GDP)	1.7 [l]	2.2 [e]	2.3 [e,b]
Education: Primary gross enrol. ratio (f/m per 100 pop.)	96.5 / 108.0 [m]	90.2 / 100.3	84.7 / 85.5 [n]
Education: Sec. gross enrol. ratio (f/m per 100 pop.)	... / ...	32.9 / 42.8	... / ...
Education: Upr. Sec. gross enrol. ratio (f/m per 100 pop.)	... / ...	25.3 / 34.5	... / ...
Intentional homicide rate (per 100 000 pop.)	3.3	3.3 [o]	...
Seats held by women in the National Parliament (%)	12.5	11.0	11.0 [p]

Environment and infrastructure indicators

	2010	2015	2022
Individuals using the Internet (per 100 inhabitants)	2.3	10.0 [e]	25.6 [e,b]
Threatened species (number)	147	158	282
Forested area (% of land area)	82.2	80.7 [e]	79.4 [e,c]
Energy production, primary (Petajoules)	64	76	87 [c]
Energy supply per capita (Gigajoules)	19	21	20 [c]
Important sites for terrestrial biodiversity protected (%)	15.8	15.8	15.8 [g]
Net Official Development Assist. received (% of GNI)	77.85	37.69	25.18 [b]

a Projected estimate (medium fertility variant). b 2020. c 2019. d Data classified according to ISIC Rev. 4. e Estimate. f 2018. g 2021. h Data refers to a 5-year period preceding the reference year. i Including refugees. j Data as at the end of December. k The country provided new Health accounts study which replaced our previous estimates, especially for the years during the Ebola virus epidemic during 2015. l 2008. m 2009. n 2017. o 2012. p Data are as at 1 January of reporting year.

Libya

Region	Northern Africa	
Population (000, 2022)	6 812[a]	
Pop. density (per km2, 2022)	4.1[a]	
Capital city	Tripoli	
Capital city pop. (000, 2022)	1 160.9[c]	

UN membership date	14 December 1955	
Surface area (km2)	1 676 198[b]	
Sex ratio (m per 100 f)	102.4[a]	
National currency	Libyan Dinar (LYD)	
Exchange rate (per US$)	1.4[c]	

Economic indicators	2010	2015	2022
GDP: Gross domestic product (million current US$)	75 418	48 522	29 153[b]
GDP growth rate (annual %, const. 2015 prices)	5.3	- 1.0	- 59.7[b]
GDP per capita (current US$)	12 168.8	7 559.9	4 242.8[b]
Economy: Agriculture (% of Gross Value Added)[d]	1.6	3.9	3.9[b]
Economy: Industry (% of Gross Value Added)[d]	69.0	31.3	38.5[b]
Economy: Services and other activity (% of GVA)[d]	29.3	64.8	57.6[b]
Employment in agriculture (% of employed)[e]	19.1	20.3	18.8[b]
Employment in industry (% of employed)[e]	27.5	22.3	21.7[b]
Employment in services & other sectors (% employed)[e]	53.4	57.4	59.5[b]
Unemployment rate (% of labour force)[e]	19.3	19.5	19.5
Labour force participation rate (female/male pop. %)[e]	33.9 / 61.3	33.9 / 61.2	34.2 / 61.1
CPI: Consumer Price Index (2010=100)	100	126[f]	...
Agricultural production index (2014-2016=100)	105	99	105[b]
International trade: exports (million current US$)	36 440	10 200[e]	40 977[e,g]
International trade: imports (million current US$)	17 674	13 000[e]	17 631[g]
International trade: balance (million current US$)	18 766	- 2 800[e]	23 346[g]
Balance of payments, current account (million US$)	16 801	- 9 346	4 125[c]

Major trading partners						2021
Export partners (% of exports)[e]	Italy	22.3	Germany	11.2	Spain	10.6
Import partners (% of imports)[e]	Türkiye	16.3	China	12.5	Italy	8.3

Social indicators	2010	2015	2022
Population growth rate (average annual %)	2.1	1.5	1.1[a]
Urban population (% of total population)	78.1	79.3	80.4[c]
Urban population growth rate (average annual %)[h]	1.5	0.5	...
Fertility rate, total (live births per woman)	2.6	2.7	2.4[a]
Life expectancy at birth (females/males, years)	74.9 / 70.2	75.4 / 68.5	74.8 / 69.7[a]
Population age distribution (0-14/60+ years old, %)	29.9 / 5.9	31.6 / 6.7	28.3 / 7.7[a]
International migrant stock (000/% of total pop.)[i,j]	687.2 / 11.1	771.1 / 12.0	826.5 / 12.0[b]
Refugees and others of concern to the UNHCR (000)	11.2[k]	471.7	321.4[g]
Infant mortality rate (per 1 000 live births)	14.2	11.9	9.1[a]
Health: Current expenditure (% of GDP)[l,m]	3.6	6.1[n]	...
Health: Physicians (per 1 000 pop.)	2.0[o]	1.9	2.1[p]
Education: Primary gross enrol. ratio (f/m per 100 pop.)	106.6 / 111.3[q]	... / ...	... / ...
Education: Sec. gross enrol. ratio (f/m per 100 pop.)	106.0 / 90.2[q]	... / ...	... / ...
Education: Upr. Sec. gross enrol. ratio (f/m per 100 pop.)	108.8 / 77.3[q]	... / ...	... / ...
Seats held by women in the National Parliament (%)	7.7	16.0	16.5[r]

Environment and infrastructure indicators	2010	2015	2022
Individuals using the Internet (per 100 inhabitants)[e]	14.0	17.8[s]	...
Threatened species (number)	44	54	94
Forested area (% of land area)[e]	0.1	0.1	0.1[c]
CO2 emission estimates (million tons/tons per capita)	51.2 / 8.2	45.7 / 7.0	46.5 / 6.8[c]
Energy production, primary (Petajoules)	4 310	1 453	3 187[c]
Energy supply per capita (Gigajoules)	140	119	134[c]
Tourist/visitor arrivals at national borders (000)	34[t,u]	...	...
Important sites for terrestrial biodiversity protected (%)	0.0	0.0	0.0[g]
Net Official Development Assist. received (% of GNI)	0.01	0.54	1.12[b]

a Projected estimate (medium fertility variant). b 2020. c 2019. d Data classified according to ISIC Rev. 4. e Estimate. f 2013. g 2021. h Data refers to a 5-year period preceding the reference year. i Including refugees. j Refers to foreign citizens. k Data as at the end of December. l Data based on calendar year (January 1 to December 31). m Estimates should be viewed with caution as these are derived from scarce data. n 2011. o 2009. p 2017. q 2006. r Data are as at 1 January of reporting year. s 2014. t Non-resident tourists staying in hotels and similar establishments. u 2008.

Liechtenstein

Region	Western Europe	UN membership date	18 September 1990
Population (000, 2022)	39[a]	Surface area (km2)	160[b]
Pop. density (per km2, 2022)	245.8[a]	Sex ratio (m per 100 f)	98.4[a]
Capital city	Vaduz	National currency	Swiss Franc (CHF)
Capital city pop. (000, 2022)	5.5[c]	Exchange rate (per US$)	0.9[d]

Economic indicators

	2010	2015	2022
GDP: Gross domestic product (million current US$)	5 621	6 269	6 872[b]
GDP growth rate (annual %, const. 2015 prices)	7.4	~0.0	- 2.2[b]
GDP per capita (current US$)	156 166.5	167 294.2	180 227.1[b]
Economy: Agriculture (% of Gross Value Added)[e,f]	0.1	0.1	0.1[b]
Economy: Industry (% of Gross Value Added)[f,g]	44.6	43.1	44.2[b]
Economy: Services and other activity (% of GVA)[f,h]	55.3	56.8	55.7[b]
Unemployment rate (% of labour force)[i]	2.6	2.6[i]	...
Labour force participation rate (female/male pop. %)	52.6 / 70.9	53.5 / 70.6[i]	... / ...

Social indicators

	2010	2015	2022
Population growth rate (average annual %)	0.6	0.6	0.7[a]
Urban population (% of total population)	14.5	14.3	14.4[k]
Urban population growth rate (average annual %)[l]	0.3	0.5	...
Fertility rate, total (live births per woman)	1.4	1.4	1.5[a]
Life expectancy at birth (females/males, years)	84.3 / 79.5	84.5 / 80.9	86.1 / 83.0[a]
Population age distribution (0-14/60+ years old, %)	16.3 / 19.7	15.0 / 22.5	14.5 / 26.6[a]
International migrant stock (000/% of total pop.)	22.3 / 62.1	23.8 / 63.5	25.9 / 67.9[b]
Refugees and others of concern to the UNHCR (000)	0.1[m]	0.2	0.1[d]
Infant mortality rate (per 1 000 live births)	6.8	6.2	5.0[a]
Education: Government expenditure (% of GDP)	2.0[n]	2.6[o]	...
Education: Primary gross enrol. ratio (f/m per 100 pop.)[p]	102.3 / 108.6	104.8 / 106.5	103.8 / 103.8[k]
Education: Sec. gross enrol. ratio (f/m per 100 pop.)[p]	100.0 / 117.6	101.7 / 130.7	110.0 / 128.0[k]
Education: Upr. Sec. gross enrol. ratio (f/m per 100 pop.)[p]	96.2 / 137.6	110.9 / 167.5	121.3 / 158.2[k]
Intentional homicide rate (per 100 000 pop.)	2.8	0.0	2.6[b]
Seats held by women in the National Parliament (%)	24.0	20.0	28.0[q]

Environment and infrastructure indicators

	2010	2015	2022
Individuals using the Internet (per 100 inhabitants)[p]	80.0	96.6	99.5[r]
Threatened species (number)	2	4	15
Forested area (% of land area)	41.9	41.9	41.9[k]
Energy production, primary (Petajoules)[p]	1	1	1[k]
Energy supply per capita (Gigajoules)	92	88	90[k]
Tourist/visitor arrivals at national borders (000)[s]	64	57	58[b]
Important sites for terrestrial biodiversity protected (%)	80.8	80.8	80.8[d]
Net Official Development Assist. disbursed (% of GNI)	...	0.64[i]	...

a Projected estimate (medium fertility variant). **b** 2020. **c** 2018. **d** 2021. **e** Excludes irrigation canals and landscaping care. **f** Data classified according to ISIC Rev. 4. **g** Excludes publishing activities. Includes irrigation and canals. **h** Includes publishing activities and landscape care. Excludes repair of personal and household goods. **i** Population aged 15 to 64 years. **j** 2013. **k** 2019. **l** Data refers to a 5-year period preceding the reference year. **m** Data as at the end of December. **n** 2008. **o** 2011. **p** Estimate. **q** Data are as at 1 January of reporting year. **r** 2017. **s** Excluding long term tourists on campgrounds and in holiday flats.

Lithuania

Region	Northern Europe
Population (000, 2022)	2 750[a]
Pop. density (per km2, 2022)	43.9[a]
Capital city	Vilnius
Capital city pop. (000, 2022)	537.6[c]

UN membership date	17 September 1991
Surface area (km2)	65 286[b]
Sex ratio (m per 100 f)	88.6[a]
National currency	Euro (EUR)
Exchange rate (per US$)	0.9[d]

Economic indicators

	2010	2015	2022
GDP: Gross domestic product (million current US$)	37 138	41 419	56 547[b]
GDP growth rate (annual %, const. 2015 prices)	1.7	2.0	- 0.1[b]
GDP per capita (current US$)	11 888.8	14 127.1	20 771.8[b]
Economy: Agriculture (% of Gross Value Added)[e,f]	3.4	3.8	3.6[b]
Economy: Industry (% of Gross Value Added)[f,g]	29.1	29.7	27.8[b]
Economy: Services and other activity (% of GVA)[f,h]	67.5	66.5	68.6[b]
Employment in agriculture (% of employed)	8.8	9.1	6.6[i,b]
Employment in industry (% of employed)	24.6	25.1	25.9[i,b]
Employment in services & other sectors (% employed)	66.6	65.9	67.4[i,b]
Unemployment rate (% of labour force)	17.8	9.1	7.7[i]
Labour force participation rate (female/male pop. %)	52.5 / 62.0	54.4 / 64.9	57.4 / 67.8[i]
CPI: Consumer Price Index (2010=100)[j]	100	108	125[d]
Agricultural production index (2014-2016=100)	73	106	108[b]
International trade: exports (million current US$)	20 814	25 411	40 814[d]
International trade: imports (million current US$)	23 378	28 176	44 550[d]
International trade: balance (million current US$)	- 2 564	- 2 765	- 3 736[d]
Balance of payments, current account (million US$)	73	- 1 014	937[d]

Major trading partners

						2021
Export partners (% of exports)	Russian Federation	10.8	Latvia	9.4	Germany	8.2
Import partners (% of imports)	Germany	12.7	Russian Federation	12.1	Poland	12.1

Social indicators

	2010	2015	2022
Population growth rate (average annual %)	- 1.3	- 1.0	- 1.4[a]
Urban population (% of total population)	66.8	67.2	67.9[c]
Urban population growth rate (average annual %)[k]	- 1.3	- 1.1	...
Fertility rate, total (live births per woman)	1.5	1.7	1.6[a]
Life expectancy at birth (females/males, years)	78.8 / 67.9	79.5 / 69.6	79.1 / 69.5[a]
Population age distribution (0-14/60+ years old, %)	14.9 / 23.3	14.5 / 25.1	15.3 / 28.5[a]
International migrant stock (000/% of total pop.)	160.8 / 5.1	136.0 / 4.6	145.2 / 5.3[b]
Refugees and others of concern to the UNHCR (000)	4.6[l]	4.7	5.0[d]
Infant mortality rate (per 1 000 live births)	4.9	4.0	2.8[a]
Health: Current expenditure (% of GDP)	6.8	6.5	7.0[c]
Health: Physicians (per 1 000 pop.)	3.9	4.3	5.1[b]
Education: Government expenditure (% of GDP)	5.3	4.2	3.9[m]
Education: Primary gross enrol. ratio (f/m per 100 pop.)[i]	99.8 / 101.0	101.9 / 102.2	102.8 / 103.2[c,]
Education: Sec. gross enrol. ratio (f/m per 100 pop.)[i]	104.1 / 106.0	105.4 / 109.8	106.6 / 110.2[c]
Education: Upr. Sec. gross enrol. ratio (f/m per 100 pop.)[i]	108.3 / 106.8	114.0 / 119.6	110.7 / 117.2[c]
Intentional homicide rate (per 100 000 pop.)	7.0	5.9	3.7[b]
Seats held by women in the National Parliament (%)	19.1	23.4	28.4[n]

Environment and infrastructure indicators

	2010	2015	2022
Individuals using the Internet (per 100 inhabitants)	62.1[o,p]	71.4[p]	83.1[b]
Research & Development expenditure (% of GDP)	0.8	1.0	1.2[q,b]
Threatened species (number)	17	22	43
Forested area (% of land area)	34.6	34.9	35.1[c]
CO2 emission estimates (million tons/tons per capita)	12.7 / 4.0	11.0 / 3.6	11.2 / 3.9[b]
Energy production, primary (Petajoules)	64	76	83[c]
Energy supply per capita (Gigajoules)	94	100	115[c]
Tourist/visitor arrivals at national borders (000)	1 507	2 071	937[b]
Important sites for terrestrial biodiversity protected (%)	91.0	91.8	91.8[d]
Pop. using safely managed drinking water (urban/rural, %)	96.9 / ...	98.8 / ...	99.3 / ...[b]
Pop. using safely managed sanitation (urban/rural %)	89.8 / 73.0	95.4 / 81.7	97.6 / 86.2[b]
Net Official Development Assist. disbursed (% of GNI)	...	0.11[r]	...

a Projected estimate (medium fertility variant). b 2020. c 2019. d 2021. e Excludes irrigation canals and landscaping care. f Data classified according to ISIC Rev. 4. g Excludes publishing activities. Includes irrigation and canals. h Excludes repair of personal and household goods. i Estimate. j Calculated by the UNSD from national indices. k Data refers to a 5-year period preceding the reference year. l Data as at the end of December. m 2018. n Data are as at 1 January of reporting year. o Users in the last 12 months. p Population aged 16 to 74 years. q Provisional data. r 2013.

Luxembourg

Region	Western Europe	UN membership date	24 October 1945
Population (000, 2022)	648[a]	Surface area (km2)	2 586[b]
Pop. density (per km2, 2022)	250.0[a]	Sex ratio (m per 100 f)	101.3[a]
Capital city	Luxembourg	National currency	Euro (EUR)
Capital city pop. (000, 2022)	119.8[c]	Exchange rate (per US$)	0.9[d]

Economic indicators

	2010	2015	2022
GDP: Gross domestic product (million current US$)	56 159	60 047	73 353[b]
GDP growth rate (annual %, const. 2015 prices)	3.8	2.3	- 1.8[b]
GDP per capita (current US$)	110 573.8	105 952.2	117 181.6[b]
Economy: Agriculture (% of Gross Value Added)[e,f]	0.3	0.2	0.2[b]
Economy: Industry (% of Gross Value Added)[f,g]	12.2	12.6	12.3[b]
Economy: Services and other activity (% of GVA)[f,h]	87.5	87.1	87.5[b]
Employment in agriculture (% of employed)	1.1	1.0	1.0[i,b]
Employment in industry (% of employed)	13.3	12.5	11.5[i,b]
Employment in services & other sectors (% employed)	85.6	86.4	87.5[i,b]
Unemployment rate (% of labour force)	4.4	6.7	4.9[i]
Labour force participation rate (female/male pop. %)	49.8 / 65.8	54.6 / 65.4	58.3 / 65.6[i]
CPI: Consumer Price Index (2010=100)[j]	100	109	119[d]
Agricultural production index (2014-2016=100)	91	102	114[b]
International trade: exports (million current US$)	13 911	12 626	16 247[d]
International trade: imports (million current US$)	20 400	19 296	25 537[d]
International trade: balance (million current US$)	- 6 489	- 6 671	- 9 290[d]
Balance of payments, current account (million US$)	3 268	2 921	4 322[d]

Major trading partners

						2021
Export partners (% of exports)	Germany	25.1	France	16.0	Belgium	12.8
Import partners (% of imports)	Germany	23.6	Belgium	23.5	France	12.2

Social indicators

	2010	2015	2022
Population growth rate (average annual %)	1.9	2.3	1.1[a]
Urban population (% of total population)	88.5	90.2	91.2[k]
Urban population growth rate (average annual %)[l]	2.5	2.6	...
Fertility rate, total (live births per woman)	1.6	1.5	1.4[a]
Life expectancy at birth (females/males, years)	83.2 / 77.9	83.9 / 79.7	84.8 / 80.4[a]
Population age distribution (0-14/60+ years old, %)	17.7 / 18.9	16.6 / 19.3	15.8 / 20.8[a]
International migrant stock (000/% of total pop.)	163.1 / 32.1	248.9 / 43.9	298.1 / 47.6[b]
Refugees and others of concern to the UNHCR (000)	4.1[m]	2.1	6.8[d]
Infant mortality rate (per 1 000 live births)	3.8	2.5	3.1[a]
Health: Current expenditure (% of GDP)	7.0	5.3	5.4[k]
Health: Physicians (per 1 000 pop.)	2.8	2.9	3.0[n]
Education: Government expenditure (% of GDP)	...	3.9	3.7[c]
Education: Primary gross enrol. ratio (f/m per 100 pop.)	98.1 / 97.1	98.9 / 99.0	104.0 / 105.3[k]
Education: Sec. gross enrol. ratio (f/m per 100 pop.)	102.8 / 99.8	104.2 / 100.5	104.5 / 104.9[k]
Education: Upr. Sec. gross enrol. ratio (f/m per 100 pop.)	92.3 / 88.5	97.3 / 92.0	97.4 / 92.2[k]
Intentional homicide rate (per 100 000 pop.)	2.0	0.9	0.2[b]
Seats held by women in the National Parliament (%)	20.0	28.3	33.3[o]

Environment and infrastructure indicators

	2010	2015	2022
Individuals using the Internet (per 100 inhabitants)	90.6[p]	96.4	98.8[b]
Research & Development expenditure (% of GDP)	1.4	1.3	1.1[b]
Threatened species (number)	5	9	17
Forested area (% of land area)	34.5	34.5	34.5[k]
CO2 emission estimates (million tons/tons per capita)	10.8 / 21.0	9.0 / 15.5	7.6 / 11.9[b]
Energy production, primary (Petajoules)	5	6	10[k]
Energy supply per capita (Gigajoules)	351	278	272[k]
Tourist/visitor arrivals at national borders (000)[q,r]	805	1 090	525[b]
Important sites for terrestrial biodiversity protected (%)	77.6	79.4	84.2[d]
Pop. using safely managed drinking water (urban/rural, %)	99.7 / 100.0	99.7 / 98.0	99.7 / 96.5[b]
Pop. using safely managed sanitation (urban/rural %)	93.3 / 85.7	96.4 / 88.4	97.5 / 89.3[b]
Net Official Development Assist. disbursed (% of GNI)[s]	1.07	0.95	1.03[b]

a Projected estimate (medium fertility variant). b 2020. c 2018. d 2021. e Excludes irrigation canals and landscaping care. f Data classified according to ISIC Rev. 4. g Excludes publishing activities. Includes irrigation and canals. h Includes publishing activities and landscape care. Excludes repair of personal and household goods. i Estimate. j Calculated by the UNSD from national indices. k 2019. l Data refers to a 5-year period preceding the reference year. m Data as at the end of December. n 2017. o Data are as at 1 January of reporting year. p Population aged 16 to 74 years. q Including youth hostels, tourist private accommodation and others. r Non-resident tourists staying in all types of accommodation establishments. s DAC member (OECD).

Madagascar

Region	Eastern Africa	UN membership date	20 September 1960	
Population (000, 2022)	29 612[a]	Surface area (km2)	587 041[b]	
Pop. density (per km2, 2022)	50.9[a]	Sex ratio (m per 100 f)	100.4[a]	
Capital city	Antananarivo	National currency	Malagasy Ariary (MGA)	
Capital city pop. (000, 2022)	3 210.4[c]	Exchange rate (per US$)	3 956.7[d]	

Economic indicators

	2010	2015	2022
GDP: Gross domestic product (million current US$)	9 983	11 323	13 008[b]
GDP growth rate (annual %, const. 2015 prices)	0.6	3.1	- 7.8[b]
GDP per capita (current US$)	472.0	467.2	469.8[b]
Economy: Agriculture (% of Gross Value Added)[e]	30.3	27.0	26.8[b]
Economy: Industry (% of Gross Value Added)[e]	18.8	19.9	20.9[b]
Economy: Services and other activity (% of GVA)[e]	50.9	53.2	52.3[b]
Employment in agriculture (% of employed)[f]	73.4	66.4	63.8[b]
Employment in industry (% of employed)[f]	6.0	8.4	9.1[b]
Employment in services & other sectors (% employed)[f]	20.6	25.1	27.1[b]
Unemployment rate (% of labour force)	4.3	1.8	2.4[f]
Labour force participation rate (female/male pop. %)	84.1 / 89.3[f]	83.6 / 89.2	82.6 / 87.8[f]
CPI: Consumer Price Index (2010=100)	100	140	137[g,h,d]
Agricultural production index (2014-2016=100)	105	99	102[b]
International trade: exports (million current US$)	1 082	2 164	2 578[f,d]
International trade: imports (million current US$)	2 546	2 961	4 176[f,d]
International trade: balance (million current US$)	- 1 464	- 796	- 1 598[d]
Balance of payments, current account (million US$)	- 893	- 256	- 718[b]

Major trading partners

							2021
Export partners (% of exports)[f]	France	23.1	United States	22.5	Germany	8.3	
Import partners (% of imports)[f]	China	25.4	India	8.6	France	7.2	

Social indicators

	2010	2015	2022
Population growth rate (average annual %)	2.8	2.6	2.4[a]
Urban population (% of total population)	31.9	35.2	37.9[c]
Urban population growth rate (average annual %)[i]	4.9	4.7	...
Fertility rate, total (live births per woman)	4.8	4.2	3.8[a]
Life expectancy at birth (females/males, years)	64.6 / 61.2	66.3 / 62.4	67.6 / 63.0[a]
Population age distribution (0-14/60+ years old, %)	43.2 / 4.3	41.3 / 4.7	39.1 / 5.3[a]
International migrant stock (000/% of total pop.)[j,k]	28.9 / 0.1	32.1 / 0.1	35.6 / 0.1[b]
Refugees and others of concern to the UNHCR (000)	~0.0[l]	~0.0	0.3[d]
Infant mortality rate (per 1 000 live births)	47.1	41.3	32.6[a]
Health: Current expenditure (% of GDP)[m]	4.7	5.0	3.7[c]
Health: Physicians (per 1 000 pop.)	0.2	0.2[n]	0.2[o]
Education: Government expenditure (% of GDP)	2.8	2.2[f]	2.9[f,c]
Education: Primary gross enrol. ratio (f/m per 100 pop.)	142.4 / 145.0	147.3 / 147.3	135.2 / 132.9[c]
Education: Sec. gross enrol. ratio (f/m per 100 pop.)	29.7 / 31.6[p]	38.3 / 38.7[f]	35.2 / 34.0[c]
Education: Upr. Sec. gross enrol. ratio (f/m per 100 pop.)	13.6 / 15.6[p]	22.1 / 23.8[f]	22.1 / 22.2[c]
Seats held by women in the National Parliament (%)	7.9[p]	20.5	18.5[q]

Environment and infrastructure indicators

	2010	2015	2022
Individuals using the Internet (per 100 inhabitants)[f]	1.7	4.2	15.0[o]
Research & Development expenditure (% of GDP)[r]	0.1	~0.0[s,t,n]	~0.0[s,u]
Threatened species (number)	663	965	3 717
Forested area (% of land area)[f]	21.6	21.5	21.4[c]
Energy production, primary (Petajoules)	174[f]	209	318[c]
Energy supply per capita (Gigajoules)	9[f]	10	14[c]
Tourist/visitor arrivals at national borders (000)[v]	196	244	68[b]
Important sites for terrestrial biodiversity protected (%)	23.8	24.6	26.6[d]
Pop. using safely managed drinking water (urban/rural, %)	28.2 / 7.0	33.0 / 8.7	38.2 / 9.5[b]
Pop. using safely managed sanitation (urban/rural %)	11.0 / 5.2	12.7 / 6.6	14.2 / 8.0[b]
Net Official Development Assist. received (% of GNI)	4.85	6.19	9.69[b]

a Projected estimate (medium fertility variant). **b** 2020. **c** 2019. **d** 2021. **e** Data classified according to ISIC Rev. 4. **f** Estimate. **g** Data refer to 7 cities only. **h** Base: 2016 = 100 **i** Data refers to a 5-year period preceding the reference year. **j** Refers to foreign citizens. **k** Including refugees. **l** Data as at the end of December. **m** Data revision. **n** 2014. **o** 2018. **p** 2009. **q** Data are as at 1 January of reporting year. **r** Partial data. **s** Government only. **t** Break in the time series. **u** 2017. **v** Arrivals of non-resident tourists by air.

Malawi

Region	Eastern Africa	
Population (000, 2022)	20 405 [a]	
Pop. density (per km2, 2022)	215.8 [a]	
Capital city	Lilongwe	
Capital city pop. (000, 2022)	1 074.7 [c]	

UN membership date	01 December 1964
Surface area (km2)	117 726 [b]
Sex ratio (m per 100 f)	94.7 [a]
National currency	Malawi Kwacha (MWK)
Exchange rate (per US$)	773.1 [b]

Economic indicators

	2010	2015	2022
GDP: Gross domestic product (million current US$)	6 960	8 216	11 762 [b]
GDP growth rate (annual %, const. 2015 prices)	6.9	8.5	0.9 [b]
GDP per capita (current US$)	478.7	490.6	614.9 [b]
Economy: Agriculture (% of Gross Value Added) [d,e]	31.9	26.5	26.7 [b]
Economy: Industry (% of Gross Value Added) [d,f]	16.4	18.4	20.2 [b]
Economy: Services and other activity (% of GVA) [d,g]	51.7	55.1	53.1 [b]
Employment in agriculture (% of employed) [h]	48.1	45.6	43.2 [b]
Employment in industry (% of employed) [h]	14.2	14.0	13.8 [b]
Employment in services & other sectors (% employed) [h]	37.7	40.4	43.0 [b]
Unemployment rate (% of labour force) [h]	5.9	5.9	7.0
Labour force participation rate (female/male pop. %) [h]	73.2 / 82.4	72.8 / 82.7	72.7 / 80.4
CPI: Consumer Price Index (2010=100) [h]	100	251	454 [b]
Agricultural production index (2014-2016=100)	67	99	129 [b]
International trade: exports (million current US$)	1 066	1 080	954 [h,i]
International trade: imports (million current US$)	2 173	2 312	3 241 [h,i]
International trade: balance (million current US$)	- 1 107	- 1 232	- 2 287 [i]
Balance of payments, current account (million US$)	- 969	- 1 064	- 1 412 [b]

Major trading partners

						2021
Export partners (% of exports) [h]	Belgium	20.8	South Africa	6.2	United Kingdom	6.0
Import partners (% of imports) [h]	South Africa	20.6	China	16.2	United Arab Emirates	10.1

Social indicators

	2010	2015	2022
Population growth rate (average annual %)	2.9	2.7	2.5 [a]
Urban population (% of total population)	15.5	16.3	17.2 [c]
Urban population growth rate (average annual %) [j]	3.7	3.9	...
Fertility rate, total (live births per woman)	5.3	4.5	3.8 [a]
Life expectancy at birth (females/males, years)	58.4 / 54.3	64.7 / 58.2	66.3 / 59.6 [a]
Population age distribution (0-14/60+ years old, %)	46.5 / 5.4	46.0 / 4.4	42.6 / 3.8 [a]
International migrant stock (000/% of total pop.) [k]	217.7 / 1.5	197.3 / 1.2	191.4 / 1.0 [b]
Refugees and others of concern to the UNHCR (000)	15.2 [l]	22.6	51.1 [i]
Infant mortality rate (per 1 000 live births)	56.9	38.5	27.5 [a]
Health: Current expenditure (% of GDP)	7.2	9.3	7.4 [c]
Health: Physicians (per 1 000 pop.)	~0.0 [m]	~0.0 [n]	~0.0 [b]
Education: Government expenditure (% of GDP)	3.5	5.6	2.9 [h,b]
Education: Primary gross enrol. ratio (f/m per 100 pop.)	140.2 / 137.3	147.9 / 144.9	147.0 / 142.7 [c]
Education: Sec. gross enrol. ratio (f/m per 100 pop.)	31.9 / 36.1	38.9 / 42.6 [h]	33.6 / 40.5 [c]
Education: Upr. Sec. gross enrol. ratio (f/m per 100 pop.)	13.5 / 18.8	20.6 / 24.7	19.3 / 21.5 [c]
Intentional homicide rate (per 100 000 pop.)	3.6	1.8 [o]	...
Seats held by women in the National Parliament (%)	20.8	16.7	22.9 [p]

Environment and infrastructure indicators

	2010	2015	2022
Individuals using the Internet (per 100 inhabitants)	2.3	6.0 [h]	9.9 [h,c]
Threatened species (number)	158	171	143
Forested area (% of land area)	28.2	26.0 [h]	24.2 [h,c]
Energy production, primary (Petajoules)	64	69	71 [c]
Energy supply per capita (Gigajoules)	5	5	5 [c]
Tourist/visitor arrivals at national borders (000) [q]	746	805	871 [h,r]
Important sites for terrestrial biodiversity protected (%)	70.8	70.8	70.8 [i]
Pop. using safely managed sanitation (urban/rural %)	26.7 / 20.8	26.8 / 22.2	27.0 / 23.6 [b]
Net Official Development Assist. received (% of GNI)	14.84	17.05	12.35 [b]

a Projected estimate (medium fertility variant). b 2020. c 2019. d Data classified according to ISIC Rev. 4. e Excludes irrigation canals and landscaping care. f Excludes publishing activities. Includes irrigation and canals. g Includes publishing activities and landscape care. Excludes repair of personal and household goods. h Estimate. i 2021. j Data refers to a 5-year period preceding the reference year. k Including refugees. l Data as at the end of December. m 2009. n 2013. o 2012. p Data are as at 1 January of reporting year. q Departures. r 2018.

Malaysia

Region	South-eastern Asia	UN membership date	17 September 1957
Population (000, 2022)	33 938[a,b]	Surface area (km2)	330 621[c]
Pop. density (per km2, 2022)	103.3[a,b]	Sex ratio (m per 100 f)	104.5[a,b]
Capital city	Kuala Lumpur[d]	National currency	Malaysian Ringgit (MYR)
Capital city pop. (000, 2022)	7 780.3[e,f]	Exchange rate (per US$)	4.2[g]

Economic indicators	2010	2015	2022
GDP: Gross domestic product (million current US$)	255 018	301 355	336 664[c]
GDP growth rate (annual %, const. 2015 prices)	7.4	5.1	- 5.6[c]
GDP per capita (current US$)	9 040.6	9 955.2	10 401.8[c]
Economy: Agriculture (% of Gross Value Added)[h,i,j]	10.2	8.4	8.3[c]
Economy: Industry (% of Gross Value Added)[h,j,k]	40.9	38.9	36.3[c]
Economy: Services and other activity (% of GVA)[h,j,l]	48.9	52.7	55.4[c]
Employment in agriculture (% of employed)	14.2	12.5	10.1[m,c]
Employment in industry (% of employed)	27.7	27.5	26.8[m,c]
Employment in services & other sectors (% employed)	58.0	60.0	63.1[m,c]
Unemployment rate (% of labour force)	3.4	3.1	4.2[m]
Labour force participation rate (female/male pop. %)	43.5 / 76.2	50.5 / 77.6	51.2 / 77.5[m]
CPI: Consumer Price Index (2010=100)	100	113	123[g]
Agricultural production index (2014-2016=100)	89	104	100[c]
International trade: exports (million current US$)	198 791	200 211	299 230[g]
International trade: imports (million current US$)	164 586	176 175	238 250[g]
International trade: balance (million current US$)	34 204	24 036	60 981[g]
Balance of payments, current account (million US$)	25 644	9 068	12 904[g]

Major trading partners						2021
Export partners (% of exports)	China	15.5	Singapore	14.0	United States	11.5
Import partners (% of imports)	China	23.2	Singapore	9.5	Other Asia, nes	7.6

Social indicators	2010	2015	2022
Population growth rate (average annual %)[b]	1.6	1.5	1.1[a]
Urban population (% of total population)[b]	70.9	74.2	76.6[f]
Urban population growth rate (average annual %)[b,n]	3.1	2.7	...
Fertility rate, total (live births per woman)[b]	2.1	2.0	1.8[a]
Life expectancy at birth (females/males, years)[b]	77.1 / 72.1	77.7 / 72.8	78.8 / 74.0[a]
Population age distribution (0-14/60+ years old, %)[b]	27.8 / 7.9	25.2 / 9.2	22.7 / 11.4[a]
International migrant stock (000/% of total pop.)[b,o,p]	2 417.4 / 8.6	3 280.7 / 10.8	3 476.6 / 10.7[c]
Refugees and others of concern to the UNHCR (000)	212.9[q]	272.0	192.2[g]
Infant mortality rate (per 1 000 live births)[b]	6.9	6.9	5.9[a]
Health: Current expenditure (% of GDP)	3.2[r]	3.8[r]	3.8[f]
Health: Physicians (per 1 000 pop.)	1.2	1.5	2.3[c]
Education: Government expenditure (% of GDP)	5.0	4.9	4.2[f]
Education: Primary gross enrol. ratio (f/m per 100 pop.)	100.2 / 99.3	104.1 / 103.5	104.9 / 103.9[f]
Education: Sec. gross enrol. ratio (f/m per 100 pop.)	80.2 / 74.5	88.7 / 81.4	87.0 / 80.7[f]
Education: Upr. Sec. gross enrol. ratio (f/m per 100 pop.)	70.0 / 60.2	86.9 / 76.2	83.8 / 73.4[f]
Intentional homicide rate (per 100 000 pop.)	1.9	2.1[s]	...
Seats held by women in the National Parliament (%)	9.9	10.4	15.0[t]

Environment and infrastructure indicators	2010	2015	2022
Individuals using the Internet (per 100 inhabitants)	56.3[u]	71.1	89.6[c]
Research & Development expenditure (% of GDP)	1.0	1.3	1.0[v]
Threatened species (number)	1 180	1 252	2 056
Forested area (% of land area)[m]	57.7	59.2	58.3[f]
CO2 emission estimates (million tons/tons per capita)	191.6 / 6.7	222.5 / 7.3	239.1 / 7.4[f]
Energy production, primary (Petajoules)[w]	3 450	3 748	4 085[f]
Energy supply per capita (Gigajoules)[w]	105	113	122[f]
Tourist/visitor arrivals at national borders (000)[x]	24 577	25 721	4 333[c]
Important sites for terrestrial biodiversity protected (%)	31.6	37.0	37.0[g]
Net Official Development Assist. received (% of GNI)	0.00	0.00	0.00[c]

a Projected estimate (medium fertility variant). **b** Including Sabah and Sarawak. **c** 2020. **d** Kuala Lumpur is the capital and Putrajaya is the administrative capital. **e** Refers to the Greater Kuala Lumpur. **f** 2019. **g** 2021. **h** At producers' prices. **i** Excludes irrigation canals and landscaping care. **j** Data classified according to ISIC Rev. 4. **k** Excludes publishing activities. Includes irrigation and canals. **l** Includes publishing activities and landscape care. Excludes repair of personal and household goods. **m** Estimate. **n** Data refers to a 5-year period preceding the reference year. **o** Including refugees. **p** Refers to foreign citizens. **q** Data as at the end of December. **r** Provisional data. **s** 2013. **t** Data are as at 1 January of reporting year. **u** Refers to total population. **v** 2018. **w** Data comprises of Peninsular Malaysia, Sabah and Sarawak. **x** Including Singapore residents crossing the frontier by road through Johore Causeway.

Maldives

Region	Southern Asia	UN membership date	21 September 1965
Population (000, 2022)	524[a]	Surface area (km2)	300[b]
Pop. density (per km2, 2022)	1 746.0[a]	Sex ratio (m per 100 f)	135.4[a]
Capital city	Male	National currency	Rufiyaa (MVR)
Capital city pop. (000, 2022)	176.9[c]	Exchange rate (per US$)	15.4[d]

Economic indicators	2010	2015	2022
GDP: Gross domestic product (million current US$)	2 588	4 109	3 743[b]
GDP growth rate (annual %, const. 2015 prices)	7.3	2.9	- 33.5[b]
GDP per capita (current US$)	7 076.7	9 033.4	6 924.1[b]
Economy: Agriculture (% of Gross Value Added)[e,f]	6.1	6.3	8.8[b]
Economy: Industry (% of Gross Value Added)[f,g]	10.2	12.1	13.1[b]
Economy: Services and other activity (% of GVA)[f,h]	83.8	81.7	78.1[b]
Employment in agriculture (% of employed)[i]	12.8	9.8	8.2[b]
Employment in industry (% of employed)[i]	20.9	19.1	18.3[b]
Employment in services & other sectors (% employed)[i]	66.4	71.2	73.4[b]
Unemployment rate (% of labour force)[i]	11.3	6.9	5.2
Labour force participation rate (female/male pop. %)[i]	36.9 / 65.8	38.3 / 68.3	35.2 / 68.3
CPI: Consumer Price Index (2010=100)	100[i]	132[i]	135[j,d]
Agricultural production index (2014-2016=100)	114	100	105[b]
International trade: exports (million current US$)[k]	74	144	151[d]
International trade: imports (million current US$)[k]	1 095	1 897	2 574[d]
International trade: balance (million current US$)[k]	- 1 021	- 1 753	- 2 422[d]
Balance of payments, current account (million US$)	- 196	- 302	- 458[d]

Major trading partners						2021
Export partners (% of exports)	Thailand	46.4	Germany	11.4	United Kingdom	6.8
Import partners (% of imports)	Oman	13.1	United Arab Emirates	13.0	China	12.6

Social indicators	2010	2015	2022
Population growth rate (average annual %)	3.5	4.3	- 0.4[a]
Urban population (% of total population)	36.4	38.5	40.2[l]
Urban population growth rate (average annual %)[m]	4.2	3.9	...
Fertility rate, total (live births per woman)	2.3	2.0	1.7[a]
Life expectancy at birth (females/males, years)	78.8 / 76.8	80.7 / 78.9	81.8 / 80.1[a]
Population age distribution (0-14/60+ years old, %)	25.7 / 6.1	22.9 / 5.9	21.7 / 7.8[a]
International migrant stock (000/% of total pop.)[n]	54.7 / 14.9	64.3 / 14.1	70.1 / 13.0[b]
Infant mortality rate (per 1 000 live births)	11.8	8.3	6.0[a]
Health: Current expenditure (% of GDP)	8.5[o,p]	8.7	8.0[l]
Health: Physicians (per 1 000 pop.)	1.4	1.8[q]	2.1[l]
Education: Government expenditure (% of GDP)	3.6	3.9	4.1[i,l]
Education: Primary gross enrol. ratio (f/m per 100 pop.)	108.6 / 112.7[r]	100.0 / 103.0	99.3 / 96.9[l]
Education: Sec. gross enrol. ratio (f/m per 100 pop.)	... / ...	... / ...	78.4 / 84.3[l]
Education: Upr. Sec. gross enrol. ratio (f/m per 100 pop.)	... / ...	... / ...	43.5 / 34.5[l]
Intentional homicide rate (per 100 000 pop.)	1.6	0.9	0.6[l]
Seats held by women in the National Parliament (%)	6.5	5.9	4.6[s]

Environment and infrastructure indicators	2010	2015	2022
Individuals using the Internet (per 100 inhabitants)	26.5[t]	54.5[i]	62.9[i,b]
Threatened species (number)	59	69	91
Forested area (% of land area)	2.7	2.7	2.7[l]
Energy production, primary (Petajoules)	0	0	0[l]
Energy supply per capita (Gigajoules)	37	41	53[l]
Tourist/visitor arrivals at national borders (000)[u]	792	1 234	555[b]
Important sites for terrestrial biodiversity protected (%)	0.0	0.0	0.0[d]
Net Official Development Assist. received (% of GNI)	3.88	0.64	8.28[b]

a Projected estimate (medium fertility variant). b 2020. c 2018. d 2021. e Excludes irrigation canals and landscaping care. f Data classified according to ISIC Rev. 4. g Excludes publishing activities. Includes irrigation and canals. h Includes publishing activities and landscape care. Excludes repair of personal and household goods. i Estimate. j Calculated by the UNSD from national indices. k As of 2011, trade in services data reflect the improvement of the coverage of balance of payments statistics that was imremented in September 2012. l 2019. m Data refers to a 5-year period preceding the reference year. n Refers to foreign citizens. o Break in the time series. p Data revision. q 2014. r 2009. s Data are as at 1 January of reporting year. t Population aged 15 years and over. u Arrivals by air.

Mali

Region	Western Africa	UN membership date		28 September 1960	
Population (000, 2022)	22 594 a	Surface area (km2)		1 240 192 b	
Pop. density (per km2, 2022)	18.5 a	Sex ratio (m per 100 f)		102.0 a	
Capital city	Bamako	National currency		CFA Franc, BCEAO (XOF) c	
Capital city pop. (000, 2022)	2 529.3 d	Exchange rate (per US$)		579.2 e	

Economic indicators	2010	2015	2022
GDP: Gross domestic product (million current US$)	10 679	13 095	17 332 b
GDP growth rate (annual %, const. 2015 prices)	10.9	7.5	- 0.1 b
GDP per capita (current US$)	709.6	750.9	855.9 b
Economy: Agriculture (% of Gross Value Added) f	34.9	39.8	38.1 b
Economy: Industry (% of Gross Value Added) f	25.3	19.3	23.7 b
Economy: Services and other activity (% of GVA) f	39.7	40.9	38.2 b
Employment in agriculture (% of employed)	68.6 g	62.3	62.3 g,b
Employment in industry (% of employed)	8.8 g	8.3	7.6 g,b
Employment in services & other sectors (% employed)	22.5 g	29.5	30.2 g,b
Unemployment rate (% of labour force)	8.1	7.7	7.5 g
Labour force participation rate (female/male pop. %)	60.5 / 80.8 g	61.4 / 80.0	58.0 / 79.9 g
CPI: Consumer Price Index (2010=100) h	100	110	113 e
Agricultural production index (2014-2016=100)	77	97	125 b
International trade: exports (million current US$)	1 996	2 530 g	4 141 g,e
International trade: imports (million current US$)	4 704	3 169 g	6 535 g,e
International trade: balance (million current US$)	- 2 707	- 639 g	- 2 394 e
Balance of payments, current account (million US$)	- 1 191	- 698	- 380 b

Major trading partners					2021
Export partners (% of exports) g	South Africa	36.5	Switzerland	35.6	Bangladesh	7.1
Import partners (% of imports) g	Senegal	22.5	China	15.8	Ivory Coast	10.6

Social indicators	2010	2015	2022
Population growth rate (average annual %)	3.3	3.1	3.1 a
Urban population (% of total population)	36.0	40.0	43.1 d
Urban population growth rate (average annual %) i	5.6	5.0	...
Fertility rate, total (live births per woman)	6.6	6.4	5.9 a
Life expectancy at birth (females/males, years)	57.3 / 55.5	59.5 / 57.3	60.8 / 58.1 a
Population age distribution (0-14/60+ years old, %)	47.2 / 4.4	48.1 / 4.1	47.2 / 3.7 a
International migrant stock (000/% of total pop.) j	341.1 / 2.3	420.5 / 2.4	485.8 / 2.4 b
Refugees and others of concern to the UNHCR (000)	15.3 k	148.3	443.4 e
Infant mortality rate (per 1 000 live births)	76.5	65.8	53.3 a
Health: Current expenditure (% of GDP)	4.7	4.1	3.9 d
Health: Physicians (per 1 000 pop.)	0.1	0.1	0.1 l
Education: Government expenditure (% of GDP)	3.3	3.8	3.4 g,d
Education: Primary gross enrol. ratio (f/m per 100 pop.)	77.0 / 89.7	71.5 / 79.7	71.6 / 79.5 l
Education: Sec. gross enrol. ratio (f/m per 100 pop.)	31.9 / 46.5	36.8 / 46.5	37.0 / 45.0 l
Education: Upr. Sec. gross enrol. ratio (f/m per 100 pop.)	20.5 / 33.4	24.1 / 35.0	23.7 / 34.0 l
Seats held by women in the National Parliament (%)	10.2	9.5	26.5 m

Environment and infrastructure indicators	2010	2015	2022
Individuals using the Internet (per 100 inhabitants) g	2.0	10.3	27.4 b
Research & Development expenditure (% of GDP) n	0.6	0.3	0.2 d
Threatened species (number)	29	39	73
Forested area (% of land area) g	10.9	10.9	10.9 d
Energy production, primary (Petajoules) g	125	153	162 d
Energy supply per capita (Gigajoules) g	10	11	11 d
Tourist/visitor arrivals at national borders (000)	169	159	75 b
Important sites for terrestrial biodiversity protected (%)	61.6	61.6	61.6 e
Pop. using safely managed sanitation (urban/rural %)	8.3 / 15.4	9.0 / 21.4	9.6 / 28.0 b
Net Official Development Assist. received (% of GNI)	10.63	9.38	9.35 b

a Projected estimate (medium fertility variant). b 2020. c African Financial Community (CFA) Franc, Central Bank of West African States (BCEAO). d 2019. e 2021. f Data classified according to ISIC Rev. 4. g Estimate. h Bamako i Data refers to a 5-year period preceding the reference year. j Including refugees. k Data as at the end of December. l 2018. m Data are as at 1 January of reporting year. n Excluding business enterprise.

Malta

Region	Southern Europe	UN membership date	01 December 1964
Population (000, 2022)	533[a]	Surface area (km2)	315[b]
Pop. density (per km2, 2022)	1 693.0[a]	Sex ratio (m per 100 f)	108.9[a]
Capital city	Valletta	National currency	Euro (EUR)
Capital city pop. (000, 2022)	212.8[c,d]	Exchange rate (per US$)	0.9[e]

Economic indicators

	2010	2015	2022
GDP: Gross domestic product (million current US$)	9 027	11 087	14 911[b]
GDP growth rate (annual %, const. 2015 prices)	5.5	9.6	- 8.3[b]
GDP per capita (current US$)	21 791.1	25 572.1	33 770.8[b]
Economy: Agriculture (% of Gross Value Added)[f,g]	1.5	1.0	0.5[b]
Economy: Industry (% of Gross Value Added)[f,h]	18.9	13.0	14.0[b]
Economy: Services and other activity (% of GVA)[f,i]	79.7	86.0	85.5[b]
Employment in agriculture (% of employed)	1.3	1.5	0.9[i,b]
Employment in industry (% of employed)	25.5	20.0	18.0[i,b]
Employment in services & other sectors (% employed)	73.1	78.5	81.0[i,b]
Unemployment rate (% of labour force)	6.8	5.4	3.1[i]
Labour force participation rate (female/male pop. %)	34.8 / 67.1	43.6 / 68.0	52.1 / 70.7[i]
CPI: Consumer Price Index (2010=100)	100	108	116[e]
Agricultural production index (2014-2016=100)	108	99	74[b]
International trade: exports (million current US$)	3 717	3 915	3 111[i,e]
International trade: imports (million current US$)	5 732	6 788	6 905[i,e]
International trade: balance (million current US$)	- 2 015	- 2 873	- 3 794[e]
Balance of payments, current account (million US$)	- 420	301	- 1 010[e]

Major trading partners

						2021
Export partners (% of exports)[j]	Germany	17.0	France	9.0	Italy	6.8
Import partners (% of imports)[j]	Italy	20.2	United Kingdom	8.3	China	7.9

Social indicators

	2010	2015	2022
Population growth rate (average annual %)	0.9	2.3	0.3[a]
Urban population (% of total population)	94.1	94.4	94.7[k]
Urban population growth rate (average annual %)[l]	0.5	0.6	...
Fertility rate, total (live births per woman)	1.4	1.4	1.2[a]
Life expectancy at birth (females/males, years)	83.7 / 79.6	85.3 / 80.4	85.7 / 81.6[a]
Population age distribution (0-14/60+ years old, %)	14.8 / 23.5	13.7 / 24.7	13.1 / 25.0[a]
International migrant stock (000/% of total pop.)	33.0 / 8.0	52.6 / 12.1	114.8 / 26.0[b]
Refugees and others of concern to the UNHCR (000)	7.4[m]	6.5	12.3[e]
Infant mortality rate (per 1 000 live births)	6.0	6.1	5.3[a]
Health: Current expenditure (% of GDP)	8.0	8.9	8.2[k]
Health: Physicians (per 1 000 pop.)	2.2	2.9	...
Education: Government expenditure (% of GDP)	6.2	5.0	4.7[n]
Education: Primary gross enrol. ratio (f/m per 100 pop.)	101.9 / 101.6	104.3 / 102.8	107.0 / 106.2[k]
Education: Sec. gross enrol. ratio (f/m per 100 pop.)	98.2 / 110.0	97.8 / 92.1	108.2 / 107.9[k]
Education: Upr. Sec. gross enrol. ratio (f/m per 100 pop.)	86.6 / 113.2	95.0 / 85.1	111.0 / 107.3[k]
Intentional homicide rate (per 100 000 pop.)	1.0	0.9	1.6[b]
Seats held by women in the National Parliament (%)	8.7	12.9	13.4[o]

Environment and infrastructure indicators

	2010	2015	2022
Individuals using the Internet (per 100 inhabitants)	63.0[p]	76.0[q]	86.9[b]
Research & Development expenditure (% of GDP)	0.6	0.7	0.7[r,b]
Threatened species (number)	26	31	67
Forested area (% of land area)	1.1	1.1	1.4[k]
CO2 emission estimates (million tons/tons per capita)	2.6 / 6.2	1.7 / 3.7	1.6 / 3.0[b]
Energy production, primary (Petajoules)	0	1	1[k]
Energy supply per capita (Gigajoules)	85	63	69[k]
Tourist/visitor arrivals at national borders (000)[s]	1 339	1 783	659[b]
Important sites for terrestrial biodiversity protected (%)	89.3	90.6	90.9[e]
Net Official Development Assist. disbursed (% of GNI)	...	0.20[t]	

a Projected estimate (medium fertility variant). b 2020. c Refers to the localities of the Northern Harbour and Southern Harbour. d 2018. e 2021. f Data classified according to ISIC Rev. 4. g Excludes irrigation canals and landscaping care. h Excludes publishing activities. Includes irrigation and canals. i Includes publishing activities and landscape care. Excludes repair of personal and household goods. j Estimate. k 2019. l Data refers to a 5-year period preceding the reference year. m Data as at the end of December. n 2017. o Data are as at 1 January of reporting year. p Population aged 16 to 74 years. q Users in the last 3 months. r Provisional data. s Departures by air and by sea. t 2014.

Marshall Islands

Region	Micronesia	UN membership date	17 September 1991
Population (000, 2022)	42[a]	Surface area (km2)	181[b]
Pop. density (per km2, 2022)	230.9[a]	Sex ratio (m per 100 f)	104.3[a]
Capital city	Majuro	National currency	US Dollar (USD)
Capital city pop. (000, 2022)	30.7[c]		

Economic indicators

	2010	2015	2022[b]
GDP: Gross domestic product (million current US$)	160	184	244[b]
GDP growth rate (annual %, const. 2015 prices)	6.4	1.7	- 2.2[b]
GDP per capita (current US$)	2 846.9	3 207.7	4 130.1[b]
Economy: Agriculture (% of Gross Value Added)[d,e]	12.0	12.1	21.4[b]
Economy: Industry (% of Gross Value Added)[e,f]	14.1	12.1	12.6[b]
Economy: Services and other activity (% of GVA)[e,g]	73.9	75.8	66.0[b]
Employment in agriculture (% of employed)	11.0[h,i]	...	...
Employment in industry (% of employed)	9.4[h,i]	...	...
Employment in services & other sectors (% employed)	79.6[h,i]	...	...
Unemployment rate (% of labour force)	...	4.7[h,j]	...
Agricultural production index (2014-2016=100)	113	90	96[b]
International trade: exports (million current US$)[k]	17	25	1 247[l]
International trade: imports (million current US$)[k]	76	84	14 571[l]
International trade: balance (million current US$)	- 60[k]	- 59[k]	- 13 324[l]
Balance of payments, current account (million US$)	- 14	- 7	53[c]

Major trading partners

						2021
Export partners (% of exports)[k]	Denmark	44.0	Poland	12.1	Germany	7.6
Import partners (% of imports)[k]	Republic of Korea	33.1	Singapore	28.1	China	17.4

Social indicators

	2010	2015	2022
Population growth rate (average annual %)	- 0.3	- 2.1	1.0[a]
Urban population (% of total population)	73.6	75.8	77.4[m]
Urban population growth rate (average annual %)[n]	0.8	0.8	...
Fertility rate, total (live births per woman)	3.6	3.1	2.7[a]
Life expectancy at birth (females/males, years)	65.1 / 61.7	65.7 / 62.3	67.1 / 63.5[a]
Population age distribution (0-14/60+ years old, %)	39.6 / 3.9	37.4 / 5.1	32.5 / 7.6[a]
International migrant stock (000/% of total pop.)	3.1 / 5.5	3.3 / 5.7	3.3 / 5.6[b]
Infant mortality rate (per 1 000 live births)	31.4	28.7	24.5[a]
Health: Current expenditure (% of GDP)[o,p]	15.9	17.0	16.3[m]
Health: Physicians (per 1 000 pop.)	0.6	0.4[q]	...
Education: Government expenditure (% of GDP)	...	...	9.6[m]
Education: Primary gross enrol. ratio (f/m per 100 pop.)	97.4 / 98.8[r]	86.5 / 88.5	73.4 / 76.3[b]
Education: Sec. gross enrol. ratio (f/m per 100 pop.)	79.3 / 75.6[r]	68.8 / 64.1	65.9 / 59.5[b]
Education: Upr. Sec. gross enrol. ratio (f/m per 100 pop.)	71.4 / 66.8[r]	59.1 / 51.9	53.9 / 48.1[b]
Seats held by women in the National Parliament (%)	3.0	3.0	6.1[s]

Environment and infrastructure indicators

	2010	2015	2022
Individuals using the Internet (per 100 inhabitants)[k]	7.0	19.3	38.7[t]
Threatened species (number)	84	95	109
Forested area (% of land area)	52.2	52.2	52.2[m]
Energy production, primary (Petajoules)[k]	0	0	0[m]
Energy supply per capita (Gigajoules)[k]	38	38	39[m]
Tourist/visitor arrivals at national borders (000)	5[u]	6[u]	1[b]
Important sites for terrestrial biodiversity protected (%)	8.4	10.1	10.1[l]
Net Official Development Assist. received (% of GNI)	12.72	23.20	22.52[m]

a Projected estimate (medium fertility variant). **b** 2020. **c** 2018. **d** Excludes irrigation canals and landscaping care. **e** Data classified according to ISIC Rev. 4. **f** Excludes publishing activities. Includes irrigation and canals. **g** Includes publishing activities and landscape care. Excludes repair of personal and household goods. **h** Break in the time series. **i** Data classified according to ISIC Rev. 3. **j** 2011. **k** Estimate. **l** 2021. **m** 2019. **n** Data refers to a 5-year period preceding the reference year. **o** Data refer to fiscal years beginning 1 October. **p** Health expenditure indicators are high as they spend a lot on health using direct funding from the United States and also from their domestic funds. Current health expenditure is mostly government. **q** 2012. **r** 2009. **s** Data are as at 1 January of reporting year. **t** 2017. **u** Arrivals by air.

Martinique

Region	Caribbean	Population (000, 2022)	368 [a,b]
Surface area (km2)	1 090 [c]	Pop. density (per km2, 2022)	346.7 [a,b]
Sex ratio (m per 100 f)	85.3 [a,b]	Capital city	Fort-de-France
National currency	Euro (EUR)	Capital city pop. (000, 2022)	79.4 [d]
Exchange rate (per US$)	0.9 [e]		

Economic indicators	2010	2015	2022
Employment in agriculture (% of employed) [f,g]	4.1	3.9 [h]	...
Employment in industry (% of employed) [f,g]	11.9	11.8 [h]	...
Employment in services & other sectors (% employed) [f,g]	65.3	69.0 [h]	...
Unemployment rate (% of labour force) [g]	21.0	22.8 [i,j]	...
Labour force participation rate (female/male pop. %)	43.3 / 49.1 [g]	52.6 / 53.8 [g,i,j]	... / ...
CPI: Consumer Price Index (2010=100) [k]	100	106	109 [l]

Social indicators	2010	2015	2022
Population growth rate (average annual %) [b]	- 0.6	- 0.8	- 0.1 [a]
Urban population (% of total population)	89.0	89.0	89.1 [l]
Urban population growth rate (average annual %) [m]	- 0.2	- 0.5	...
Fertility rate, total (live births per woman) [b]	2.0	2.0	1.9 [a]
Life expectancy at birth (females/males, years) [b]	84.7 / 78.1	84.9 / 79.2	86.0 / 80.3 [a]
Population age distribution (0-14/60+ years old, %) [b]	19.7 / 20.3	18.1 / 24.3	15.9 / 30.6 [a]
International migrant stock (000/% of total pop.) [n]	59.6 / 15.1	69.2 / 18.3	68.6 / 18.3 [c]
Infant mortality rate (per 1 000 live births) [b]	7.3	7.1	6.2 [a]
Intentional homicide rate (per 100 000 pop.)	2.8 [o]	...	...

Environment and infrastructure indicators	2010	2015	2022
Individuals using the Internet (per 100 inhabitants)	42.0 [p,o]	...	...
Threatened species (number)	31	45	76
Forested area (% of land area) [p]	47.4	48.4	49.1 [l]
Energy production, primary (Petajoules)	1 [p,q]	...	...
Tourist/visitor arrivals at national borders (000)	478	487	312 [c]
Important sites for terrestrial biodiversity protected (%)	97.2	97.2	97.2 [e]

a Projected estimate (medium fertility variant). b For statistical purposes, the data for France do not include this area. c 2020. d 2018. e 2021. f Population aged 15 to 64 years. g Excluding the institutional population. h 2012. i Break in the time series. j 2013. k Calculated by the UNSD from national indices. l 2019. m Data refers to a 5-year period preceding the reference year. n Including refugees. o 2009. p Estimate. q Data after 2010 are included in France.

Mauritania

Region	Western Africa	UN membership date	27 October 1961
Population (000, 2022)	4 736[a]	Surface area (km2)	1 030 700[b]
Pop. density (per km2, 2022)	4.6[a]	Sex ratio (m per 100 f)	96.1[a]
Capital city	Nouakchott	National currency	Ouguiya (MRU)
Capital city pop. (000, 2022)	1 259.0[c]	Exchange rate (per US$)	36.7[b]

Economic indicators

	2010	2015	2022
GDP: Gross domestic product (million current US$)	5 629	6 167	7 916[b]
GDP growth rate (annual %, const. 2015 prices)	2.6	5.4	- 1.8[b]
GDP per capita (current US$)	1 610.9	1 524.1	1 702.5[b]
Economy: Agriculture (% of Gross Value Added)[d,e]	17.6	23.0	22.1[b]
Economy: Industry (% of Gross Value Added)[e,f]	40.3	25.3	31.5[b]
Economy: Services and other activity (% of GVA)[e,g]	42.1	51.7	46.4[b]
Employment in agriculture (% of employed)[h]	56.9	53.8	50.6[b]
Employment in industry (% of employed)[h]	11.9	12.5	13.1[b]
Employment in services & other sectors (% employed)[h]	31.2	33.7	36.3[b]
Unemployment rate (% of labour force)[h]	9.9	10.1	11.2
Labour force participation rate (female/male pop. %)[h]	28.2 / 64.7	27.9 / 63.0	27.5 / 62.3
CPI: Consumer Price Index (2010=100)	...	...	117[i,j]
Agricultural production index (2014-2016=100)	86	100	110[b]
International trade: exports (million current US$)	1 819	1 832	3 326[h,j]
International trade: imports (million current US$)	1 708	3 703	3 335[h,j]
International trade: balance (million current US$)	111	- 1 872	- 9[j]
Balance of payments, current account (million US$)	...	- 956	- 576[b]

Major trading partners

							2021
Export partners (% of exports)[h]	China	33.9	Switzerland	17.1	Canada	10.0
Import partners (% of imports)[h]	Spain	14.6	United Arab Emirates	14.2	France	8.4

Social indicators

	2010	2015	2022
Population growth rate (average annual %)	2.9	2.6	2.6[a]
Urban population (% of total population)	46.6	51.1	54.5[c]
Urban population growth rate (average annual %)[k]	4.9	4.8	...
Fertility rate, total (live births per woman)	5.0	4.8	4.3[a]
Life expectancy at birth (females/males, years)	64.7 / 61.5	66.3 / 62.8	66.4 / 63.0[a]
Population age distribution (0-14/60+ years old, %)	43.3 / 5.3	43.7 / 5.3	41.6 / 5.1[a]
International migrant stock (000/% of total pop.)[l,m]	84.9 / 2.4	166.6 / 4.1	182.3 / 3.9[b]
Refugees and others of concern to the UNHCR (000)	27.0[n]	77.3	101.8[j]
Infant mortality rate (per 1 000 live births)	59.8	53.0	43.6[a]
Health: Current expenditure (% of GDP)	2.6	3.7	3.3[c]
Health: Physicians (per 1 000 pop.)	0.2	0.2	0.2[o]
Education: Government expenditure (% of GDP)	2.0[p]	2.3[q]	1.9[b]
Education: Primary gross enrol. ratio (f/m per 100 pop.)	102.0 / 97.5	107.0 / 102.0	103.5 / 97.4[c]
Education: Sec. gross enrol. ratio (f/m per 100 pop.)	19.1 / 22.4[h]	30.3 / 32.5	40.4 / 38.4[c]
Education: Upr. Sec. gross enrol. ratio (f/m per 100 pop.)	12.8 / 16.5[h]	20.0 / 23.0	29.9 / 28.5[c]
Seats held by women in the National Parliament (%)	22.1	25.2	20.3[r]

Environment and infrastructure indicators

	2010	2015	2022
Individuals using the Internet (per 100 inhabitants)[h]	4.0	17.6	40.8[b]
Research & Development expenditure (% of GDP)	...	...	~0.0[s,t,o]
Threatened species (number)	58	69	131
Forested area (% of land area)	0.4	0.3	0.3[h,c]
Energy production, primary (Petajoules)	34	30	21[c]
Energy supply per capita (Gigajoules)	13	15[h]	17[c]
Important sites for terrestrial biodiversity protected (%)	11.2	11.2	11.2[j]
Net Official Development Assist. received (% of GNI)	6.72	5.50	8.32[b]

a Projected estimate (medium fertility variant). b 2020. c 2019. d Excludes irrigation canals and landscaping care. e Data classified according to ISIC Rev. 4. f Excludes publishing activities. Includes irrigation and canals. g Includes publishing activities and landscape care. Excludes repair of personal and household goods. h Estimate. i Index base: 2014=100. j 2021. k Data refers to a 5-year period preceding the reference year. l Including refugees. m Refers to foreign citizens. n Data as at the end of December. o 2018. p 2006. q 2013. r Data are as at 1 January of reporting year. s Higher Education only. t Partial data.

Mauritius

Region	Eastern Africa	UN membership date	24 April 1968
Population (000, 2022)	1 300 [a,b]	Surface area (km2)	1 979 [c,d]
Pop. density (per km2, 2022)	640.1 [a,b]	Sex ratio (m per 100 f)	97.3 [a,b]
Capital city	Port Louis	National currency	Mauritius Rupee (MUR)
Capital city pop. (000, 2022)	149.4 [e]	Exchange rate (per US$)	43.5 [f]

Economic indicators

	2010	2015	2022
GDP: Gross domestic product (million current US$)	10 004	11 692	10 921 [d]
GDP growth rate (annual %, const. 2015 prices)	4.4	3.6	- 14.9 [d]
GDP per capita (current US$)	8 016.1	9 283.6	8 586.9 [d]
Economy: Agriculture (% of Gross Value Added) [g,h]	4.1	3.6	3.9 [d]
Economy: Industry (% of Gross Value Added) [g,i]	25.3	21.7	18.8 [d]
Economy: Services and other activity (% of GVA) [g,j]	70.7	74.7	77.3 [d]
Employment in agriculture (% of employed)	8.6	6.9 [k]	5.9 [k,d]
Employment in industry (% of employed)	28.7	26.6 [k]	25.1 [k,d]
Employment in services & other sectors (% employed)	62.7	66.5 [k]	69.0 [k,d]
Unemployment rate (% of labour force)	7.6	7.4	6.9 [k]
Labour force participation rate (female/male pop. %)	42.8 / 73.9	45.4 / 73.2	44.1 / 70.9 [k]
CPI: Consumer Price Index (2010=100) [l]	100	120	139 [f]
Agricultural production index (2014-2016=100)	106	100	81 [d]
International trade: exports (million current US$)	1 850	2 481	1 672 [f]
International trade: imports (million current US$)	4 402	4 458	5 147 [f]
International trade: balance (million current US$)	- 2 553	- 1 977	- 3 476 [f]
Balance of payments, current account (million US$)	- 1 006	- 417	- 1 365 [d]

Major trading partners

						2021
Export partners (% of exports)	South Africa	13.9	France	13.5	United Kingdom	9.1
Import partners (% of imports)	China	17.8	India	15.6	United Arab Emirates	8.6

Social indicators

	2010	2015	2022
Population growth rate (average annual %) [b]	0.3	0.1	0.1 [a]
Urban population (% of total population) [b]	41.6	41.0	40.8 [m]
Urban population growth rate (average annual %) [b,n]	0.2	- 0.1	...
Fertility rate, total (live births per woman) [b]	1.6	1.4	1.4 [a]
Life expectancy at birth (females/males, years) [b]	77.6 / 70.6	78.2 / 71.8	77.1 / 71.0 [a]
Population age distribution (0-14/60+ years old, %) [b]	21.9 / 11.6	19.5 / 14.6	16.3 / 19.0 [a]
International migrant stock (000/% of total pop.) [b,o]	24.8 / 2.0	28.6 / 2.3	28.9 / 2.3 [d]
Refugees and others of concern to the UNHCR (000)	...	...	-0.0 [f]
Infant mortality rate (per 1 000 live births) [b]	12.3	12.3	13.4 [a]
Health: Current expenditure (% of GDP)	4.6	5.7	6.2 [m]
Health: Physicians (per 1 000 pop.)	1.2	2.0	2.7 [d]
Education: Government expenditure (% of GDP)	3.6	4.9	4.6 [d]
Education: Primary gross enrol. ratio (f/m per 100 pop.)	103.1 / 102.5	103.8 / 102.0	99.6 / 97.3 [f]
Education: Sec. gross enrol. ratio (f/m per 100 pop.)	91.3 / 87.2 [k]	99.5 / 95.3	96.0 / 91.5 [f]
Education: Upr. Sec. gross enrol. ratio (f/m per 100 pop.)	84.8 / 79.3 [k]	91.9 / 82.8	84.8 / 76.0 [f]
Intentional homicide rate (per 100 000 pop.)	2.6	1.7	2.8 [d]
Seats held by women in the National Parliament (%)	17.1	11.6	20.0 [p]

Environment and infrastructure indicators

	2010	2015	2022
Individuals using the Internet (per 100 inhabitants)	28.3 [q]	50.1 [k]	64.9 [d]
Research & Development expenditure (% of GDP)	0.4 [r,s,t]	0.2 [u,v,w]	0.4 [d]
Threatened species (number)	222	249	292
Forested area (% of land area)	18.9	18.9	19.1 [m]
CO2 emission estimates (million tons/tons per capita)	3.7 / 2.9	4.0 / 3.1	3.8 / 2.9 [d]
Energy production, primary (Petajoules)	11	12	10 [m]
Energy supply per capita (Gigajoules)	50	53	55 [m]
Tourist/visitor arrivals at national borders (000)	935	1 151	309 [d]
Important sites for terrestrial biodiversity protected (%)	9.0	9.6	9.6 [f]
Net Official Development Assist. received (% of GNI)	1.26	0.62	2.82 [d]

a Projected estimate (medium fertility variant). b Including Agalega, Rodrigues and Saint Brandon. c Excluding the islands of Saint Brandon and Agalega. d 2020. e 2018. f 2021. g Data classified according to ISIC Rev. 4. h Excludes irrigation canals and landscaping care. i Excludes publishing activities. Includes irrigation and canals. j Includes publishing activities and landscape care. Excludes repair of personal and household goods. k Estimate. l Calculated by the UNSD from national indices. m 2019. n Data refers to a 5-year period preceding the reference year. o Refers to foreign citizens. p Data are as at 1 January of reporting year. q Population aged 5 years and over. r Based on R&D budget instead of R&D expenditure. s Overestimated or based on overestimated data. t 2005. u Excluding business enterprise. v Break in the time series. w 2012.

Mayotte

Region	Eastern Africa	Population (000, 2022)	326[a,b]	
Pop. density (per km2, 2022)	869.6[a,b]	Sex ratio (m per 100 f)	90.0[a,b]	
Capital city	Mamoudzou	National currency	Euro (EUR)	
Capital city pop. (000, 2022)	6.2[c]	Exchange rate (per US$)	0.9[d]	

Economic indicators	2010	2015	2022
International trade: exports (million current US$)	6[e]	...	...
International trade: imports (million current US$)	309[e]	...	...
International trade: balance (million current US$)	- 303[e]	...	...

Social indicators	2010	2015	2022
Population growth rate (average annual %)[a]	2.6	4.1	3.0[b]
Urban population (% of total population)	49.0	47.0	45.9[f]
Urban population growth rate (average annual %)[g]	2.7	2.0	...
Fertility rate, total (live births per woman)[a]	4.4	4.9	4.4[b]
Life expectancy at birth (females/males, years)[a]	80.4 / 74.6	80.9 / 74.3	78.5 / 71.9[b]
Population age distribution (0-14/60+ years old, %)[a]	44.7 / 3.9	43.9 / 4.4	44.2 / 4.6[b]
International migrant stock (000/% of total pop.)[h]	72.8 / 34.9	81.4 / 33.9	111.5 / 40.9[i]
Infant mortality rate (per 1 000 live births)[a]	4.8	4.1	3.7[b]
Intentional homicide rate (per 100 000 pop.)	5.9[j]	...	...

Environment and infrastructure indicators	2010	2015	2022
Threatened species (number)	69	84	116
Forested area (% of land area)	38.5	37.8	37.3[f]
Important sites for terrestrial biodiversity protected (%)	63.1	63.1	63.6[d]

a For statistical purposes, the data for France do not include this area. b Projected estimate (medium fertility variant). c 2018. d 2021. e 2005. f 2019. g Data refers to a 5-year period preceding the reference year. h Including refugees. i 2020. j 2009.

Mexico

Region	Central America	UN membership date	07 November 1945
Population (000, 2022)	127 504 [a]	Surface area (km2)	1 964 375 [b]
Pop. density (per km2, 2022)	65.1 [a]	Sex ratio (m per 100 f)	95.2 [a]
Capital city	Mexico City	National currency	Mexican Peso (MXN)
Capital city pop. (000, 2022)	21 671.9 [c,d]	Exchange rate (per US$)	20.6 [e]

Economic indicators

	2010	2015	2022
GDP: Gross domestic product (million current US$)	1 057 801	1 171 870	1 073 439 [b]
GDP growth rate (annual %, const. 2015 prices)	5.1	3.3	- 8.3 [b]
GDP per capita (current US$)	9 271.4	9 616.7	8 325.6 [b]
Economy: Agriculture (% of Gross Value Added) [f,g]	3.4	3.4	4.1 [b]
Economy: Industry (% of Gross Value Added) [f,h]	33.7	31.8	31.7 [b]
Economy: Services and other activity (% of GVA) [f,i]	62.9	64.8	64.3 [b]
Employment in agriculture (% of employed)	13.9	13.4	12.4 [j,b]
Employment in industry (% of employed)	24.4	25.2	26.2 [j,b]
Employment in services & other sectors (% employed)	61.7	61.4	61.4 [j,b]
Unemployment rate (% of labour force)	5.3	4.3	3.9 [j]
Labour force participation rate (female/male pop. %)	42.3 / 78.4	43.2 / 77.7	44.0 / 75.1 [j]
CPI: Consumer Price Index (2010=100) [k]	100	119	155 [e]
Agricultural production index (2014-2016=100)	89	98	113 [b]
International trade: exports (million current US$)	298 305	380 550	494 596 [e]
International trade: imports (million current US$)	301 482	395 234	506 565 [e]
International trade: balance (million current US$)	- 3 177	- 14 684	- 11 970 [e]
Balance of payments, current account (million US$)	- 4 737	- 30 906	- 4 866 [e]

Major trading partners

						2021
Export partners (% of exports)	United States	78.1	Americas n.e.s	2.8	Canada	2.6
Import partners (% of imports)	United States	43.7	China	19.9	Republic of Korea	3.7

Social indicators

	2010	2015	2022
Population growth rate (average annual %)	1.4	1.1	0.8 [a]
Urban population (% of total population)	77.8	79.3	80.4 [d]
Urban population growth rate (average annual %) [l]	2.0	1.8	...
Fertility rate, total (live births per woman)	2.3	2.1	1.8 [a]
Life expectancy at birth (females/males, years)	77.1 / 71.3	77.7 / 71.7	78.2 / 71.5 [a]
Population age distribution (0-14/60+ years old, %)	29.9 / 8.9	27.6 / 10.2	24.5 / 12.2 [a]
International migrant stock (000/% of total pop.) [m]	969.7 / 0.8	1 013.7 / 0.8	1 197.6 / 0.9 [b]
Refugees and others of concern to the UNHCR (000)	1.6 [n]	2.2	311.1 [e]
Infant mortality rate (per 1 000 live births)	16.1	13.7	10.9 [a]
Health: Current expenditure (% of GDP) [o]	5.7	5.7	5.4 [d]
Health: Physicians (per 1 000 pop.)	2.0	2.3	2.4 [d]
Education: Government expenditure (% of GDP)	5.2	5.2	4.3 [p]
Education: Primary gross enrol. ratio (f/m per 100 pop.)	109.8 / 111.4	106.5 / 106.7	105.1 / 104.2 [d]
Education: Sec. gross enrol. ratio (f/m per 100 pop.)	90.4 / 83.8	104.1 / 97.6	109.5 / 99.9 [d]
Education: Upr. Sec. gross enrol. ratio (f/m per 100 pop.)	62.4 / 58.6	73.3 / 72.0	86.0 / 80.5 [d]
Intentional homicide rate (per 100 000 pop.)	22.6	17.0	28.4 [b]
Seats held by women in the National Parliament (%)	27.6	38.0	50.0 [q]

Environment and infrastructure indicators

	2010	2015	2022
Individuals using the Internet (per 100 inhabitants)	31.0 [r]	57.4 [s]	72.0 [b]
Research & Development expenditure (% of GDP)	0.5	0.4	0.3 [j,b]
Threatened species (number)	943	1 109	2 219
Forested area (% of land area)	34.4	34.1	33.9 [d]
CO2 emission estimates (million tons/tons per capita)	448.1 / 3.9	450.1 / 3.7	387.7 / 3.0 [b]
Energy production, primary (Petajoules)	9 403	8 031	6 328 [d]
Energy supply per capita (Gigajoules)	66	64	61 [d]
Tourist/visitor arrivals at national borders (000) [t]	23 290	32 093	24 824 [b]
Important sites for terrestrial biodiversity protected (%)	34.2	35.5	37.0 [b]
Pop. using safely managed sanitation (urban/rural %)	35.5 / ...	47.2 / ...	59.7 / ... [b]
Net Official Development Assist. received (% of GNI)	0.04	0.03	0.09 [b]

a Projected estimate (medium fertility variant). b 2020. c Refers to the total population in 76 municipalities of the Metropolitan Area of Mexico City. d 2019. e 2021. f Data classified according to ISIC Rev. 4. g Excludes irrigation canals and landscaping care. h Excludes publishing activities. Includes irrigation and canals. i Includes publishing activities and landscape care. Excludes repair of personal and household goods. j Estimate. k Calculated by the UNSD from national indices. l Data refers to a 5-year period preceding the reference year. m Including refugees. n Data as at the end of December. o Data based on calendar year (January 1 to December 31). p 2018. q Data are as at 1 January of reporting year. r Estimate to December based on ENDUTIH survey. Refers to total population. s Population aged 6 years and over. t Including nationals residing abroad.

Micronesia (Federated States of)

Region	Micronesia	UN membership date	17 September 1991
Population (000, 2022)	114[a]	Surface area (km2)	702[b]
Pop. density (per km2, 2022)	163.1[a]	Sex ratio (m per 100 f)	101.1[a]
Capital city	Palikir	National currency	US Dollar (USD)
Capital city pop. (000, 2022)	7.0[c]		

Economic indicators	2010	2015	2022
GDP: Gross domestic product (million current US$)	297	316	403[b]
GDP growth rate (annual %, const. 2015 prices)	2.3	4.6	- 1.8[b]
GDP per capita (current US$)	2 885.4	2 906.4	3 499.9[b]
Economy: Agriculture (% of Gross Value Added)[d]	26.7	27.8	25.8[b]
Economy: Industry (% of Gross Value Added)[d]	7.8	6.5	5.4[b]
Economy: Services and other activity (% of GVA)[d]	65.5	65.7	68.8[b]
CPI: Consumer Price Index (2010=100)	100	113	114[c]
Agricultural production index (2014-2016=100)	83	100	100[b]
International trade: exports (million current US$)	23	40[e]	227[e,f]
International trade: imports (million current US$)	168	160[e]	570[e,f]
International trade: balance (million current US$)	- 145	- 121[e]	- 343[f]
Balance of payments, current account (million US$)	- 25	22[g]	...

Major trading partners						2021
Export partners (% of exports)[e]	Thailand	74.5	China	10.1	Japan	8.2
Import partners (% of imports)[e]	United States	35.7	China	14.6	Japan	10.9

Social indicators	2010	2015	2022
Population growth rate (average annual %)	0.3	0.4	0.9[a]
Urban population (% of total population)	22.3	22.5	22.8[h]
Urban population growth rate (average annual %)[i]	- 0.5	0.3	...
Fertility rate, total (live births per woman)	3.2	3.0	2.7[a]
Life expectancy at birth (females/males, years)	74.4 / 68.2	74.8 / 68.2	74.8 / 67.3[a]
Population age distribution (0-14/60+ years old, %)	35.5 / 5.5	33.1 / 7.2	30.3 / 9.8[a]
International migrant stock (000/% of total pop.)	2.8 / 2.7	2.8 / 2.5	2.8 / 2.5[b]
Refugees and others of concern to the UNHCR (000)	...	~0.0	~0.0[j]
Infant mortality rate (per 1 000 live births)	27.0	24.0	18.9[a]
Health: Current expenditure (% of GDP)[k]	13.1	12.5	11.4[h]
Health: Physicians (per 1 000 pop.)	0.2[l]	...	0.9[b]
Education: Government expenditure (% of GDP)	...	12.4	9.7[e,c]
Education: Primary gross enrol. ratio (f/m per 100 pop.)	113.8 / 112.4[m]	96.0 / 98.3	89.8 / 90.2[b]
Education: Sec. gross enrol. ratio (f/m per 100 pop.)	86.6 / 79.9[n]	... / ...	... / ...
Education: Upr. Sec. gross enrol. ratio (f/m per 100 pop.)	77.5 / 72.7[n]	... / ...	... / ...
Intentional homicide rate (per 100 000 pop.)	...	...	0.9[h]
Seats held by women in the National Parliament (%)	0.0	0.0	7.1[o]

Environment and infrastructure indicators	2010	2015	2022
Individuals using the Internet (per 100 inhabitants)[e]	20.0	31.5	35.3[j]
Threatened species (number)	148	163	186
Forested area (% of land area)	91.6	91.8	92.0[h]
Energy production, primary (Petajoules)	0	0	0[h]
Energy supply per capita (Gigajoules)	15	19	19[e,h]
Tourist/visitor arrivals at national borders (000)[p]	45	31	18[h]
Important sites for terrestrial biodiversity protected (%)	~0.0	~0.0	~0.0[f]

a Projected estimate (medium fertility variant). b 2020. c 2018. d Data classified according to ISIC Rev. 4. e Estimate. f 2021. g 2014. h 2019. i Data refers to a 5-year period preceding the reference year. j 2017. k Data refer to fiscal years beginning 1 October. l 2009. m 2007. n 2005. o Data are as at 1 January of reporting year. p Arrivals in the States of Kosrae, Chuuk, Pohnpei and Yap; excluding FSM citizens.

Monaco

Region	Western Europe	UN membership date	28 May 1993
Population (000, 2022)	36[a]	Surface area (km2)	2[b]
Pop. density (per km2, 2022)	24 475.8[a]	Sex ratio (m per 100 f)	96.1[a]
Capital city	Monaco	National currency	Euro (EUR)
Capital city pop. (000, 2022)	38.9[c]	Exchange rate (per US$)	0.9[d]

Economic indicators	2010	2015	2022
GDP: Gross domestic product (million current US$)	5 362	6 259	6 816[b]
GDP growth rate (annual %, const. 2015 prices)	2.1	4.9	- 11.8[b]
GDP per capita (current US$)	150 577.0	165 945.5	173 695.8[b]
Economy: Industry (% of Gross Value Added)[e,f]	12.9	17.6	14.9[b]
Economy: Services and other activity (% of GVA)[e,f]	87.1	82.4	85.1[b]

Social indicators	2010	2015	2022
Population growth rate (average annual %)	2.3	1.7	- 0.5[a]
Urban population (% of total population)	100.0	100.0	100.0[g]
Urban population growth rate (average annual %)[h]	1.9	0.6	...
Fertility rate, total (live births per woman)	2.2	2.2	2.1[a]
Life expectancy at birth (females/males, years)	86.7 / 82.5	88.2 / 82.7	88.9 / 85.1[a]
Population age distribution (0-14/60+ years old, %)	13.0 / 34.6	12.1 / 41.0	13.0 / 43.7[a]
International migrant stock (000/% of total pop.)	21.1 / 59.3	26.0 / 68.9	26.6 / 67.8[b]
Refugees and others of concern to the UNHCR (000)	~0.0[i]	~0.0	~0.0[d]
Infant mortality rate (per 1 000 live births)	5.0	4.5	3.6[a]
Health: Current expenditure (% of GDP)	2.3	2.0	1.5[g]
Health: Physicians (per 1 000 pop.)	...	7.5[j]	...
Education: Government expenditure (% of GDP)	1.3	1.0[j]	1.2[g]
Intentional homicide rate (per 100 000 pop.)	0.0[k]	...	...
Seats held by women in the National Parliament (%)	26.1	20.8	33.3[l]

Environment and infrastructure indicators	2010	2015	2022
Individuals using the Internet (per 100 inhabitants)	75.0	93.4[m]	97.1[m,n]
Research & Development expenditure (% of GDP)	~0.0[o,p]	...	...
Threatened species (number)	11	16	46
Forested area (% of land area)[m]	0.0	0.0	0.0[g]
Tourist/visitor arrivals at national borders (000)	279	331	159[b]
Pop. using safely managed drinking water (urban/rural, %)	100.0 / ...	100.0 / ...	100.0 / ...[b]
Pop. using safely managed sanitation (urban/rural %)	100.0 / ...	100.0 / ...	100.0 / ...[b]

a Projected estimate (medium fertility variant). b 2020. c 2018. d 2021. e At producers' prices. f Data classified according to ISIC Rev. 4. g 2019. h Data refers to a 5-year period preceding the reference year. i Data as at the end of December. j 2014. k 2008. l Data are as at 1 January of reporting year. m Estimate. n 2017. o Partial data. p 2005.

Mongolia

Region	Eastern Asia
Population (000, 2022)	3 398[a]
Pop. density (per km2, 2022)	2.2[a]
Capital city	Ulaanbaatar
Capital city pop. (000, 2022)	1 552.7[c]

UN membership date	27 October 1961
Surface area (km2)	1 564 116[b]
Sex ratio (m per 100 f)	98.4[a]
National currency	Tugrik (MNT)
Exchange rate (per US$)	2 849.3[d]

Economic indicators

	2010	2015	2022
GDP: Gross domestic product (million current US$)	7 189	11 750	13 137[b]
GDP growth rate (annual %, const. 2015 prices)	6.4	2.4	- 5.3[b]
GDP per capita (current US$)	2 643.3	3 918.6	4 007.3[b]
Economy: Agriculture (% of Gross Value Added)[e,f]	13.1	14.5	13.3[b]
Economy: Industry (% of Gross Value Added)[f,g]	37.0	33.8	42.3[b]
Economy: Services and other activity (% of GVA)[f,h]	50.0	51.7	44.3[b]
Employment in agriculture (% of employed)	33.5	28.5	26.9[i,b]
Employment in industry (% of employed)	16.2	20.3	19.5[i,b]
Employment in services & other sectors (% employed)	50.2	51.3	53.6[i,b]
Unemployment rate (% of labour force)	6.6	4.9	6.2[i]
Labour force participation rate (female/male pop. %)	54.2 / 64.7	53.9 / 66.0	52.3 / 67.1[i]
CPI: Consumer Price Index (2010=100)	100[j]	164[j]	134[k,d]
Agricultural production index (2014-2016=100)	63	110	172[b]
International trade: exports (million current US$)	2 908[i]	4 669	9 241[d]
International trade: imports (million current US$)	3 200[i]	3 797	6 844[d]
International trade: balance (million current US$)	- 291[i]	873	2 397[d]
Balance of payments, current account (million US$)	- 885	- 948	- 675[b]

Major trading partners

						2021
Export partners (% of exports)	China	82.6	Switzerland	9.4	Singapore	2.7
Import partners (% of imports)	China	36.4	Russian Federation	28.6	Japan	6.6

Social indicators

	2010	2015	2022
Population growth rate (average annual %)	1.3	2.2	1.5[a]
Urban population (% of total population)	67.6	68.2	68.5[c]
Urban population growth rate (average annual %)[l]	3.0	2.1	...
Fertility rate, total (live births per woman)	2.5	3.0	2.8[a]
Life expectancy at birth (females/males, years)	71.8 / 63.0	73.7 / 65.5	77.4 / 68.1[a]
Population age distribution (0-14/60+ years old, %)	28.1 / 5.6	29.3 / 6.1	32.5 / 8.0[a]
International migrant stock (000/% of total pop.)[m,n]	16.1 / 0.6	19.9 / 0.7	21.3 / 0.7[b]
Refugees and others of concern to the UNHCR (000)	0.3[o]	~0.0	~0.0[d]
Infant mortality rate (per 1 000 live births)	21.7	16.3	8.8[a]
Health: Current expenditure (% of GDP)	3.7	4.2	3.8[c]
Health: Physicians (per 1 000 pop.)	2.8	3.2	3.9[p]
Education: Government expenditure (% of GDP)	4.6	4.2	4.9[i,c]
Education: Primary gross enrol. ratio (f/m per 100 pop.)	124.3 / 127.2	99.4 / 101.3	102.3 / 104.5[c]
Education: Sec. gross enrol. ratio (f/m per 100 pop.)	94.8 / 88.3	... / ...	91.9 / 91.1[c]
Education: Upr. Sec. gross enrol. ratio (f/m per 100 pop.)	96.0 / 84.8	92.2 / 87.1	87.0 / 86.6[c]
Intentional homicide rate (per 100 000 pop.)	8.8	7.1	6.0[b]
Seats held by women in the National Parliament (%)	3.9	14.9	17.1[q]

Environment and infrastructure indicators

	2010	2015	2022
Individuals using the Internet (per 100 inhabitants)	10.2[r]	22.5[s]	62.5[b]
Research & Development expenditure (% of GDP)	0.2[t]	0.2[t]	0.1[u,b]
Threatened species (number)	36	36	43
Forested area (% of land area)	9.1[i]	9.1	9.1[c]
CO2 emission estimates (million tons/tons per capita)	14.4 / 5.2	17.4 / 5.7	23.1 / 7.0[c]
Energy production, primary (Petajoules)	655	655	1 409[c]
Energy supply per capita (Gigajoules)	60	91	168[c]
Tourist/visitor arrivals at national borders (000)	456	386	59[b]
Important sites for terrestrial biodiversity protected (%)	40.4	40.4	45.0[d]
Pop. using safely managed drinking water (urban/rural, %)	36.9 / 5.3	37.7 / 8.1	38.6 / 11.4[b]
Pop. using safely managed sanitation (urban/rural %)	45.0 / 34.1	52.0 / 41.1	58.7 / 48.7[b]
Net Official Development Assist. received (% of GNI)	4.34	2.19	5.89[b]

a Projected estimate (medium fertility variant). b 2020. c 2019. d 2021. e Excludes irrigation canals and landscaping care. f Data classified according to ISIC Rev. 4. g Excludes publishing activities. Includes irrigation and canals. h Includes publishing activities and landscape care. Excludes repair of personal and household goods. i Estimate. j Calculated by the UNSD from national indices. k Index base: 2015=100. l Data refers to a 5-year period preceding the reference year. m Refers to foreign citizens. n Including refugees. o Data as at the end of December. p 2018. q Data are as at 1 January of reporting year. r Refers to total population. s All population. t Partial data. u Break in the time series.

Montenegro

Region	Southern Europe	UN membership date	28 June 2006
Population (000, 2022)	627[a]	Surface area (km2)	13 812[b]
Pop. density (per km2, 2022)	45.4[a]	Sex ratio (m per 100 f)	94.9[a]
Capital city	Podgorica	National currency	Euro (EUR)
Capital city pop. (000, 2022)	177.2[c,d]	Exchange rate (per US$)	0.9[e]

Economic indicators

	2010	2015	2022
GDP: Gross domestic product (million current US$)	4 139	4 053	4 789[b]
GDP growth rate (annual %, const. 2015 prices)	2.7	3.4	- 15.2[b]
GDP per capita (current US$)	6 630.0	6 464.7	7 625.7[b]
Economy: Agriculture (% of Gross Value Added)[f,g]	9.2	9.8	8.2[b]
Economy: Industry (% of Gross Value Added)[g,h]	20.5	17.4	19.2[b]
Economy: Services and other activity (% of GVA)[g,i]	70.3	72.9	72.7[b]
Employment in agriculture (% of employed)	6.2[j]	7.7	7.8[j,b]
Employment in industry (% of employed)	18.7[j]	17.5	19.2[j,b]
Employment in services & other sectors (% employed)	75.1[j]	74.8	73.0[j,b]
Unemployment rate (% of labour force)	19.6	17.5	16.7[j]
Labour force participation rate (female/male pop. %)	42.2 / 55.8[j]	47.6 / 60.1	49.1 / 63.0[j]
CPI: Consumer Price Index (2010=100)	100	111	119[k,e]
Agricultural production index (2014-2016=100)	93	98	103[b]
International trade: exports (million current US$)	437	353	516[e]
International trade: imports (million current US$)	2 182	2 050	2 946[e]
International trade: balance (million current US$)	- 1 745	- 1 697	- 2 430[e]
Balance of payments, current account (million US$)	- 852	- 443	- 538[e]

Major trading partners

2021

Export partners (% of exports)	Serbia	24.6	Switzerland	11.5	Bosnia Herzegovina	7.7
Import partners (% of imports)	Serbia	20.1	China	9.8	Germany	9.3

Social indicators

	2010	2015	2022
Population growth rate (average annual %)	~0.0	- 0.1	- 0.1[a]
Urban population (% of total population)	64.1	65.8	67.2[l]
Urban population growth rate (average annual %)[m]	0.8	0.6	...
Fertility rate, total (live births per woman)	1.7	1.7	1.7[a]
Life expectancy at birth (females/males, years)	78.9 / 73.3	79.4 / 74.0	80.3 / 73.5[a]
Population age distribution (0-14/60+ years old, %)	19.3 / 18.0	18.5 / 20.2	18.1 / 22.9[a]
International migrant stock (000/% of total pop.)	78.5 / 12.6	71.7 / 11.4	71.0 / 11.3[b]
Refugees and others of concern to the UNHCR (000)	18.3[n]	19.8	1.9[e]
Infant mortality rate (per 1 000 live births)	5.7	2.6	1.2[a]
Health: Current expenditure (% of GDP)	...	9.0	8.3[l]
Health: Physicians (per 1 000 pop.)	2.0	2.4	2.7[b]
Education: Primary gross enrol. ratio (f/m per 100 pop.)	110.6 / 110.3	95.5 / 95.3	101.6 / 101.7[b]
Education: Sec. gross enrol. ratio (f/m per 100 pop.)	101.9 / 99.0	93.5 / 92.0	91.3 / 89.5[b]
Education: Upr. Sec. gross enrol. ratio (f/m per 100 pop.)	90.9 / 85.8	88.3 / 87.2	89.9 / 86.3[b]
Intentional homicide rate (per 100 000 pop.)	2.4	2.7	2.9[b]
Seats held by women in the National Parliament (%)	11.1	17.3	27.2[o]

Environment and infrastructure indicators

	2010	2015	2022
Individuals using the Internet (per 100 inhabitants)	37.5[j]	68.1	77.6[b]
Research & Development expenditure (% of GDP)	1.1[p]	0.4	0.4[l]
Threatened species (number)	72	85	163
Forested area (% of land area)[j]	61.5	61.5	61.5[l]
CO2 emission estimates (million tons/tons per capita)	2.7 / 4.2	2.4 / 3.8	2.7 / 4.2[l]
Energy production, primary (Petajoules)	35	30	32[l]
Energy supply per capita (Gigajoules)	77	67	75[l]
Tourist/visitor arrivals at national borders (000)	1 088	1 560	351[b]
Important sites for terrestrial biodiversity protected (%)	17.7	17.7	25.9[e]
Pop. using safely managed drinking water (urban/rural, %)	87.0 / ...	87.2 / ...	87.3 / ...[b]
Pop. using safely managed sanitation (urban/rural %)	32.9 / 35.6	42.2 / 37.9	48.6 / 38.9[b]
Net Official Development Assist. received (% of GNI)	1.95	2.41	4.21[b]

a Projected estimate (medium fertility variant). b 2020. c Refers to the urban population of Podgorica municipality. d 2018. e 2021. f Excludes irrigation canals and landscaping care. g Data classified according to ISIC Rev. 4. h Excludes publishing activities. Includes irrigation and canals. i Includes publishing activities and landscape care. Excludes repair of personal and household goods. j Estimate. k Calculated by the UNSD from national indices. l 2019. m Data refers to a 5-year period preceding the reference year. n Data as at the end of December. o Data are as at 1 January of reporting year. p 2007.

Montserrat

Region	Caribbean
Surface area (km2)	103[c]
Sex ratio (m per 100 f)	111.7[a,b]
National currency	E. Caribbean Dollar (XCD)[d]
Exchange rate (per US$)	2.7[f]

Population (000, 2022)	4[a,b]
Pop. density (per km2, 2022)	42.6[a,b]
Capital city	Brades Estate
Capital city pop. (000, 2022)	0.5[e]

Economic indicators	2010	2015	2022
GDP: Gross domestic product (million current US$)	56	61	68[c]
GDP growth rate (annual %, const. 2015 prices)	- 2.8	1.1	- 5.3[c]
GDP per capita (current US$)	11 331.1	12 348.9	13 523.1[c]
Economy: Agriculture (% of Gross Value Added)[g]	1.1	1.4	0.8[c]
Economy: Industry (% of Gross Value Added)[g]	13.3	12.4	13.1[c]
Economy: Services and other activity (% of GVA)[g]	85.7	86.3	86.1[c]
Unemployment rate (% of labour force)	...	5.6[h]	...
CPI: Consumer Price Index (2010=100)[i]	100	108	109[f]
International trade: exports (million current US$)	1	3[i]	2[i,f]
International trade: imports (million current US$)[i]	29	39	31[f]
International trade: balance (million current US$)	- 28[i]	- 36[i]	- 29[f]
Balance of payments, current account (million US$)	- 19	- 1	- 13[f]

Major trading partners						2021
Export partners (% of exports)[i]	France	27.7	Antigua and Barbuda	25.3	Areas nes[j]	9.0
Import partners (% of imports)[i]	United States	67.8	Trinidad and Tobago	6.1	United Kingdom	5.5

Social indicators	2010	2015	2022
Population growth rate (average annual %)[b]	1.4	- 0.9	-0.0[a]
Urban population (% of total population)	9.2	9.0	9.1[k]
Urban population growth rate (average annual %)[l]	0.3	0.5	...
Fertility rate, total (live births per woman)[b]	1.4	1.5	1.6[a]
Life expectancy at birth (females/males, years)[b]	75.5 / 73.3	76.3 / 73.9	77.5 / 74.5[a]
Population age distribution (0-14/60+ years old, %)[b]	19.8 / 18.5	18.2 / 20.0	12.8 / 24.4[a]
International migrant stock (000/% of total pop.)	1.3 / 26.4	1.4 / 27.2	1.4 / 27.6[c]
Refugees and others of concern to the UNHCR (000)	~0.0[m]	...	...
Infant mortality rate (per 1 000 live births)[b]	15.7	13.1	10.3[a]
Education: Government expenditure (% of GDP)	5.1[n]	...	9.1[k]
Education: Primary gross enrol. ratio (f/m per 100 pop.)	163.4 / 154.0[n]	96.0 / 92.9[o]	112.4 / 99.1[k]
Education: Sec. gross enrol. ratio (f/m per 100 pop.)	123.7 / 124.0[n]	180.4 / 173.5[o]	101.9 / 94.1[k]
Education: Upr. Sec. gross enrol. ratio (f/m per 100 pop.)	86.2 / 87.1[n]	160.0 / 208.8[o]	88.9 / 89.6[k]
Intentional homicide rate (per 100 000 pop.)	20.4[p]	20.3[q]	...

Environment and infrastructure indicators	2010	2015	2022
Individuals using the Internet (per 100 inhabitants)	35.0	54.6[h]	...
Threatened species (number)	35	54	74
Forested area (% of land area)[l]	25.0	25.0	25.0[k]
Energy production, primary (Petajoules)	...	...	0[k]
Energy supply per capita (Gigajoules)	168	149	70[k]
Tourist/visitor arrivals at national borders (000)	6	9	4[c]
Important sites for terrestrial biodiversity protected (%)	0.0	30.6	30.6[f]

a Projected estimate (medium fertility variant). b For statistical purposes, the data for United Kingdom do not include this area. c 2020. d East Caribbean Dollar. e 2018. f 2021. g Data classified according to ISIC Rev. 4. h 2011. i Estimate. j Areas nes k 2019. l Data refers to a 5-year period preceding the reference year. m Data as at the end of December. n 2009. o 2014. p 2008. q 2012.

Morocco

Region	Northern Africa	UN membership date	12 November 1956
Population (000, 2022)	37 458[a]	Surface area (km2)	446 550[b]
Pop. density (per km2, 2022)	83.9[a]	Sex ratio (m per 100 f)	101.3[a]
Capital city	Rabat	National currency	Moroccan Dirham (MAD)
Capital city pop. (000, 2022)	1 864.9[c,d]	Exchange rate (per US$)	9.3[e]

Economic indicators

	2010	2015	2022
GDP: Gross domestic product (million current US$)[f]	93 217	101 179	114 724[b]
GDP growth rate (annual %, const. 2015 prices)[f]	4.0	4.9	- 5.0[b]
GDP per capita (current US$)[f]	2 882.1	2 918.9	3 108.2[b]
Economy: Agriculture (% of Gross Value Added)	14.4	14.3	13.2[b]
Economy: Industry (% of Gross Value Added)	28.6	29.5	29.5[b]
Economy: Services and other activity (% of GVA)	56.9	56.2	57.3[b]
Employment in agriculture (% of employed)[g]	40.5	37.2	34.1[b]
Employment in industry (% of employed)[g]	21.5	21.7	21.8[b]
Employment in services & other sectors (% employed)[g]	38.0	41.1	44.0[b]
Unemployment rate (% of labour force)	9.1	9.5	11.2[g]
Labour force participation rate (female/male pop. %)	25.9 / 74.8	24.7 / 71.4	22.4 / 66.5[g]
CPI: Consumer Price Index (2010=100)	100[h]	106[h]	104[i,e]
Agricultural production index (2014-2016=100)	93	108	101[b]
International trade: exports (million current US$)	17 765	22 337	34 328[g,e]
International trade: imports (million current US$)	35 379	38 146	57 016[g,e]
International trade: balance (million current US$)	- 17 614	- 15 809	- 22 688[e]
Balance of payments, current account (million US$)	- 3 925	- 2 161	- 3 262[e]

Major trading partners

						2021
Export partners (% of exports)[g]	Spain	23.9	France	22.0	Italy	4.4
Import partners (% of imports)[g]	Spain	15.4	China	12.2	France	12.0

Social indicators

	2010	2015	2022
Population growth rate (average annual %)	1.3	1.2	1.0[a]
Urban population (% of total population)	58.0	60.8	63.0[d]
Urban population growth rate (average annual %)[j]	2.2	2.4	...
Fertility rate, total (live births per woman)	2.6	2.5	2.3[a]
Life expectancy at birth (females/males, years)	72.5 / 69.2	74.8 / 71.2	77.2 / 72.9[a]
Population age distribution (0-14/60+ years old, %)	28.9 / 7.9	28.0 / 9.3	26.6 / 11.9[a]
International migrant stock (000/% of total pop.)[k,l]	71.2 / 0.2	92.4 / 0.3	102.4 / 0.3[b]
Refugees and others of concern to the UNHCR (000)	1.1[m]	4.4	14.9[e]
Infant mortality rate (per 1 000 live births)	25.9	19.8	14.4[a]
Health: Current expenditure (% of GDP)[n]	5.9	5.1	5.3[g,d]
Health: Physicians (per 1 000 pop.)	0.6[o]	0.9[p]	0.7[q]
Education: Government expenditure (% of GDP)	5.3[o]	...	...
Education: Primary gross enrol. ratio (f/m per 100 pop.)	106.3 / 113.0	106.6 / 112.3	113.4 / 116.8[b]
Education: Sec. gross enrol. ratio (f/m per 100 pop.)	58.8 / 67.6	64.1 / 75.1[r]	80.3 / 84.5[b]
Education: Upr. Sec. gross enrol. ratio (f/m per 100 pop.)	46.8 / 49.2	52.5 / 57.5[r]	63.8 / 61.5[b]
Intentional homicide rate (per 100 000 pop.)	1.4	1.2	1.2[b]
Seats held by women in the National Parliament (%)	10.5	17.0	24.1[s]

Environment and infrastructure indicators

	2010	2015	2022
Individuals using the Internet (per 100 inhabitants)	52.0[t,u]	57.1	84.1[b]
Research & Development expenditure (% of GDP)	0.7	...	...
Threatened species (number)	157	176	269
Forested area (% of land area)[g]	12.7	12.7	12.8[b]
CO2 emission estimates (million tons/tons per capita)	47.3 / 1.4	56.0 / 1.6	63.4 / 1.7[b]
Energy production, primary (Petajoules)	84	62	105[d]
Energy supply per capita (Gigajoules)	23	23	25[d]
Tourist/visitor arrivals at national borders (000)[v]	9 288	10 177	2 778[b]
Important sites for terrestrial biodiversity protected (%)	34.5	34.5	59.5[e]
Pop. using safely managed drinking water (urban/rural, %)	88.2 / 30.7	89.8 / 44.6	90.7 / 61.2[b]
Pop. using safely managed sanitation (urban/rural %)	39.1 / ...	40.3 / ...	41.5 / ...[b]
Net Official Development Assist. received (% of GNI)	1.07	1.53	1.65[b]

a Projected estimate (medium fertility variant). b 2020. c Including Salé and Temara. d 2019. e 2021. f Including Western Sahara. g Estimate. h Calculated by the UNSD from national indices. i Base 2017 = 100. j Data refers to a 5-year period preceding the reference year. k Refers to foreign citizens. l Including refugees. m Data as at the end of December. n Data based on calendar year (January 1 to December 31). o 2009. p 2014. q 2017. r 2012. s Data are as at 1 January of reporting year. t Living in electrified areas. u Population aged 6 to 74 years. v Including nationals residing abroad.

Mozambique

Region	Eastern Africa	UN membership date	16 September 1975	
Population (000, 2022)	32 970[a]	Surface area (km2)	799 380[b]	
Pop. density (per km2, 2022)	41.9[a]	Sex ratio (m per 100 f)	96.3[a]	
Capital city	Maputo	National currency	Mozambique Metical (MZN)	
Capital city pop. (000, 2022)	1 104.3[c]	Exchange rate (per US$)	63.8[d]	

Economic indicators

	2010	2015	2022
GDP: Gross domestic product (million current US$)	11 105	15 951	14 029[b]
GDP growth rate (annual %, const. 2015 prices)	6.5	6.7	- 1.2[b]
GDP per capita (current US$)	471.9	589.9	448.8[b]
Economy: Agriculture (% of Gross Value Added)[e,f]	29.8	25.9	28.8[b]
Economy: Industry (% of Gross Value Added)[e,g]	18.2	20.5	24.5[b]
Economy: Services and other activity (% of GVA)[e,h]	52.0	53.6	46.7[b]
Employment in agriculture (% of employed)	76.4[i]	72.1	69.9[i,b]
Employment in industry (% of employed)	5.3[i]	7.7	8.6[i,b]
Employment in services & other sectors (% employed)	18.3[i]	20.1	21.5[i,b]
Unemployment rate (% of labour force)	3.2[i]	3.4	3.8[i]
Labour force participation rate (female/male pop. %)	82.7 / 81.7[i]	78.1 / 80.1	78.0 / 79.0[i]
CPI: Consumer Price Index (2010=100)[j]	100	126	199[d]
Agricultural production index (2014-2016=100)	109	96	133[b]
International trade: exports (million current US$)	2 243	3 649[i]	4 877[i,d]
International trade: imports (million current US$)	3 564	7 852[i]	9 702[i,d]
International trade: balance (million current US$)	- 1 321	- 4 203[i]	- 4 824[d]
Balance of payments, current account (million US$)	- 1 679	- 5 968	- 3 616[b]

Major trading partners

						2021
Export partners (% of exports)[i]	South Africa	21.1	India	12.2	United Kingdom	10.8
Import partners (% of imports)[i]	South Africa	29.3	China	10.8	India	9.6

Social indicators

	2010	2015	2022
Population growth rate (average annual %)	2.9	3.0	2.7[a]
Urban population (% of total population)	31.8	34.4	36.5[c]
Urban population growth rate (average annual %)[k]	4.1	4.5	...
Fertility rate, total (live births per woman)	5.6	5.1	4.6[a]
Life expectancy at birth (females/males, years)	55.8 / 52.4	60.4 / 55.7	62.7 / 56.5[a]
Population age distribution (0-14/60+ years old, %)	45.4 / 4.3	45.0 / 4.2	43.5 / 4.2[a]
International migrant stock (000/% of total pop.)[l]	306.5 / 1.3	321.8 / 1.2	338.8 / 1.1[b]
Refugees and others of concern to the UNHCR (000)	10.0[m]	18.8	816.3[d]
Infant mortality rate (per 1 000 live births)	75.8	62.3	52.8[a]
Health: Current expenditure (% of GDP)	5.4	6.7	7.8[c]
Health: Physicians (per 1 000 pop.)	~0.0	0.1[n]	0.1[b]
Education: Government expenditure (% of GDP)	6.0	6.0[i]	6.2[i,c]
Education: Primary gross enrol. ratio (f/m per 100 pop.)	105.9 / 119.2	103.4 / 113.8[i]	114.9 / 121.9[b]
Education: Sec. gross enrol. ratio (f/m per 100 pop.)	22.5 / 28.0	31.9 / 35.2[i]	33.4 / 37.4[o]
Education: Upr. Sec. gross enrol. ratio (f/m per 100 pop.)	9.8 / 13.3	21.3 / 23.5[i]	28.0 / 34.5[o]
Intentional homicide rate (per 100 000 pop.)	3.7	3.5[p]	...
Seats held by women in the National Parliament (%)	39.2	39.6	42.4[q]

Environment and infrastructure indicators

	2010	2015	2022
Individuals using the Internet (per 100 inhabitants)	4.2	6.5[i]	16.5[i,b]
Research & Development expenditure (% of GDP)	0.4[r,s]	0.3	...
Threatened species (number)	209	268	511
Forested area (% of land area)	49.6	48.2	47.0[c]
CO2 emission estimates (million tons/tons per capita)	3.6 / 0.1	6.6 / 0.2	8.4 / 0.2[c]
Energy production, primary (Petajoules)	397	716	835[c]
Energy supply per capita (Gigajoules)	13	17	15[c]
Tourist/visitor arrivals at national borders (000)[t]	1 718[s]	1 552	952[b]
Important sites for terrestrial biodiversity protected (%)	36.2	41.2	41.2[d]
Pop. using safely managed sanitation (urban/rural %)	... / 10.1	... / 15.5	... / 21.3[b]
Net Official Development Assist. received (% of GNI)	18.08	11.57	18.79[b]

a Projected estimate (medium fertility variant). b 2020. c 2019. d 2021. e Data classified according to ISIC Rev. 4. f Excludes irrigation canals and landscaping care. g Excludes publishing activities. Includes irrigation and canals. h Includes publishing activities and landscape care. Excludes repair of personal and household goods. i Estimate. j Calculated by the UNSD from national indices. k Data refers to a 5-year period preceding the reference year. l Including refugees. m Data as at the end of December. n 2013. o 2017. p 2011. q Data are as at 1 January of reporting year. r Excluding business enterprise. s Break in the time series. t The data of all the border posts of the country are used.

Myanmar

Region	South-eastern Asia		UN membership date	19 April 1948	
Population (000, 2022)	54 179 [a]		Surface area (km2)	676 577 [b]	
Pop. density (per km2, 2022)	82.9 [a]		Sex ratio (m per 100 f)	99.1 [a]	
Capital city	Nay Pyi Taw		National currency	Kyat (MMK)	
Capital city pop. (000, 2022)	546.5 [c]		Exchange rate (per US$)	1 329.1 [b]	

Economic indicators

	2010	2015	2022
GDP: Gross domestic product (million current US$) [d]	44 847	63 835	70 284 [b]
GDP growth rate (annual %, const. 2015 prices) [d]	7.8	6.4	- 17.9 [b]
GDP per capita (current US$) [d]	886.3	1 211.7	1 291.7 [b]
Economy: Agriculture (% of Gross Value Added) [e,f]	35.3	26.7	21.5 [b]
Economy: Industry (% of Gross Value Added) [e,f]	28.3	33.9	38.5 [b]
Economy: Services and other activity (% of GVA) [e,f,g]	36.5	39.4	40.0 [b]
Employment in agriculture (% of employed)	53.5 [h]	51.7	48.1 [h,b]
Employment in industry (% of employed)	17.7 [h]	16.8	16.3 [h,b]
Employment in services & other sectors (% employed)	28.8 [h]	31.5	35.6 [h,b]
Unemployment rate (% of labour force)	0.7 [h]	0.8	2.3 [h]
Labour force participation rate (female/male pop. %)	52.6 / 80.3 [h]	51.2 / 79.7	42.6 / 71.2 [h]
CPI: Consumer Price Index (2010=100)	100	129	168 [c]
Agricultural production index (2014-2016=100)	98	101	103 [b]
International trade: exports (million current US$)	8 873	11 432	15 145 [i]
International trade: imports (million current US$)	4 866	16 913	14 322 [i]
International trade: balance (million current US$)	4 008	- 5 481	823 [i]
Balance of payments, current account (million US$)	1 574	- 3 109	68 [c]

Major trading partners

						2021
Export partners (% of exports)	China	29.5	Thailand	23.1	Japan	6.0
Import partners (% of imports)	China	29.4	Singapore	19.1	Thailand	14.4

Social indicators

	2010	2015	2022
Population growth rate (average annual %)	0.8	0.8	0.7 [a]
Urban population (% of total population)	28.9	29.9	30.9 [c]
Urban population growth rate (average annual %) [j]	1.3	1.5	...
Fertility rate, total (live births per woman)	2.3	2.2	2.1 [a]
Life expectancy at birth (females/males, years)	66.2 / 60.6	68.7 / 62.5	70.5 / 64.2 [a]
Population age distribution (0-14/60+ years old, %)	28.3 / 7.9	26.6 / 9.0	24.6 / 10.8 [a]
International migrant stock (000/% of total pop.) [k]	76.4 / 0.2	73.3 / 0.1	76.4 / 0.1 [b]
Refugees and others of concern to the UNHCR (000)	859.4 [l]	1 466.5	1 030.0 [i]
Infant mortality rate (per 1 000 live births)	48.7	40.7	32.7 [a]
Health: Current expenditure (% of GDP) [m,n,o]	2.0	5.5	4.7 [c]
Health: Physicians (per 1 000 pop.)	0.5	0.6 [p]	0.7 [c]
Education: Government expenditure (% of GDP)	0.9	2.1	2.0 [c]
Education: Primary gross enrol. ratio (f/m per 100 pop.)	97.6 / 98.6	100.3 / 103.3 [q]	109.7 / 114.8 [r]
Education: Sec. gross enrol. ratio (f/m per 100 pop.)	49.2 / 47.1	52.3 / 51.3 [q]	71.3 / 65.6 [r]
Education: Upr. Sec. gross enrol. ratio (f/m per 100 pop.)	36.7 / 33.2	36.1 / 32.4 [q]	59.2 / 49.7 [r]
Intentional homicide rate (per 100 000 pop.)	1.6	2.2	~0.0 [b]
Seats held by women in the National Parliament (%)	...	6.2	15.3 [s,t]

Environment and infrastructure indicators

	2010	2015	2022
Individuals using the Internet (per 100 inhabitants)	0.2	10.9 [h]	35.1 [h,b]
Research & Development expenditure (% of GDP)	...	...	0.1 [u,v,b]
Threatened species (number)	249	301	431
Forested area (% of land area)	48.1	45.9 [h]	44.2 [c]
CO2 emission estimates (million tons/tons per capita) [o]	11.7 / 0.2	22.7 / 0.4	39.3 / 0.6 [c]
Energy production, primary (Petajoules)	967	1 177	1 214 [c]
Energy supply per capita (Gigajoules)	13	16	18 [c]
Tourist/visitor arrivals at national borders (000)	792	4 681	903 [b]
Important sites for terrestrial biodiversity protected (%)	18.8	20.9	22.3 [i]
Pop. using safely managed drinking water (urban/rural, %)	68.5 / 33.6	71.5 / 42.7	73.8 / 52.1 [b]
Pop. using safely managed sanitation (urban/rural %)	60.8 / 61.1	57.1 / 62.6	53.4 / 64.0 [b]
Net Official Development Assist. received (% of GNI)	0.69	2.00	3.88 [b]

a Projected estimate (medium fertility variant). b 2020. c 2019. d Data compiled in accordance with the System of National Accounts 1968 (1968 SNA). e Data classified according to ISIC Rev. 4. f At producers' prices. g Including restaurants and hotels. h Estimate. i 2021. j Data refers to a 5-year period preceding the reference year. k Refers to foreign citizens. l Data as at the end of December. n Country is still reporting data based on SHA 1.0. o Data refer to fiscal years beginning 1 April. p 2012. q 2014. r 2018. s Figures correspond to members elected at or appointed following the 2020 elections. The new parliament was unable to hold its first sitting in February 2021 due to a military take over. t Data are as at 1 January of reporting year. u Excluding private non-profit. v Excluding business enterprise.

Namibia

Region	Southern Africa	UN membership date	23 April 1990
Population (000, 2022)	2 567 [a]	Surface area (km2)	825 229 [b]
Pop. density (per km2, 2022)	3.1 [a]	Sex ratio (m per 100 f)	93.2 [a]
Capital city	Windhoek	National currency	Namibia Dollar (NAD)
Capital city pop. (000, 2022)	417.4 [c]	Exchange rate (per US$)	15.9 [d]

Economic indicators

	2010	2015	2022
GDP: Gross domestic product (million current US$)	11 282	11 335	10 710 [b]
GDP growth rate (annual %, const. 2015 prices)	6.0	4.3	- 8.0 [b]
GDP per capita (current US$)	5 324.6	4 896.6	4 215.2 [b]
Economy: Agriculture (% of Gross Value Added) [e,f]	9.1	7.2	9.7 [b]
Economy: Industry (% of Gross Value Added) [f,g]	29.7	29.9	28.4 [b]
Economy: Services and other activity (% of GVA) [f,h]	61.2	62.9	62.0 [b]
Employment in agriculture (% of employed) [i]	28.1	24.5	21.8 [b]
Employment in industry (% of employed) [i]	13.9	17.0	16.4 [b]
Employment in services & other sectors (% employed) [i]	57.9	58.5	61.8 [b]
Unemployment rate (% of labour force)	22.1	20.9 [i]	21.1 [i]
Labour force participation rate (female/male pop. %) [i]	52.1 / 62.3	56.4 / 65.4	55.1 / 62.4
CPI: Consumer Price Index (2010=100) [j]	100	129	167 [d]
Agricultural production index (2014-2016=100)	100	100	103 [b]
International trade: exports (million current US$)	5 848	4 628	6 474 [i,d]
International trade: imports (million current US$)	5 980	7 697	8 105 [i,d]
International trade: balance (million current US$)	- 131	- 3 069	- 1 631 [d]
Balance of payments, current account (million US$)	- 448	- 1 559	- 1 120 [d]

Major trading partners

						2021
Export partners (% of exports) [i]	China	34.1	South Africa	14.5	Botswana	8.0
Import partners (% of imports) [i]	South Africa	36.2	Zambia	19.1	Areas nes [k]	6.5

Social indicators

	2010	2015	2022
Population growth rate (average annual %)	1.5	1.8	1.4 [a]
Urban population (% of total population)	41.6	46.9	51.0 [c]
Urban population growth rate (average annual %) [l]	3.9	4.6	...
Fertility rate, total (live births per woman)	3.6	3.6	3.2 [a]
Life expectancy at birth (females/males, years)	58.7 / 53.3	64.0 / 57.3	61.7 / 54.6 [a]
Population age distribution (0-14/60+ years old, %)	37.0 / 5.3	36.3 / 5.7	36.2 / 6.1 [a]
International migrant stock (000/% of total pop.) [m]	103.8 / 4.9	101.6 / 4.4	109.4 / 4.3 [b]
Refugees and others of concern to the UNHCR (000)	8.8 [n]	4.4	5.8 [d]
Infant mortality rate (per 1 000 live births)	34.3	33.4	29.8 [a]
Health: Current expenditure (% of GDP)	9.7	10.0	8.5 [c]
Health: Physicians (per 1 000 pop.)	0.4 [o]	...	0.6 [p]
Education: Government expenditure (% of GDP)	8.2	9.9 [i]	9.4 [i,b]
Education: Primary gross enrol. ratio (f/m per 100 pop.)	112.9 / 117.5	118.4 / 123.7 [q]	122.1 / 126.4 [p]
Education: Sec. gross enrol. ratio (f/m per 100 pop.)	70.0 / 61.5 [o]	... / ...	... / ...
Education: Upr. Sec. gross enrol. ratio (f/m per 100 pop.)	38.3 / 34.0 [o]	... / ...	... / ...
Intentional homicide rate (per 100 000 pop.)	14.8	17.7 [r]	11.9 [b]
Seats held by women in the National Parliament (%)	26.9	41.3	44.2 [s]

Environment and infrastructure indicators

	2010	2015	2022
Individuals using the Internet (per 100 inhabitants)	11.6	25.7 [i]	41.0 [i,b]
Research & Development expenditure (% of GDP) [u]	0.1 [t]	0.3 [v]	...
Threatened species (number)	92	105	136
Forested area (% of land area) [i]	8.9	8.5	8.2 [c]
CO2 emission estimates (million tons/tons per capita)	3.2 / 1.5	4.0 / 1.7	3.9 / 1.5 [c]
Energy production, primary (Petajoules)	17	21	24 [c]
Energy supply per capita (Gigajoules)	30	34	34 [c]
Tourist/visitor arrivals at national borders (000)	984	1 388	170 [b]
Important sites for terrestrial biodiversity protected (%)	83.5	86.2	86.2 [d]
Net Official Development Assist. received (% of GNI)	2.41	1.26	1.71 [b]

a Projected estimate (medium fertility variant). b 2020. c 2019. d 2021. e Excludes irrigation canals and landscaping care. f Data classified according to ISIC Rev. 4. g Excludes publishing activities. Includes irrigation and canals. h Includes publishing activities and landscape care. Excludes repair of personal and household goods. i Estimate. j Calculated by the UNSD from national indices. k Areas nes l Data refers to a 5-year period preceding the reference year. m Including refugees. n Data as at the end of December. o 2007. p 2018. q 2013. r 2012. s Data are as at 1 January of reporting year. t Excluding government. u Partial data. v 2014.

Nauru

Region	Micronesia	UN membership date	14 September 1999
Population (000, 2022)	13[a]	Surface area (km2)	21[b]
Pop. density (per km2, 2022)	633.4[a]	Sex ratio (m per 100 f)	103.2[a]
Capital city	Yaren	National currency	Australian Dollar (AUD)
Capital city pop. (000, 2022)	11.3[c,d]	Exchange rate (per US$)	1.4[e]

Economic indicators	2010	2015	2022
GDP: Gross domestic product (million current US$)	59	104	135[b]
GDP growth rate (annual %, const. 2015 prices)	13.6	36.5	1.0[b]
GDP per capita (current US$)	5 924.8	10 050.4	12 510.4[b]
Economy: Agriculture (% of Gross Value Added)[f,g]	4.2	2.4	2.4[b]
Economy: Industry (% of Gross Value Added)[f,g]	43.6	40.7	36.4[b]
Economy: Services and other activity (% of GVA)[f,g]	52.2	56.9	61.2[b]
Unemployment rate (% of labour force)	...	23.0[h,i]	...
Labour force participation rate (female/male pop. %)	... / ...	49.3 / 78.9[i]	... / ...
CPI: Consumer Price Index (2010=100)	100	100[i]	
Agricultural production index (2014-2016=100)	100	100	101[b]
Balance of payments, current account (million US$)	24	- 17	8[d]

Social indicators	2010	2015	2022
Population growth rate (average annual %)	0.2	2.2	0.9[a]
Urban population (% of total population)	100.0	100.0	100.0[k]
Urban population growth rate (average annual %)[l]	- 0.2	2.3	
Fertility rate, total (live births per woman)	3.9	3.8	3.5[a]
Life expectancy at birth (females/males, years)	63.5 / 56.5	66.0 / 59.0	67.8 / 60.5[a]
Population age distribution (0-14/60+ years old, %)	36.5 / 2.9	38.5 / 3.4	38.8 / 4.6[a]
International migrant stock (000/% of total pop.)[m,n]	0.9 / 9.1	1.8 / 17.7	2.2 / 20.3[b]
Refugees and others of concern to the UNHCR (000)	...	0.8	1.0[e]
Infant mortality rate (per 1 000 live births)	26.1	19.8	15.3[a]
Health: Current expenditure (% of GDP)[o,p,q]	12.7	13.7	9.8[k]
Health: Physicians (per 1 000 pop.)	1.1	1.3	...
Education: Government expenditure (% of GDP)	4.2[r,s]	...	...
Education: Primary gross enrol. ratio (f/m per 100 pop.)	93.4 / 93.8[t]	111.6 / 121.3[u]	97.1 / 94.2[b]
Education: Sec. gross enrol. ratio (f/m per 100 pop.)	67.9 / 63.9[t]	83.2 / 86.0[u]	98.4 / 95.0[k]
Education: Upr. Sec. gross enrol. ratio (f/m per 100 pop.)	55.7 / 50.3[s]	90.5 / 93.1[u]	96.4 / 111.9[k]
Seats held by women in the National Parliament (%)	0.0	5.3	10.5[v]

Environment and infrastructure indicators	2010	2015	2022
Individuals using the Internet (per 100 inhabitants)	...	54.0[w,i]	62.4[r,x]
Threatened species (number)	74	80	92
Forested area (% of land area)[r]	0.0	0.0	0.0[k]
Energy production, primary (Petajoules)	0	0	0[k]
Energy supply per capita (Gigajoules)	58	73[r]	68[r,k]
Important sites for terrestrial biodiversity protected (%)	0.0	0.0	0.0[e]
Net Official Development Assist. received (% of GNI)	48.74	26.48	31.22[k]

a Projected estimate (medium fertility variant). **b** 2020. **c** Refers to Nauru. **d** 2018. **e** 2021. **f** Data classified according to ISIC Rev. 4. **g** At producers' prices. **h** Break in the time series. **i** 2011. **j** 2012. **k** 2019. **l** Data refers to a 5-year period preceding the reference year. **m** Refers to foreign citizens. **n** Including refugees. **o** Indicators are sensitive to external funds flowing in to the country. **p** Data refer to fiscal years beginning 1 July. **q** General government expenditure (GGE) can be larger than the Gross domestic product (GDP) because government accounts for a very large part of domestic consumption and because a large part of domestic consumption in the country is accounted for by imports. **r** Estimate. **s** 2007. **t** 2008. **u** 2014. **v** Data are as at 1 January of reporting year. **w** Population aged 15 years and over. **x** 2017.

Nepal

Region	Southern Asia	UN membership date	14 December 1955
Population (000, 2022)	30 548[a]	Surface area (km2)	147 181[b]
Pop. density (per km2, 2022)	207.6[a]	Sex ratio (m per 100 f)	92.1[a]
Capital city	Kathmandu	National currency	Nepalese Rupee (NPR)
Capital city pop. (000, 2022)	1 376.1[c,d]	Exchange rate (per US$)	121.4[e]

Economic indicators	2010	2015	2022
GDP: Gross domestic product (million current US$)	18 365	23 667	33 079[b]
GDP growth rate (annual %, const. 2015 prices)	6.2	4.0	- 2.1[b]
GDP per capita (current US$)	679.8	876.1	1 135.3[b]
Economy: Agriculture (% of Gross Value Added)[f]	32.2	29.4[g]	26.2[g,b]
Economy: Industry (% of Gross Value Added)[f]	15.0	14.6[h]	13.4[h,b]
Economy: Services and other activity (% of GVA)[f]	52.8	56.0[i]	60.4[i,b]
Employment in agriculture (% of employed)[j]	70.2	67.3	64.5[b]
Employment in industry (% of employed)[j]	13.3	14.3	15.3[b]
Employment in services & other sectors (% employed)[j]	16.5	18.5	20.2[b]
Unemployment rate (% of labour force)	1.8[j]	3.1	5.2[j]
Labour force participation rate (female/male pop. %)[j]	79.7 / 87.0	81.6 / 85.5	81.5 / 81.9
CPI: Consumer Price Index (2010=100)[k]	...	104	140[e]
Agricultural production index (2014-2016=100)	83	99	115[b]
International trade: exports (million current US$)[l]	874	660	1 749[j,e]
International trade: imports (million current US$)[l]	5 116	6 612	16 332[j,e]
International trade: balance (million current US$)[l]	- 4 242	- 5 952	- 14 583[e]
Balance of payments, current account (million US$)	- 128	2 447	- 5 379[e]

Major trading partners					2021
Export partners (% of exports)[j]	India	68.7	United States	10.3	Germany	3.0
Import partners (% of imports)[j]	India	63.1	China	15.7	Indonesia	2.1

Social indicators	2010	2015	2022
Population growth rate (average annual %)	0.5	0.7	1.2[a]
Urban population (% of total population)	16.8	18.6	20.2[d]
Urban population growth rate (average annual %)[m]	3.1	3.2	...
Fertility rate, total (live births per woman)	2.5	2.2	2.0[a]
Life expectancy at birth (females/males, years)	68.6 / 65.1	69.1 / 65.8	72.4 / 68.6[a]
Population age distribution (0-14/60+ years old, %)	36.2 / 7.4	33.4 / 8.5	28.9 / 9.0[a]
International migrant stock (000/% of total pop.)[n]	581.9 / 2.2	509.5 / 1.9	487.6 / 1.7[b]
Refugees and others of concern to the UNHCR (000)	891.3[o]	36.8	20.2[e]
Infant mortality rate (per 1 000 live births)	36.7	29.6	20.3[a]
Health: Current expenditure (% of GDP)[p]	4.4	5.5	4.4[d]
Health: Physicians (per 1 000 pop.)	...	0.6[q]	0.9[b]
Education: Government expenditure (% of GDP)	3.6	3.3	4.4[r]
Education: Primary gross enrol. ratio (f/m per 100 pop.)	149.9 / 139.3	148.6 / 139.9	143.5 / 140.8[d]
Education: Sec. gross enrol. ratio (f/m per 100 pop.)	56.9 / 58.3[i]	69.4 / 66.3[i]	86.9 / 84.2[b]
Education: Upr. Sec. gross enrol. ratio (f/m per 100 pop.)	41.5 / 43.9[i]	49.6 / 48.7[i]	75.0 / 70.5[b]
Intentional homicide rate (per 100 000 pop.)	3.0	2.1[s]	...
Seats held by women in the National Parliament (%)	33.2	29.5	33.6[t]

Environment and infrastructure indicators	2010	2015	2022
Individuals using the Internet (per 100 inhabitants)	7.9[u]	17.6[i]	37.7[j,b]
Research & Development expenditure (% of GDP)	0.3[v,w]	...	...
Threatened species (number)	93	105	127
Forested area (% of land area)	41.6	41.6	41.6[d]
CO2 emission estimates (million tons/tons per capita)	7.3 / 0.2	9.1 / 0.2	13.7 / 0.4[d]
Energy production, primary (Petajoules)	384	424	457[d]
Energy supply per capita (Gigajoules)	16	19	21[d]
Tourist/visitor arrivals at national borders (000)[x]	603	539	230[b]
Important sites for terrestrial biodiversity protected (%)	51.7	51.7	51.7[e]
Pop. using safely managed drinking water (urban/rural, %)	37.9 / 27.5	32.9 / 23.6	24.7 / 15.7[b]
Pop. using safely managed sanitation (urban/rural %)	28.3 / 26.6	35.0 / 37.3	42.5 / 50.2[b]
Net Official Development Assist. received (% of GNI)	4.76	4.96	5.16[b]

a Projected estimate (medium fertility variant). b 2020. c Refers to the municipality. d 2019. e 2021. f Data classified according to ISIC Rev. 4. g Excludes irrigation canals and landscaping care. h Excludes publishing activities. Includes irrigation and canals. i Includes publishing activities and landscape care. Excludes repair of personal and household goods. j Estimate. k Index base: 2014/2015=100. l Merchandise trade data up to 2009 reported by fiscal year and beginning 2010 reported by calendar year. m Data refers to a 5-year period preceding the reference year. n Including refugees. o Data as at the end of December. p Data refer to fiscal years beginning 16 July. q 2013. r 2018. s 2014. t Data are as at 1 January of reporting year. u December. v Partial data. w Based on R&D budget instead of R&D expenditure. x Including arrivals from India.

Netherlands

Region	Western Europe	
Population (000, 2022)	17 564[a,b]	
Pop. density (per km2, 2022)	521.6[a,b]	
Capital city	Amsterdam[d]	
Capital city pop. (000, 2022)	1 140.3[e]	

UN membership date	10 December 1945	
Surface area (km2)	41 543[c]	
Sex ratio (m per 100 f)	98.8[a,b]	
National currency	Euro (EUR)	
Exchange rate (per US$)	0.9[f]	

Economic indicators

	2010	2015	2022
GDP: Gross domestic product (million current US$)	846 555	765 265	913 865[c]
GDP growth rate (annual %, const. 2015 prices)	1.3	2.0	- 3.8[c]
GDP per capita (current US$)	50 743.8	45 179.0	53 333.7[c]
Economy: Agriculture (% of Gross Value Added)[g,h]	2.0	1.9	1.8[c]
Economy: Industry (% of Gross Value Added)[g,i]	21.9	20.2	19.9[c]
Economy: Services and other activity (% of GVA)[g,j]	76.1	77.9	78.3[c]
Employment in agriculture (% of employed)	3.1	2.3	2.0[k,c]
Employment in industry (% of employed)	17.7	16.4	15.8[k,c]
Employment in services & other sectors (% employed)	79.2	81.2	82.2[k,c]
Unemployment rate (% of labour force)	5.0	6.9	3.5[k]
Labour force participation rate (female/male pop. %)	58.7 / 71.2	58.8 / 70.1	62.0 / 71.0[k]
CPI: Consumer Price Index (2010=100)	100	109	121[f]
Agricultural production index (2014-2016=100)	90	101	102[c]
International trade: exports (million current US$)	492 646	464 697	693 800[f]
International trade: imports (million current US$)	439 987	412 644	623 247[f]
International trade: balance (million current US$)	52 659	52 053	70 554[f]
Balance of payments, current account (million US$)	61 803	48 583	96 623[f]

Major trading partners

						2021
Export partners (% of exports)	Germany	22.7	Belgium	10.7	France	8.1
Import partners (% of imports)	Germany	17.4	China	10.2	Belgium	9.9

Social indicators

	2010	2015	2022
Population growth rate (average annual %)[a]	0.5	0.5	0.3[b]
Urban population (% of total population)	87.1	90.2	91.9[e]
Urban population growth rate (average annual %)[l]	1.4	1.0	...
Fertility rate, total (live births per woman)[a]	1.8	1.7	1.6[b]
Life expectancy at birth (females/males, years)[a]	82.7 / 78.8	83.1 / 79.7	83.9 / 80.9[b]
Population age distribution (0-14/60+ years old, %)[a]	17.5 / 22.0	16.6 / 24.1	15.4 / 27.0[b]
International migrant stock (000/% of total pop.)	1 832.5 / 11.0	1 996.3 / 11.8	2 358.3 / 13.8[c]
Refugees and others of concern to the UNHCR (000)	90.1[m]	92.5	107.0[f]
Infant mortality rate (per 1 000 live births)[a]	3.8	3.2	3.0[b]
Health: Current expenditure (% of GDP)	10.2	10.3	10.1[e]
Health: Physicians (per 1 000 pop.)	3.0	3.5	4.1[c]
Education: Government expenditure (% of GDP)	5.5	5.3	5.4[n]
Education: Primary gross enrol. ratio (f/m per 100 pop.)	108.1 / 108.5	102.7 / 102.7	106.1 / 106.1[e]
Education: Sec. gross enrol. ratio (f/m per 100 pop.)	121.2 / 122.9	134.6 / 132.6	135.2 / 133.6[e]
Education: Upr. Sec. gross enrol. ratio (f/m per 100 pop.)	118.4 / 115.4	137.2 / 128.6	141.2 / 131.9[e]
Intentional homicide rate (per 100 000 pop.)	0.9	0.6	0.6[c]
Seats held by women in the National Parliament (%)	42.0	37.3	40.7[o]

Environment and infrastructure indicators

	2010	2015	2022
Individuals using the Internet (per 100 inhabitants)	90.7[p,q]	91.7	91.3[c]
Research & Development expenditure (% of GDP)	1.7	2.1	2.3[c]
Threatened species (number)	24	29	82
Forested area (% of land area)	11.1	10.8	10.9[k,e]
CO2 emission estimates (million tons/tons per capita)	172.3 / 10.3	158.6 / 9.3	136.3 / 7.7[c]
Energy production, primary (Petajoules)[r]	2 979	2 012	1 376[e]
Energy supply per capita (Gigajoules)[r]	206	177	174[e]
Tourist/visitor arrivals at national borders (000)	10 883	15 007	7 265[c]
Important sites for terrestrial biodiversity protected (%)	73.0	76.2	79.6[f]
Pop. using safely managed sanitation (urban/rural %)	97.5 / 97.4	97.5 / 97.5	97.5 / 97.5[c]
Net Official Development Assist. disbursed (% of GNI)[s]	1.67	8.91	1.47[c]

a For statistical purposes, the data for Netherlands do not include Aruba, Bonaire, Sint Eustatius and Saba, Curaçao, and Sint Maarten (Dutch part). b Projected estimate (medium fertility variant). c 2020. d Amsterdam is the capital and The Hague is the seat of government. e 2019. f 2021. g Data classified according to ISIC Rev. 4. h Excludes irrigation canals and landscaping care. i Excludes publishing activities. Includes irrigation and canals. j Includes publishing activities and landscape care. Excludes repair of personal and household goods. k Estimate. l Data refers to a 5-year period preceding the reference year. m Data as at the end of December. n 2018. o Data are as at 1 January of reporting year. p Users in the last 12 months. q Population aged 16 to 74 years. r Data exclude Suriname and the Netherlands Antilles (former) s DAC member (OECD).

New Caledonia

Region	Melanesia
Surface area (km2)	19 100 [c]
Sex ratio (m per 100 f)	98.9 [a,b]
National currency	CFP Franc (XPF) [d]
Exchange rate (per US$)	105.4 [f]

Population (000, 2022)	290 [a,b]
Pop. density (per km2, 2022)	15.9 [a,b]
Capital city	Nouméa
Capital city pop. (000, 2022)	197.8 [e]

Economic indicators	2010	2015	2022
GDP: Gross domestic product (million current US$)	9 355	8 735	9 709 [c]
GDP growth rate (annual %, const. 2015 prices)	6.9	0.8	0.2 [c]
GDP per capita (current US$)	36 900.3	32 223.6	34 006.3 [c]
Economy: Agriculture (% of Gross Value Added) [g]	1.5	2.1	2.2 [c]
Economy: Industry (% of Gross Value Added) [g]	28.3	24.0	23.0 [c]
Economy: Services and other activity (% of GVA) [g,h]	70.2	73.9	74.9 [c]
Employment in agriculture (% of employed) [i]	2.6	2.2	1.9 [c]
Employment in industry (% of employed) [i]	22.0	21.6	20.7 [c]
Employment in services & other sectors (% employed) [i]	75.5	76.2	77.5 [c]
Unemployment rate (% of labour force) [i]	13.8	14.7	16.3
Labour force participation rate (female/male pop. %) [i]	60.9 / 72.5	58.9 / 69.1	57.7 / 68.4
CPI: Consumer Price Index (2010=100) [i]	100	106	110 [f]
Agricultural production index (2014-2016=100)	86	110	100 [c]
International trade: exports (million current US$)	1 268	1 239	1 296 [i,f]
International trade: imports (million current US$)	3 303	2 529	2 647 [i,f]
International trade: balance (million current US$)	- 2 036	- 1 291	- 1 351 [f]
Balance of payments, current account (million US$)	- 1 360	- 1 119	- 654 [k]

Major trading partners						2021
Export partners (% of exports) [i]	China	54.5	Republic of Korea	16.5	Japan	11.4
Import partners (% of imports) [i]	France	36.0	Singapore	14.9	Australia	13.4

Social indicators	2010	2015	2022
Population growth rate (average annual %) [a]	1.8	0.3	1.1 [b]
Urban population (% of total population)	67.1	69.4	71.1 [l]
Urban population growth rate (average annual %) [m]	2.5	2.1	...
Fertility rate, total (live births per woman) [a]	2.2	2.1	2.0 [b]
Life expectancy at birth (females/males, years) [a]	82.6 / 74.3	82.7 / 74.9	84.6 / 77.5 [b]
Population age distribution (0-14/60+ years old, %) [a]	25.8 / 11.3	24.1 / 12.6	22.2 / 15.8 [b]
International migrant stock (000/% of total pop.)	61.2 / 24.1	68.9 / 25.4	73.1 / 25.6 [c]
Infant mortality rate (per 1 000 live births) [a]	14.0	12.2	9.4 [b]
Intentional homicide rate (per 100 000 pop.)	3.2 [n]	...	...

Environment and infrastructure indicators	2010	2015	2022
Individuals using the Internet (per 100 inhabitants) [i]	42.0	74.0	82.0 [o]
Threatened species (number)	415	493	936
Forested area (% of land area) [i]	45.9	45.9	45.8 [l]
Energy production, primary (Petajoules)	1	2	2 [l]
Energy supply per capita (Gigajoules)	183	226	232 [l]
Tourist/visitor arrivals at national borders (000) [p]	99	114	31 [c]
Important sites for terrestrial biodiversity protected (%)	27.9	37.8	42.2 [f]

a For statistical purposes, the data for France do not include this area. b Projected estimate (medium fertility variant). c 2020. d Communauté financière du Pacifique (CFP) Franc. e 2018. f 2021. g Data classified according to ISIC Rev. 4. h Including restaurants and hotels. i Estimate. j Calculated by the UNSD from national indices. k 2016. l 2019. m Data refers to a 5-year period preceding the reference year. n 2009. o 2017. p Including nationals residing abroad.

New Zealand

Region	Oceania	UN membership date	24 October 1945
Population (000, 2022)	5 185[a,b]	Surface area (km2)	268 107[c]
Pop. density (per km2, 2022)	19.6[a,b]	Sex ratio (m per 100 f)	98.3[a,b]
Capital city	Wellington	National currency	New Zealand Dollar (NZD)
Capital city pop. (000, 2022)	413.0[d]	Exchange rate (per US$)	1.5[e]

Economic indicators	2010	2015	2022
GDP: Gross domestic product (million current US$)	146 518	178 064	212 044[c]
GDP growth rate (annual %, const. 2015 prices)	0.9	4.4	- 0.3[c]
GDP per capita (current US$)	33 527.6	38 587.8	43 972.1[c]
Economy: Agriculture (% of Gross Value Added)[f,g]	7.1	4.9	6.3[c]
Economy: Industry (% of Gross Value Added)[f,h]	23.0	23.1	22.3[c]
Economy: Services and other activity (% of GVA)[f,i]	69.9	72.0	71.5[c]
Employment in agriculture (% of employed)	6.7	6.1	5.6[j,c]
Employment in industry (% of employed)	20.6	21.6	19.4[j,c]
Employment in services & other sectors (% employed)	72.6	72.3	75.1[j,c]
Unemployment rate (% of labour force)	6.6	5.4	3.9[j]
Labour force participation rate (female/male pop. %)	61.6 / 74.1	63.4 / 74.4	64.7 / 74.9[j]
CPI: Consumer Price Index (2010=100)[k]	100	108	121[e]
Agricultural production index (2014-2016=100)	87	101	103[c]
International trade: exports (million current US$)	31 393	34 357	73 366[e]
International trade: imports (million current US$)	30 616	36 528	49 882[e]
International trade: balance (million current US$)	777	- 2 171	23 484[e]
Balance of payments, current account (million US$)	- 3 429	- 4 686	- 14 214[e]

Major trading partners						2021
Export partners (% of exports)	China	31.1	Australia	12.8	United States	10.8
Import partners (% of imports)	China	29.7	Australia	11.3	United States	8.5

Social indicators	2010	2015	2022
Population growth rate (average annual %)[a]	0.9	1.7	0.8[b]
Urban population (% of total population)	86.2	86.3	86.6[d]
Urban population growth rate (average annual %)[l]	1.1	1.1	...
Fertility rate, total (live births per woman)[a]	2.2	2.0	1.8[b]
Life expectancy at birth (females/males, years)[a]	83.0 / 79.2	83.7 / 80.1	84.7 / 81.3[b]
Population age distribution (0-14/60+ years old, %)[a]	20.9 / 18.3	20.0 / 20.0	18.7 / 22.2[b]
International migrant stock (000/% of total pop.)	947.4 / 21.7	1 039.7 / 22.5	1 381.7 / 28.7[c]
Refugees and others of concern to the UNHCR (000)	2.5[m]	1.6	2.4[c]
Infant mortality rate (per 1 000 live births)[a]	5.0	4.4	3.5[b]
Health: Current expenditure (% of GDP)	9.6	9.3	9.7[d]
Health: Physicians (per 1 000 pop.)	2.6	3.0	3.6[c]
Education: Government expenditure (% of GDP)	7.0	6.3	6.0[n]
Education: Primary gross enrol. ratio (f/m per 100 pop.)	101.3 / 101.0	98.2 / 97.7	101.8 / 101.6[d]
Education: Sec. gross enrol. ratio (f/m per 100 pop.)	121.8 / 116.4	118.1 / 111.5	126.5 / 119.9[d]
Education: Upr. Sec. gross enrol. ratio (f/m per 100 pop.)	144.6 / 130.7	138.6 / 122.9	158.3 / 142.4[d]
Intentional homicide rate (per 100 000 pop.)	1.0	1.0	2.6[d]
Seats held by women in the National Parliament (%)	33.6	31.4	49.2[o]

Environment and infrastructure indicators	2010	2015	2022
Individuals using the Internet (per 100 inhabitants)[i]	80.5	85.2	91.5[c]
Research & Development expenditure (% of GDP)	1.3[p]	1.2	1.4[q,d]
Threatened species (number)	153	197	276
Forested area (% of land area)	37.4	37.4	37.5[d]
CO2 emission estimates (million tons/tons per capita)	31.0 / 7.0	32.0 / 6.8	33.7 / 6.5[c]
Energy production, primary (Petajoules)	775	784	744[d]
Energy supply per capita (Gigajoules)	192	207	201[d]
Tourist/visitor arrivals at national borders (000)	2 435	3 039	948[c]
Important sites for terrestrial biodiversity protected (%)	45.4	46.2	46.2[e]
Net Official Development Assist. disbursed (% of GNI)[r]	0.32	0.37	0.34[c]

a For statistical purposes, the data for New Zealand do not include Cook Islands, Niue, and Tokelau. b Projected estimate (medium fertility variant). c 2020. d 2019. e 2021. f Data classified according to ISIC Rev. 4. g Excludes irrigation canals and landscaping care. h Excludes publishing activities. Includes irrigation and canals. i Includes publishing activities and landscape care. Excludes repair of personal and household goods. j Estimate. k Calculated by the UNSD from national indices. l Data refers to a 5-year period preceding the reference year. m Data as at the end of December. n 2018. o Data are as at 1 January of reporting year. p 2009. q Provisional data. r DAC member (OECD).

Nicaragua

Region	Central America	UN membership date	24 October 1945		
Population (000, 2022)	6 948[a]	Surface area (km2)	130 374[b]		
Pop. density (per km2, 2022)	57.7[a]	Sex ratio (m per 100 f)	97.1[a]		
Capital city	Managua	National currency	Cordoba Oro (NIO)		
Capital city pop. (000, 2022)	1 055.5[c]	Exchange rate (per US$)	35.5[d]		

Economic indicators

	2010	2015	2022
GDP: Gross domestic product (million current US$)	8 759	12 757	12 621[b]
GDP growth rate (annual %, const. 2015 prices)	4.4	4.8	- 2.0[b]
GDP per capita (current US$)	1 503.9	2 049.8	1 905.3[b]
Economy: Agriculture (% of Gross Value Added)[e]	18.7	17.8	17.5[b]
Economy: Industry (% of Gross Value Added)[e]	24.2	28.5	27.8[b]
Economy: Services and other activity (% of GVA)[e]	57.0	53.7	54.7[b]
Employment in agriculture (% of employed)[f]	29.4	31.0	30.6[b]
Employment in industry (% of employed)[f]	18.4	17.6	15.6[b]
Employment in services & other sectors (% employed)[f]	52.2	51.4	53.8[b]
Unemployment rate (% of labour force)	7.8	4.7	5.7[f]
Labour force participation rate (female/male pop. %)[f]	44.4 / 84.2	48.4 / 83.0	47.4 / 81.7
CPI: Consumer Price Index (2010=100)	100	137	177[d]
Agricultural production index (2014-2016=100)	89	98	134[b]
International trade: exports (million current US$)	1 848	4 667	6 495[d]
International trade: imports (million current US$)	4 191	5 866	9 826[d]
International trade: balance (million current US$)	- 2 343	- 1 199	- 3 331[d]
Balance of payments, current account (million US$)	- 777	- 1 260	958[b]

Major trading partners

					2021
Export partners (% of exports)	United States	56.5	Mexico	11.8	El Salvador	5.9
Import partners (% of imports)	United States	24.9	China	12.5	Mexico	8.8

Social indicators

	2010	2015	2022
Population growth rate (average annual %)	1.5	1.4	1.4[a]
Urban population (% of total population)	56.9	57.9	58.8[c]
Urban population growth rate (average annual %)[g]	1.6	1.5	
Fertility rate, total (live births per woman)	2.6	2.5	2.3[a]
Life expectancy at birth (females/males, years)	75.1 / 68.9	75.9 / 70.0	77.6 / 71.6[a]
Population age distribution (0-14/60+ years old, %)	34.4 / 5.9	32.1 / 6.8	29.7 / 7.9[a]
International migrant stock (000/% of total pop.)[h]	37.3 / 0.6	40.3 / 0.6	42.2 / 0.6[b]
Refugees and others of concern to the UNHCR (000)	0.1[i]	0.4	1.0[d]
Infant mortality rate (per 1 000 live births)	20.0	16.3	12.3[a]
Health: Current expenditure (% of GDP)[f,j]	7.7	8.0	8.4[c]
Health: Physicians (per 1 000 pop.)	0.7	0.9	1.7[k]
Education: Government expenditure (% of GDP)	4.5	4.1	3.4[f,c]
Education: Primary gross enrol. ratio (f/m per 100 pop.)	120.1 / 121.1	... / ...	... / ...
Education: Sec. gross enrol. ratio (f/m per 100 pop.)	78.0 / 69.1	... / ...	... / ...
Education: Upr. Sec. gross enrol. ratio (f/m per 100 pop.)	64.4 / 50.6	... / ...	... / ...
Intentional homicide rate (per 100 000 pop.)	13.5	8.4	7.9[c]
Seats held by women in the National Parliament (%)	20.7	39.1	50.6[l]

Environment and infrastructure indicators

	2010	2015	2022
Individuals using the Internet (per 100 inhabitants)[f]	10.0	19.7	45.2[b]
Research & Development expenditure (% of GDP)	...	0.1[m]	...
Threatened species (number)	121	141	244
Forested area (% of land area)	34.8	32.5	29.1[c]
CO2 emission estimates (million tons/tons per capita)	4.7 / 0.7	5.5 / 0.8	5.4 / 0.7[c]
Energy production, primary (Petajoules)	69	88	96[c]
Energy supply per capita (Gigajoules)	22	26	26[c]
Tourist/visitor arrivals at national borders (000)[n]	1 011	1 386	384[b]
Important sites for terrestrial biodiversity protected (%)	68.1	69.7	69.7[d]
Pop. using safely managed drinking water (urban/rural, %)	66.6 / 31.9	67.2 / 38.6	67.3 / 38.5[b]
Net Official Development Assist. received (% of GNI)	6.00	3.69	4.89[b]

a Projected estimate (medium fertility variant). **b** 2020. **c** 2019. **d** 2021. **e** Data classified according to ISIC Rev. 4. **f** Estimate. **g** Data refers to a 5-year period preceding the reference year. **h** Including refugees. **i** Data as at the end of December. **j** Data based on calendar year (January 1 to December 31). **k** 2018. **l** Data are as at 1 January of reporting year. **m** Higher Education only. **n** Including nationals residing abroad.

Niger

Region	Western Africa	UN membership date	20 September 1960	
Population (000, 2022)	26 208 [a]	Surface area (km2)	1 267 000 [b]	
Pop. density (per km2, 2022)	20.7 [a]	Sex ratio (m per 100 f)	102.9 [a]	
Capital city	Niamey	National currency	CFA Franc, BCEAO (XOF) [c]	
Capital city pop. (000, 2022)	1 251.5 [d]	Exchange rate (per US$)	579.2 [e]	

Economic indicators

	2010	2015	2022
GDP: Gross domestic product (million current US$)	7 631	9 677	13 741 [b]
GDP growth rate (annual %, const. 2015 prices)	8.7	4.8	3.6 [b]
GDP per capita (current US$)	463.5	483.8	567.7 [b]
Economy: Agriculture (% of Gross Value Added) [f,g]	39.5	34.7	40.5 [b]
Economy: Industry (% of Gross Value Added) [g,h]	20.9	24.1	21.3 [b]
Economy: Services and other activity (% of GVA) [g,i]	39.7	41.2	38.2 [b]
Employment in agriculture (% of employed) [j]	77.1	75.9	74.8 [b]
Employment in industry (% of employed) [j]	7.5	7.4	7.2 [b]
Employment in services & other sectors (% employed) [j]	15.4	16.7	18.0 [b]
Unemployment rate (% of labour force) [j]	0.8	0.5	0.8
Labour force participation rate (female/male pop. %) [j]	68.8 / 90.5	62.3 / 85.1	62.0 / 84.4
CPI: Consumer Price Index (2010=100) [l]	...	107 [k,m]	102 [n,d]
Agricultural production index (2014-2016=100)	86	102	129 [b]
International trade: exports (million current US$)	479	790	4 444 [j,e]
International trade: imports (million current US$)	2 273	2 458	4 064 [j,e]
International trade: balance (million current US$)	- 1 794	- 1 669	380 [e]
Balance of payments, current account (million US$)	- 1 137	- 1 486	- 1 816 [b]

Major trading partners

							2021
Export partners (% of exports) [j]	Areas nes [o]	49.5	France	17.1	Mali	8.7
Import partners (% of imports) [j]	France	22.3	China	18.4	United States	6.6

Social indicators

	2010	2015	2022
Population growth rate (average annual %)	3.7	3.9	3.7 [a]
Urban population (% of total population)	16.2	16.2	16.5 [d]
Urban population growth rate (average annual %) [p]	3.7	3.9	...
Fertility rate, total (live births per woman)	7.5	7.2	6.7 [a]
Life expectancy at birth (females/males, years)	59.0 / 57.7	62.1 / 60.1	63.4 / 60.8 [a]
Population age distribution (0-14/60+ years old, %)	49.1 / 3.8	49.1 / 3.9	48.8 / 3.9 [a]
International migrant stock (000/% of total pop.) [q]	126.5 / 0.8	253.0 / 1.3	348.1 / 1.4 [b]
Refugees and others of concern to the UNHCR (000)	0.3 [r]	202.2	611.6 [e]
Infant mortality rate (per 1 000 live births)	61.8	50.4	40.1 [a]
Health: Current expenditure (% of GDP)	5.0	5.3	5.7 [d]
Health: Physicians (per 1 000 pop.)	~0.0 [s]	~0.0	~0.0 [b]
Education: Government expenditure (% of GDP)	2.7	4.5	3.5 [j,d]
Education: Primary gross enrol. ratio (f/m per 100 pop.)	55.9 / 69.2	65.6 / 77.4	62.0 / 70.7 [d]
Education: Sec. gross enrol. ratio (f/m per 100 pop.)	10.7 / 15.3	17.0 / 23.1	20.7 / 27.7 [t]
Education: Upr. Sec. gross enrol. ratio (f/m per 100 pop.)	3.1 / 5.5	8.7 / 11.0	9.1 / 13.6 [t]
Intentional homicide rate (per 100 000 pop.)	...	4.4 [u]	...
Seats held by women in the National Parliament (%)	9.7	13.3	25.9 [v]

Environment and infrastructure indicators

	2010	2015	2022
Individuals using the Internet (per 100 inhabitants)	0.8 [j]	2.5 [j]	10.2 [w,t]
Threatened species (number)	26	31	43
Forested area (% of land area) [j]	1.0	0.9	0.9 [d]
CO2 emission estimates (million tons/tons per capita)	2.0 / 0.1	2.8 / 0.1	3.0 / 0.1 [d]
Energy production, primary (Petajoules)	56	100	112 [j,d]
Energy supply per capita (Gigajoules)	4	5	5 [j,d]
Tourist/visitor arrivals at national borders (000)	74	135	85 [b]
Important sites for terrestrial biodiversity protected (%)	23.4	23.4	54.7 [e]
Pop. using safely managed sanitation (urban/rural %)	33.4 / 7.7	38.0 / 9.5	43.0 / 10.8 [b]
Net Official Development Assist. received (% of GNI)	8.95	8.55	14.66 [b]

a Projected estimate (medium fertility variant). b 2020. c African Financial Community (CFA) Franc, Central Bank of West African States (BCEAO). d 2019. e 2021. f Excludes irrigation canals and landscaping care. g Data classified according to ISIC Rev. 4. h Excludes publishing activities. Includes irrigation and canals. i Includes publishing activities and landscape care. Excludes repair of personal and household goods. j Estimate. k Index base: 2008=100. l WAEMU harmonized consumer price index. m Niamey n Index base: 2014=100. o Areas nes p Data refers to a 5-year period preceding the reference year. q Including refugees. r Data as at the end of December. s 2009. t 2017. u 2012. v Data are as at 1 January of reporting year. w Population aged 15 years and over.

Nigeria

Region	Western Africa	UN membership date	07 October 1960
Population (000, 2022)	218 541 [a]	Surface area (km2)	923 768 [b]
Pop. density (per km2, 2022)	240.0 [a]	Sex ratio (m per 100 f)	102.2 [a]
Capital city	Abuja	National currency	Naira (NGN)
Capital city pop. (000, 2022)	3 095.1 [c,d]	Exchange rate (per US$)	381.0 [b]

Economic indicators

	2010	2015	2022
GDP: Gross domestic product (million current US$)	363 360	494 583	429 899 [b]
GDP growth rate (annual %, const. 2015 prices)	8.0	2.7	- 1.8 [b]
GDP per capita (current US$)	2 292.4	2 730.4	2 085.5 [b]
Economy: Agriculture (% of Gross Value Added) [e,f]	23.9	20.9	24.4 [b]
Economy: Industry (% of Gross Value Added) [f,g]	25.3	20.4	28.6 [b]
Economy: Services and other activity (% of GVA) [f,h]	50.8	58.8	47.0 [b]
Employment in agriculture (% of employed) [i]	41.4	36.9	34.7 [b]
Employment in industry (% of employed) [i]	10.3	12.2	12.2 [b]
Employment in services & other sectors (% employed) [i]	48.4	50.9	53.1 [b]
Unemployment rate (% of labour force)	3.8 [i]	4.3	9.6 [i]
Labour force participation rate (female/male pop. %) [i]	56.8 / 63.9	50.8 / 59.5	48.4 / 59.9
CPI: Consumer Price Index (2010=100) [j]	100	159	354 [k,l]
Agricultural production index (2014-2016=100)	87	99	106 [b]
International trade: exports (million current US$)	86 568	48 433	47 232 [l]
International trade: imports (million current US$)	44 235	33 831	52 068 [l]
International trade: balance (million current US$)	42 333	14 602	- 4 837 [l]
Balance of payments, current account (million US$)	13 111	- 15 439	- 16 976 [b]

Major trading partners

							2021
Export partners (% of exports)	India	16.4	Spain	11.8	France	6.3
Import partners (% of imports)	China	24.7	Netherlands	10.3	India	8.8

Social indicators

	2010	2015	2022
Population growth rate (average annual %)	2.8	2.5	2.4 [a]
Urban population (% of total population)	43.5	47.8	51.2 [d]
Urban population growth rate (average annual %) [m]	4.8	4.6	...
Fertility rate, total (live births per woman)	6.0	5.6	5.1 [a]
Life expectancy at birth (females/males, years)	51.4 / 50.5	52.2 / 51.5	54.0 / 53.3 [a]
Population age distribution (0-14/60+ years old, %)	44.3 / 4.9	44.3 / 4.8	43.0 / 4.7 [a]
International migrant stock (000/% of total pop.) [n,o]	990.5 / 0.6	1 199.1 / 0.7	1 308.6 / 0.6 [b]
Refugees and others of concern to the UNHCR (000)	10.6 [p]	1 510.2	2 847.1 [l]
Infant mortality rate (per 1 000 live births)	86.4	81.6	71.9 [a]
Health: Current expenditure (% of GDP)	3.3	3.6	3.0 [d]
Health: Physicians (per 1 000 pop.)	0.4 [q]	0.4 [r]	0.4 [s]
Education: Primary gross enrol. ratio (f/m per 100 pop.)	81.0 / 89.1 [i]	89.4 / 90.8 [t]	86.5 / 88.4 [s]
Education: Sec. gross enrol. ratio (f/m per 100 pop.)	41.2 / 47.2	44.7 / 48.8	42.4 / 44.6 [s]
Education: Upr. Sec. gross enrol. ratio (f/m per 100 pop.)	38.4 / 44.5	41.6 / 46.3	35.2 / 38.1 [s]
Intentional homicide rate (per 100 000 pop.)	...	...	22.0 [d]
Seats held by women in the National Parliament (%)	7.0	6.7	3.6 [u]

Environment and infrastructure indicators

	2010	2015	2022
Individuals using the Internet (per 100 inhabitants) [i]	11.5	24.5	35.5 [b]
Research & Development expenditure (% of GDP)	0.1 [v,w]	...	...
Threatened species (number)	297	333	455
Forested area (% of land area) [i]	25.5	24.6	23.9 [d]
CO2 emission estimates (million tons/tons per capita)	89.0 / 0.4	121.8 / 0.5	131.8 / 0.5 [d]
Energy production, primary (Petajoules)	10 591	10 634	10 795 [d]
Energy supply per capita (Gigajoules)	34	33	33 [d]
Tourist/visitor arrivals at national borders (000)	1 555	1 255	1 889 [x]
Important sites for terrestrial biodiversity protected (%)	79.9	79.9	79.9 [l]
Pop. using safely managed drinking water (urban/rural, %)	23.5 / 13.7	24.4 / 15.7	25.4 / 17.7 [b]
Pop. using safely managed sanitation (urban/rural %)	26.9 / 23.7	30.9 / 24.6	35.1 / 25.6 [b]
Net Official Development Assist. received (% of GNI)	0.60	0.51	0.81 [b]

a Projected estimate (medium fertility variant). b 2020. c Data refers to the urban agglomeration. d 2019. e Excludes irrigation canals and landscaping care. f Data classified according to ISIC Rev. 4. g Excludes publishing activities. Includes irrigation and canals. h Includes publishing activities and landscape care. Excludes repair of personal and household goods. i Estimate. j Rural and urban areas. k Calculated by the UNSD from national indices. l 2021. m Data refers to a 5-year period preceding the reference year. n Refers to foreign citizens. o Including refugees. p Data as at the end of December. q 2009. r 2013. s 2018. t 2014. u Data are as at 1 January of reporting year. v Excluding business enterprise. w 2007. x 2016.

Niue

Region	Polynesia	Population (000, 2022)	2[a,b]
Surface area (km2)	260[c]	Pop. density (per km2, 2022)	7.4[a,b]
Sex ratio (m per 100 f)	88.4[a,b]	Capital city	Alofi
National currency	New Zealand Dollar (NZD)	Capital city pop. (000, 2022)	0.7[d]
Exchange rate (per US$)	1.5[e]		

Economic indicators	2010	2015	2022
Agricultural production index (2014-2016=100)	99	97	100[c]

Social indicators	2010	2015	2022
Population growth rate (average annual %)[b]	0.2	1.2	0.3[a]
Urban population (% of total population)	38.7	42.6	45.5[f]
Urban population growth rate (average annual %)[g]	1.2	1.9	...
Fertility rate, total (live births per woman)[b]	2.9	2.7	2.4[a]
Life expectancy at birth (females/males, years)[b]	70.5 / 66.6	71.6 / 68.7	72.9 / 69.5[a]
Population age distribution (0-14/60+ years old, %)[b]	26.2 / 16.6	27.0 / 18.6	26.1 / 21.0[a]
International migrant stock (000/% of total pop.)	0.6 / 36.3	0.6 / 36.5	0.6 / 36.3[c]
Infant mortality rate (per 1 000 live births)[b]	27.4	23.9	18.4[a]
Health: Current expenditure (% of GDP)[h,i,j]	15.5	8.7	5.3[f]
Health: Physicians (per 1 000 pop.)	1.9[k]	...	...
Education: Primary gross enrol. ratio (f/m per 100 pop.)	100.0 / 103.5[l]	127.8 / 127.7	138.8 / 138.3[c]
Education: Sec. gross enrol. ratio (f/m per 100 pop.)	90.8 / 82.9[l]	109.4 / 89.5	129.7 / 128.6[c]
Education: Upr. Sec. gross enrol. ratio (f/m per 100 pop.)	... / ...	80.0 / 88.6	165.9 / 167.6[c]

Environment and infrastructure indicators	2010	2015	2022
Individuals using the Internet (per 100 inhabitants)[m]	77.0	79.6[n]	...
Threatened species (number)	43	50	61
Forested area (% of land area)	72.2	72.4	72.5[f]
Energy production, primary (Petajoules)	0	0	0[m,f]
Energy supply per capita (Gigajoules)	53	64	66[m,f]
Tourist/visitor arrivals at national borders (000)[o]	6	8	1[c]
Important sites for terrestrial biodiversity protected (%)	95.3	95.3	95.3[e]

a Projected estimate (medium fertility variant). b For statistical purposes, the data for New Zealand do not include this area. c 2020. d 2018. e 2021. f 2019. g Data refers to a 5-year period preceding the reference year. h General government expenditure (GGE) can be larger than the Gross domestic product (GDP) because government accounts for a very large part of domestic consumption and because a large part of domestic consumption in the country is accounted for by imports. i Data refer to fiscal years beginning 1 July. j Indicators are sensitive to external funds flowing in to the country. k 2008. l 2005. m Estimate. n 2011. o Including Niueans residing usually in New Zealand.

North Macedonia

Region	Southern Europe	UN membership date	08 April 1993
Population (000, 2022)	2 094 [a]	Surface area (km2)	25 713 [b]
Pop. density (per km2, 2022)	84.0 [a]	Sex ratio (m per 100 f)	99.4 [a]
Capital city	Skopje	National currency	Denar (MKD)
Capital city pop. (000, 2022)	589.8 [c]	Exchange rate (per US$)	54.4 [d]

Economic indicators

	2010	2015	2022
GDP: Gross domestic product (million current US$)	9 407	10 065	12 264 [b]
GDP growth rate (annual %, const. 2015 prices)	3.4	3.9	- 4.5 [b]
GDP per capita (current US$)	4 542.9	4 840.3	5 886.5 [b]
Economy: Agriculture (% of Gross Value Added) [e,f]	11.7	11.1	10.8 [b]
Economy: Industry (% of Gross Value Added) [f,g]	24.4	27.4	21.6 [b]
Economy: Services and other activity (% of GVA) [f,h]	63.9	61.5	67.6 [b]
Employment in agriculture (% of employed)	18.6 [i]	17.9	15.1 [i,b]
Employment in industry (% of employed)	30.3 [i]	30.5	31.4 [i,b]
Employment in services & other sectors (% employed)	51.1 [i]	51.6	53.5 [i,b]
Unemployment rate (% of labour force)	32.0	26.1	16.1 [i]
Labour force participation rate (female/male pop. %)	42.9 / 68.6	43.5 / 67.4	43.5 / 64.4 [i]
CPI: Consumer Price Index (2010=100)	100	110	118 [d]
Agricultural production index (2014-2016=100)	97	102	102 [b]
International trade: exports (million current US$)	3 351	4 530	8 145 [i,d]
International trade: imports (million current US$)	5 474	6 427	11 696 [i,d]
International trade: balance (million current US$)	- 2 123	- 1 897	- 3 551 [d]
Balance of payments, current account (million US$)	- 198	- 193	- 479 [d]

Major trading partners

						2021
Export partners (% of exports) [i]	Germany	47.2	Serbia	7.9	Bulgaria	4.7
Import partners (% of imports) [i]	United Kingdom	15.6	Germany	10.7	Serbia	7.8

Social indicators

	2010	2015	2022
Population growth rate (average annual %)	0.2	0.1	- 0.5 [a]
Urban population (% of total population)	57.1	57.4	58.2 [c]
Urban population growth rate (average annual %) [j]	- 0.1	0.2	...
Fertility rate, total (live births per woman)	1.5	1.5	1.4 [a]
Life expectancy at birth (females/males, years)	77.5 / 72.8	78.2 / 73.8	76.2 / 71.7 [a]
Population age distribution (0-14/60+ years old, %)	18.5 / 16.5	17.1 / 18.6	16.0 / 21.3 [a]
International migrant stock (000/% of total pop.)	129.7 / 6.3	130.7 / 6.3	131.3 / 6.3 [b]
Refugees and others of concern to the UNHCR (000)	3.3 [k]	1.6	3.7 [d]
Infant mortality rate (per 1 000 live births)	6.8	6.9	4.9 [a]
Health: Current expenditure (% of GDP)	6.7	6.3	7.3 [c]
Health: Physicians (per 1 000 pop.)	2.7	2.9	...
Education: Primary gross enrol. ratio (f/m per 100 pop.)	86.7 / 88.0	94.0 / 93.7	98.1 / 98.3 [i]
Education: Sec. gross enrol. ratio (f/m per 100 pop.)	81.0 / 83.3	81.2 / 82.6	79.1 / 80.8 [i]
Education: Upr. Sec. gross enrol. ratio (f/m per 100 pop.)	74.6 / 77.1	78.1 / 79.5	70.3 / 73.5 [i]
Intentional homicide rate (per 100 000 pop.)	2.1	1.2	1.2 [c]
Seats held by women in the National Parliament (%)	32.5	33.3	41.7 [m]

Environment and infrastructure indicators

	2010	2015	2022
Individuals using the Internet (per 100 inhabitants)	51.9 [n]	70.4 [o]	81.4 [b]
Research & Development expenditure (% of GDP)	0.2	0.4	0.4 [b]
Threatened species (number)	90	100	148
Forested area (% of land area) [i]	38.1	39.4	39.7 [c]
CO2 emission estimates (million tons/tons per capita)	8.5 / 4.0	7.3 / 3.4	7.3 / 3.4 [b]
Energy production, primary (Petajoules)	68	58	51 [c]
Energy supply per capita (Gigajoules)	58	56	58 [c]
Tourist/visitor arrivals at national borders (000)	262	486	118 [b]
Important sites for terrestrial biodiversity protected (%)	24.4	24.4	24.4 [d]
Pop. using safely managed drinking water (urban/rural, %)	84.7 / 74.5	84.6 / 74.6	84.6 / 65.9 [b]
Pop. using safely managed sanitation (urban/rural %)	9.3 / 17.2	8.7 / 17.6	8.2 / 17.9 [b]
Net Official Development Assist. received (% of GNI)	2.09	2.20	2.39 [b]

a Projected estimate (medium fertility variant). b 2020. c 2019. d 2021. e Excludes irrigation canals and landscaping care. f Data classified according to ISIC Rev. 4. g Excludes publishing activities. h Includes publishing activities and landscape care. Excludes repair of personal and household goods. i Estimate. j Data refers to a 5-year period preceding the reference year. k Data as at the end of December. l 2018. m Data are as at 1 January of reporting year. n Population aged 15 to 74 years. o Users in the last 3 months.

Northern Mariana Islands

Region	Micronesia	Population (000, 2022)	50[a,b]
Surface area (km2)	457[c]	Pop. density (per km2, 2022)	108.4[a,b]
Sex ratio (m per 100 f)	116.2[a,b]	Capital city	Garapan
National currency	US Dollar (USD)	Capital city pop. (000, 2022)	4.0[d]

Economic indicators

	2010	2015	2022
Unemployment rate (% of labour force)	11.2[e,f]	...	...
Labour force participation rate (female/male pop. %)	66.6 / 77.6[e,f]	... / ...	... / ...
International trade: exports (million current US$)[g]	1 453	1 685	2 011[h]
International trade: imports (million current US$)[g]	2 867	4 215	6 690[h]
International trade: balance (million current US$)	- 1 414[g]	- 2 530[g]	- 4 678[h]

Major trading partners

					2021
Export partners (% of exports)[g]	Republic of Korea	42.7	Iceland	22.4	Other Asia, nes	11.3
Import partners (% of imports)[g]	Singapore	52.4	Japan	15.5	Republic of Korea	15.0

Social indicators

	2010	2015	2022
Population growth rate (average annual %)[a]	- 5.5	- 0.7	0.5[b]
Urban population (% of total population)	90.9	91.4	91.7[i]
Urban population growth rate (average annual %)[j]	- 3.1	0.2	...
Fertility rate, total (live births per woman)[a]	2.9	2.5	2.1[b]
Life expectancy at birth (females/males, years)[a]	79.4 / 75.8	78.8 / 75.3	79.5 / 75.9[b]
Population age distribution (0-14/60+ years old, %)[a]	27.3 / 6.0	24.2 / 9.9	21.2 / 18.8[b]
International migrant stock (000/% of total pop.)	24.2 / 44.8	21.6 / 38.8	21.8 / 38.0[c]
Infant mortality rate (per 1 000 live births)[a]	5.7	7.3	5.9[b]

Environment and infrastructure indicators

	2010	2015	2022
Threatened species (number)	85	99	109
Forested area (% of land area)	65.9	64.1	53.0[i]
Energy supply per capita (Gigajoules)[g]	138	139	134[i]
Tourist/visitor arrivals at national borders (000)[k]	375	475	87[c]
Important sites for terrestrial biodiversity protected (%)	40.6	40.6	40.6[h]

a For statistical purposes, the data for United States of America do not include this area. b Projected estimate (medium fertility variant). c 2020. d 2010. e Population aged 16 years and over. f Break in the time series. g Estimate. h 2021. i 2019. j Data refers to a 5-year period preceding the reference year. k Arrivals by air.

Norway

Region	Northern Europe	UN membership date	27 November 1945
Population (000, 2022)	5 434[a,b]	Surface area (km2)	323 772[c]
Pop. density (per km2, 2022)	17.9[a,b]	Sex ratio (m per 100 f)	101.9[a,b]
Capital city	Oslo	National currency	Norwegian Krone (NOK)
Capital city pop. (000, 2022)	1 026.8[d]	Exchange rate (per US$)	8.8[e]

Economic indicators

	2010	2015	2022
GDP: Gross domestic product (million current US$)	428 757	385 802	362 522[c]
GDP growth rate (annual %, const. 2015 prices)	0.7	2.0	- 0.8[c]
GDP per capita (current US$)	87 754.3	74 194.9	66 870.7[c]
Economy: Agriculture (% of Gross Value Added)[f,g]	1.8	1.7	2.1[c]
Economy: Industry (% of Gross Value Added)[g,h]	39.0	34.8	29.4[c]
Economy: Services and other activity (% of GVA)[g,i]	59.2	63.4	68.5[c]
Employment in agriculture (% of employed)	2.5	2.0	2.0[j,c]
Employment in industry (% of employed)	19.7	20.1	19.1[j,c]
Employment in services & other sectors (% employed)	77.8	77.9	78.9[j,c]
Unemployment rate (% of labour force)	3.5	4.3	4.8[j]
Labour force participation rate (female/male pop. %)	61.8 / 69.6	62.3 / 67.7	61.2 / 71.8[j]
CPI: Consumer Price Index (2010=100)	100	109	126[e]
Agricultural production index (2014-2016=100)	97	100	100[c]
International trade: exports (million current US$)	130 657	103 785	161 687[e]
International trade: imports (million current US$)	77 330	76 399	99 193[e]
International trade: balance (million current US$)	53 327	27 386	62 493[e]
Balance of payments, current account (million US$)	50 258	31 106	73 459[e]

Major trading partners

							2021
Export partners (% of exports)	United Kingdom	20.5	Germany	19.1	Netherlands	7.9
Import partners (% of imports)	China	13.2	Sweden	11.3	Germany	11.1

Social indicators

	2010	2015	2022
Population growth rate (average annual %)[b]	1.3	0.9	0.7[a]
Urban population (% of total population)[b]	79.1	81.1	82.6[d]
Urban population growth rate (average annual %)[b,k]	1.4	1.7	...
Fertility rate, total (live births per woman)[b]	1.9	1.7	1.5[a]
Life expectancy at birth (females/males, years)[b]	83.2 / 78.8	84.1 / 80.4	85.1 / 81.7[a]
Population age distribution (0-14/60+ years old, %)[b]	18.8 / 21.0	18.0 / 21.9	16.7 / 24.2[a]
International migrant stock (000/% of total pop.)[b]	524.6[l] / 10.7	746.4 / 14.4	852.1 / 15.7[c]
Refugees and others of concern to the UNHCR (000)	55.9[l]	54.9	50.4[e]
Infant mortality rate (per 1 000 live births)[b]	2.8	2.3	1.9[a]
Health: Current expenditure (% of GDP)	8.9	10.1	10.5[d]
Health: Physicians (per 1 000 pop.)	4.1	4.4	5.0[c]
Education: Government expenditure (% of GDP)	6.7	7.6	7.6[m]
Education: Primary gross enrol. ratio (f/m per 100 pop.)	99.2 / 98.9	99.8 / 100.0	100.2 / 100.2[d]
Education: Sec. gross enrol. ratio (f/m per 100 pop.)	111.7 / 113.5	113.2 / 116.0	115.6 / 121.5[d]
Education: Upr. Sec. gross enrol. ratio (f/m per 100 pop.)	124.1 / 127.8	122.1 / 129.4	125.8 / 137.0[d]
Intentional homicide rate (per 100 000 pop.)	0.6	0.5	0.6[c]
Seats held by women in the National Parliament (%)	39.6	39.6	45.0[n]

Environment and infrastructure indicators

	2010	2015	2022
Individuals using the Internet (per 100 inhabitants)	93.4[o]	96.8[p]	97.0[c]
Research & Development expenditure (% of GDP)	1.6	1.9	2.3[c]
Threatened species (number)	36	44	134
Forested area (% of land area)	33.1	33.2	33.3[d]
CO2 emission estimates (million tons/tons per capita)	40.7 / 8.2	38.7 / 7.3	36.8 / 6.7[c]
Energy production, primary (Petajoules)[b]	8 672	8 689	8 188[d]
Energy supply per capita (Gigajoules)[b]	277	234	216[d]
Tourist/visitor arrivals at national borders (000)	4 767[q]	5 361[r]	1 397[t,c]
Important sites for terrestrial biodiversity protected (%)	51.0	53.6	56.5[e]
Net Official Development Assist. disbursed (% of GNI)[s]	1.41	1.12	1.11[c]

a Projected estimate (medium fertility variant). b Including Svalbard and Jan Mayen Islands. c 2020. d 2019. e 2021. f Excludes irrigation canals and landscaping care. g Data classified according to ISIC Rev. 4. h Excludes publishing activities. Includes irrigation and canals. i Includes publishing activities and landscape care. Excludes repair of personal and household goods. j Estimate. k Data refers to a 5-year period preceding the reference year. l Data as at the end of December. m 2018. n Data are as at 1 January of reporting year. o Population aged 16 to 74 years. p Users in the last 3 months. q Arrivals of non-resident tourists at national borders. r Non-resident tourists staying in all types of accommodation establishments. s DAC member (OECD).

Oman

Region	Western Asia	UN membership date	07 October 1971
Population (000, 2022)	4 576[a]	Surface area (km2)	309 980[b]
Pop. density (per km2, 2022)	14.8[a]	Sex ratio (m per 100 f)	155.5[a]
Capital city	Muscat	National currency	Rial Omani (OMR)
Capital city pop. (000, 2022)	1 501.6[c,d]	Exchange rate (per US$)	0.4[e]

Economic indicators

	2010	2015	2022
GDP: Gross domestic product (million current US$)	56 913	68 400	63 368[b]
GDP growth rate (annual %, const. 2015 prices)	1.7	4.6	- 2.8[b]
GDP per capita (current US$)	18 712.6	16 028.6	12 408.9[b]
Economy: Agriculture (% of Gross Value Added)[f]	1.4	1.9	2.2[b]
Economy: Industry (% of Gross Value Added)[f]	62.6	50.6	50.9[b]
Economy: Services and other activity (% of GVA)[f]	36.0	47.5	47.0[b]
Employment in agriculture (% of employed)	5.2	4.9[g]	4.4[g,b]
Employment in industry (% of employed)	36.9	33.6[g]	32.8[g,b]
Employment in services & other sectors (% employed)	58.0	61.4[g]	62.7[g,b]
Unemployment rate (% of labour force)[g]	4.0	3.4	3.1
Labour force participation rate (female/male pop. %)[g]	27.8 / 84.9	29.5 / 87.6	30.2 / 86.9
CPI: Consumer Price Index (2010=100)	100	109	114[e]
Agricultural production index (2014-2016=100)	84	101	153[b]
International trade: exports (million current US$)	36 600	35 686	43 092[g,e]
International trade: imports (million current US$)	19 775	29 007	24 633[g,e]
International trade: balance (million current US$)	16 825	6 679	18 460[e]
Balance of payments, current account (million US$)	4 634	- 10 954	- 8 660[b]

Major trading partners

						2021
Export partners (% of exports)[g]	China	49.2	India	10.0	Republic of Korea	4.9
Import partners (% of imports)[g]	United Arab Emirates	38.0	China	10.1	India	7.1

Social indicators

	2010	2015	2022
Population growth rate (average annual %)	11.2	5.1	1.4[a]
Urban population (% of total population)	75.2	81.4	85.4[d]
Urban population growth rate (average annual %)[h]	4.6	8.0	...
Fertility rate, total (live births per woman)	2.9	3.0	2.6[a]
Life expectancy at birth (females/males, years)	78.5 / 74.6	79.5 / 76.3	76.0 / 72.4[a]
Population age distribution (0-14/60+ years old, %)	26.9 / 3.9	22.3 / 3.9	27.0 / 4.5[a]
International migrant stock (000/% of total pop.)[i,j]	816.2 / 26.8	1 856.2 / 43.5	2 372.8 / 46.5[b]
Refugees and others of concern to the UNHCR (000)	0.1[k]	0.4	0.6[e]
Infant mortality rate (per 1 000 live births)	10.0	9.6	8.6[a]
Health: Current expenditure (% of GDP)[l]	2.8	4.3	4.1[g,d]
Health: Physicians (per 1 000 pop.)	1.9	2.1	1.8[b]
Education: Government expenditure (% of GDP)	4.2[m]	5.0[n]	5.4[g,d]
Education: Primary gross enrol. ratio (f/m per 100 pop.)	100.8 / 105.4[m]	110.7 / 106.0	107.8 / 101.4[b]
Education: Sec. gross enrol. ratio (f/m per 100 pop.)	97.2 / 102.3[m]	102.4 / 104.2	102.6 / 111.6[b]
Education: Upr. Sec. gross enrol. ratio (f/m per 100 pop.)	92.8 / 93.1[m]	98.3 / 98.6	96.5 / 130.5[b]
Intentional homicide rate (per 100 000 pop.)	1.6	0.4	0.3[b]
Seats held by women in the National Parliament (%)	0.0	1.2	2.3[o]

Environment and infrastructure indicators

	2010	2015	2022
Individuals using the Internet (per 100 inhabitants)	35.8[p]	73.5[g]	95.2[b]
Research & Development expenditure (% of GDP)	...	0.3	0.4[b]
Threatened species (number)	79	90	142
Forested area (% of land area)	~0.0	~0.0	~0.0[g,d]
CO2 emission estimates (million tons/tons per capita)	42.8 / 14.0	64.2 / 14.9	69.5 / 13.9[d]
Energy production, primary (Petajoules)	2 793	3 228	3 448[d]
Energy supply per capita (Gigajoules)	271	258	205[d]
Tourist/visitor arrivals at national borders (000)	1 441	1 909	622[b]
Important sites for terrestrial biodiversity protected (%)	19.8	22.8	23.3[e]
Net Official Development Assist. received (% of GNI)	- 0.04	...	...

a Projected estimate (medium fertility variant). b 2020. c Refers to Muscat governorate. d 2019. e 2021. f Data classified according to ISIC Rev. 4. g Estimate. h Data refers to a 5-year period preceding the reference year. i Refers to foreign citizens. j Including refugees. k Data as at the end of December. l Data based on calendar year (January 1 to December 31). m 2009. n 2013. o Data are as at 1 January of reporting year. p Population aged 5 years and over.

Pakistan

Region	Southern Asia	UN membership date	30 September 1947
Population (000, 2022)	235 825 [a]	Surface area (km2)	796 095 [b]
Pop. density (per km2, 2022)	305.9 [a]	Sex ratio (m per 100 f)	101.8 [a]
Capital city	Islamabad	National currency	Pakistan Rupee (PKR)
Capital city pop. (000, 2022)	1 095.1 [c]	Exchange rate (per US$)	176.5 [d]

Economic indicators

	2010	2015	2022
GDP: Gross domestic product (million current US$)	174 508	267 035	257 829 [b]
GDP growth rate (annual %, const. 2015 prices)	1.6	4.7	0.5 [b]
GDP per capita (current US$)	972.6	1 339.0	1 167.2 [b]
Economy: Agriculture (% of Gross Value Added) [e,f]	24.3	25.1	24.4 [b]
Economy: Industry (% of Gross Value Added) [f,g]	20.6	20.1	19.0 [b]
Economy: Services and other activity (% of GVA) [f,h]	55.1	54.9	56.7 [b]
Employment in agriculture (% of employed)	43.4	41.0	35.9 [i,b]
Employment in industry (% of employed)	21.4	24.0	25.8 [i,b]
Employment in services & other sectors (% employed)	35.2	35.0	38.3 [i,b]
Unemployment rate (% of labour force)	0.6	3.6	4.2 [i]
Labour force participation (female/male pop. %)	22.0 / 78.6	23.9 / 78.8	21.0 / 78.5 [i]
CPI: Consumer Price Index (2010=100)	100 [j]	145	219 [d]
Agricultural production index (2014-2016=100)	81	99	114 [b]
International trade: exports (million current US$)	21 413	22 089	28 795 [d]
International trade: imports (million current US$)	37 537	43 990	72 892 [d]
International trade: balance (million current US$)	- 16 124	- 21 901	- 44 096 [d]
Balance of payments, current account (million US$)	- 1 354	- 2 803	- 12 262 [d]

Major trading partners

					2021
Export partners (% of exports)	United States	21.1	China	10.5	United Kingdom 7.3
Import partners (% of imports)	China	28.3	United Arab Emirates	10.1	Indonesia 5.8

Social indicators

	2010	2015	2022
Population growth rate (average annual %)	2.2	1.2	2.0 [a]
Urban population (% of total population)	35.0	36.0	36.9 [c]
Urban population growth rate (average annual %) [k]	2.6	2.7	...
Fertility rate, total (live births per woman)	4.3	3.9	3.4 [a]
Life expectancy at birth (females/males, years)	66.9 / 62.3	68.2 / 63.5	68.9 / 64.1 [a]
Population age distribution (0-14/60+ years old, %)	39.2 / 5.7	38.4 / 6.0	36.6 / 6.8 [a]
International migrant stock (000/% of total pop.) [l]	3 943.7 / 2.2	3 506.5 / 1.8	3 276.6 / 1.5 [b]
Refugees and others of concern to the UNHCR (000)	4 151.0 [m]	3 440.0	1 547.7 [d]
Infant mortality rate (per 1 000 live births)	70.5	62.1	51.8 [a]
Health: Current expenditure (% of GDP) [n,o]	2.6	2.7	3.4 [i,c]
Health: Physicians (per 1 000 pop.)	0.8	0.9	1.1 [c]
Education: Government expenditure (% of GDP)	2.3	2.6	2.5 [c]
Education: Primary gross enrol. ratio (f/m per 100 pop.)	77.6 / 91.0	78.3 / 91.4	89.2 / 101.3 [c]
Education: Sec. gross enrol. ratio (f/m per 100 pop.)	28.8 / 37.3	34.9 / 44.0	41.6 / 47.9 [c]
Education: Upr. Sec. gross enrol. ratio (f/m per 100 pop.)	21.8 / 29.0	27.4 / 36.2	34.0 / 39.7 [c]
Intentional homicide rate (per 100 000 pop.)	7.4	4.8	3.8 [b]
Seats held by women in the National Parliament (%)	22.2	20.7	20.5 [p]

Environment and infrastructure indicators

	2010	2015	2022
Individuals using the Internet (per 100 inhabitants) [i]	8.0	11.0	25.0 [b]
Research & Development expenditure (% of GDP)	0.4 [q,r,s]	0.2 [q,r]	0.2 [c]
Threatened species (number)	109	129	221
Forested area (% of land area) [i]	5.3	5.1	4.9 [c]
CO2 emission estimates (million tons/tons per capita)	140.3 / 0.7	163.3 / 0.8	188.4 / 0.8 [c]
Energy production, primary (Petajoules)	2 252	2 302	2 366 [c]
Energy supply per capita (Gigajoules)	17	17	18 [c]
Tourist/visitor arrivals at national borders (000)	907	966 [t]	...
Important sites for terrestrial biodiversity protected (%)	34.8	34.8	34.8 [d]
Pop. using safely managed drinking water (urban/rural, %)	45.7 / 32.3	42.2 / 32.8	40.2 / 33.3 [b]
Net Official Development Assist. received (% of GNI)	1.69	1.01	1.00 [b]

a Projected estimate (medium fertility variant). b 2020. c 2019. d 2021. e Excludes irrigation canals and landscaping care. f Data classified according to ISIC Rev. 4. g Excludes publishing activities. Includes irrigation and canals. h Includes publishing activities and landscape care. Excludes repair of personal and household goods. i Estimate. j Break in the time series. k Data refers to a 5-year period preceding the reference year. l Including refugees. m Data as at the end of December. n Data refer to fiscal years beginning 1 July. o Health expenditure data for even years (2006, 2008, 2010, 2012, 2014, 2016 and 2018) are based on SHA 1.0 health accounts produced by the country, adjusted to separate current health expenditure from capital health expenditure. p Data are as at 1 January of reporting year. q Excluding business enterprise. r Excluding private non-profit. s 2009. t 2012.

Palau

Region	Micronesia	UN membership date	15 December 1994	
Population (000, 2022)	18[a]	Surface area (km2)	459[b]	
Pop. density (per km2, 2022)	39.2[a]	Sex ratio (m per 100 f)	108.0[a]	
Capital city	Melekeok	National currency	US Dollar (USD)	
Capital city pop. (000, 2022)	11.4[c,d]			

Economic indicators

	2010	2015	2022
GDP: Gross domestic product (million current US$)	184	279	264[b]
GDP growth rate (annual %, const. 2015 prices)	0.1	5.0	- 9.7[b]
GDP per capita (current US$)	10 230.6	15 784.0	14 566.9[b]
Economy: Agriculture (% of Gross Value Added)[e,f]	4.2	3.3	3.3[b]
Economy: Industry (% of Gross Value Added)[f,g]	11.0	8.9	14.4[b]
Economy: Services and other activity (% of GVA)[f,h]	84.8	87.8	82.3[b]
Employment in agriculture (% of employed)	2.4[i,j,k]	...	...
Employment in industry (% of employed)	11.8[i,j,k]	...	...
Employment in services & other sectors (% employed)	85.9[i,j,k]	...	...
Unemployment rate (% of labour force)	4.2[i,l]	...	...
Labour force participation rate (female/male pop. %)	58.1 / 75.4[i,l]	... / ...	... / ...
CPI: Consumer Price Index (2010=100)	100	118	125[m]
International trade: exports (million current US$)	12[n]	6	4[n,m]
International trade: imports (million current US$)	107	150	217[n,m]
International trade: balance (million current US$)	- 96	- 144	- 213[m]
Balance of payments, current account (million US$)	- 19	- 24	- 52[o]

Major trading partners

						2021
Export partners (% of exports)[n]	Japan	31.5	Türkiye	16.6	Other Asia, nes	15.8
Import partners (% of imports)[n]	China	32.3	United States	23.5	Japan	8.3

Social indicators

	2010	2015	2022
Population growth rate (average annual %)	- 1.6	0.1	~0.0[a]
Urban population (% of total population)	74.8	78.2	80.5[p]
Urban population growth rate (average annual %)[q]	1.6	1.7	...
Fertility rate, total (live births per woman)	2.0	2.1	2.4[a]
Life expectancy at birth (females/males, years)	68.7 / 63.0	66.7 / 61.3	69.3 / 62.2[a]
Population age distribution (0-14/60+ years old, %)	21.3 / 9.8	20.6 / 12.2	21.0 / 15.6[a]
International migrant stock (000/% of total pop.)	5.5 / 30.6	4.9 / 27.9	5.1 / 28.1[b]
Refugees and others of concern to the UNHCR (000)	...	~0.0	~0.0[o]
Infant mortality rate (per 1 000 live births)	20.8	17.9	14.6[a]
Health: Current expenditure (% of GDP)[r,s]	11.5	11.4	15.2[p]
Health: Physicians (per 1 000 pop.)	1.6	1.4[l]	1.8[b]
Education: Primary gross enrol. ratio (f/m per 100 pop.)	... / ...	105.2 / 119.6[t]	106.1 / 98.9[b]
Education: Sec. gross enrol. ratio (f/m per 100 pop.)	... / ...	122.9 / 110.8[t]	158.0 / 157.4[b]
Education: Upr. Sec. gross enrol. ratio (f/m per 100 pop.)	89.4 / 86.0[u]	129.8 / 112.9[t]	171.5 / 173.6[b]
Intentional homicide rate (per 100 000 pop.)	...	17.0	11.2[d]
Seats held by women in the National Parliament (%)	0.0	0.0	6.3[v]

Environment and infrastructure indicators

	2010	2015	2022
Threatened species (number)	128	177	197
Forested area (% of land area)[n]	88.2	89.1	89.8[p]
Energy production, primary (Petajoules)	...	...	0[p]
Energy supply per capita (Gigajoules)	161	160[n]	169[n,p]
Tourist/visitor arrivals at national borders (000)[w]	85	162	18[b]
Important sites for terrestrial biodiversity protected (%)	42.7	48.1	48.1[m]
Pop. using safely managed drinking water (urban/rural, %)	84.9 / 62.8	93.0 / 68.2	96.2 / 70.3[b]
Net Official Development Assist. received (% of GNI)	14.24	4.61	8.72[p]

a Projected estimate (medium fertility variant). b 2020. c Refers to Koror. d 2018. e Excludes irrigation canals and landscaping care. f Data classified according to ISIC Rev. 4. g Excludes publishing activities. Includes irrigation and canals. h Includes publishing activities and landscape care. Excludes repair of personal and household goods. i Population aged 16 years and over. j Data classified according to ISIC Rev. 3. k 2008. l 2005. m 2021. n Estimate. o 2017. p 2019. q Data refers to a 5-year period preceding the reference year. r Data refer to fiscal years beginning 1 October. s Data revision. t 2014. u 2007. v Data are as at 1 January of reporting year. w Air arrivals (Palau International Airport).

Panama

Region	Central America	UN membership date		13 November 1945
Population (000, 2022)	4 409 a	Surface area (km2)		75 320 b
Pop. density (per km2, 2022)	59.4 a	Sex ratio (m per 100 f)		100.0 a
Capital city	Panama City	National currency		Balboa (PAB)
Capital city pop. (000, 2022)	1 821.7 c,d	Exchange rate (per US$)		1.0 e

Economic indicators

	2010	2015	2022
GDP: Gross domestic product (million current US$)	29 440	54 092	52 938 b
GDP growth rate (annual %, const. 2015 prices)	5.8	5.7	- 17.9 b
GDP per capita (current US$)	8 082.0	13 630.3	12 269.0 b
Economy: Agriculture (% of Gross Value Added) f	3.8	2.9	2.8 b
Economy: Industry (% of Gross Value Added) f	20.1	28.7	24.2 b
Economy: Services and other activity (% of GVA) f	76.2	68.4	72.9 b
Employment in agriculture (% of employed)	17.4	14.7	13.7 g,b
Employment in industry (% of employed)	18.7	18.7	18.8 g,b
Employment in services & other sectors (% employed)	63.9	66.6	67.5 g,b
Unemployment rate (% of labour force)	3.7	3.0	11.7 g
Labour force participation rate (female/male pop. %)	45.5 / 77.9	49.3 / 76.4	52.8 / 74.6 g
CPI: Consumer Price Index (2010=100) h	100	120	122 e
Agricultural production index (2014-2016=100)	90	100	107 b
International trade: exports (million current US$) i	10 987	11 348	3 782 e
International trade: imports (million current US$) i	16 737	10 375	13 313 e
International trade: balance (million current US$) i	- 5 751	973	- 9 531 e
Balance of payments, current account (million US$)	- 3 113	- 4 848	- 1 412 e

Major trading partners

						2021
Export partners (% of exports)	China	31.7	Japan	13.2	Republic of Korea	10.2
Import partners (% of imports)	United States	25.5	Free Zones	22.9	China	11.9

Social indicators

	2010	2015	2022
Population growth rate (average annual %)	1.8	1.7	1.3 a
Urban population (% of total population)	65.1	66.7	68.1 d
Urban population growth rate (average annual %) j	2.2	2.2	...
Fertility rate, total (live births per woman)	2.6	2.6	2.3 a
Life expectancy at birth (females/males, years)	79.7 / 73.3	80.5 / 74.5	80.1 / 73.7 a
Population age distribution (0-14/60+ years old, %)	29.2 / 9.4	28.0 / 10.6	26.1 / 12.7 a
International migrant stock (000/% of total pop.) k	157.8 / 4.3	184.7 / 4.7	313.2 / 7.3 b
Refugees and others of concern to the UNHCR (000)	17.6 l	19.3	136.0 e
Infant mortality rate (per 1 000 live births)	16.9	15.1	12.7 a
Health: Current expenditure (% of GDP) g,m	7.1	6.8	7.6 d
Health: Physicians (per 1 000 pop.)	1.4	1.6	1.6 d
Education: Government expenditure (% of GDP)	3.5 n	2.8 g	3.1 g,d
Education: Primary gross enrol. ratio (f/m per 100 pop.)	103.1 / 107.0	94.9 / 97.2	93.0 / 93.5 b
Education: Sec. gross enrol. ratio (f/m per 100 pop.)	73.5 / 69.2	77.9 / 73.9	79.5 / 77.5 b
Education: Upr. Sec. gross enrol. ratio (f/m per 100 pop.)	56.3 / 48.3	62.5 / 55.3	72.3 / 67.0 b
Intentional homicide rate (per 100 000 pop.)	12.6	11.9	11.6 b
Seats held by women in the National Parliament (%)	8.5	19.3	22.5 o

Environment and infrastructure indicators

	2010	2015	2022
Individuals using the Internet (per 100 inhabitants)	40.1 p	51.2	64.2 g,b
Research & Development expenditure (% of GDP)	0.1	0.1	0.1 q
Threatened species (number)	347	373	514
Forested area (% of land area)	58.2 g	57.6	57.0 d
CO2 emission estimates (million tons/tons per capita)	8.8 / 2.4	10.1 / 2.5	12.8 / 3.0 d
Energy production, primary (Petajoules)	26	36	34 d
Energy supply per capita (Gigajoules)	39	43	49 d
Tourist/visitor arrivals at national borders (000)	1 324	2 110	414 b
Important sites for terrestrial biodiversity protected (%)	55.3	55.3	55.9 e
Net Official Development Assist. received (% of GNI)	0.48	0.02	0.80 b

a Projected estimate (medium fertility variant). b 2020. c Refers to the metropolitan area of Panama City. d 2019. e 2021. f Data classified according to ISIC Rev. 4. g Estimate. h Urban areas. i From 2004 to 2020 merchandise data including Zona Libre de Colon. j Data refers to a 5-year period preceding the reference year. k Including refugees. l Data as at the end of December. m Data based on calendar year (January 1 to December 31). n 2008. o Data are as at 1 January of reporting year. p Multipliers were applied to residential and commercial subscriptions, taking into account the average size of households and employees per business. q 2017.

Papua New Guinea

Region	Melanesia	UN membership date	10 October 1975	
Population (000, 2022)	10 143[a]	Surface area (km2)	462 840[b]	
Pop. density (per km2, 2022)	22.4[a]	Sex ratio (m per 100 f)	106.6[a]	
Capital city	Port Moresby	National currency	Kina (PGK)	
Capital city pop. (000, 2022)	374.5[c]	Exchange rate (per US$)	3.5[d]	

Economic indicators

	2010	2015	2022
GDP: Gross domestic product (million current US$)	14 251	21 723	23 619[b]
GDP growth rate (annual %, const. 2015 prices)	10.1	6.6	- 3.9[b]
GDP per capita (current US$)	1 949.4	2 679.3	2 639.9[b]
Economy: Agriculture (% of Gross Value Added)[e,f]	20.2	18.3	18.2[b]
Economy: Industry (% of Gross Value Added)[e,g]	34.2	36.4	38.1[b]
Economy: Services and other activity (% of GVA)[e,h]	45.5	45.3	43.7[b]
Employment in agriculture (% of employed)[i]	66.4	61.3	57.8[b]
Employment in industry (% of employed)[i]	4.8	6.4	6.7[b]
Employment in services & other sectors (% employed)[i]	28.8	32.3	35.5[b]
Unemployment rate (% of labour force)	2.0	2.5[i]	2.6[i]
Labour force participation rate (female/male pop. %)	47.7 / 49.0	47.0 / 48.6[i]	46.4 / 48.2[i]
CPI: Consumer Price Index (2010=100)	100[j]	128	171[d]
Agricultural production index (2014-2016=100)	90	100	102[b]
International trade: exports (million current US$)[i]	5 742	8 425	9 139[d]
International trade: imports (million current US$)[i]	3 950	2 537	5 329[d]
International trade: balance (million current US$)	1 792[i]	5 888[i]	3 811[d]
Balance of payments, current account (million US$)	- 642	4 407	5 451[k]

Major trading partners

						2021
Export partners (% of exports)[i]	Japan	25.0	China	24.6	Australia	14.1
Import partners (% of imports)[i]	Australia	25.8	China	22.2	Singapore	19.0

Social indicators

	2010	2015	2022
Population growth rate (average annual %)	3.0	2.5	1.9[a]
Urban population (% of total population)	13.0	13.0	13.2[c]
Urban population growth rate (average annual %)[l]	2.2	2.2	...
Fertility rate, total (live births per woman)	3.9	3.6	3.2[a]
Life expectancy at birth (females/males, years)	65.3 / 61.3	67.8 / 62.3	69.2 / 63.4[a]
Population age distribution (0-14/60+ years old, %)	37.9 / 4.3	36.5 / 4.6	34.2 / 5.5[a]
International migrant stock (000/% of total pop.)[m,n]	30.4 / 0.4	30.9 / 0.4	31.1 / 0.3[b]
Refugees and others of concern to the UNHCR (000)	9.7[o]	9.9	26.0[d]
Infant mortality rate (per 1 000 live births)	44.9	40.0	33.8[a]
Health: Current expenditure (% of GDP)	2.1	1.8	2.3[c]
Health: Physicians (per 1 000 pop.)	0.1	...	0.1[c]
Education: Government expenditure (% of GDP)	...	...	1.9[i,k]
Education: Primary gross enrol. ratio (f/m per 100 pop.)	54.3 / 61.4[p]	95.7 / 107.7[q]	111.8 / 119.9[k]
Education: Sec. gross enrol. ratio (f/m per 100 pop.)	... / ...	33.0 / 44.0[q]	41.6 / 52.0[k]
Education: Upr. Sec. gross enrol. ratio (f/m per 100 pop.)	... / ...	17.2 / 25.4[q]	15.6 / 23.1[k]
Intentional homicide rate (per 100 000 pop.)	9.8	...	...
Seats held by women in the National Parliament (%)	0.9	2.7	0.0[r]

Environment and infrastructure indicators

	2010	2015	2022
Individuals using the Internet (per 100 inhabitants)	1.3[s]	7.9[i]	11.2[i,t]
Research & Development expenditure (% of GDP)	...	...	~0.0[u,v,w]
Threatened species (number)	453	478	1 088
Forested area (% of land area)[i]	79.9	79.5	79.3[c]
Energy production, primary (Petajoules)	95	240	240[i,c]
Energy supply per capita (Gigajoules)	19	22	23[i,c]
Tourist/visitor arrivals at national borders (000)	140	183	39[b]
Important sites for terrestrial biodiversity protected (%)	7.2	7.2	7.3[d]
Pop. using safely managed sanitation (urban/rural %)	29.8 / ...	29.1 / ...	28.3 / ...[b]
Net Official Development Assist. received (% of GNI)	3.90	2.77	4.56[b]

a Projected estimate (medium fertility variant). **b** 2020. **c** 2019. **d** 2021. **e** Data classified according to ISIC Rev. 4. **f** Excludes irrigation canals and landscaping care. **g** Excludes publishing activities. Includes irrigation and canals. **h** Includes publishing activities and landscape care. Excludes repair of personal and household goods. **i** Estimate. **j** Break in the time series. **k** 2018. **l** Data refers to a 5-year period preceding the reference year. **m** Refers to foreign citizens. **n** Including refugees. **o** Data as at the end of December. **p** 2008. **q** 2012. **r** Data are as at 1 January of reporting year. **s** Population aged 10 years and over. **t** 2017. **u** Partial data. **v** Excluding business enterprise. **w** 2016.

Paraguay

Region	South America	UN membership date	24 October 1945	
Population (000, 2022)	6 781 a	Surface area (km2)	406 752 b	
Pop. density (per km2, 2022)	16.8 a	Sex ratio (m per 100 f)	100.7 a	
Capital city	Asunción	National currency	Guarani (PYG)	
Capital city pop. (000, 2022)	3 279.2 c,d	Exchange rate (per US$)	6 879.1 e	

Economic indicators	2010	2015	2022
GDP: Gross domestic product (million current US$)	27 261	36 211	35 304 b
GDP growth rate (annual %, const. 2015 prices)	11.1	3.0	- 1.0 b
GDP per capita (current US$)	4 363.1	5 413.8	4 949.7 b
Economy: Agriculture (% of Gross Value Added) f,g	14.0	10.2	11.3 b
Economy: Industry (% of Gross Value Added) f,h	37.2	37.3	36.2 b
Economy: Services and other activity (% of GVA) f,i	48.8	52.5	52.5 b
Employment in agriculture (% of employed)	25.6	19.7	19.9 i,b
Employment in industry (% of employed)	19.2	19.7	17.9 j,b
Employment in services & other sectors (% employed)	55.2	60.6	62.1 j,b
Unemployment rate (% of labour force)	4.6	4.6	7.1 j
Labour force participation rate (female/male pop. %)	52.9 / 82.2	54.7 / 80.8	59.8 / 84.0 j
CPI: Consumer Price Index (2010=100) k,l	100	125	153 e
Agricultural production index (2014-2016=100)	81	99	117 b
International trade: exports (million current US$)	6 517	8 328	10 560 e
International trade: imports (million current US$)	10 033	10 291	13 560 e
International trade: balance (million current US$)	- 3 517	- 1 964	- 2 999 e
Balance of payments, current account (million US$)	6	- 78	311 e

Major trading partners						2021
Export partners (% of exports)	Brazil	33.6	Argentina	25.0	Chile	9.5
Import partners (% of imports)	China	30.0	Brazil	23.7	Argentina	9.5

Social indicators	2010	2015	2022
Population growth rate (average annual %)	1.3	1.4	1.1 a
Urban population (% of total population)	59.3	60.8	61.9 d
Urban population growth rate (average annual %) m	1.9	1.8	...
Fertility rate, total (live births per woman)	2.7	2.6	2.4 a
Life expectancy at birth (females/males, years)	74.8 / 69.2	76.0 / 70.5	73.6 / 67.6 a
Population age distribution (0-14/60+ years old, %)	33.0 / 7.5	30.5 / 8.2	28.9 / 9.4 a
International migrant stock (000/% of total pop.) j,n	160.3 / 2.6	156.5 / 2.3	169.6 / 2.4 b
Refugees and others of concern to the UNHCR (000)	0.1 o	0.2	6.7 e
Infant mortality rate (per 1 000 live births)	21.7	18.6	16.4 a
Health: Current expenditure (% of GDP) j,p,q	5.5	6.7	7.2 d
Health: Physicians (per 1 000 pop.)	...	1.3 r	1.1 b
Education: Government expenditure (% of GDP)	2.8	3.3 j	3.5 j,d
Education: Primary gross enrol. ratio (f/m per 100 pop.)	100.9 / 104.3	103.0 / 105.7 r	83.6 / 85.6 b
Education: Sec. gross enrol. ratio (f/m per 100 pop.)	69.8 / 65.7	78.6 / 73.3 r	79.7 / 74.1 b
Education: Upr. Sec. gross enrol. ratio (f/m per 100 pop.)	58.7 / 53.9	71.8 / 64.9 r	79.6 / 70.4 b
Intentional homicide rate (per 100 000 pop.)	11.9	9.2	6.7 b
Seats held by women in the National Parliament (%)	12.5	15.0	17.5 s

Environment and infrastructure indicators	2010	2015	2022
Individuals using the Internet (per 100 inhabitants)	19.8 t,u	49.7	74.0 b
Research & Development expenditure (% of GDP)	~0.0 v	0.1 w	0.1 w,d
Threatened species (number)	48	58	75
Forested area (% of land area) j	49.3	44.0	41.2 d
CO2 emission estimates (million tons/tons per capita)	5.3 / 0.8	6.6 / 0.9	8.5 / 1.1 d
Energy production, primary (Petajoules)	352	350	309 d
Energy supply per capita (Gigajoules)	41	42	43 d
Tourist/visitor arrivals at national borders (000) x,y	465	1 215	252 b
Important sites for terrestrial biodiversity protected (%)	36.2	36.3	36.3 e
Pop. using safely managed drinking water (urban/rural, %)	70.3 / 40.8	71.6 / 47.7	72.2 / 50.7 b
Pop. using safely managed sanitation (urban/rural %)	51.8 / 54.1	52.8 / 62.6	53.7 / 70.7 b
Net Official Development Assist. received (% of GNI)	0.43	0.17	0.89 b

a Projected estimate (medium fertility variant). b 2020. c Refers to the district of Asunción and the 19 districts of Central Department. d 2019. e 2021. f Data classified according to ISIC Rev. 4. g Excludes irrigation canals and landscaping care. h Excludes publishing activities. Includes irrigation and canals. i Includes publishing activities and landscape care. Excludes repair of personal and household goods. j Estimate. k Calculated by the UNSD from national indices. l For Greater Asuncion only. m Data refers to a 5-year period preceding the reference year. n Including refugees. o Data as at the end of December. p Data are based on SHA2011. q Data based on calendar year (January 1 to December 31). r 2012. s Data are as at 1 January of reporting year. t Population aged 10 years and over. u Users in the last 3 months. v 2008. w Excluding business enterprise. x Excluding nationals residing abroad and crew members. y E/D cards in the "Silvio Petirossi" airport and passenger counts at the national border crossings - National Police and SENATUR.

Peru

Region	South America
Population (000, 2022)	34 050[a]
Pop. density (per km2, 2022)	26.6[a]
Capital city	Lima
Capital city pop. (000, 2022)	10 554.7[c,d]

UN membership date	31 October 1945
Surface area (km2)	1 285 216[b]
Sex ratio (m per 100 f)	98.0[a]
National currency	Sol (PEN)
Exchange rate (per US$)	4.0[e]

Economic indicators

	2010	2015	2022
GDP: Gross domestic product (million current US$)	147 528	189 803	203 196[b]
GDP growth rate (annual %, const. 2015 prices)	8.3	3.3	- 11.1[b]
GDP per capita (current US$)	5 082.3	6 229.0	6 162.7[b]
Economy: Agriculture (% of Gross Value Added)[f,g]	7.5	7.7	8.2[b]
Economy: Industry (% of Gross Value Added)[f,h]	39.1	33.2	33.1[b]
Economy: Services and other activity (% of GVA)[f,i]	53.5	59.1	58.7[b]
Employment in agriculture (% of employed)	27.7	28.3	27.2[j,b]
Employment in industry (% of employed)	16.9	16.6	15.3[j,b]
Employment in services & other sectors (% employed)	55.4	55.2	57.5[j,b]
Unemployment rate (% of labour force)	3.6	3.3	4.2[j]
Labour force participation rate (female/male pop. %)	72.6 / 87.1	67.7 / 84.4	67.4 / 82.5[j]
CPI: Consumer Price Index (2010=100)[k]	100	118	139[e]
Agricultural production index (2014-2016=100)	84	100	119[b]
International trade: exports (million current US$)	35 807	33 667	57 559[j,e]
International trade: imports (million current US$)	29 966	38 026	47 584[j,e]
International trade: balance (million current US$)	5 842	- 4 359	9 975[e]
Balance of payments, current account (million US$)	- 3 564	- 8 938	- 5 273[e]

Major trading partners

							2021
Export partners (% of exports)[j]	China	28.3	United States	16.1	Canada	6.2
Import partners (% of imports)[j]	China	28.6	United States	18.5	Brazil	5.5

Social indicators

	2010	2015	2022
Population growth rate (average annual %)	0.8	1.2	0.8[a]
Urban population (% of total population)	76.4	77.4	78.1[d]
Urban population growth rate (average annual %)[l]	1.6	1.6	...
Fertility rate, total (live births per woman)	2.6	2.3	2.2[a]
Life expectancy at birth (females/males, years)	75.9 / 71.6	77.7 / 73.6	75.5 / 71.3[a]
Population age distribution (0-14/60+ years old, %)	29.8 / 10.1	28.4 / 11.2	26.0 / 12.0[a]
International migrant stock (000/% of total pop.)[m]	104.7 / 0.4	154.8 / 0.5	1 224.5 / 3.7[b]
Refugees and others of concern to the UNHCR (000)	1.4[n]	1.8	1 557.2[e]
Infant mortality rate (per 1 000 live births)	15.7	12.6	9.7[a]
Health: Current expenditure (% of GDP)[p]	4.7[o]	5.0[q]	5.2[q,d]
Health: Physicians (per 1 000 pop.)	0.9[r]	1.1[s]	1.4[t]
Education: Government expenditure (% of GDP)	2.9	4.0	4.2[b]
Education: Primary gross enrol. ratio (f/m per 100 pop.)	110.0 / 109.8	100.3 / 100.2	118.7 / 123.3[b]
Education: Sec. gross enrol. ratio (f/m per 100 pop.)	93.5 / 91.1	97.4 / 97.8	106.9 / 114.4[b]
Education: Upr. Sec. gross enrol. ratio (f/m per 100 pop.)	80.2 / 73.5	91.4 / 90.9	109.2 / 115.5[b]
Intentional homicide rate (per 100 000 pop.)	...	7.4	7.7[t]
Seats held by women in the National Parliament (%)	27.5	22.3	40.0[u]

Environment and infrastructure indicators

	2010	2015	2022
Individuals using the Internet (per 100 inhabitants)	34.8[v]	40.9	65.2[b]
Research & Development expenditure (% of GDP)	...	0.1	0.2[b]
Threatened species (number)	551	643	967
Forested area (% of land area)[j]	57.9	57.2	56.6[d]
CO2 emission estimates (million tons/tons per capita)	43.1 / 1.4	51.1 / 1.6	53.8 / 1.6[d]
Energy production, primary (Petajoules)	810	953	964[d]
Energy supply per capita (Gigajoules)	28	30	32[d]
Tourist/visitor arrivals at national borders (000)[w,x]	2 299	3 456	897[b]
Important sites for terrestrial biodiversity protected (%)	25.6	27.5	29.1[e]
Pop. using safely managed drinking water (urban/rural, %)	57.9 / 18.0	58.6 / 20.1	59.4 / 22.1[b]
Pop. using safely managed sanitation (urban/rural %)	36.0 / ...	49.3 / ...	63.5 / ...[b]
Net Official Development Assist. received (% of GNI)	- 0.22	0.18	0.25[b]

a Projected estimate (medium fertility variant). b 2020. c Refers to the Province of Lima and the Constitutional Province of Callao. d 2019. e 2021. f Data classified according to ISIC Rev. 4. g Excludes irrigation canals and landscaping care. h Excludes publishing activities. Includes irrigation and canals. i Includes publishing activities and landscape care. Excludes repair of personal and household goods. j Estimate. k Metropolitan Lima. l Data refers to a 5-year period preceding the reference year. m Including refugees. n Data as at the end of December. o Country is still reporting data based on SHA 1.0. p Data based on calendar year (January 1 to December 31). q Data are based on SHA2011. r 2009. s 2012. t 2018. u Data are as at 1 January of reporting year. v Population aged 6 years and over. w Including tourists with identity document other than a passport. x Including nationals residing abroad.

Philippines

Region	South-eastern Asia	UN membership date	24 October 1945
Population (000, 2022)	115 559[a]	Surface area (km2)	300 000[b]
Pop. density (per km2, 2022)	385.2[a]	Sex ratio (m per 100 f)	103.2[a]
Capital city	Manila	National currency	Philippine Piso (PHP)
Capital city pop. (000, 2022)	13 698.9[c,d]	Exchange rate (per US$)	50.8[e]

Economic indicators

	2010	2015	2022
GDP: Gross domestic product (million current US$)	208 369	306 446	361 489[b]
GDP growth rate (annual %, const. 2015 prices)	7.3	6.3	- 9.6[b]
GDP per capita (current US$)	2 217.5	3 001.0	3 298.8[b]
Economy: Agriculture (% of Gross Value Added)[f,g,h]	13.7	11.0	10.2[b]
Economy: Industry (% of Gross Value Added)[h,i,j]	32.3	30.5	28.4[b]
Economy: Services and other activity (% of GVA)[h,i,k]	53.9	58.5	61.4[b]
Employment in agriculture (% of employed)	32.8[l]	29.2	22.5[l,b]
Employment in industry (% of employed)	15.5[l]	16.2	19.8[l,b]
Employment in services & other sectors (% employed)	51.6[l]	54.6	57.6[l,b]
Unemployment rate (% of labour force)	3.6	3.1	2.3[l]
Labour force participation rate (female/male pop. %)	48.0 / 74.9	48.6 / 74.3	45.4 / 69.8[l]
CPI: Consumer Price Index (2010=100)[m]	...	107	129[e]
Agricultural production index (2014-2016=100)	92	101	101[b]
International trade: exports (million current US$)	51 498	58 648	74 620[e]
International trade: imports (million current US$)	58 468	70 153	124 390[e]
International trade: balance (million current US$)	- 6 970	- 11 505	- 49 771[e]
Balance of payments, current account (million US$)	7 179	7 266	- 6 922[e]

Major trading partners

						2021
Export partners (% of exports)	United States	15.9	China	15.5	Japan	14.4
Import partners (% of imports)	China	22.7	Japan	9.5	Republic of Korea	7.7

Social indicators

	2010	2015	2022
Population growth rate (average annual %)	1.8	1.8	1.5[a]
Urban population (% of total population)	45.3	46.3	47.1[d]
Urban population growth rate (average annual %)[n]	1.5	2.1	...
Fertility rate, total (live births per woman)	3.3	3.0	2.7[a]
Life expectancy at birth (females/males, years)	72.4 / 69.1	73.0 / 69.5	74.2 / 70.2[a]
Population age distribution (0-14/60+ years old, %)	34.5 / 6.6	32.6 / 7.4	30.3 / 8.6[a]
International migrant stock (000/% of total pop.)[o,p]	208.6 / 0.2	211.9 / 0.2	225.5 / 0.2[b]
Refugees and others of concern to the UNHCR (000)	139.9[q]	386.2	384.2[e]
Infant mortality rate (per 1 000 live births)	26.3	24.7	21.6[a]
Health: Current expenditure (% of GDP)	4.1[r]	3.9	4.1[d]
Health: Physicians (per 1 000 pop.)	1.3	...	0.8[b]
Education: Government expenditure (% of GDP)	2.3	3.3	3.2[l,d]
Education: Primary gross enrol. ratio (f/m per 100 pop.)	107.1 / 108.3[s]	110.5 / 113.9	97.6 / 100.6[d]
Education: Sec. gross enrol. ratio (f/m per 100 pop.)	87.5 / 80.9[s]	91.5 / 84.4	93.9 / 85.9[d]
Education: Upr. Sec. gross enrol. ratio (f/m per 100 pop.)	78.2 / 68.1	83.1 / 74.3	79.0 / 66.9[d]
Intentional homicide rate (per 100 000 pop.)	9.2	8.7[t]	4.4[d]
Seats held by women in the National Parliament (%)	21.0	27.2	27.7[u]

Environment and infrastructure indicators

	2010	2015	2022
Individuals using the Internet (per 100 inhabitants)	25.0	36.9[l]	49.8[l,b]
Research & Development expenditure (% of GDP)	0.1[s]	0.2	0.3[v]
Threatened species (number)	697	767	1 561
Forested area (% of land area)	22.9	23.5	24.0[d]
CO2 emission estimates (million tons/tons per capita)	78.6 / 0.8	104.7 / 1.0	138.8 / 1.3[d]
Energy production, primary (Petajoules)	999	1 092	1 274[d]
Energy supply per capita (Gigajoules)	18	21	23[d]
Tourist/visitor arrivals at national borders (000)[w]	3 520	5 361	1 483[b]
Important sites for terrestrial biodiversity protected (%)	24.8	26.3	42.8[e]
Pop. using safely managed drinking water (urban/rural, %)	60.8 / 32.4	61.3 / 33.5	61.8 / 34.5[b]
Pop. using safely managed sanitation (urban/rural %)	47.9 / 50.2	51.3 / 57.8	54.9 / 65.8[b]
Net Official Development Assist. received (% of GNI)	0.25	0.15	0.37[b]

a Projected estimate (medium fertility variant). b 2020. c Refers to the National Capital Region. d 2019. e 2021. f Including taxes less subsidies on production. g Excludes irrigation canals and landscaping care. h Data classified according to ISIC Rev. 4. i Including taxes less subsidies on production and imports. j Excludes publishing activities. Includes irrigation and canals. k Includes publishing activities and landscape care. Excludes repair of personal and household goods. l Estimate. m Base: 2012=100. n Data refers to a 5-year period preceding the reference year. o Including refugees. p Refers to foreign citizens. q Data as at the end of December. r Data revision. s 2009. t 2012. u Data are as at 1 January of reporting year. v 2018. w Including nationals residing abroad.

Poland

Region	Eastern Europe		UN membership date	24 October 1945	
Population (000, 2022)	39 857 [a]		Surface area (km2)	312 679 [b]	
Pop. density (per km2, 2022)	130.2 [a]		Sex ratio (m per 100 f)	93.8 [a]	
Capital city	Warsaw		National currency	Zloty (PLN)	
Capital city pop. (000, 2022)	1 775.9 [c]		Exchange rate (per US$)	4.1 [d]	

Economic indicators	2010	2015	2022
GDP: Gross domestic product (million current US$)	479 834	477 812	596 618 [b]
GDP growth rate (annual %, const. 2015 prices)	3.7	4.2	- 2.5 [b]
GDP per capita (current US$)	12 518.6	12 562.7	15 764.1 [b]
Economy: Agriculture (% of Gross Value Added) [e,f]	3.2	2.7	2.8 [b]
Economy: Industry (% of Gross Value Added) [f,g]	32.8	34.0	31.4 [b]
Economy: Services and other activity (% of GVA) [f,h]	64.0	63.4	65.7 [b]
Employment in agriculture (% of employed)	13.1	11.5	8.9 [i,b]
Employment in industry (% of employed)	30.3	30.5	32.0 [i,b]
Employment in services & other sectors (% employed)	56.6	57.9	59.1 [i,b]
Unemployment rate (% of labour force)	9.6	7.5	2.8 [i]
Labour force participation rate (female/male pop. %)	47.6 / 63.7	48.4 / 64.6	48.7 / 65.1 [i]
CPI: Consumer Price Index (2010=100) [j]	100	108	124 [d]
Agricultural production index (2014-2016=100)	91	97	111 [b]
International trade: exports (million current US$)	157 065	194 461	317 832 [d]
International trade: imports (million current US$)	174 128	189 696	335 451 [d]
International trade: balance (million current US$)	- 17 063	4 765	- 17 619 [d]
Balance of payments, current account (million US$)	- 26 660	- 4 347	- 3 895 [d]

Major trading partners					2021
Export partners (% of exports)	Germany	28.6	Czechia	6.0	France	5.7
Import partners (% of imports)	Germany	21.1	China	14.8	Russian Federation	6.0

Social indicators	2010	2015	2022
Population growth rate (average annual %)	0.1	- 0.1	8.1 [a]
Urban population (% of total population)	60.9	60.3	60.0 [c]
Urban population growth rate (average annual %) [k]	- 0.2	- 0.2	...
Fertility rate, total (live births per woman)	1.4	1.3	1.5 [a]
Life expectancy at birth (females/males, years)	80.5 / 72.2	81.3 / 73.5	80.8 / 73.2 [a]
Population age distribution (0-14/60+ years old, %)	15.2 / 19.3	15.0 / 22.6	15.2 / 25.0 [a]
International migrant stock (000/% of total pop.)	642.4 / 1.7	611.9 / 1.6	817.3 / 2.2 [b]
Refugees and others of concern to the UNHCR (000)	18.4 [l]	29.0	8.4 [d]
Infant mortality rate (per 1 000 live births)	4.9	4.0	3.4 [a]
Health: Current expenditure (% of GDP)	6.4	6.4	6.4 [c]
Health: Physicians (per 1 000 pop.)	2.2	2.3	3.8 [b]
Education: Government expenditure (% of GDP)	5.1	4.8	4.6 [m]
Education: Primary gross enrol. ratio (f/m per 100 pop.)	96.1 / 96.9	100.3 / 100.0 [n]	96.5 / 97.8 [c]
Education: Sec. gross enrol. ratio (f/m per 100 pop.)	95.7 / 96.2	105.7 / 109.7	110.1 / 113.4 [c]
Education: Upr. Sec. gross enrol. ratio (f/m per 100 pop.)	96.8 / 96.1	112.1 / 116.6	116.4 / 121.7 [c]
Intentional homicide rate (per 100 000 pop.)	1.0	0.8	0.7 [b]
Seats held by women in the National Parliament (%)	20.0	24.1	28.3 [o]

Environment and infrastructure indicators	2010	2015	2022
Individuals using the Internet (per 100 inhabitants)	62.3 [p]	68.0 [p,q]	83.2 [b]
Research & Development expenditure (% of GDP)	0.7	1.0	1.4 [b]
Threatened species (number)	37	51	110
Forested area (% of land area)	30.5	30.8	30.9 [c]
CO2 emission estimates (million tons/tons per capita)	314.3 / 8.0	288.7 / 7.4	273.3 / 7.0 [b]
Energy production, primary (Petajoules)	2 809	2 843	2 484 [c]
Energy supply per capita (Gigajoules)	111	105	114 [c]
Tourist/visitor arrivals at national borders (000)	12 470 [r]	16 728	8 418 [b]
Important sites for terrestrial biodiversity protected (%)	85.5	88.5	88.5 [b]
Pop. using safely managed sanitation (urban/rural %)	90.9 / ...	92.6 / ...	93.8 / ... [b]
Net Official Development Assist. disbursed (% of GNI) [s]	0.08	0.11	0.14 [b]

a Projected estimate (medium fertility variant). b 2020. c 2019. d 2021. e Excludes irrigation canals and landscaping care. f Data classified according to ISIC Rev. 4. g Excludes publishing activities. Includes irrigation and canals. h Includes publishing activities and landscape care. Excludes repair of personal and household goods. i Estimate. j Calculated by the UNSD from national indices. k Data refers to a 5-year period preceding the reference year. l Data as at the end of December. m 2018. n 2014. o Data are as at 1 January of reporting year. p Population aged 16 to 74 years. q Users in the last 3 months. r Based on surveys by the Institute of Tourism. s DAC member (OECD).

Portugal

Region	Southern Europe	UN membership date		14 December 1955	
Population (000, 2022)	10 271 [a]	Surface area (km2)		92 226 [b]	
Pop. density (per km2, 2022)	111.7 [a]	Sex ratio (m per 100 f)		89.3 [a]	
Capital city	Lisbon	National currency		Euro (EUR)	
Capital city pop. (000, 2022)	2 942.1 [c,d]	Exchange rate (per US$)		0.9 [e]	

Economic indicators	2010	2015	2022
GDP: Gross domestic product (million current US$)	237 881	199 314	228 539 [b]
GDP growth rate (annual %, const. 2015 prices)	1.7	1.8	- 8.4 [b]
GDP per capita (current US$)	22 449.9	19 223.3	22 413.0 [b]
Economy: Agriculture (% of Gross Value Added) [f,g]	2.2	2.4	2.4 [b]
Economy: Industry (% of Gross Value Added) [g,h]	22.7	22.3	22.2 [b]
Economy: Services and other activity (% of GVA) [g,i]	75.1	75.2	75.4 [b]
Employment in agriculture (% of employed)	11.2	7.5	5.7 [j,b]
Employment in industry (% of employed)	27.3	24.3	24.6 [j,b]
Employment in services & other sectors (% employed)	61.5	68.1	69.8 [j,b]
Unemployment rate (% of labour force)	10.8	12.4	6.0 [j]
Labour force participation rate (female/male pop. %)	55.9 / 67.2	53.8 / 64.1	54.2 / 62.6 [j]
CPI: Consumer Price Index (2010=100) [k,l]	100	107	112 [e]
Agricultural production index (2014-2016=100)	97	108	107 [b]
International trade: exports (million current US$)	49 414	55 045	75 196 [e]
International trade: imports (million current US$)	77 682	66 909	97 857 [e]
International trade: balance (million current US$)	- 28 268	- 11 864	- 22 661 [e]
Balance of payments, current account (million US$)	- 24 407	471	- 2 848 [e]

Major trading partners					2021
Export partners (% of exports)	Spain	26.7	France	13.1	Germany	11.0
Import partners (% of imports)	Spain	32.8	Germany	12.4	France	6.7

Social indicators	2010	2015	2022
Population growth rate (average annual %)	- 0.2	- 0.3	- 0.2 [a]
Urban population (% of total population)	60.6	63.5	65.8 [d]
Urban population growth rate (average annual %) [m]	1.2	0.5	...
Fertility rate, total (live births per woman)	1.4	1.3	1.4 [a]
Life expectancy at birth (females/males, years)	83.1 / 76.8	84.1 / 78.1	84.9 / 79.3 [a]
Population age distribution (0-14/60+ years old, %)	15.2 / 24.4	14.2 / 26.8	13.2 / 29.7 [a]
International migrant stock (000/% of total pop.)	762.8 / 7.2	864.8 / 8.3	1 002.0 / 9.8 [b]
Refugees and others of concern to the UNHCR (000)	0.5 [n]	1.4	3.0 [e]
Infant mortality rate (per 1 000 live births)	2.6	3.0	2.4 [a]
Health: Current expenditure (% of GDP)	10.0	9.3	9.5 [d]
Health: Physicians (per 1 000 pop.)	4.0	4.7	5.5 [d]
Education: Government expenditure (% of GDP)	5.4	4.9	4.7 [o]
Education: Primary gross enrol. ratio (f/m per 100 pop.)	109.9 / 113.2	104.9 / 109.0	106.2 / 108.5 [d]
Education: Sec. gross enrol. ratio (f/m per 100 pop.)	108.3 / 105.3	116.9 / 120.6	120.9 / 120.3 [d]
Education: Upr. Sec. gross enrol. ratio (f/m per 100 pop.)	105.2 / 96.6	117.7 / 120.1	126.8 / 123.6 [d]
Intentional homicide rate (per 100 000 pop.)	1.3 [p]	...	0.9 [b]
Seats held by women in the National Parliament (%)	27.4	31.3	40.0 [q]

Environment and infrastructure indicators	2010	2015	2022
Individuals using the Internet (per 100 inhabitants)	53.3 [r]	68.6	78.3 [b]
Research & Development expenditure (% of GDP)	1.5	1.2	1.6 [b]
Threatened species (number)	171	256	539
Forested area (% of land area) [j]	35.5	36.2	36.2 [d]
CO2 emission estimates (million tons/tons per capita) [s]	48.5 / 4.5	47.9 / 4.5	38.2 / 3.6 [b]
Energy production, primary (Petajoules) [t]	242	222	246 [d]
Energy supply per capita (Gigajoules) [t]	93	89	89 [d]
Tourist/visitor arrivals at national borders (000) [u]	6 756	11 723 [v]	4 208 [v,b]
Important sites for terrestrial biodiversity protected (%)	73.0	75.9	76.1 [e]
Pop. using safely managed drinking water (urban/rural, %)	97.7 / 90.2	97.5 / 91.5	96.8 / 92.5 [b]
Pop. using safely managed sanitation (urban/rural %)	72.7 / ...	85.3 / ...	92.7 / ... [b]
Net Official Development Assist. disbursed (% of GNI) [w]	0.07	0.27	- 0.23 [b]

a Projected estimate (medium fertility variant). b 2020. c Refers to Grande Lisboa, the Peninsula of Setúbal, and the municipality Azambuja. d 2019. e 2021. f Excludes irrigation canals and landscaping care. g Data classified according to ISIC Rev. 4. h Excludes publishing activities. Includes irrigation and canals. i Includes publishing activities and landscape care. Excludes repair of personal and household goods. j Estimate. k Excluding rent. l Calculated by the UNSD from national indices. m Data refers to a 5-year period preceding the reference year. n Data as at the end of December. o 2018. p 2005. q Data are as at 1 January of reporting year. r Population aged 16 to 74 years. s Data includes the Azores and Madeira. t Including the Azores and Madeira Islands. u Non-resident tourists staying in all types of accommodation establishments. v Include hotels, apartment hotels, "pousadas", tourist apartments, tourist villages, camping sites, recreation centres, tourism in rural areas and local accommodation. w DAC member (OECD).

Puerto Rico

Region	Caribbean	Population (000, 2022)	3 252[a]
Surface area (km2)	8 868[b]	Pop. density (per km2, 2022)	374.2[a]
Sex ratio (m per 100 f)	89.3[a]	Capital city	San Juan
National currency	US Dollar (USD)	Capital city pop. (000, 2022)	2 451.4[c,d]

Economic indicators	2010	2015	2022
GDP: Gross domestic product (million current US$)[e]	98 381	103 376	103 138[b]
GDP growth rate (annual %, const. 2015 prices)[e]	- 0.4	- 1.0	- 3.9[b]
GDP per capita (current US$)[e]	27 482.0	30 570.7	36 051.6[b]
Economy: Agriculture (% of Gross Value Added)[f,g]	0.8	0.8	0.6[b]
Economy: Industry (% of Gross Value Added)[f,g]	50.7	51.1	50.8[b]
Economy: Services and other activity (% of GVA)[f,g]	48.4	48.0	48.6[b]
Employment in agriculture (% of employed)[h]	1.4	1.2	1.0[b]
Employment in industry (% of employed)[h]	17.4	16.3	15.5[b]
Employment in services & other sectors (% employed)[h]	81.3	82.5	83.5[b]
Unemployment rate (% of labour force)	16.1	12.0	8.1[h]
Labour force participation rate (female/male pop. %)	33.6 / 50.6	32.7 / 49.0	32.5 / 49.7[h]
CPI: Consumer Price Index (2010=100)[i]	100	105	107[j]
Agricultural production index (2014-2016=100)	117	100	93[b]

Social indicators	2010	2015	2022
Population growth rate (average annual %)	- 0.6	- 1.8	0.2[a]
Urban population (% of total population)	93.8	93.6	93.6[d]
Urban population growth rate (average annual %)[k]	- 0.3	- 0.3	...
Fertility rate, total (live births per woman)	1.6	1.4	1.3[a]
Life expectancy at birth (females/males, years)	82.1 / 74.0	83.8 / 75.7	83.9 / 75.6[a]
Population age distribution (0-14/60+ years old, %)	19.6 / 20.5	16.7 / 24.3	13.4 / 30.0[a]
International migrant stock (000/% of total pop.)	305.0 / 8.5	280.5 / 8.3	247.1 / 8.6[b]
Infant mortality rate (per 1 000 live births)	7.2	6.8	6.8[a]
Education: Government expenditure (% of GDP)	...	6.1[l]	...
Education: Primary gross enrol. ratio (f/m per 100 pop.)	99.3 / 95.7	91.6 / 90.2[m]	... / ...
Education: Sec. gross enrol. ratio (f/m per 100 pop.)	88.3 / 83.6	89.8 / 83.5[m]	... / ...
Education: Upr. Sec. gross enrol. ratio (f/m per 100 pop.)	81.1 / 75.0	83.8 / 76.2[m]	... / ...
Intentional homicide rate (per 100 000 pop.)	28.8	20.4[l]	18.5[b]

Environment and infrastructure indicators	2010	2015	2022
Individuals using the Internet (per 100 inhabitants)	45.3[n]	63.5	77.7[d]
Research & Development expenditure (% of GDP)	0.5[o]	0.4	...
Threatened species (number)	103	127	164
Forested area (% of land area)[h]	55.4	55.7	55.9[d]
Energy production, primary (Petajoules)	1	1	2[d]
Energy supply per capita (Gigajoules)	8	17	24[d]
Tourist/visitor arrivals at national borders (000)[p,q]	3 186	3 542	2 617[b]
Important sites for terrestrial biodiversity protected (%)	33.0	33.0	33.0[r]

a Projected estimate (medium fertility variant). b 2020. c Refers to the Metropolitan Statistical Area. d 2019. e Data compiled in accordance with the System of National Accounts 1968 (1968 SNA). f At producers' prices. g Data classified according to ISIC Rev. 4. h Estimate. i Calculated by the UNSD from national indices. j 2017. k Data refers to a 5-year period preceding the reference year. l 2014. m 2013. n Population aged 12 years and over. o 2009. p Arrivals of non-resident tourists by air. q Data refer to fiscal years beginning 1 July. r 2021.

Qatar

Region	Western Asia	UN membership date	21 September 1971
Population (000, 2022)	2 695[a]	Surface area (km2)	11 627[b]
Pop. density (per km2, 2022)	232.6[a]	Sex ratio (m per 100 f)	263.8[a]
Capital city	Doha	National currency	Qatari Rial (QAR)
Capital city pop. (000, 2022)	637.3[c,d]	Exchange rate (per US$)	3.6[e]

Economic indicators

	2010	2015	2022
GDP: Gross domestic product (million current US$)	125 122	161 740	146 401[b]
GDP growth rate (annual %, const. 2015 prices)	16.7	4.8	- 3.7[b]
GDP per capita (current US$)	67 403.2	63 039.1	50 814.9[b]
Economy: Agriculture (% of Gross Value Added)[f,g,h]	0.1	0.2	0.3[b]
Economy: Industry (% of Gross Value Added)[f,g,i]	67.5	55.4	48.6[b]
Economy: Services and other activity (% of GVA)[f,g,j]	32.4	44.4	51.1[b]
Employment in agriculture (% of employed)	1.5[k]	1.2	1.2[k,b]
Employment in industry (% of employed)	56.4[k]	54.1	54.4[k,b]
Employment in services & other sectors (% employed)	42.1[k]	44.6	44.5[k,b]
Unemployment rate (% of labour force)	0.4	0.2	0.1[k]
Labour force participation rate (female/male pop. %)	51.1 / 96.1	58.2 / 95.8	57.7 / 95.8[k]
CPI: Consumer Price Index (2010=100)	...	105[l]	99[m,e]
Agricultural production index (2014-2016=100)	76	116	146[b]
International trade: exports (million current US$)	74 964	77 971	87 061[k,e]
International trade: imports (million current US$)	23 240	32 610	28 006[k,e]
International trade: balance (million current US$)	51 725	45 361	59 054[e]
Balance of payments, current account (million US$)	...	13 751	26 288[e]

Major trading partners

						2021
Export partners (% of exports)[k]	Japan	15.5	China	15.2	India	14.3
Import partners (% of imports)[k]	United States	15.7	China	14.9	United Kingdom	7.0

Social indicators

	2010	2015	2022
Population growth rate (average annual %)	4.7	8.3	0.8[a]
Urban population (% of total population)	98.5	98.9	99.2[d]
Urban population growth rate (average annual %)[n]	14.7	6.7	...
Fertility rate, total (live births per woman)	2.1	1.9	1.8[a]
Life expectancy at birth (females/males, years)	80.5 / 77.4	81.7 / 79.2	83.1 / 80.6[a]
Population age distribution (0-14/60+ years old, %)	13.8 / 1.8	13.9 / 2.2	15.8 / 3.3[a]
International migrant stock (000/% of total pop.)[o]	1 456.4 / 78.5	1 687.6 / 65.8	2 226.2 / 77.3[b]
Refugees and others of concern to the UNHCR (000)	1.3[p]	1.4	1.6[e]
Infant mortality rate (per 1 000 live births)	7.8	6.7	5.0[a]
Health: Current expenditure (% of GDP)[q,r]	1.9	3.0[k]	2.9[k,d]
Health: Physicians (per 1 000 pop.)	3.7	1.7[s]	2.5[t]
Education: Government expenditure (% of GDP)	4.5	3.6[s]	3.2[b]
Education: Primary gross enrol. ratio (f/m per 100 pop.)	104.4 / 100.9	103.0 / 102.2	105.7 / 102.2[b]
Education: Sec. gross enrol. ratio (f/m per 100 pop.)	102.7 / 108.3	... / ...	... / ...
Education: Upr. Sec. gross enrol. ratio (f/m per 100 pop.)	100.9 / 100.3	... / ...	... / ...
Intentional homicide rate (per 100 000 pop.)	0.2	0.2	0.4[b]
Seats held by women in the National Parliament (%)	0.0	0.0	4.4[u]

Environment and infrastructure indicators

	2010	2015	2022
Individuals using the Internet (per 100 inhabitants)	69.0[v]	92.9	99.7[b]
Research & Development expenditure (% of GDP)	...	0.5	0.5[t]
Threatened species (number)	32	35	71
Forested area (% of land area)[k]	0.0	0.0	0.0[d]
CO2 emission estimates (million tons/tons per capita)	55.8 / 29.9	80.4 / 31.2	87.3 / 30.7[d]
Energy production, primary (Petajoules)	7 428	9 402	9 363[d]
Energy supply per capita (Gigajoules)	628	603	608[d]
Tourist/visitor arrivals at national borders (000)	1 700	2 941	582[b]
Important sites for terrestrial biodiversity protected (%)	60.0	60.0	60.0[e]

a Projected estimate (medium fertility variant). b 2020. c Does not include the populations from the industrial area and zone 58. d 2019. e 2021. f At producers' prices. g Data classified according to ISIC Rev. 4. h Excludes irrigation canals and landscaping care. i Excludes publishing activities. Includes irrigation and canals. j Includes publishing activities and landscape care. Excludes repair of personal and household goods. k Estimate. l Index base: 2013=100. m Base: 2018=100. n Data refers to a 5-year period preceding the reference year. o Refers to foreign citizens. p Data as at the end of December. q Data based on calendar year (January 1 to December 31). r Estimates should be viewed with caution as these are derived from scarce data. s 2014. t 2018. u Data are as at 1 January of reporting year. v Refers to total population.

Republic of Korea

Region	Eastern Asia	UN membership date	17 September 1991
Population (000, 2022)	51 816[a]	Surface area (km2)	100 401[b]
Pop. density (per km2, 2022)	523.7[a]	Sex ratio (m per 100 f)	99.7[a]
Capital city	Seoul	National currency	South Korean Won (KRW)
Capital city pop. (000, 2022)	9 962.4[c,d]	Exchange rate (per US$)	1 186.6[e]

Economic indicators

	2010	2015	2022
GDP: Gross domestic product (million current US$)	1 144 067	1 465 773	1 637 896[b]
GDP growth rate (annual %, const. 2015 prices)	6.8	2.8	- 0.9[b]
GDP per capita (current US$)	23 091.2	28 840.7	31 947.0[b]
Economy: Agriculture (% of Gross Value Added)[f,g]	2.4	2.2	2.0[b]
Economy: Industry (% of Gross Value Added)[g,h]	37.5	37.2	35.6[b]
Economy: Services and other activity (% of GVA)[g,i]	60.1	60.6	62.4[b]
Employment in agriculture (% of employed)	6.6	5.1	4.8[j,b]
Employment in industry (% of employed)	25.0	25.2	25.0[j,b]
Employment in services & other sectors (% employed)	68.4	69.7	70.2[j,b]
Unemployment rate (% of labour force)	3.3	3.6	3.1[j]
Labour force participation rate (female/male pop. %)	49.9 / 73.0	52.3 / 74.1	53.5 / 72.5[j]
CPI: Consumer Price Index (2010=100)[k]	100	110	119[e]
Agricultural production index (2014-2016=100)	94	100	98[b]
International trade: exports (million current US$)	466 381	526 753	644 479[j,e]
International trade: imports (million current US$)	425 208	436 487	614 900[j,e]
International trade: balance (million current US$)	41 173	90 266	29 579[e]
Balance of payments, current account (million US$)	27 950	105 119	88 302[e]

Major trading partners

						2021
Export partners (% of exports)[j]	China	25.9	United States	14.5	Viet Nam	9.5
Import partners (% of imports)[j]	China	23.3	United States	12.4	Japan	9.8

Social indicators

	2010	2015	2022
Population growth rate (average annual %)	0.5	0.8	- 0.1[a]
Urban population (% of total population)	81.9	81.6	81.4[d]
Urban population growth rate (average annual %)[l]	0.5	0.3	...
Fertility rate, total (live births per woman)	1.2	1.2	0.9[a]
Life expectancy at birth (females/males, years)	84.2 / 77.1	85.8 / 79.0	87.1 / 80.7[a]
Population age distribution (0-14/60+ years old, %)	16.4 / 15.5	13.8 / 18.3	11.6 / 25.5[a]
International migrant stock (000/% of total pop.)[m,n]	920.0 / 1.9	1 370.9 / 2.7	1 728.2 / 3.4[b]
Refugees and others of concern to the UNHCR (000)	1.2[o]	6.6	17.8[e]
Infant mortality rate (per 1 000 live births)	3.5	2.9	2.3[a]
Health: Current expenditure (% of GDP)	5.9	6.7	8.2[d]
Health: Physicians (per 1 000 pop.)	2.0	2.2	2.5[d]
Education: Government expenditure (% of GDP)	...	...	4.5[p]
Education: Primary gross enrol. ratio (f/m per 100 pop.)	101.8 / 101.7	98.7 / 98.9	100.9 / 101.1[d]
Education: Sec. gross enrol. ratio (f/m per 100 pop.)	96.1 / 96.6	99.7 / 100.3	95.6 / 96.2[d]
Education: Upr. Sec. gross enrol. ratio (f/m per 100 pop.)	92.2 / 93.0	96.6 / 97.1	96.6 / 97.5[d]
Intentional homicide rate (per 100 000 pop.)	1.0	0.7	0.6[b]
Seats held by women in the National Parliament (%)	14.7	16.3	18.6[q]

Environment and infrastructure indicators

	2010	2015	2022
Individuals using the Internet (per 100 inhabitants)	83.7[r]	89.9[s]	96.5[b]
Research & Development expenditure (% of GDP)	3.3	4.0	4.8[b]
Threatened species (number)	64	76	170
Forested area (% of land area)[j]	65.7	65.0	64.5[d]
CO2 emission estimates (million tons/tons per capita)	555.4 / 2.0	587.2 / 0.9	575.6 / 2.1[d]
Energy production, primary (Petajoules)	1 863	2 125	1 992[d]
Energy supply per capita (Gigajoules)	212	225	229[d]
Tourist/visitor arrivals at national borders (000)[t]	8 798	13 232	2 519[b]
Important sites for terrestrial biodiversity protected (%)	33.8	36.4	37.6[e]
Net Official Development Assist. disbursed (% of GNI)[u]	1.17	0.89	0.74[b]

a Projected estimate (medium fertility variant). b 2020. c Refers to Seoul Special City. d 2019. e 2021. f Excludes irrigation canals and landscaping care. g Data classified according to ISIC Rev. 4. h Excludes publishing activities. i Includes publishing activities and landscape care. Excludes repair of personal and household goods. j Estimate. k Calculated by the UNSD from national indices. l Data refers to a 5-year period preceding the reference year. m Refers to foreign citizens. n Including refugees. o Data as at the end of December. p 2018. q Data are as at 1 January of reporting year. r Population aged 3 years and over. s Population aged 16 to 74 years. t Including nationals residing abroad and crew members. u DAC member (OECD).

Republic of Moldova

Region	Eastern Europe	UN membership date	02 March 1992
Population (000, 2022)	3 273[a,b]	Surface area (km2)	33 847[c]
Pop. density (per km2, 2022)	99.5[a,b]	Sex ratio (m per 100 f)	90.9[a,b]
Capital city	Chisinau	National currency	Moldovan Leu (MDL)
Capital city pop. (000, 2022)	504.3[d]	Exchange rate (per US$)	17.7[e]

Economic indicators

	2010	2015	2022
GDP: Gross domestic product (million current US$)	6 975	7 745	11 914[c]
GDP growth rate (annual %, const. 2015 prices)	7.1	- 0.3	- 7.0[c]
GDP per capita (current US$)	1 707.0	1 902.7	2 953.5[c]
Economy: Agriculture (% of Gross Value Added)[f,g]	13.0	13.2	11.0[c]
Economy: Industry (% of Gross Value Added)[g,h]	23.7	26.0	26.4[c]
Economy: Services and other activity (% of GVA)[g,i]	63.3	60.8	62.5[c]
Employment in agriculture (% of employed)	27.5	34.2	35.4[j,c]
Employment in industry (% of employed)	18.7	17.8	17.1[j,c]
Employment in services & other sectors (% employed)	53.8	48.0	47.5[j,c]
Unemployment rate (% of labour force)	7.4	4.7	3.7[j]
Labour force participation rate (female/male pop. %)	38.6 / 44.9	41.2 / 48.2	33.7 / 43.4[j]
CPI: Consumer Price Index (2010=100)[k,l]	100	136	181[e]
Agricultural production index (2014-2016=100)	88	91	82[c]
International trade: exports (million current US$)	1 541	1 967	3 144[e]
International trade: imports (million current US$)	3 855	3 987	7 177[e]
International trade: balance (million current US$)	- 2 314	- 2 020	- 4 032[e]
Balance of payments, current account (million US$)	- 481	- 463	- 1 590[e]

Major trading partners

							2021
Export partners (% of exports)	Romania	26.5	Türkiye	10.0	Russian Federation	8.8
Import partners (% of imports)	Russian Federation	14.7	China	11.7	Romania	11.6

Social indicators

	2010	2015	2022
Population growth rate (average annual %)[a]	- 2.2	- 1.7	13.7[b]
Urban population (% of total population)[a]	42.6	42.5	42.7[d]
Urban population growth rate (average annual %)[a,m]	- 0.4	- 0.2	...
Fertility rate, total (live births per woman)[a]	1.7	1.9	1.8[b]
Life expectancy at birth (females/males, years)[a]	73.8 / 65.0	73.8 / 64.8	73.3 / 64.2[b]
Population age distribution (0-14/60+ years old, %)[a]	18.0 / 15.1	18.2 / 17.7	19.3 / 19.4[b]
International migrant stock (000/% of total pop.)[a]	129.5 / 3.2	106.4 / 2.6	104.4 / 2.6[c]
Refugees and others of concern to the UNHCR (000)	2.3[n]	6.8	3.8[e]
Infant mortality rate (per 1 000 live births)[a]	14.6	13.4	12.4[b]
Health: Current expenditure (% of GDP)	10.1	8.6	6.4[d]
Health: Physicians (per 1 000 pop.)	2.4	2.5	3.1[c]
Education: Government expenditure (% of GDP)	7.6	5.8	6.1[d]
Education: Primary gross enrol. ratio (f/m per 100 pop.)[j]	... / ...	105.1 / 106.2	105.3 / 107.2[c]
Education: Sec. gross enrol. ratio (f/m per 100 pop.)[j]	... / ...	105.8 / 104.4	108.1 / 108.8[c]
Education: Upr. Sec. gross enrol. ratio (f/m per 100 pop.)[j]	... / ...	105.7 / 101.2	120.1 / 116.4[c]
Intentional homicide rate (per 100 000 pop.)	6.5	4.6	2.3[c]
Seats held by women in the National Parliament (%)	23.8	20.8	40.6[o]

Environment and infrastructure indicators

	2010	2015	2022
Individuals using the Internet (per 100 inhabitants)	32.3[j]	69.0	76.1[j,p]
Research & Development expenditure (% of GDP)	0.4	0.3	0.2[c]
Threatened species (number)	27	29	36
Forested area (% of land area)	11.4	11.8	11.8[d]
CO2 emission estimates (million tons/tons per capita)	8.2 / 2.8	7.9 / 2.7	10.3 / 3.8[c]
Energy production, primary (Petajoules)[q]	8	28	30[d]
Energy supply per capita (Gigajoules)[q]	22	27	29[d]
Tourist/visitor arrivals at national borders (000)[l,r]	64	94	29[c]
Important sites for terrestrial biodiversity protected (%)	71.8	83.9	86.0[e]
Pop. using safely managed sanitation (urban/rural %)	75.2 / ...	76.7 / ...	78.9 / ...[c]
Net Official Development Assist. received (% of GNI)	6.32	3.81	4.19[c]

a Including the Transnistria region. b Projected estimate (medium fertility variant). c 2020. d 2019. e 2021. f Excludes irrigation canals and landscaping care. g Data classified according to ISIC Rev. 4. h Excludes publishing activities. Includes irrigation and canals. i Includes publishing activities and landscape care. Excludes repair of personal and household goods. j Estimate. k Data refer to 8 cities only. l Excluding the left side of the river Nistru and the municipality of Bender. m Data refers to a 5-year period preceding the reference year. n Data as at the end of December. o Data are as at 1 January of reporting year. p 2017. q Data exclude Transnistria and the municipality of Bender. r Non-resident tourists staying in all types of accommodation establishments.

Réunion

Region	Eastern Africa
Surface area (km2)	2 510[c]
Sex ratio (m per 100 f)	93.2[a,b]
National currency	Euro (EUR)
Exchange rate (per US$)	0.9[e]

Population (000, 2022)	974[a,b]
Pop. density (per km2, 2022)	389.6[a,b]
Capital city	Saint-Denis
Capital city pop. (000, 2022)	147.2[d]

Economic indicators	2010	2015	2022
Employment in agriculture (% of employed)[g]	4.2[f]	4.3[h,i]	...
Employment in industry (% of employed)[g]	14.1[f]	12.7[h,i]	...
Employment in services & other sectors (% employed)[g]	67.1[f]	81.7[h,i]	...
Unemployment rate (% of labour force)[g]	28.9	28.9[h,i]	...
Labour force participation rate (female/male pop. %)	45.3 / 59.9[g]	49.1 / 61.3[g,h,i]	... / ...
CPI: Consumer Price Index (2010=100)[k]	100	105	108[l,c]

Social indicators	2010	2015	2022
Population growth rate (average annual %)[b]	0.7	0.5	0.8[a]
Urban population (% of total population)	98.5	99.3	99.6[m]
Urban population growth rate (average annual %)[n]	1.4	0.9	
Fertility rate, total (live births per woman)[b]	2.4	2.5	2.2[a]
Life expectancy at birth (females/males, years)[b]	83.4 / 76.3	84.3 / 78.1	85.4 / 79.7[a]
Population age distribution (0-14/60+ years old, %)[b]	26.4 / 12.2	25.0 / 14.8	22.8 / 18.8[a]
International migrant stock (000/% of total pop.)	123.0 / 14.8	127.2 / 14.7	131.8 / 14.7[c]
Infant mortality rate (per 1 000 live births)[b]	6.5	5.6	4.7[a]
Intentional homicide rate (per 100 000 pop.)	1.8[o]	...	...

Environment and infrastructure indicators	2010	2015	2022
Individuals using the Internet (per 100 inhabitants)	36.3[p,o]	...	...
Threatened species (number)	104	126	157
Forested area (% of land area)[p]	37.6	38.3	39.0[m]
Energy production, primary (Petajoules)	8[q]	...	...
Tourist/visitor arrivals at national borders (000)[r]	420	426	217[c]
Important sites for terrestrial biodiversity protected (%)	47.1	47.1	47.1[e]

a Projected estimate (medium fertility variant). b For statistical purposes, the data for France do not include this area. c 2020. d 2018. e 2021. f Population aged 15 to 64 years. g Excluding the institutional population. h Break in the time series. i 2012. j 2013. k Calculated by the UNSD from national indices. l Average for 10 months excluding data for April and May. m 2019. n Data refers to a 5-year period preceding the reference year. o 2009. p Estimate. q Data after 2010 are included in France. r Arrivals by air only.

Romania

Region	Eastern Europe	UN membership date	14 December 1955
Population (000, 2022)	19 659[a]	Surface area (km2)	238 391[b]
Pop. density (per km2, 2022)	85.4[a]	Sex ratio (m per 100 f)	93.7[a]
Capital city	Bucharest	National currency	Romanian Leu (RON)
Capital city pop. (000, 2022)	1 812.3[c]	Exchange rate (per US$)	4.4[d]

Economic indicators

	2010	2015	2022
GDP: Gross domestic product (million current US$)	166 309	177 731	248 716[b]
GDP growth rate (annual %, const. 2015 prices)	- 3.9	3.0	- 3.9[b]
GDP per capita (current US$)	8 123.8	8 919.9	12 928.6[b]
Economy: Agriculture (% of Gross Value Added)[e,f]	5.6	4.8	4.2[b]
Economy: Industry (% of Gross Value Added)[f,g]	42.6	34.3	28.9[b]
Economy: Services and other activity (% of GVA)[f,h]	51.8	61.0	66.8[b]
Employment in agriculture (% of employed)	31.0	25.6	21.3[i,b]
Employment in industry (% of employed)	28.3	28.5	30.1[i,b]
Employment in services & other sectors (% employed)	40.7	46.0	48.6[i,b]
Unemployment rate (% of labour force)	7.0	6.8	4.7[i]
Labour force participation rate (female/male pop. %)	46.2 / 64.2	45.3 / 64.5	43.4 / 63.1[i]
CPI: Consumer Price Index (2010=100)	100[j]	114[j]	133[k,d]
Agricultural production index (2014-2016=100)	93	96	91[b]
International trade: exports (million current US$)	49 413	60 605	88 390[d]
International trade: imports (million current US$)	62 007	69 858	116 402[d]
International trade: balance (million current US$)	- 12 593	- 9 253	- 28 012[d]
Balance of payments, current account (million US$)	- 8 478	- 1 396	- 19 751[d]

Major trading partners

						2021
Export partners (% of exports)	Germany	20.5	Italy	10.4	France	6.4
Import partners (% of imports)	Germany	20.2	Italy	8.9	Hungary	6.9

Social indicators

	2010	2015	2022
Population growth rate (average annual %)	- 0.7	- 0.5	4.0[a]
Urban population (% of total population)	53.8	53.9	54.1[c]
Urban population growth rate (average annual %)[l]	- 0.7	- 0.5	...
Fertility rate, total (live births per woman)	1.6	1.6	1.7[a]
Life expectancy at birth (females/males, years)	77.7 / 70.4	78.2 / 71.4	77.6 / 70.7[a]
Population age distribution (0-14/60+ years old, %)	15.8 / 21.3	15.7 / 23.5	15.9 / 24.5[a]
International migrant stock (000/% of total pop.)	177.2 / 0.9	281.0 / 1.4	705.3 / 3.7[b]
Refugees and others of concern to the UNHCR (000)	1.7[m]	2.9	5.7[d]
Infant mortality rate (per 1 000 live births)	10.3	7.9	5.4[a]
Health: Current expenditure (% of GDP)	5.8	4.9	5.7[n,c]
Health: Physicians (per 1 000 pop.)	2.5	2.6[o]	3.0[p]
Education: Government expenditure (% of GDP)	3.5	3.1	3.3[q]
Education: Primary gross enrol. ratio (f/m per 100 pop.)	99.1 / 100.8	88.5 / 89.8	87.1 / 87.9[c]
Education: Sec. gross enrol. ratio (f/m per 100 pop.)	97.2 / 98.1	92.9 / 92.9	88.2 / 87.9[c]
Education: Upr. Sec. gross enrol. ratio (f/m per 100 pop.)	97.1 / 97.7	91.0 / 89.1	91.6 / 89.0[c]
Intentional homicide rate (per 100 000 pop.)	1.3	1.7	1.5[b]
Seats held by women in the National Parliament (%)	11.4	13.7	19.1[r]

Environment and infrastructure indicators

	2010	2015	2022
Individuals using the Internet (per 100 inhabitants)	39.9[s]	55.8[t]	78.5[b]
Research & Development expenditure (% of GDP)	0.5	0.5	0.5[b]
Threatened species (number)	64	85	169
Forested area (% of land area)	28.3	30.0	30.1[c]
CO2 emission estimates (million tons/tons per capita)	76.7 / 3.7	71.7 / 3.5	68.5 / 3.5[b]
Energy production, primary (Petajoules)	1 155	1 116	1 031[c]
Energy supply per capita (Gigajoules)	72	67	72[c]
Tourist/visitor arrivals at national borders (000)	7 498	9 331	5 023[b]
Important sites for terrestrial biodiversity protected (%)	65.0	75.9	76.0[d]
Pop. using safely managed drinking water (urban/rural, %)	95.0 / 66.7	95.0 / 66.7	95.0 / 66.7[b]
Net Official Development Assist. disbursed (% of GNI)	...	0.07[o]	...

a Projected estimate (medium fertility variant). **b** 2020. **c** 2019. **d** 2021. **e** Excludes irrigation canals and landscaping care. **f** Data classified according to ISIC Rev. 4. **g** Excludes publishing activities. Includes irrigation and canals. **h** Includes publishing activities and landscape care. Excludes repair of personal and household goods. **i** Estimate. **j** Break in the time series. **k** Calculated by the UNSD from national indices. **l** Data refers to a 5-year period preceding the reference year. **m** Data as at the end of December. **n** Beginning with 2016, the legislative norms in the insurance field changed in order to comply with Solvency II EU Directive. As a result, the data reported by health services and providers showed an increase in insurance benefits sum. **o** 2013. **p** 2017. **q** 2018. **r** Data are as at 1 January of reporting year. **s** Population aged 16 to 74 years. **t** Users in the last 3 months.

Russian Federation

Region	Eastern Europe	UN membership date	24 October 1945
Population (000, 2022)	144 713[a]	Surface area (km2)	17 098 246[b]
Pop. density (per km2, 2022)	8.8[a]	Sex ratio (m per 100 f)	86.7[a]
Capital city	Moscow	National currency	Russian Ruble (RUB)
Capital city pop. (000, 2022)	12 476.2[c]	Exchange rate (per US$)	74.3[d]

Economic indicators

	2010	2015	2022
GDP: Gross domestic product (million current US$)	1 539 845	1 363 482	1 483 498[b]
GDP growth rate (annual %, const. 2015 prices)	4.5	- 2.0	- 3.0[b]
GDP per capita (current US$)	10 732.2	9 404.3	10 165.5[b]
Economy: Agriculture (% of Gross Value Added)[e]	3.8	4.3	4.1[b]
Economy: Industry (% of Gross Value Added)[e]	34.8	33.3	33.4[b]
Economy: Services and other activity (% of GVA)[e]	61.4	62.4	62.5[b]
Employment in agriculture (% of employed)	7.7	6.7	5.6[f,b]
Employment in industry (% of employed)	27.8	27.3	26.6[f,b]
Employment in services & other sectors (% employed)	64.5	66.0	67.8[f,b]
Unemployment rate (% of labour force)	7.4	5.6	4.7[f]
Labour force participation rate (female/male pop. %)	55.9 / 70.3	55.5 / 71.2	54.3 / 69.5[f]
CPI: Consumer Price Index (2010=100)	100	152	199[d]
Agricultural production index (2014-2016=100)	74	100	112[b]
International trade: exports (million current US$)[g]	397 068	343 908	505 616[f,d]
International trade: imports (million current US$)[g]	228 912	182 782	297 634[f,d]
International trade: balance (million current US$)[g]	168 156	161 126	207 982[d]
Balance of payments, current account (million US$)	67 452	67 777	122 040[d]

Major trading partners

							2021
Export partners (% of exports)[g,f]	China	14.6	Netherlands	7.4	United Kingdom	6.9
Import partners (% of imports)[g,f]	China	23.7	Germany	10.1	United States	5.7

Social indicators

	2010	2015	2022
Population growth rate (average annual %)	~0.0	0.3	~-0.0[a]
Urban population (% of total population)	73.7	74.0	74.6[c]
Urban population growth rate (average annual %)[h]	~0.0	0.2	...
Fertility rate, total (live births per woman)	1.6	1.8	1.5[a]
Life expectancy at birth (females/males, years)	75.3 / 63.5	77.4 / 66.6	75.7 / 64.7[a]
Population age distribution (0-14/60+ years old, %)	15.2 / 18.1	16.9 / 20.0	17.7 / 22.8[a]
International migrant stock (000/% of total pop.)	11 194.7 / /.8	11 643.3 / 8.0	11 636.9 / 8.0[b]
Refugees and others of concern to the UNHCR (000)	132.6[i]	431.2	73.1[d]
Infant mortality rate (per 1 000 live births)	7.9	6.0	4.0[a]
Health: Current expenditure (% of GDP)	5.0	5.3	5.6[c]
Health: Physicians (per 1 000 pop.)	5.0	3.9	3.8[b]
Education: Government expenditure (% of GDP)	4.1[j]	3.8	4.7[k]
Education: Primary gross enrol. ratio (f/m per 100 pop.)	99.6 / 99.1[l]	99.5 / 98.7	103.7 / 104.7[c]
Education: Sec. gross enrol. ratio (f/m per 100 pop.)	84.1 / 85.4[l]	101.0 / 103.4	102.1 / 105.0[c]
Education: Upr. Sec. gross enrol. ratio (f/m per 100 pop.)	78.3 / 85.9[l]	104.2 / 115.3	106.5 / 114.9[c]
Intentional homicide rate (per 100 000 pop.)	11.6	11.5	7.3[b]
Seats held by women in the National Parliament (%)	14.0	13.6	16.2[m]

Environment and infrastructure indicators

	2010	2015	2022
Individuals using the Internet (per 100 inhabitants)	49.0[n]	70.1[o,p]	85.0[b]
Research & Development expenditure (% of GDP)	1.1	1.1	1.1[b]
Threatened species (number)	126	217	311
Forested area (% of land area)[f]	49.8	49.8	49.8[c]
CO2 emission estimates (million tons/tons per capita)	1 538.7 / 10.7	1 543.5 / 10.6	1 566.8 / 10.8[b]
Energy production, primary (Petajoules)	53 679	56 024	64 239[c]
Energy supply per capita (Gigajoules)	202	200	217[c]
Tourist/visitor arrivals at national borders (000)	22 281	33 729	6 359[b]
Important sites for terrestrial biodiversity protected (%)	22.7	24.6	25.5[d]
Pop. using safely managed sanitation (urban/rural %)	62.3 / 46.7	63.1 / 49.5	63.7 / 52.2[b]

a Projected estimate (medium fertility variant). b 2020. c 2019. d 2021. e Data classified according to ISIC Rev. 4. f Estimate. g Russian data provided by the Russian Federation. Includes statistical data for the Autonomous Republic of Crimea and the city of Sevastopol, Ukraine, temporarily occupied by the Russian Federation. h Data refers to a 5-year period preceding the reference year. i Data as at the end of December. j 2008. k 2018. l 2009. m Data are as at 1 January of reporting year. n Population aged 16 to 74 years. o Users in the last 3 months. p Population aged 15 to 72 years.

Rwanda

Region	Eastern Africa	UN membership date	18 September 1962
Population (000, 2022)	13 777[a]	Surface area (km2)	26 338[b]
Pop. density (per km2, 2022)	569.0[a]	Sex ratio (m per 100 f)	95.8[a]
Capital city	Kigali	National currency	Rwanda Franc (RWF)
Capital city pop. (000, 2022)	1 094.8[c]	Exchange rate (per US$)	1 009.6[d]

Economic indicators

	2010	2015	2022
GDP: Gross domestic product (million current US$)	6 120	8 526	10 332[b]
GDP growth rate (annual %, const. 2015 prices)	7.3	8.9	- 3.4[b]
GDP per capita (current US$)	609.6	749.9	797.7[b]
Economy: Agriculture (% of Gross Value Added)[e,f]	26.9	26.3	28.5[b]
Economy: Industry (% of Gross Value Added)[e,g]	18.0	19.1	21.0[b]
Economy: Services and other activity (% of GVA)[e,h]	55.1	54.5	50.5[b]
Employment in agriculture (% of employed)[i]	79.5	66.7	61.7[b]
Employment in industry (% of employed)[i]	5.7	8.3	9.1[b]
Employment in services & other sectors (% employed)[i]	14.8	25.0	29.2[b]
Unemployment rate (% of labour force)[i]	1.1	1.1	1.5
Labour force participation rate (female/male pop. %)[i]	84.0 / 84.3	83.8 / 83.3	83.1 / 82.3
CPI: Consumer Price Index (2010=100)[j,k]	100	122	153[d]
Agricultural production index (2014-2016=100)	107	101	112[b]
International trade: exports (million current US$)	242	594	2 195[i,d]
International trade: imports (million current US$)	1 405	2 370	5 342[i,d]
International trade: balance (million current US$)	- 1 163	- 1 777	- 3 147[d]
Balance of payments, current account (million US$)	- 399	- 1 084	- 1 235[b]

Major trading partners

						2021
Export partners (% of exports)[i]	Dem. Rep. of Congo	32.1	United Arab Emirates	29.6	Uganda	5.3
Import partners (% of imports)[i]	China	19.9	India	8.8	Kenya	8.7

Social indicators

	2010	2015	2022
Population growth rate (average annual %)	2.6	2.4	2.3[a]
Urban population (% of total population)	16.9	17.0	17.3[c]
Urban population growth rate (average annual %)[l]	2.6	2.6	...
Fertility rate, total (live births per woman)	4.5	4.1	3.7[a]
Life expectancy at birth (females/males, years)	64.2 / 60.7	67.2 / 63.2	69.2 / 64.8[a]
Population age distribution (0-14/60+ years old, %)	42.2 / 4.6	41.2 / 4.8	38.5 / 5.2[a]
International migrant stock (000/% of total pop.)[m]	426.9 / 4.3	514.6 / 4.5	513.9 / 4.0[b]
Refugees and others of concern to the UNHCR (000)	55.7[n]	135.6	146.8[d]
Infant mortality rate (per 1 000 live births)	44.9	34.8	28.3[a]
Health: Current expenditure (% of GDP)[o]	8.1	6.6[p]	6.4[c]
Health: Physicians (per 1 000 pop.)	...	0.1	0.1[c]
Education: Government expenditure (% of GDP)	4.6	3.6[i]	3.4[i,b]
Education: Primary gross enrol. ratio (f/m per 100 pop.)	150.1 / 146.4	140.6 / 138.7	130.0 / 132.7[c]
Education: Sec. gross enrol. ratio (f/m per 100 pop.)	31.6 / 31.6	39.4 / 36.3	47.0 / 41.6[c]
Education: Upr. Sec. gross enrol. ratio (f/m per 100 pop.)	18.4 / 20.6	32.1 / 31.9	32.5 / 31.0[c]
Intentional homicide rate (per 100 000 pop.)	2.9	2.6	...
Seats held by women in the National Parliament (%)	56.2	63.8	61.3[q]

Environment and infrastructure indicators

	2010	2015	2022
Individuals using the Internet (per 100 inhabitants)	8.0	18.0[i]	26.5[i,b]
Research & Development expenditure (% of GDP)	...	...	0.8[c]
Threatened species (number)	55	61	176
Forested area (% of land area)[i]	10.7	10.9	11.1[c]
Energy production, primary (Petajoules)	76	86[i]	88[i,c]
Energy supply per capita (Gigajoules)	8	9[i]	9[i,c]
Tourist/visitor arrivals at national borders (000)	605	1 217	1 544[c]
Important sites for terrestrial biodiversity protected (%)	47.1	51.2	51.2[d]
Pop. using safely managed drinking water (urban/rural, %)	35.1 / 2.6	40.8 / 3.9	45.5 / 5.0[b]
Pop. using safely managed sanitation (urban/rural %)	... / 43.3	... / 49.2	... / 53.8[b]
Net Official Development Assist. received (% of GNI)	17.02	12.99	16.09[b]

a Projected estimate (medium fertility variant). b 2020. c 2019. d 2021. e Data classified according to ISIC Rev. 4. f Excludes irrigation canals and landscaping care. g Excludes publishing activities. Includes irrigation and canals. h Includes publishing activities and landscape care. Excludes repair of personal and household goods. i Estimate. j Calculated by the UNSD from national indices. k For urban population only. l Data refers to a 5-year period preceding the reference year. m Including refugees. n Data as at the end of December. o Data revision. p Break in the time series. q Data are as at 1 January of reporting year.

Saint Helena

Region	Western Africa	Population (000, 2022)	5[a,b]
Surface area (km2)	309[c,d,e]	Pop. density (per km2, 2022)	13.8[a,b]
Sex ratio (m per 100 f)	93.4[a,b]	Capital city	Jamestown
National currency	Saint Helena Pound (SHP)	Capital city pop. (000, 2022)	0.6[f]
Exchange rate (per US$)	0.7[g]		

Economic indicators

	2010	2015	2022
Employment in agriculture (% of employed)	7.3[h,i,j]	...	...
Employment in industry (% of employed)	20.0[h,i,j]	...	...
Employment in services & other sectors (% employed)	72.7[h,i,j]	...	...
Unemployment rate (% of labour force)	2.0	...	...
International trade: exports (million current US$)[k]	~0	~0	~0[g]
International trade: imports (million current US$)[k]	20	41	93[g]
International trade: balance (million current US$)	- 20[k]	- 40[k]	- 93[g]

Major trading partners

						2021
Export partners (% of exports)[k]	United States	84.1	Japan	5.2	Greece	2.1
Import partners (% of imports)[k]	United Kingdom	44.3	United States	24.8	South Africa	19.1

Social indicators

	2010	2015	2022
Population growth rate (average annual %)[a]	0.7	0.7	- 1.0[b]
Urban population (% of total population)[c]	39.5	39.5	39.9[l]
Urban population growth rate (average annual %)[c,m]	- 0.7	- 0.7	...
Fertility rate, total (live births per woman)[a]	1.6	1.6	1.6[b]
Life expectancy at birth (females/males, years)[a]	80.3 / 73.4	78.6 / 72.6	80.9 / 74.4[b]
Population age distribution (0-14/60+ years old, %)[a]	14.3 / 26.8	13.6 / 27.9	14.1 / 38.2[b]
International migrant stock (000/% of total pop.)[a,n]	0.2 / 4.8	0.4 / 6.4	0.4 / 7.2[e]
Infant mortality rate (per 1 000 live births)[a]	12.8	14.6	11.1[b]
Intentional homicide rate (per 100 000 pop.)	0.0[o]	...	...

Environment and infrastructure indicators

	2010	2015	2022
Individuals using the Internet (per 100 inhabitants)	24.9	37.6[k,p]	...
Threatened species (number)[c]	60	80	188
Forested area (% of land area)[k]	5.1	5.1	5.1[l]
Energy production, primary (Petajoules)	0	0	0[l]
Energy supply per capita (Gigajoules)	30	27	34[l]
Important sites for terrestrial biodiversity protected (%)	15.4	38.5	38.5[g]

a Including Ascension and Tristan da Cunha. For statistical purposes, the data for United Kingdom do not include this area. b Projected estimate (medium fertility variant). c Including Ascension and Tristan da Cunha. d St. Helena Island has no substantial natural inland waters however there are 15 reservoirs and similar open water storage features on island. e 2020. f 2018. g 2021. h Population aged 15 to 69 years. i Data classified according to ISIC Rev. 3. j 2008. k Estimate. l 2019. m Data refers to a 5-year period preceding the reference year. n Refers to foreign citizens. o 2009. p 2012.

Saint Kitts and Nevis

Region	Caribbean	UN membership date	23 September 1983
Population (000, 2022)	48[a]	Surface area (km2)	261[b]
Pop. density (per km2, 2022)	183.3[a]	Sex ratio (m per 100 f)	93.4[a]
Capital city	Basseterre	National currency	E. Caribbean Dollar (XCD)[c]
Capital city pop. (000, 2022)	14.4[d]	Exchange rate (per US$)	2.7[e]

Economic indicators	2010	2015	2022
GDP: Gross domestic product (million current US$)	760	923	927[b]
GDP growth rate (annual %, const. 2015 prices)	- 0.6	1.0	- 10.7[b]
GDP per capita (current US$)	15 508.6	18 029.3	17 433.6[b]
Economy: Agriculture (% of Gross Value Added)[f]	1.4	1.1	1.4[b]
Economy: Industry (% of Gross Value Added)[f]	25.2	26.1	28.2[b]
Economy: Services and other activity (% of GVA)[f]	73.4	72.8	70.4[b]
CPI: Consumer Price Index (2010=100)[g]	100	106	104[e]
Agricultural production index (2014-2016=100)	105	100	91[b]
International trade: exports (million current US$)	32	32	44[h,e]
International trade: imports (million current US$)	270	297	263[h,e]
International trade: balance (million current US$)	- 238	- 265	- 219[e]
Balance of payments, current account (million US$)	- 139	- 80	- 61[e]

Major trading partners						2021
Export partners (% of exports)[h]	United States	57.2	Italy	16.4	Canada	3.3
Import partners (% of imports)[h]	United States	47.0	Republic of Korea	13.3	Trinidad and Tobago	8.5

Social indicators	2010	2015	2022
Population growth rate (average annual %)	0.2	--0.0	0.2[a]
Urban population (% of total population)	31.3	30.8	30.8[i]
Urban population growth rate (average annual %)[j]	0.7	0.8	...
Fertility rate, total (live births per woman)	1.8	1.6	1.5[a]
Life expectancy at birth (females/males, years)	74.4 / 68.4	74.9 / 67.1	75.7 / 68.7[a]
Population age distribution (0-14/60+ years old, %)	23.7 / 10.3	21.4 / 11.8	19.5 / 16.0[a]
International migrant stock (000/% of total pop.)[k]	7.2 / 14.8	7.4 / 14.5	7.7 / 14.5[b]
Refugees and others of concern to the UNHCR (000)	...	--0.0	~0.0[e]
Infant mortality rate (per 1 000 live births)	12.8	14.6	7.8[a]
Health: Current expenditure (% of GDP)[h,l]	5.3	5.3	5.4[i]
Health: Physicians (per 1 000 pop.)	...	2.7	2.8[d]
Education: Government expenditure (% of GDP)	4.2[m]	2.6	...
Education: Primary gross enrol. ratio (f/m per 100 pop.)	110.6 / 116.5	107.9 / 108.7	107.1 / 110.4[n]
Education: Sec. gross enrol. ratio (f/m per 100 pop.)	105.2 / 107.4[h]	107.5 / 108.3	108.7 / 105.1[n]
Education: Upr. Sec. gross enrol. ratio (f/m per 100 pop.)	100.0 / 92.8[h]	99.9 / 100.1	103.5 / 98.1[n]
Intentional homicide rate (per 100 000 pop.)	42.8	36.1[o]	18.8[b]
Seats held by women in the National Parliament (%)	6.7	6.7	25.0[p]

Environment and infrastructure indicators	2010	2015	2022
Individuals using the Internet (per 100 inhabitants)	63.0	75.7[h]	80.7[h,q]
Threatened species (number)	36	51	72
Forested area (% of land area)[h]	42.3	42.3	42.3[i]
Energy production, primary (Petajoules)	0	0	0[h,i]
Energy supply per capita (Gigajoules)	65	65[h]	68[h,i]
Tourist/visitor arrivals at national borders (000)[r]	98	118	29[b]
Important sites for terrestrial biodiversity protected (%)	22.3	23.3	56.8[e]
Net Official Development Assist. received (% of GNI)	1.57	3.64[s]	...

a Projected estimate (medium fertility variant). b 2020. c East Caribbean Dollar. d 2018. e 2021. f Data classified according to ISIC Rev. 4. g Calculated by the UNSD from national indices. h Estimate. i 2019. j Data refers to a 5-year period preceding the reference year. k Including refugees. l Data based on calendar year (January 1 to December 31). m 2007. n 2016. o 2012. p Data are as at 1 January of reporting year. q 2017. r Arrivals of non-resident tourists by air. s 2013.

Saint Lucia

Region	Caribbean	UN membership date	18 September 1979
Population (000, 2022)	180[a]	Surface area (km2)	616[b]
Pop. density (per km2, 2022)	292.0[a]	Sex ratio (m per 100 f)	97.8[a]
Capital city	Castries	National currency	E. Caribbean Dollar (XCD)[c]
Capital city pop. (000, 2022)	22.3[d]	Exchange rate (per US$)	2.7[e]

Economic indicators

	2010	2015	2022
GDP: Gross domestic product (million current US$)	1 487	1 810	1 617[b]
GDP growth rate (annual %, const. 2015 prices)	0.5	0.1	- 20.4[b]
GDP per capita (current US$)	8 539.7	10 104.5	8 804.7[b]
Economy: Agriculture (% of Gross Value Added)[f,g]	3.0	2.5	2.6[b]
Economy: Industry (% of Gross Value Added)[g,h]	13.5	12.7	12.8[b]
Economy: Services and other activity (% of GVA)[g,i]	83.4	84.8	84.6[b]
Employment in agriculture (% of employed)[j]	19.8	18.5	17.0[b]
Employment in industry (% of employed)[j]	18.6	17.9	18.3[b]
Employment in services & other sectors (% employed)[j]	61.7	63.7	64.7[b]
Unemployment rate (% of labour force)[j]	17.1	20.6	15.8
Labour force participation rate (female/male pop. %)[j]	60.9 / 72.9	64.0 / 75.8	63.9 / 73.4
CPI: Consumer Price Index (2010=100)[k]	100	111	111[e]
Agricultural production index (2014-2016=100)	107	101	86[b]
International trade: exports (million current US$)	215	181	157[j,e]
International trade: imports (million current US$)	647	583	1 141[j,e]
International trade: balance (million current US$)	- 432	- 403	- 984[e]
Balance of payments, current account (million US$)	- 203	- 12	- 2[e]

Major trading partners

							2021
Export partners (% of exports)[j]	United States	33.9	Barbados	10.7	Trinidad and Tobago	8.3
Import partners (% of imports)[j]	United States	42.7	Trinidad and Tobago	16.0	China	5.4

Social indicators

	2010	2015	2022
Population growth rate (average annual %)	0.8	0.5	0.1[a]
Urban population (% of total population)	18.4	18.5	18.8[l]
Urban population growth rate (average annual %)[m]	- 3.4	0.6	...
Fertility rate, total (live births per woman)	1.5	1.5	1.4[a]
Life expectancy at birth (females/males, years)	75.7 / 69.9	76.4 / 70.1	74.9 / 68.0[a]
Population age distribution (0-14/60+ years old, %)	24.1 / 11.1	20.6 / 11.9	18.0 / 14.2[a]
International migrant stock (000/% of total pop.)[n]	9.0 / 5.2	8.7 / 4.8	8.3 / 4.5[b]
Refugees and others of concern to the UNHCR (000)	~0.0[o]	0.1	~0.0[b]
Infant mortality rate (per 1 000 live births)	16.5	14.6	11.9[a]
Health: Current expenditure (% of GDP)[j,p]	5.0	4.6	4.3[l]
Health: Physicians (per 1 000 pop.)	1.6	1.9[q]	0.6[r]
Education: Government expenditure (% of GDP)	3.5[j]	3.9	3.6[b]
Education: Primary gross enrol. ratio (f/m per 100 pop.)	98.0 / 103.2[s]	99.5 / 102.8	102.4 / 99.9[b]
Education: Sec. gross enrol. ratio (f/m per 100 pop.)	93.3 / 94.4	88.1 / 88.9	91.0 / 92.8[b]
Education: Upr. Sec. gross enrol. ratio (f/m per 100 pop.)	93.6 / 89.1	83.3 / 81.5	86.7 / 92.0[b]
Intentional homicide rate (per 100 000 pop.)	25.3	15.6	28.3[b]
Seats held by women in the National Parliament (%)	11.1	16.7	11.1[t]

Environment and infrastructure indicators

	2010	2015	2022
Individuals using the Internet (per 100 inhabitants)[j]	32.5	41.7	53.3[b]
Threatened species (number)	46	58	87
Forested area (% of land area)[j]	34.0	34.0	34.0[l]
Energy production, primary (Petajoules)[j]	1	1	1[l]
Energy supply per capita (Gigajoules)[j]	45	43	44[l]
Tourist/visitor arrivals at national borders (000)[u]	306	345	131[b]
Important sites for terrestrial biodiversity protected (%)	45.6	45.6	45.6[e]
Net Official Development Assist. received (% of GNI)	2.84	0.83	6.11[b]

a Projected estimate (medium fertility variant). b 2020. c East Caribbean Dollar. d 2018. e 2021, f Excludes irrigation canals and landscaping care. g Data classified according to ISIC Rev. 4. h Excludes publishing activities. Includes irrigation and canals. i Includes publishing activities and landscape care. Excludes repair of personal and household goods. j Estimate. k Calculated by the UNSD from national indices. l 2019. m Data refers to a 5-year period preceding the reference year. n Including refugees. o Data as at the end of December. p Data refer to fiscal years beginning 1 April. q 2014. r 2017. s 2007. t Data are as at 1 January of reporting year. u Excluding nationals residing abroad.

Saint Pierre and Miquelon

Region	Northern America	Population (000, 2022)	6[a,b]
Surface area (km2)	242[c]	Pop. density (per km2, 2022)	25.5[a,b]
Sex ratio (m per 100 f)	98.9[a,b]	Capital city	Saint-Pierre
National currency	Euro (EUR)	Capital city pop. (000, 2022)	5.7[d]
Exchange rate (per US$)	0.9[e]		

Economic indicators		2010	2015	2022
International trade: exports (million current US$)[f]		137	533	1 587[e]
International trade: imports (million current US$)[f]		747	2 259	5 008[e]
International trade: balance (million current US$)		- 610[f]	- 1 726[f]	- 3 421[e]

Major trading partners							2021
Export partners (% of exports)[f]	Canada	78.7	France	9.8	Ireland	5.9
Import partners (% of imports)[f]	France	57.7	Canada	36.9	Netherlands	2.2

Social indicators	2010	2015	2022
Population growth rate (average annual %)[b]	0.0	- 0.2	- 0.3[a]
Urban population (% of total population)	89.9	89.9	89.9[g]
Urban population growth rate (average annual %)[h]	~0.0	0.1	...
Fertility rate, total (live births per woman)[b]	1.8	1.6	1.6[a]
Life expectancy at birth (females/males, years)[b]	81.0 / 72.9	81.2 / 73.1	81.7 / 74.0[a]
Population age distribution (0-14/60+ years old, %)[b]	17.9 / 20.2	17.6 / 23.1	16.9 / 23.8[a]
International migrant stock (000/% of total pop.)	1.0 / 16.0	1.0 / 16.5	1.0 / 17.2[c]
Infant mortality rate (per 1 000 live births)[b]	9.2	8.8	7.8[a]
Intentional homicide rate (per 100 000 pop.)	15.8[i]	...	...

Environment and infrastructure indicators	2010	2015	2022
Threatened species (number)	4	7	23
Forested area (% of land area)[f]	6.3	5.8	5.4[g]
Energy production, primary (Petajoules)	0	0	0[g]
Energy supply per capita (Gigajoules)[f]	143	153	159[g]
Important sites for terrestrial biodiversity protected (%)	0.8	1.6	1.6[e]

a Projected estimate (medium fertility variant). b For statistical purposes, the data for France do not include this area. c 2020. d 2018. e 2021. f Estimate. g 2019. h Data refers to a 5-year period preceding the reference year. i 2009.

Saint Vincent and the Grenadines

Region	Caribbean	UN membership date	16 September 1980
Population (000, 2022)	104 [a]	Surface area (km2)	389 [b]
Pop. density (per km2, 2022)	266.5 [a]	Sex ratio (m per 100 f)	103.7 [a]
Capital city	Kingstown	National currency	E. Caribbean Dollar (XCD) [c]
Capital city pop. (000, 2022)	26.6 [d]	Exchange rate (per US$)	2.7 [e]

Economic indicators

	2010	2015	2022
GDP: Gross domestic product (million current US$)	681	755	810 [b]
GDP growth rate (annual %, const. 2015 prices)	- 3.3	1.3	- 2.7 [b]
GDP per capita (current US$)	6 292.8	6 920.9	7 298.4 [b]
Economy: Agriculture (% of Gross Value Added) [f]	7.1	7.3	8.0 [b]
Economy: Industry (% of Gross Value Added) [f]	19.2	18.0	16.6 [b]
Economy: Services and other activity (% of GVA) [f]	73.7	74.6	75.5 [b]
Employment in agriculture (% of employed) [g]	12.9	11.7	10.5 [b]
Employment in industry (% of employed) [g]	20.5	20.0	19.9 [b]
Employment in services & other sectors (% employed) [g]	66.6	68.4	69.5 [b]
Unemployment rate (% of labour force) [g]	19.0	19.1	21.0
Labour force participation rate (female/male pop. %) [g]	53.0 / 75.5	53.7 / 75.1	53.5 / 74.3
CPI: Consumer Price Index (2010=100) [g]	100 [h]	105	112 [e]
Agricultural production index (2014-2016=100)	94	100	106 [e]
International trade: exports (million current US$)	42	47	35 [e]
International trade: imports (million current US$)	379	334	372 [e]
International trade: balance (million current US$)	- 338	- 287	- 338 [e]
Balance of payments, current account (million US$)	- 208	- 116	- 212 [e]

Major trading partners

							2021
Export partners (% of exports)	Barbados	16.5	Saint Lucia	16.3	United States	14.6
Import partners (% of imports)	United States	46.8	Trinidad and Tobago	9.4	China	6.6

Social indicators

	2010	2015	2022
Population growth rate (average annual %)	- 0.5	- 0.4	- 0.3 [a]
Urban population (% of total population)	49.0	51.0	52.6 [i]
Urban population growth rate (average annual %) [j]	0.9	0.8	...
Fertility rate, total (live births per woman)	2.1	2.1	1.8 [a]
Life expectancy at birth (females/males, years)	77.6 / 72.2	77.3 / 72.0	71.7 / 66.7 [a]
Population age distribution (0-14/60+ years old, %)	25.7 / 11.6	23.6 / 13.5	21.9 / 16.2 [a]
International migrant stock (000/% of total pop.) [k]	4.6 / 4.2	4.6 / 4.2	4.7 / 4.3 [b]
Refugees and others of concern to the UNHCR (000)	...	...	~0.0 [a]
Infant mortality rate (per 1 000 live births)	16.8	14.3	12.5 [a]
Health: Current expenditure (% of GDP) [g,l,m]	4.6	4.1	4.8 [i]
Health: Physicians (per 1 000 pop.)	0.7	0.9 [n]	...
Education: Government expenditure (% of GDP)	5.1	...	5.7 [d]
Education: Primary gross enrol. ratio (f/m per 100 pop.)	106.2 / 111.9	109.7 / 110.7	112.7 / 114.1 [d]
Education: Sec. gross enrol. ratio (f/m per 100 pop.)	110.7 / 105.5	107.7 / 107.1	108.7 / 105.9 [d]
Education: Upr. Sec. gross enrol. ratio (f/m per 100 pop.)	102.5 / 81.6	94.0 / 80.9	102.8 / 85.3 [d]
Intentional homicide rate (per 100 000 pop.)	23.1	...	17.2 [i]
Seats held by women in the National Parliament (%)	21.7	13.0	18.2 [o]

Environment and infrastructure indicators

	2010	2015	2022
Individuals using the Internet (per 100 inhabitants) [g]	33.7	49.4	56.0 [d]
Threatened species (number)	38	54	80
Forested area (% of land area)	73.2	73.2	73.2 [i]
Energy production, primary (Petajoules)	0	0	0 [g,i]
Energy supply per capita (Gigajoules)	31	33	31 [i]
Tourist/visitor arrivals at national borders (000) [p]	72	75	27 [b]
Important sites for terrestrial biodiversity protected (%)	45.6	45.6	45.6 [o]
Net Official Development Assist. received (% of GNI)	2.52	1.83	9.34 [b]

a Projected estimate (medium fertility variant). **b** 2020. **c** East Caribbean Dollar. **d** 2018. **e** 2021. **f** Data classified according to ISIC Rev. 4. **g** Estimate. **h** Break in the time series. **i** 2019. **j** Data refers to a 5-year period preceding the reference year. **k** Including refugees. **l** Estimates should be viewed with caution as these are derived from scarce data. **m** Data based on calendar year (January 1 to December 31). **n** 2012. **o** Data are as at 1 January of reporting year. **p** Arrivals of non-resident tourists by air.

Samoa

Region	Polynesia	UN membership date	15 December 1976
Population (000, 2022)	222[a]	Surface area (km2)	2 842[b]
Pop. density (per km2, 2022)	78.6[a]	Sex ratio (m per 100 f)	104.0[a]
Capital city	Apia	National currency	Tala (WST)
Capital city pop. (000, 2022)	36.1[c]	Exchange rate (per US$)	2.6[d]

Economic indicators

	2010	2015	2022
GDP: Gross domestic product (million current US$)	692	787	772[b]
GDP growth rate (annual %, const. 2015 prices)	2.4	6.7	- 9.2[b]
GDP per capita (current US$)	3 722.1	4 066.3	3 890.0[b]
Economy: Agriculture (% of Gross Value Added)[e,f,g,h]	9.1	8.9	10.5[b]
Economy: Industry (% of Gross Value Added)[h,i]	18.1[e]	18.1[e]	15.2[j,b]
Economy: Services and other activity (% of GVA)[e,h,j,k]	72.8	73.0	74.3[b]
Employment in agriculture (% of employed)[l]	34.5	32.3	29.9[b]
Employment in industry (% of employed)[l]	23.1	22.6	23.3[b]
Employment in services & other sectors (% employed)[l]	42.4	45.1	46.9[b]
Unemployment rate (% of labour force)[l]	5.7	8.5	9.9
Labour force participation rate (female/male pop. %)[l]	31.5 / 55.0	31.4 / 54.9	30.7 / 54.1
CPI: Consumer Price Index (2010=100)[l,m]	100	108	119[d]
Agricultural production index (2014-2016=100)	98	102	95[b]
International trade: exports (million current US$)	70	59	29[d]
International trade: imports (million current US$)	310	371	368[d]
International trade: balance (million current US$)	- 240	- 312	- 339[d]
Balance of payments, current account (million US$)	- 62	- 13	- 116[d]

Major trading partners

							2021
Export partners (% of exports)	New Zealand	23.3	American Samoa	21.1	United States	18.6
Import partners (% of imports)	New Zealand	23.2	Singapore	16.0	China	13.5

Social indicators

	2010	2015	2022
Population growth rate (average annual %)	0.8	0.9	1.5[a]
Urban population (% of total population)	20.1	18.9	18.1[n]
Urban population growth rate (average annual %)[o]	- 0.4	- 0.4	...
Fertility rate, total (live births per woman)	4.6	4.4	3.9[a]
Life expectancy at birth (females/males, years)	75.0 / 69.7	75.2 / 70.1	75.3 / 70.1[a]
Population age distribution (0-14/60+ years old, %)	39.0 / 6.8	38.4 / 7.2	37.6 / 8.1[a]
International migrant stock (000/% of total pop.)[p]	5.1 / 2.8	4.3 / 2.2	4.0 / 2.0[b]
Refugees and others of concern to the UNHCR (000)	...	...	~0.0[b]
Infant mortality rate (per 1 000 live births)	16.3	15.7	15.1[a]
Health: Current expenditure (% of GDP)[q]	5.3	5.8	6.4[n]
Health: Physicians (per 1 000 pop.)	0.3	0.5[r]	0.6[b]
Education: Government expenditure (% of GDP)	5.1[s]	4.9[l]	4.8[l,b]
Education: Primary gross enrol. ratio (f/m per 100 pop.)	109.9 / 111.5	106.4 / 106.4	117.1 / 118.6[b]
Education: Sec. gross enrol. ratio (f/m per 100 pop.)	93.6 / 82.3	99.1 / 89.3	98.0 / 88.8[t]
Education: Upr. Sec. gross enrol. ratio (f/m per 100 pop.)	87.3 / 70.3	94.5 / 79.0	92.3 / 79.6[t]
Intentional homicide rate (per 100 000 pop.)	8.6	3.1[r]	6.6[c]
Seats held by women in the National Parliament (%)	8.2	6.1	7.8[u]

Environment and infrastructure indicators

	2010	2015	2022
Individuals using the Internet (per 100 inhabitants)[l]	7.0	25.4	33.6[v]
Threatened species (number)	78	90	110
Forested area (% of land area)[l]	58.8	58.0	57.3[n]
Energy production, primary (Petajoules)	2	2	2[l,n]
Energy supply per capita (Gigajoules)	23	26	29[n]
Tourist/visitor arrivals at national borders (000)	122	128	23[b]
Important sites for terrestrial biodiversity protected (%)	47.0	47.0	47.1[d]
Pop. using safely managed sanitation (urban/rural %)	38.1 / 50.7	37.2 / 50.4	36.6 / 50.1[b]
Net Official Development Assist. received (% of GNI)	19.35	12.14	21.25[b]

a Projected estimate (medium fertility variant). b 2020. c 2018. d 2021. e At producers' prices. f Including taxes less subsidies on production. g Excludes irrigation canals and landscaping care. h Data classified according to ISIC Rev. 4. i Excludes publishing activities. Includes irrigation and canals. j Including taxes less subsidies on production and imports. k Includes publishing activities and landscape care. Excludes repair of personal and household goods. l Estimate. m Excluding rent. n 2019. o Data refers to a 5-year period preceding the reference year. p Including refugees. q Data refer to fiscal years beginning 1 July. r 2013. s 2008. t 2016. u Data are as at 1 January of reporting year. v 2017.

San Marino

Region	Southern Europe	UN membership date	02 March 1992
Population (000, 2022)	34[a]	Surface area (km2)	61[b]
Pop. density (per km2, 2022)	551.8[a]	Sex ratio (m per 100 f)	94.8[a]
Capital city	San Marino	National currency	Euro (EUR)
Capital city pop. (000, 2022)	4.5[c]	Exchange rate (per US$)	0.9[d]

Economic indicators	2010	2015	2022
GDP: Gross domestic product (million current US$)	2 139	1 419	1 555[b]
GDP growth rate (annual %, const. 2015 prices)	- 4.6	- 6.2	- 6.5[b]
GDP per capita (current US$)	68 505.8	42 643.4	45 832.2[b]
Economy: Agriculture (% of Gross Value Added)[e,f]	0.0	0.0	0.0[b]
Economy: Industry (% of Gross Value Added)[e,g]	36.1	35.1	37.2[b]
Economy: Services and other activity (% of GVA)[e,h]	63.9	64.9	62.8[b]
Employment in agriculture (% of employed)	0.3[i]	...	...
Employment in industry (% of employed)	34.3[i]	...	...
Employment in services & other sectors (% employed)	65.4[i]	...	...
Unemployment rate (% of labour force)	4.4	6.6[i,j,k]	...
CPI: Consumer Price Index (2010=100)[l]	...	108	115[d]

Social indicators	2010	2015	2022
Population growth rate (average annual %)	2.2	0.8	- 0.1[a]
Urban population (% of total population)	95.7	96.7	97.4[m]
Urban population growth rate (average annual %)[n]	1.5	1.4	...
Fertility rate, total (live births per woman)	1.5	1.2	1.1[a]
Life expectancy at birth (females/males, years)	84.3 / 80.9	84.3 / 81.4	84.7 / 82.0[a]
Population age distribution (0-14/60+ years old, %)	15.4 / 23.0	14.9 / 24.1	12.7 / 27.8[a]
International migrant stock (000/% of total pop.)[o]	4.9 / 15.6	5.2 / 15.6	5.5 / 16.3[b]
Infant mortality rate (per 1 000 live births)	3.0	2.8	2.4[a]
Health: Current expenditure (% of GDP)	6.6	7.2	6.4[m]
Health: Physicians (per 1 000 pop.)	...	6.1[k]	...
Education: Government expenditure (% of GDP)	2.6	2.7[p]	3.4[m]
Education: Primary gross enrol. ratio (f/m per 100 pop.)	... / ...	... / ...	95.0 / 97.4[q,b]
Education: Sec. gross enrol. ratio (f/m per 100 pop.)	... / ...	... / ...	60.7 / 63.5[q,b]
Education: Upr. Sec. gross enrol. ratio (f/m per 100 pop.)	... / ...	... / ...	37.6 / 46.4[q,b]
Intentional homicide rate (per 100 000 pop.)	0.0	0.0[p]	...
Seats held by women in the National Parliament (%)	16.7	16.7	33.3[r]

Environment and infrastructure indicators	2010	2015	2022
Individuals using the Internet (per 100 inhabitants)	54.2[s]	49.6[p]	60.2[q,t]
Threatened species (number)	0	1	5
Forested area (% of land area)[q]	16.7	16.7	16.7[m]
Tourist/visitor arrivals at national borders (000)[u]	120	54	58[b]

a Projected estimate (medium fertility variant). b 2020. c 2018. d 2021. e Data classified according to ISIC Rev. 4. f Excludes irrigation canals and landscaping care. g Excludes publishing activities. Includes irrigation and canals. h Includes publishing activities and landscape care. Excludes repair of personal and household goods. i Break in the time series. j Population aged 14 years and over. k 2014. l Index base: December 2010=100. m 2019. n Data refers to a 5-year period preceding the reference year. o Refers to foreign citizens. p 2011. q Estimate. r Data are as at 1 January of reporting year. s 2009. t 2017. u Including Italian visitors.

Sao Tome and Principe

Region	Middle Africa	UN membership date	16 September 1975
Population (000, 2022)	227[a]	Surface area (km2)	964[b]
Pop. density (per km2, 2022)	236.9[a]	Sex ratio (m per 100 f)	99.5[a]
Capital city	Sao Tome	National currency	Dobra (STN)
Capital city pop. (000, 2022)	80.1[c]	Exchange rate (per US$)	19.9[b]

Economic indicators

	2010	2015	2022
GDP: Gross domestic product (million current US$)	197	318	476[b]
GDP growth rate (annual %, const. 2015 prices)	6.7	3.9	3.1[b]
GDP per capita (current US$)	1 094.7	1 595.8	2 174.0[b]
Economy: Agriculture (% of Gross Value Added)[d]	11.8	12.2	14.3[b]
Economy: Industry (% of Gross Value Added)[d]	18.2	15.7	13.5[b]
Economy: Services and other activity (% of GVA)[d]	70.1	72.1	72.2[b]
Employment in agriculture (% of employed)[e]	24.3	21.1	18.7[b]
Employment in industry (% of employed)[e]	17.8	18.3	18.5[b]
Employment in services & other sectors (% employed)[e]	57.9	60.5	62.9[b]
Unemployment rate (% of labour force)[e]	14.6	13.8	15.7
Labour force participation rate (female/male pop. %)[e]	37.8 / 72.0	37.9 / 71.9	37.6 / 70.1
CPI: Consumer Price Index (2010=100)	100	154	185[c]
Agricultural production index (2014-2016=100)	104	90	103[b]
International trade: exports (million current US$)	6	9	19[f]
International trade: imports (million current US$)	112	142	166[f]
International trade: balance (million current US$)	- 106	- 133	- 147[f]
Balance of payments, current account (million US$)	- 88	- 69	- 60[b]

Major trading partners

						2021
Export partners (% of exports)	Netherlands	45.1	Belgium	21.3	Portugal	13.1
Import partners (% of imports)	Portugal	49.3	Angola	12.0	Togo	9.4

Social indicators

	2010	2015	2022
Population growth rate (average annual %)	2.2	1.8	2.0[a]
Urban population (% of total population)	65.0	70.2	73.6[g]
Urban population growth rate (average annual %)[h]	4.2	3.8	...
Fertility rate, total (live births per woman)	4.7	4.4	3.8[a]
Life expectancy at birth (females/males, years)	67.8 / 62.9	70.2 / 64.6	71.9 / 66.1[a]
Population age distribution (0-14/60+ years old, %)	42.1 / 5.1	42.3 / 5.2	39.5 / 5.9[a]
International migrant stock (000/% of total pop.)[i]	2.7 / 1.5	2.4 / 1.2	2.1 / 1.0[b]
Infant mortality rate (per 1 000 live births)	26.8	17.8	12.6[a]
Health: Current expenditure (% of GDP)[j]	6.8	5.3	5.5[g]
Health: Physicians (per 1 000 pop.)	...	0.3	0.5[g]
Education: Government expenditure (% of GDP)	9.7	3.9	5.9[e,g]
Education: Primary gross enrol. ratio (f/m per 100 pop.)	116.2 / 117.0	103.2 / 107.3	105.0 / 108.5[k]
Education: Sec. gross enrol. ratio (f/m per 100 pop.)	52.3 / 51.2	86.9 / 78.2	95.9 / 82.9[k]
Education: Upr. Sec. gross enrol. ratio (f/m per 100 pop.)	17.8 / 22.6	64.3 / 56.4	78.2 / 63.0[k]
Intentional homicide rate (per 100 000 pop.)	3.3	3.3[l]	...
Seats held by women in the National Parliament (%)	7.3	18.2	23.6[m]

Environment and infrastructure indicators

	2010	2015	2022
Individuals using the Internet (per 100 inhabitants)	18.8	25.8[e]	33.0[e,b]
Threatened species (number)	70	81	140
Forested area (% of land area)[e]	60.5	57.3	54.7[g]
Energy production, primary (Petajoules)	1	1	1[g]
Energy supply per capita (Gigajoules)	13	14[e]	14[e,g]
Tourist/visitor arrivals at national borders (000)	8	26	11[b]
Important sites for terrestrial biodiversity protected (%)	86.3	86.3	86.3[f]
Pop. using safely managed drinking water (urban/rural, %)	36.3 / 21.4	38.6 / 23.1	40.1 / 24.7[b]
Pop. using safely managed sanitation (urban/rural %)	26.1 / 18.8	31.1 / 24.3	36.1 / 30.3[b]
Net Official Development Assist. received (% of GNI)	25.48	15.54	19.46[b]

a Projected estimate (medium fertility variant). **b** 2020. **c** 2018. **d** Data classified according to ISIC Rev. 4. **e** Estimate. **f** 2021. **g** 2019. **h** Data refers to a 5-year period preceding the reference year. **i** Refers to foreign citizens. **j** Data revision. **k** 2017. **l** 2011. **m** Data are as at 1 January of reporting year.

Saudi Arabia

Region	Western Asia
Population (000, 2022)	36 409[a]
Pop. density (per km2, 2022)	16.9[a]
Capital city	Riyadh
Capital city pop. (000, 2022)	7 070.7[c]

UN membership date	24 October 1945
Surface area (km2)	2 206 714[b]
Sex ratio (m per 100 f)	136.0[a]
National currency	Saudi Riyal (SAR)
Exchange rate (per US$)	3.8[d]

Economic indicators	2010	2015	2022
GDP: Gross domestic product (million current US$)	528 207	654 270	700 118[b]
GDP growth rate (annual %, const. 2015 prices)	5.0	4.1	- 4.1[b]
GDP per capita (current US$)	19 262.6	20 627.9	20 110.3[b]
Economy: Agriculture (% of Gross Value Added)[e]	2.6	2.6	2.6[b]
Economy: Industry (% of Gross Value Added)[f]	58.2	45.3	41.3[b]
Economy: Services and other activity (% of GVA)[g,h]	39.1	52.0	56.1[b]
Employment in agriculture (% of employed)	4.2[i]	6.1	2.3[i,b]
Employment in industry (% of employed)	21.1[i]	22.7	24.8[i,b]
Employment in services & other sectors (% employed)	74.7[i]	71.2	72.9[i,b]
Unemployment rate (% of labour force)	5.6	5.6	6.7[i]
Labour force participation rate (female/male pop. %)	18.4 / 74.9[i]	21.2 / 76.8	30.8 / 81.2[i]
CPI: Consumer Price Index (2010=100)	100[j]	96[k]	104[k,d]
Agricultural production index (2014-2016=100)	101	101	151[b]
International trade: exports (million current US$)[l]	250 577	203 689	298 163[i,d]
International trade: imports (million current US$)[l]	103 622	174 786	146 700[i,d]
International trade: balance (million current US$)[l]	146 955	28 903	151 463[d]
Balance of payments, current account (million US$)	66 751	- 56 724	44 324[d]

Major trading partners						2021
Export partners (% of exports)[i]	Areas nes	71.1	United Arab Emirates	4.8	China	4.4
Import partners (% of imports)[i]	China	20.2	United States	10.7	United Arab Emirates	6.8

Social indicators	2010	2015	2022
Population growth rate (average annual %)	2.7	1.9	1.5[a]
Urban population (% of total population)	82.1	83.2	84.1[c]
Urban population growth rate (average annual %)[m]	3.0	3.1	...
Fertility rate, total (live births per woman)	2.9	2.6	2.4[a]
Life expectancy at birth (females/males, years)	77.6 / 74.5	78.6 / 75.8	79.5 / 76.7[a]
Population age distribution (0-14/60+ years old, %)	29.5 / 3.2	27.5 / 4.1	25.9 / 5.3[a]
International migrant stock (000/% of total pop.)[n,o]	8 430.0 / 30.7	10 771.4 / 34.0	13 454.8 / 38.6[b]
Refugees and others of concern to the UNHCR (000)	70.7	70.3	80.5[d]
Infant mortality rate (per 1 000 live births)	10.5	7.8	5.5[a]
Health: Current expenditure (% of GDP)[p]	3.6	6.0	5.7[i,c]
Health: Physicians (per 1 000 pop.)	2.4	2.6[q]	2.7[b]
Education: Government expenditure (% of GDP)	5.1[r]	...	...
Education: Primary gross enrol. ratio (f/m per 100 pop.)	106.2 / 107.1	112.1 / 108.7	101.2 / 99.3[b]
Education: Sec. gross enrol. ratio (f/m per 100 pop.)	89.0 / 100.4[i,s]	115.0 / 117.9	108.3 / 116.7[b]
Education: Upr. Sec. gross enrol. ratio (f/m per 100 pop.)	83.1 / 92.8[s]	116.5 / 122.7	109.6 / 126.5[b]
Intentional homicide rate (per 100 000 pop.)	1.1[t]	...	0.8[c]
Seats held by women in the National Parliament (%)	0.0	19.9	19.9[u]

Environment and infrastructure indicators	2010	2015	2022
Individuals using the Internet (per 100 inhabitants)	41.0	69.6[v]	97.9[b]
Research & Development expenditure (% of GDP)	0.9[w,x]	0.8[w,y,z]	0.5[b]
Threatened species (number)	103	119	168
Forested area (% of land area)[i]	0.5	0.5	0.5[c]
CO2 emission estimates (million tons/tons per capita)	421.7 / 15.3	536.1 / 16.8	499.4 / 14.4[c]
Energy production, primary (Petajoules)	22 115	27 723	27 418[c]
Energy supply per capita (Gigajoules)	281	325	296[c]
Tourist/visitor arrivals at national borders (000)	10 850	17 994	4 138[b]
Important sites for terrestrial biodiversity protected (%)	22.0	22.0	22.0[d]
Net Official Development Assist. received (% of GNI)	- 0.03[t]	...	...

a Projected estimate (medium fertility variant). **b** 2020. **c** 2019. **d** 2021. **e** Excludes irrigation canals and landscaping care. Data classified according to ISIC Rev. 4. **f** Data classified according to ISIC Rev. 4. Includes publishing activities and landscape care. Excludes repair of personal and household goods. **g** Includes publishing activities and landscape care. Excludes repair of personal and household goods. **h** Data classified according to ISIC Rev. 4. **i** Estimate. **j** Calculated by the UNSD from national indices. **k** Base: 2018=100. **l** Major export partners were confidential or unknown (denoted Areas nes) and resulted in high partner concentration for exports in graph 5. **m** Data refers to a 5-year period preceding the reference year. **n** Including refugees. **o** Refers to foreign citizens. **p** Data based on calendar year (January 1 to December 31). **q** 2014. **r** 2008. **s** 2009. **t** 2007. **u** Data are as at 1 January of reporting year. **v** This number is reflecting the whole population, based on the age range 12-65 years for the study it is 70% of the population. **w** Based on R&D budget instead of R&D expenditure. **x** Overestimated or based on overestimated data. Break in the time series. **y** Overestimated or based on overestimated data. **z** 2013.

Senegal

Region	Western Africa	UN membership date	28 September 1960
Population (000, 2022)	17 316[a]	Surface area (km2)	196 712[b]
Pop. density (per km2, 2022)	89.9[a]	Sex ratio (m per 100 f)	96.8[a]
Capital city	Dakar	National currency	CFA Franc, BCEAO (XOF)[c]
Capital city pop. (000, 2022)	3 057.1[d,e]	Exchange rate (per US$)	579.2[f]

Economic indicators

	2010	2015	2022
GDP: Gross domestic product (million current US$)	16 725	17 761	24 412[b]
GDP growth rate (annual %, const. 2015 prices)	4.2	6.4	0.8[b]
GDP per capita (current US$)	1 319.2	1 218.3	1 458.0[b]
Economy: Agriculture (% of Gross Value Added)[g,h]	16.6	16.0	16.6[b]
Economy: Industry (% of Gross Value Added)[h,i]	25.6	26.4	26.0[b]
Economy: Services and other activity (% of GVA)[h,j]	57.8	57.6	57.4[b]
Employment in agriculture (% of employed)	38.2[k]	33.3	29.4[k,b]
Employment in industry (% of employed)	12.8[k]	13.0	13.6[k,b]
Employment in services & other sectors (% employed)	49.0[k]	53.7	56.9[k,b]
Unemployment rate (% of labour force)	10.3[k]	6.8	3.6[k]
Labour force participation rate (female/male pop. %)	34.0 / 63.7[k]	34.4 / 57.9	33.9 / 56.9[k]
CPI: Consumer Price Index (2010=100)[l]	100	105	115[m,f]
Agricultural production index (2014-2016=100)	98	112	180[b]
International trade: exports (million current US$)	2 086	2 612	5 202[f]
International trade: imports (million current US$)	4 777	5 595	9 699[f]
International trade: balance (million current US$)	- 2 691	- 2 984	- 4 497[f]
Balance of payments, current account (million US$)	- 589	- 945	- 2 215[n]

Major trading partners

						2021
Export partners (% of exports)	Mali	20.2	Switzerland	14.4	India	9.8
Import partners (% of imports)	France	11.8	China	9.7	India	7.1

Social indicators

	2010	2015	2022
Population growth rate (average annual %)	2.7	2.7	2.5[a]
Urban population (% of total population)	43.8	45.9	47.7[e]
Urban population growth rate (average annual %)[o]	3.7	3.9	...
Fertility rate, total (live births per woman)	5.1	4.8	4.3[a]
Life expectancy at birth (females/males, years)	66.3 / 62.8	69.1 / 64.5	70.2 / 65.5[a]
Population age distribution (0-14/60+ years old, %)	43.2 / 4.9	43.1 / 4.8	41.5 / 4.9[a]
International migrant stock (000/% of total pop.)[p]	256.1 / 2.0	266.5 / 1.8	274.9 / 1.6[b]
Refugees and others of concern to the UNHCR (000)	24.2[q]	17.3	16.5[f]
Infant mortality rate (per 1 000 live births)	40.0	31.5	21.0[a]
Health: Current expenditure (% of GDP)	4.0	4.4	4.1[e]
Health: Physicians (per 1 000 pop.)	0.1[f]	0.2	0.1[e]
Education: Government expenditure (% of GDP)	5.2	5.5	5.3[k,e]
Education: Primary gross enrol. ratio (f/m per 100 pop.)	86.4 / 81.7	89.8 / 80.2	88.9 / 77.3[b]
Education: Sec. gross enrol. ratio (f/m per 100 pop.)	33.8 / 38.7	50.1 / 50.4[s]	50.1 / 43.1[b]
Education: Upr. Sec. gross enrol. ratio (f/m per 100 pop.)	13.4 / 19.9[r]	32.4 / 37.3[k,s]	37.3 / 34.7[b]
Intentional homicide rate (per 100 000 pop.)	...	0.3	...
Seats held by women in the National Parliament (%)	22.7	42.7	42.7[t]

Environment and infrastructure indicators

	2010	2015	2022
Individuals using the Internet (per 100 inhabitants)[k]	8.0[u]	21.7	42.6[b]
Research & Development expenditure (% of GDP)	0.4	0.6[v]	...
Threatened species (number)	82	106	182
Forested area (% of land area)[k]	44.0	42.9	42.1[e]
CO2 emission estimates (million tons/tons per capita)	5.9 / 0.4	7.9 / 0.5	8.9 / 0.5[e]
Energy production, primary (Petajoules)	86	69	75[e]
Energy supply per capita (Gigajoules)	13	12	13[e]
Tourist/visitor arrivals at national borders (000)[k]	900	1 007	1 365[w]
Important sites for terrestrial biodiversity protected (%)	42.1	42.5	45.4[f]
Pop. using safely managed sanitation (urban/rural %)	17.0 / 18.2	20.9 / 21.0	24.4 / 23.9[b]
Net Official Development Assist. received (% of GNI)	5.86	5.00	6.63[b]

a Projected estimate (medium fertility variant). b 2020. c African Financial Community (CFA) Franc, Central Bank of West African States (BCEAO). d Refers to the sum of the Departments of Dakar, Pikinie and Guédiawaye, in Dakar Region. e 2019. f 2021. g Excludes irrigation canals and landscaping care. h Data classified according to ISIC Rev. 4. i Excludes publishing activities. Includes irrigation and canals. j Includes publishing activities and landscape care. Excludes repair of personal and household goods. k Estimate. l WAEMU harmonized consumer price index. m Calculated by the UNSD from national indices. n 2018. o Data refers to a 5-year period preceding the reference year. p Including refugees. q Data as at the end of December. r 2008. s 2014. t Data are as at 1 January of reporting year. u Refers to total population. Survey result: 16% for population age 12+. v Excluding business enterprise. w 2017.

Serbia

Region	Southern Europe	UN membership date	01 November 2000
Population (000, 2022)	7 221 [a,b]	Surface area (km2)	88 444 [c]
Pop. density (per km2, 2022)	94.1 [a,b]	Sex ratio (m per 100 f)	92.1 [a,b]
Capital city	Belgrade	National currency	Serbian Dinar (RSD)
Capital city pop. (000, 2022)	1 393.7 [d,e]	Exchange rate (per US$)	103.9 [f]

Economic indicators	2010	2015	2022
GDP: Gross domestic product (million current US$) [g]	41 819	39 656	53 335 [c]
GDP growth rate (annual %, const. 2015 prices) [g]	0.7	1.8	- 0.9 [c]
GDP per capita (current US$) [g]	5 735.4	5 589.0	7 655.7 [c]
Economy: Agriculture (% of Gross Value Added) [h,i]	7.9	8.1	7.6 [c]
Economy: Industry (% of Gross Value Added) [i,j]	30.3	30.9	30.0 [c]
Economy: Services and other activity (% of GVA) [i,k]	61.8	61.0	62.4 [c]
Employment in agriculture (% of employed)	22.3	19.4	15.1 [l,c]
Employment in industry (% of employed)	25.6	24.5	27.4 [l,c]
Employment in services & other sectors (% employed)	52.1	56.1	57.6 [l,c]
Unemployment rate (% of labour force)	19.2	17.7	10.6 [l]
Labour force participation rate (female/male pop. %)	39.0 / 55.4	43.4 / 60.3	46.5 / 62.0 [l]
CPI: Consumer Price Index (2010=100)	100	133	152 [f]
Agricultural production index (2014-2016=100)	100	94	111 [c]
International trade: exports (million current US$) [m]	9 795	13 379	25 564 [f]
International trade: imports (million current US$) [m]	16 735	18 210	33 791 [f]
International trade: balance (million current US$) [m]	- 6 940	- 4 831	- 8 228 [f]
Balance of payments, current account (million US$)	- 2 692	- 1 370	- 2 742 [f]

Major trading partners						2021
Export partners (% of exports)	Germany	12.7	Italy	8.5	Bosnia Herzegovina	7.2
Import partners (% of imports)	Germany	13.2	China	12.8	Italy	8.1

Social indicators	2010	2015	2022
Population growth rate (average annual %) [a]	- 0.4	- 0.3	- 1.1 [b]
Urban population (% of total population) [n]	55.0	55.7	56.3 [e]
Urban population growth rate (average annual %) [n,o]	–0.0	- 0.1	...
Fertility rate, total (live births per woman) [a]	1.4	1.5	1.5 [b]
Life expectancy at birth (females/males, years) [a]	77.3 / 71.4	78.7 / 72.8	77.0 / 71.3 [b]
Population age distribution (0-14/60+ years old, %) [a]	14.3 / 24.5	14.3 / 26.4	14.4 / 27.1 [b]
International migrant stock (000/% of total pop.) [n]	826.3 / 9.2	807.4 / 9.1	823.0 / 9.4 [c]
Refugees and others of concern to the UNHCR (000)	312.6 [n,p]	259.7 [n]	243.9 [f]
Infant mortality rate (per 1 000 live births) [a]	5.9	4.6	4.4 [b]
Health: Current expenditure (% of GDP)	9.5	8.8	8.7 [e]
Health: Physicians (per 1 000 pop.)	2.5	2.5	3.1 [q]
Education: Government expenditure (% of GDP)	4.3	3.8	3.6 [e]
Education: Primary gross enrol. ratio (f/m per 100 pop.) [l]	95.6 / 96.1	101.2 / 101.5	97.6 / 97.8 [c]
Education: Sec. gross enrol. ratio (f/m per 100 pop.) [l]	92.4 / 90.5	97.4 / 96.0	92.9 / 91.6 [c]
Education: Upr. Sec. gross enrol. ratio (f/m per 100 pop.) [l]	86.9 / 83.1	93.1 / 89.7	89.0 / 86.3 [c]
Intentional homicide rate (per 100 000 pop.)	1.4	1.2	1.0 [c]
Seats held by women in the National Parliament (%)	21.6	34.0	40.0 [r]

Environment and infrastructure indicators	2010	2015	2022
Individuals using the Internet (per 100 inhabitants)	40.9	65.3	78.4 [c]
Research & Development expenditure (% of GDP) [s]	0.7	0.8	0.9 [c]
Threatened species (number)	46	56	121
Forested area (% of land area) [l]	31.0	31.1	31.1 [e]
CO2 emission estimates (million tons/tons per capita)	46.8 / 6.3	45.4 / 6.3	46.2 / 6.3 [c]
Energy production, primary (Petajoules) [a]	440	449	426 [e]
Energy supply per capita (Gigajoules) [a]	90	86	91 [e]
Tourist/visitor arrivals at national borders (000) [t,u]	683	1 132	446 [c]
Important sites for terrestrial biodiversity protected (%)	21.0	26.2	28.8 [f]
Pop. using safely managed drinking water (urban/rural, %)	81.5 / 66.6	81.5 / 66.6	81.5 / 66.6 [c]
Pop. using safely managed sanitation (urban/rural %)	14.8 / 25.6	15.9 / 22.1	17.2 / 19.9 [c]
Net Official Development Assist. received (% of GNI)	1.62	0.80	0.94 [c]

a Excluding Kosovo. b Projected estimate (medium fertility variant). c 2020. d Refers to the urban population of Belgrade area. e 2019. f 2021. g Including Kosovo and Metohija. h Excludes irrigation canals and landscaping care. i Data classified according to ISIC Rev. 4. j Excludes publishing activities. Includes irrigation and canals. k Includes publishing activities and landscape care. Excludes repair of personal and household goods. l Estimate. m Special trade system up to 2008. n Including Kosovo. o Data refers to a 5-year period preceding the reference year. p Data as at the end of December. q 2016. r Data are as at 1 January of reporting year. s Excluding data from some regions, provinces or states. t Tourists staying in visitor accommodation establishments. u Excluding Kosovo and Metohija.

Seychelles

Region	Eastern Africa	UN membership date	21 September 1976
Population (000, 2022)	107[a]	Surface area (km2)	457[b]
Pop. density (per km2, 2022)	234.4[a]	Sex ratio (m per 100 f)	111.2[a]
Capital city	Victoria	National currency	Seychelles Rupee (SCR)
Capital city pop. (000, 2022)	28.1[c]	Exchange rate (per US$)	14.7[d]

Economic indicators

	2010	2015	2022
GDP: Gross domestic product (million current US$)	970	1 377	1 059[b]
GDP growth rate (annual %, const. 2015 prices)	5.9	4.9	- 10.8[b]
GDP per capita (current US$)	10 628.1	14 503.3	10 766.8[b]
Economy: Agriculture (% of Gross Value Added)[e,f]	2.7	2.4	2.2[b]
Economy: Industry (% of Gross Value Added)[f,g]	16.5	14.0	16.4[b]
Economy: Services and other activity (% of GVA)[f,h]	80.8	83.6	81.4[b]
Employment in agriculture (% of employed)	...	3.6[i,j,k]	...
Employment in industry (% of employed)	...	17.9[i,j,k]	...
Employment in services & other sectors (% employed)	...	78.2[i,j,k]	...
Unemployment rate (% of labour force)	5.5[l]	4.1[i,j,m,k]	...
Labour force participation rate (female/male pop. %)	... / ...	61.9 / 68.3[i,j,m,k]	... / ...
CPI: Consumer Price Index (2010=100)[n]	100	121	144[d]
Agricultural production index (2014-2016=100)	100	99	98[b]
International trade: exports (million current US$)[o]	418	474	1 075[p,d]
International trade: imports (million current US$)[o]	1 180	975	1 132[p,d]
International trade: balance (million current US$)[o]	- 763	- 501	- 58[d]
Balance of payments, current account (million US$)	- 214	- 256	- 312[b]

Major trading partners

					2021
Export partners (% of exports)[p]	Bermuda 19.4	France 15.5	Cayman Islands 12.2
Import partners (% of imports)[p]	United Arab Emirates 19.2	British Virgin Islands 11.9	Germany 9.3

Social indicators

	2010	2015	2022
Population growth rate (average annual %)	1.5	1.2	0.4[a]
Urban population (% of total population)	53.3	55.4	57.1[q]
Urban population growth rate (average annual %)[r]	1.2	1.3	...
Fertility rate, total (live births per woman)	2.2	2.3	2.3[a]
Life expectancy at birth (females/males, years)	77.6 / 68.8	78.3 / 69.7	76.0 / 68.2[a]
Population age distribution (0-14/60+ years old, %)	24.3 / 9.2	23.3 / 10.2	23.1 / 13.1[a]
International migrant stock (000/% of total pop.)	11.4 / 12.5	12.8 / 13.5	13.0 / 13.3[b]
Refugees and others of concern to the UNHCR (000)	...	...	~0.0[c]
Infant mortality rate (per 1 000 live births)	12.0	12.6	11.4[a]
Health: Current expenditure (% of GDP)	4.8	4.6	5.2[q]
Health: Physicians (per 1 000 pop.)	1.1	1.0[s]	2.3[q]
Education: Government expenditure (% of GDP)	3.5	4.2	3.9[p,q]
Education: Primary gross enrol. ratio (f/m per 100 pop.)	112.1 / 108.8	106.0 / 102.8	103.0 / 98.7[b]
Education: Sec. gross enrol. ratio (f/m per 100 pop.)	77.1 / 72.5[p]	84.4 / 78.6	81.6 / 75.2[b]
Education: Upr. Sec. gross enrol. ratio (f/m per 100 pop.)	56.0 / 47.5[p]	63.3 / 55.9	63.4 / 54.4[b]
Intentional homicide rate (per 100 000 pop.)	9.9	7.4	10.2[q]
Seats held by women in the National Parliament (%)	23.5	43.8	22.9[t]

Environment and infrastructure indicators

	2010	2015	2022
Individuals using the Internet (per 100 inhabitants)[p]	41.0	54.3	79.0[b]
Research & Development expenditure (% of GDP)	0.3[l]	...	0.2[m,u]
Threatened species (number)	190	435	461
Forested area (% of land area)[p]	73.3	73.3	73.3[q]
Energy production, primary (Petajoules)	0	0	0[q]
Energy supply per capita (Gigajoules)	67	73	85[q]
Tourist/visitor arrivals at national borders (000)	175	276	115[b]
Important sites for terrestrial biodiversity protected (%)	24.3	24.3	52.8[d]
Net Official Development Assist. received (% of GNI)	5.88	0.52	1.15[v]

a Projected estimate (medium fertility variant). b 2020. c 2018. d 2021. e Excludes irrigation canals and landscaping care. f Data classified according to ISIC Rev. 4. g Excludes publishing activities. Includes irrigation and canals. h Includes publishing activities and landscape care. Excludes repair of personal and household goods. i Excluding some areas. j Excluding the institutional population. k 2011. l 2005. m Break in the time series. n Calculated by the UNSD from national indices. o As of 2010, trade in services data reflect improvement of the coverage of balance of payment statistics. p Estimate. q 2019. r Data refers to a 5-year period preceding the reference year. s 2012. t Data are as at 1 January of reporting year. u 2016. v 2017.

Sierra Leone

Region	Western Africa	UN membership date	27 September 1961
Population (000, 2022)	8 606 [a]	Surface area (km2)	72 300 [b]
Pop. density (per km2, 2022)	120.0 [a]	Sex ratio (m per 100 f)	100.4 [a]
Capital city	Freetown	National currency	Leone (SLL)
Capital city pop. (000, 2022)	1 168.4 [c]	Exchange rate (per US$)	11 224.6 [d]

Economic indicators	2010	2015	2022
GDP: Gross domestic product (million current US$)	2 578	4 248	3 787 [b]
GDP growth rate (annual %, const. 2015 prices)	5.3	- 20.5	- 2.2 [b]
GDP per capita (current US$)	401.8	592.3	474.7 [b]
Economy: Agriculture (% of Gross Value Added) [e]	55.2	60.5	63.3 [b]
Economy: Industry (% of Gross Value Added) [e]	8.1	4.6	4.7 [b]
Economy: Services and other activity (% of GVA) [e]	36.7	34.9	32.0 [b]
Employment in agriculture (% of employed) [f]	63.9	57.9	54.4 [b]
Employment in industry (% of employed) [f]	5.3	5.8	6.5 [b]
Employment in services & other sectors (% employed) [f]	30.8	36.3	39.1 [b]
Unemployment rate (% of labour force) [f]	4.2	4.7	5.0
Labour force participation rate (female/male pop. %) [f]	60.2 / 61.2	56.4 / 57.3	56.3 / 55.9
CPI: Consumer Price Index (2010=100) [g]	100	134	297 [d]
Agricultural production index (2014-2016=100)	101	96	108 [b]
International trade: exports (million current US$)	319 [f]	93	263 [f,d]
International trade: imports (million current US$)	776 [f]	1 759	1 939 [f,d]
International trade: balance (million current US$)	- 457 [f]	- 1 666	- 1 677 [d]
Balance of payments, current account (million US$)	- 585	- 1 003	- 276 [b]

Major trading partners						2021
Export partners (% of exports) [f]	China	42.6	Belgium	14.3	Germany	8.2
Import partners (% of imports) [f]	China	29.1	India	11.4	Türkiye	8.0

Social indicators	2010	2015	2022
Population growth rate (average annual %)	2.7	2.4	2.1 [a]
Urban population (% of total population)	38.9	40.8	42.5 [c]
Urban population growth rate (average annual %) [h]	3.7	3.3	...
Fertility rate, total (live births per woman)	5.3	4.5	3.9 [a]
Life expectancy at birth (females/males, years)	54.5 / 52.9	58.2 / 56.2	61.7 / 59.1 [a]
Population age distribution (0-14/60+ years old, %)	43.2 / 5.0	41.8 / 4.9	39.0 / 5.1 [a]
International migrant stock (000/% of total pop.) [i]	79.3 / 1.2	58.8 / 0.8	53.7 / 0.7 [b]
Refugees and others of concern to the UNHCR (000)	8.6 [i]	1.4	0.3 [d]
Infant mortality rate (per 1 000 live births)	104.4	88.1	70.0 [a]
Health: Current expenditure (% of GDP) [k]	10.9	20.4	8.7 [c]
Health: Physicians (per 1 000 pop.)	~0.0	~0.0 [l]	0.1 [m]
Education: Government expenditure (% of GDP)	2.6	3.1 [f]	9.3 [b]
Education: Primary gross enrol. ratio (f/m per 100 pop.)	... / ...	116.9 / 115.3	143.7 / 139.0 [b]
Education: Sec. gross enrol. ratio (f/m per 100 pop.)	... / ...	36.5 / 41.6	41.1 / 42.5 [b]
Education: Upr. Sec. gross enrol. ratio (f/m per 100 pop.)	... / ...	22.3 / 28.5	26.4 / 29.2 [n]
Intentional homicide rate (per 100 000 pop.)	2.5	1.7	...
Seats held by women in the National Parliament (%)	13.2	12.4	12.3 [o]

Environment and infrastructure indicators	2010	2015	2022
Individuals using the Internet (per 100 inhabitants) [f]	0.6	6.3	18.0 [b]
Threatened species (number)	131	158	292
Forested area (% of land area) [f]	37.9	36.5	35.4 [c]
Energy production, primary (Petajoules)	52	54	56 [c]
Energy supply per capita (Gigajoules)	9	10	9 [c]
Tourist/visitor arrivals at national borders (000) [p]	39	24	24 [b]
Important sites for terrestrial biodiversity protected (%)	62.1	65.3	65.3 [d]
Pop. using safely managed drinking water (urban/rural, %)	11.5 / 4.6	12.0 / 6.7	12.5 / 9.2 [b]
Pop. using safely managed sanitation (urban/rural, %)	18.6 / 6.8	19.2 / 8.2	19.8 / 9.7 [b]
Net Official Development Assist. received (% of GNI)	17.59	22.69	22.49 [b]

a Projected estimate (medium fertility variant). b 2020. c 2019. d 2021. e Data classified according to ISIC Rev. 4. f Estimate. g Calculated by the UNSD from national indices. h Data refers to a 5-year period preceding the reference year. i Including refugees. j Data as at the end of December. k Data revision. l 2011. m 2018. n 2017. o Data are as at 1 January of reporting year. p Arrivals by air.

Singapore

Region	South-eastern Asia	UN membership date	21 September 1965
Population (000, 2022)	5 976[a]	Surface area (km2)	728[b,c]
Pop. density (per km2, 2022)	8 749.2[a]	Sex ratio (m per 100 f)	109.6[a]
Capital city	Singapore	National currency	Singapore Dollar (SGD)
Capital city pop. (000, 2022)	5 868.1[d]	Exchange rate (per US$)	1.4[e]

Economic indicators

	2010	2015	2022
GDP: Gross domestic product (million current US$)	239 808	307 999	339 988[c]
GDP growth rate (annual %, const. 2015 prices)	14.5	3.0	- 5.4[c]
GDP per capita (current US$)	46 735.5	55 076.9	58 114.2[c]
Economy: Agriculture (% of Gross Value Added)[f,g,h]	0.0	0.0	0.0[c]
Economy: Industry (% of Gross Value Added)[g,i,j]	28.2	25.8	25.6[c]
Economy: Services and other activity (% of GVA)[g,k]	71.8	74.2	74.4[c]
Employment in agriculture (% of employed)[l]	0.9	0.8	0.7[c]
Employment in industry (% of employed)[l]	21.6	17.3	15.2[c]
Employment in services & other sectors (% employed)[l]	77.5	81.9	84.1[c]
Unemployment rate (% of labour force)	4.1	3.8	3.9[l]
Labour force participation rate (female/male pop. %)	58.1 / 78.6	62.6 / 79.4	60.1 / 77.1[l]
CPI: Consumer Price Index (2010=100)	100	113	117[e]
Agricultural production index (2014-2016=100)	76	99	160[c]
International trade: exports (million current US$)	353 240	357 941	643 131[l,e]
International trade: imports (million current US$)	313 071	308 122	555 098[l,e]
International trade: balance (million current US$)	40 169	49 820	88 033[e]
Balance of payments, current account (million US$)	54 996	57 574	71 926[e]

Major trading partners

						2021
Export partners (% of exports)[l]	China	13.7	China, Hong Kong SAR	12.4	United States	10.8
Import partners (% of imports)[l]	China	14.4	Malaysia	12.7	Other Asia, nes	11.0

Social indicators

	2010	2015	2022
Population growth rate (average annual %)	2.6	1.2	0.7[a]
Urban population (% of total population)	100.0	100.0	100.0[d]
Urban population growth rate (average annual %)[m]	2.4	1.7	...
Fertility rate, total (live births per woman)	1.2	1.2	1.0[a]
Life expectancy at birth (females/males, years)	84.0 / 79.3	85.0 / 80.6	86.3 / 82.0[a]
Population age distribution (0-14/60+ years old, %)	14.3 / 12.4	12.7 / 15.5	11.8 / 23.0[a]
International migrant stock (000/% of total pop.)	2 164.8 / 42.2	2 483.4 / 44.4	2 523.6 / 43.1[c]
Refugees and others of concern to the UNHCR (000)	~0.0[n]	~0.0	1.1[e]
Infant mortality rate (per 1 000 live births)	2.2	2.1	1.7[a]
Health: Current expenditure (% of GDP)[o,p]	3.2	4.2	4.4[d]
Health: Physicians (per 1 000 pop.)	1.8	2.2	2.5[d]
Education: Government expenditure (% of GDP)	3.1	2.9	2.5[l,c]
Education: Primary gross enrol. ratio (f/m per 100 pop.)	... / ...	... / ...	100.7 / 100.7[l,d]
Education: Sec. gross enrol. ratio (f/m per 100 pop.)	... / ...	... / ...	104.3 / 105.1[l,d]
Education: Upr. Sec. gross enrol. ratio (f/m per 100 pop.)	... / ...	... / ...	107.5 / 109.3[l,d]
Intentional homicide rate (per 100 000 pop.)	0.4	0.3	0.2[c]
Seats held by women in the National Parliament (%)	23.4	25.3	29.1[q]

Environment and infrastructure indicators

	2010	2015	2022
Individuals using the Internet (per 100 inhabitants)	71.0[r]	83.2	92.0[c]
Research & Development expenditure (% of GDP)	1.9	2.2	1.9[d]
Threatened species (number)	277	287	361
Forested area (% of land area)[l]	25.3	23.2	22.0[d]
CO2 emission estimates (million tons/tons per capita)	42.7 / 8.4	45.7 / 8.2	47.6 / 8.3[d]
Energy production, primary (Petajoules)	25	26	27[d]
Energy supply per capita (Gigajoules)	211	209	142[d]
Tourist/visitor arrivals at national borders (000)[s]	9 161	12 052	2 086[c]
Important sites for terrestrial biodiversity protected (%)	21.1	21.1	21.1[e]
Pop. using safely managed drinking water (urban/rural, %)	100.0 / ...	100.0 / ...	100.0 / ...[c]
Pop. using safely managed sanitation (urban/rural %)	100.0 / ...	100.0 / ...	100.0 / ...[c]

a Projected estimate (medium fertility variant). b The land area of Singapore comprises the mainland and other islands. c 2020. d 2019. e 2021. f Includes quarrying. g Data classified according to ISIC Rev. 4. h Excludes irrigation canals and landscaping care. i Excluding quarrying. j Excludes publishing activities. Includes irrigation and canals. k Includes publishing activities and landscape care. Excludes repair of personal and household goods. l Estimate. m Data refers to a 5-year period preceding the reference year. n Data as at the end of December. o Medisave is classified as Social insurance scheme, considering that it is a compulsory payment. p Data refer to fiscal years beginning 1 April. q Data are as at 1 January of reporting year. r Population aged 7 years and over. s Excluding Malaysian citizens arriving by land.

Sint Maarten (Dutch part)

Region	Caribbean	Population (000, 2022)	44 a,b
Surface area (km2)	34 c	Pop. density (per km2, 2022)	1 299.3 a,b
Sex ratio (m per 100 f)	115.2 a,b	Capital city	Philipsburg
National currency	Neth. Ant. Guilder (ANG) d	Capital city pop. (000, 2022)	40.6 e,f
Exchange rate (per US$)	0.9 g		

Economic indicators	2010	2015	2022
GDP: Gross domestic product (million current US$)	896	1 066	858 c
GDP growth rate (annual %, const. 2015 prices)	1.1	0.5	- 24.0 c
GDP per capita (current US$)	26 237.8	26 682.0	20 000.1 c
Economy: Agriculture (% of Gross Value Added)	0.1	0.1	0.1 c
Economy: Industry (% of Gross Value Added)	13.4	9.8	10.3 c
Economy: Services and other activity (% of GVA)	86.5	90.1	89.6 c
Balance of payments, current account (million US$)	...	18	- 286 c

Social indicators	2010	2015	2022
Population growth rate (average annual %) a	0.7	2.9	~0.0 b
Urban population (% of total population)	100.0	100.0	100.0 h
Urban population growth rate (average annual %) i	0.4	3.1	...
Fertility rate, total (live births per woman) a	1.8	1.7	1.6 b
Life expectancy at birth (females/males, years) a	78.0 / 72.5	80.6 / 74.0	77.1 / 72.0 b
Population age distribution (0-14/60+ years old, %) a	22.6 / 9.2	19.2 / 11.3	11.0 / 19.7 b
International migrant stock (000/% of total pop.) j	26.2 / 76.7	27.3 / 68.3	28.8 / 67.3 c
Refugees and others of concern to the UNHCR (000)	~0.0 k	~0.0	~0.0 g
Infant mortality rate (per 1 000 live births) a	15.1	11.9	13.9 b
Education: Primary gross enrol. ratio (f/m per 100 pop.)	... / ...	128.9 / 127.5 l	... / ...
Education: Sec. gross enrol. ratio (f/m per 100 pop.)	... / ...	88.5 / 92.7 l	... / ...
Education: Upr. Sec. gross enrol. ratio (f/m per 100 pop.)	... / ...	76.4 / 84.9 l	... / ...

Environment and infrastructure indicators	2010	2015	2022
Threatened species (number)	...	49	66
Forested area (% of land area) m	...	2.3	10.9 h
Energy supply per capita (Gigajoules) m	...	291	256 h
Tourist/visitor arrivals at national borders (000) n	443	505	106 c
Important sites for terrestrial biodiversity protected (%)	5.1	5.1	5.1 g

a For statistical purposes, the data for Netherlands do not include this area. b Projected estimate (medium fertility variant). c 2020. d Netherlands Antillean Guilder. e Refers to the total population of Sint Maarten. f 2018. g 2021. h 2019. i Data refers to a 5-year period preceding the reference year. j Including refugees. k Data as at the end of December. l 2014. m Estimate. n Arrivals by air. Including arrivals to Saint Martin (French part).

Slovakia

Region	Eastern Europe
Population (000, 2022)	5 644[a]
Pop. density (per km2, 2022)	115.1[a]
Capital city	Bratislava
Capital city pop. (000, 2022)	432.5[c]

UN membership date	19 January 1993
Surface area (km2)	49 035[b]
Sex ratio (m per 100 f)	95.6[a]
National currency	Euro (EUR)
Exchange rate (per US$)	0.9[d]

Economic indicators	2010	2015	2022
GDP: Gross domestic product (million current US$)	90 713	88 601	105 173[b]
GDP growth rate (annual %, const. 2015 prices)	6.3	5.2	- 4.4[b]
GDP per capita (current US$)	16 785.3	16 300.2	19 263.6[b]
Economy: Agriculture (% of Gross Value Added)[e,f]	1.7	2.4	2.0[b]
Economy: Industry (% of Gross Value Added)[f,g]	33.8	34.0	30.6[b]
Economy: Services and other activity (% of GVA)[f,h]	64.5	63.6	67.5[b]
Employment in agriculture (% of employed)	3.2	3.2	2.1[i,b]
Employment in industry (% of employed)	37.1	36.1	36.1[i,b]
Employment in services & other sectors (% employed)	59.7	60.7	61.8[i,b]
Unemployment rate (% of labour force)	14.4	11.5	6.2[i]
Labour force participation rate (female/male pop. %)	50.8 / 67.8	52.0 / 67.9	54.5 / 66.6[i]
CPI: Consumer Price Index (2010=100)	100	109	121[d]
Agricultural production index (2014-2016=100)	87	90	101[d]
International trade: exports (million current US$)	65 306	74 970	104 360[d]
International trade: imports (million current US$)	65 644	73 053	104 682[d]
International trade: balance (million current US$)	- 338	1 916	- 322[d]
Balance of payments, current account (million US$)	- 4 210	- 1 849	- 2 220[d]

Major trading partners						2021
Export partners (% of exports)	Germany	21.9	Czechia	11.7	Poland	8.3
Import partners (% of imports)	Germany	19.0	Czechia	9.6	Other Europe, nes	8.0

Social indicators	2010	2015	2022
Population growth rate (average annual %)	0.1	0.1	7.2[a]
Urban population (% of total population)	54.7	53.9	53.7[c]
Urban population growth rate (average annual %)[j]	- 0.3	- 0.2	...
Fertility rate, total (live births per woman)	1.4	1.4	1.6[a]
Life expectancy at birth (females/males, years)	79.2 / 71.7	80.1 / 73.1	78.8 / 71.9[a]
Population age distribution (0-14/60+ years old, %)	15.4 / 18.0	15.3 / 20.9	15.7 / 23.1[a]
International migrant stock (000/% of total pop.)	146.3 / 2.7	177.6 / 3.3	197.2 / 3.6[b]
Refugees and others of concern to the UNHCR (000)	1.6[k]	2.5	2.6[d]
Infant mortality rate (per 1 000 live births)	5.7	5.1	4.7[a]
Health: Current expenditure (% of GDP)	7.7	6.8	7.0[c]
Health: Physicians (per 1 000 pop.)	3.4	3.4	3.6[c]
Education: Government expenditure (% of GDP)	4.1	4.6	4.0[l]
Education: Primary gross enrol. ratio (f/m per 100 pop.)	101.0 / 101.9	98.1 / 98.9	100.6 / 101.1[c]
Education: Sec. gross enrol. ratio (f/m per 100 pop.)	92.8 / 91.8	91.5 / 90.5	91.4 / 90.2[c]
Education: Upr. Sec. gross enrol. ratio (f/m per 100 pop.)	93.0 / 89.5	86.8 / 83.5	88.3 / 84.6[c]
Intentional homicide rate (per 100 000 pop.)	1.5	0.8	1.2[b]
Seats held by women in the National Parliament (%)	18.0	18.7	21.3[m]

Environment and infrastructure indicators	2010	2015	2022
Individuals using the Internet (per 100 inhabitants)	75.7[n,o]	77.6[n,o]	89.9[b]
Research & Development expenditure (% of GDP)	0.6	1.2	0.9[b]
Threatened species (number)	34	45	131
Forested area (% of land area)	39.9	40.0	40.1[c]
CO2 emission estimates (million tons/tons per capita)	34.9 / 6.4	29.8 / 5.4	26.9 / 4.9[b]
Energy production, primary (Petajoules)	250	265	287[c]
Energy supply per capita (Gigajoules)	136	124	129[c]
Tourist/visitor arrivals at national borders (000)[p]	1 327	4 869	5 630[c]
Important sites for terrestrial biodiversity protected (%)	76.3	84.3	85.8[d]
Pop. using safely managed sanitation (urban/rural %)	89.2 / 76.7	88.3 / 75.3	87.9 / 75.0[b]
Net Official Development Assist. disbursed (% of GNI)[q]	0.09	0.10	0.16[b]

a Projected estimate (medium fertility variant). b 2020. c 2019. d 2021. e Excludes irrigation canals and landscaping care. f Data classified according to ISIC Rev. 4. g Excludes publishing activities. Includes irrigation and canals. h Includes publishing activities and landscape care. Excludes repair of personal and household goods. i Estimate. j Data refers to a 5-year period preceding the reference year. k Data as at the end of December. l 2018. m Data are as at 1 January of reporting year. n Users in the last 3 months. o Population aged 16 to 74 years. p The number of inbound arrivals is based on a combination of accommodation statistics and border survey statistics (as calculated within Tourism Satellite Account). q DAC member (OECD).

Slovenia

Region	Southern Europe	UN membership date	22 May 1992
Population (000, 2022)	2 120[a]	Surface area (km2)	20 273[b]
Pop. density (per km2, 2022)	105.3[a]	Sex ratio (m per 100 f)	101.1[a]
Capital city	Ljubljana	National currency	Euro (EUR)
Capital city pop. (000, 2022)	286.5[c]	Exchange rate (per US$)	0.9[d]

Economic indicators

	2010	2015	2022
GDP: Gross domestic product (million current US$)	48 181	43 090	53 590[b]
GDP growth rate (annual %, const. 2015 prices)	1.3	2.2	- 4.2[b]
GDP per capita (current US$)	23 569.9	20 804.5	25 777.4[b]
Economy: Agriculture (% of Gross Value Added)[e,f]	2.2	2.4	2.4[b]
Economy: Industry (% of Gross Value Added)[f,g]	30.4	32.4	33.2[b]
Economy: Services and other activity (% of GVA)[f,h]	67.4	65.2	64.4[b]
Employment in agriculture (% of employed)	8.8	7.1	5.1[i,b]
Employment in industry (% of employed)	32.6	32.0	33.5[i,b]
Employment in services & other sectors (% employed)	58.6	60.9	61.5[i,b]
Unemployment rate (% of labour force)	7.2	9.0	3.7[i]
Labour force participation rate (female/male pop. %)	53.2 / 65.3	51.9 / 62.9	53.4 / 61.8[i]
CPI: Consumer Price Index (2010=100)	100	106	113[d]
Agricultural production index (2014-2016=100)	104	102	105[b]
International trade: exports (million current US$)	24 435	26 587	46 773[d]
International trade: imports (million current US$)	26 592	25 870	49 607[d]
International trade: balance (million current US$)	- 2 157	717	- 2 834[d]
Balance of payments, current account (million US$)	- 366	1 646	2 073[d]

Major trading partners

						2021
Export partners (% of exports)	Germany	17.3	Switzerland	13.4	Italy	10.6
Import partners (% of imports)	China	13.1	Germany	12.9	Switzerland	10.9

Social indicators

	2010	2015	2022
Population growth rate (average annual %)	0.6	0.5	~0.0[a]
Urban population (% of total population)	52.7	53.8	54.8[i]
Urban population growth rate (average annual %)[k]	0.9	0.7	...
Fertility rate, total (live births per woman)	1.6	1.6	1.6[a]
Life expectancy at birth (females/males, years)	82.7 / 76.5	83.6 / 78.0	84.6 / 79.6[a]
Population age distribution (0-14/60+ years old, %)	14.2 / 21.9	14.9 / 24.7	15.1 / 27.7[a]
International migrant stock (000/% of total pop.)	253.8 / 12.4	237.6 / 11.5	278.0 / 13.4[b]
Refugees and others of concern to the UNHCR (000)	4.6[l]	0.3	1.1[d]
Infant mortality rate (per 1 000 live births)	2.5	1.7	1.4[a]
Health: Current expenditure (% of GDP)	8.6	8.5	8.5[j]
Health: Physicians (per 1 000 pop.)	2.4	2.8	3.3[i]
Education: Government expenditure (% of GDP)	5.5	4.9	4.9[c]
Education: Primary gross enrol. ratio (f/m per 100 pop.)	99.5 / 99.5	100.3 / 99.6	102.9 / 103.1[i]
Education: Sec. gross enrol. ratio (f/m per 100 pop.)	98.6 / 99.3	111.0 / 109.7	114.1 / 112.0[i]
Education: Upr. Sec. gross enrol. ratio (f/m per 100 pop.)	99.8 / 101.0	117.7 / 115.7	126.3 / 123.0[i]
Intentional homicide rate (per 100 000 pop.)	0.7	1.0	0.5[b]
Seats held by women in the National Parliament (%)	14.4	36.7	28.9[m]

Environment and infrastructure indicators

	2010	2015	2022
Individuals using the Internet (per 100 inhabitants)	70.0[n]	73.1	86.6[b]
Research & Development expenditure (% of GDP)	2.1	2.2	2.1[b]
Threatened species (number)	95	125	208
Forested area (% of land area)	61.9	62.0	61.6[i,j]
CO2 emission estimates (million tons/tons per capita)	15.8 / 0.0	13.1 / 0.0	12.1 / 0.0[b]
Energy production, primary (Petajoules)	158	143	145[j]
Energy supply per capita (Gigajoules)	150	133	137[j]
Tourist/visitor arrivals at national borders (000)	2 049	3 022	1 216[b]
Important sites for terrestrial biodiversity protected (%)	70.9	73.2	73.7[d]
Net Official Development Assist. disbursed (% of GNI)[o]	0.13	0.37	1.15[b]

a Projected estimate (medium fertility variant). b 2020. c 2018. d 2021. e Excludes irrigation canals and landscaping care. f Data classified according to ISIC Rev. 4. g Excludes publishing activities. Includes irrigation and canals. h Includes publishing activities and landscape care. Excludes repair of personal and household goods. i Estimate. j 2019. k Data refers to a 5-year period preceding the reference year. l Data as at the end of December. m Data are as at 1 January of reporting year. n Population aged 16 to 74 years. o DAC member (OECD).

Solomon Islands

Region	Melanesia	UN membership date	19 September 1978
Population (000, 2022)	724[a]	Surface area (km2)	28 896[b]
Pop. density (per km2, 2022)	25.2[a]	Sex ratio (m per 100 f)	104.4[a]
Capital city	Honiara	National currency	Solomon Is. Dollar (SBD)[c]
Capital city pop. (000, 2022)	81.8[d]	Exchange rate (per US$)	8.1[e]

Economic indicators

	2010	2015	2022
GDP: Gross domestic product (million current US$)	903	1 307	1 546[b]
GDP growth rate (annual %, const. 2015 prices)	9.7	1.4	- 4.3[b]
GDP per capita (current US$)	1 709.8	2 167.2	2 250.6[b]
Economy: Agriculture (% of Gross Value Added)[f]	34.8	33.3	33.6[b]
Economy: Industry (% of Gross Value Added)[f]	13.8	15.6	16.7[b]
Economy: Services and other activity (% of GVA)[f]	51.4	51.1	49.7[b]
Employment in agriculture (% of employed)[g]	44.8	39.9	37.1[b]
Employment in industry (% of employed)[g]	8.2	9.4	9.6[b]
Employment in services & other sectors (% employed)[g]	47.0	50.7	53.4[b]
Unemployment rate (% of labour force)[g]	1.6	0.7	0.9
Labour force participation rate (female/male pop. %)[g]	84.3 / 88.0	84.0 / 87.9	83.4 / 87.5
CPI: Consumer Price Index (2010=100)	100	125	137[e]
Agricultural production index (2014-2016=100)	92	100	105[b]
International trade: exports (million current US$)	215	400	356[g,e]
International trade: imports (million current US$)	328	466	574[g,e]
International trade: balance (million current US$)	- 112	- 65	- 218[e]
Balance of payments, current account (million US$)	- 144	- 36	- 25[b]

Major trading partners

						2021
Export partners (% of exports)[g]	China	58.0	Italy	7.5	India	6.0
Import partners (% of imports)[g]	China	31.9	Australia	12.1	Singapore	10.3

Social indicators

	2010	2015	2022
Population growth rate (average annual %)	2.4	2.5	2.2[a]
Urban population (% of total population)	20.0	22.4	24.2[h]
Urban population growth rate (average annual %)[i]	4.7	4.3	...
Fertility rate, total (live births per woman)	4.4	4.4	3.9[a]
Life expectancy at birth (females/males, years)	70.6 / 67.1	71.2 / 68.1	72.4 / 69.3[a]
Population age distribution (0-14/60+ years old, %)	41.2 / 5.2	40.5 / 5.2	39.1 / 5.5[a]
International migrant stock (000/% of total pop.)[j]	2.8 / 0.5	2.6 / 0.4	2.5 / 0.4[b]
Refugees and others of concern to the UNHCR (000)	...	~0.0	~0.0[h]
Infant mortality rate (per 1 000 live births)	22.0	19.1	15.6[a]
Health: Current expenditure (% of GDP)	8.4	4.6	4.8[h]
Health: Physicians (per 1 000 pop.)	0.2[k]	0.2[l]	0.2[m]
Education: Government expenditure (% of GDP)	7.9	10.1	
Education: Primary gross enrol. ratio (f/m per 100 pop.)	113.2 / 116.0	113.0 / 114.2	103.9 / 104.7[h]
Education: Sec. gross enrol. ratio (f/m per 100 pop.)	44.9 / 51.9	47.0 / 49.5[n]	... / ...
Education: Upr. Sec. gross enrol. ratio (f/m per 100 pop.)	26.4 / 36.6	26.5 / 30.7[n]	... / ...
Intentional homicide rate (per 100 000 pop.)	3.8[k]	...	...
Seats held by women in the National Parliament (%)	0.0	2.0	8.0[o]

Environment and infrastructure indicators

	2010	2015	2022
Individuals using the Internet (per 100 inhabitants)[g]	5.0	10.0	11.9[p]
Threatened species (number)	220	238	291
Forested area (% of land area)[g]	90.4	90.3	90.2[h]
Energy production, primary (Petajoules)[g]	3	3	3[h]
Energy supply per capita (Gigajoules)	15[g]	13	11[g,h]
Tourist/visitor arrivals at national borders (000)[q]	20	22	4[b]
Important sites for terrestrial biodiversity protected (%)	4.5	4.6	4.6[e]
Net Official Development Assist. received (% of GNI)	41.45	14.81	13.49[b]

a Projected estimate (medium fertility variant). b 2020. c Solomon Islands Dollar. d 2018. e 2021. f Data classified according to ISIC Rev. 4. g Estimate. h 2019. i Data refers to a 5-year period preceding the reference year. j Including refugees. k 2008. l 2013. m 2016. n 2012. o Data are as at 1 January of reporting year. p 2017. q Arrivals by air.

Somalia

Region	Eastern Africa	UN membership date	20 September 1960
Population (000, 2022)	17 598[a]	Surface area (km2)	637 657[b]
Pop. density (per km2, 2022)	28.1[a]	Sex ratio (m per 100 f)	100.5[a]
Capital city	Mogadishu	National currency	Somali Shilling (SOS)
Capital city pop. (000, 2022)	2 179.9[c,d]	Exchange rate (per US$)	24 300.0[e,f]

Economic indicators	2010	2015	2022
GDP: Gross domestic product (million current US$)	1 093	1 455	1 873[b]
GDP growth rate (annual %, const. 2015 prices)	2.6	2.7	- 1.5[b]
GDP per capita (current US$)	90.7	105.4	117.9[b]
Economy: Agriculture (% of Gross Value Added)[g]	60.2	60.2	60.2[b]
Economy: Industry (% of Gross Value Added)[g]	7.4	7.4	7.4[b]
Economy: Services and other activity (% of GVA)[g]	32.5	32.5	32.5[b]
Employment in agriculture (% of employed)[h]	83.8	83.4	83.0[b]
Employment in industry (% of employed)[h]	4.1	3.8	3.5[b]
Employment in services & other sectors (% employed)[h]	12.1	12.8	13.4[b]
Unemployment rate (% of labour force)[h]	19.0	18.9	19.6
Labour force participation rate (female/male pop. %)[h]	20.5 / 48.7	20.8 / 47.9	21.0 / 47.1
Agricultural production index (2014-2016=100)	107	102	100[b]
International trade: exports (million current US$)[h]	568	853	610[f]
International trade: imports (million current US$)[h]	496	525	3 675[f]
International trade: balance (million current US$)	72[h]	328[h]	- 3 065[f]

Major trading partners						2021
Export partners (% of exports)[h]	United Arab Emirates	49.5	Saudi Arabia	11.3	Yemen	4.6
Import partners (% of imports)[h]	United Arab Emirates	35.5	China	20.0	India	14.0

Social indicators	2010	2015	2022
Population growth rate (average annual %)	2.5	3.3	3.0[a]
Urban population (% of total population)	39.3	43.2	45.6[d]
Urban population growth rate (average annual %)[i]	4.5	4.8	...
Fertility rate, total (live births per woman)	7.3	7.0	6.2[a]
Life expectancy at birth (females/males, years)	52.5 / 48.7	56.9 / 52.9	58.2 / 54.1[a]
Population age distribution (0-14/60+ years old, %)	48.3 / 4.0	47.8 / 4.1	47.2 / 4.1[a]
International migrant stock (000/% of total pop.)[h,j]	48.1 / 0.4	41.0 / 0.3	58.6 / 0.4[b]
Refugees and others of concern to the UNHCR (000)	1 489.8[k]	1 165.0	2 994.5[f]
Infant mortality rate (per 1 000 live births)	102.5	83.9	66.2[a]
Health: Physicians (per 1 000 pop.)	~0.0[l]	~0.0[m]	...
Education: Primary gross enrol. ratio (f/m per 100 pop.)	16.6 / 30.1[n]	... / ...	... / ...
Education: Sec. gross enrol. ratio (f/m per 100 pop.)	3.7 / 8.1[n]	... / ...	... / ...
Education: Upr. Sec. gross enrol. ratio (f/m per 100 pop.)	3.2 / 6.9[n]	... / ...	... / ...
Seats held by women in the National Parliament (%)	6.9	13.8	24.4[o,p]

Environment and infrastructure indicators	2010	2015	2022
Individuals using the Internet (per 100 inhabitants)[h]	1.2[q]	1.8	2.0[r]
Threatened species (number)	128	165	221
Forested area (% of land area)[h]	10.8	10.1	9.7[d]
Energy production, primary (Petajoules)	124	129	147[d]
Energy supply per capita (Gigajoules)	10	10	10[d]
Important sites for terrestrial biodiversity protected (%)	0.0	0.0	0.0[f]
Pop. using safely managed sanitation (urban/rural %)	38.4 / 12.5	41.1 / 16.4	43.9 / 20.9[b]
Net Official Development Assist. received (% of GNI)	...	31.36	62.26[b]

a Projected estimate (medium fertility variant). b 2020. c Data refers to the urban agglomeration. d 2019. e UN operational exchange rate. f 2021. g Data classified according to ISIC Rev. 4. h Estimate. i Data refers to a 5-year period preceding the reference year. j Including refugees. k Data as at the end of December. l 2006. m 2014. n 2007. o The figures correspond to the lower house prior to the elections that began in November 2021. As at February 2022, elections were still ongoing for the lower house. p Data arc as at 1 January of reporting year. q 2009. r 2017.

South Africa

Region	Southern Africa	UN membership date	07 November 1945
Population (000, 2022)	59 894 [a]	Surface area (km2)	1 221 037 [b]
Pop. density (per km2, 2022)	49.1 [a]	Sex ratio (m per 100 f)	94.9 [a]
Capital city	Pretoria [c]	National currency	Rand (ZAR)
Capital city pop. (000, 2022)	2 472.6 [d]	Exchange rate (per US$)	15.9 [e]

Economic indicators

	2010	2015	2022
GDP: Gross domestic product (million current US$)	375 348	317 416	302 141 [b]
GDP growth rate (annual %, const. 2015 prices)	3.0	1.2	- 7.0 [b]
GDP per capita (current US$)	7 328.6	5 730.9	5 094.4 [b]
Economy: Agriculture (% of Gross Value Added)	2.6	2.3	2.7 [b]
Economy: Industry (% of Gross Value Added)	30.2	29.1	28.3 [b]
Economy: Services and other activity (% of GVA)	67.2	68.6	69.0 [b]
Employment in agriculture (% of employed)	4.9	5.6	5.0 [f,b]
Employment in industry (% of employed)	24.4	23.8	22.7 [f,b]
Employment in services & other sectors (% employed)	70.7	70.6	72.3 [f,b]
Unemployment rate (% of labour force)	24.7	25.2	33.5 [f]
Labour force participation rate (female/male pop. %)	44.5 / 60.4	47.6 / 61.9	47.4 / 61.0 [f]
CPI: Consumer Price Index (2010=100) [g,h]	100	130	171 [e]
Agricultural production index (2014-2016=100)	90	101	111 [b]
International trade: exports (million current US$)	82 631	80 264	125 189 [f,e]
International trade: imports (million current US$)	83 100	85 511	96 726 [f,e]
International trade: balance (million current US$)	- 469	- 5 246	28 462 [e]
Balance of payments, current account (million US$)	- 5 422	- 14 944	15 529 [e]

Major trading partners

						2021
Export partners (% of exports) [f]	China	11.5	United States	8.4	Areas nes [i]	8.1
Import partners (% of imports) [f]	China	20.8	Germany	9.1	United States	6.4

Social indicators

	2010	2015	2022
Population growth rate (average annual %)	1.2	2.4	0.8 [a]
Urban population (% of total population)	62.2	64.8	66.9 [d]
Urban population growth rate (average annual %) [j]	2.0	2.2	...
Fertility rate, total (live births per woman)	2.4	2.4	2.3 [a]
Life expectancy at birth (females/males, years)	61.3 / 56.1	66.8 / 60.7	64.2 / 58.6 [a]
Population age distribution (0-14/60+ years old, %)	28.7 / 7.6	28.3 / 8.1	28.6 / 8.7 [a]
International migrant stock (000/% of total pop.) [k]	2 114.8 / 4.1	3 231.7 / 5.8	2 860.5 / 4.8 [b]
Refugees and others of concern to the UNHCR (000)	229.7 [l]	912.6	250.2 [e]
Infant mortality rate (per 1 000 live births)	35.1	27.8	28.1 [a]
Health: Current expenditure (% of GDP)	8.7	8.8	9.1 [d]
Health: Physicians (per 1 000 pop.)	...	...	0.8 [d]
Education: Government expenditure (% of GDP)	5.7	6.0	6.8 [b]
Education: Primary gross enrol. ratio (f/m per 100 pop.)	102.7 / 106.8	101.9 / 109.2	96.6 / 100.1 [d]
Education: Sec. gross enrol. ratio (f/m per 100 pop.)	96.6 / 91.0	108.8 / 110.1	105.7 / 99.5 [d]
Education: Upr. Sec. gross enrol. ratio (f/m per 100 pop.)	92.3 / 83.9	110.2 / 113.2	107.5 / 97.6 [d]
Intentional homicide rate (per 100 000 pop.)	31.0	33.7	33.5 [b]
Seats held by women in the National Parliament (%)	44.5	41.5	46.7 [m]

Environment and infrastructure indicators

	2010	2015	2022
Individuals using the Internet (per 100 inhabitants) [f]	24.0	51.9	70.0 [b]
Research & Development expenditure (% of GDP)	0.7	0.7	0.6 [d]
Threatened species (number)	441	527	796
Forested area (% of land area)	14.4	14.2 [f]	14.1 [f,d]
CO2 emission estimates (million tons/tons per capita)	425.7 / 8.2	425.4 / 7.6	440.0 / 7.4 [d]
Energy production, primary (Petajoules)	6 659	6 564	6 712 [d]
Energy supply per capita (Gigajoules)	115	103	102 [d]
Tourist/visitor arrivals at national borders (000)	8 074 [n]	8 904 [n,o]	2 802 [o,b]
Important sites for terrestrial biodiversity protected (%)	30.5	32.4	35.5 [e]
Pop. using safely managed drinking water (urban/rural, %)	87.4 / ...	84.3 / ...	81.1 / ... [b]
Net Official Development Assist. received (% of GNI)	0.28	0.46	0.41 [b]

a Projected estimate (medium fertility variant). b 2020. c Pretoria is the administrative capital, Cape Town is the legislative capital and Bloemfontein is the judiciary capital. d 2019. e 2021. f Estimate. g For urban population only. h Calculated by the UNSD from national indices. i Areas nes j Data refers to a 5-year period preceding the reference year. k Including refugees. l Data as at the end of December. m Data are as at 1 January of reporting year. n Break in the time series. o Excluding transit.

South Sudan

Region	Eastern Africa	UN membership date	14 July 2011	
Population (000, 2022)	10 913[a]	Surface area (km2)	658 841[b]	
Pop. density (per km2, 2022)	19.3[a]	Sex ratio (m per 100 f)	98.1[a]	
Capital city	Juba	National currency	S. Sudanese Pound (SSP)[c]	
Capital city pop. (000, 2022)	385.8[d]	Exchange rate (per US$)	432.0[e]	

Economic indicators

	2010	2015	2022
GDP: Gross domestic product (million current US$)	14 925	6 231	15 903[f]
GDP growth rate (annual %, const. 2015 prices)	- 0.5	6.9	- 6.6[f]
GDP per capita (current US$)	1 569.7	581.5	1 420.7[f]
Economy: Agriculture (% of Gross Value Added)[g]	5.1	4.2	5.8[f]
Economy: Industry (% of Gross Value Added)[g]	55.4	45.0	40.6[f]
Economy: Services and other activity (% of GVA)[g]	39.4	50.9	53.6[f]
Employment in agriculture (% of employed)[h]	56.4	56.8	56.1[f]
Employment in industry (% of employed)[h]	16.8	15.2	14.1[f]
Employment in services & other sectors (% employed)[h]	26.8	28.0	29.7[f]
Unemployment rate (% of labour force)[h]	12.2	12.3	13.3
Labour force participation rate (female/male pop. %)[h]	71.8 / 76.4	72.1 / 75.6	71.9 / 74.0
CPI: Consumer Price Index (2010=100)	100	332	22 571[e]
Agricultural production index (2014-2016=100)	...	100	103[f]
International trade: exports (million current US$)[h]	...	3 103	490[e]
International trade: imports (million current US$)[h]	...	635	1 082[e]
International trade: balance (million current US$)	...	2 468[h]	- 593[e]
Balance of payments, current account (million US$)	...	- 500	- 1 718[f]

Major trading partners

2021

Export partners (% of exports)[h]	China	46.9	Uganda	15.9	Italy	13.9
Import partners (% of imports)[h]	Uganda	28.7	United Arab Emirates	22.9	Kenya	13.3

Social indicators

	2010	2015	2022
Population growth rate (average annual %)	5.9	1.1	1.5[a]
Urban population (% of total population)	17.9	18.9	19.9[d]
Urban population growth rate (average annual %)[i]	5.1	4.4	...
Fertility rate, total (live births per woman)	5.4	4.9	4.3[a]
Life expectancy at birth (females/males, years)	55.8 / 53.7	57.2 / 53.9	57.0 / 54.0[a]
Population age distribution (0-14/60+ years old, %)	43.0 / 4.0	43.5 / 4.1	43.9 / 4.8[a]
International migrant stock (000/% of total pop.)[j]	230.7 / 2.4	844.1 / 7.9	882.3 / 7.9[f]
Refugees and others of concern to the UNHCR (000)	...	2 058.5	2 401.4[e]
Infant mortality rate (per 1 000 live births)	69.4	63.8	60.7[a]
Health: Current expenditure (% of GDP)	...	...	6.0[k,d]
Health: Physicians (per 1 000 pop.)	...	...	~0.0[l]
Education: Government expenditure (% of GDP)	...	1.5	1.5[m]
Education: Primary gross enrol. ratio (f/m per 100 pop.)	... / ...	60.4 / 85.3	... / ...
Education: Sec. gross enrol. ratio (f/m per 100 pop.)	... / ...	7.7 / 14.3	... / ...
Education: Upr. Sec. gross enrol. ratio (f/m per 100 pop.)	... / ...	3.6 / 8.0	... / ...
Intentional homicide rate (per 100 000 pop.)	...	14.9[n]	...
Seats held by women in the National Parliament (%)	...	26.5	32.4[o]

Environment and infrastructure indicators

	2010	2015	2022
Individuals using the Internet (per 100 inhabitants)[h]	...	3.0	6.5[f]
Threatened species (number)	...	42	64
Forested area (% of land area)	...	41.6	11.3[d]
CO2 emission estimates (million tons/tons per capita)	... / ...	2.0 / 0.2	1.8 / 0.2[d]
Energy production, primary (Petajoules)	...	321	371[d]
Energy supply per capita (Gigajoules)	...	3	3[d]
Important sites for terrestrial biodiversity protected (%)	33.6	33.6	33.6[e]
Net Official Development Assist. received (% of GNI)	...	15.92	...

a Projected estimate (medium fertility variant). b 2017. c South Sudanese Pound. d 2019. e 2021. f 2020. g Data classified according to ISIC Rev. 4. h Estimate. i Data refers to a 5-year period preceding the reference year. j Including refugees. k The country did not exist before 2012 (independence from Sudan on July 9, 2011, which corresponds to fiscal year 2011/12, converted in 2012). l 2018. m 2016. n 2012. o Data are as at 1 January of reporting year.

Spain

Region	Southern Europe	UN membership date	14 December 1955
Population (000, 2022)	47 559[a,b]	Surface area (km2)	506 008[c]
Pop. density (per km2, 2022)	94.7[a,b]	Sex ratio (m per 100 f)	96.1[a,b]
Capital city	Madrid	National currency	Euro (EUR)
Capital city pop. (000, 2022)	6 559.0[d]	Exchange rate (per US$)	0.9[e]

Economic indicators	2010	2015	2022
GDP: Gross domestic product (million current US$)	1 420 722	1 195 119	1 281 485[c]
GDP growth rate (annual %, const. 2015 prices)	0.2	3.8	- 10.8[c]
GDP per capita (current US$)	30 272.6	25 606.8	27 408.6[c]
Economy: Agriculture (% of Gross Value Added)[f,g]	2.6	3.0	3.4[c]
Economy: Industry (% of Gross Value Added)[f,h]	25.2	22.1	22.3[c]
Economy: Services and other activity (% of GVA)[f,i]	72.1	74.9	74.2[c]
Employment in agriculture (% of employed)	4.2	4.1	4.0[j,c]
Employment in industry (% of employed)	23.0	19.9	20.2[j,c]
Employment in services & other sectors (% employed)	72.8	76.0	75.8[j,c]
Unemployment rate (% of labour force)	19.9	22.1	13.5[j]
Labour force participation rate (female/male pop. %)	52.2 / 67.3	53.1 / 64.8	52.2 / 62.0[j]
CPI: Consumer Price Index (2010=100)[k]	100	107	114[e]
Agricultural production index (2014-2016=100)	95	99	117[c]
International trade: exports (million current US$)	246 265	276 959	391 559[e]
International trade: imports (million current US$)	315 547	304 708	426 060[e]
International trade: balance (million current US$)	- 69 282	- 27 750	- 34 501[e]
Balance of payments, current account (million US$)	- 52 250	24 108	13 263[e]

Major trading partners						2021
Export partners (% of exports)	France	15.2	Germany	9.8	Italy	8.0
Import partners (% of imports)	Germany	10.6	China	9.7	France	9.5

Social indicators	2010	2015	2022
Population growth rate (average annual %)[b]	0.4	--0.0	- 0.1[a]
Urban population (% of total population)[b]	78.4	79.6	80.6[d]
Urban population growth rate (average annual %)[b,l]	1.5	0.1	...
Fertility rate, total (live births per woman)[b]	1.4	1.3	1.3[a]
Life expectancy at birth (females/males, years)[b]	85.0 / 79.0	85.4 / 79.9	86.5 / 81.2[a]
Population age distribution (0-14/60+ years old, %)[b]	15.0 / 22.2	15.2 / 24.1	13.8 / 26.8[a]
International migrant stock (000/% of total pop.)[b]	6 280.1 / 13.4	5 891.2 / 12.6	6 842.2 / 14.6[c]
Refugees and others of concern to the UNHCR (000)	6.6[m]	17.3	212.9[e]
Infant mortality rate (per 1 000 live births)[b]	3.2	2.6	2.2[e]
Health: Current expenditure (% of GDP)	9.1	9.1	9.1[d]
Health: Physicians (per 1 000 pop.)	3.7	3.8	4.4[d]
Education: Government expenditure (% of GDP)	4.9	4.3	4.2[n]
Education: Primary gross enrol. ratio (f/m per 100 pop.)	103.6 / 104.4	107.2 / 105.6	103.1 / 101.8[d]
Education: Sec. gross enrol. ratio (f/m per 100 pop.)	120.7 / 117.6	124.6 / 125.3	127.8 / 124.2[d]
Education: Upr. Sec. gross enrol. ratio (f/m per 100 pop.)	134.3 / 123.1	128.0 / 124.7	137.1 / 128.6[d]
Intentional homicide rate (per 100 000 pop.)	0.9	0.6	0.6[c]
Seats held by women in the National Parliament (%)	36.6	41.1	43.0[o]

Environment and infrastructure indicators	2010	2015	2022
Individuals using the Internet (per 100 inhabitants)	65.8[p]	78.7[q]	93.2[c]
Research & Development expenditure (% of GDP)	1.4	1.2	1.4[c]
Threatened species (number)	240	551	852
Forested area (% of land area)	37.1	37.1	37.2[d]
CO2 emission estimates (million tons/tons per capita)	266.1 / 5.6	250.7 / 5.3	198.2 / 4.1[c]
Energy production, primary (Petajoules)[r]	1 419	1 367	1 387[d]
Energy supply per capita (Gigajoules)[r]	114	105	108[d]
Tourist/visitor arrivals at national borders (000)	52 677	68 175	18 933[c]
Important sites for terrestrial biodiversity protected (%)	53.4	57.5	57.6[e]
Pop. using safely managed drinking water (urban/rural, %)	99.9 / 98.7	99.8 / 98.7	99.8 / 98.7[c]
Net Official Development Assist. disbursed (% of GNI)[s]	0.74	1.84	1.08[c]

a Projected estimate (medium fertility variant). b Including Canary Islands, Ceuta and Melilla. c 2020. d 2019. e 2021. f Data classified according to ISIC Rev. 4. g Excludes irrigation canals and landscaping care. h Excludes publishing activities. Includes irrigation and canals. i Includes publishing activities and landscape care. Excludes repair of personal and household goods. j Estimate. k Calculated by the UNSD from national indices. l Data refers to a 5-year period preceding the reference year. m Data as at the end of December. n 2018. o Data are as at 1 January of reporting year. p Population aged 10 years and over. q Users in the last 3 months. r Data include the Canary Islands. s DAC member (OECD).

Region	Southern Asia	UN membership date	14 December 1955
Population (000, 2022)	21 832[a]	Surface area (km2)	65 610[b]
Pop. density (per km2, 2022)	348.2[a]	Sex ratio (m per 100 f)	92.9[a]
Capital city	Colombo[c]	National currency	Sri Lanka Rupee (LKR)
Capital city pop. (000, 2022)	606.2[d]	Exchange rate (per US$)	186.4[b]

Economic indicators

	2010	2015	2022
GDP: Gross domestic product (million current US$)	56 726	80 604	80 677[b]
GDP growth rate (annual %, const. 2015 prices)	8.0	5.0	- 3.6[b]
GDP per capita (current US$)	2 799.6	3 855.2	3 767.6[b]
Economy: Agriculture (% of Gross Value Added)[e,f]	9.5	8.8	8.9[b]
Economy: Industry (% of Gross Value Added)[e,g]	29.7	29.3	27.8[b]
Economy: Services and other activity (% of GVA)[e,h]	60.9	61.9	63.3[b]
Employment in agriculture (% of employed)	31.8	28.7	23.7[i,b]
Employment in industry (% of employed)	25.5	25.8	30.4[i,b]
Employment in services & other sectors (% employed)	42.6	45.6	45.9[i,b]
Unemployment rate (% of labour force)	4.8	4.5	4.9[i]
Labour force participation rate (female/male pop. %)	34.0 / 74.2	35.4 / 73.9	31.4 / 69.0[i]
CPI: Consumer Price Index (2010=100)	100[j,k]	110[l]	147[l,m]
Agricultural production index (2014-2016=100)	93	104	119[b]
International trade: exports (million current US$)	8 304	10 440	13 331[m]
International trade: imports (million current US$)	12 354	18 967	21 502[m]
International trade: balance (million current US$)	- 4 050	- 8 528	- 8 171[m]
Balance of payments, current account (million US$)	- 1 075	- 1 883	- 1 083[b]

Major trading partners

					2021
Export partners (% of exports)	United States	24.7	United Kingdom 7.5	India	6.7
Import partners (% of imports)	China	23.7	India 22.0	United Arab Emirates	6.6

Social indicators

	2010	2015	2022
Population growth rate (average annual %)	0.9	0.4	0.3[a]
Urban population (% of total population)	18.2	18.3	18.6[d]
Urban population growth rate (average annual %)[n]	0.6	0.5	...
Fertility rate, total (live births per woman)	2.2	2.1	2.0[a]
Life expectancy at birth (females/males, years)	77.6 / 69.2	79.0 / 71.0	80.2 / 72.9[a]
Population age distribution (0-14/60+ years old, %)	25.5 / 11.8	25.0 / 13.6	22.8 / 16.7[a]
International migrant stock (000/% of total pop.)[o]	39.0 / 0.2	39.7 / 0.2	40.3 / 0.2[b]
Refugees and others of concern to the UNHCR (000)	435.3[p]	51.8	26.2[m]
Infant mortality rate (per 1 000 live births)	9.7	7.5	5.5[a]
Health: Current expenditure (% of GDP)	3.9	3.9	4.1[d]
Health: Physicians (per 1 000 pop.)	0.7	0.9	1.2[b]
Education: Government expenditure (% of GDP)	1.7	2.2	2.1[q]
Education: Primary gross enrol. ratio (f/m per 100 pop.)	98.2 / 100.7	100.6 / 102.7	100.0 / 100.5[d]
Education: Sec. gross enrol. ratio (f/m per 100 pop.)	97.5 / 96.3	101.8 / 97.2[r]	102.6 / 98.0[q]
Education: Upr. Sec. gross enrol. ratio (f/m per 100 pop.)	98.2 / 91.7	103.9 / 94.0[r]	105.3 / 95.2[q]
Intentional homicide rate (per 100 000 pop.)	3.8	2.3	3.5[d]
Seats held by women in the National Parliament (%)	5.8	5.8	5.3[s]

Environment and infrastructure indicators

	2010	2015	2022
Individuals using the Internet (per 100 inhabitants)	3.9[t]	12.1[i,u,v]	35.0[b]
Research & Development expenditure (% of GDP)	0.1	0.1	0.1[q]
Threatened species (number)	552	580	820
Forested area (% of land area)	33.5	34.4	34.2[d]
CO2 emission estimates (million tons/tons per capita)	14.0 / 0.6	21.0 / 0.9	24.2 / 1.0[d]
Energy production, primary (Petajoules)	184	181	178[i,d]
Energy supply per capita (Gigajoules)	18	21	21[d]
Tourist/visitor arrivals at national borders (000)[w]	654	1 798	508[b]
Important sites for terrestrial biodiversity protected (%)	41.4	43.7	43.7[m]
Pop. using safely managed drinking water (urban/rural, %)	88.4 / ...	91.5 / ...	93.3 / ...[b]
Net Official Development Assist. received (% of GNI)	1.00	0.57	0.28[b]

a Projected estimate (medium fertility variant). b 2020. c Colombo is the capital and Sri Jayewardenepura Kotte is the legislative capital. d 2019. e Data classified according to ISIC Rev. 4. f Excludes irrigation canals and landscaping care. g Excludes publishing activities. Includes irrigation and canals. h Includes publishing activities and landscape care. Excludes repair of personal and household goods. i Estimate. j Colombo k Calculated by the UNSD from national indices. l Index base: 2013=100. m 2021. n Data refers to a 5-year period preceding the reference year. o Including refugees. p Data as at the end of December. q 2018. r 2013. s Data are as at 1 January of reporting year. t 2007. u Users in the last 12 months. v Population aged 5 to 69 years. w Excluding nationals residing abroad.

State of Palestine

Region	Western Asia	Population (000, 2022)	5 250 [a,b]
Surface area (km2)	6 025 [c]	Pop. density (per km2, 2022)	872.1 [a,b]
Sex ratio (m per 100 f)	99.6 [a,b]	Capital city	East Jerusalem [d]
Capital city pop. (000, 2022)	275.1 [d,e]		

Economic indicators	2010	2015	2022
GDP: Gross domestic product (million current US$)	9 682	13 972	15 561 [c]
GDP growth rate (annual %, const. 2015 prices)	5.8	3.7	- 11.5 [c]
GDP per capita (current US$)	2 387.2	3 085.0	3 050.4 [c]
Economy: Agriculture (% of Gross Value Added) [f,g]	10.6	8.7	8.3 [c]
Economy: Industry (% of Gross Value Added) [f,h]	21.8	19.2	22.0 [c]
Economy: Services and other activity (% of GVA) [f,i]	67.6	72.1	69.6 [c]
Employment in agriculture (% of employed)	11.8	8.7	5.9 [j,c]
Employment in industry (% of employed)	24.7	28.7	31.7 [j,c]
Employment in services & other sectors (% employed)	63.5	62.6	62.4 [j,c]
Unemployment rate (% of labour force)	21.4	23.0	24.5 [j]
Labour force participation rate (female/male pop. %)	13.8 / 65.6	17.7 / 69.7	17.5 / 68.0 [j]
CPI: Consumer Price Index (2010=100)	100	111	113 [k,l]
Agricultural production index (2014-2016=100)	101	90	108 [c]
International trade: exports (million current US$)	576	958	1 379 [j,l]
International trade: imports (million current US$)	3 959	5 225	6 526 [j,l]
International trade: balance (million current US$)	- 3 383	- 4 268	- 5 147 [l]
Balance of payments, current account (million US$)	- 1 307	- 1 939	- 1 903 [c]

Major trading partners							2021
Export partners (% of exports) [j]	Israel	84.0	Jordan	5.4	United Arab Emirates	1.7
Import partners (% of imports) [j]	Israel	55.1	Türkiye	10.1	China	6.6

Social indicators	2010	2015	2022
Population growth rate (average annual %) [b]	2.4	2.4	2.3 [a]
Urban population (% of total population) [b]	74.1	75.4	76.4 [m]
Urban population growth rate (average annual %) [b,n]	2.9	3.1	...
Fertility rate, total (live births per woman) [b]	4.4	4.0	3.4 [a]
Life expectancy at birth (females/males, years) [b]	75.1 / 70.9	76.4 / 72.4	75.9 / 71.0 [a]
Population age distribution (0-14/60+ years old, %) [b]	42.4 / 4.3	40.6 / 4.8	38.8 / 5.5 [a]
International migrant stock (000/% of total pop.) [b]	273.8 / 6.8	273.2 / 6.0	272.8 / 5.3 [c]
Refugees and others of concern to the UNHCR (000)	...	~0.0	...
Infant mortality rate (per 1 000 live births) [b]	18.6	16.4	13.9 [a]
Education: Government expenditure (% of GDP)	6.2	4.7	5.3 [j,e]
Education: Primary gross enrol. ratio (f/m per 100 pop.)	90.4 / 92.2	97.5 / 97.5	96.2 / 96.6 [c]
Education: Sec. gross enrol. ratio (f/m per 100 pop.)	89.1 / 82.5	89.9 / 81.9	95.5 / 86.8 [c]
Education: Upr. Sec. gross enrol. ratio (f/m per 100 pop.)	85.9 / 70.2	77.4 / 59.0	89.5 / 70.7 [c]
Intentional homicide rate (per 100 000 pop.)	0.8	1.2	0.9 [c]

Environment and infrastructure indicators	2010	2015	2022
Individuals using the Internet (per 100 inhabitants) [j]	37.4 [o]	56.7	74.6 [c]
Research & Development expenditure (% of GDP) [p]	0.4	0.5 [q]	...
Threatened species (number)	18	24	55
Forested area (% of land area) [j]	1.7	1.7	1.7 [m]
Energy production, primary (Petajoules)	9	9	10 [m]
Energy supply per capita (Gigajoules)	13	16	16 [m]
Tourist/visitor arrivals at national borders (000)	522	432 [r]	93 [r,c]
Important sites for terrestrial biodiversity protected (%)	18.1	19.9	20.9 [l]
Pop. using safely managed drinking water (urban/rural, %)	78.1 / 71.6	79.5 / 73.6	80.9 / 75.6 [c]
Pop. using safely managed sanitation (urban/rural %)	60.8 / 24.9	66.5 / 36.1	72.4 / 48.0 [c]
Net Official Development Assist. received (% of GNI)	24.44	11.94	11.21 [c]

a Projected estimate (medium fertility variant). b Including East Jerusalem. c 2020. d Designation and data provided by the State of Palestine. The position of the UN on Jerusalem is stated in A/RES/181 (II) and subsequent General Assembly and Security Council resolutions. e 2018. f Data classified according to ISIC Rev. 4. g Excludes irrigation canals and landscaping care. h Excludes publishing activities. Includes irrigation and canals. i Includes publishing activities and landscape care. Excludes repair of personal and household goods. j Estimate. k Calculated by the UNSD from national indices. l 2021. m 2019. n Data refers to a 5-year period preceding the reference year. o Refers to total population. p Excluding business enterprise. q 2013. r Represent the data on hotel activity in the West Bank only.

Region	Northern Africa	UN membership date	12 November 1956
Population (000, 2022)	46 874[a]	Pop. density (per km2, 2022)	26.6[a]
Sex ratio (m per 100 f)	99.9[a]	Capital city	Khartoum
National currency	Sudanese Pound (SDG)	Capital city pop. (000, 2022)	5 677.9[b]
Exchange rate (per US$)	55.0[c]		

Economic indicators

	2010	2015	2022
GDP: Gross domestic product (million current US$)[d]	54 740	83 933	62 057[c]
GDP growth rate (annual %, const. 2015 prices)[d]	8.3	4.0	- 1.6[c]
GDP per capita (current US$)[d]	1 584.6	2 157.5	1 415.2[c]
Economy: Agriculture (% of Gross Value Added)[e]	42.6	32.0	21.5[c]
Economy: Industry (% of Gross Value Added)[e]	14.1	16.3	21.0[c]
Economy: Services and other activity (% of GVA)[e]	43.4	51.8	57.5[c]
Employment in agriculture (% of employed)[f]	45.6	41.5	39.7[c]
Employment in industry (% of employed)[f]	14.7	16.8	15.9[c]
Employment in services & other sectors (% employed)[f]	39.8	41.7	44.4[c]
Unemployment rate (% of labour force)[f]	15.2	17.5	19.5
Labour force participation rate (female/male pop. %)[f]	28.9 / 71.6	29.2 / 70.2	29.1 / 68.3
CPI: Consumer Price Index (2010=100)[f]	100	350	18 895[g]
Agricultural production index (2014-2016=100)	...	92	116[c]
International trade: exports (million current US$)[h]	...	5 588	1 913[f,g]
International trade: imports (million current US$)[h]	...	8 413	9 676[f,g]
International trade: balance (million current US$)[h]	...	- 2 826	- 7 763[g]
Balance of payments, current account (million US$)	- 1 725	- 5 461	- 5 841[c]

Major trading partners

						2021
Export partners (% of exports)[f]	United Arab Emirates	50.5	China	15.9	Saudi Arabia	5.5
Import partners (% of imports)[f]	China	19.2	United Arab Emirates	16.7	Saudi Arabia	11.1

Social indicators

	2010	2015	2022
Population growth rate (average annual %)	2.0	3.1	2.6[a]
Urban population (% of total population)	33.1	33.9	34.9[b]
Urban population growth rate (average annual %)[i]	2.3	2.8	...
Fertility rate, total (live births per woman)	5.0	4.9	4.4[a]
Life expectancy at birth (females/males, years)	65.5 / 60.7	67.3 / 62.1	68.2 / 63.0[a]
Population age distribution (0-14/60+ years old, %)	42.1 / 4.1	42.0 / 4.9	40.9 / 5.5[a]
International migrant stock (000/% of total pop.)[j]	618.7 / 1.8	620.5 / 1.6	1 379.1 / 3.1[c]
Refugees and others of concern to the UNHCR (000)	1 951.5[k]	2 767.9	3 649.4[g]
Infant mortality rate (per 1 000 live births)	50.7	45.3	37.5[a]
Health: Current expenditure (% of GDP)[m,n]	5.1[l]	7.3	4.6[f,b]
Health: Physicians (per 1 000 pop.)	0.3[o]	0.4	0.3[p]
Education: Government expenditure (% of GDP)	2.2[q]	...	...
Education: Primary gross enrol. ratio (f/m per 100 pop.)	67.8 / 75.6	69.8 / 76.4	76.1 / 81.7[r]
Education: Sec. gross enrol. ratio (f/m per 100 pop.)	39.4 / 45.5	45.3 / 46.0	46.3 / 45.4[r]
Education: Upr. Sec. gross enrol. ratio (f/m per 100 pop.)	31.5 / 34.0	40.3 / 38.2	40.6 / 37.6[r]
Seats held by women in the National Parliament (%)	...	24.3	27.7[b]

Environment and infrastructure indicators

	2010	2015	2022
Individuals using the Internet (per 100 inhabitants)	8.7[s]	...	28.4[f,c]
Research & Development expenditure (% of GDP)	0.2[f,t,u]	...	...
Threatened species (number)	112	123	168
Forested area (% of land area)	...	903.7	10.0[b]
CO2 emission estimates (million tons/tons per capita)	17.4 / 0.3	18.7 / 0.4	20.9 / 0.4[b]
Energy production, primary (Petajoules)	...	461	408[b]
Energy supply per capita (Gigajoules)	...	13	12[f,b]
Tourist/visitor arrivals at national borders (000)[v]	495	741	836[f]
Important sites for terrestrial biodiversity protected (%)	9.1	9.1	17.8[g]
Net Official Development Assist. received (% of GNI)	3.12	1.52	9.62[c]

a Projected estimate (medium fertility variant). **b** 2019. **c** 2020. **d** Data compiled in accordance with the System of National Accounts 1968 (1968 SNA). **e** Data classified according to ISIC Rev. 4. **f** Estimate. **g** 2021. **h** Data up to 2011 refer to former Sudan (including South Sudan) and data beginning 2012 is attributed to Sudan without South Sudan. **i** Data refers to a 5-year period preceding the reference year. **j** Including refugees. **k** Data as at the end of December. **l** Including South Sudan. **m** Estimates should be viewed with caution as these are derived from scarce data. **n** Data based on calendar year (January 1 to December 31). **o** 2008. **p** 2017. **q** 2009. **r** 2018. **s** 2007. **t** Overestimated or based on overestimated data. **u** 2005. **v** Including nationals residing abroad.

Suriname

Region	South America
Population (000, 2022)	618[a]
Pop. density (per km2, 2022)	4.0[a]
Capital city	Paramaribo
Capital city pop. (000, 2022)	239.5[c,d]

UN membership date	04 December 1975
Surface area (km2)	163 820[b]
Sex ratio (m per 100 f)	99.1[a]
National currency	Surinam Dollar (SRD)
Exchange rate (per US$)	21.1[e]

Economic indicators	2010	2015	2022
GDP: Gross domestic product (million current US$)	4 482	5 126	4 120[b]
GDP growth rate (annual %, const. 2015 prices)	6.1	- 2.6	- 15.9[b]
GDP per capita (current US$)	8 470.2	9 168.0	7 022.8[b]
Economy: Agriculture (% of Gross Value Added)[f]	10.7	11.3[g]	8.5[g,b]
Economy: Industry (% of Gross Value Added)[f]	39.2	29.6[h]	36.5[h,b]
Economy: Services and other activity (% of GVA)[f]	50.1	59.1[i]	55.0[i,b]
Employment in agriculture (% of employed)[j]	7.6	7.4	7.4[b]
Employment in industry (% of employed)[j]	24.3	23.9	23.5[b]
Employment in services & other sectors (% employed)[j]	68.1	68.7	69.1[b]
Unemployment rate (% of labour force)	7.2	7.2	9.9[j]
Labour force participation rate (female/male pop. %)[j]	40.7 / 64.9	44.5 / 66.8	44.6 / 66.0
CPI: Consumer Price Index (2010=100)[k]	100	139	633[e]
Agricultural production index (2014-2016=100)	92	98	100[b]
International trade: exports (million current US$)	2 026	1 814	1 513[e]
International trade: imports (million current US$)	1 397	1 904	1 381[e]
International trade: balance (million current US$)	628	- 90	132[e]
Balance of payments, current account (million US$)	651	- 786	261[b]

Major trading partners						2021
Export partners (% of exports)	United Arab Emirates	39.5	Switzerland	23.4	Belgium	6.4
Import partners (% of imports)	United States	24.6	Netherlands	14.6	Trinidad and Tobago	12.8

Social indicators	2010	2015	2022
Population growth rate (average annual %)	1.1	1.0	0.8[a]
Urban population (% of total population)	66.3	66.1	66.1[l]
Urban population growth rate (average annual %)[m]	1.0	0.9	...
Fertility rate, total (live births per woman)	2.6	2.5	2.3[a]
Life expectancy at birth (females/males, years)	73.6 / 66.5	74.2 / 67.6	73.6 / 67.2[a]
Population age distribution (0-14/60+ years old, %)	29.9 / 8.6	28.5 / 9.5	26.2 / 11.4[a]
International migrant stock (000/% of total pop.)[n,o]	39.7 / 7.5	43.1 / 7.7	47.8 / 8.1[b]
Refugees and others of concern to the UNHCR (000)	~0.0[p]	~0.0	2.0[e]
Infant mortality rate (per 1 000 live births)	20.5	18.1	16.1[a]
Health: Current expenditure (% of GDP)[j,r]	5.0[q]	6.2[q]	9.7[l]
Health: Physicians (per 1 000 pop.)	0.7[s]	1.0	0.8[d]
Education: Government expenditure (% of GDP)[j]	...	5.9	7.2[l]
Education: Primary gross enrol. ratio (f/m per 100 pop.)	113.8 / 114.2	116.4 / 115.2	109.2 / 109.3[l]
Education: Sec. gross enrol. ratio (f/m per 100 pop.)	80.7 / 62.6	88.6 / 67.1	... / ...
Education: Upr. Sec. gross enrol. ratio (f/m per 100 pop.)	67.7 / 37.8	66.9 / 36.8	... / ...
Intentional homicide rate (per 100 000 pop.)	8.3[t]	6.1	9.4[b]
Seats held by women in the National Parliament (%)	25.5	11.8	29.4[u]

Environment and infrastructure indicators	2010	2015	2022
Individuals using the Internet (per 100 inhabitants)	31.6	42.8[i]	70.1[j,b]
Threatened species (number)	65	76	123
Forested area (% of land area)[j]	98.1	97.8	97.5[l]
CO2 emission estimates (million tons/tons per capita)	1.8 / 3.3	2.7 / 4.8	2.7 / 4.5[l]
Energy production, primary (Petajoules)	43	40	40[l]
Energy supply per capita (Gigajoules)	75	69	74[l]
Tourist/visitor arrivals at national borders (000)	205	228	278[v]
Important sites for terrestrial biodiversity protected (%)	51.2	51.2	51.2[e]
Pop. using safely managed drinking water (urban/rural, %)	62.9 / 35.6	63.1 / 38.2	63.4 / 40.8[b]
Pop. using safely managed sanitation (urban/rural %)	23.6 / 38.3	22.0 / 36.2	20.7 / 33.9[b]
Net Official Development Assist. received (% of GNI)	2.36	0.31	0.81[b]

a Projected estimate (medium fertility variant). **b** 2020. **c** Refers to the total population of the District of Paramaribo. **d** 2018. **e** 2021. **f** Data classified according to ISIC Rev. 4. **g** Excludes irrigation canals and landscaping care. **h** Excludes publishing activities. Includes irrigation and canals. **i** Includes publishing activities and landscape care. **j** Estimate. **k** Calculated by the UNSD from national indices. **l** 2019. **m** Data refers to a 5-year period preceding the reference year. **n** Refers to foreign citizens. **o** Including refugees. **p** Data as at the end of December. **q** Estimates should be viewed with caution as these are derived from scarce data. **r** Data based on calendar year (January 1 to December 31). **s** 2009. **t** 2008. **u** Data are as at 1 January of reporting year. **v** 2017.

Sweden

Region	Northern Europe
Population (000, 2022)	10 549[a]
Pop. density (per km2, 2022)	25.9[a]
Capital city	Stockholm
Capital city pop. (000, 2022)	1 608.0[c,d]

UN membership date	19 November 1946
Surface area (km2)	438 574[b]
Sex ratio (m per 100 f)	101.6[a]
National currency	Swedish Krona (SEK)
Exchange rate (per US$)	9.0[e]

Economic indicators

	2010	2015	2022
GDP: Gross domestic product (million current US$)	495 813	505 104	541 064[b]
GDP growth rate (annual %, const. 2015 prices)	6.0	4.5	- 2.8[b]
GDP per capita (current US$)	52 801.2	51 726.2	53 574.6[b]
Economy: Agriculture (% of Gross Value Added)[f,g]	1.9	1.6	1.6[b]
Economy: Industry (% of Gross Value Added)[f,h]	26.9	24.9	23.8[b]
Economy: Services and other activity (% of GVA)[f,i]	71.2	73.4	74.6[b]
Employment in agriculture (% of employed)	2.1	2.0	1.6[i,b]
Employment in industry (% of employed)	19.9	18.3	17.7[j,b]
Employment in services & other sectors (% employed)	78.0	79.7	80.7[j,b]
Unemployment rate (% of labour force)	8.6	7.4	7.7[j]
Labour force participation rate (female/male pop. %)	58.9 / 67.4	60.7 / 67.4	61.6 / 67.8[j]
CPI: Consumer Price Index (2010=100)	100	104	113[e]
Agricultural production index (2014-2016=100)	91	102	101[b]
International trade: exports (million current US$)	158 411	140 001	189 845[e]
International trade: imports (million current US$)	148 788	138 361	187 116[e]
International trade: balance (million current US$)	9 622	1 641	2 729[e]
Balance of payments, current account (million US$)	29 196	16 750	34 684[e]

Major trading partners   2021

Export partners (% of exports)	Norway	10.7	Germany	10.3	United States	8.1
Import partners (% of imports)	Germany	17.0	Norway	10.2	Netherlands	10.0

Social indicators

	2010	2015	2022
Population growth rate (average annual %)	0.9	1.0	0.6[a]
Urban population (% of total population)	85.1	86.6	87.7[d]
Urban population growth rate (average annual %)[k]	0.9	1.1	...
Fertility rate, total (live births per woman)	2.0	1.8	1.7[a]
Life expectancy at birth (females/males, years)	83.5 / 79.5	84.0 / 80.3	85.1 / 81.9[a]
Population age distribution (0-14/60+ years old, %)	16.6 / 24.9	17.4 / 25.3	17.6 / 25.7[a]
International migrant stock (000/% of total pop.)	1 337.2 / 14.2	1 602.5 / 16.4	2 003.9 / 19.8[b]
Refugees and others of concern to the UNHCR (000)	110.8[i]	225.5	286.9[e]
Infant mortality rate (per 1 000 live births)	2.6	2.4	1.8[a]
Health: Current expenditure (% of GDP)	8.3	10.8	10.9[d]
Health: Physicians (per 1 000 pop.)	3.8	4.2	7.1[d]
Education: Government expenditure (% of GDP)	6.5	7.4	7.6[m]
Education: Primary gross enrol. ratio (f/m per 100 pop.)	101.2 / 101.7	125.5 / 120.5	128.7 / 123.8[d]
Education: Sec. gross enrol. ratio (f/m per 100 pop.)	97.6 / 98.6	150.0 / 131.5	151.2 / 141.6[d]
Education: Upr. Sec. gross enrol. ratio (f/m per 100 pop.)	99.1 / 100.5	179.1 / 149.2	184.6 / 167.2[d]
Intentional homicide rate (per 100 000 pop.)	1.0	1.1	1.2[b]
Seats held by women in the National Parliament (%)	46.4	43.6	46.1[n]

Environment and infrastructure indicators

	2010	2015	2022
Individuals using the Internet (per 100 inhabitants)	90.0[o]	90.6	94.5[b]
Research & Development expenditure (% of GDP)	3.2[i]	3.2[p]	3.5[b]
Threatened species (number)	29	36	115
Forested area (% of land area)	68.9[i]	68.7	68.7[d]
CO2 emission estimates (million tons/tons per capita)	48.5 / 5.0	39.5 / 3.8	34.0 / 3.1[b]
Energy production, primary (Petajoules)	1 343	1 398	1 513[d]
Energy supply per capita (Gigajoules)	223	188	199[d]
Tourist/visitor arrivals at national borders (000)	5 183	6 482	1 957[b]
Important sites for terrestrial biodiversity protected (%)	57.3	58.0	59.1[e]
Pop. using safely managed sanitation (urban/rural %)	94.8 / 88.7	95.3 / 89.9	95.5 / 90.6[b]
Net Official Development Assist. disbursed (% of GNI)[q]	1.10	2.05	0.91[b]

a Projected estimate (medium fertility variant). b 2020. c Refers to "tätort" (according to the administrative divisions of 2005). d 2019. e 2021. f Data classified according to ISIC Rev. 4. g Excludes irrigation canals and landscaping care. h Excludes publishing activities. Includes irrigation and canals. i Includes publishing activities and landscape care. Excludes repair of personal and household goods. j Estimate. k Data refers to a 5-year period preceding the reference year. l Data as at the end of December. m 2018. n Data are as at 1 January of reporting year. o Population aged 16 to 75 years. p The sum of the breakdown does not add to the total. q DAC member (OECD).

Switzerland

Region	Western Europe	UN membership date	10 September 2002
Population (000, 2022)	8 740[a]	Surface area (km2)	41 291[b]
Pop. density (per km2, 2022)	218.6[a]	Sex ratio (m per 100 f)	98.6[a]
Capital city	Bern	National currency	Swiss Franc (CHF)
Capital city pop. (000, 2022)	426.0[c]	Exchange rate (per US$)	0.9[d]

Economic indicators

	2010	2015	2022
GDP: Gross domestic product (million current US$)	603 434	702 150	752 248[b]
GDP growth rate (annual %, const. 2015 prices)	3.3	1.7	- 2.4[b]
GDP per capita (current US$)	77 277.5	84 629.2	86 918.6[b]
Economy: Agriculture (% of Gross Value Added)[e,f]	0.7	0.6	0.7[b]
Economy: Industry (% of Gross Value Added)[e,g]	25.8	25.3	26.0[b]
Economy: Services and other activity (% of GVA)[e,h]	73.5	74.1	73.3[b]
Employment in agriculture (% of employed)	3.5	3.4	2.9[i,b]
Employment in industry (% of employed)	22.4	20.8	20.0[i,b]
Employment in services & other sectors (% employed)	74.1	75.8	77.2[i,b]
Unemployment rate (% of labour force)	4.8	4.8	4.9[i]
Labour force participation rate (female/male pop. %)	60.0 / 74.3	62.3 / 74.2	62.0 / 73.0[i]
CPI: Consumer Price Index (2010=100)[j]	100	98	99[d]
Agricultural production index (2014-2016=100)	99	99	98[b]
International trade: exports (million current US$)	195 609	291 959	379 457[d]
International trade: imports (million current US$)	176 281	253 152	321 934[d]
International trade: balance (million current US$)	19 329	38 807	57 523[d]
Balance of payments, current account (million US$)	81 748	66 360	75 502[d]

Major trading partners

						2021
Export partners (% of exports)	United States	16.5	Germany	14.5	China	8.7
Import partners (% of imports)	Germany	19.3	United Kingdom	11.2	United States	7.5

Social indicators

	2010	2015	2022
Population growth rate (average annual %)	1.2	1.1	0.7[a]
Urban population (% of total population)	73.6	73.7	73.8[c]
Urban population growth rate (average annual %)[k]	1.1	1.2	...
Fertility rate, total (live births per woman)	1.5	1.5	1.5[a]
Life expectancy at birth (females/males, years)	84.4 / 80.0	84.9 / 80.7	85.9 / 82.5[a]
Population age distribution (0-14/60+ years old, %)	15.2 / 22.7	14.9 / 23.5	15.0 / 25.7[a]
International migrant stock (000/% of total pop.)	2 075.2 / 26.6	2 258.2 / 27.2	2 491.2 / 28.8[b]
Refugees and others of concern to the UNHCR (000)	61.9[l]	86.6	122.8[d]
Infant mortality rate (per 1 000 live births)	3.9	4.0	3.1[a]
Health: Current expenditure (% of GDP)	9.9	11.0	11.3[c]
Health: Physicians (per 1 000 pop.)	3.8	4.2	4.4[b]
Education: Government expenditure (% of GDP)	4.8	4.9	4.9[m]
Education: Primary gross enrol. ratio (f/m per 100 pop.)	102.6 / 103.1	104.0 / 104.3	105.5 / 106.0[c]
Education: Sec. gross enrol. ratio (f/m per 100 pop.)	94.6 / 97.5	99.6 / 103.2	99.5 / 105.1[c]
Education: Upr. Sec. gross enrol. ratio (f/m per 100 pop.)	82.6 / 89.5	95.3 / 100.8	95.8 / 104.9[c]
Intentional homicide rate (per 100 000 pop.)	0.7	0.7	0.5[b]
Seats held by women in the National Parliament (%)	29.0	30.5	42.5[n]

Environment and infrastructure indicators

	2010	2015	2022
Individuals using the Internet (per 100 inhabitants)	83.9[o,p]	87.5	94.2[i,b]
Research & Development expenditure (% of GDP)	2.6[q]	3.0	3.1[c]
Threatened species (number)	45	62	170
Forested area (% of land area)	31.2	31.7	32.0[c]
CO2 emission estimates (million tons/tons per capita)	44.2 / 5.5	38.3 / 4.5	35.0 / 3.9[b]
Energy production, primary (Petajoules)[r]	515	495	544[c]
Energy supply per capita (Gigajoules)[r]	139	122	119[c]
Tourist/visitor arrivals at national borders (000)	8 628[s]	9 305[s]	3 690[t,b]
Important sites for terrestrial biodiversity protected (%)	34.8	34.9	37.0[d]
Pop. using safely managed sanitation (urban/rural %)	99.9 / 98.8	99.9 / 98.9	99.9 / 98.9[b]
Net Official Development Assist. disbursed (% of GNI)[u]	4.01	0.94	0.45[b]

a Projected estimate (medium fertility variant). b 2020. c 2019. d 2021. e Data classified according to ISIC Rev. 4. f Excludes irrigation canals and landscaping care. g Excludes publishing activities. Includes irrigation and canals. h Includes publishing activities and landscape care. Excludes repair of personal and household goods. i Estimate. j Calculated by the UNSD from national indices. k Data refers to a 5-year period preceding the reference year. l Data as at the end of December. m 2018. n Data are as at 1 January of reporting year. o Population aged 14 years and over. p Users in the last 6 months. q 2008. r Including Liechtenstein. s Hotels and similar establishments (including health establishments). t All collective tourism establishments. u DAC member (OECD).

Syrian Arab Republic

Region	Western Asia	UN membership date	24 October 1945
Population (000, 2022)	22 125[a]	Surface area (km2)	185 180[b]
Pop. density (per km2, 2022)	120.4[a]	Sex ratio (m per 100 f)	100.3[a]
Capital city	Damascus	National currency	Syrian Pound (SYP)
Capital city pop. (000, 2022)	2 353.6[c,d]	Exchange rate (per US$)	2 500.0[e,f]

Economic indicators

	2010	2015	2022
GDP: Gross domestic product (million current US$)	60 465	19 967	15 572[b]
GDP growth rate (annual %, const. 2015 prices)	3.4	- 3.2	5.0[b]
GDP per capita (current US$)	2 830.4	1 109.4	889.8[b]
Economy: Agriculture (% of Gross Value Added)[g,h]	19.7	20.7	20.6[b]
Economy: Industry (% of Gross Value Added)[g,i]	30.7	30.0	30.1[b]
Economy: Services and other activity (% of GVA)[g,i]	49.6	49.3	49.3[b]
Employment in agriculture (% of employed)[j]	14.5	12.0	10.5[b]
Employment in industry (% of employed)[j]	31.0	28.3	26.5[b]
Employment in services & other sectors (% employed)[j]	54.4	59.7	63.0[b]
Unemployment rate (% of labour force)	8.6	8.7[j]	10.0[j]
Labour force participation rate (female/male pop. %)	13.0 / 72.3	15.8 / 71.9[j]	16.1 / 71.5[j]
CPI: Consumer Price Index (2010=100)	100	449	896[d]
Agricultural production index (2014-2016=100)	127	107	122[b]
International trade: exports (million current US$)	11 353	1 688[j]	821[j,f]
International trade: imports (million current US$)	17 562	3 206[j]	6 448[j,f]
International trade: balance (million current US$)	- 6 209	- 1 518[j]	- 5 628[f]
Balance of payments, current account (million US$)	- 367	...	...

Major trading partners

					2021
Export partners (% of exports)[j]	Saudi Arabia	23.8	Türkiye	19.5	Lebanon 13.4
Import partners (% of imports)[j]	Türkiye	39.7	United Arab Emirates	17.4	China 9.1

Social indicators

	2010	2015	2022
Population growth rate (average annual %)	2.3	- 3.0	4.8[a]
Urban population (% of total population)	55.6	52.2	54.8[d]
Urban population growth rate (average annual %)[k]	3.4	- 3.6	...
Fertility rate, total (live births per woman)	3.4	3.0	2.7[a]
Life expectancy at birth (females/males, years)	76.7 / 71.4	70.4 / 60.6	76.1 / 68.7[a]
Population age distribution (0-14/60+ years old, %)	36.4 / 5.2	41.1 / 6.3	31.4 / 7.2[a]
International migrant stock (000/% of total pop.)[l,m]	1 783.6 / 8.3	835.7 / 4.6	868.7 / 5.0[b]
Refugees and others of concern to the UNHCR (000)	1 308.1[n]	7 946.5	7 078.6[f]
Infant mortality rate (per 1 000 live births)	15.9	25.1	16.3[a]
Health: Current expenditure (% of GDP)[o]	3.3	3.6[p]	...
Health: Physicians (per 1 000 pop.)	1.5	1.6[q]	1.3[r]
Education: Government expenditure (% of GDP)	5.1[s]	...	...
Education: Primary gross enrol. ratio (f/m per 100 pop.)	114.7 / 118.8	80.2 / 83.1[t]	... / ...
Education: Sec. gross enrol. ratio (f/m per 100 pop.)	72.3 / 72.1	52.4 / 52.7[t]	... / ...
Education: Upr. Sec. gross enrol. ratio (f/m per 100 pop.)	38.8 / 35.8	33.7 / 30.5[t]	... / ...
Intentional homicide rate (per 100 000 pop.)	2.2	...	...
Seats held by women in the National Parliament (%)	12.4	12.4	11.2[u]

Environment and infrastructure indicators

	2010	2015	2022
Individuals using the Internet (per 100 inhabitants)	20.7	30.0[j]	35.8[j,b]
Research & Development expenditure (% of GDP)	...	~0.0[v,w]	...
Threatened species (number)	78	108	172
Forested area (% of land area)	2.7	2.8[j]	2.8[j,d]
CO2 emission estimates (million tons/tons per capita)	57.7 / 2.7	23.9 / 1.3	23.8 / 1.4[d]
Energy production, primary (Petajoules)	1 165	197	186[d]
Energy supply per capita (Gigajoules)	43	24	23[d]
Tourist/visitor arrivals at national borders (000)[x]	8 546	5 070[y]	...
Important sites for terrestrial biodiversity protected (%)	0.0	0.0	0.0[f]
Net Official Development Assist. received (% of GNI)	0.21[z]	...	...

a Projected estimate (medium fertility variant). b 2020. c Estimates should be viewed with caution as these are derived from scarce data. d 2019. e UN operational exchange rate. f 2021. g Data classified according to ISIC Rev. 4. h Including taxes less subsidies on production. i Including taxes less subsidies on production and imports. j Estimate. k Data refers to a 5-year period preceding the reference year. l Including refugees. m Refers to foreign citizens. n Data as at the end of December. o Data based on calendar year (January 1 to December 31). p 2012. q 2014. r 2016. s 2009. t 2013. u Data are as at 1 January of reporting year. v Excluding private non-profit. w Excluding business enterprise. x Including Iraqi nationals. y 2011. z 2007.

Tajikistan

Region	Central Asia	UN membership date	02 March 1992
Population (000, 2022)	9 953[a]	Surface area (km2)	141 400[b]
Pop. density (per km2, 2022)	69.6[a]	Sex ratio (m per 100 f)	101.3[a]
Capital city	Dushanbe	National currency	Somoni (TJS)
Capital city pop. (000, 2022)	893.8[c]	Exchange rate (per US$)	11.3[d]

Economic indicators

	2010	2015	2022
GDP: Gross domestic product (million current US$)	5 642	8 271	7 997[b]
GDP growth rate (annual %, const. 2015 prices)	6.5	8.8	4.5[b]
GDP per capita (current US$)	749.6	978.4	838.5[b]
Economy: Agriculture (% of Gross Value Added)[e]	21.8	23.9	24.9[f,b]
Economy: Industry (% of Gross Value Added)[e]	27.9	30.8	27.4[g,b]
Economy: Services and other activity (% of GVA)[e]	50.3	45.3	47.8[h,b]
Employment in agriculture (% of employed)[i]	52.4	48.3	44.2[b]
Employment in industry (% of employed)[i]	15.6	15.6	16.0[b]
Employment in services & other sectors (% employed)[i]	31.9	36.1	39.9[b]
Unemployment rate (% of labour force)[i]	10.9	7.6	7.7
Labour force participation rate (female/male pop. %)[i]	29.2 / 54.8	31.8 / 52.8	30.2 / 50.4
CPI: Consumer Price Index (2010=100)[j]	100	140	211[b]
Agricultural production index (2014-2016=100)	76	102	135[b]
International trade: exports (million current US$)[i]	1 206	891	1 091[d]
International trade: imports (million current US$)[i]	2 659	3 435	4 356[d]
International trade: balance (million current US$)	- 1 453[i]	- 2 544[i]	- 3 264[d]
Balance of payments, current account (million US$)	- 581	- 477	735[d]

Major trading partners

						2021
Export partners (% of exports)[i]	Türkiye	28.3	Kazakhstan	21.2	Uzbekistan	11.5
Import partners (% of imports)[i]	Russian Federation	29.7	Kazakhstan	24.1	China	14.0

Social indicators

	2010	2015	2022
Population growth rate (average annual %)	2.1	2.4	1.9[a]
Urban population (% of total population)	26.5	26.7	27.3[c]
Urban population growth rate (average annual %)[k]	2.2	2.4	...
Fertility rate, total (live births per woman)	3.5	3.5	3.1[a]
Life expectancy at birth (females/males, years)	70.4 / 65.4	71.9 / 67.0	73.5 / 69.2[a]
Population age distribution (0-14/60+ years old, %)	36.8 / 4.6	36.6 / 4.9	36.3 / 6.2[a]
International migrant stock (000/% of total pop.)[i]	279.8 / 3.7	275.1 / 3.3	276.0 / 2.9[b]
Refugees and others of concern to the UNHCR (000)	7.1[m]	11.9	15.4[d]
Infant mortality rate (per 1 000 live births)	36.5	32.1	23.4[a]
Health: Current expenditure (% of GDP)	5.7	6.9	7.1[c]
Health: Physicians (per 1 000 pop.)	1.7	1.7[n]	...
Education: Government expenditure (% of GDP)	4.0	5.2	5.7[i,c]
Education: Primary gross enrol. ratio (f/m per 100 pop.)	100.2 / 102.7	97.1 / 98.1	100.3 / 101.4[o]
Education: Sec. gross enrol. ratio (f/m per 100 pop.)	78.9 / 90.4	83.8 / 93.0[p]	... / ...
Education: Upr. Sec. gross enrol. ratio (f/m per 100 pop.)	47.8 / 71.0	58.5 / 77.7[p]	... / ...
Intentional homicide rate (per 100 000 pop.)	2.4	1.6[q]	0.9[b]
Seats held by women in the National Parliament (%)	17.5	16.9	27.0[r]

Environment and infrastructure indicators

	2010	2015	2022
Individuals using the Internet (per 100 inhabitants)[i]	11.6	19.0	22.0[o]
Research & Development expenditure (% of GDP)[s,t]	0.1	0.1	0.1[b]
Threatened species (number)	40	41	50
Forested area (% of land area)[i]	2.9	3.0	3.0[c]
CO2 emission estimates (million tons/tons per capita)	2.3 / 0.3	4.3 / 0.5	7.7 / 0.8[c]
Energy production, primary (Petajoules)	115	131[i]	170[c]
Energy supply per capita (Gigajoules)	19	20	22[c]
Tourist/visitor arrivals at national borders (000)	160	414	351[b]
Important sites for terrestrial biodiversity protected (%)	15.8	16.8	16.8[d]
Pop. using safely managed sanitation (urban/rural %)	... / 57.4	... / 58.4	... / 59.3[b]
Net Official Development Assist. received (% of GNI)	5.57	4.19	7.86[b]

a Projected estimate (medium fertility variant). b 2020. c 2019. d 2021. e Data classified according to ISIC Rev. 4. f Excludes irrigation canals and landscaping care. g Excludes publishing activities. Includes irrigation and canals. h Includes publishing activities and landscape care. Excludes repair of personal and household goods. i Estimate. j Calculated by the UNSD from national indices. k Data refers to a 5-year period preceding the reference year. l Including refugees. m Data as at the end of December. n 2014. o 2017. p 2013. q 2011. r Data are as at 1 January of reporting year. s Excluding business enterprise. t Excluding private non-profit.

Thailand

Region	South-eastern Asia	
Population (000, 2022)	71 697[a]	
Pop. density (per km2, 2022)	140.3[a]	
Capital city	Bangkok	
Capital city pop. (000, 2022)	10 350.2[c]	

UN membership date	16 December 1946
Surface area (km2)	513 140[b]
Sex ratio (m per 100 f)	94.3[a]
National currency	Baht (THB)
Exchange rate (per US$)	33.4[d]

Economic indicators

	2010	2015	2022
GDP: Gross domestic product (million current US$)	341 105	401 296	501 795[b]
GDP growth rate (annual %, const. 2015 prices)	7.5	3.1	- 6.1[b]
GDP per capita (current US$)	5 076.3	5 840.1	7 189.0[b]
Economy: Agriculture (% of Gross Value Added)[e,f,g]	10.5	8.9	8.6[b]
Economy: Industry (% of Gross Value Added)[e,f,h]	39.9	36.2	33.1[b]
Economy: Services and other activity (% of GVA)[e,f,i]	49.6	54.9	58.3[b]
Employment in agriculture (% of employed)	38.2	32.3	31.2[j,b]
Employment in industry (% of employed)	20.6	23.7	22.5[j,b]
Employment in services & other sectors (% employed)	41.1	44.0	46.3[j,b]
Unemployment rate (% of labour force)	0.6	0.6	1.0[j]
Labour force participation rate (female/male pop. %)	63.7 / 80.0	61.1 / 77.9	58.0 / 74.1[i]
CPI: Consumer Price Index (2010=100)[k]	100	110	114[d]
Agricultural production index (2014-2016=100)	90	97	97[b]
International trade: exports (million current US$)	195 312	214 309	265 034[j,d]
International trade: imports (million current US$)	182 393	202 642	274 271[j,d]
International trade: balance (million current US$)	12 918	11 667	- 9 237[d]
Balance of payments, current account (million US$)	11 486	27 753	- 10 582[d]

Major trading partners

							2021
Export partners (% of exports)[j]	United States	14.9	China	12.9	Japan	9.9
Import partners (% of imports)[j]	China	24.0	Japan	13.3	United States	7.3

Social indicators

	2010	2015	2022
Population growth rate (average annual %)	0.6	0.4	0.2[a]
Urban population (% of total population)	43.9	47.7	50.7[c]
Urban population growth rate (average annual %)[l]	3.7	2.1	...
Fertility rate, total (live births per woman)	1.6	1.5	1.3[a]
Life expectancy at birth (females/males, years)	80.4 / 72.1	82.0 / 73.5	83.9 / 75.5[a]
Population age distribution (0-14/60+ years old, %)	19.3 / 13.2	17.4 / 16.3	15.5 / 22.0[a]
International migrant stock (000/% of total pop.)[m]	3 234.4 / 4.8	3 470.2 / 5.1	3 632.5 / 5.2[b]
Refugees and others of concern to the UNHCR (000)	649.4[n]	625.3	651.0[d]
Infant mortality rate (per 1 000 live births)	11.6	9.2	7.1[a]
Health: Current expenditure (% of GDP)[o]	3.4	3.7	3.8[c]
Health: Physicians (per 1 000 pop.)	0.4	0.5	1.0[b]
Education: Government expenditure (% of GDP)	3.5	3.8	3.0[c]
Education: Primary gross enrol. ratio (f/m per 100 pop.)	96.3 / 97.4	97.6 / 103.5	102.3 / 102.2[b]
Education: Sec. gross enrol. ratio (f/m per 100 pop.)	85.3 / 79.6	118.2 / 123.0	112.3 / 115.2[b]
Education: Upr. Sec. gross enrol. ratio (f/m per 100 pop.)	73.5 / 62.4	120.2 / 120.3	110.5 / 107.9[b]
Intentional homicide rate (per 100 000 pop.)	5.4	4.9[p]	...
Seats held by women in the National Parliament (%)	13.3	6.1	15.8[q]

Environment and infrastructure indicators

	2010	2015	2022
Individuals using the Internet (per 100 inhabitants)	22.4	39.3[r]	77.8[b]
Research & Development expenditure (% of GDP)	0.2[s]	0.6	1.1[c]
Threatened species (number)	477	595	782
Forested area (% of land area)[j]	39.3	39.3	39.0[c]
CO2 emission estimates (million tons/tons per capita)	226.7 / 3.3	253.4 / 3.6	256.9 / 3.6[c]
Energy production, primary (Petajoules)	2 952	3 131	3 125[c]
Energy supply per capita (Gigajoules)	73	82	83[o]
Tourist/visitor arrivals at national borders (000)	15 936	29 923	6 702[b]
Important sites for terrestrial biodiversity protected (%)	66.7	67.6	68.0[d]
Pop. using safely managed sanitation (urban/rural %)	25.9 / 20.0	27.7 / 21.1	29.6 / 22.1[b]
Net Official Development Assist. disbursed (% of GNI)	...	0.02[t]	...
Net Official Development Assist. received (% of GNI)	- 0.01	0.02	0.04[b]

a Projected estimate (medium fertility variant). b 2020. c 2019. d 2021. e At producers' prices. f Data classified according to ISIC Rev. 4. g Excludes irrigation canals and landscaping care. h Excludes publishing activities. Includes irrigation and canals. i Includes publishing activities and landscape care. Excludes repair of personal and household goods. j Estimate. k Calculated by the UNSD from national indices. l Data refers to a 5-year period preceding the reference year. m Including refugees. n Data as at the end of December. o Data refer to fiscal years beginning 1 October. p 2011. q Data are as at 1 January of reporting year. r Population aged 6 years and over. s 2009. t 2014.

Timor-Leste

Region	South-eastern Asia	UN membership date	27 September 2002
Population (000, 2022)	1 341 a	Surface area (km2)	14 919 b
Pop. density (per km2, 2022)	90.2 a	Sex ratio (m per 100 f)	104.0 a
Capital city	Dili	National currency	US Dollar (USD)
Capital city pop. (000, 2022)	281.1 c		

Economic indicators	2010	2015	2022
GDP: Gross domestic product (million current US$)	882	1 594	1 902 b
GDP growth rate (annual %, const. 2015 prices)	9.3	2.8	11.3 b
GDP per capita (current US$)	806.4	1 332.8	1 442.7 b
Economy: Agriculture (% of Gross Value Added) d,e	24.7	17.8	16.1 b
Economy: Industry (% of Gross Value Added) e,f	8.8	18.4	26.4 b
Economy: Services and other activity (% of GVA) e,g	66.5	63.8	57.5 b
Employment in agriculture (% of employed)	50.8	47.4 h	43.7 h,b
Employment in industry (% of employed)	9.3	10.0 h	9.8 h,b
Employment in services & other sectors (% employed)	39.9	42.6 h	46.4 h,b
Unemployment rate (% of labour force)	3.3	4.4 h	4.8 h
Labour force participation rate (female/male pop. %) h	62.0 / 72.8	61.5 / 72.7	61.4 / 72.5
CPI: Consumer Price Index (2010=100) h	100	143	146 i
Agricultural production index (2014-2016=100)	117	103	100 b
International trade: exports (million current US$) h	42	45	507 j
International trade: imports (million current US$) h	246	578	1 094 j
International trade: balance (million current US$)	- 205 h	- 533 h	- 587 i
Balance of payments, current account (million US$)	1 671	225	- 308 b

Major trading partners						2021
Export partners (% of exports) h	China	33.2	Singapore	22.2	Japan	19.6
Import partners (% of imports) h	China	31.6	Indonesia	30.2	Singapore	13.7

Social indicators	2010	2015	2022
Population growth rate (average annual %)	2.2	1.6	1.4 a
Urban population (% of total population)	27.7	29.5	30.9 i
Urban population growth rate (average annual %) k	2.8	3.5	...
Fertility rate, total (live births per woman)	4.8	3.9	3.0 a
Life expectancy at birth (females/males, years)	67.0 / 63.8	68.9 / 65.5	70.8 / 67.4 a
Population age distribution (0-14/60+ years old, %)	41.4 / 7.6	39.0 / 7.9	34.7 / 7.3 a
International migrant stock (000/% of total pop.) l	11.5 / 1.1	8.5 / 0.7	8.4 / 0.6 b
Refugees and others of concern to the UNHCR (000)	~0.0 m	~0.0	~0.0 i
Infant mortality rate (per 1 000 live births)	47.3	39.8	30.9 a
Health: Current expenditure (% of GDP)	6.5	7.7 n	7.2 n,i
Health: Physicians (per 1 000 pop.)	...	0.7	0.8 b
Education: Government expenditure (% of GDP)	11.1	8.4	6.8 h,c
Education: Primary gross enrol. ratio (f/m per 100 pop.)	119.2 / 126.1	126.6 / 129.8	111.2 / 113.7 i
Education: Sec. gross enrol. ratio (f/m per 100 pop.)	62.1 / 62.6	74.4 / 70.5	90.5 / 82.7 i
Education: Upr. Sec. gross enrol. ratio (f/m per 100 pop.)	50.6 / 52.5	62.5 / 59.2	81.5 / 71.9 i
Intentional homicide rate (per 100 000 pop.)	3.6	4.1	...
Seats held by women in the National Parliament (%)	29.2	38.5	40.0 o

Environment and infrastructure indicators	2010	2015	2022
Individuals using the Internet (per 100 inhabitants) h	3.0	18.6	29.1 b
Threatened species (number)	18	21	56
Forested area (% of land area) h	62.9	62.4	62.0 i
Energy production, primary (Petajoules)	367	345	224 i
Energy supply per capita (Gigajoules)	4	6	8 i
Tourist/visitor arrivals at national borders (000) p	40	62	18 b
Important sites for terrestrial biodiversity protected (%)	40.7	40.7	45.6 i
Net Official Development Assist. received (% of GNI)	8.72	7.60	10.24 b

a Projected estimate (medium fertility variant). b 2020. c 2018. d Excludes irrigation canals and landscaping care. e Data classified according to ISIC Rev. 4. f Excludes publishing activities. Includes irrigation and canals. g Includes publishing activities and landscape care. Excludes repair of personal and household goods. h Estimate. i 2019. j 2021. k Data refers to a 5-year period preceding the reference year. l Including refugees. m Data as at the end of December. n Data revision. o Data are as at 1 January of reporting year. p Arrivals by air at Dili Airport.

Togo

Region	Western Africa	UN membership date	20 September 1960	
Population (000, 2022)	8 849[a]	Surface area (km2)	56 785[b]	
Pop. density (per km2, 2022)	162.7[a]	Sex ratio (m per 100 f)	101.1[a]	
Capital city	Lomé	National currency	CFA Franc, BCEAO (XOF)[c]	
Capital city pop. (000, 2022)	1 785.3[d]	Exchange rate (per US$)	579.2[e]	

Economic indicators	2010	2015	2022
GDP: Gross domestic product (million current US$)	3 426	5 346	7 146[b]
GDP growth rate (annual %, const. 2015 prices)	6.1	11.1	0.7[b]
GDP per capita (current US$)	533.5	730.0	863.1[b]
Economy: Agriculture (% of Gross Value Added)[f,g]	33.8	24.2	22.0[b]
Economy: Industry (% of Gross Value Added)[f,h,i]	16.0	20.1	22.9[b]
Economy: Services and other activity (% of GVA)[f,j,k]	50.3	55.6	55.1[b]
Employment in agriculture (% of employed)[l]	44.0	40.2	37.2[b]
Employment in industry (% of employed)[l]	12.4	12.8	12.9[b]
Employment in services & other sectors (% employed)[l]	43.6	47.0	49.9[b]
Unemployment rate (% of labour force)	2.4[l]	2.2	3.9[l]
Labour force participation rate (female/male pop. %)[l]	55.3 / 61.6	55.6 / 60.9	55.8 / 59.5
CPI: Consumer Price Index (2010=100)	100	111	115[b]
Agricultural production index (2014-2016=100)	89	98	111[b]
International trade: exports (million current US$)	741	792	1 080[e]
International trade: imports (million current US$)	1 350	1 877	2 863[e]
International trade: balance (million current US$)	- 609	- 1 085	- 1 784[e]
Balance of payments, current account (million US$)	- 200	- 461	- 21[b]

Major trading partners						2021
Export partners (% of exports)	Burkina Faso	14.3	Mali	11.1	Benin	10.8
Import partners (% of imports)	China	19.7	France	8.8	India	6.3

Social indicators	2010	2015	2022
Population growth rate (average annual %)	2.7	2.5	2.3[a]
Urban population (% of total population)	37.5	40.1	42.2[d]
Urban population growth rate (average annual %)[m]	4.0	4.0	...
Fertility rate, total (live births per woman)	5.0	4.6	4.2[a]
Life expectancy at birth (females/males, years)	57.4 / 57.2	59.6 / 59.2	62.2 / 60.9[a]
Population age distribution (0-14/60+ years old, %)	41.8 / 4.6	41.4 / 4.7	40.0 / 5.1[a]
International migrant stock (000/% of total pop.)[n,o]	255.6 / 4.0	277.4 / 3.8	279.9 / 3.4[b]
Refugees and others of concern to the UNHCR (000)	14.2[p]	22.6	11.6[e]
Infant mortality rate (per 1 000 live births)	60.2	52.4	43.9[a]
Health: Current expenditure (% of GDP)	4.5	5.0	5.7[d]
Health: Physicians (per 1 000 pop.)	0.1	~0.0	0.1[b]
Education: Government expenditure (% of GDP)	4.1	5.1	5.0[l,d]
Education: Primary gross enrol. ratio (f/m per 100 pop.)	120.8 / 133.9	124.9 / 131.2	124.4 / 128.1[b]
Education: Sec. gross enrol. ratio (f/m per 100 pop.)	31.4 / 59.4[l,q]	... / ...	52.1 / 71.6[r]
Education: Upr. Sec. gross enrol. ratio (f/m per 100 pop.)	17.2 / 41.1[l,q]	... / ...	34.8 / 54.2[b]
Seats held by women in the National Parliament (%)	11.1	17.6	18.7[s]

Environment and infrastructure indicators	2010	2015	2022
Individuals using the Internet (per 100 inhabitants)[l]	3.0	7.1	24.0[b]
Research & Development expenditure (% of GDP)[t]	0.2	0.3[u,v]	...
Threatened species (number)	54	66	128
Forested area (% of land area)[l]	22.8	22.5	22.3[d]
CO2 emission estimates (million tons/tons per capita)	2.5 / 0.3	1.5 / 0.1	2.0 / 0.2[d]
Energy production, primary (Petajoules)	99	112	114[d]
Energy supply per capita (Gigajoules)	20	18	17[d]
Tourist/visitor arrivals at national borders (000)	202	273[w]	482[w,b]
Important sites for terrestrial biodiversity protected (%)	79.5	79.5	79.5[e]
Pop. using safely managed drinking water (urban/rural, %)	29.3 / 5.6	33.3 / 6.2	36.8 / 6.7[b]
Pop. using safely managed sanitation (urban/rural %)	12.2 / 4.4	12.3 / 5.7	12.3 / 6.8[b]
Net Official Development Assist. received (% of GNI)	11.84	4.61	7.39[b]

a Projected estimate (medium fertility variant). b 2020. c African Financial Community (CFA) Franc, Central Bank of West African States (BCEAO). d 2019. e 2021. f Data classified according to ISIC Rev. 4. g Excludes irrigation canals and landscaping care. h Refers to buildings and public works. i Excludes publishing activities. Includes irrigation and canals. j Refers to trade only. k Includes publishing activities and landscape care. Excludes repair of personal and household goods. l Estimate. m Data refers to a 5-year period preceding the reference year. n Refers to foreign citizens. o Including refugees. p Data as at the end of December. q 2007. r 2017. s Data are as at 1 January of reporting year. t Excluding business enterprise. u Excluding private non-profit. v 2014. w Including nationals residing abroad.

Tokelau

Region	Polynesia	Population (000, 2022)	2[a,b]	
Surface area (km2)	12[c]	Pop. density (per km2, 2022)	155.9[a,b]	
Sex ratio (m per 100 f)	99.8[a,b]	Capital city	Tokelau[d]	
National currency	New Zealand Dollar (NZD)	Exchange rate (per US$)	1.5[e]	

Economic indicators	2010	2015	2022
Agricultural production index (2014-2016=100)	97	101	97[c]
International trade: exports (million current US$)[f]	~0	~0	~0[e]
International trade: imports (million current US$)[f]	1	1	1[e]
International trade: balance (million current US$)	- 1[f]	- 1[f]	- 1[e]

Major trading partners						2021
Export partners (% of exports)[f]	Singapore	54.0	Nigeria	16.5	South Africa	8.9
Import partners (% of imports)[f]	New Zealand	30.6	Germany	18.3	Ireland	14.0

Social indicators	2010	2015	2022
Population growth rate (average annual %)[a]	0.9	- 2.7	1.1[b]
Urban population (% of total population)	0.0	0.0	0.0[g]
Urban population growth rate (average annual %)[h]	0.0	0.0	...
Fertility rate, total (live births per woman)[a]	3.3	3.0	2.7[b]
Life expectancy at birth (females/males, years)[a]	74.6 / 72.8	75.3 / 73.8	76.2 / 74.4[b]
Population age distribution (0-14/60+ years old, %)[a]	30.4 / 14.6	30.1 / 14.6	28.5 / 12.9[b]
International migrant stock (000/% of total pop.)[i]	1.1 / 99.9	1.2 / 95.0	1.2 / 91.7[c]
Infant mortality rate (per 1 000 live births)[a]	7.8	6.0	4.7[b]
Education: Primary gross enrol. ratio (f/m per 100 pop.)	... / ...	... / ...	136.1 / 136.4[c]
Education: Sec. gross enrol. ratio (f/m per 100 pop.)	... / ...	... / ...	132.9 / 137.5[c]
Education: Upr. Sec. gross enrol. ratio (f/m per 100 pop.)	... / ...	... / ...	74.3 / 36.1[c]

Environment and infrastructure indicators	2010	2015	2022
Threatened species (number)	41	46	60
Forested area (% of land area)[f]	0.0	0.0	0.0[g]
Important sites for terrestrial biodiversity protected (%)	0.0	0.0	0.0[e]

a For statistical purposes, the data for New Zealand do not include this area. b Projected estimate (medium fertility variant). c 2020. d The "capital" rotates yearly between the three atolls of Atafu, Fakaofo and Nukunomu, each with fewer than 500 inhabitants in 2011. e 2021. f Estimate. g 2019. h Data refers to a 5-year period preceding the reference year. i Including refugees.

Tonga

Region	Polynesia	UN membership date		14 September 1999
Population (000, 2022)	107[a]	Surface area (km2)		747[b]
Pop. density (per km2, 2022)	164.4[a]	Sex ratio (m per 100 f)		97.8[a]
Capital city	Nuku'alofa	National currency		Pa'anga (TOP)
Capital city pop. (000, 2022)	22.9[c]	Exchange rate (per US$)		2.3[d]

Economic indicators

	2010	2015	2022
GDP: Gross domestic product (million current US$)	371	403	491[b]
GDP growth rate (annual %, const. 2015 prices)	0.8	1.2	0.7[b]
GDP per capita (current US$)	3 570.2	4 001.2	4 646.1[b]
Economy: Agriculture (% of Gross Value Added)[e,f]	18.7	19.7	21.1[b]
Economy: Industry (% of Gross Value Added)[e,g]	20.5	18.1	17.6[b]
Economy: Services and other activity (% of GVA)[e,h]	60.9	62.3	61.2[b]
Employment in agriculture (% of employed)[i]	27.9	26.3	23.7[b]
Employment in industry (% of employed)[i]	29.7	28.9	29.2[b]
Employment in services & other sectors (% employed)[i]	42.3	44.8	47.1[b]
Unemployment rate (% of labour force)[i]	1.7	2.6	3.8
Labour force participation rate (female/male pop. %)[i]	40.3 / 62.1	38.9 / 58.2	37.3 / 55.1
CPI: Consumer Price Index (2010=100)[i]	100	110	113[j]
Agricultural production index (2014-2016=100)	140	101	94[b]
International trade: exports (million current US$)	8	15[i]	311[i,d]
International trade: imports (million current US$)	159	208[i]	168[i,d]
International trade: balance (million current US$)	- 151	- 193[i]	143[d]
Balance of payments, current account (million US$)	- 87	- 44	- 19[d]

Major trading partners

						2021
Export partners (% of exports)[i]	United States	28.6	New Zealand	17.4	Australia	15.2
Import partners (% of imports)[i]	New Zealand	33.7	China	18.8	Fiji	16.5

Social indicators

	2010	2015	2022
Population growth rate (average annual %)	0.3	- 0.5	0.9[a]
Urban population (% of total population)	23.4	23.3	23.1[k]
Urban population growth rate (average annual %)[l]	0.8	0.3	...
Fertility rate, total (live births per woman)	3.9	3.6	3.2[a]
Life expectancy at birth (females/males, years)	73.4 / 67.6	73.5 / 67.9	74.1 / 68.6[a]
Population age distribution (0-14/60+ years old, %)	37.6 / 8.2	36.8 / 8.6	34.3 / 9.0[a]
International migrant stock (000/% of total pop.)[m]	4.6 / 4.4	4.0 / 3.9	3.7 / 3.5[b]
Refugees and others of concern to the UNHCR (000)	~0.0[n]	...	~0.0[b]
Infant mortality rate (per 1 000 live births)	11.3	10.7	9.2[a]
Health: Current expenditure (% of GDP)[o]	5.0	4.7	5.0[k]
Health: Physicians (per 1 000 pop.)	0.6	0.5[p]	0.9[b]
Education: Government expenditure (% of GDP)	...	...	8.0[i,k]
Education: Primary gross enrol. ratio (f/m per 100 pop.)	107.3 / 109.4	116.0 / 116.7	112.1 / 117.4[b]
Education: Sec. gross enrol. ratio (f/m per 100 pop.)	107.2 / 100.4	102.4 / 99.4	95.6 / 81.3[b]
Education: Upr. Sec. gross enrol. ratio (f/m per 100 pop.)	93.4 / 84.8[q]	76.9 / 64.5	67.6 / 55.7[b]
Intentional homicide rate (per 100 000 pop.)	1.0	1.0[r]	2.9[s]
Seats held by women in the National Parliament (%)	3.1	0.0	3.7[s]

Environment and infrastructure indicators

	2010	2015	2022
Individuals using the Internet (per 100 inhabitants)[i]	16.0	38.7	41.2[t]
Threatened species (number)	58	74	115
Forested area (% of land area)	12.4	12.4[i]	12.4[i,k]
Energy production, primary (Petajoules)	0	0	0[k]
Energy supply per capita (Gigajoules)	16	16	22[k]
Tourist/visitor arrivals at national borders (000)[u]	47	54	9[b]
Important sites for terrestrial biodiversity protected (%)	26.1	26.1	26.1[d]
Pop. using safely managed drinking water (urban/rural, %)	50.2 / 23.1	50.5 / 23.1	50.8 / 23.1[b]
Pop. using safely managed sanitation (urban/rural %)	28.9 / 38.7	26.0 / 38.1	23.2 / 37.0[b]
Net Official Development Assist. received (% of GNI)	17.50	15.47	20.06[k]

a Projected estimate (medium fertility variant). b 2020. c 2018. d 2021. e Data classified according to ISIC Rev. 4. f Excludes irrigation canals and landscaping care. g Excludes publishing activities. Includes irrigation and canals. h Includes publishing activities and landscape care. Excludes repair of personal and household goods. i Estimate. j 2016. k 2019. l Data refers to a 5-year period preceding the reference year. m Including refugees. n Data as at the end of December. o Data refer to fiscal years beginning 1 July. p 2013. q 2006. r 2012. s Data are as at 1 January of reporting year. t 2017. u Arrivals by air.

Trinidad and Tobago

Region	Caribbean	UN membership date		18 September 1962	
Population (000, 2022)	1 531 [a]	Surface area (km2)		5 127 [b]	
Pop. density (per km2, 2022)	298.4 [a]	Sex ratio (m per 100 f)		97.3 [a]	
Capital city	Port of Spain	National currency		TT Dollar (TTD) [c]	
Capital city pop. (000, 2022)	544.3 [d,e]	Exchange rate (per US$)		6.8 [f]	

Economic indicators	2010	2015	2022
GDP: Gross domestic product (million current US$)	22 198	25 192	21 393 [b]
GDP growth rate (annual %, const. 2015 prices)	3.3	1.8	- 7.4 [b]
GDP per capita (current US$)	16 713.8	18 383.6	15 286.0 [b]
Economy: Agriculture (% of Gross Value Added) [g,h]	0.7	1.1	1.1 [b]
Economy: Industry (% of Gross Value Added) [h,i]	52.3	40.4	34.9 [b]
Economy: Services and other activity (% of GVA) [h,j]	47.0	58.5	64.0 [b]
Employment in agriculture (% of employed)	3.8 [k]	3.4	2.9 [k,b]
Employment in industry (% of employed)	29.8 [k]	27.9	26.6 [k,b]
Employment in services & other sectors (% employed)	66.5 [k]	68.6	70.5 [k,b]
Unemployment rate (% of labour force)	4.0	2.4	4.3 [k]
Labour force participation rate (female/male pop. %)	49.7 / 72.4	49.5 / 70.8	47.5 / 68.6 [k]
CPI: Consumer Price Index (2010=100) [l]	100	134	144 [b]
Agricultural production index (2014-2016=100)	110	89	104 [b]
International trade: exports (million current US$)	10 982	10 756	8 620 [f]
International trade: imports (million current US$)	6 480	9 298	5 761 [f]
International trade: balance (million current US$)	4 502	1 458	2 860 [f]
Balance of payments, current account (million US$)	4 172	2 057	- 136 [b]

Major trading partners					2021
Export partners (% of exports)	United States	41.6	Guyana	6.7	Mexico	4.3
Import partners (% of imports)	United States	34.6	China	10.5	Mexico	7.0

Social indicators	2010	2015	2022
Population growth rate (average annual %)	0.7	0.6	0.3 [a]
Urban population (% of total population)	54.0	53.3	53.2 [e]
Urban population growth rate (average annual %) [m]	0.1	0.2	...
Fertility rate, total (live births per woman)	1.7	1.7	1.6 [a]
Life expectancy at birth (females/males, years)	76.1 / 69.3	77.9 / 71.1	78.2 / 71.3 [a]
Population age distribution (0-14/60+ years old, %)	20.8 / 10.7	20.4 / 13.4	19.0 / 17.2 [a]
International migrant stock (000/% of total pop.) [n]	48.2 / 3.6	50.0 / 3.7	78.8 / 5.6 [b]
Refugees and others of concern to the UNHCR (000)	0.1 [o]	0.2	29.6 [f]
Infant mortality rate (per 1 000 live births)	19.9	17.2	15.0 [a]
Health: Current expenditure (% of GDP) [k,p]	5.1	6.1	7.0 [e]
Health: Physicians (per 1 000 pop.)	1.8	2.6	4.5 [e]
Education: Government expenditure (% of GDP) [k]	...	3.4	3.6 [e]
Education: Primary gross enrol. ratio (f/m per 100 pop.)	104.4 / 108.0	... / ...	... / ...
Intentional homicide rate (per 100 000 pop.)	35.6	30.6	38.6 [e]
Seats held by women in the National Parliament (%)	26.8	28.6	26.2 [q]

Environment and infrastructure indicators	2010	2015	2022
Individuals using the Internet (per 100 inhabitants)	48.5 [k]	65.1 [k]	70.6 [r]
Research & Development expenditure (% of GDP)	~0.0	0.1	0.1 [s,e]
Threatened species (number)	48	65	145
Forested area (% of land area)	45.3	44.9	44.6 [e]
CO2 emission estimates (million tons/tons per capita)	21.1 / 15.8	20.7 / 15.0	16.7 / 11.9 [e]
Energy production, primary (Petajoules)	1 786	1 557	1 444 [e]
Energy supply per capita (Gigajoules)	627	582	515 [e]
Tourist/visitor arrivals at national borders (000) [t]	388	440	95 [b]
Important sites for terrestrial biodiversity protected (%)	32.0	32.0	32.0 [f]
Net Official Development Assist. received (% of GNI)	0.02	...	...

a Projected estimate (medium fertility variant). b 2020. c Trinidad and Tobago Dollar. d Data refers to the urban agglomeration. e 2019. f 2021. g Excludes irrigation canals and landscaping care. h Data classified according to ISIC Rev. 4. i Excludes publishing activities. Includes irrigation and canals. j Includes publishing activities and landscape care. Excludes repair of personal and household goods. k Estimate. l Data refer to the Retail Price Index. m Data refers to a 5-year period preceding the reference year. n Including refugees. o Data as at the end of December. p Data refer to fiscal years beginning 1 October. q Data are as at 1 January of reporting year. r 2017. s Excluding business enterprise. t Arrivals by air.

Tunisia

Region	Northern Africa
Population (000, 2022)	12 356[a]
Pop. density (per km2, 2022)	79.5[a]
Capital city	Tunis
Capital city pop. (000, 2022)	2 327.8[c,d]

UN membership date	12 November 1956
Surface area (km2)	163 610[b]
Sex ratio (m per 100 f)	97.5[a]
National currency	Tunisian Dinar (TND)
Exchange rate (per US$)	2.9[e]

Economic indicators

	2010	2015	2022
GDP: Gross domestic product (million current US$)	44 051	43 173	39 218[b]
GDP growth rate (annual %, const. 2015 prices)	3.5	1.2	- 8.6[b]
GDP per capita (current US$)	4 142.0	3 861.6	3 318.3[b]
Economy: Agriculture (% of Gross Value Added)[f,g]	8.1	10.9	12.4[b]
Economy: Industry (% of Gross Value Added)[f,g]	31.1	26.6	22.9[b]
Economy: Services and other activity (% of GVA)[f,g]	60.8	62.5	64.7[b]
Employment in agriculture (% of employed)	17.9	14.5[h]	12.7[h,b]
Employment in industry (% of employed)	33.4	33.3[h]	32.5[h,b]
Employment in services & other sectors (% employed)	48.6	52.2[h]	54.8[h,b]
Unemployment rate (% of labour force)	13.0	15.2	16.2[h]
Labour force participation rate (female/male pop. %)	24.9 / 69.6	26.1 / 69.0	25.7 / 67.3[h]
CPI: Consumer Price Index (2010=100)	100[h,i]	127[h]	177[e]
Agricultural production index (2014-2016=100)	85	115	122[b]
International trade: exports (million current US$)	16 427	14 073	16 604[h,e]
International trade: imports (million current US$)	22 215	20 223	22 489[h,e]
International trade: balance (million current US$)	- 5 789	- 6 149	- 5 885[e]
Balance of payments, current account (million US$)	- 2 104	- 3 850	- 2 530[b]

Major trading partners

						2021
Export partners (% of exports)[h]	France	29.1	Italy	16.2	Germany	12.8
Import partners (% of imports)[h]	Italy	15.4	France	14.2	China	9.5

Social indicators

	2010	2015	2022
Population growth rate (average annual %)	1.1	1.1	0.8[a]
Urban population (% of total population)	66.7	68.1	69.3[d]
Urban population growth rate (average annual %)[j]	1.5	1.6	...
Fertility rate, total (live births per woman)	2.1	2.3	2.1[a]
Life expectancy at birth (females/males, years)	78.6 / 72.6	78.9 / 72.8	77.4 / 71.4[a]
Population age distribution (0-14/60+ years old, %)	23.8 / 9.8	24.2 / 11.2	24.8 / 13.7[a]
International migrant stock (000/% of total pop.)[k,l]	43.2 / 0.4	56.5 / 0.5	60.1 / 0.5[b]
Refugees and others of concern to the UNHCR (000)	0.1[m]	1.0	8.5[e]
Infant mortality rate (per 1 000 live births)	15.6	14.6	13.5[a]
Health: Current expenditure (% of GDP)[n]	5.9	6.6[o]	7.0[h,p,d]
Health: Physicians (per 1 000 pop.)	1.2	1.3	1.3[q]
Education: Government expenditure (% of GDP)	6.3	6.6	7.3[r]
Education: Primary gross enrol. ratio (f/m per 100 pop.)	107.0 / 107.4	114.6 / 114.5	112.5 / 114.3[b]
Education: Sec. gross enrol. ratio (f/m per 100 pop.)	94.5 / 86.2	95.3 / 88.6[s]	99.3 / 86.9[r]
Education: Upr. Sec. gross enrol. ratio (f/m per 100 pop.)	84.2 / 67.6	84.9 / 69.1[s]	89.8 / 68.9[r]
Intentional homicide rate (per 100 000 pop.)	2.7	3.1[t]	4.8[b]
Seats held by women in the National Parliament (%)	27.6	31.3	26.3[u]

Environment and infrastructure indicators

	2010	2015	2022
Individuals using the Internet (per 100 inhabitants)	36.8	46.5	71.9[h,b]
Research & Development expenditure (% of GDP)	0.7	0.6	0.7[d]
Threatened species (number)	75	83	128
Forested area (% of land area)	4.4	4.5[h]	4.5[h,d]
CO2 emission estimates (million tons/tons per capita)	23.8 / 2.2	26.1 / 2.3	26.7 / 2.2[d]
Energy production, primary (Petajoules)	341	269	218[d]
Energy supply per capita (Gigajoules)	40	41	41[d]
Tourist/visitor arrivals at national borders (000)[v]	7 828	5 359	2 012[b]
Important sites for terrestrial biodiversity protected (%)	26.0	39.8	39.8[e]
Pop. using safely managed drinking water (urban/rural, %)	83.4 / 63.0	83.8 / 65.8	83.9 / 68.7[b]
Pop. using safely managed sanitation (urban/rural %)	79.8 / 41.8	84.9 / 51.9	88.6 / 62.9[b]
Net Official Development Assist. received (% of GNI)	1.31	1.18	2.55[b]

a Projected estimate (medium fertility variant). b 2020. c Refers to Grand Tunis. d 2019. e 2021. f At factor cost. g Data classified according to ISIC Rev. 4. h Estimate. i Break in the time series. j Data refers to a 5-year period preceding the reference year. k Including refugees. l Refers to foreign citizens. m Data as at the end of December. n Data based on calendar year (January 1 to December 31). o Data are based on SHA2011. p Estimates should be viewed with caution as these are derived from scarce data. q 2017. r 2016. s 2011. t 2012. u Data are as at 1 January of reporting year. v Including nationals residing abroad.

Türkiye

Region	Western Asia		UN membership date		24 October 1945
Population (000, 2022)	85 341[a]		Surface area (km2)		783 562[b]
Pop. density (per km2, 2022)	110.9[a]		Sex ratio (m per 100 f)		100.4[a]
Capital city	Ankara		National currency		Turkish Lira (TRY)
Capital city pop. (000, 2022)	5 018.0[c,d]		Exchange rate (per US$)		13.0[e]

Economic indicators	2010	2015	2022
GDP: Gross domestic product (million current US$)	776 967	864 314	720 098[b]
GDP growth rate (annual %, const. 2015 prices)	8.4	6.1	1.8[b]
GDP per capita (current US$)	10 742.4	11 006.2	8 538.1[b]
Economy: Agriculture (% of Gross Value Added)[f,g]	10.2	7.8	7.5[b]
Economy: Industry (% of Gross Value Added)[g,h]	27.8	31.6	31.5[b]
Economy: Services and other activity (% of GVA)[g,i]	62.0	60.6	61.0[b]
Employment in agriculture (% of employed)	23.7	20.4	18.0[j,b]
Employment in industry (% of employed)	26.2	27.2	26.1[j,b]
Employment in services & other sectors (% employed)	50.1	52.4	55.9[j,b]
Unemployment rate (% of labour force)	10.7	10.2	14.0[j]
Labour force participation rate (female/male pop. %)	27.3 / 70.3	31.6 / 72.0	32.8 / 70.3[j]
CPI: Consumer Price Index (2010=100)	100[j]	146[j]	315[e]
Agricultural production index (2014-2016=100)	86	102	114[b]
International trade: exports (million current US$)[k]	113 883	143 850	225 219[e]
International trade: imports (million current US$)[k]	185 544	207 207	271 423[e]
International trade: balance (million current US$)[k]	- 71 661	- 63 356	- 46 204[e]
Balance of payments, current account (million US$)	- 44 620	- 27 314	- 13 693[e]

Major trading partners						2021
Export partners (% of exports)	Germany	8.6	United States	6.5	United Kingdom	6.1
Import partners (% of imports)	China	11.9	Russian Federation	10.7	Undisclosed[l]	9.0

Social indicators	2010	2015	2022
Population growth rate (average annual %)	1.3	1.7	0.6[a]
Urban population (% of total population)	70.8	73.6	75.6[d]
Urban population growth rate (average annual %)[m]	2.1	2.4	...
Fertility rate, total (live births per woman)	2.1	2.2	1.9[a]
Life expectancy at birth (females/males, years)	78.2 / 71.9	79.8 / 73.5	81.5 / 75.4[a]
Population age distribution (0-14/60+ years old, %)	26.7 / 9.5	24.6 / 10.6	23.2 / 12.7[a]
International migrant stock (000/% of total pop.)[n]	1 373.7 / 1.9	4 346.2 / 5.5	6 052.7 / 7.2[b]
Refugees and others of concern to the UNHCR (000)	17.8[o]	1 985.3	4 019.0[e]
Infant mortality rate (per 1 000 live births)	15.3	11.0	7.7[a]
Health: Current expenditure (% of GDP)	5.0	4.1	4.3[d]
Health: Physicians (per 1 000 pop.)	1.7	1.8	1.9[d]
Education: Government expenditure (% of GDP)	2.7[p]	...	4.3[q]
Education: Primary gross enrol. ratio (f/m per 100 pop.)	100.6 / 102.0	102.7 / 103.4	96.5 / 97.6[b]
Education: Sec. gross enrol. ratio (f/m per 100 pop.)	80.5 / 87.9	101.5 / 104.2	102.0 / 106.1[d]
Education: Upr. Sec. gross enrol. ratio (f/m per 100 pop.)	67.5 / 77.4	102.9 / 109.8	99.1 / 108.5[d]
Intentional homicide rate (per 100 000 pop.)	4.2	2.8	2.5[b]
Seats held by women in the National Parliament (%)	9.1	14.4	17.4[r]

Environment and infrastructure indicators	2010	2015	2022
Individuals using the Internet (per 100 inhabitants)	39.8[s,t]	53.7[t]	77.7[b]
Research & Development expenditure (% of GDP)	0.8	0.9	1.1[b]
Threatened species (number)	150	370	453
Forested area (% of land area)	27.4	28.1	28.7[d]
CO2 emission estimates (million tons/tons per capita)	272.3 / 3.7	322.9 / 4.1	370.0 / 4.4[b]
Energy production, primary (Petajoules)	1 355	1 317	1 891[d]
Energy supply per capita (Gigajoules)	61	69	73[d]
Tourist/visitor arrivals at national borders (000)[u]	31 364	39 478	15 894[b]
Important sites for terrestrial biodiversity protected (%)	2.3	2.3	2.3[e]
Pop. using safely managed sanitation (urban/rural %)	69.8 / 64.9	74.7 / 72.6	78.0 / 79.9[b]
Net Official Development Assist. disbursed (% of GNI)[v]	0.23	0.65	1.10[w]
Net Official Development Assist. received (% of GNI)	0.14	0.25	0.08[b]

a Projected estimate (medium fertility variant). b 2020. c Refers to Altindag, Cankaya, Etimesgut, Golbasi, Keçioren, Mamak, Sincan and Yenimahalle. d 2019. e 2021. f Excludes irrigation canals and landscaping care. g Data classified according to ISIC Rev. 4. h Excludes publishing activities. Includes irrigation and canals. i Includes publishing activities and landscape care. Excludes repair of personal and household goods. j Estimate. k Special trade system up to 2012. l Undisclosed (Special categories). m Data refers to a 5-year period preceding the reference year. n Including refugees. o Data as at the end of December. p 2006. q 2018. r Data are as at 1 January of reporting year. s Population aged 16 to 74 years. t Users in the last 12 months. u Turkish citizens resident abroad are included. v Türkiye reports support to refugees in Türkiye against type of aid C01 "project-type interventions" instead of H02 "in-donor refugee costs". w 2017.

Turkmenistan

Region	Central Asia
Population (000, 2022)	6 431 [a]
Pop. density (per km2, 2022)	13.7 [a]
Capital city	Ashgabat
Capital city pop. (000, 2022)	828.1 [d]

UN membership date	02 March 1992
Surface area (km2)	488 100 [b]
Sex ratio (m per 100 f)	98.2 [a]
National currency	Turkmen. Manat (TMT) [c]
Exchange rate (per US$)	3.5 [e,f]

Economic indicators

	2010	2015	2022
GDP: Gross domestic product (million current US$)	22 583	36 052	42 845 [b]
GDP growth rate (annual %, const. 2015 prices)	14.6	1.5	- 3.4 [b]
GDP per capita (current US$)	4 439.2	6 477.9	7 103.9 [b]
Economy: Agriculture (% of Gross Value Added) [g]	11.5	9.4	11.4 [b]
Economy: Industry (% of Gross Value Added) [g]	60.0	55.1	46.5 [b]
Economy: Services and other activity (% of GVA) [g]	28.5	35.5	42.1 [b]
Employment in agriculture (% of employed) [h]	24.8	21.9	19.5 [b]
Employment in industry (% of employed) [h]	39.2	41.2	42.6 [b]
Employment in services & other sectors (% employed) [h]	36.0	36.9	37.9 [b]
Unemployment rate (% of labour force)	4.0	4.1 [h]	5.1 [h]
Labour force participation rate (female/male pop. %) [h]	39.7 / 58.7	37.9 / 56.7	36.6 / 55.5
Agricultural production index (2014-2016=100)	109	102	96 [b]
International trade: exports (million current US$) [h]	3 335	3 670	8 699 [f]
International trade: imports (million current US$) [h]	2 400	2 596	3 933 [f]
International trade: balance (million current US$)	935 [h]	1 074 [h]	4 766 [f]

Major trading partners

						2021
Export partners (% of exports) [h]	China	62.6	Türkiye	8.0	Uzbekistan	7.8
Import partners (% of imports) [h]	Türkiye	23.7	Russian Federation	23.5	China	12.4

Social indicators

	2010	2015	2022
Population growth rate (average annual %)	1.7	1.8	1.4 [a]
Urban population (% of total population)	48.5	50.3	52.0 [d]
Urban population growth rate (average annual %) [i]	2.0	2.5	...
Fertility rate, total (live births per woman)	2.8	2.9	2.6 [a]
Life expectancy at birth (females/males, years)	71.6 / 64.9	72.2 / 65.4	72.9 / 65.9 [a]
Population age distribution (0-14/60+ years old, %)	30.2 / 6.0	30.4 / 6.8	31.1 / 8.8 [a]
International migrant stock (000/% of total pop.) [j]	198.0 / 3.9	196.4 / 3.5	194.9 / 3.2 [b]
Refugees and others of concern to the UNHCR (000)	20.1 [k]	7.2	4.1 [f]
Infant mortality rate (per 1 000 live births)	36.8	36.1	32.9 [a]
Health: Current expenditure (% of GDP)	5.0	6.3	6.6 [d]
Health: Physicians (per 1 000 pop.)	2.3	2.2 [l]	
Education: Government expenditure (% of GDP)	...	3.0 [m]	3.1 [d]
Education: Primary gross enrol. ratio (f/m per 100 pop.)	... / ...	... / ...	115.9 / 118.0 [b]
Education: Sec. gross enrol. ratio (f/m per 100 pop.)	... / ...	... / ...	92.4 / 94.1 [b]
Education: Upr. Sec. gross enrol. ratio (f/m per 100 pop.)	... / ...	... / ...	80.0 / 81.4 [b]
Intentional homicide rate (per 100 000 pop.)	4.2 [n]	...	...
Seats held by women in the National Parliament (%)	16.8	25.8	25.9 [o]

Environment and infrastructure indicators

	2010	2015	2022
Individuals using the Internet (per 100 inhabitants) [h]	3.0	15.0	21.3 [p]
Threatened species (number)	45	49	59
Forested area (% of land area) [h]	8.8	8.8	8.8 [d]
CO2 emission estimates (million tons/tons per capita)	57.2 / 11.2	69.5 / 12.4	69.6 / 11.6 [d]
Energy production, primary (Petajoules)	1 982	3 407	3 399 [d]
Energy supply per capita (Gigajoules)	187	208	200 [d]
Tourist/visitor arrivals at national borders (000)	8 [q]	...	...
Important sites for terrestrial biodiversity protected (%)	14.0	14.0	14.0 [f]
Pop. using safely managed drinking water (urban/rural, %)	91.5 / 72.7	96.4 / 85.1	97.1 / 92.3 [b]
Net Official Development Assist. received (% of GNI)	0.21	0.07	0.06 [d]

a Projected estimate (medium fertility variant). b 2020. c Turkmenistan New Manat. d 2019. e UN operational exchange rate. f 2021. g Data classified according to ISIC Rev. 4. h Estimate. i Data refers to a 5-year period preceding the reference year. j Including refugees. k Data as at the end of December. l 2014. m 2012. n 2006. o Data are as at 1 January of reporting year. p 2017. q 2007.

Turks and Caicos Islands

Region	Caribbean	Population (000, 2022)	46 [a,b]
Surface area (km2)	948 [c,d]	Pop. density (per km2, 2022)	48.1 [a,b]
Sex ratio (m per 100 f)	101.4 [a,b]	Capital city	Cockburn Town
National currency	US Dollar (USD)	Capital city pop. (000, 2022)	0.1 [e]

Economic indicators

	2010	2015	2022
GDP: Gross domestic product (million current US$)	687	942	925 [d]
GDP growth rate (annual %, const. 2015 prices)	1.0	11.3	- 26.8 [d]
GDP per capita (current US$)	21 028.4	26 182.4	23 880.5 [d]
Economy: Agriculture (% of Gross Value Added) [f]	0.6	0.6	0.5 [d]
Economy: Industry (% of Gross Value Added) [f]	12.4	11.1	17.6 [d]
Economy: Services and other activity (% of GVA) [f]	86.9	88.3	81.9 [d]
Employment in agriculture (% of employed)	1.2 [g,h,i]	...	...
Employment in industry (% of employed)	23.1 [g,h,i]	...	...
Employment in services & other sectors (% employed)	74.0 [g,h,i]	...	...
Unemployment rate (% of labour force)	8.3 [h,i]	...	...
International trade: exports (million current US$) [j]	16	5	3 [k]
International trade: imports (million current US$) [j]	302	410	257 [k]
International trade: balance (million current US$)	- 286 [j]	- 405 [j]	- 254 [k]
Balance of payments, current account (million US$)	...	154	173 [l]

Major trading partners

						2021
Export partners (% of exports) [j]	United States	48.0	Singapore	6.5	Ireland	5.9
Import partners (% of imports) [j]	United States	84.8	Dominican Rep.	2.9	United Kingdom	1.9

Social indicators

	2010	2015	2022
Population growth rate (average annual %) [b]	3.8	5.1	0.8 [a]
Urban population (% of total population)	90.2	92.2	93.4 [m]
Urban population growth rate (average annual %) [n]	3.7	2.5	...
Fertility rate, total (live births per woman) [b]	1.7	1.7	1.7 [a]
Life expectancy at birth (females/males, years) [b]	79.1 / 73.7	79.6 / 74.5	78.0 / 72.2 [a]
Population age distribution (0-14/60+ years old, %) [b]	22.9 / 9.5	18.8 / 12.5	16.7 / 15.6 [a]
International migrant stock (000/% of total pop.) [o]	17.2 / 52.7	22.7 / 63.2	25.7 / 66.5 [d]
Refugees and others of concern to the UNHCR (000)	...	~0.0	~0.0 [k]
Infant mortality rate (per 1 000 live births) [b]	10.5	7.2	11.4 [a]
Education: Government expenditure (% of GDP)	2.5 [p]	3.1	3.5 [j,m]
Education: Primary gross enrol. ratio (f/m per 100 pop.)	84.2 / 77.7 [p]	... / ...	116.4 / 116.7 [l]
Education: Sec. gross enrol. ratio (f/m per 100 pop.)	95.5 / 86.3 [q]	76.2 / 69.0	77.6 / 75.5 [l]
Education: Upr. Sec. gross enrol. ratio (f/m per 100 pop.)	53.7 / 54.6 [q]	87.1 / 67.4	69.9 / 65.0 [l]
Intentional homicide rate (per 100 000 pop.)	6.3 [q]	5.7 [r]	...

Environment and infrastructure indicators

	2010	2015	2022
Threatened species (number)	34	56	79
Forested area (% of land area) [j]	11.1	11.1	11.1 [m]
Energy production, primary (Petajoules)	0	0	0 [m]
Energy supply per capita (Gigajoules) [j]	125	127	138 [m]
Tourist/visitor arrivals at national borders (000)	281	386	164 [d]
Important sites for terrestrial biodiversity protected (%)	27.9	27.9	27.9 [k]

a Projected estimate (medium fertility variant). b For statistical purposes, the data for United Kingdom do not include this area. c Including low water level for all islands (area to shoreline). d 2020. e 2001. f Data classified according to ISIC Rev. 4. g Data classified according to ISIC Rev. 3. h Break in the time series. i 2008. j Estimate. k 2021. l 2018. m 2019. n Data refers to a 5-year period preceding the reference year. o Including refugees. p 2005. q 2009. r 2014.

Tuvalu

Region	Polynesia	UN membership date	05 September 2000
Population (000, 2022)	11[a]	Surface area (km2)	26[b]
Pop. density (per km2, 2022)	377.0[a]	Sex ratio (m per 100 f)	105.2[a]
Capital city	Funafuti	National currency	Australian Dollar (AUD)
Capital city pop. (000, 2022)	7.0[c]	Exchange rate (per US$)	1.4[d]

Economic indicators

	2010	2015	2022
GDP: Gross domestic product (million current US$)	31	36	55[b]
GDP growth rate (annual %, const. 2015 prices)	- 3.3	10.4	1.0[b]
GDP per capita (current US$)	2 981.5	3 261.0	4 648.3[b]
Economy: Agriculture (% of Gross Value Added)[e]	27.3	13.9	11.3[b]
Economy: Industry (% of Gross Value Added)[e,f]	5.7	12.4	15.3[b]
Economy: Services and other activity (% of GVA)[e]	67.0	73.7	73.4[b]
CPI: Consumer Price Index (2010=100)	100	101[g]	...
Agricultural production index (2014-2016=100)	94	100	102[b]
International trade: exports (million current US$)[h]	~0	~0	30[d]
International trade: imports (million current US$)[h]	12	12	84[d]
International trade: balance (million current US$)	- 12[h]	- 12[h]	- 54[d]
Balance of payments, current account (million US$)	- 14	- 26	- 9[i]

Major trading partners

						2021
Export partners (% of exports)[h]	Thailand	38.3	Nigeria	26.9	Philippines	16.9
Import partners (% of imports)[h]	Singapore	32.0	China	24.3	Japan	22.0

Social indicators

	2010	2015	2022
Population growth rate (average annual %)	1.3	- 0.2	0.8[a]
Urban population (% of total population)	54.8	59.7	63.2[i]
Urban population growth rate (average annual %)[j]	2.9	2.6	...
Fertility rate, total (live births per woman)	3.5	3.2	3.1[a]
Life expectancy at birth (females/males, years)	67.7 / 60.6	68.3 / 60.5	69.4 / 61.1[a]
Population age distribution (0-14/60+ years old, %)	32.5 / 8.4	31.6 / 8.9	31.7 / 11.1[a]
International migrant stock (000/% of total pop.)[k]	0.2 / 2.1	0.2 / 2.1	0.2 / 2.0[b]
Infant mortality rate (per 1 000 live births)	25.6	21.5	17.6[a]
Health: Current expenditure (% of GDP)[l]	16.9	16.7	24.0[i]
Health: Physicians (per 1 000 pop.)	1.2[m]	0.9[n]	1.2[b]
Education: Primary gross enrol. ratio (f/m per 100 pop.)	108.4 / 112.6[o]	97.8 / 101.7	86.0 / 85.1[b]
Education: Sec. gross enrol. ratio (f/m per 100 pop.)	... / ...	90.9 / 75.2	63.0 / 62.2[b]
Education: Upr. Sec. gross enrol. ratio (f/m per 100 pop.)	... / ...	71.6 / 42.1[n]	54.8 / 46.4[b]
Intentional homicide rate (per 100 000 pop.)	9.5	18.6[p]	0.0[i]
Seats held by women in the National Parliament (%)	0.0	6.7	6.3[q]

Environment and infrastructure indicators

	2010	2015	2022
Individuals using the Internet (per 100 inhabitants)[h]	14.6	27.3	35.2[r]
Threatened species (number)	85	93	105
Forested area (% of land area)	33.3	33.3	33.3[i]
Energy production, primary (Petajoules)	0	0	0[i]
Energy supply per capita (Gigajoules)	13	10[h]	11[h,i]
Tourist/visitor arrivals at national borders (000)	2	2	1[b]
Pop. using safely managed drinking water (urban/rural, %)	49.7 / ...	50.0 / ...	50.0 / ...[b]
Pop. using safely managed sanitation (urban/rural %)	5.3 / 7.1	5.3 / 7.5	5.3 / 7.5[c]
Net Official Development Assist. received (% of GNI)	27.27	88.66	63.12[b]

a Projected estimate (medium fertility variant). b 2020. c 2018. d 2021. e Data classified according to ISIC Rev. 4. f Includes Electricity, gas and water supply. g 2011. h Estimate. i 2019. j Data refers to a 5-year period preceding the reference year. k Refers to foreign citizens. l General government expenditure (GGE) can be larger than the Gross domestic product (GDP) because government accounts for a very large part of domestic consumption and because a large part of domestic consumption in the country is accounted for by imports. m 2009. n 2014. o 2006. p 2012. q Data are as at 1 January of reporting year. r 2017.

Uganda

Region	Eastern Africa	UN membership date	25 October 1962
Population (000, 2022)	47 250 [a]	Surface area (km2)	241 550 [b]
Pop. density (per km2, 2022)	236.5 [a]	Sex ratio (m per 100 f)	98.1 [a]
Capital city	Kampala	National currency	Uganda Shilling (UGX)
Capital city pop. (000, 2022)	3 137.7 [c,d]	Exchange rate (per US$)	3 544.4 [e]

Economic indicators	2010	2015	2022
GDP: Gross domestic product (million current US$)	30 701	29 297	38 702 [b]
GDP growth rate (annual %, const. 2015 prices)	19.9	6.4	- 0.8 [b]
GDP per capita (current US$)	946.7	766.4	846.1 [b]
Economy: Agriculture (% of Gross Value Added) [f,g]	27.3	23.3	25.6 [b]
Economy: Industry (% of Gross Value Added) [g,h]	26.6	29.4	29.3 [b]
Economy: Services and other activity (% of GVA) [g,i]	46.1	47.3	45.1 [b]
Employment in agriculture (% of employed) [j]	66.8	72.6	72.4 [b]
Employment in industry (% of employed) [j]	7.8	6.8	6.6 [b]
Employment in services & other sectors (% employed) [j]	25.4	20.6	20.9 [b]
Unemployment rate (% of labour force) [j]	3.6	1.9	2.9
Labour force participation rate (female/male pop. %) [j]	65.4 / 75.1	66.0 / 74.2	65.5 / 71.8
CPI: Consumer Price Index (2010=100)	...	151 [k]	113 [l,e]
Agricultural production index (2014-2016=100)	96	104	117 [b]
International trade: exports (million current US$)	1 619	2 267	3 890 [j,e]
International trade: imports (million current US$)	4 664	5 528	9 686 [j,e]
International trade: balance (million current US$)	- 3 046	- 3 261	- 5 796 [e]
Balance of payments, current account (million US$)	- 1 610	- 1 671	- 3 488 [b]

Major trading partners						2021
Export partners (% of exports) [j]	United Arab Emirates	44.5	Kenya	11.2	South Sudan	8.6
Import partners (% of imports) [j]	China	16.4	India	11.6	Kenya	9.4

Social indicators	2010	2015	2022
Population growth rate (average annual %)	2.9	3.1	2.8 [a]
Urban population (% of total population)	19.4	22.1	24.4 [d]
Urban population growth rate (average annual %) [m]	6.1	6.0	...
Fertility rate, total (live births per woman)	6.1	5.3	4.5 [a]
Life expectancy at birth (females/males, years)	58.8 / 55.2	63.0 / 59.1	65.7 / 61.5 [a]
Population age distribution (0-14/60+ years old, %)	49.9 / 2.6	48.5 / 2.7	44.8 / 2.9 [a]
International migrant stock (000/% of total pop.) [n]	492.9 / 1.5	851.2 / 2.2	1 720.3 / 3.8 [b]
Refugees and others of concern to the UNHCR (000)	594.4 [o]	646.5	4 007.8 [e]
Infant mortality rate (per 1 000 live births)	51.8	39.4	30.4 [a]
Health: Current expenditure (% of GDP)	6.8	5.1	3.8 [d]
Health: Physicians (per 1 000 pop.)	0.1 [p]	0.1	0.2 [b]
Education: Government expenditure (% of GDP)	1.7	2.3 [i]	3.0 [j,b]
Education: Primary gross enrol. ratio (f/m per 100 pop.)	122.4 / 121.5	103.7 / 101.6	104.1 / 101.3 [q]
Education: Sec. gross enrol. ratio (f/m per 100 pop.)	21.8 / 27.5 [r]	... / ...	... / ...
Education: Upr. Sec. gross enrol. ratio (f/m per 100 pop.)	12.0 / 16.5 [s]	... / ...	... / ...
Intentional homicide rate (per 100 000 pop.)	9.7	12.1 [t]	9.8 [b]
Seats held by women in the National Parliament (%)	31.5	35.0	33.8 [u]

Environment and infrastructure indicators	2010	2015	2022
Individuals using the Internet (per 100 inhabitants) [j]	4.3	5.7	19.9 [b]
Research & Development expenditure (% of GDP)	0.4	0.1 [v,t]	...
Threatened species (number)	166	188	278
Forested area (% of land area)	13.7	12.7 [i]	11.9 [j,d]
Energy production, primary (Petajoules)	599	745	889 [d]
Energy supply per capita (Gigajoules)	20	21	22 [d]
Tourist/visitor arrivals at national borders (000)	946	1 303	473 [b]
Important sites for terrestrial biodiversity protected (%)	72.2	72.2	72.2 [e]
Pop. using safely managed drinking water (urban/rural, %)	28.9 / 3.4	35.8 / 5.5	42.8 / 8.0 [b]
Pop. using safely managed sanitation (urban/rural %)	... / 14.5	... / 15.1	... / 15.6 [b]
Net Official Development Assist. received (% of GNI)	6.44	5.16	8.39 [b]

a Projected estimate (medium fertility variant). b 2020. c Data includes Kira, Makindye Ssabagabo and Nansana. d 2019. e 2021. f Excludes irrigation canals and landscaping care. g Data classified according to ISIC Rev. 4. h Excludes publishing activities. Includes irrigation and canals. i Includes publishing activities and landscape care. Excludes repair of personal and household goods. j Estimate. k Base: 1 July 2009 - 30 June 2010=100. l Base: 1 July 2016 - 30 June 2017=100. m Data refers to a 5-year period preceding the reference year. n Including refugees. o Data as at the end of December. p 2005. q 2017. r 2007. s 2008. t 2014. u Data are as at 1 January of reporting year. v Break in the time series.

Ukraine

Region	Eastern Europe	UN membership date	24 October 1945
Population (000, 2022)	39 702[a,b]	Surface area (km2)	603 500[c]
Pop. density (per km2, 2022)	68.5[a,b]	Sex ratio (m per 100 f)	84.9[a,b]
Capital city	Kyiv	National currency	Hryvnia (UAH)
Capital city pop. (000, 2022)	2 973.3[d]	Exchange rate (per US$)	27.3[e,f]

Economic indicators

	2010	2015	2022
GDP: Gross domestic product (million current US$)	136 012	91 031[e]	155 582[e,c]
GDP growth rate (annual %, const. 2015 prices)[e]	0.3	- 9.8	- 4.0[c]
GDP per capita (current US$)[e]	2 970.2	2 026.4	3 557.5[c]
Economy: Agriculture (% of Gross Value Added)[e,g,h]	8.4	14.2	10.8[c]
Economy: Industry (% of Gross Value Added)[e,g,i]	29.3	25.6	24.3[c]
Economy: Services and other activity (% of GVA)[e,g,j]	62.3	60.2	64.9[c]
Employment in agriculture (% of employed)	20.3	15.3	14.1[k,c]
Employment in industry (% of employed)	25.7	24.7	24.8[k,c]
Employment in services & other sectors (% employed)	54.0	60.1	61.1[k,c]
Unemployment rate (% of labour force)	8.1	9.1	8.5[k]
Labour force participation rate (female/male pop. %)[k]	51.8 / 61.6	50.4 / 63.4	48.5 / 63.9
CPI: Consumer Price Index (2010=100)	100	180	317[f]
Agricultural production index (2014-2016=100)	78	97	99[c]
International trade: exports (million current US$)[e]	51 430	38 127	65 870[f]
International trade: imports (million current US$)[e]	60 737	37 516	69 963[f]
International trade: balance (million current US$)[e]	- 9 307	611	- 4 093[f]
Balance of payments, current account (million US$)	- 3 016	5 035	- 2 639[f]

Major trading partners

						2021
Export partners (% of exports)[e]	China	12.1	Poland	7.6	Türkiye	6.1
Import partners (% of imports)[e]	China	15.2	Germany	8.7	Russian Federation	8.4

Social indicators

	2010	2015	2022
Population growth rate (average annual %)[b]	- 0.4	- 0.3	- 18.4[a]
Urban population (% of total population)[b]	68.6	69.1	69.5[d]
Urban population growth rate (average annual %)[b,l]	- 0.2	- 0.4	...
Fertility rate, total (live births per woman)[b]	1.4	1.5	1.3[a]
Life expectancy at birth (females/males, years)[b]	75.4 / 65.7	78.4 / 68.2	73.9 / 63.5[a]
Population age distribution (0-14/60+ years old, %)[b]	14.2 / 20.8	15.2 / 22.0	15.4 / 26.5[a]
International migrant stock (000/% of total pop.)[b]	4 818.8 / 10.5	4 915.1 / 10.9	4 997.4 / 11.4[c]
Refugees and others of concern to the UNHCR (000)	46.4[m]	1 426.6	2 394.8[f]
Infant mortality rate (per 1 000 live births)[b]	8.4	6.7	7.1[a]
Health: Current expenditure (% of GDP)	6.8	7.8	7.1[d]
Health: Physicians (per 1 000 pop.)	3.5	3.0[n]	...
Education: Government expenditure (% of GDP)	7.4	5.7	5.4[d]
Education: Primary gross enrol. ratio (f/m per 100 pop.)	99.1 / 98.5	100.1 / 98.0[n]	... / ...
Education: Sec. gross enrol. ratio (f/m per 100 pop.)	94.4 / 96.7[k]	95.0 / 96.9[n]	... / ...
Education: Upr. Sec. gross enrol. ratio (f/m per 100 pop.)	76.4 / 83.6[k]	89.0 / 96.6[n]	... / ...
Intentional homicide rate (per 100 000 pop.)	4.3	6.3[n]	6.2[o]
Seats held by women in the National Parliament (%)	8.0	11.8	20.3[p]

Environment and infrastructure indicators

	2010	2015	2022
Individuals using the Internet (per 100 inhabitants)	23.3	48.9[q]	75.0[c]
Research & Development expenditure (% of GDP)	0.8	0.6[r]	0.4[r,c]
Threatened species (number)	61	87	146
Forested area (% of land area)	16.5	16.7	16.7[d]
CO2 emission estimates (million tons/tons per capita)	268.0 / 5.8	189.0 / 4.2[e]	164.3 / 3.2[e,c]
Energy production, primary (Petajoules)[e]	3 238	2 552	2 503[d]
Energy supply per capita (Gigajoules)[e]	120	04	85[d]
Tourist/visitor arrivals at national borders (000)	21 203	12 428	3 141[c]
Important sites for terrestrial biodiversity protected (%)	57.1	58.2	59.8[f]
Pop. using safely managed drinking water (urban/rural, %)	91.0 / 71.2	88.8 / 88.7	88.7 / 89.8[c]
Pop. using safely managed sanitation (urban/rural %)	46.1 / ...	60.9 / ...	68.9 / ...[c]
Net Official Development Assist. received (% of GNI)[e]	0.49	1.61	1.48[c]

a Projected estimate (medium fertility variant). b Including Crimea. c 2020. d 2019. e The Government of Ukraine has informed the United Nations that it is not in a position to provide statistical data concerning the Autonomous Republic of Crimea and the city of Sevastopol. f 2021. g Data classified according to ISIC Rev. 4. h Excludes irrigation canals and landscaping care. i Excludes publishing activities. Includes irrigation and canals. j Includes publishing activities and landscape care. Excludes repair of personal and household goods. k Estimate. l Data refers to a 5-year period preceding the reference year. m Data as at the end of December. n 2014. o 2017. p Data are as at 1 January of reporting year. q Users in the last 12 months. r Excluding data from some regions, provinces or states.

United Arab Emirates

Region	Western Asia	UN membership date	09 December 1971
Population (000, 2022)	9 441[a]	Surface area (km2)	71 024[b,c]
Pop. density (per km2, 2022)	132.9[a]	Sex ratio (m per 100 f)	226.3[a]
Capital city	Abu Dhabi	National currency	UAE Dirham (AED)[d]
Capital city pop. (000, 2022)	1 452.1[e]	Exchange rate (per US$)	3.7[f]

Economic indicators	2010	2015	2022
GDP: Gross domestic product (million current US$)	289 787	358 135	358 869[c]
GDP growth rate (annual %, const. 2015 prices)	1.6	5.1	- 6.1[c]
GDP per capita (current US$)	33 893.3	38 663.4	36 284.5[c]
Economy: Agriculture (% of Gross Value Added)	0.8	0.7	0.9[c]
Economy: Industry (% of Gross Value Added)	52.5	43.9	40.9[c]
Economy: Services and other activity (% of GVA)	46.7	55.4	58.2[c]
Employment in agriculture (% of employed)[g]	3.4	2.0	1.4[c]
Employment in industry (% of employed)[g]	37.2	35.7	34.2[c]
Employment in services & other sectors (% employed)[g]	59.4	62.4	64.4[c]
Unemployment rate (% of labour force)[g]	2.5	1.8	3.3
Labour force participation rate (female/male pop. %)[g]	42.0 / 89.1	49.1 / 91.5	47.7 / 89.0
CPI: Consumer Price Index (2010=100)	100[h]	109	112[c]
Agricultural production index (2014-2016=100)	132	98	108[c]
International trade: exports (million current US$)	198 362	300 479	464 039[g,f]
International trade: imports (million current US$)	187 001	287 025	329 066[g,f]
International trade: balance (million current US$)	11 361	13 454	134 972[f]

Major trading partners						2021
Export partners (% of exports)[g]	Areas nes[i]	49.7	Saudi Arabia	6.5	Iraq	3.9
Import partners (% of imports)[g]	China	16.0	Areas nes	12.8	United States	6.7

Social indicators	2010	2015	2022
Population growth rate (average annual %)	1.1	0.9	0.8[a]
Urban population (% of total population)	84.1	85.7	86.8[e]
Urban population growth rate (average annual %)[j]	12.3	2.4	...
Fertility rate, total (live births per woman)	1.8	1.5	1.4[a]
Life expectancy at birth (females/males, years)	80.2 / 76.5	81.2 / 77.6	81.4 / 77.7[a]
Population age distribution (0-14/60+ years old, %)	13.7 / 0.3	14.3 / 1.1	15.2 / 3.5[a]
International migrant stock (000/% of total pop.)[k,l]	7 316.7 / 85.6	7 995.1 / 86.3	8 716.3 / 88.1[c]
Refugees and others of concern to the UNHCR (000)	0.6[m]	0.8	8.7[f]
Infant mortality rate (per 1 000 live births)	7.4	6.5	5.2[a]
Health: Current expenditure (% of GDP)[n]	3.9	3.6	4.3[g,a]
Health: Physicians (per 1 000 pop.)	1.4	2.2	2.6[e]
Education: Government expenditure (% of GDP)	...	...	3.1[e]
Education: Primary gross enrol. ratio (f/m per 100 pop.)	102.1 / 101.1[o]	111.6 / 111.4	115.9 / 114.8[c]
Education: Sec. gross enrol. ratio (f/m per 100 pop.)	... / ...	... / ...	104.0 / 102.7[c]
Education: Upr. Sec. gross enrol. ratio (f/m per 100 pop.)	... / ...	... / ...	107.9 / 105.8[c]
Intentional homicide rate (per 100 000 pop.)	0.8	0.6	0.7[e]
Seats held by women in the National Parliament (%)	22.5	17.5	50.0[p]

Environment and infrastructure indicators	2010	2015	2022
Individuals using the Internet (per 100 inhabitants)	68.0[q]	90.5[g]	100.0[c]
Research & Development expenditure (% of GDP)	...	0.9	1.4[c]
Threatened species (number)	48	48	93
Forested area (% of land area)[g]	4.5	4.5	4.5[e]
CO2 emission estimates (million tons/tons per capita)	155.6 / 18.1	187.3 / 20.1	179.2 / 18.2[e]
Energy production, primary (Petajoules)	7 849	9 995	9 723[e]
Energy supply per capita (Gigajoules)	348	386	224[e]
Tourist/visitor arrivals at national borders (000)	7 126[r,s]	16 842[h]	7 165[t,c]
Important sites for terrestrial biodiversity protected (%)	28.6	42.8	51.6[f]
Net Official Development Assist. disbursed (% of GNI)	0.38[u,v]	...	...

a Projected estimate (medium fertility variant). b Land area only. c 2020. d United Arab Emirates Dirham. e 2019. f 2021. g Estimate. h Break in the time series. i Areas nes j Data refers to a 5-year period preceding the reference year. k Refers to foreign citizens. l Including refugees. m Data as at the end of December. n Data based on calendar year (January 1 to December 31). o 2007. p Data are as at 1 January of reporting year. q Refers to total population. r Non-resident tourists staying in hotels and similar establishments. s 2005. t Non-resident tourists staying in all types of accommodation establishments. u Data reported at activity level, represent flows from all government agencies. v 2009.

United Kingdom

Region	Northern Europe	UN membership date	24 October 1945
Population (000, 2022)	67 509 [a,b]	Surface area (km2)	242 495 [c,d]
Pop. density (per km2, 2022)	278.1 [a,b]	Sex ratio (m per 100 f)	97.7 [a,b]
Capital city	London	National currency	Pound Sterling (GBP)
Capital city pop. (000, 2022)	9 176.5 [e,f]	Exchange rate (per US$)	0.7 [g]

Economic indicators

	2010	2015	2022
GDP: Gross domestic product (million current US$)	2 491 110	2 956 574	2 764 198 [d]
GDP growth rate (annual %, const. 2015 prices)	2.1	2.6	- 9.7 [d]
GDP per capita (current US$)	39 254.9	44 891.7	40 718.2 [d]
Economy: Agriculture (% of Gross Value Added) [h,i]	0.7	0.7	0.6 [d]
Economy: Industry (% of Gross Value Added) [i,j]	21.0	20.3	18.8 [d]
Economy: Services and other activity (% of GVA) [i,k]	78.4	78.9	80.5 [d]
Employment in agriculture (% of employed)	1.2	1.1	1.0 [l,d]
Employment in industry (% of employed)	19.2	18.7	17.7 [l,d]
Employment in services & other sectors (% employed)	79.6	80.2	81.3 [l,d]
Unemployment rate (% of labour force)	7.8	5.3	4.0 [l]
Labour force participation rate (female/male pop. %)	56.1 / 69.0	57.2 / 68.6	58.3 / 67.3 [l]
CPI: Consumer Price Index (2010=100) [m]	100	112	125 [g]
Agricultural production index (2014-2016=100)	94	101	97 [g]
International trade: exports (million current US$)	422 014	466 296	467 783 [g]
International trade: imports (million current US$)	627 618	630 251	688 251 [g]
International trade: balance (million current US$)	- 205 603	- 163 955	- 220 468 [g]
Balance of payments, current account (million US$)	- 76 851	- 152 636	- 82 534 [g]

Major trading partners

						2021
Export partners (% of exports)	United States	12.8	Germany	8.7	Switzerland	8.5
Import partners (% of imports)	China	13.2	Germany	11.0	United States	8.7

Social indicators

	2010	2015	2022
Population growth rate (average annual %) [a]	0.8	0.7	0.3 [b]
Urban population (% of total population)	81.3	82.6	83.7 [f]
Urban population growth rate (average annual %) [n]	1.3	1.0	...
Fertility rate, total (live births per woman) [a]	1.9	1.8	1.6 [b]
Life expectancy at birth (females/males, years) [a]	82.3 / 78.4	82.7 / 79.1	83.8 / 80.4 [b]
Population age distribution (0-14/60+ years old, %) [a]	17.6 / 22.3	17.7 / 23.2	17.5 / 25.2 [b]
International migrant stock (000/% of total pop.)	7 119.7 / 11.2	8 407.0 / 12.8	9 359.6 / 13.8 [d]
Refugees and others of concern to the UNHCR (000)	253.3 [o]	155.1	219.6 [g]
Infant mortality rate (per 1 000 live births) [a]	4.4	3.9	3.2 [b]
Health: Current expenditure (% of GDP)	9.8	9.9	10.2 [f]
Health: Physicians (per 1 000 pop.)	2.6	2.7	3.0 [d]
Education: Government expenditure (% of GDP)	5.7	5.6	5.2 [p]
Education: Primary gross enrol. ratio (f/m per 100 pop.)	104.3 / 104.0	101.9 / 102.0	100.4 / 100.6 [f]
Education: Sec. gross enrol. ratio (f/m per 100 pop.)	103.1 / 102.7	126.4 / 122.8	120.1 / 117.4 [f]
Education: Upr. Sec. gross enrol. ratio (f/m per 100 pop.)	99.6 / 96.0	138.5 / 130.2	123.1 / 117.0 [f]
Intentional homicide rate (per 100 000 pop.)	1.2	1.0	1.1 [p]
Seats held by women in the National Parliament (%)	19.5	22.8	34.4 [q]

Environment and infrastructure indicators

	2010	2015	2022
Individuals using the Internet (per 100 inhabitants)	85.0 [r]	92.0 [r,s]	94.8 [d]
Research & Development expenditure (% of GDP)	1.6 [l]	1.6	1.7 [f]
Threatened species (number)	73	87	191
Forested area (% of land area)	12.6	13.0	13.2 [f]
CO2 emission estimates (million tons/tons per capita)	481.8 / 7.6	399.2 / 6.1	311.1 / 4.6 [d]
Energy production, primary (Petajoules) [t]	6 217	4 939	5 087 [f]
Energy supply per capita (Gigajoules) [t]	134	115	108 [f]
Tourist/visitor arrivals at national borders (000)	28 911	35 149	10 714 [d]
Important sites for terrestrial biodiversity protected (%)	85.8	85.9	86.3 [g]
Pop. using safely managed sanitation (urban/rural %)	98.9 / 93.6	99.0 / 93.6	99.0 / 93.6 [d]
Net Official Development Assist. disbursed (% of GNI) [u]	1.12	0.70	0.69 [f]

a Refers to the United Kingdom of Great Britain and Northern Ireland. For statistical purposes, the data for United Kingdom do not include Anguilla, Bermuda, British Virgin Islands, Cayman Islands, Channel Islands, Falkland Islands (Malvinas), Gibraltar, Isle of Man, Montserrat, Saint Helena, Turks and Caicos Islands. b Projected estimate (medium fertility variant). c Excluding Channel Islands (Guernsey and Jersey) and Isle of Man, shown separately, if available. d 2020. e Data refer to "Urban area" (Greater London). f 2019. g 2021. h Excludes irrigation canals and landscaping care. i Data classified according to ISIC Rev. 4. j Excludes publishing activities. Includes irrigation and canals. k Includes publishing activities and landscape care. Excludes repair of personal and household goods. l Estimate. m Calculated by the UNSD from national indices. n Data refers to a 5-year period preceding the reference year. o Data as at the end of December. p 2018. q Data are as at 1 January of reporting year. r Population aged 16 to 74 years. s Users in the last 3 months. t Shipments of coal and oil to Jersey, Guernsey and the Isle of Man from the United Kingdom are not classed as exports. Supplies of coal and oil to these islands are, therefore, included as part of UK supply. Exports of natural gas to the Isle of Man included with the exports to Ireland. u DAC member (OECD).

United Republic of Tanzania

Region	Eastern Africa	
Population (000, 2022)	65 498 [a,b]	
Pop. density (per km2, 2022)	73.9 [a,b]	
Capital city	Dodoma	
Capital city pop. (000, 2022)	261.6 [d]	
UN membership date	14 December 1961	
Surface area (km2)	947 303 [c]	
Sex ratio (m per 100 f)	97.7 [a,b]	
National currency	Tanzanian Shilling (TZS)	
Exchange rate (per US$)	2 297.6 [e]	

Economic indicators	2010	2015	2022
GDP: Gross domestic product (million current US$) [f]	31 553	47 379	64 740 [c]
GDP growth rate (annual %, const. 2015 prices) [f]	6.4	6.2	4.8 [c]
GDP per capita (current US$) [f]	732.2	946.8	1 115.0 [c]
Economy: Agriculture (% of Gross Value Added) [g,h]	27.6	29.2	28.5 [c]
Economy: Industry (% of Gross Value Added) [g,i]	25.6	26.7	32.1 [c]
Economy: Services and other activity (% of GVA) [g,j]	46.8	44.1	39.4 [c]
Employment in agriculture (% of employed) [k]	70.4	67.5	64.9 [c]
Employment in industry (% of employed) [k]	5.8	6.4	6.8 [c]
Employment in services & other sectors (% employed) [k]	23.8	26.1	28.3 [c]
Unemployment rate (% of labour force) [k]	3.0	2.1	2.6
Labour force participation rate (female/male pop. %) [k]	83.9 / 88.8	80.0 / 88.0	79.8 / 87.2
CPI: Consumer Price Index (2010=100) [l]	100	158 [m]	194 [c]
Agricultural production index (2014-2016=100)	77	103	116 [c]
International trade: exports (million current US$)	4 051	5 854	6 391 [e]
International trade: imports (million current US$)	8 013	14 706	10 873 [e]
International trade: balance (million current US$)	- 3 962	- 8 852	- 4 482 [e]
Balance of payments, current account (million US$)	- 2 211	- 4 477	- 1 122 [c]

Major trading partners					2021
Export partners (% of exports)	United Arab Emirates 16.5	India 15.8	South Africa 14.3
Import partners (% of imports)	China 24.8	United Arab Emirates 12.5	India 11.1

Social indicators	2010	2015	2022
Population growth rate (average annual %) [b]	2.8	3.6	2.9 [a]
Urban population (% of total population) [b]	28.1	31.6	34.5 [n]
Urban population growth rate (average annual %) [b,o]	5.6	5.5	...
Fertility rate, total (live births per woman) [b]	5.3	5.1	4.7 [a]
Life expectancy at birth (females/males, years) [b]	61.9 / 58.4	67.0 / 62.4	68.9 / 64.7 [a]
Population age distribution (0-14/60+ years old, %) [b]	45.1 / 4.7	44.8 / 4.8	43.4 / 4.7 [a]
International migrant stock (000/% of total pop.) [b,p]	309.8 / 0.7	384.6 / 0.7	426.0 / 0.7 [c]
Refugees and others of concern to the UNHCR (000)	273.8 [q]	328.2	253.0 [e]
Infant mortality rate (per 1 000 live births) [b]	49.5	41.1	31.8 [a]
Health: Current expenditure (% of GDP) [f,r]	5.2	3.6	3.8 [n]
Health: Physicians (per 1 000 pop.)	...	0.1 [s]	0.1 [d]
Education: Government expenditure (% of GDP)	4.5	4.2 [k]	3.1 [k,c]
Education: Primary gross enrol. ratio (f/m per 100 pop.)	103.8 / 101.9	87.0 / 82.5	98.4 / 95.5 [c]
Education: Sec. gross enrol. ratio (f/m per 100 pop.)	28.5 / 34.8	27.0 / 27.3	32.9 / 30.0 [c]
Education: Upr. Sec. gross enrol. ratio (f/m per 100 pop.)	7.4 / 9.8	5.0 / 7.4	5.5 / 7.0 [c]
Intentional homicide rate (per 100 000 pop.)	8.8	7.3	6.5 [t]
Seats held by women in the National Parliament (%)	30.7	36.0	36.9 [u]

Environment and infrastructure indicators	2010	2015	2022
Individuals using the Internet (per 100 inhabitants) [k]	2.9	10.0	22.0 [c]
Research & Development expenditure (% of GDP) [v]	0.4	0.5 [w]	...
Threatened species (number)	691	1 077	1 464
Forested area (% of land area) [k]	56.4	54.3	52.2 [n]
CO2 emission estimates (million tons/tons per capita)	10.8 / 0.1	15.6 / 0.2	16.0 / 0.2 [n]
Energy production, primary (Petajoules)	727	780	834 [n]
Energy supply per capita (Gigajoules)	18	17	16 [n]
Tourist/visitor arrivals at national borders (000)	754	1 104	592 [c]
Important sites for terrestrial biodiversity protected (%)	56.4	56.4	62.6 [e]
Pop. using safely managed sanitation (urban/rural %)	24.1 / 14.2	29.9 / 18.4	34.8 / 21.7 [c]
Net Official Development Assist. received (% of GNI)	9.42	5.56	3.67 [c]

a Projected estimate (medium fertility variant). b Including Zanzibar. c 2020. d 2018. e 2021. f Tanzania mainland only, excluding Zanzibar. g Data classified according to ISIC Rev. 4. h Excludes irrigation canals and landscaping care. i Excludes publishing activities. Includes irrigation and canals. j Includes publishing activities and landscape care. Excludes repair of personal and household goods. k Estimate. l For Tanganyika only. m Break in the time series. n 2019. o Data refers to a 5-year period preceding the reference year. p Including refugees. q Data as at the end of December. r Data revision. s 2014. t 2016. u Data are as at 1 January of reporting year. v Excluding business enterprise. w 2013.

United States of America

Region	Northern America	UN membership date	24 October 1945
Population (000, 2022)	338 290[a,b]	Surface area (km2)	9 833 517[c]
Pop. density (per km2, 2022)	37.0[a,b]	Sex ratio (m per 100 f)	98.1[a,b]
Capital city	Washington, D.C.	National currency	US Dollar (USD)
Capital city pop. (000, 2022)	5 264.5[d]		

Economic indicators	2010	2015	2022
GDP: Gross domestic product (million current US$)	15 048 970	18 206 023	20 893 746[c]
GDP growth rate (annual %, const. 2015 prices)	2.7	2.7	- 3.4[c]
GDP per capita (current US$)	48 700.4	56 738.1	63 122.6[c]
Economy: Agriculture (% of Gross Value Added)[e,f,g]	1.0	1.0	0.8[c]
Economy: Industry (% of Gross Value Added)[f,g,h]	19.7	18.9	18.0[c]
Economy: Services and other activity (% of GVA)[f,g,i]	79.4	80.1	81.2[c]
Employment in agriculture (% of employed)	1.4	1.4	1.3[j,c]
Employment in industry (% of employed)	19.6	19.9	19.7[j,c]
Employment in services & other sectors (% employed)	78.9	78.7	79.0[j,c]
Unemployment rate (% of labour force)	9.6	5.3	4.1[j]
Labour force participation rate (female/male pop. %)	57.7 / 69.9	55.8 / 67.9	55.2 / 66.4[j]
CPI: Consumer Price Index (2010=100)[k]	100	109	124[l]
Agricultural production index (2014-2016=100)	92	97	104[c]
International trade: exports (million current US$)	1 278 099	1 501 846	1 430 254[c]
International trade: imports (million current US$)	1 968 260	2 313 425	2 405 382[c]
International trade: balance (million current US$)	- 690 161	- 811 579	1 179 839[l]
Balance of payments, current account (million US$)	- 432 002	- 408 884	- 821 645[l]

Major trading partners						2021
Export partners (% of exports)	Canada	17.5	Mexico	15.8	China	8.6
Import partners (% of imports)	China	18.5	Mexico	13.2	Canada	12.4

Social indicators	2010	2015	2022
Population growth rate (average annual %)[b]	0.8	0.8	0.5[a]
Urban population (% of total population)	80.8	81.7	82.5[d]
Urban population growth rate (average annual %)[m]	1.1	0.9	...
Fertility rate, total (live births per woman)[b]	1.9	1.8	1.7[a]
Life expectancy at birth (females/males, years)[b]	81.2 / 76.3	81.3 / 76.4	81.0 / 75.5[a]
Population age distribution (0-14/60+ years old, %)[b]	19.9 / 18.3	19.3 / 20.3	18.0 / 23.4[a]
International migrant stock (000/% of total pop.)[b]	44 183.6 / 14.3	48 178.9 / 15.0	50 632.8 / 15.3[c]
Refugees and others of concern to the UNHCR (000)	270.9	491.7	1 585.1[l]
Infant mortality rate (per 1 000 live births)[b]	6.2	5.9	5.0[a]
Health: Current expenditure (% of GDP)[n,o]	16.3	16.5	16.8[d]
Health: Physicians (per 1 000 pop.)	...	...	2.6[p]
Education: Primary gross enrol. ratio (f/m per 100 pop.)[j]	101.3 / 102.4[q]	100.3 / 100.3	101.3 / 100.6[d]
Education: Sec. gross enrol. ratio (f/m per 100 pop.)[j]	95.9 / 94.2[q]	98.2 / 97.2	99.2 / 100.9[d]
Education: Upr. Sec. gross enrol. ratio (f/m per 100 pop.)[j]	91.7 / 86.6[q]	95.6 / 93.9	96.3 / 99.1[d]
Intentional homicide rate (per 100 000 pop.)	4.8	4.9	6.5[c]
Seats held by women in the National Parliament (%)	16.8	19.4	27.7[r]

Environment and infrastructure indicators	2010	2015	2022
Individuals using the Internet (per 100 inhabitants)	71.7[s]	74.6[s,t]	90.9[j,c]
Research & Development expenditure (% of GDP)	2.7[u]	2.8[u,v]	3.5[w,c]
Threatened species (number)	1 152	1 299	1 877
Forested area (% of land area)	33.7	33.9[i]	33.9[i,d]
CO2 emission estimates (million tons/tons per capita)[x]	5 428.2 / 17.3	5 004.5 / 15.4	4 354.2 / 13.0[c]
Energy production, primary (Petajoules)	72 292	84 620	96 539[d]
Energy supply per capita (Gigajoules)	301	285	281[d]
Tourist/visitor arrivals at national borders (000)	60 010	77 774[v]	19 457[c]
Important sites for terrestrial biodiversity protected (%)	36.8	38.0	38.3[l]
Pop. using safely managed drinking water (urban/rural, %)	96.5 / ...	97.0 / ...	97.5 / ...[c]
Pop. using safely managed sanitation (urban/rural %)	96.9 / ...	97.2 / ...	97.3 / ...[c]
Net Official Development Assist. disbursed (% of GNI)[y]	1.48	0.21	0.02[c]

a Projected estimate (medium fertility variant). **b** For statistical purposes, the data for United States of America do not include American Samoa, Guam, Northern Mariana Islands, Puerto Rico, and United States Virgin Islands. **c** 2020. **d** 2019. **e** Excludes irrigation canals and landscaping care. **f** Data classified according to ISIC Rev. 4. **g** Including taxes less subsidies on production and imports. **h** Excludes publishing activities. Includes irrigation and canals. **i** Includes publishing activities and landscape care. Excludes repair of personal and household goods. **j** Estimate. **k** For urban population only. **l** 2021. **m** Data refers to a 5-year period preceding the reference year. **n** Data revision. **o** Data based on calendar year (January 1 to December 31). **p** 2018. **q** 2005. **r** Data are as at 1 January of reporting year. **s** Population aged 3 years and over. **t** Users in the last 6 months. **u** Do not correspond exactly to Frascati Manual recommendations. **v** Break in the time series. **w** Provisional data. **x** Including overseas territories. **y** DAC member (OECD).

United States Virgin Islands

Region	Caribbean	Population (000, 2022)	100[a,b]
Surface area (km2)	347[c]	Pop. density (per km2, 2022)	284.2[a,b]
Sex ratio (m per 100 f)	87.3[a,b]	Capital city	Charlotte Amalie
National currency	US Dollar (USD)	Capital city pop. (000, 2022)	52.3[d]

Economic indicators	2010	2015	2022
Employment in agriculture (% of employed)[e]	4.2	3.7	3.2[c]
Employment in industry (% of employed)[e]	23.2	20.3	19.6[c]
Employment in services & other sectors (% employed)[e]	72.6	76.0	77.2[c]
Unemployment rate (% of labour force)[e]	11.7	12.6	12.7
Labour force participation rate (female/male pop. %)[e]	55.6 / 67.0	49.2 / 68.0	40.0 / 58.5

Social indicators	2010	2015	2022
Population growth rate (average annual %)[b]	- 0.6	- 0.5	- 0.8[a]
Urban population (% of total population)	94.6	95.4	95.8[f]
Urban population growth rate (average annual %)[g]	- 0.1	- 0.1	...
Fertility rate, total (live births per woman)[b]	2.5	2.2	2.1[a]
Life expectancy at birth (females/males, years)[b]	77.8 / 69.2	80.3 / 69.9	80.9 / 69.8[a]
Population age distribution (0-14/60+ years old, %)[b]	20.7 / 20.6	19.5 / 23.9	19.2 / 27.7[a]
International migrant stock (000/% of total pop.)	56.7 / 53.4	56.7 / 54.0	56.8 / 54.3[c]
Infant mortality rate (per 1 000 live births)[b]	7.6	6.4	5.3[a]
Intentional homicide rate (per 100 000 pop.)	52.8	49.3[h]	...

Environment and infrastructure indicators	2010	2015	2022
Individuals using the Internet (per 100 inhabitants)[e]	31.2	54.8	64.4[i]
Research & Development expenditure (% of GDP)	~0.0[j,k]	...	...
Threatened species (number)	33	53	89
Forested area (% of land area)	52.7	54.7	56.5[f]
Energy production, primary (Petajoules)[e]	...	0	0[f]
Energy supply per capita (Gigajoules)[e]	...	1	1[f]
Tourist/visitor arrivals at national borders (000)	572	642	303[c]
Important sites for terrestrial biodiversity protected (%)	43.0	43.4	43.4[i]

a Projected estimate (medium fertility variant). b For statistical purposes, the data for United States of America do not include this area. c 2020. d 2018. e Estimate. f 2019. g Data refers to a 5-year period preceding the reference year. h 2012. i 2017. j Partial data. k 2007. l 2021.

Uruguay

Region	South America	UN membership date	18 December 1945
Population (000, 2022)	3 423[a]	Surface area (km2)	173 626[b]
Pop. density (per km2, 2022)	19.8[a]	Sex ratio (m per 100 f)	94.0[a]
Capital city	Montevideo	National currency	Peso Uruguayo (UYU)
Capital city pop. (000, 2022)	1 744.7[c,d]	Exchange rate (per US$)	44.7[b]

Economic indicators	2010	2015	2022
GDP: Gross domestic product (million current US$)	40 285	57 081	53 629[b]
GDP growth rate (annual %, const. 2015 prices)	7.8	1.8	- 5.9[b]
GDP per capita (current US$)	11 992.0	16 729.4	15 438.4[b]
Economy: Agriculture (% of Gross Value Added)[f]	8.0	7.7	8.5[b]
Economy: Industry (% of Gross Value Added)[f]	27.3	22.1	20.2[b]
Economy: Services and other activity (% of GVA)[f]	64.7	70.3	71.2[b]
Employment in agriculture (% of employed)	11.6	8.8	7.9[g,b]
Employment in industry (% of employed)	21.4	20.5	18.7[g,b]
Employment in services & other sectors (% employed)	67.0	70.7	73.4[g,b]
Unemployment rate (% of labour force)	7.2	7.5	10.3[g]
Labour force participation rate (female/male pop. %)	54.9 / 74.6	56.3 / 74.4	55.5 / 69.8[g]
CPI: Consumer Price Index (2010=100)[h]	100	150	240[e]
Agricultural production index (2014-2016=100)	93	101	92[b]
International trade: exports (million current US$)	6 724	7 670	9 045[g,e]
International trade: imports (million current US$)	8 622	9 489	10 602[g,e]
International trade: balance (million current US$)	- 1 898	- 1 820	- 1 557[e]
Balance of payments, current account (million US$)	- 731	- 147	- 1 092[e]

Major trading partners						2021
Export partners (% of exports)[g]	China	20.3	Free Zones	16.4	Brazil	15.4
Import partners (% of imports)[g]	Brazil	21.1	China	19.0	Argentina	13.0

Social indicators	2010	2015	2022
Population growth rate (average annual %)	0.3	0.3	~0.0[a]
Urban population (% of total population)	94.4	95.0	95.4[d]
Urban population growth rate (average annual %)[i]	0.5	0.5	...
Fertility rate, total (live births per woman)	2.0	2.0	1.5[a]
Life expectancy at birth (females/males, years)	80.9 / 72.6	81.4 / 73.4	81.7 / 74.1[a]
Population age distribution (0-14/60+ years old, %)	22.3 / 18.8	21.1 / 19.4	19.1 / 20.8[a]
International migrant stock (000/% of total pop.)[j]	76.3 / 2.3	78.8 / 2.3	108.3 / 3.1[b]
Refugees and others of concern to the UNHCR (000)	0.2[k]	0.4	26.8[e]
Infant mortality rate (per 1 000 live births)	9.3	7.6	5.8[a]
Health: Current expenditure (% of GDP)[m]	7.9[l]	8.3[n]	9.3[n,d]
Health: Physicians (per 1 000 pop.)	4.0[o]	...	4.9[p]
Education: Government expenditure (% of GDP)	2.9[q]	4.4[r]	4.7[d]
Education: Primary gross enrol. ratio (f/m per 100 pop.)	110.9 / 114.6	109.8 / 112.2	104.0 / 104.6[d]
Education: Sec. gross enrol. ratio (f/m per 100 pop.)	109.5 / 93.2	... / ...	129.7 / 116.6[d]
Education: Upr. Sec. gross enrol. ratio (f/m per 100 pop.)	104.6 / 79.4	... / ...	132.4 / 108.7[d]
Intentional homicide rate (per 100 000 pop.)	6.1	8.6	9.7[b]
Seats held by women in the National Parliament (%)	14.1	13.1	25.3[s]

Environment and infrastructure indicators	2010	2015	2022
Individuals using the Internet (per 100 inhabitants)	46.4[t]	64.6	86.1[g,b]
Research & Development expenditure (% of GDP)	0.3	0.4	0.5[d]
Threatened species (number)	80	103	139
Forested area (% of land area)	9.9	11.0	11.5[d]
CO2 emission estimates (million tons/tons per capita)	6.2 / 1.8	6.7 / 1.8	6.8 / 1.8[b]
Energy production, primary (Petajoules)	89	127	142[d]
Energy supply per capita (Gigajoules)	52	62	64[d]
Tourist/visitor arrivals at national borders (000)	2 353	2 773	3 059[d]
Important sites for terrestrial biodiversity protected (%)	12.0	21.5	23.3[e]
Pop. using safely managed drinking water (urban/rural, %)	94.2 / ...	94.5 / ...	94.6 / ...[b]
Net Official Development Assist. received (% of GNI)	0.12	0.05	0.07[p]

a Projected estimate (medium fertility variant). b 2020. c Data refer to the department of Montevideo and localities of the departments of Canelones and San José (Cerámicas del Sur and Ciudad del Plata). d 2019. e 2021. f Data classified according to ISIC Rev. 4. g Estimate. h Calculated by the UNSD from national indices. i Data refers to a 5-year period preceding the reference year. j Including refugees. k Data as at the end of December. l Country is still reporting data based on SHA 1.0. m Data based on calendar year (January 1 to December 31). n Data are based on SHA2011. o 2008. p 2017. q 2006. r 2011. s Data are as at 1 January of reporting year. t Population aged 6 years and over.

Uzbekistan

Region	Central Asia	UN membership date	02 March 1992
Population (000, 2022)	34 628 [a]	Surface area (km2)	448 969 [b]
Pop. density (per km2, 2022)	81.4 [a]	Sex ratio (m per 100 f)	100.2 [a]
Capital city	Tashkent	National currency	Uzbekistan Sum (UZS)
Capital city pop. (000, 2022)	2 490.3 [c]	Exchange rate (per US$)	10 785.0 [d,e]

Economic indicators

	2010	2015	2022
GDP: Gross domestic product (million current US$)	46 909	81 847	57 707 [b]
GDP growth rate (annual %, const. 2015 prices)	8.5	7.4	1.6 [b]
GDP per capita (current US$)	1 645.0	2 646.3	1 724.2 [b]
Economy: Agriculture (% of Gross Value Added) [f,g]	32.6	33.6	27.3 [b]
Economy: Industry (% of Gross Value Added) [f,h]	25.7	25.9	34.4 [b]
Economy: Services and other activity (% of GVA) [f,i]	41.7	40.5	38.3 [b]
Employment in agriculture (% of employed) [j]	30.9	26.7	23.3 [b]
Employment in industry (% of employed) [j]	25.4	27.7	29.9 [b]
Employment in services & other sectors (% employed) [j]	43.6	45.6	46.8 [b]
Unemployment rate (% of labour force)	5.4	5.2	7.0 [j]
Labour force participation rate (female/male pop. %) [j]	50.3 / 74.9	47.8 / 73.1	45.2 / 71.0
CPI: Consumer Price Index (2010=100)	...	...	192 [k,l,e]
Agricultural production index (2014-2016=100)	74	101	105 [b]
International trade: exports (million current US$)	11 688 [j]	12 871 [j]	14 092 [e]
International trade: imports (million current US$)	8 680 [j]	12 416 [j]	23 886 [e]
International trade: balance (million current US$)	3 008 [j]	455 [j]	- 9 794 [e]
Balance of payments, current account (million US$)	2 279	896	- 4 810 [e]

Major trading partners

						2021
Export partners (% of exports)	Areas nes [m]	32.9	China	12.4	Russian Federation	12.1
Import partners (% of imports)	Russian Federation	22.4	China	20.4	Kazakhstan	11.4

Social indicators

	2010	2015	2022
Population growth rate (average annual %)	1.6	1.6	1.6 [a]
Urban population (% of total population)	51.0	50.8	50.4 [c]
Urban population growth rate (average annual %) [n]	2.5	1.5	...
Fertility rate, total (live births per woman)	2.4	2.5	2.8 [a]
Life expectancy at birth (females/males, years)	71.8 / 66.7	73.3 / 67.7	74.3 / 69.0 [a]
Population age distribution (0-14/60+ years old, %)	29.2 / 6.5	28.5 / 7.1	30.2 / 8.6 [a]
International migrant stock (000/% of total pop.) [o]	1 220.1 / 4.3	1 170.9 / 3.8	1 162.0 / 3.5 [b]
Refugees and others of concern to the UNHCR (000)	0.3 [p]	86.8	59.1 [e]
Infant mortality rate (per 1 000 live births)	25.1	17.1	12.4 [a]
Health: Current expenditure (% of GDP)	5.2	5.0	5.6 [c]
Health: Physicians (per 1 000 pop.)	2.5	2.4 [q]	5.1 [b]
Education: Government expenditure (% of GDP)	...	5.8 [j]	5.1 [b]
Education: Primary gross enrol. ratio (f/m per 100 pop.)	93.1 / 94.7	99.2 / 100.6	99.1 / 101.0 [b]
Education: Sec. gross enrol. ratio (f/m per 100 pop.)	89.9 / 89.8	91.3 / 92.4	97.1 / 97.7 [c]
Education: Upr. Sec. gross enrol. ratio (f/m per 100 pop.)	82.3 / 81.4	89.6 / 90.4	96.6 / 94.0 [c]
Intentional homicide rate (per 100 000 pop.)	3.0 [r]	1.6	1.2 [c]
Seats held by women in the National Parliament (%)	22.0	16.0	33.3 [s]

Environment and infrastructure indicators

	2010	2015	2022
Individuals using the Internet (per 100 inhabitants)	15.9 [j]	42.8 [j]	71.1 [b]
Research & Development expenditure (% of GDP)	0.2	0.2	0.1 [b]
Threatened species (number)	50	54	65
Forested area (% of land area)	7.7	8.1	8.3 [c]
CO_2 emission estimates (million tons/tons per capita)	120.4 / 4.2	94.3 / 3.0	112.7 / 3.3 [c]
Energy production, primary (Petajoules)	2 324	2 058	2 286 [c]
Energy supply per capita (Gigajoules)	64	56	61 [c]
Tourist/visitor arrivals at national borders (000)	975	1 918	1 504 [b]
Important sites for terrestrial biodiversity protected (%)	15.4	15.4	17.7 [e]
Pop. using safely managed drinking water (urban/rural, %)	85.4 / 30.2	85.9 / 30.9	86.1 / 31.1 [b]
Net Official Development Assist. received (% of GNI)	0.42	0.54	2.54 [b]

a Projected estimate (medium fertility variant). b 2020. c 2019. d UN operational exchange rate. e 2021. f Data classified according to ISIC Rev. 4. g Excludes irrigation canals and landscaping care. h Excludes publishing activities. Includes irrigation and canals. i Includes publishing activities and landscape care. Excludes repair of personal and household goods. j Estimate. k Calculated by the UNSD from national indices. l Base: 2016 = 100 m Areas nes n Data refers to a 5-year period preceding the reference year. o Including refugees. p Data as at the end of December. q 2014. r 2008. s Data are as at 1 January of reporting year.

Vanuatu

Region	Melanesia	UN membership date	15 September 1981		
Population (000, 2022)	327[a]	Surface area (km2)	12 189[b]		
Pop. density (per km2, 2022)	26.8[a]	Sex ratio (m per 100 f)	101.2[a]		
Capital city	Port Vila	National currency	Vatu (VUV)		
Capital city pop. (000, 2022)	52.7[c]	Exchange rate (per US$)	112.2[d]		

Economic indicators

	2010	2015	2022
GDP: Gross domestic product (million current US$)	701	760	855[b]
GDP growth rate (annual %, const. 2015 prices)	1.6	0.2	- 9.2[b]
GDP per capita (current US$)	2 966.9	2 801.9	2 783.0[b]
Economy: Agriculture (% of Gross Value Added)[e,f]	21.9	23.1	23.1[b]
Economy: Industry (% of Gross Value Added)[a,g]	13.0	11.5	11.1[b]
Economy: Services and other activity (% of GVA)[e,h]	65.0	65.4	65.8[b]
Employment in agriculture (% of employed)[i]	60.2	58.3	55.3[b]
Employment in industry (% of employed)[i]	6.9	6.1	6.3[b]
Employment in services & other sectors (% employed)[i]	32.9	35.6	38.4[b]
Unemployment rate (% of labour force)	1.8	1.9[i]	2.1[i]
Labour force participation rate (female/male pop. %)[i]	60.3 / 78.2	60.5 / 78.3	60.1 / 78.1
CPI: Consumer Price Index (2010=100)	100	107	126[j,k,d]
Agricultural production index (2014-2016=100)	114	98	90[b]
International trade: exports (million current US$)	46	39[i]	637[i,d]
International trade: imports (million current US$)	276	354[i]	252[i,d]
International trade: balance (million current US$)	- 230	- 316[i]	385[d]
Balance of payments, current account (million US$)	- 42	2	24[b]

Major trading partners

						2021
Export partners (% of exports)[i]	Thailand	38.5	Japan	22.1	Cyprus	7.0
Import partners (% of imports)[i]	China	24.0	Australia	16.9	New Zealand	14.4

Social indicators

	2010	2015	2022
Population growth rate (average annual %)	2.3	2.4	2.4[a]
Urban population (% of total population)	24.5	25.0	25.4[l]
Urban population growth rate (average annual %)[m]	3.6	2.7	...
Fertility rate, total (live births per woman)	4.2	4.0	3.7[a]
Life expectancy at birth (females/males, years)	72.1 / 67.6	71.9 / 67.6	73.1 / 68.3[a]
Population age distribution (0-14/60+ years old, %)	38.9 / 5.5	39.6 / 5.6	39.4 / 5.8[a]
International migrant stock (000/% of total pop.)[n]	3.0 / 1.3	3.2 / 1.2	3.3 / 1.1[b]
Refugees and others of concern to the UNHCR (000)	~0.0[o]	~0.0	~0.0[d]
Infant mortality rate (per 1 000 live births)	24.1	23.5	18.8[a]
Health: Current expenditure (% of GDP)[p]	3.5	4.3	3.4[l]
Health: Physicians (per 1 000 pop.)	0.1[q]	0.2[r]	0.2[s]
Education: Government expenditure (% of GDP)	5.2[t]	5.6	2.3[b]
Education: Primary gross enrol. ratio (f/m per 100 pop.)	121.9 / 123.0	107.8 / 110.7	120.4 / 123.3[b]
Education: Sec. gross enrol. ratio (f/m per 100 pop.)	59.5 / 59.6	54.9 / 53.5	55.3 / 48.3[b]
Education: Upr. Sec. gross enrol. ratio (f/m per 100 pop.)	43.3 / 51.3	35.4 / 33.7	34.8 / 26.7[b]
Intentional homicide rate (per 100 000 pop.)	...	...	0.3[b]
Seats held by women in the National Parliament (%)	3.8	0.0	0.0[u]

Environment and infrastructure indicators

	2010	2015	2022
Individuals using the Internet (per 100 inhabitants)	8.0	22.4[i]	25.7[i,v]
Threatened species (number)	121	137	156
Forested area (% of land area)[i]	36.3	36.3	36.3[l]
Energy production, primary (Petajoules)	1	1	1[l]
Energy supply per capita (Gigajoules)	11	11	11[l]
Tourist/visitor arrivals at national borders (000)	97	90	22[b]
Important sites for terrestrial biodiversity protected (%)	2.8	2.8	2.8[d]
Pop. using safely managed drinking water (urban/rural, %)	55.5 / ...	56.3 / ...	56.6 / ...[b]
Net Official Development Assist. received (% of GNI)	16.87	25.10	18.22[b]

a Projected estimate (medium fertility variant). **b** 2020. **c** 2018. **d** 2021. **e** Data classified according to ISIC Rev. 4. **f** Excludes irrigation canals and landscaping care. **g** Excludes publishing activities. Includes irrigation and canals. **h** Includes publishing activities and landscape care. Excludes repair of personal and household goods. **i** Estimate. **j** Calculated by the UNSD from national indices. **k** Monthly average for quarter or index for quarter. **l** 2019. **m** Data refers to a 5-year period preceding the reference year. **n** Including refugees. **o** Data as at the end of December. **p** Government expenditures show fluctuations due to variations in capital investment. **q** 2008. **r** 2012. **s** 2016. **t** 2009. **u** Data are as at 1 January of reporting year. **v** 2017.

Venezuela (Bolivarian Republic of)

Region	South America	UN membership date	15 November 1945
Population (000, 2022)	28 302[a]	Surface area (km2)	929 690[b]
Pop. density (per km2, 2022)	30.9[a]	Sex ratio (m per 100 f)	97.8[a]
Capital city	Caracas	National currency	Bolívar (VES)
Capital city pop. (000, 2022)	2 935.5[c,d]	Exchange rate (per US$)	10.0[e]

Economic indicators

	2010	2015	2022
GDP: Gross domestic product (million current US$)	393 806	344 343	106 359[b]
GDP growth rate (annual %, const. 2015 prices)	- 1.5	- 6.2	- 30.0[b]
GDP per capita (current US$)	13 846.9	11 446.9	3 740.3[b]
Economy: Agriculture (% of Gross Value Added)[f]	5.7	4.6	5.2[b]
Economy: Industry (% of Gross Value Added)[f]	51.0	49.1	48.4[b]
Economy: Services and other activity (% of GVA)[f]	43.4	46.3	46.3[b]
Employment in agriculture (% of employed)[g]	8.3	7.4	8.4[b]
Employment in industry (% of employed)[g]	21.8	20.3	16.1[b]
Employment in services & other sectors (% employed)[g]	69.9	72.3	75.5[b]
Unemployment rate (% of labour force)	7.1	6.1[g]	5.5[g]
Labour force participation rate (female/male pop. %)	49.6 / 78.5	48.9 / 76.1[g]	34.4 / 67.9[g]
CPI: Consumer Price Index (2010=100)[h]	100	772	801[i,j]
Agricultural production index (2014-2016=100)	104	101	86[b]
International trade: exports (million current US$)	66 963	37 236[g]	3 283[g,j]
International trade: imports (million current US$)	32 343	40 146[g]	10 287[g,j]
International trade: balance (million current US$)	34 620	- 2 910[g]	- 7 003[j]
Balance of payments, current account (million US$)	5 585	- 16 051	- 3 870[k]

Major trading partners

							2021
Export partners (% of exports)[g]	China	27.9	Türkiye	15.4	United States	9.1
Import partners (% of imports)[g]	China	28.9	United States	21.9	Brazil	14.4

Social indicators

	2010	2015	2022
Population growth rate (average annual %)	1.3	1.1	1.8[a]
Urban population (% of total population)	88.1	88.2	88.2[d]
Urban population growth rate (average annual %)[l]	1.6	1.4	...
Fertility rate, total (live births per woman)	2.5	2.3	2.2[a]
Life expectancy at birth (females/males, years)	77.1 / 68.9	77.2 / 69.0	75.7 / 66.9[a]
Population age distribution (0-14/60+ years old, %)	30.0 / 8.5	28.5 / 9.7	27.6 / 12.9[a]
International migrant stock (000/% of total pop.)[m]	1 347.3 / 4.7	1 404.4 / 4.7	1 324.2 / 4.7[b]
Refugees and others of concern to the UNHCR (000)	217.4[n]	174.9	1 087.4[j]
Infant mortality rate (per 1 000 live births)	14.5	15.5	14.8[a]
Health: Current expenditure (% of GDP)[g,o,p,q]	6.8	4.3	5.4[d]
Health: Physicians (per 1 000 pop.)	...	...	1.7[e]
Education: Government expenditure (% of GDP)	6.9[r]	1.9[g]	1.3[g,e]
Education: Primary gross enrol. ratio (f/m per 100 pop.)	101.3 / 104.2	99.8 / 102.0	96.0 / 98.3[e]
Education: Sec. gross enrol. ratio (f/m per 100 pop.)	86.6 / 79.0	94.5 / 87.7	91.6 / 84.7[e]
Education: Upr. Sec. gross enrol. ratio (f/m per 100 pop.)	77.6 / 66.0	85.7 / 74.7	86.0 / 75.2[e]
Intentional homicide rate (per 100 000 pop.)	46.0	52.0	49.9[e]
Seats held by women in the National Parliament (%)	17.5	17.0	22.2[s,t,j]

Environment and infrastructure indicators

	2010	2015	2022
Individuals using the Internet (per 100 inhabitants)	37.4[g]	58.0	61.6[g,e]
Research & Development expenditure (% of GDP)	0.2	0.3[u]	...
Threatened species (number)	270	312	826
Forested area (% of land area)[g]	53.9	52.9	52.5[d]
CO2 emission estimates (million tons/tons per capita)	157.5 / 5.5	142.6 / 4.7	91.2 / 3.2[d]
Energy production, primary (Petajoules)	7 948	7 390	3 238[d]
Energy supply per capita (Gigajoules)	109	87	48[d]
Tourist/visitor arrivals at national borders (000)	526	789	427[e]
Important sites for terrestrial biodiversity protected (%)	78.8	78.8	78.8[j]
Net Official Development Assist. received (% of GNI)	0.01	0.01[u]	...

a Projected estimate (medium fertility variant). b 2020. c Refers to multiple municipalities and parishes (see source). d 2019. e 2017. f Data classified according to ISIC Rev. 4. g Estimate. h Calculated by the UNSD from national indices. i Figures in billions. j 2021. k 2016. l Data refers to a 5-year period preceding the reference year. m Including refugees. n Data as at the end of December. o The National Currency Unit (NCU) used for Venezuela data 2000-2019 is the Bolívar Soberano (VES), which replaced the Bolívar Fuerte (VEF) in August 2018 (1 VES = 100000 VEF). Also, WHO is using United Nations' exchange rate for NCU to USD, which differs from the official exchange rate. p Data based on calendar year (January 1 to December 31). q Estimates should be viewed with caution as these are derived from scarce data. r 2009. s Data are as at 1 January of reporting year. t Figures correspond to the legislature elected in 2015 as data for the 2020 election had not been confirmed by the time of reporting. u 2014.

Viet Nam

Region	South-eastern Asia
Population (000, 2022)	98 187 [a]
Pop. density (per km2, 2022)	313.3 [a]
Capital city	Hanoi
Capital city pop. (000, 2022)	4 479.6 [c,d]

UN membership date	20 September 1977
Surface area (km2)	331 317 [b]
Sex ratio (m per 100 f)	97.6 [a]
National currency	Dong (VND)
Exchange rate (per US$)	23 145.0 [e]

Economic indicators

	2010	2015	2022
GDP: Gross domestic product (million current US$)	115 932	193 241	271 158 [b]
GDP growth rate (annual %, const. 2015 prices)	6.4	6.7	2.9 [b]
GDP per capita (current US$)	1 317.9	2 085.1	2 785.7 [b]
Economy: Agriculture (% of Gross Value Added) [f,g]	21.0	18.9	16.5 [b]
Economy: Industry (% of Gross Value Added) [g,h]	36.7 [i]	37.0 [i]	37.4 [b]
Economy: Services and other activity (% of GVA) [g,j]	42.2	44.2	46.1 [b]
Employment in agriculture (% of employed)	48.7	44.0	36.2 [k,b]
Employment in industry (% of employed)	21.7	22.7	28.4 [k,b]
Employment in services & other sectors (% employed)	29.6	33.2	35.4 [k,b]
Unemployment rate (% of labour force)	1.1	1.8	2.3 [k]
Labour force participation rate (female/male pop. %)	71.5 / 81.0	72.4 / 82.1	69.1 / 79.2 [k]
CPI: Consumer Price Index (2010=100)	100	145	172 [e]
Agricultural production index (2014-2016=100)	84	100	107 [b]
International trade: exports (million current US$)	72 237	162 017	324 165 [k,e]
International trade: imports (million current US$)	84 839	165 776	304 468 [k,e]
International trade: balance (million current US$)	- 12 602	- 3 759	19 697 [e]
Balance of payments, current account (million US$)	- 4 276	- 2 041	- 3 812 [e]

Major trading partners

						2021
Export partners (% of exports) [k]	United States	27.4	China	17.4	Japan	6.8
Import partners (% of imports) [k]	China	32.2	Republic of Korea	17.9	Japan	7.8

Social indicators

	2010	2015	2022
Population growth rate (average annual %)	1.1	1.0	0.7 [a]
Urban population (% of total population)	30.4	33.8	36.6 [d]
Urban population growth rate (average annual %) [l]	3.1	3.2	...
Fertility rate, total (live births per woman)	1.9	2.0	1.9 [a]
Life expectancy at birth (females/males, years)	78.3 / 68.8	78.7 / 69.1	79.3 / 69.9 [a]
Population age distribution (0-14/60+ years old, %)	24.3 / 9.3	23.4 / 10.9	22.4 / 13.8 [a]
International migrant stock (000/% of total pop.) [m,n]	61.8 / 0.1	72.8 / 0.1	76.8 / 0.1 [b]
Refugees and others of concern to the UNHCR (000)	12.1 [o]	11.0	30.6 [e]
Infant mortality rate (per 1 000 live births)	18.0	17.2	15.0 [a]
Health: Current expenditure (% of GDP)	4.7	4.6	5.2 [d]
Health: Physicians (per 1 000 pop.)	0.7	0.8	0.8 [p]
Education: Government expenditure (% of GDP)	5.1	4.5 [k]	4.1 [k,d]
Education: Primary gross enrol. ratio (f/m per 100 pop.)	103.2 / 108.1	110.1 / 109.7	118.6 / 115.9 [b]
Intentional homicide rate (per 100 000 pop.)	1.5	1.5 [q]	...
Seats held by women in the National Parliament (%)	25.8	24.3	30.3 [r]

Environment and infrastructure indicators

	2010	2015	2022
Individuals using the Internet (per 100 inhabitants)	30.6	45.0 [k,s]	70.3 [b]
Research & Development expenditure (% of GDP)	...	0.4	0.5 [d]
Threatened species (number)	424	565	880
Forested area (% of land area)	42.7	44.9	46.5 [k,d]
CO2 emission estimates (million tons/tons per capita)	132.5 / 1.4	188.6 / 2.0	285.5 / 2.9 [d]
Energy production, primary (Petajoules)	2 747	3 035	2 776 [d]
Energy supply per capita (Gigajoules)	27	35	46 [d]
Tourist/visitor arrivals at national borders (000) [t]	5 050	7 944	3 687 [b]
Important sites for terrestrial biodiversity protected (%)	31.1	40.0	40.0 [e]
Net Official Development Assist. received (% of GNI)	2.48	1.73	0.46 [b]

a Projected estimate (medium fertility variant). b 2020. c Refers to urban population in the city districts. d 2019. e 2021. f Excludes irrigation canals and landscaping care. g Data classified according to ISIC Rev. 4. h Excludes publishing activities. Includes irrigation and canals. i At producers' prices. j Includes publishing activities and landscape care. Excludes repair of personal and household goods. k Estimate. l Data refers to a 5-year period preceding the reference year. m Refers to foreign citizens. n Including refugees. o Data as at the end of December. p 2016. q 2011. r Data are as at 1 January of reporting year. s Population aged 18 years and over. t Including nationals residing abroad.

Wallis and Futuna Islands

Region	Polynesia	Population (000, 2022)	12 a,b
Surface area (km2)	142 c	Pop. density (per km2, 2022)	82.7 a,b
Sex ratio (m per 100 f)	92.2 a,b	Capital city	Matu-Utu
National currency	CFP Franc (XPF) d	Capital city pop. (000, 2022)	1.0 e
Exchange rate (per US$)	105.4 f		

Economic indicators	2010	2015	2022
International trade: exports (million current US$) g	1	1	2 f
International trade: imports (million current US$) g	35	49	74 f
International trade: balance (million current US$)	- 34 g	- 48 g	- 73 f

Major trading partners						2021
Export partners (% of exports) g	Singapore	23.5	United States	13.2	Sweden	10.7
Import partners (% of imports) g	France	37.8	Fiji	18.4	New Zealand	17.1

Social indicators	2010	2015	2022
Population growth rate (average annual %) e	- 1.9	- 1.0	- 0.7 b
Urban population (% of total population)	0.0	0.0	0.0 h
Urban population growth rate (average annual %) i	0.0	0.0	...
Fertility rate, total (live births per woman) a	2.1	2.1	1.9 b
Life expectancy at birth (females/males, years) a	78.7 / 72.8	78.5 / 77.4	81.0 / 79.0 b
Population age distribution (0-14/60+ years old, %) a	28.9 / 12.7	26.7 / 15.4	22.7 / 19.1 b
International migrant stock (000/% of total pop.) j	2.1 / 16.6	2.0 / 16.7	2.0 / 18.1 c
Infant mortality rate (per 1 000 live births) a	14.7	11.9	9.8 b

Environment and infrastructure indicators	2010	2015	2022
Individuals using the Internet (per 100 inhabitants)	8.2	9.0 g,k	...
Threatened species (number)	74	88	95
Forested area (% of land area) g	41.6	41.6	41.6 h
Energy production, primary (Petajoules) g	0	0	0 h
Energy supply per capita (Gigajoules)	29	28	32 h
Important sites for terrestrial biodiversity protected (%)	0.0	0.0	0.0 f
Pop. using safely managed drinking water (urban/rural, %)	... / 59.0	... / 58.9	... / 58.8 c

a For statistical purposes, the data for France do not include this area. **b** Projected estimate (medium fertility variant). **c** 2020. **d** Communauté financière du Pacifique (CFP) Franc. **e** 2018. **f** 2021. **g** Estimate. **h** 2019. **i** Data refers to a 5-year period preceding the reference year. **j** Including refugees. **k** 2012.

Western Sahara

Region	Northern Africa	Population (000, 2022)	576[a]
Surface area (km2)	266 000[b,c]	Pop. density (per km2, 2022)	2.2[a]
Sex ratio (m per 100 f)	123.2[a]	Capital city	El Aaiún
National currency	Moroccan Dirham (MAD)	Capital city pop. (000, 2022)	232.4[d]
Exchange rate (per US$)	9.3[e]		

Economic indicators	2010	2015	2022
Employment in agriculture (% of employed)[f]	24.4	21.9	19.8[c]
Employment in industry (% of employed)[f]	24.0	25.1	25.7[c]
Employment in services & other sectors (% employed)[f]	51.5	53.0	54.5[c]
Unemployment rate (% of labour force)[f]	6.9	7.4	8.3
Labour force participation rate (female/male pop. %)[f]	24.3 / 71.9	24.6 / 71.4	24.7 / 70.7

Social indicators	2010	2015	2022
Population growth rate (average annual %)	3.8	2.8	2.0[a]
Urban population (% of total population)	86.3	86.5	86.8[g]
Urban population growth rate (average annual %)[h]	1.9	1.9	...
Fertility rate, total (live births per woman)	2.9	2.5	2.3[a]
Life expectancy at birth (females/males, years)	69.4 / 66.0	71.3 / 67.7	73.1 / 69.3[a]
Population age distribution (0-14/60+ years old, %)	27.0 / 6.3	26.0 / 7.5	24.3 / 9.4[a]
International migrant stock (000/% of total pop.)[f]	4.5 / 0.9	5.2 / 1.0	5.4 / 0.9[c]
Infant mortality rate (per 1 000 live births)	37.9	30.8	23.7[a]

Environment and infrastructure indicators	2010	2015	2022
Threatened species (number)	39	39	85
Forested area (% of land area)[f]	2.5	2.5	2.5[g]

a Projected estimate (medium fertility variant). **b** Comprising the Northern Region (former Saguia el Hamra) and Southern Region (former Río de Oro). **c** 2020. **d** 2018. **e** 2021. **f** Estimate. **g** 2019. **h** Data refers to a 5-year period preceding the reference year.

Yemen

Region	Western Asia	UN membership date	30 September 1947
Population (000, 2022)	33 697 [a]	Surface area (km2)	527 968 [b]
Pop. density (per km2, 2022)	63.8 [a]	Sex ratio (m per 100 f)	102.1 [a]
Capital city	Sana'a	National currency	Yemeni Rial (YER)
Capital city pop. (000, 2022)	2 874.4 [c,d]	Exchange rate (per US$)	952.0 [e]

Economic indicators

	2010	2015	2022
GDP: Gross domestic product (million current US$)	30 907	26 660	27 958 [b]
GDP growth rate (annual %, const. 2015 prices)	4.1	- 36.1	1.2 [b]
GDP per capita (current US$)	1 334.8	1 006.1	937.4 [b]
Economy: Agriculture (% of Gross Value Added) [f]	12.1	18.2	19.6 [b]
Economy: Industry (% of Gross Value Added) [f]	38.7	20.1	20.9 [b]
Economy: Services and other activity (% of GVA) [f]	49.2	61.7	59.5 [b]
Employment in agriculture (% of employed)	24.1	29.2 [g]	28.6 [g,b]
Employment in industry (% of employed)	19.0	12.8 [g]	10.0 [g,b]
Employment in services & other sectors (% employed)	56.9	58.0 [g]	61.4 [g,b]
Unemployment rate (% of labour force) [g]	12.8	13.8	13.3
Labour force participation rate (female/male pop. %)	10.0 / 67.5	6.1 / 67.0 [g]	6.0 / 67.8 [g]
CPI: Consumer Price Index (2010=100)	100	158 [h]	...
Agricultural production index (2014-2016=100)	101	100	105 [b]
International trade: exports (million current US$)	6 437	510	86 [g,e]
International trade: imports (million current US$)	9 255	6 573	5 174 [g,e]
International trade: balance (million current US$)	- 2 818	- 6 063	- 5 088 [e]
Balance of payments, current account (million US$)	- 1 054	- 3 026	- 2 419 [i]

Major trading partners

						2021
Export partners (% of exports) [g]	Egypt	49.6	Türkiye	28.0	Oman	10.5
Import partners (% of imports) [g]	United Arab Emirates	24.0	China	10.4	Saudi Arabia	6.5

Social indicators

	2010	2015	2022
Population growth rate (average annual %)	2.9	2.6	2.2 [a]
Urban population (% of total population)	31.8	34.8	37.3 [d]
Urban population growth rate (average annual %) [j]	4.6	4.4	...
Fertility rate, total (live births per woman)	4.9	4.3	3.7 [a]
Life expectancy at birth (females/males, years)	69.4 / 65.2	68.9 / 63.0	67.2 / 60.5 [a]
Population age distribution (0-14/60+ years old, %)	43.6 / 4.2	41.7 / 4.1	39.5 / 4.1 [a]
International migrant stock (000/% of total pop.) [k,l]	288.4 / 1.2	379.9 / 1.4	387.1 / 1.3 [b]
Refugees and others of concern to the UNHCR (000)	508.6 [m]	1 540.5	4 183.6 [e]
Infant mortality rate (per 1 000 live births)	45.7	46.3	46.8 [a]
Health: Current expenditure (% of GDP) [n,o]	5.2	4.3	...
Health: Physicians (per 1 000 pop.)	0.3 [p]	0.5 [h]	...
Education: Government expenditure (% of GDP)	5.2 [q]		...
Education: Primary gross enrol. ratio (f/m per 100 pop.)	82.3 / 100.9	89.4 / 106.6 [r]	87.1 / 99.9 [i]
Education: Sec. gross enrol. ratio (f/m per 100 pop.)	33.6 / 54.2	40.0 / 58.2 [r]	43.3 / 59.6 [i]
Education: Upr. Sec. gross enrol. ratio (f/m per 100 pop.)	24.6 / 41.8	31.6 / 47.2 [r]	34.5 / 49.5 [i]
Intentional homicide rate (per 100 000 pop.)	4.7	6.8 [r]	...
Seats held by women in the National Parliament (%)	0.3	0.3	0.0 [s,t]

Environment and infrastructure indicators

	2010	2015	2022
Individuals using the Internet (per 100 inhabitants)	12.4	24.1 [g]	26.7 [g,u]
Threatened species (number)	269	287	336
Forested area (% of land area) [g]	1.0	1.0	1.0 [d]
CO2 emission estimates (million tons/tons per capita)	22.6 / 1.0	11.6 / 0.4	9.7 / 0.3 [d]
Energy production, primary (Petajoules)	804	173	113 [d]
Energy supply per capita (Gigajoules)	14	7	5 [d]
Tourist/visitor arrivals at national borders (000) [v]	1 025	367	...
Important sites for terrestrial biodiversity protected (%)	27.9	27.9	27.9 [e]
Pop. using safely managed sanitation (urban/rural %)	64.3 / ...	61.4 / ...	60.6 / ... [b]
Net Official Development Assist. received (% of GNI)	2.29	4.32	34.02 [w]

a Projected estimate (medium fertility variant). b 2020. c Data refers to the urban agglomeration. d 2019. e 2021. f Data classified according to ISIC Rev. 4. g Estimate. h 2014. i 2016. j Data refers to a 5-year period preceding the reference year. k Including refugees. l Refers to foreign citizens. m Data as at the end of December. n Data based on calendar year (January 1 to December 31). o Estimates should be viewed with caution as these are derived from scarce data. p 2009. q 2008. r 2013. s Data corresponds to the composition of the House of Representatives elected in 2003. t Data are as at 1 January of reporting year. u 2017. v Including nationals residing abroad. w 2018.

Zambia

Region	Eastern Africa	UN membership date	01 December 1964
Population (000, 2022)	20 018 [a]	Surface area (km2)	752 612 [b]
Pop. density (per km2, 2022)	26.9 [a]	Sex ratio (m per 100 f)	97.4 [a]
Capital city	Lusaka	National currency	Zambian Kwacha (ZMW)
Capital city pop. (000, 2022)	2 646.6 [c]	Exchange rate (per US$)	16.7 [d]

Economic indicators

	2010	2015	2022
GDP: Gross domestic product (million current US$)	20 265	20 859	18 111 [b]
GDP growth rate (annual %, const. 2015 prices)	10.3	2.9	- 2.8 [b]
GDP per capita (current US$)	1 489.4	1 313.6	985.1 [b]
Economy: Agriculture (% of Gross Value Added) [e,f]	10.0	5.3	3.1 [b]
Economy: Industry (% of Gross Value Added) [e,g]	34.1	35.3	41.6 [b]
Economy: Services and other activity (% of GVA) [e,h]	55.9	59.4	55.4 [b]
Employment in agriculture (% of employed) [i]	64.3	51.7	48.5 [b]
Employment in industry (% of employed) [i]	8.8	10.7	10.8 [b]
Employment in services & other sectors (% employed) [i]	26.9	37.7	40.7 [b]
Unemployment rate (% of labour force)	13.2	10.1 [i]	13.0 [i]
Labour force participation rate (female/male pop. %) [i]	70.6 / 81.9	69.5 / 79.6	69.5 / 77.9
CPI: Consumer Price Index (2010=100)	100 [j]	144	246 [b]
Agricultural production index (2014-2016=100)	95	91	116 [b]
International trade: exports (million current US$)	7 200	6 607	11 895 [i,d]
International trade: imports (million current US$)	5 321	7 934	7 311 [i,d]
International trade: balance (million current US$)	1 879	- 1 328	4 584 [d]
Balance of payments, current account (million US$)	1 525	- 768	2 352 [d]

Major trading partners

							2021
Export partners (% of exports) [i]	Switzerland	44.3	China	18.7	Dem. Rep. of Congo	12.4
Import partners (% of imports) [i]	South Africa	33.2	China	16.8	United Arab Emirates	8.8

Social indicators

	2010	2015	2022
Population growth rate (average annual %)	3.4	3.2	2.7 [a]
Urban population (% of total population)	39.4	41.9	44.1 [c]
Urban population growth rate (average annual %) [k]	4.1	4.3	...
Fertility rate, total (live births per woman)	5.4	4.8	4.2 [a]
Life expectancy at birth (females/males, years)	58.5 / 54.9	63.5 / 58.8	64.5 / 59.1 [a]
Population age distribution (0-14/60+ years old, %)	46.6 / 2.7	45.5 / 2.7	42.9 / 3.0 [a]
International migrant stock (000/% of total pop.) [l]	150.0 / 1.1	132.1 / 0.8	188.0 / 1.0 [b]
Refugees and others of concern to the UNHCR (000)	57.9 [m]	51.8	100.0 [d]
Infant mortality rate (per 1 000 live births)	52.9	46.3	38.2 [a]
Health: Current expenditure (% of GDP) [n]	3.7	4.4	5.3 [c]
Health: Physicians (per 1 000 pop.)	0.1	...	0.1 [o]
Education: Government expenditure (% of GDP)	3.7	4.6	4.5 [i,c]
Education: Primary gross enrol. ratio (f/m per 100 pop.)	107.3 / 106.6	101.6 / 101.3	99.9 / 97.5 [p]
Intentional homicide rate (per 100 000 pop.)	6.0	5.4	...
Seats held by women in the National Parliament (%)	14.0	12.7	15.1 [q]

Environment and infrastructure indicators

	2010	2015	2022
Individuals using the Internet (per 100 inhabitants)	3.0 [i]	8.8 [r]	19.8 [i,b]
Research & Development expenditure (% of GDP)	0.3 [j,s]	...	...
Threatened species (number)	67	83	129
Forested area (% of land area) [i]	62.8	61.5	60.5 [c]
CO2 emission estimates (million tons/tons per capita)	3.7 / 0.2	6.0 / 0.3	7.6 / 0.3 [c]
Energy production, primary (Petajoules)	303	351	391 [c]
Energy supply per capita (Gigajoules)	25	26	25 [c]
Tourist/visitor arrivals at national borders (000)	815	932	502 [b]
Important sites for terrestrial biodiversity protected (%)	46.1	46.1	46.1 [d]
Pop. using safely managed drinking water (urban/rural, %)	49.6 / ...	50.1 / ...	50.5 / ... [b]
Pop. using safely managed sanitation (urban/rural, %)	... / 15.7	... / 19.6	... / 23.8 [b]
Net Official Development Assist. received (% of GNI)	4.86	3.82	5.40 [b]

a Projected estimate (medium fertility variant). b 2020. c 2019. d 2021. e Data classified according to ISIC Rev. 4. f Excludes irrigation canals and landscaping care. g Excludes publishing activities. Includes irrigation and canals. h Includes publishing activities and landscape care. Excludes repair of personal and household goods. i Estimate. j Break in the time series. k Data refers to a 5-year period preceding the reference year. l Including refugees. m Data as at the end of December. n Data revision. o 2018. p 2017. q Data are as at 1 January of reporting year. r Population aged 11 years and over. s 2008.

Zimbabwe

Region	Eastern Africa
Population (000, 2022)	16 320[a]
Pop. density (per km2, 2022)	42.2[a]
Capital city	Harare
Capital city pop. (000, 2022)	1 521.3[c]

UN membership date	25 August 1980
Surface area (km2)	390 757[b]
Sex ratio (m per 100 f)	89.4[a]
National currency	Zimbabwe Dollar (ZWL)

Economic indicators

	2010	2015	2022
GDP: Gross domestic product (million current US$)	12 042	19 963	21 787[b]
GDP growth rate (annual %, const. 2015 prices)	19.7	1.8	0.8[b]
GDP per capita (current US$)	948.3	1 445.1	1 465.8[b]
Economy: Agriculture (% of Gross Value Added)[d]	10.9	9.3	9.2[b]
Economy: Industry (% of Gross Value Added)[d]	23.5	25.0	23.4[b]
Economy: Services and other activity (% of GVA)[d]	65.6	65.7	67.4[b]
Employment in agriculture (% of employed)[e]	65.5	67.2	66.3[b]
Employment in industry (% of employed)[e]	9.2	7.1	6.5[b]
Employment in services & other sectors (% employed)[e]	25.2	25.7	27.2[b]
Unemployment rate (% of labour force)[e]	5.2	4.8	5.0
Labour force participation rate (female/male pop. %)[e]	77.5 / 88.2	80.3 / 89.6	79.9 / 89.1
CPI: Consumer Price Index (2010=100)	100	106	5 411[f]
Agricultural production index (2014-2016=100)	105	97	113[b]
International trade: exports (million current US$)	3 199	3 411	5 622[e,f]
International trade: imports (million current US$)	5 852	6 053	6 323[e,f]
International trade: balance (million current US$)	- 2 653	- 2 642	- 700[f]
Balance of payments, current account (million US$)	- 1 655	- 1 597	1 096[b]

Major trading partners

					2021
Export partners (% of exports)[e]	South Africa	39.4	Undisclosed[g] 22.0	United Arab Emirates	20.3
Import partners (% of imports)[e]	South Africa	49.3	Singapore 10.9	China	9.3

Social indicators

	2010	2015	2022
Population growth rate (average annual %)	1.4	2.1	2.1[a]
Urban population (% of total population)	33.2	32.4	32.2[c]
Urban population growth rate (average annual %)[h]	1.2	1.8	...
Fertility rate, total (live births per woman)	4.0	3.8	3.4[a]
Life expectancy at birth (females/males, years)	52.2 / 48.9	61.6 / 57.3	62.1 / 56.4[a]
Population age distribution (0-14/60+ years old, %)	43.2 / 4.6	42.9 / 4.9	40.6 / 4.8[a]
International migrant stock (000/% of total pop.)[i]	398.3 / 3.1	400.5 / 2.9	416.1 / 2.8[b]
Refugees and others of concern to the UNHCR (000)	4.9[j]	308.1	22.7[f]
Infant mortality rate (per 1 000 live births)	55.0	41.1	37.4[a]
Health: Current expenditure (% of GDP)	10.5	7.5	7.7[c]
Health: Physicians (per 1 000 pop.)	0.1	0.2	0.2[b]
Education: Government expenditure (% of GDP)	1.5	5.8[e]	3.6[e,k]
Education: Primary gross enrol. ratio (f/m per 100 pop.)	... / ...	102.8 / 104.9	97.6 / 97.1[b]
Education: Sec. gross enrol. ratio (f/m per 100 pop.)	... / ...	51.3 / 53.5[l]	... / ...
Education: Upr. Sec. gross enrol. ratio (f/m per 100 pop.)	... / ...	38.9 / 43.2[l]	... / ...
Intentional homicide rate (per 100 000 pop.)	5.6	7.5[m]	...
Seats held by women in the National Parliament (%)	15.0	31.5	30.6[n]

Environment and infrastructure indicators

	2010	2015	2022
Individuals using the Internet (per 100 inhabitants)	6.4[e]	22.7[e]	29.3[b]
Threatened species (number)	55	60	131
Forested area (% of land area)[e]	46.3	45.7	45.2[c]
CO2 emission estimates (million tons/tons per capita)	11.8 / 0.7	14.5 / 0.9	13.9 / 0.8[c]
Energy production, primary (Petajoules)	372	434	415[c]
Energy supply per capita (Gigajoules)	31	33	32[c]
Tourist/visitor arrivals at national borders (000)	2 239	2 057	639[b]
Important sites for terrestrial biodiversity protected (%)	76.1	81.2	81.2[f]
Pop. using safely managed drinking water (urban/rural, %)	64.5 / 15.2	64.5 / 14.0	64.6 / 12.9[b]
Pop. using safely managed sanitation (urban/rural %)	22.0 / 32.0	19.0 / 31.1	16.0 / 30.2[b]
Net Official Development Assist. received (% of GNI)	6.71	4.38	5.97[b]

a Projected estimate (medium fertility variant). **b** 2020. **c** 2019. **d** Data classified according to ISIC Rev. 4. **e** Estimate. **f** 2021. **g** Undisclosed (Special categories). **h** Data refers to a 5-year period preceding the reference year. **i** Including refugees. **j** Data as at the end of December. **k** 2018. **l** 2013. **m** 2012. **n** Data are as at 1 January of reporting year.

Technical notes

Below are brief descriptions of the indicators presented in the world, regional and country profiles. The terms are arranged in alphabetical order.

Agricultural production index is calculated by the Laspeyres formula based on the sum of price-weighted quantities of different agricultural commodities produced. The commodities covered in the computation of indices of agricultural production are all crops and livestock products originating in each country. Practically all products are covered, with the main exception of fodder crops. Production quantities of each commodity are weighted by the average international commodity prices in the base period and summed for each year. To obtain the index, the aggregate for a given year is divided by the average aggregate for the base period 2014-2016. Indices are calculated without any deductions for feed and seed and are referred to as "gross" by the Food and Agriculture Organization of the United Nations (FAO).
Source of the data: Food and Agriculture Organization of the United Nations (FAO), Rome, FAOSTAT database, last accessed June 2022.

Balance of payments is a statement summarizing the economic transactions between the residents of a country and non-residents during a specific period, usually a year. It includes transactions in goods, services, income, transfers and financial assets and liabilities. Generally, the balance of payments is divided into two major components: the current account and the capital and financial account. The data on balance of payments correspond to the current account category. The current account is a record of all transactions in the balance of payments covering the exports and imports of goods and services, payments of income, and current transfers between residents of a country and non-residents.
Source of the data: International Monetary Fund (IMF), Washington, D.C., Balance of Payment (BOP) Statistics database, last accessed June 2022.

Capital city and capital city population is the designation of any specific city as a capital city as reported by the country or area. The city can be the seat of the government as determined by the country. Some countries designate more than one city to be a capital city with a specific title function (e.g., administrative and/or legislative capital). The data refer to the year 2022, unless otherwise stated in a footnote.
Source of the data: United Nations Population Division (UNPD), New York, "World Urbanization Prospects (WUP): The 2018 Revision", last accessed May 2018.

CO_2 emission estimates represent total CO_2 emissions from fuel combustion. This includes CO_2 emissions from fuel combustion in IPCC Source/Sink Category 1 A Fuel Combustion Activities and those which may be reallocated to IPCC Source/Sink Category 2 Industrial Processes and Product Use under the 2006 GLs.
Source of the data: International Energy Agency, IEA World Energy Balances 2020 and 2006 IPCC Guidelines for Greenhouse Gas Inventories, last accessed June 2022.

Technical notes (*continued*)

CPI: Consumer price index measures the period-to-period proportional change in the prices of a fixed set of consumer goods and services of constant quantity and characteristics, acquired, used or paid for by the reference population. The index is constructed as a weighted average of a large number of elementary aggregate indices. Each of the elementary aggregate indices is estimated using a sample of prices for a defined set of goods and services obtained in, or by residents of, a specific region from a given set of outlets or other sources of consumption. The indices here generally refer to "all items" and to the country as a whole, unless otherwise stated in a footnote.

Source of the data: United Nations Statistics Division (UNSD), New York, Monthly Bulletin of Statistics (MBS), last accessed June 2022.

Economy: agriculture, industry and services and other activity presents the shares of the components of Gross Value Added (GVA) at current prices by kind of economic activity; agriculture (agriculture, hunting, forestry and fishing), industry (mining and quarrying, manufacturing, electricity, gas and water supply; and construction) and in services and other sectors based on the sections of the International Standard Industrial Classification of All Economic Activities (ISIC), Revision 3, unless a different revision is stated in a footnote.

Source of the data: United Nations Statistics Division (UNSD), New York, National Accounts Statistics: Analysis of Main Aggregates (AMA) database, last accessed March 2022.

Education: Government expenditure shows the trends in general government expenditures for educational affairs and services at primary, secondary and upper secondary levels and subsidiary services to education, expressed as a percentage of the gross domestic product.

Source of the data: United Nations Educational, Scientific and Cultural Organization (UNESCO), Montreal, the UNESCO Institute for Statistics (UIS) statistics database, last accessed May 2022.

Education: Primary, secondary and upper secondary gross enrolment ratio is the total enrolment in the primary, secondary and upper secondary levels of education, regardless of age, expressed as a percentage of the eligible official school-age population corresponding to the same level of education in a given school year. Education at the primary level provides the basic elements of education (e.g. at elementary school or primary school). Education at the secondary level is provided at middle school, secondary school, high school, teacher-training school at this level and schools of a vocational or technical nature. Education at the upper secondary level is the second or final stage of general and vocational secondary education. Programmes at upper secondary education, are typically designed to complete secondary education in preparation for tertiary education or provide skills relevant to employment, or both. The programmes offered are more varied, specialised and in-depth instruction than programmes in lower secondary education. Programmes are more differentiated, with an increased range of options and streams available. Enrolment is measured at the beginning of the school or academic year. The gross enrolment ratio at each level will include all pupils whatever their ages, whereas the population is limited to the range of official school ages. Therefore, for countries with almost universal education among the school-age population, the gross enrolment ratio can exceed 100 if the actual age distribution of pupils extends beyond the official school ages.

Source of the data: United Nations Educational, Scientific and Cultural Organization (UNESCO), Montreal, the UNESCO Institute for Statistics (UIS) statistics database, last accessed May 2022.

Employment in agricultural, industrial and services and other sectors: The "employed" comprise all persons above a specified age who, during a specified brief period, either one week or one day, were in "paid employment" or in "self-employment", see ILO's Current International Recommendations on Labour Statistics. The data refer to those 15 years and over, unless otherwise stated in a footnote, who perform any work at all in the reference period, for pay or profit in agriculture (agriculture, forestry and fishing), industry (mining and quarrying; manufacturing; electricity, gas, steam and air conditioning supply; water supply, sewerage, waste management and remediation activities; and construction) and in services and other sectors based on the sections of the International Standard Industrial Classification of All Economic Activities (ISIC), Revision 4, unless an earlier revision is stated in a footnote.

Source of the data: International Labour Organization (ILO), Geneva, Key Indicators of the Labour Market (KILM 9th edition) and the ILOSTAT database, last accessed January 2020.

Energy production, primary, is the capture or extraction of fuels or energy from natural energy flows, the biosphere and natural reserves of fossil fuels within the national territory in a form suitable for use. Inert matter removed from the extracted fuels and quantities reinjected, flared or vented are not included. The resulting products are referred to as "primary" products. It excludes secondary production, that is, the manufacture of energy products through the process of transforming primary and/or other secondary fuels or energy. Data are provided in a common energy unit (Petajoule) and refer to the following primary energy sources: hard coal, brown coal, peat, oil shale, conventional crude oil, natural gas liquids (NGL), other hydrocarbons, additives and oxygenates, natural gas, fuelwood, wood residues and by-products, bagasse, animal waste, black liquor, other vegetal material and residues, biogasoline, biodiesels, bio jet kerosene, other liquid biofuels, biogases, industrial waste, municipal waste, nuclear, solar photovoltaic, solar thermal, hydro, wind, geothermal, and tide, wave and other marine sources. Peat, biomass and wastes are included only when the production is for energy purposes. See International Recommendations for Energy Statistics (2011) and the UN publication Energy Balances for a complete description of the methodology.

Technical notes (*continued*)

Source of the data: United Nations Statistics Division (UNSD), New York, Energy Statistics Yearbook 2019, last accessed March 2022.

Energy supply per capita is defined as primary energy production plus imports minus exports minus international marine bunkers minus international aviation bunkers minus stock changes divided by the population. For imports, exports, international bunkers and stock changes, it includes secondary energy products, in addition to primary products.

Source of the data: United Nations Statistics Division (UNSD), New York, Energy Statistics Yearbook 2019, last accessed March 2022.

Exchange rate in units of national currency per US dollar refers to end-of-period quotations. The exchange rates are classified into broad categories, reflecting both the role of the authorities in the determination of the exchange and/or the multiplicity of exchange rates in a country. The market rate is used to describe exchange rates determined largely by market forces; the official rate is an exchange rate determined by the authorities, sometimes in a flexible manner. For countries maintaining multiple exchange arrangements, the rates are labelled principal rate, secondary rate, and tertiary rate.

Source of the data: International Monetary Fund (IMF), Washington, D.C., the International Financial Statistics (IFS) database supplemented by United Nations Department of Management (DM), UN Treasury operational rates of exchange, last accessed June 2022.

Fertility rate is the total fertility rate, a widely used summary indicator of fertility. It refers to the number of children that would be born per woman, assuming no female mortality at child bearing ages and the age-specific fertility rates of a specified country and reference period. The data are an average over five-year ranges; 2005-2010 data are labelled "2010", 2011-2015 data are labelled "2015" and 2016-2022 data are labelled "2022", unless otherwise stated in a footnote.

Source of the data: United Nations Population Division (UNPD), New York, "World Population Prospects (WPP): The 2022 Revision"; supplemented by data from the United Nations Statistics Division (UNSD), New York, Demographic Yearbook 2020 and the Pacific Community (SPC) Statistics and Demography Programme for small countries or areas, last accessed July 2022.

Forested area refers to the percentage of land area occupied by forest. Forest is defined in the Food and Agriculture Organization's Global Forest Resources Assessment as land spanning more than 0.5 hectares with trees higher than 5 metres and a canopy cover of more than 10 percent, or trees able to reach these thresholds in situ. It does not include land that is predominantly under agricultural or urban land use. Data are calculated from the forest estimates divided by the land area.

Source of the data: Food and Agriculture Organization of the United Nations (FAO), Rome, FAOSTAT database, last accessed March 2022.

GDP: Gross domestic product is an aggregate measure of production equal to the sum of gross value added of all resident producer units plus that part (possibly the total) of taxes on products, less subsidies on products, that is not included in the valuation of output. It is also equal to the sum of the final uses of goods and services (all uses except intermediate consumption) measured at purchasers' prices, less the value of imports of goods and services, and equal to the sum of primary incomes distributed by resident producer units (see System of National Accounts 2008). The data are in current United States (US) dollars and are estimates of the total production of goods and services of the countries represented in economic terms, not as a measure of the standard of living of their inhabitants. To have comparable coverage for as many countries as possible, these US dollar estimates are based on official GDP data in national currency, supplemented by national currency estimates prepared by the Statistics Division using additional data from national and international sources. The estimates given here are in most cases those accepted by the United Nations General Assembly's Committee on Contributions for determining United Nations members' contributions to the United Nations regular budget. The exchange rates for the conversion of GDP national currency data into US dollars are the average market rates published by the International Monetary Fund, in International Financial Statistics (IFS). Official exchange rates are used only when free market rates are not available. For non-members of the Fund, the conversion rates used are the average of UN Treasury rates of exchange. It should be noted that the conversion from local currency into US dollars introduces deficiencies in comparability over time and among countries which should be considered when using the data. For example, comparability over time is distorted when exchange rate fluctuations differ substantially from domestic inflation rates.
Source of the data: United Nations Statistics Division (UNSD), New York, National Accounts Statistics: Analysis of Main Aggregates (AMA) database, last accessed March 2022.

GDP growth rate is derived on the basis of constant 2015 price series in national currency. The figures are annual rates of growth expressed in percentages.
Source of the data: United Nations Statistics Division (UNSD), New York, National Accounts Statistics: Analysis of Main Aggregates (AMA) database, last accessed March 2022.

GDP per capita estimates are the value of all goods and services produced in the economy divided by the population.
Source of the data: United Nations Statistics Division (UNSD), New York, National Accounts Statistics: Analysis of Main Aggregates (AMA) database, last accessed March 2022.

Health: Physicians includes generalist medical practitioners and specialist medical practitioners, expressed as the number of physicians per 1 000 population. The classification of health workers used is based on criteria for vocational education and training, regulation of health professions, and activities and tasks of jobs, i.e. a framework for categorizing key workforce variables according to shared characteristics.

Source of the data: World Health Organisation (WHO), Geneva, WHO Global Health Workforce statistics database, last accessed June 2022.

Health: Current expenditure refers to all health care goods and services used or consumed during a year excluding capital spending, or rather "gross capital formation", which is the purchase of new assets used repeatedly over several years. These estimates are in line with the 2011 System of Health Accounts (SHA). Current expenditure is expressed as a proportion of Gross Domestic Product (GDP).

Source of the data: World Health Organization (WHO), Geneva, WHO Global Health Expenditure database, last accessed April 2022.

Important sites for terrestrial biodiversity protected shows land which contributes significantly to the global persistence of biodiversity measured as a proportion of which is wholly covered by a designated protected area. Data are based on spatial overlap between polygons for Key Biodiversity Areas from the World Database of key Biodiversity Areas and polygons for protected areas from the World Database on Protected Areas. Figures for each region are calculated as the proportion of each Key Biodiversity Area covered by protected areas, averaged (i.e. calculated as the mean) across all Key Biodiversity Areas within the region.

Source of the data: United Nations Environment Programme (UNEP) World Conservation Monitoring Centre (WCMC), Cambridge, Sustainable Development Goals (SDGs) statistics database, last accessed March 2022.

Individuals using the Internet refer to the percentage of people who used the Internet from any location and for any purpose, irrespective of the device and network used. It can be via a computer (i.e. desktop or laptop computer, tablet or similar handheld computer), mobile phone, games machine, digital TV, etc. Access can be via a fixed or mobile network. There are certain data limits to this indicator, insofar as estimates have to be calculated for many developing countries which do not yet collect information and communications technology household statistics.

Source of the data: International Telecommunication Union (ITU), Geneva, the ITU database, last accessed March 2022.

Infant mortality rate is the ratio of infant deaths (the deaths of children under one year of age) in a given year to the total number of live births in the same year, expressed as a rate per 1 000 live births. The data are an average over five-year ranges; 2005-2010 data are labelled "2010", 2011-2015 data are labelled "2015" and 2016-2022 data are labelled "2022", unless otherwise stated in a footnote.

Source of the data: United Nations Population Division (UNPD), New York, "World Population Prospects (WPP): The 2022 Revision"; supplemented by data from the

United Nations Statistics Division (UNSD), New York, Demographic Yearbook 2020 and the Pacific Community (SPC) Statistics and Demography Programme for small countries or areas, last accessed July 2022.

Intentional homicide rate: The rates are the annual number of unlawful deaths purposefully inflicted on a person by another person, reported for the year per 100 000. For most countries, country information on causes of death is not available for most causes. Estimates are therefore based on cause of death modelling and death registration data from other countries in the region. Further country-level information and data on specific causes was also used.
Source of the data: United Nations Office on Drugs and Crime (UNODC), Vienna, UNODC Statistics database, last accessed June 2022.

International migrant stock generally represents the number of persons born in a country other than that in which they live. When information on country of birth was not recorded, data on the number of persons having foreign citizenship was used instead. In the absence of any empirical data, estimates were imputed. Data refer to mid-year. Figures for international migrant stock as a percentage of the population are the outcome of dividing the estimated international migrant stock by the estimated total population and multiplying the result by 100.
Source of the data: United Nations Population Division (UNPD), New York, "International migrant stock: The 2020 Revision", last accessed January 2021.

International trade: Exports, imports and balance show the movement of goods out of and into a country. Goods simply being transported through a country (goods in transit) or temporarily admitted (except for goods for inward processing) do not add to the stock of material resources of a country and are not included in the international merchandise trade statistics. In the "general trade system", the definition of the statistical territory of a country coincides with its economic territory. In the "special trade system", the definition of the statistical territory comprises only a particular part of the economic territory, mainly that part which coincides with the free circulation area for goods. "The free circulation area" is a part of the economic territory of a country within which goods "may be disposed of without Customs restrictions". In the case of exports, the transaction value is the value at which the goods were sold by the exporter, including the cost of transportation and insurance, to bring the goods onto the transporting vehicle at the frontier of the exporting country (an FOB-type valuation). In the case of imports, the transaction value is the value at which the goods were purchased by the importer plus the cost of transportation and insurance to the frontier of the importing country (a CIF-type valuation). Both imports and exports are shown in United States dollars. Conversion from national currencies is made by means of currency conversion factors based on official exchange rates (par values or weighted averages). All regional aggregations are calculated as the sum of their components.

Technical notes (*continued*)

Source of the data: United Nations Statistics Division (UNSD), New York, Commodity Trade Statistics Database (UN COMTRADE), last accessed June 2022.

Labour force participation rate is calculated by expressing the number of persons in the labour force as a percentage of the working-age population. The labour force is the sum of the number of persons employed and the number of unemployed (see ILO's current International Recommendations on Labour Statistics). The working-age population is the population above a certain age, prescribed for the measurement of economic characteristics. The data refer to the age group of 15 years and over and are based on ILO's modelled estimates, unless otherwise stated in a footnote.
Source of the data: International Labour Organization (ILO), Geneva, Key Indicators of the Labour Market (KILM 9th edition) and the ILOSTAT database, last accessed January 2022.

Life expectancy at birth is the average number of years of life at birth (age 0) for males and females according to the expected mortality rates by age estimated for the reference year and population. The data are an average over five-year ranges; 2005-2010 data are labelled "2010", 2011-2015 data are labelled "2015" and 2016-2022 data are labelled "2022", unless otherwise stated in a footnote.
Source of the data: United Nations Population Division (UNPD), New York, "World Population Prospects (WPP): The 2022 Revision"; supplemented by data from the United Nations Statistics Division (UNSD), New York, Demographic Yearbook 2020 and the Pacific Community (SPC) Statistics and Demography Programme for small countries or areas, last accessed July 2022.

Major trading partners show the three largest trade partners (countries of last known destination and origin or consignment) in international merchandise trade transactions. In some cases a special partner is shown (i.e. Areas nes, bunkers, etc.) instead of a country and refers to one of the following special categories. Areas not elsewhere specified (i.e. Areas nes) is used (a) for low value trade, (b) if the partner designation was unknown to the country or if an error was made in the partner assignment and (c) for reasons of confidentiality. If a specific geographical location can be identified within Areas nes, then they are recorded accordingly (i.e. Asia nes). Bunkers are ship stores and aircraft supplies, which consists mostly of fuels and food. Free zones belong to the geographical and economic territory of a country but not to its customs territory. For the purposes of trade statistics, the transactions between the customs territory and the free zones are recorded, if the reporting country uses the Special Trade System. Free zones can be commercial free zones (duty free shops) or industrial free zones. Data are expressed as percentages of total exports and of total imports of the country, area or special partner.
Source of the data: United Nations Statistics Division (UNSD), New York, Commodity Trade Statistics Database (UN COMTRADE), last accessed June 2022.

National currency refers to those notes and coins in circulation that are commonly used to make payments. The official currency names and the ISO currency codes are those officially in use, and may be subject to change.
Source of the data: International Organisation for Standardization (ISO), Geneva, Currency Code Services – ISO 4217 Maintenance Agency, last accessed May 2018.

Net Official Development Assistance received or disbursed is defined as those flows to developing countries and multilateral institutions provided by official agencies, including state and local governments, or by their executive agencies, each transaction of which meets the following tests: i) it is administered with the promotion of the economic development and welfare of developing countries as its main objective; and ii) it is concessional in character and conveys a grant element of at least 25 per cent. It is expressed as a percentage of Gross National Income of either the donor or recipient. The multilateral institutions include the World Bank Group, regional banks, financial institutions of the European Union and a number of United Nations institutions, programmes and trust funds.
Source of the data: Organisation for Economic Co-operation and Development (OECD), Paris, the OECD Development Assistance Committee (DAC) statistics database, last accessed June 2022.

Population refers to the medium fertility projected de facto population as of 1 July 2022, unless otherwise stated in a footnote. The total population of a country may comprise either all usual residents of the country (de jure population) or all persons present in the country (de facto population) at the time of the census; for purposes of international comparisons, the de facto definition is used, unless otherwise stated in a footnote.
Source of the data: United Nations Population Division (UNPD), New York, "World Population Prospects (WPP): The 2022 Revision", last accessed July 2022.

Population age distribution refers to the percentage of the population aged 0-14 years and aged 60 years and older at the mid-year unless otherwise stated in a footnote.
Source of the data: United Nations Population Division (UNPD), New York, "World Population Prospects (WPP): The 2022 Revision"; supplemented by data from the United Nations Statistics Division (UNSD), New York, Demographic Yearbook 2020 and the Pacific Community (SPC) Statistics and Demography Programme for small countries or areas, last accessed July 2022.

Population density refers to the medium fertility projected population as of 1 July 2022 per square kilometre of surface area, unless otherwise stated in a footnote.
Source of the data: United Nations Population Division (UNPD), New York, "World Population Prospects (WPP): The 2022 Revision", last accessed July 2022.

Technical notes (*continued*)

Population growth rate is the average annual percentage change in total population size. The data are an average over five-year ranges; 2010-2015 data are labelled "2010", 2011-2015 data are labelled "2015" and 2016-2022 data are labelled "2022", unless otherwise stated in a footnote.
Source of the data: United Nations Population Division (UNPD), New York, "World Population Prospects (WPP): The 2022 Revision", last accessed July 2022.

Refugees and others of concern to the UNHCR: The 1951 United Nations Convention relating to the Status of Refugees states that a refugee is someone who, owing to a well-founded fear of being persecuted for reasons of race, religion, nationality, political opinion or membership in a particular social group, is outside the country of his or her nationality and is unable to, or owing to such fear, is unwilling to avail himself or herself of the protection of that country; or who, not having a nationality and being outside the country of his or her former habitual residence, is unable or, owing to such fear, unwilling to return to it. In this series, refugees refer to persons granted a humanitarian status and/or those granted temporary protection. Included are persons who have been granted temporary protection on a group basis. The series also includes returned refugees, asylum-seekers, stateless persons and persons displaced internally within their own country and others of concern to UNHCR.
Source of the data: United Nations High Commissioner for Refugees (UNHCR), Geneva, UNHCR population statistics database, last accessed May 2022.

Region is based on macro geographical regions arranged according to continents and component geographical regions used for statistical purposes as at 31 July 2017.
Source of the data: United Nations Statistics Division (UNSD), New York, Statistical Yearbook 2017 edition (60th issue) Annex I - Country and area nomenclature, regional and other groupings (based on Series M49: Standard Country or Area codes and Geographical Regions for Statistical Use), last accessed October 2017.

Research & Development expenditure refers to expenditure on creative work undertaken on a systematic basis in order to increase the stock of knowledge, including knowledge of humanity, culture and society, and the use of this stock of knowledge to devise new applications, expressed as a percentage of Gross Domestic Product (GDP). It is the total intramural expenditure on R&D performed on the national territory during a given period. It includes R&D performed within a country and funded from abroad but excludes payments made abroad for R&D.
Source of the data: United Nations Educational, Scientific and Cultural Organization (UNESCO), Montreal, the UNESCO Institute for Statistics (UIS) statistics database, last accessed June 2022.

Safely managed water and sanitation: population using safely managed drinking water sources is currently being measured by the proportion of population in urban and rural areas, according to national definitions, meeting the criteria for using safely

managed drinking water sources (SDG 6.1.1) by using an improved basic drinking water source which is located on premises, available when needed and free of faecal and priority chemical contamination. Improved drinking water sources are those that have the potential to deliver safe water by nature of their design and construction, and include: piped water, boreholes or tubewells, protected dug wells, protected springs, rainwater, and packaged or delivered water. Population using safely managed sanitation facilities is currently being measured by the proportion of the population in urban and rural areas, according to national definitions, meeting the criteria for having a safely managed sanitation service (SDG 6.2.1a) by using a basic sanitation facility which is not shared with other households and where excreta is safely disposed in situ or transported and treated off-site. Improved sanitation facilities are those designed to hygienically separate excreta from human contact, and include: flush/pour flush to piped sewer system, septic tanks or pit latrines; ventilated improved pit latrines, composting toilets or pit latrines with slabs.
Source of the data: World Health Organization (WHO) and the United Nations Children's Fund (UNICEF), Geneva and New York, the WHO/UNICEF Joint Monitoring Programme (JMP) for Water and Sanitation database, last accessed July 2021.

Seats held by women in the National Parliament refer to the number of women in the lower chamber of the National Parliament expressed as a percentage of total occupied seats in the lower or single House, situation as of 1 January 2022.
Source of the data: Inter-Parliamentary Union (IPU), Geneva, Women in National Parliament dataset and the Sustainable Development Goals (SDGs) statistics database, last accessed March 2022.

Sex ratio is calculated as the ratio of the medium fertility projected population of men to that of 100 women as of 1 July 2022, unless otherwise stated in a footnote.
Source of the data: United Nations Population Division (UNPD), New York, "World Population Prospects (WPP): The 2022 Revision"; supplemented by data from the United Nations Statistics Division (UNSD), New York, Demographic Yearbook 2020 and the Pacific Community (SPC) Statistics and Demography Programme for small countries or areas, last accessed July 2022.

Surface area refers to land area excluding inland water.
Source of the data: United Nations Statistics Division (UNSD), New York, Demographic Yearbook 2020 and the demographic statistics database, last accessed June 2022.

Threatened species represents the number of plants and animals that are most in need of conservation attention and are compiled by the World Conservation Union IUCN/ Species Survival Commission (SSC).

Technical notes (*continued*)

Source of the data: International Union for Conservation of Nature (IUCN), Gland and Cambridge, IUCN Red List of Threatened Species publication, last accessed March 2022.

Tourist/visitor arrivals at national borders is any person who travels to a country other than that in which he or she has his or her usual residence but outside his/her usual environment for a period not exceeding 12 months and whose main purpose of visit is other than the exercise of an activity remunerated from with the country visited, and who stays at least one night in a collective or private accommodation in the country visited (see Recommendations on Tourism Statistics of the United Nations and the World Tourism Organization). The data refer to arrivals of non-resident tourists at national borders, unless otherwise stated in a footnote.
Source of the data: World Tourism Organization (UNWTO), Madrid, the UNWTO statistics database, last accessed June 2022.

UN membership date: The United Nations (UN) is an intergovernmental organization whose members are the countries of the world. Currently there are 193 Member States of the United Nations, some of which joined the UN by signing and ratifying the Charter of the United Nations in 1945; the other countries joined the UN later, through the adoption of a resolution admitting them to membership. The process usually follows these steps: first, the country applies for membership and makes a declaration accepting the obligations of the Charter; second, the Security Council adopts a resolution recommending that the General Assembly admit the country to membership and finally the General Assembly adopts a resolution admitting the country.
Source of the data: United Nations (UN), Department of Public Information (DPI), News and Media Division, New York, Member states and date of admission, last accessed May 2018.

Unemployment refers to persons above a specified age who during a specified reference period were: "without work", i.e. were not in paid employment or self-employment as defined under employment; "currently available for work", i.e. were available for paid employment or self-employment during the reference period; and "seeking work", i.e. had taken specific steps in a specified recent period to seek paid employment or self-employment (see ILO's current International Recommendations on Labour Statistics). The data refer to the 15 years and over age group and are based on ILO's modelled estimates, unless otherwise stated in a footnote.
Source of the data: International Labour Organization (ILO), Geneva, Key Indicators of the Labour Market (KILM 9th edition) and the ILOSTAT database, last accessed January 2022.

Urban population is based on the number of persons at the mid-year defined as urban according to national definitions of this concept. In most cases these definitions are those used in the most recent population census.

Source of the data: United Nations Population Division (UNPD), New York, "World Urbanization Prospects (WUP): The 2018 Revision", last accessed May 2018.

Urban population growth rate is based on the number of persons defined as urban according to national definitions of this concept. In most cases these definitions are those used in the most recent population census. The data are an average over five-year ranges; 2005-2010 data are labelled "2010", 2011-2015 data are labelled "2015" and 2016-2022 data are labelled "2022", unless otherwise stated in a footnote.

Source of the data: United Nations Population Division (UNPD), New York, "World Urbanization Prospects (WUP): The 2018 Revision", last accessed May 2018.

Statistical sources and references

Statistical sources

Food and Agriculture Organization of the United Nations (FAO), Rome, FAOSTAT database, available at http://www.fao.org/faostat/en/#home.

International Energy Agency (IEA), Paris, available at https://www.iea.org/data-and-statistics?country=WORLD&fuel=Energy supply&indicator=Total primary energy supply (TPES) by source

International Labour Organization (ILO), Geneva, the ILOSTAT database, available at http://www.ilo.org/ilostat.
_____, Key Indicators of the Labour Market (KILM 9th edition), available at http://www.ilo.org/global/statistics-and-databases/research-and-databases/kilm/lang--en/index.htm.

International Monetary Fund (IMF), Washington, D.C., Balance of Payment (BOP) Statistics database, available at http://data.imf.org/bop.
_____, the International Financial Statistics (IFS) database, available at http://data.imf.org/ifs.

International Organisation for Standardization (ISO), Geneva, Currency Code Services – ISO 4217 Maintenance Agency, available at https://www.iso.org/iso-4217-currency-codes.html.

International Telecommunication Union (ITU), Geneva, the ITU Database, available at http://www.itu.int/en/ITU-D/statistics/Pages/default.aspx.

International Union for Conservation of Nature (IUCN), Gland and Cambridge, IUCN Red List of Threatened Species publication, available at http://www.iucnredlist.org/about/summary-statistics.

Inter-Parliamentary Union (IPU), Geneva, Women in National Parliament dataset, available at https://data.ipu.org/women-ranking.

Organisation for Economic Co-operation and Development (OECD), Paris, the OECD Development Assistance Committee (DAC) statistics database, available at http://stats.oecd.org/.

Pacific Community (SPC) Statistics and Demography Programme, Nouméa, Population and demographic indicators, available at http://sdd.spc.int/en/.

United Nations (UN), Department of Economic and Social Affairs (DESA), Population Division (UNPD), New York, "International migrant stock: The 2020 Revision", available at http://www.un.org/en/development/desa/population/migration/data/index.shtml.
_____, "World Population Prospects (WPP): The 2022 Revision", available at https://esa.un.org/unpd/wpp/.
_____, "World Urbanization Prospects (WUP): The 2018 Revision", available at https://esa.un.org/unpd/wup/.

Statistical sources and references (*continued*)

United Nations (UN), Department of Economic and Social Affairs (DESA), Statistics Division (UNSD), New York, Commodity Trade statistics database (UN COMTRADE), available at https://comtrade.un.org/.

_____, Demographic Yearbook (Series R, United Nations publication), available at https://unstats.un.org/unsd/demographic-social/products/dyb/.

_____, Energy Statistics Yearbook (Series J, United Nations publication), available at http://unstats.un.org/unsd/energy/yearbook/default.htm.

_____, Monthly Bulletin of Statistics (Series Q, United Nations publication), available at http://unstats.un.org/unsd/mbs/.

_____, National Accounts Statistics: Analysis of Main Aggregates (AMA) database (Series X, United Nations publication), available at http://unstats.un.org/unsd/snaama/introduction.asp.

_____, Statistical Yearbook (Series S, United Nations publication), available at https://unstats.un.org/unsd/publications/statistical-yearbook/.

_____, Sustainable Development Goals (SDGs) statistics database, available at https://unstats.un.org/sdgs/indicators/database.

United Nations (UN), Department of Management (DM), Office of Programme Planning, Budget and Accounts (OPPBA), New York, UN Treasury operational rates of exchange, available at https://treasury.un.org/operationalrates/OperationalRates.php

United Nations (UN), Department of Public Information (DPI), News and Media Division, New York, Member states and date of admission, available at https://www.un.org/en/about-us/member-states.

United Nations Educational, Scientific and Cultural Organization (UNESCO), Montreal, the UNESCO Institute for Statistics (UIS) statistics database, available at http://data.uis.unesco.org/.

United Nations High Commissioner for Refugees (UNHCR), Geneva, UNHCR population statistics database, available at https://www.unhcr.org/refugee-statistics

United Nations Office on Drugs and Crime (UNODC), Vienna, UNODC Statistics database, available at https://dataunodc.un.org.

World Health Organization (WHO) and the United Nations Children's Fund (UNICEF), Geneva and New York, the WHO/UNICEF Joint Monitoring Programme (JMP) for Water and Sanitation database, available at https://washdata.org/monitoring/sanitation.

World Health Organization (WHO), Geneva, WHO Global Health Expenditure database, available at http://apps.who.int/nha/database.

_____, WHO Global Health Workforce statistics database, available at https://www.who.int/data/gho.

Statistical sources and references (*continued*)

World Tourism Organization (UNWTO), Madrid, the UNWTO statistics database, available at http://www.e-unwto.org/loi/unwtotfb.

References

Food and Agriculture Organization of the United Nations (2015). Global Forest Resources Assessment 2020, available at http://www.fao.org/forest-resources-assessment/en/.

International Labour Organization (2000). Current International Recommendations on Labour Statistics, 2000 Edition, available at http://www.ilo.org/global/publications/ilo-bookstore/order-online/books/WCMS_PUBL_9221108465_EN/lang--en/index.htm.

International Monetary Fund (2009). Balance of Payments and International Investment Position Manual, Sixth Edition, available at https://www.imf.org/external/pubs/ft/bop/2007/bopman6.htm.

United Nations (1951 and 1967). Convention relating to the Status of Refugees of 1951 (United Nations, Treaty Series, vol. 189 (1954), No. 2545, p. 137), art. 1) and Protocol relating to the Status of Refugees of 1967 (United Nations, Treaty Series, vol. 606 (1967), No. 8791, p. 267), available at https://treaties.un.org/doc/Publication/UNTS/Volume%20189/volume-189-I-2545-English.pdf and https://treaties.un.org/doc/Publication/UNTS/Volume%20606/volume-606-I-8791-English.pdf.

United Nations (1982). Concepts and Methods in Energy Statistics, with Special Reference to Energy Accounts and Balances: A Technical Report. Statistical Office, Series F, No. 29 and Corr. 1 (United Nations publication, Sales No. E.82.XVII.13 and corrigendum), available at http://unstats.un.org/unsd/publication/SeriesF/SeriesF_29E.pdf.

United Nations (2008). International Standard Industrial Classification of All Economic Activities (ISIC), Rev. 4. Statistics Division, Series M, No. 4, Rev.4 (United Nations publication, Sales No. E.08.XVII.25), available at http://unstats.un.org/unsd/publication/SeriesM/seriesm_4rev4e.pdf.

United Nations (2017). Principles and Recommendations for Population and Housing Censuses Rev. 3. Statistics Division, Series M, No. 67, Rev. 3 (United Nations publication, Sales No. 15.XVII.10), available at https://unstats.un.org/unsd/demographic-social/Standards-and-Methods/files/Principles_and_Recommendations/Population-and-Housing-Censuses/Series_M67rev3-E.pdf.

United Nations (2010). International Merchandise Trade Statistics: Concepts and Definitions, Statistics Division, Series M, No.52, Rev.3, (United Nations publication, Sales No. E.10.XVII.13), available at http://unstats.un.org/unsd/publication/SeriesM/SeriesM_52rev3E.pdf.

Statistical sources and references (*continued*)

United Nations (2011). International Recommendations for Energy Statistics (IRES), Statistics Division, available at http://unstats.un.org/unsd/statcom/doc11/BG-IRES.pdf.

United Nations (2013). International Merchandise Trade Statistics: Compilers Manual Revision 1 (IMTS 2010-CM), Statistics Division , Series F, No. 87, Rev.1 (United Nations publication, Sales No. E.13.XVII.8), available at https://unstats.un.org/unsd/trade/publications/seriesf_87Rev1_e_cover.pdf.

United Nations (2018). Standard Country or Area Codes for Statistical Use, Statistics Division, Series M, No. 49, available at http://unstats.un.org/unsd/methods/m49/m49.htm

United Nations, European Commission, International Monetary Fund, Organisation for Economic Cooperation and Development and World Bank (2009). System of National Accounts 2008, Statistics Division, Series M, No. 2, Rev.5 (United Nations publication, Sales No. E.08.XVII.29), available at http://unstats.un.org/unsd/nationalaccount/sna2008.asp.

World Health Organization (2019), International Statistical Classification of Diseases and Related Health Problems, Eleventh Revision (ICD-11), (Geneva) available at http://www.who.int/classifications/icd/en/.

United Nations and World Tourism Organization (2008). International Recommendations for Tourism Statistics 2008, Statistics Division, Series M, No. 83/Rev.1 (United Nations publication, Sales No. E.08.XVII.28), available at http://unstats.un.org/unsd/publication/SeriesM/SeriesM_83rev1e.pdf.

Related statistical products

The World Statistics Pocketbook can also be viewed online in PDF format as well as an app for Android and Apple devices at http://unstats.un.org/unsd/publications/pocketbook/ and in UNdata at http://data.un.org/en/index.html.

Other statistical publications offering a broad cross-section of information which may be of interest to users of the World Statistics Pocketbook include:

1. The Monthly Bulletin of Statistics (MBS) in print and the Monthly Bulletin of Statistics Online, available at http://unstats.un.org/unsd/mbs/.
2. The Statistical Yearbook (SYB) in print and online in PDF format, available at http://unstats.un.org/unsd/publications/statistical-yearbook/.

Both publications are available for sale in print format (see below for instructions on how to order). For more information about other publications and online databases prepared by the United Nations Statistics Division, please visit: https://unstats.un.org/unsd/publications/. For additional information about the work of the United Nations Statistics Division, please visit http://unstats.un.org/unsd. To order United Nations publications, please visit https://shop.un.org or contact:

United Nations Publications
300 East 42nd Street
New York, NY 10017
Tel: 1-888-254-4286 / Fax: 1-800-338-4550 / E-mail: publications@un.org

Please provide the Development Data Section – which is responsible for producing the World Statistics Pocketbook, the Monthly Bulletin of Statistics and the Statistical Yearbook – your feedback and suggestions regarding these statistical products, as well as the utility of the data, by contacting statistics@un.org.